BETWEEN TWO WORLDS

✧

BETWEEN TWO WORLDS

�֍

A Reading of Descartes's *Meditations*

JOHN CARRIERO

PRINCETON UNIVERSITY PRESS

PRINCETON AND OXFORD

Copyright © 2009 by Princeton University Press
Published by Princeton University Press, 41 William Street,
Princeton, New Jersey 08540

In the United Kingdom: Princeton University Press, 6 Oxford Street,
Woodstock, Oxfordshire OX20 1TW

Library of Congress Cataloging-in-Publication Data

Carriero, John Peter.
Between two worlds : a reading of Descartes's Meditations / John Carriero.
p. cm.
Includes bibliographical references and index.
ISBN 978-0-691-13560-1 (cloth : alk. paper) — ISBN 978-0-691-13561-8 (pbk. : alk. paper)
1. Descartes, René, 1596–1650. Meditationes de prima philosophia.   2. First
philosophy.   I. Title.
B1854.C36   2009
194—dc22   2008036732

British Library Cataloging-in-Publication Data is available

This book has been composed in Dante Typeface
Printed on acid-free paper. ∞
press.princeton.edu

Printed in the United States of America

1   3   5   7   9   10   8   6   4   2

For Katya

✦

Contents

→←

Preface

><

C AN SOMEONE today take up a work of philosophy written over
350 years ago and engage with it on its own terms? This book is an
attempt to do so with Descartes's *Meditations concerning First Philosophy*.
My goal is to work through the text as it appears and to confront it in an
unfiltered way. When I draw on material other than the *Meditations*—
historical background, other writings of Descartes, or, occasionally, other
scholars' interpretations—it is because I have found it necessary for making philosophical sense of Descartes's thought. I hope that these excur-
sions away from the *Meditations* will be justified by making his argument
more understandable when I return.

There is much to be gained by working through the text of *Meditations*, with care, in a relatively unmediated way. I am encouraged in this
thought by my experience reading Thomas Aquinas's commentaries on
Aristotle, which are based on lectures he gave one and a half millennia
after Aristotle lived. Aquinas, working through Aristotle's text line by
line, gradually develops a philosophically powerful picture of Aristotle's
thought. To be sure, Aquinas's commentaries benefit from a long tradition of response to Aristotle's texts, especially by Averroes (referred to by
Aquinas simply as "the commentator"); and Aquinas occasionally provides some (ancient) historical context and sometimes takes up the positions of other interpreters. All the same, his lectures are squarely focused
on Aristotle's text and comparatively uncluttered by other matters. Such
an approach is well suited to Aristotle because he is a systematic thinker,
as a sustained reading of his texts brings out. This kind of approach
makes it natural to draw maps of the individual works and chapters,
posting on them "you are here" flags; it also encourages reflection on the
flow of Aristotle's discussion—why he takes up the topics he does, why
he treats them in the order that he does, and how they are interrelated.

Descartes's *Meditations* is systematic and philosophically rich enough
to merit similar treatment. I say similar, because I do not try to give the
text the line-by-line treatment one finds in the tradition of Aristotelian
commentary; I also allow myself more latitude to draw on other materials that I think are necessary for understanding Descartes's text or at least
can significantly enhance our understanding of it. But I do usually work

through the text in a paragraph-by-paragraph manner, and devote a fair amount of attention to how the different moments hang together in the overall scheme of a meditation, or in the overall scheme of the *Meditations* as a whole. By proceeding in this way, we can locate systematic themes that would otherwise be hard to discern. In addition, a leisurely stroll through the text (leisurely by contemporary standards) allows one to spot nuances and important details, develop questions and issues, and register an occasional twist or bump in the road, a way of proceeding that would be all but impossible within the confines of a standard journal article. For example, as a reader of Descartes I have found it a luxury to be able to pursue the ins and outs of the entire wax discussion, from start to finish, in the Second Meditation: having the opportunity to do so allows one to get a grip on certain subtleties and complexities in his text.

Although I have generally tried to make sense of Descartes's text as it stands, in the order in which it appears, I have made one significant exception, concerning Descartes's proof for the existence of body. It seems to me that this proof is supposed to be read against a failed line of thought developed in the Third Meditation (¶¶8–12), and it seems best to discuss the failed argument in light of the argument Descartes accepts. Rather than delay my discussion of the passage in the Third Meditation until we get to the Sixth, I have moved up my discussion of the argument from the Sixth Meditation. This treatment comprises the bulk of chapter 3 (I).

Descartes wrote the *Meditations* in the hope that it would be adopted as a textbook. This gives the work an accessibility not often found in major works in philosophy. (This is particularly true of the first two meditations; things become more technical, at least on the surface, when we get to the Third Meditation, where Descartes introduces notions like material falsity and formal and objective reality.) The immediacy of the work helps to explain why even today the *Meditations* continues to be read alongside much more recent works in courses introducing students to the theory of knowledge.

Because Descartes intended the *Meditations* to be accessible in this way, I believe a thoroughgoing treatment of it will hold something of value for a wide range of students. I assume that many of this book's readers will have relatively little familiarity with the *Meditations*, perhaps only some exposure to the First or Second Meditation in a class on epistemology or the history of philosophy. I recommend that readers not familiar with the overall plan of the *Meditations* read the entire work first. In addition, most readers will find it helpful to reread the relevant meditation as they begin each chapter and to have the text of the *Meditations* at their side throughout (just as one would have a copy of Aristotle's text nearby when one reads Aquinas's commentaries). I suggest that readers number the paragraphs of each meditation, since I refer to the text in this way; for example, III.¶4 is the fourth paragraph of the Third Medita-tion, and V.¶¶5–6 are the fifth and sixth paragraphs of the Fifth Medita-tion. Despite the intimidating appearance this apparatus can give, I am not assuming that readers will be able to recall such passages immediately. I simply have found this a useful device for finding one's way around in the *Meditations'* (relatively manageable) text and eventually coming to know it well. (The paragraph structure does not seem to have originated with Des-cartes, but whoever did introduce it had a good grasp of the flow of the argument.) I also sometimes refer to various landmarks in the *Meditations* ("the cogito," "the ontological argument," etc.) as if the reader already knew her way around the text; but, again, an in-depth familiarity with the text and the location of its key discussions is not something I am presupposing, but rather something that I hope will develop as the reader becomes more closely acquainted with the *Meditations*. Finally, in the inter-est of accessibility, I have done what I could to make each of the chapters freestanding, so that a reader with an interest in a particular meditation can simply read the chapter on that one; in some cases this has resulted in my covering the same ground more than once. I did this in part because each of the meditations has an integrity of its own, which one wants to unearth as far as one can: for several of the meditations, the question, What is this meditation about? is a good place to start.

I began work on this project while on leave during the 2002–3 academic year. That leave was supported in part by a University of California Presi-dential Fellowship in the Humanities. During that year I drafted the chap-ters on the Third and Sixth Meditations. I wrote the chapter on the Second Meditation the following year. I had a second leave during the 2005–6 academic year, which was supported in part by a grant from the National Endowment for the Humanities. During that year I wrote drafts of the chapters on the Fourth, Fifth, and First Meditations (in that order). I am grateful to the UC President's Office and the NEH; without their support it would not have been possible to see this project through to completion. I acknowledge with gratitude the financial and administrative support that Dean Pauline Yu and Dean Gabrielle Spiegel and Assistant Dean Lori Stein provided. The last third of chapter 5 was published, in slightly different form, as "The Cartesian Circle and the Foundations of Knowledge," in *A Companion to Descartes*, edited by Janet Broughton and John Carriero, pub-lished in 2008 by Blackwell Publishing. I thank the publisher for granting permission to reprint this material.

I have had a lot of help with this project. Joseph Almog was more often than not the first person to read a draft of a chapter and invariably provided philosophically rigorous and supportive feedback. He influ-enced my treatment of Descartes's theory on sensation and my thinking about Descartes's theory of the human being (although I believe we still disagree somewhat about the latter). Paul Hoffman also read most of the manuscript and provided detailed, helpful comments, leading to numerous substantial revisions (more, I think, than he intended). Tyler Burge provided detailed, insightful written comments on about half the manuscript near the end of the project, which were of great use for getting the manuscript into final form. Barbara Herman has been a frequent source of advice and helped me rework the introduction in particular. Sean Greenberg provided perceptive comments on the chapters on the Fourth and Sixth Meditations, as did Marleen Rozemond on the Sixth.

Lilli Alanen, who served as a reader for Princeton University Press, provided an extremely valuable report that led me to make a number of significant revisions, particularly in the chapter on the Fourth Meditation. She also supported the project in numerous other ways. A second, anonymous reader also had important suggestions, and I have tried to implement them.

Calvin Normore has been a terrific sounding board for the project over the years; I am grateful to him for our very many discussions, which often helped me give shape to inchoate ideas. I also learned quite a bit from my conversations with Deborah Brown, as well as from her talks and papers, especially about objective reality and material falsity. Very early versions of many of the chapters were given on different occasions at the University of Turku. I would like to thank the audiences there, especially Olli Koistinen and Arto Repo, for their insightful feedback. I would also like to express my gratitude to Janet Broughton for her special support and encouragement, and for the many phone conversations during which she generously allowed us to drift over into something connected with my project, when we were supposed to be working on something else.

Toward the end of the project, Houston Smit and David Owen organized a small reading group at the University of Arizona on the manuscript; I would like to thank them for a day of very stimulating discussion. At UCLA a reading group on the will took up the chapter on the Fourth Meditation; that session, along with Alanen's comments, led to a substantial reworking of the central sections of that chapter. I am grateful to its participants, Mandel Cabrera, David Goldman, David Meriwether, Calvin Normore, Jesse Summers, and Stephen White.

I have had many helpful conversations about various aspects of this book with friends, students, and colleagues over the years, which not only helped me to develop and clarify my ideas but did much to keep the project fun. Much of this material was tried out on undergraduates in a course on the *Meditations* that I regularly teach at UCLA; I learned a great deal from their unjaded and candid responses. I would like to thank friends and colleagues with whom I can specifically remember discussing aspects of the project (and to apologize to those whom I may have forgotten): Marilyn Adams, Donald Ainslie, Talia Bettcher, Martha Bolton, Brian Copenhaver, Michael Della Rocca, Erin Eaker, David Ebrey, Stephen Engstrom, Roger Florka, Samuel Freeman, Michelle Gallagher, Hannah Ginsborg, Warren Goldfarb, David Goldman, Pamela Hieronymi, Andrew Hsu, Joseph Hwang, Jeremy Hyman, David Kaplan, Sean Kelsey, Gavin Lawrence, Ed McCann, Henry Mendell, Susan Meyer, David Owens, Charles Parsons, Sarah Patterson, Elliot Paul, Tom Ricketts, Marleen Rozemond, Amy Schmitter, Lisa Shapiro, Alison Simmons, Chris Smeenk, Daniel Warren, Catherine Wilson, Ken Winkler, and Moriel Zelikowsky. I would also like to thank Robert Adams, Michael Friedman, and Robert Sleigh for the special support they provided.

Jesse Summers assisted with the preparation of the bibliography. Joe Hwang checked the quotations and translations with special care and gave me many helpful suggestions. Katya Rice, Rob Watson, and Dana Cairns Watson aided with proofreading and editing. I am grateful to Ian Malcolm of Princeton University Press for his support, encouragement, and (most of all) patience, to Richard Isomaki for his thoughtful copyediting, and to Carol Roberts for her careful work on the indexes. Finally, I would like to thank Stephan Chambers, who, some two decades ago, first suggested the title to me.

Note on Translations

✦

I HAVE used the standard Cottingham, Stoothoff, and Murdoch (CSM) edition of Descartes's writings as the starting point for my translations. (See the bibliography for publication details.) I sometimes depart from it in small ways to make the translation more literal. When I do so, I often report the original Latin in the quotation. On a few occasions, when the translation matters, I raise translation issues in the main text. I have frequently consulted Anscombe and Geach's translation when I found myself puzzled by Descartes's Latin.

In addition to referring to the text of the *Meditations* by Adam and Tannery (AT) page number (see the bibliography for publication details) and CSM page number, I usually cite by meditation number and paragraph number (e.g., I.¶2 is the second paragraph of the First Meditation). It is useful to have a scheme for finding one's way around in the text that is responsive to its argumentative articulation.

I have meddled less frequently with the translations of scholastic authors (usually Aquinas). I don't have the same feel for these texts, and nuance is less important given the use I make of them.

BETWEEN TWO WORLDS

✕

Introduction

➤✦

THE *Meditationes de Prima Philosophia* is a truly revolutionary work, one that radically reshaped the landscape of metaphysics and epistemology. The three main topics taken up in the *Meditations*—the mind and its nature, body and its nature, and God—would become the focal points for subsequent metaphysics, especially for the rationalist side of early modern philosophy and for Kant. The broad idea that philosophy ought to begin with an account of mind and knowledge would also prove extremely influential, especially for the subsequent empiricist tradition and, again, for Kant. Indeed, it does not seem too much of an exaggeration to say, paraphrasing Whitehead, that early modern philosophy consists largely of footnotes to Descartes.

Revolutionary though it is, the *Meditations* is remarkably engaging and short. In seventy-five pages—not much longer than a journal article—Descartes takes up questions that almost every reflective person thinks about at some point. What can I know with certainty? Is there an external world? What is the nature of my mind? Does God exist? What is the nature of body? What is knowledge? How is my mind related to my body? Descartes's exploration of these questions proceeds in an intimate, almost conversational, manner. His bold and original answers continue to occupy our attention.

One of the factors contributing to the work's accessibility is Descartes's wish to make a clean start in philosophy (the first in a series of clean starts that philosophers will make, as it happens). The work is addressed to a reader—a meditator—relying only on her native faculties; it is not intended to require prior exposure to the philosophical tradition. I believe that Descartes's relation to the tradition is more complicated than he seems to think, because (as will emerge) he is as much reshaping it as extricating himself from it. Still, one can open the *Meditations* to almost any page and soon find oneself drawn in and absorbed in his discussion of the world and our place in it. He was an absolute master: he knew how to approach fundamental matters in a direct and nontechnical manner.

Like others of his time, Descartes had confidence in the ability of the human mind to fruitfully pursue questions about God, the nature or essence of the mind, and the nature or essence of the physical world. We don't have that same confidence today. I don't think this is because we know more than Descartes, or because we have, in our sophistication, seen through his naïveté. Rather, too much water has passed under the bridge for us to be able to enter fully, let alone adopt, the perspective of a seventeenth-century thinker; the philosophical conversation has moved on. It is not necessary, however, to recover that confidence in order to appreciate Descartes's thought. Powerful philosophical minds have a way of making their presence felt even across a vast intellectual divide of differences in starting points, basic questions, methods, and general worldview. Exploring the thought of a major figure of the past, such as Plato, Aristotle, Aquinas, or Descartes, has the paradoxical effect of reinforcing its foreignness while at the same time helping us to appreciate its attraction and power. If one can't go home again to the seventeenth century, one can still find a visit enlightening.

Although the *Meditations* occupies a pivotal place in the history of philosophy, it has received unbalanced scholarly attention. For much of the twentieth century, scholars tended to read the work through an epistemological lens, with a focus on its handling of skepticism, certainty, justification of belief, and knowledge. Scholars offered sustained, often quite intricate, accounts of the First Meditation's skeptical arguments and the Second Meditation's cogito argument. Often, however, they have proceeded to take up remaining topics in the work—the wax passage, the various arguments for the existence of God, the proof that mind and body are really distinct, the proof that body exists, and so on—in a more occasional and less systematic way.

Behind this way of proceeding is a familiar picture of Descartes's place in the history of philosophy. Descartes is credited with ushering in a modern conception of mind and knowledge, where the mental is characterized as the seat of consciousness or (an incorrigible) subjectivity. The skeptical arguments and the cogito argument are of central importance because they help us appreciate that the mind is what, as it were, lies behind the veil of ideas, beyond the reach of the skeptical doubt. (Not infrequently, of course, this conception of mind is seen as harboring disastrous mistakes for subsequent tradition.) On this picture, most of the exciting work takes place early in the *Meditations*. Descartes's resolution of the skeptical doubt feels anticlimactic, almost disappointing: a curious and unpersuasive argument for the existence of God in the Third (which is supposed to afford our best hope of securing the certainty that two and three together make five), another unconvincing argument for the existence of God in the Fifth (coupled with the troubling claim that all of my knowledge depends on my knowledge of God), an intriguing but dubious argument for the claim that my mind and my body are different things (different enough that my mind cannot exist without my body), and a disappointing argument for the existence of body (again trading heavily on the existence of God) in the Sixth to try to bring back the external world. On this approach, we wonder how Descartes thought he could get so much metaphysics past the careful standards of inquiry implicit in the skeptical doubt (prove that God exists, tell us what the natures of mind and body are, prove that mind and body are distinct substances).

More recently, scholars have been moving away from this picture of Descartes and emphasizing the metaphysical side of his thought. I agree that excessive focus on skepticism—in particular, a misunderstanding of what Descartes is using the skepticism for—has distorted our understanding of his thought. A reading that seeks to leverage Descartes's conception of mind out of external-world skepticism leaves as irrelevant or desperate too much of what is going on in the *Meditations*. Still, I don't think an alternative picture that orients us to the *Meditations* as a whole has emerged. I would like to suggest a candidate.

Very roughly, for reasons that go back to the scientific revolution, it became untenable in the seventeenth century to think of human knowledge the way Descartes's scholastic Aristotelian teachers did. They thought of human understanding as basically a form of universal cognition, abstracted from sensory experience. As a famous scholastic slogan has it, there is nothing in the intellect that was not first in the senses. Descartes did not find this a plausible way of thinking about what he regarded as the three main areas of human knowledge: the mind, God, and body. Descartes thought that our understanding of the mind, as something that affirms, denies, doubts, understands, and so forth, owes very little to the senses. He believed that our basic understanding of God, as, for example, an unlimited being that sustains everything in existence from one moment to the next, could not possibly have come to us through the senses. And he thought that our basic grasp of a body, as extended substance in motion, transcends anything that we acquire through our senses.

Therefore, in the *Meditations*, Descartes develops a new conception of the human mind and its situation in the universe that it knows. In the Second Meditation, he explains its essence or nature. The mind, on Descartes's telling, turns out to be quite a bit more independent from the rest of the human being than it is on an Aristotelian telling. In particular, it no longer requires the senses in order to operate naturally. It is not merely a power (the intellect) of some more fundamental thing (a human being). It is a thing in its own right, a "substance." In the Third Meditation, Descartes argues that the mind was created by a supremely perfect being (God). In the Fourth Meditation, he explains how, even so, it is possible for it to go wrong, as well as what it can do to avoid going wrong; in the Fifth Meditation, he tells us something about the truth or reality (certain "true and immutable natures") to which the mind is related when it knows, and he offers an account of the highest form of knowledge, what Descartes calls *scientia*. Finally, in the Sixth Meditation, he attempts to position the mind vis-à-vis its body.

I would like to describe in somewhat more detail some of the main themes emerging from my reading of the text, indicate some of my methodological commitments, and position my interpretation vis-à-vis a prevalent picture of Descartes. Because here I am only sketching and charting out, not developing or explaining in detail, some of what follows will be opaque to readers not already familiar with the main contours of the *Meditations* or some of the main currents in Descartes scholarship; still, I believe that even for these readers the following discussion will provide a useful first pass at the important framing issues and orienting ideas to come, even if my summary remarks contain what are for them placeholders that will need to be filled in later. Descartes tried, in the *Meditations*, to proceed strictly in a manner where nothing that came earlier depended on something to come later, but in this case I find myself unable to follow his example.

In the First Meditation Descartes presents skeptical arguments that are supposed to leave us in a condition of total bewilderment, causing us to wonder whether it is in our power to know any truth at all. As we enter the Second Meditation, under the spell of this uncertainty, we begin to doubt whether there even *is* a truth or reality for us to know: "So what remains true? Perhaps just this one thing, that nothing is certain" (¶2; 7:24; 2:16). Then something quite remarkable happens: I come to see (through the so-called cogito argument) that, come what may, I *do* know that at least this much is true: I exist. That is, I come to see not only that there is (at least) one reality for me to know (namely myself) but also that this real thing that I know to exist has the ability to *see that at least some things are true*. This being is usually called the mind; however, for reasons I will explain in chapter 2, I sometimes prefer to call this being—namely, me insofar as I am a cognitive being (see, e.g., III.¶32; 7:49; 2:33–34)—the *cogito being*.

The discovery of the cogito being provides Descartes with an Archimedean point (II.¶1) from which he levers a systematic exploration of the being's nature, its proper functioning, and its metaphysical preconditions. What is the nature of this being? What is its origin? When does it understand well and judge properly? When it understands well and judges properly, what are the "somethings," "not nothings," to which its cognition relates it? And, finally, why is it that when this being understands well and judges properly, it reaches truth or reality?

The rest of the Second Meditation contains an account of the nature of the cogito being and explains how it is better known and understood than body. At the beginning of the Third Meditation, the meditator, reflecting on what went well in the Second Meditation, hypothesizes that this being gets to truth or reality when it perceives clearly and distinctly (III.¶2). In order to discover whether this hypothesis is itself true, we need to find out who or what created the cogito being (the main subject of the Third Meditation) and to understand the nature of judgment and error (a goal of the Fourth Meditation). At the beginning of the Fifth Meditation, Descartes introduces the notion of a true and immutable nature: a true and immutable nature is a locus of understanding; it is the reality that the cogito being is characteristically related to when it understands. These true and immutable natures, he explains, do not require real existence; for example, the true and immutable nature that the cogito being understands when it sees that the three angles of a triangle sum to two right angles, is not a "nothing" but a "something," and is independent of the cogito being, even if it should turn out that no triangles exist anywhere outside its thought. Finally, at the end of the Fifth Meditation, Descartes explains why the cogito being must recognize the author of its nature, God, if it is to have *scientia* (knowledge in its fullest sense). The Sixth Meditation unfolds a new chapter in the story. Up to that point, we have been concerned with only the cogito being itself. In the Sixth Meditation, Descartes undertakes to position the cogito being with respect to physical reality, a project that is necessarily original inasmuch as Descartes's conceptions of the cogito being (or "mind") and body (as simply extension) are both novel.

This book follows this story across the *Meditations*. It is something of a cross between a running commentary and a thematically organized series of essays. Because my goal is to provide a sustained reading of the *Meditations*, I focus on the text itself. I look to other of Descartes's writings (especially the Replies and Objections, and sometimes his correspondence) mainly when the text of the *Meditations* resists direct treatment. As noted earlier, I believe that Descartes attempted to write the *Meditations* in an intuitive and accessible way that encourages this sort of direct encounter.

All the same, Descartes's intentions notwithstanding, the text, for all its surface familiarity, was written in an alien philosophical landscape (a landscape that it did much to reshape). We will need to be comfortable with that terrain—perhaps even more than is first apparent—in order to recognize what Descartes's larger argument is all about and so to locate its originality. What I have in mind here is not so much the technical scholastic notions that crop up from time to time (e.g., objective and formal reality, formal and eminent causation, material falsity, and so forth), but rather more central and fundamental differences between Descartes's intellectual milieu and our own. There are two large impediments, in particular, that I think can stand in the way of our entering Descartes's thought.

First, the *Meditations* presupposes a familiarity with the project of scholastic philosophical theology that few readers have today. Philosophical theology is absolutely central to Meditations Three through Six. In the Third Meditation, Descartes twice argues that the cogito being could have been caused only by God; in the Fourth Meditation, Descartes explains how the mind's liability to error is compatible with its being created by a supremely perfect being; in the Fifth Meditation, Descartes presents an argument for the existence of God and an explanation of how *scientia* depends on the recognition of God's existence; and in the last third of the Sixth Meditation, he explains how a certain kind of instinctual error, belonging to the composite of mind and body, is compatible with God's having designed the union of the mind and body. To the extent that we are uncomfortable with traditional philosophical theology, we will have to hold these discussions—which seem to me to lie at the heart of the *Meditations*—at arm's length.

Second, and less obviously, lying in the immediate background to much of the *Meditations* is a general picture of human cognition, which Descartes set his face against and against which much of his argument takes shape. According to this picture, all human cognition arises out of sensation and remains essentially dependent on it. While this picture has an affinity with some modern versions of empiricism, it differs in certain fundamental ways that matter for understanding the *Meditations'* argument and for appreciating the originality of Descartes's position.[1]

For help with both these aspects of the intellectual setting of the *Meditations*, I have turned to Thomas Aquinas. Of course Descartes did not compose the *Meditations* with Thomas's *Summa Theologiae* in front of him; after all, almost five centuries separate the two thinkers. I believe, though, that broad lines of Thomistic Aristotelianism helped to shape Descartes's discussion and set the stage for much of his major philosophical innovation—more so than did other forms of Aristotelianism, or other traditions of thought. I assume (this is not controversial) that Descartes's Jesuit teachers at La Flèche gave him a good feel for Thomistic Aristotelianism, and (this may be more controversial) that that training provided him with something that functioned as a sort of standard view against which he developed his own philosophy, somewhat in the way that his own thought would provide Spinoza and Locke with a starting point for their philosophy (or that Locke would provide Berkeley with one). In the case of his account of the mind, Descartes self-consciously departed from what he learned at La Flèche in fundamental ways. There is, I think, more continuity between Descartes and Aquinas with respect to philosophical theology, but even here Descartes innovated in very significant ways—ways that are decisive for the subsequent rationalist tradition. Confronting Descartes's philosophical theology with that of Aquinas is made easier by the fact that Caterus, the Thomistically inclined author of the First Set of Objections, practically staged the confrontation for us.

My decision to focus on the text of the *Meditations* itself and to use Aquinas as the primary background for understanding Descartes's thought brings with it methodological limitations. For one thing, this commitment—the sustained reading of the text in light of Thomistic Aristotelianism—limits my ability to engage with the contemporary secondary literature. To be sure, there is a wealth of insightful and valuable literature on Descartes that touches on the aspects of the *Meditations* that I write about. However, most articles on Descartes are organized around themes or topics (e.g., Descartes's attitude toward substance, or his argument for the mind-body distinction, or his view of sensory qualities), and not around the text of the *Meditations*. Moreover, articles that are devoted to parts of that text—the First Meditation and the discussion of the piece of wax in the Second Meditation, for instance, have come in for much discussion over the years—are not concerned with working out the import of those parts against the context of a broadly speaking Thomistic Aristotelian outlook, nor do they aim to place them in the context of an overall, sustained reading of the *Meditations*. My engagement with the secondary literature is occasional because I did not see a way to treat it in a more consistent and systematic manner that would still allow me to work through Descartes's text continuously, in a direct and uncluttered way.[2]

My focus on Aquinas, to the neglect of scholastic authors much more contemporary to Descartes, will strike some as curious. I have not tried to take account of the many scholastic sources, both direct and indirect, that influenced (or may have influenced) Descartes's thought. In part, this is because I believe that Descartes was a truly revolutionary figure and that his originality can more readily be appreciated if one concentrates on certain fundamental themes (e.g., the place of the senses in human cognition, or certain framing commitments in philosophical theology and what sort of cognition of God is supposed to be available to us in this life) than if one focuses on more technical matters. While I do believe Descartes won the revolution he initiated, I don't think he gained the victory through hand-to-hand combat. Moreover, in my view, the most important payoff of contextualizing Descartes's thought would be a better *philosophical* understanding of that thought. Noting that others in the period held similar or different views, as the case may be, does not of itself take us very far toward that goal. If, for example, we discover that others held views like the one Descartes adopts, but we have no real sense of why they found those views philosophically attractive, then we have deferred rather than illuminated a question. Or if we learn that others held a position that differs from one that Descartes adopts, but we have no real sense of how that position hangs together philosophically, then our understanding of what the disagreement is really about is still deficient. So it has seemed more important to try to get a philosophical feel for a few especially central commitments in Thomistic Aristotelian thinking about cognition and philosophical theology than to canvass the many fascinating estuaries, tributaries, and streams that fed into Descartes's thought and which a more properly historical treatment of it would have taken account of.

In the remainder of this chapter, I first provide an overview of Descartes's main enduring innovation in philosophical theology. I then sketch a Thomistic theory of cognition that I believe serves as background for much of the argument of the *Meditations*. Descartes, as noted earlier, took himself to be making a clean break with the philosophical tradition he inherited, especially Thomistic Aristotelianism, and we will want to understand something about the position he is rejecting in order to appreciate what he is arguing about and how his argument is supposed to work. This will allow me to introduce some of the main ideas in my interpretation of the *Meditations*. I conclude with a brief account of a prevalent contemporary picture of Descartes's achievement that, in my view, gets us off on the wrong foot.

PHILOSOPHICAL THEOLOGY

Of special importance to Descartes, as he develops his novel account of mind, is our cognitive relation to God. Both of Descartes's arguments for the existence of God are based on the thought that we start out with some cognitive purchase on God's essence or nature, that is, some positive knowledge of what God is, as opposed to a merely negative and relative knowledge (e.g., as the first mover unmoved of the motion we see in the world). The need for such a starting position is more obvious in the case of the Fifth Meditation's argument, which requires that we have some grasp of God's nature (some grasp of *what* God is) that enables us to see that God's nature contains existence. But it is equally true of the Third Meditation's argument. The argument presented there, at bottom, is that we couldn't have the cognition of God that we have unless God had a direct role in bringing it about. Descartes holds this position, I will suggest, only because he thinks our cognition of God reaches to God's very essence or nature, and so goes much beyond what Aquinas thought was available to us in this life. As Aquinas would have been the first to agree, we could not arrive at cognition of what God is by abstracting from, and reasoning about, materials provided by the senses. Indeed, Descartes thinks (as he hints in the final paragraph of the Third Meditation) that our cognition of God in this life approaches the *visio dei* vouchsafed to the blessed in the next, a cognitive achievement that Aquinas believed requires special assistance from God.

Let me say something about the place of philosophical theology in Descartes's thought. Philosophical theology pervades the *Meditations*. As noted above, it is important not only for the Third and Fifth Meditations' discussions of God's existence but also for the Fourth's account of error and the Sixth's account of instinctual misfire; in any reasonable accounting, it takes up well over half of the work. Moreover, I believe Descartes's specific approach to philosophical theology, as well as the centrality that he gives it for metaphysics and epistemology, was decisive for the subsequent pre-Kantian rationalist tradition. This newfound centrality of philosophical theology to philosophy is, I believe, one of Descartes's principal legacies to his rationalist successors. Indeed, it is one of the primary ways by which the rationalist tradition differs from the empiricist tradition: Locke and Hume (Berkeley is an exception) assign a less central place to philosophical theology than do Descartes, Spinoza, and Leibniz. Let me explain.

There is a sense in which philosophical theology is more integral to Descartes's metaphysics and epistemology than it was to Aquinas's. For Aquinas there is a path that leads gradually from natural philosophy and metaphysics to natural theology, but one can, and indeed must, learn a considerable amount of philosophy before one is ready to take up natural theology.[3] For example, one needs to be familiar with Aristotelian ways of thinking about change, form, matter, and causation before one is ready to understand what is going on in the "Five Ways" (the five demonstrations of God's existence that Aquinas offers in the *Summa Theologiae*). By way of contrast, one can hardly take a step in the metaphysics and epistemology of Descartes (the Third Meditation, if not the First) before finding oneself knee-deep in philosophical theology. The same is true of the metaphysics and epistemology of his rationalist successors: consider, for example, Spinoza's doctrine that there is no substance besides God, or Malebranche's occasionalism, or Leibniz's theory of preestablished harmony. None of these philosophers think we can get very far in understanding the basic structure of the world and our place in it without theorizing about God.

Further, Spinoza's and Leibniz's ways of thinking about demonstrations of God's existence are closer to Descartes's arguments than to Aquinas's Aristotelian-style cosmological arguments; both seem to believe that we have the unproblematic access to God's essence or nature that Descartes thinks we have. This is so much the case that Kant—who did more than anyone else to sow the seeds of doubt about the viability of the rationalist project in philosophical theology—holds that even the rationalist cosmological (causal) arguments for the existence of God (which were current in his time) were really, at bottom, disguised ontological arguments. Part of what is going on here, of course, is that Aristotelian ways of thinking about causation are coming under significant pressure with the advent of the new science, and the Five Ways are deeply indebted to Aristotelian ways of thinking about causation. (The first two of the Five Ways are based on the Aristotelian efficient cause, and the remaining three are based on the material, formal, and final cause, respectively.) But there is something else that is going on here as well, I believe. Spinoza and Leibniz also share with Descartes the idea that our cognitive access to God, to God's essence or nature in particular, is much less complicated than thinkers in the high Aristotelian scholastic tradition took it to be.

Although Descartes's philosophical theology is important to the *Meditations*, and important to his influence on the subsequent rationalist tradition, it can be difficult to keep this aspect of his philosophy squarely in view. Philosophical theology is not an enterprise in which the larger philosophical culture, especially that found in the world of analytic philosophy, places a great deal of confidence these days. (I offer this as a general proposition; obviously there are exceptions.) Many scholars, working from their sense of what might be valuable and enduring in Descartes's thought, have not wanted to emphasize this side of it. To be sure, they haven't ignored his philosophical theology completely—his demonstrations of the existence of God and his doctrine of the creation of the eternal truths have received their share of attention over the years—but commentators have tended to work around these commitments where they felt they could, often contenting themselves with pointing out where this or that demonstration of God's existence fails or begs the question. Since we now seem to know that such a demonstration is doomed from the start—carrying it through would be like trisecting the angle—the serious questions that remain are along the lines of "Where is the fallacy?" or perhaps "How did such a great mind get taken in?" In our more humble moments, we realize that this cannot be the last word, and that there is something deserving of intellectual respect going on here, even if it is difficult to recover and we can no longer take it at face value (in the same way that many scholars find it difficult to take at face value Marxist philosophy or Freudian psychology but still find value and interest in these traditions).

In any event, because of the centrality of philosophical theology to the *Meditations*, one cannot attempt a serious reading of that text without engaging with this aspect of Descartes's thought. In order to recover

Descartes's philosophical theology, I have found myself leaning on the contextual background more at this juncture than elsewhere, drawing extensively on the Replies and Objections as well as on Aquinas himself. By doing so, at least we can become more sophisticated students of Descartes's thought. For example, although his second argument for the existence of God—based on the inability to hold oneself in existence from one moment to the next—is often viewed, both by Descartes's contemporaries and by modern scholars,[4] as little more than a reprise of one of Aquinas's cosmological arguments, this assessment seems superficial. The superficiality becomes apparent when one reflects that the causal principles that Aquinas employs lead to something *un*caused (an *un*moved mover or *un*caused cause), whereas Descartes's principles lead (much to Arnauld's chagrin) to something that supports itself in existence, that is, something *self*-caused rather than not caused. (Descartes's way of thinking about this matter seems to have influenced Spinoza, who characterizes God as *causa sui*.)

This difference seems to reflect a more fundamental difference between Descartes and Aquinas over how human beings come to have cognition about God. For Aquinas, we arrive at our conception of God by reflecting on natural processes in the world and reasoning about them. This path leads gradually to a first mover unmoved and, from there, to the idea of a being whose essence is its *esse*. For Descartes, our cognitive approach to God is more immediate. We begin not with the question "What, if anything, is ultimately responsible for the change and motion that we find around us?" but rather a question that is more overtly metaphysical, "What keeps me in existence from one moment to the next?" (or, for that matter, "What holds me in existence at the present moment?"). Descartes does not find it plausible that we could reach this sort of question using materials acquired from sensory experience; rather, he thinks our ability to understand and operate with such questions shows us that we already have in place a robust idea of God (an "innate idea" that makes available something of God's essence or nature).

AQUINAS ON HUMAN COGNITION

Aristotle famously writes in *De Anima* that the soul becomes, in a way, all things.[5] In the Aristotelian tradition, knowledge is a matter of the assimilation of the known by the knower. An Aristotelian account of knowledge sets out to characterize this relation between knower and known and to detail how that relationship came about. In order for one thing to know another, the knower must have something in common with the thing known. This commonality is understood in terms of formal identity: the knower assimilates a form of the thing that is known. In the case of human natural knowledge, this assimilation takes place through the cooperation of our lower, sensory faculties and higher, intellectual faculties. So, Aquinas holds, with respect to human cognition, *nihil est in intellectu nisi prius fuerit in sensu*, that is, nothing is in the intellect unless it was first in the senses. In particular, although cognizing universally is an immaterial process, it requires (in the case of human beings) the presence of corporeal images ("phantasms"), which come from *species* acquired by the senses. We abstract from these phantasms when we cognize universally.

On this theory, structure that is initially found in the world is imported into the soul through the senses, where it is refined and stored as phantasms in the imagination (which includes the memory). This material is further refined, through abstraction, into intellectual cognition. Put slightly more technically, our sensory faculties take in sensory forms (*sensible species*) from the world, which are further processed and stored in the imagination as phantasms. The intellect proceeds to refine this material by abstracting away from what belongs to the sensed things as individuals, pulling out what they have in common so as to arrive at something universal; when this happens, a second, intellectual form (*intelligible species*) is produced, thereby bringing about an intellectual assimilation (via the *intelligible species*) of known by knower. When one cognizes intellectually, one must "turn toward the phantasms" from which one is abstracting. We never, then, leave the phantasms behind in our intellectual cognition; they provide us with, as it were, our portal to the world. It is only through the possession of phantasms (and the species from which the phantasms come) that the soul (in this life, according to its natural mode of cognition) has access to truth or reality; the natural functioning of the human intellect is such that the intellect must employ these stored images in order to cognize truth or reality. Thus, if someone were to lose all of her phantasms, her intellect would lose its access to the world. She would not only be unable to remember and imagine particular things, she would also be unable to abstract, to cognize universally, to understand.

It is easy enough to see why someone might hold that it is impossible to cognize the natural world, that is, to do natural philosophy, which is about material things, without working with some structure acquired from the world through the senses. It is perhaps more difficult to see why someone would think that the same holds true of our knowledge of mathematics, which is not an overtly empirical discipline, and more difficult still to see why someone would think the same of our knowledge of immaterial things, such as God and our own intellect, which do not fall under the senses at all. So let's briefly review how Aquinas worked out this picture in the context of these three domains of cognition.

According to Aquinas, mathematics is concerned with intelligible matter. Intelligible matter is sensible matter considered only with the accident quantity. We conceive mathematical things, such as circles or triangles, by considering matter only under those accidents associated with the accident quantity; when we do so, we abstract[6] in particular from those accidents involving change and motion. Since the mathematician neglects change and efficient causation, her concern is much simpler and more tractable than that of the natural philosopher. On account of this, the mathematician is able to reason in an *a priori* manner, in the traditional sense of *a priori*, from cause to effect, that is, from definitions of various kinds of quantified matter to the consequences of those definitions, whereas the natural philosopher must reason in an *a posteriori* manner, from effects to causes, that is, from the sensible effects to the underlying essences or natures responsible for those effects. Notwithstanding this important methodological difference between mathematics and natural philosophy, the mathematician no less than the natural philosopher depends on the senses in order to receive forms from the world, which forms (when suitably refined) give her cognitive access to the object of her discipline, intelligible matter.[7]

The story with the knowledge of immaterial things is different. Since the human soul's acquisition of forms takes place through the senses, the natural object of human knowledge, that is, what human beings are by nature best suited to know, is sensible things. It does not follow, however, that human beings have no knowledge of immaterial things; it follows only that what knowledge they do have of immaterial things is more circuitous than the knowledge that they have of sensible, material things. This obliqueness is felt differently in the case of human knowledge of God from the way it is felt in the case of intellectual self-knowledge.[8]

According to Aquinas, the human mind cannot grasp the essence of God, that is, cannot grasp *what* God is. Rather, we are able to infer certain things about God, including that he exists. There are three principal routes to such knowledge, "by way of negation, by way of causality, and by way of transcendence" (*In Boetium de Trinitate* Q. 6, A. 3). We know, for example, that God exists, that he is the first cause of all bodies "by way of causality," that he is immaterial, that is, not a body "by way of negation," and that he is more perfect than any body "by way of transcendence." The point of departure for each of these paths is our knowledge of body; hence, our knowledge of divinity works through images acquired from sensory experience.[9] Now, the dependence of human knowledge of God on the senses envisioned here is not simply genetic: the human intellect understands God *through* the images that enable it to understand body. When we understand, we must always turn to the phantasms that contain structure imported from the world. So, for example, if a human being were to lose her phantasms, she would lose her cognitive access to the nature of body; and if she lost that, she would also lose her conception of God as a being that causes bodies, is not a body, and transcends body. This is why Aquinas compares the way images ground human knowledge to the way the principles of demonstration ground "the whole process of science."[10]

Intellectual self-knowledge also presents a difficult challenge to the principle *nihil est in intellectu nisi prius fuerit in sensu*. How can it be that likenesses obtained from the senses are relevant to our understanding of our own intellect? Indeed, it might seem that the intellect is specially aware of itself in a way that ought to suffice for intellectual self-knowledge. Aquinas responds to such concerns by maintaining that, since in general a power is understood through its activity and "in this life our intellect has material and sensible things for its proper natural object," the intellect "understands itself according as it is made actual by the species abstracted from sensible things" (ST I, Q. 87, A. 1). Now, when the intellect is made actual through the acquisition of intelligible species abstracted from sensible phantasms, it comes to know itself in two ways, first, "singularly," as "when Socrates or Plato perceives that he has an intellectual soul because he perceives that he understands," and second, "universally," as "when we consider the nature of the human mind from the act of the intellect [*ex actu intellectus*]." Aquinas goes on to note that while "the mere presence of the mind suffices for the first" sort of self-knowledge, the second is more difficult, requiring "a careful and subtle inquiry." Aquinas outlines this "careful and subtle inquiry" in his treatment of a similar question in *De Veritate*:

> Hence, our mind cannot so understand itself that it immediately apprehends itself. Rather, it comes to a knowledge of itself through apprehension of other things, just as the nature of the first matter is known from its receptivity for forms of a certain kind. This becomes apparent when we look at the manner in which philosophers have investigated the nature of the soul.
>
> For, from the fact that the human soul knows the universal natures of things, they have perceived that the species by which we understand is immaterial. Otherwise, it would be individuated and so would not lead to knowledge of the universal. From the immateriality of the species by which we understand, philosophers have understood that the intellect is a thing independent of matter. And from this they have proceeded to a knowledge of the other properties of the intellective soul. (DV Q. 10, A. 8)[11]

We understand the intellect to be that faculty which knows the universal natures of material things. This understanding of the intellect serves as the basis for our knowledge of other properties of the intellect, such as its independence of matter and its incorruptibility. As our knowledge that the intellect is a faculty that knows the universal nature of material things depends on the senses, so too does the entire edifice of intellectual self-knowledge.

In Aquinas's view, what is distinctive of human—as opposed to (non-human) animal—cognition is our ability to understand. Aquinas saw understanding as fundamentally a matter of cognizing universally: we, unlike (the other) animals, are able to grasp the universal nature *cow*, and not merely this cow or that cow; similarly, we, unlike animals, are responsive to good in general, and not merely this good or that good. Further, according to Aquinas, cognizing universally is an immaterial process, taking place in an immaterial subject, the human intellect. The human intellect does not have a location in the body in the way that our faculty of digestion or faculty of vision does. It is in virtue of its possession of this immaterial power that the human soul can, according to Aquinas, survive the dissolution of its body.

To be clear, the preceding concerns Aquinas's views on the human intellect's *natural* functioning. There are other modes of cognition open to the human intellect that take it beyond its nature in certain respects. One, available to every human intellect between death and bodily resurrection, involves the infusion of special species or likenesses by God. Without the body, the intellect would not have phantasms from which to abstract; so if the intellect is to be able to function at all in this condition, it must receive some assistance from above. Over the course of his career, Aquinas changed his view from regarding this mode of cognition as in some way preferable to the human intellect's natural mode of cognition (because it is similar to that enjoyed by higher, purely intellectual beings) to regarding it as second best, a sort of stopgap (because it is unsuited to the human intellect, which is not powerful enough to make good use of the infused species).[12] And a second mode of cognition beyond our natural function is available only to the blessed; this requires the special strengthening of the created intellect by God's divine light ("the light of glory").

These qualifications aside, however, the nature of the human intellect is to understand truth or reality only by abstracting from phantasms, originally acquired through senses; and the intellect must turn to these phantasms whenever it functions according to its natural mode of operation. Although it is sometimes thought that Aquinas's allowing for the soul to have some cognition without the body brings his position close to Descartes's in certain ways, it is Aquinas's account of the intellect's natural mode of cognition that I believe matters most for our understanding of the *Meditations*, since that is a work about the natural functioning of the human mind.

It is worth pausing to consider the sense in which Aquinas's account of human cognition counts as a philosophical account of human knowledge. It is not (directly) an account of how our beliefs or knowledge claims are justified, although it may have consequences for this. Nor is it an *a priori* "first philosophy"—quite clearly Aquinas's theory is available only after we have learned quite a bit about the world. But it is an explanation of how human cognition is related to reality, and in particular, how reality is given to human cognition. As such, the account sets limits to human cognition: for example, since the essence of God cannot be recovered from God's sensible effects, the account tells us we cannot (in this life) grasp God's essence.

As an account of the various ways in which reality is given to our cognition, Aquinas's account, it seems to me, stands in a line with accounts offered by Locke and Kant. They, too, were interested in how the world and its structure is made available to our cognition, and thought that careful reflection on this topic served to show our cognitive limits. Locke, for example, argued that materials for human cognition come through experience (sensation and reflection) and that these materials simply do not provide the human mind with the wherewithal to address many metaphysical questions (e.g., Can matter think? What is the nature of substance?). Kant argued that objects are given to the human mind only through (sensible) intuition, and this fact dooms the rationalist's metaphysical project. Neither Aquinas nor Locke, nor for that matter Descartes, has, of course, a Kantian conception of an object, but they do ask to what extent the world's "structure" (form, essence, nature) is given to us, and they connect this question to a general theory of how such structure is given to our thought. I find it sometimes useful to place Aquinas's account of cognition, along with Descartes's nativist alternative, in a line of philosophical reflection that includes Locke's and Kant's theories, the very obvious and significant philosophical differences among them notwithstanding, in order to help draw out the philosophical character of the former.

Now, Descartes parts company with Aquinas in a very fundamental way over the question of how structure is given to human cognition. He holds that the mind does not depend on the senses for its access to reality, but rather is naturally endowed by God with such access. This break brings with it a new understanding of the relation between intellectual and sensory cognition (as clear and distinct versus obscure and confused), of the relation between the intellect (the "mind alone") and body. It also brings with it a new, fundamental characterization of the mind according to which what is fundamental is not the ability to cognize universally (to abstract universals) but to see that something is true (to make judgments).[13]

As the story of the cogito being unfolds, it quickly emerges that its connection to the truth or reality that it cognizes does not depend on the senses, phantasms, or the body. Thus, early in the Second Meditation, immediately after establishing that the cogito being's essence is to think, Descartes warns the meditator against using the imagination in her attempt to understand better the nature of the cogito being (II.¶7). Later in that meditation, in the well-known discussion of a piece of wax, he argues that the cogito being's grasp of what an extended thing is outstrips what the cogito being can imagine or sense. In that discussion, understanding the piece of wax turns out to be a matter of using one's mental vision to penetrate to the wax's deep structure—of "distinguish[ing] the wax from its outward forms and, as it were, strip it and consider it naked" (II.¶14; 7:32; 2:22)—rather than of pulling out some common nature. On this telling, the distinguishing mark of human cognition is not the ability to cognize universally. As the *Meditations* continues, we come to see that we have a sort of cognitive access to God that even Aquinas would have agreed could not have come from corporeal phantasms (as noted in our discussion of philosophical theology, the demonstrations of God's existence in the Third and Fifth Meditations rest on this). Finally, Descartes claims, near the beginning of the Fifth Meditation, that our geometrical cognition does not depend on our having acquired from the senses ideas of the figures that we make judgments about; and, near the beginning of the Sixth Meditation, that we can draw conclusions about figures that cannot be perspicuously represented by our imagination.

Because the cogito being does not depend on its lower, corporeal faculties—sense and imagination—for its access to truth and reality, it is, by its nature, less wedded to its body than the human intellect is on Aquinas's theory. This, it seems to me, is the fulcrum for Descartes's well-known claim that the mind and body are metaphysically independent of one another, that is, two "really distinct" beings. The cogito being (the mind) does not require the body in order to function according to its natural mode of operation, and so body does not enter (even obliquely) into an account of its essence or nature. So, in Descartes's view, the human mind depends less on the body than Aquinas thought.[14]

Descartes holds that the converse is true as well—the body depends less on the mind—in the following sense. According to Aquinas, the human soul (which includes the intellectual soul) is related to the human body as substantial form is to matter. Now, in order for matter to exist, it must be actualized by form; so, on Aquinas's theory, the human body is made actual by the human soul. In contrast, Descartes understands the physical world—*res extensa*—as consisting of a fluidlike plenum, extending indefinitely in all directions. Individual bodies are mechanisms holding the status of relatively stable patterns of motion within this plenum, roughly analogous to a tornado or the jet stream, although often more enduring and, especially in the case of plants and animals, much more complex. The plenum is self-sufficient; it does not require form in order to exist. The same is true of the various individual mechanistic systems within the plenum: they are not actualized by form. So, in particular, in Descartes's view, the systems of matter that count as human bodies are not "actualized" by human minds (even if it is the case that for those systems to count as human bodies, they must be united to human minds). Thus, Descartes finds himself faced with the task of positioning (what would be from the point of view of his Thomistic education) two new entities, an autonomous mind and a self-sufficient mechanistic system, vis-à-vis each other. Although metaphysically independent, these beings are somehow intimately related. Articulating their relationship is an important task of the Sixth Meditation.[15]

Even though Descartes breaks with Aquinas over the doctrine of abstraction, there remains an important continuity between his way of thinking about cognition and Aquinas's. This point of continuity has to do with the tricky subject of how "intentionality" plays out within Descartes's philosophy, and the little I have to say on this topic revolves around it.

In the Aristotelian tradition, cognition is understood as the existence of some mind-independent structure, form, in the soul. There has to be form (or nature or essence) first before there can be form (or nature or essence) in the soul. Whether this form, nature, or essence exists in the world, whether it exists in the mind of God, or whether it has some other "ontological status" (perhaps as the effect of some decrees that God makes) does not matter for the point I am making here, which is that whatever its ontological status, human cognition involves form or structure, which is independent of and prior to the soul, coming to exist in the soul.

Now, it might be thought that Descartes, perhaps through his theory of innate ideas, takes a step away from this picture of human cognition toward Kant, where basic forms of human thought are not essentially dependent on an objective order or reality from which they are taken but rather are used to generate such an order or reality. Such an interpretation is encouraged by Descartes's use of skeptical doubt, which can make it seem as if my ideas depend only on me, without any other metaphysical presuppositions (at least if we drop well-placed scruples about sliding from my certainty that I am having an idea while in doubt about other things to an account of the nature of the idea).

Nevertheless, it seems clear to me that Descartes is, on this point, still thinking of cognition in a more or less traditional way. A point that Aquinas makes when treating the cognition of God is that the Latin *forma* is the term traditionally used to translate the Greek *idea*.[16] So the term *idea* carries with it overtones of a thing's structure. I believe that this overtone continues with Descartes, so that for him, too, an idea is some form or structure—some "reality"—existing objectively in the mind (hence Descartes denies that the idea of nothing is an idea in the proper sense [5:153; 3:338]). As with his scholastic predecessors, that structure is prior to my cognition at least to the extent that it "determines" my cognition (and not the other way around). So, in his discussion of true and immutable natures in the Fifth Meditation, Descartes writes concerning his cognition of a triangle that "even if perhaps no such figure exists, or has ever existed, anywhere outside my thought, there is still a determinate nature, or essence, or form of the triangle which is immutable and eternal, and not invented by me or dependent on my mind" (V.¶5; 7:64; 2:45). This is in line with the explanation of objective reality Descartes gives to Caterus in the First Replies (7:102; 2:75), where he writes as if there is some single thing—the sun—with two modes of existence (in a way that suggests that the sun is prior to the modes of existence rather than posterior to them, as it would be if, for example, it were extracted from what the two modes of existence have in common).[17] Descartes's (and Aquinas's) outlook may run against the grain of a modern tendency to think of ideas as primary and the "objective order" as (co-?)dependent on the ideas. However, the general thought that the objective order is somehow built up out of our ideas, as opposed to the position that an idea is a trace or image of a prior objective order coming to exist in us, seems to me to belong to a later moment in the history of philosophy. Perhaps this general thought occurs in one way in an empiricist like Hume (who seems to disavow any important distinction between an idea and its object) and in a very different way in Kant. But for Descartes, as for the Aristotelian tradition, ideas are best thought of as vehicles through which some reality or structure (i.e., some "nature, or essence, or form") comes to exist in the mind and is made available to cognition: since the idea of a triangle is just the true and immutable nature of triangle existing objectively within me, without the true and immutable nature (or essence or form) of triangle there could be no idea (or essence or form) of triangle.

Now, one might agree with what I have just claimed with respect to intellectual ideas but harbor doubts about whether this could be right about sensory ideas. Perhaps, for Descartes, sensory ideas are brute ("arbitrary") effects of the physical world on the mind, and not structures imported from the physical world into the mind (his attack on the Aristotelian claim that sensory ideas "resemble" their objects might seem to point in this direction, toward a "brute effect" view). However, I think it is the same story with sensory ideas.[18] They, too, involve the existence of structure (presumably some corporeal configuration) in the mind. What Descartes says about sensory ideas is that the structure (the "reality") that is found objectively in them is obscure and confused. This vocabulary is easily understood if we think of sensory ideas as depositing structure into the mind: the point would be that while they deposit structure, they do so in such a way that it is made available only obscurely and confusedly. By way of contrast, this vocabulary is harder to understand (as Locke in effect noted) if we think of sensory ideas as brute impingements of the physical world on the mind. On that model, vocabulary like "obscure and confused" seems out of place, inasmuch as it is hard to understand what it would be for a brute impingement to be either clear or obscure, either distinct or confused. Soon enough the philosophical tradition will move away from thinking of the difference between sensation and intellection in terms of (what Kant will term) the "logical" difference between clarity and distinctness, on the one hand, and obscurity and confusedness, on the other, to making a distinction based on the genesis or origin of the idea—but that, too, is a subsequent development. (One can raise questions about defective ideas, e.g., materially false ideas; even these, I think, should be measured against a paradigm of an idea as an imported reality.)[19]

The view I am attributing to Descartes clashes with a picture of him as a certain sort of epistemologist.[20] Many are accustomed to thinking of a Cartesian idea as consisting of precisely whatever is made available to the mind (perhaps after some careful attention) for the purposes of reflectively grounding our beliefs, so that the structure found in an idea is exhausted by whatever can be brought to explicit awareness. Sensory ideas come to be, as it were, the epistemological surfaces of a thing. This makes difficult the thought, at least suggested by language like "obscure" and "confused," that sensory ideas should have a metaphysical backside,[21] that is, contain some additional structure we cannot get at by contemplating the idea because that structure is present in the idea only obscurely or confusedly. Indeed, many find it natural to think that one of the primary purposes of the First Meditation's skeptical doubt is to teach us how to lift these epistemological surfaces off of bodies. I don't think Descartes was interested in these epistemological surfaces. To be sure, there are things he says that could be read as espousing such a view, but quite a bit of what he says, at least if taken at face value, runs against the grain of such a view. Certainly his basic cognitive framework, where ideas are realities existing objectively, and a sensory idea is confused and obscure, does not encourage the view that ideas, by their nature, must be epistemically transparent in such a way that an idea cannot contain more than meets (or can meet) the eye, so to speak. (For example, if my sensory idea of white is a certain surface texture existing in a confused manner in my mind, then it seems that the idea contains more structure than I have access to.) Further, one does not find in his writings the sort of developed theory of these surfaces and their relation to the objects to which they belong that one would hope for if he were advancing such a position. And what is perhaps most important, none of his major undertakings in the *Meditations* has much, if anything, to do with these epistemological surfaces (by his major undertakings, I have in mind providing an account of the nature of the human mind, its origin, its relation to truth or reality, and the truth or reality to which it is related). Things run more smoothly if we do not read Descartes as an epistemological-surface theorist and instead see him as sharing with his scholastic predecessors the basic tenet that cognition involves a common reality, form, or structure existing both in the mind ("objectively") and in the world ("formally"), even at the level of sensory cognition.

A Familiar View of Descartes's Conception of the Mind

The picture of Descartes as working with epistemological surfaces is, of course, part of a larger conception of him as a certain sort of epistemologist; this conception has, to my mind, often obscured Descartes's own philosophical agenda.

The First Meditation has been looked to as a *locus classicus* for questions of skepticism, knowledge, and certainty, topics that have been of considerable interest to philosophers in the twentieth and twenty-first centuries. It is credited for moving these questions to the center of philosophy, and for raising in a particularly forceful way, and perhaps for the first time in its full generality, the question, Can I really know that there *is* an external world? Notice that this focus already subtly directs our attention away from Descartes's ambitious substantive metaphysics. For example, if I have trouble knowing that there is a table in front of me, it seems a tall order to know what the essence of the mind is or whether God exists. Apparently he let his guard down somewhere along the line, and now the task becomes to figure out where.

Moreover, readers have sometimes taken Descartes's characterization of the mind to fall more or less directly out of the First Meditation's external-world skepticism. The mind and its states reach as far as, but no farther than, what is left unchallenged by the dreaming doubt—the epistemological surfaces just alluded to. So, for example, I can use the dreaming doubt (or some suitably similar device) to factor those aspects of my current encounter with the keyboard I take to be under my fingers into two metaphysically independent components, one that belongs to the mind and one that belongs to the physical world: I think to myself, "I see and feel a keyboard in front of me." But what if I were dreaming or hallucinating (or whatever)? Well, in any case, there are "keyboard ideas" or "keyboard experiences" (or "keyboard sense data"?) of which I am indisputably aware, even if it should turn out that there is no keyboard (or, for that matter, no external world). These epistemological surfaces, be they "keyboard ideas" or "keyboard experiences" or whatnot, belong to the mind; and the mind is, fundamentally, the locus of such conscious "states" (to use a word that Descartes does not himself use), which states are sufficiently distinct from body that they could occur in me if I had no body.

This view is naturally combined with two other positions. First, when I sense, say, a red truck, what I am in immediate epistemic contact with is not the physical truck but instead certain mental items, for example, red sensory ideas, which stand in some special (usually causal in nature) relation with the truck. In other words, I start my cognitive life from behind a veil of sensory perception, and must find a means of arguing my way out, to an external physical world. Second, consciousness is the distinguishing feature of the mind: my mind extends as far as my certainty, in the face of a doubt based on the idea that I might, for all I know, be dreaming or hallucinating, and that certainty extends only to that of which I am consciously aware (the "keyboard ideas" or "keyboard experiences"). Thus, when Descartes says that the essence of the mind is to think, what he really means is that the essence of the mind is to be conscious, and that the mind is fundamentally the seat of consciousness, the subject of my conscious states—that is, those states which I can know that I am having even while assuming that I am dreaming or hallucinating.

Obviously the foregoing is not a very carefully developed or complete account, but I hope it is familiar. In calling the view familiar, I do not mean to imply that it represents a consensus among Descartes scholars today. Indeed, many have begun to wonder about the place of consciousness in Descartes's conception of mind, especially as he presents it in the *Meditations*.[22] And there are very able Descartes scholars on both sides (and, I think, in the middle) of the question of whether he was committed to a veil of ideas.[23] Still, this picture of Descartes has enough currency within a wider philosophical audience that I think it is not misleading to call it the familiar view.

I have not found that the familiar view is something that emerges from a patient consideration of the text. Nor have I found it a useful guide to bring to the text in order to illuminate it. It leaves too much of what is going on (for example, most of the philosophical theology mentioned earlier) out of the picture and, to my mind, where the view is supposed to apply, does too little to motivate the very substantive philosophical claims that Descartes is depicted as advancing. More often than not, these claims and the reasoning on which they rest turn out to be "instructive mistakes." This feeling can be traced back to the fact that so little of the familiar view is explicitly worked out (rather than simply assumed or presupposed) in the text of the *Meditations*. If the point of the *Meditations* is to advance the familiar view, Descartes has left most of the important philosophical work to the reader.[24] So, for the most part, I have ignored the familiar view, as distracting us from the concerns that, it seems to me, Descartes is plainly and centrally advancing and developing in the text.

I have not been able to ignore the familiar view completely, however. Although I think it mostly false, it is not obviously so. Indeed, it is hard not to bring the familiar view to the text and to suppose that Descartes held some such view in the back of his mind when he wrote the *Meditations*, even if it is very difficult to read his text as the working out of such a view. And, I agree, there are some things that Descartes says along the way that (at least on their face) encourage the idea that he held some of the commitments attributed to him by the familiar view. To mention three examples: First, Descartes makes a remark in the Second Meditation about the senses that has suggested to many that he factors sensation into mental and physical components and identifies sensation with the mental side, treating the physical side as not essential to the activity (II.¶9). Second, when he does this, he seems to be using consciousness (or indubitability under external-world skepticism) as a criterion of the mental, thus lending support to the view that he identifies the essence of mind with consciousness. Finally, the fact that Descartes sees a need to prove that bodies exist, coupled with a comment he makes in the Sixth Meditation about what he regards as the proper object of the senses (III.¶6), can be taken as evidence that he embraces some sort of "veil of ideas" theory of perception.[25] We will examine all of this later *in situ*, but I would like to indicate here in a general way why these moments don't seem to me to go very far toward showing that Descartes held the familiar view. (When treating issues connected with the familiar view, I am sometimes more resolute than I perhaps should be, giving the impression that the rejection of the familiar view is a considered commitment on Descartes's part. It seems to me, rather, that for the most part it is not on his radar screen, which, I must admit, makes it unclear exactly what he would want to say if confronted with a question such as "Do you mean to say that we could sense even if we had no bodies?" or "Do you mean to say that we perceive only ideas 'directly' and not bodies or their qualities?")

Let's begin with consciousness. Consciousness is probably at some level important to Descartes's conception of the mind, even if this importance is not especially emphasized in the *Meditations*. (The Latin word for consciousness, *conscius*, appears only once in the *Meditations*. Other cognitive terminology—for example, *cognoscere* and *cognitio*—can carry connotations of consciousness or awareness, but as Descartes does not draw explicit attention to such connotations, it is hard to know to what extent he means to be invoking them.)[26] But what is important here is that if consciousness does enter into Descartes's account of mind, it does not lie at the heart of it. Rather, what is fundamental is the ability *to see that something is so*, to make judgments and (at times) to know the truth, to penetrate beneath the surface of things to the underlying structure. Consciousness enters the picture (to the extent that it does) through its connection with these activities: Descartes understands seeing that something is so as paradigmatically an occurrent, conscious activity, which is why he thinks that we can be conscious of the mind's exercise of its powers; and, conversely, when we are conscious of the exercise of a power, as when we sense or imagine, that activity becomes available to assist us in our judgments, and so the relevant power, at least to that extent, belongs to the mind.

This is what, I think, leads Descartes to associate the mental with the conscious and, in some settings, to use consciousness (or indubitability under external-world skepticism) as a sort of criterion by which to distinguish between those aspects of a given complex activity (especially sensing) that belong to the mind and those aspects that do not (which usually belong instead to the body). But—and this seems to me important—when Descartes uses consciousness (or indubitability under external-world skepticism) in this way, he is employing the criterion to settle the question of the relationship between the different (i.e., mental, corporeal) aspects of the activity to one another, or their relation to the larger activity itself. In particular, I do not see him as implying that the aspect of sensing singled out by consciousness or indubitability—the mental aspect—could somehow exist in reality without the rest of the package. Nothing along these lines would follow from the fact that, even under external-world skepticism, I am certain about the mental aspects that have occurred but uncertain whether the corporeal aspects have occurred. Indeed, for him to have to assume that this did follow—that is, that because I can be certain that mental aspects associated with sensation have taken place while I am in doubt about whether there have been any corporeal goings-on in the universe, it follows that the mental aspects could take place without any corporeal goings-on—would be for Descartes to make, at the level of sensation, a mistake that he has often been (unfairly) accused of making when he argues that the mind can exist without the body. In the latter case, he is often accused of inferring that my mind can exist without my body from the fact that I can be certain that my mind exists while I am in doubt that my body exists; in the case of sensation, he would be arguing that sensing, or the mental aspects of sensing, can exist without body because I can be certain that sensing, or the mental aspects of sensing, is going on while I am in doubt that my body exists. Neither argument, as it stands, seems very compelling, and I do not believe that Descartes offers either of them. In the case of mind and body, he does hold the conclusion (i.e., that the mind can exist without the body), but offers a different argument for it (roughly, that the mind does not need corporeal phantasms in order to function successfully cognitively, in order to make true judgments about reality). In the case of sensation, I do not think Descartes even holds the conclusion (i.e., that beings without bodies can have sensory ideas).

Rather, when Descartes uses consciousness (or indubitability) as a criterion to show that sensation, or some aspect of it, belongs to the mind, I think his point is that I can see beyond doubt that there is something going on in me that is at least in the vicinity of sensation—call this something that is going on, as Descartes himself sometimes does, "as it were sensing"; exactly what it is awaits a fuller account. So, for example, I can tell that there is something going on in me right now—call it "seeming to see a keyboard" or "as it were seeing a keyboard"—even while, under the spell of the First Meditation, I find myself doubting that keyboards exist (or that I have a body). But under these circumstances, I would have only a very partial view of this "seeming to see." A fuller characterization of what this seeing is, including an account of the place of body in seeing, awaits a more complete view of the situation.[27]

Finally, I don't read Descartes as holding that I am (immediately) aware only of my sensory ideas and only subsequently (and perhaps indirectly) aware of bodies or their qualities. (To be sure, the ground here is difficult because of the variety of things that philosophers have wanted to mean by "immediately," "subsequently," and "indirectly.")[28] Part of my reason for thinking this is based on the scholastic picture of cognition sketched above. On that picture, I become cognizant of the red in a body simply by having the form of red exist in me (in some "cognitive" or "spiritual" or "objective" mode of existence); in order to sense a body, I don't need to first direct my attention to some mode of the mind. In other words, what a sensory idea does is to make me (immediately) cognizant of, aware of, or conscious of a quality in a body, some physical structure in the keyboard.

But, one might object, if this is so, why does Descartes feel obliged to offer an argument for the existence of body? Wouldn't it suffice to show that one has a sensory idea, coupled with the thesis that sensory ideas function so as to import reality transmitted from currently existing bodies, and be done with it? Well, before the argument for the existence of body, the meditator does not know what sensory ideas do, how they function; she does not know that her possession of a sensory idea makes her cognizant of something existing in a body. She has her suspicions, of course. So we might put it thus: before the argument she does not know that sensory ideas function in the way she suspects they do, in the way she finds herself naturally inclined to believe they do. And the point of the argument is simply to show that sensory ideas *do* function more or less in the way she naturally (i.e., has "a great propensity to") thinks they function. The argument (as I understand it) is not intended to get us from a realm of inner mental objects ("sensory ideas") to some other realm of outer, physical objects ("bodies"); rather, it is to confirm our instinctive feeling that we have been receiving information ("directly") from outer objects, bodies, all along.

Some will, no doubt, disagree with my tendency to distance Descartes from the familiar view. For much of what follows, it will not matter very much, because the familiar view seems to be more in the line of something that one might bring to the text in order to attempt to illuminate it, rather than something that emerges from the text. As things turn out, we can make much headway in understanding the text without becoming very involved with the familiar view.

→ 1 ←

The First Meditation

THE FIRST MEDITATION consists of twelve paragraphs. In ¶¶1–2, Descartes introduces the metaphor that knowledge has "foundations." In the first sentence of ¶3, he presents a putative candidate for the foundations of knowledge, and immediately proceeds to criticize it; that criticism culminates in the dreaming doubt (¶5). At this juncture the discussion seems to take a detour, and Descartes presents an extended comparison between thought and painting (¶¶6–8). That discussion (somehow) brings the meditator to a second doubt (¶¶9–10), the evil-genius doubt or, as I will sometimes call it, the imperfect-nature doubt. In the concluding paragraphs of the meditation (¶¶11–12), Descartes describes how the meditator should conduct herself epistemically over the immediate course of the subsequent meditations.

In what follows, I will try to explain how what seem to me to be the central moments of the First Meditation—(1) the targeting of the foundations, (2) the dreaming doubt, (3) the extended comparison between thought and painting, and, finally, (4) the evil-genius doubt—hang together to form a continuous discussion. In my view, many accounts of the First Meditation fail to do justice to this continuity, often breaking down around (3), the comparison between thought and painting, just where, it seems to me, the discussion is gathering steam. When I say break down, I do not mean that commentators are unable to offer readings of this obscure discussion that are consistent with their overall take on what is happening in the First Meditation. Rather, their readings do not explain how this moment in the discussion advances an overall argument. That is, they lose hold of the continuous thread of argument running from the foundations and the dreaming doubt through these three paragraphs (¶¶6–8) and ultimately to the evil-genius doubt.

¶¶1–3. FOUNDATIONS OF KNOWLEDGE

The first sentence of the *Meditations* reads, "Some years ago I was struck by the large number of falsehoods that I had accepted as true in my childhood, and by the highly doubtful nature of the whole edifice that I had subsequently based on them" (7:17; 2:12). Although the *Meditations* is written in the first person, it is often convenient to distinguish two points of view, or two personae, a narrator or person guiding the meditation and a reader or person following the guide's directions. It is convenient to refer to the narrator as Descartes (even though this can be misleading because the *Meditations* is not a work of autobiography) and to refer to the reader as the meditator. I usually use the feminine pronoun to refer to the meditator, because this provides an easy means of distinguishing between the point of view of the person undergoing the meditation and that of the person leading the meditation.

In the first paragraph, Descartes attempts to provide a motivation for the project that he is about to ask the meditator to undertake. I do not believe he expects this motivation to be fully available to the meditator.[1] It seems unlikely that he expects most of his readers to recognize themselves in the description given in the first sentence; that is, it seems unlikely that he expects most of them to have been struck by the large number of falsehoods that they have accepted since childhood or by the doubtful nature of the edifice that they subsequently based on those falsehoods. Indeed, he does not give any examples of these falsehoods, leaving that instead to the meditator's imagination.

It is not obvious that this presents a problem for Descartes's way of proceeding, because it is not obvious that the motivation for undertaking the *Meditations* needs to be fully available to the meditator, especially at the beginning. Perhaps it is enough that her curiosity is piqued. What is clear, I think, is that in any case the project of the *Meditations* presupposes a good deal of cooperation on the part of the meditator.[2] Externally, this comes out in Descartes's indications in his other writings that he does not think he can make progress with a certain sort of stubborn reader (see 7:159). Internally, it comes out in some of the language he uses surrounding skeptical doubt, in particular in his frequent use of first-person resolutions to quasi-imperative effect, as in these examples from the last three paragraphs of the First Meditation:

> So in the future I must withhold my assent from these former beliefs just as carefully as I would from obvious false things, if I want to discover any certainty. (¶10; 7:21–22; 2:15)

> But it is not enough merely to have noticed this; I must make an effort to remember it. . . . In view of this, I think it will be a good plan to turn my will in completely the opposite direction and deceive myself, by pretending that these former opinions are utterly false and imaginary. (¶11; 7:22; 2:15)

I will suppose therefore that not God, who is supremely good and the source of truth, but rather some malicious demon of the utmost power and cunning has employed all his energies in order to deceive me. I shall think that the sky, the air, the earth, colours, shapes, sounds and all external things are the delusions of dreams which he has devised to ensnare my judgement. I shall consider myself as not having hands or eyes, or flesh, or blood, or senses, but as falsely believing that I have all these things. I shall stubbornly and firmly persist in this meditation. (¶12; 7:22–23; 2:15)

Quasi-imperative resolutions of this sort also appear at the beginning of the Second Meditation (II.¶3) and the Third Meditation (III.¶1). (Apparently Descartes thinks that the meditator has made sufficient progress by the Fourth Meditation that it is no longer necessary to issue such instructions [see IV.¶1].)

The skeptical considerations that Descartes is about to present not only embody arguments that need to be addressed, then, but also provide the basis for instructions to be followed. I believe this speaks to the meditator's motivation in taking them up. She is, I think, to a certain extent, especially at the beginning, simply trusting the narrator (that is, the agent issuing the quasi-imperatives or making the resolutions—whom I'm referring to as Descartes), following his instructions, and supposing that if she complies with them she too will find that she has accepted a number of falsehoods since childhood and built a doubtful edifice on the basis of them.

In order for the exercise to work, however, the meditator must at least find the skeptical instructions intelligible, and here, it seems to me, there is a *prima facie* difficulty, having to do not with the inducement of coming to discover that one has been in some fundamental way in error, but rather with the suggestion that one's beliefs have a "foundation." It is important that the meditator *already* be able to recognize herself in that description, because shortly she will be asked to cast all of her beliefs into doubt by overturning this foundation. If she does not know what to make of the suggestion that her beliefs have a foundation, it will be difficult for her to follow Descartes's instructions. Let me elaborate.

The foundational imagery is pronounced in the first two paragraphs:

Some years ago I was struck by the large number of falsehoods that I had accepted as true in my childhood, and by the highly doubtful nature of what I had subsequently erected [*superextruxi*] upon them. I realized that it was necessary, once in the course of my life, to overthrow [*evertenda*] everything completely and start again right from the foundations [*fundamentis*]. . . . I am here quite alone, and at least I will devote myself sincerely and without reservation to the overthrow [*eversione*] of all my opinions. (¶1; 7:17; 2:12)

> Once the foundations [*fundamentis*] of a building are undermined [*suffo-sis*], anything built on [*superaedificatum*] them collapses of its own accord; so I will go straight for the basic principles on which all my former beliefs rested. (¶2; 7:18; 2:12)

Now, what is the meditator to make of this foundational metaphor? It is not obvious—is it?—that it is part of a naive, ordinary conception of our cognition that our beliefs or opinions have foundations. Nor is it clear, for that matter, what a more sophisticated Aristotelian scholastic would make of this suggestion. Yet, as I have just said, it is important for the meditator, already in her current position, to be able to see her beliefs as having a foundation, because if what Descartes is asking her to do is to work, she must think that there are basic principles such that if they were "undermined," everything would fall with them. To make matters worse, Descartes suggests that all of her beliefs rest on only one foundational principle. In the next paragraph, he provides the following as the apparently sole principle:

> Whatever I have up till now accepted as most true I have acquired either from the senses or through senses. (¶3; 7:18; 2:12)

So the meditator has to be able somehow to see all of her beliefs as resting on this principle. But how?

We might start by considering what, in Descartes's view, the foundations of knowledge (correctly understood) look like. According to Descartes, the foundations are what we might call the metaphysical underpinnings of cognition; they provide an account of my place as a cognizer within the universe that I cognize. These foundations include the fact that insofar as I am a cognitive being, I have been created by God in such a way that everything that I clearly perceive is true. They also include the fact that my primary cognitive relation to truth or reality runs directly from my intellect to the world (circumventing the senses): Two of the ideas that afford me clear and distinct perception, my ideas of the self and God, are purely intellectual and innate (i.e., not acquired from the senses); and my most distinct cognition of any particular body contains a purely intellectual factor—the idea of extension—that is prior to and independent of the sensory elements found in my cognition of that body (II.¶11–12). So my primary cognitive relation to reality has been brought about by God, the author of my nature, who has made me so that ideas that belong to my mind innately make available to me truth and reality (or, in the terminology of the Fifth Meditation, true and immutable natures) for my consideration and judgment.[3]

Now, it may sound odd to describe this constellation of commitments as a "foundation of knowledge." But notice that getting these commitments right has in Descartes's view far-reaching consequences that are closely entwined with the central goals of the *Meditations*. To anticipate: A correct account of these matters enables me to recognize, contrary to what I might naively have thought, that the existence and nature of the mind is better known than that of any body (Second Meditation). It helps me realize that my cognition that two plus three sum to five is on a different footing from my cognition that body exists, because whereas as I can simply see that the former is true (it is revealed to me by the natural light), the latter is based on a powerful instinct given to me by God (it is a teaching of nature) (Third and Sixth Meditations). It enables me to recognize that my cognition of God is not constructed out of sensory materials but reaches God's essence, and is such that it could have come only from God himself (Third Meditation). A correct understanding of the metaphysical underpinnings of cognition is necessary in order for me to achieve *scientia* and thereby to be freed from the episodic, transient nature of clear perception (Fifth Meditation). Finally, it paves the way for Descartes's argument from distinct cognition of something to the nature of what is cognized (in his handling of the essence of material things, Fifth Meditation, ¶¶1–4) and, again, in Descartes's movement from distinct perception to claims about what is open to the essence of mind and the essence of body (Sixth Meditation, ¶9).

Of course, none of this is available to the meditator back here in the First Meditation, but it does tell us something about how Descartes is thinking of a foundation of knowledge. For example (as would be widely agreed), it is unlikely that we are supposed to be thinking in terms of some set of basic axioms from which all beliefs can be derived. But also (as perhaps would be more controversial), the suggestion that Descartes is exploring some set of "evidential policies"[4] through appeal to which our beliefs are justified does not jibe well with the foundations that he eventually provides. Viewing Descartes's foundations in this way has sometimes led interpreters to read him as implicitly defining knowledge through specially articulated standards for reasonable doubt, so that knowledge turns out to be what cannot be reasonably doubted. I think this way of reading the *Meditations* underestimates the differences in the way epistemology was done in his time and our own (in large part as a result of the *Meditations*). For instance, the juridical terminology that seems to have originated with Kant and is still prevalent in much current epistemology—evidence, warrant, justification, and so forth—hardly appears in the *Meditations*. (Descartes does write of making things evident to ourselves and the evidence of his arguments, but he rarely (if at all) writes of something's being evidence *for* something.) Again, the so-called truth rule, "Everything I clearly and distinctly perceive is true," has a methodological dimension, but even so it does not function as a rule of evidence: in general, when trying to understand, I should be focused on what Descartes terms in III.¶4 "the things themselves [*ipsas res*]" (as opposed to the quality of my perception of them). The primary "evidential" use of the rule seems to be retrospective: I can use it, as Descartes explains, to be sure that if I *previously* perceived something clearly, I got it right.

Neither of the two foundations that Descartes discusses—the initial Aristotelian, sensory one, which he wishes to discard, and the one having to do with the origin of the human mind in a supremely perfect being, which he wishes to defend—is easily thought of as the articulation of a set of principles telling us when a given belief is sufficiently grounded by the evidence (or sufficiently impervious to skeptical challenge) to count as knowledge or be worthy of rational credence. Descartes's foundations are epistemological in a different way. He is working with the idea that one can begin philosophy with a general survey of the mind and its resources for knowing, assess one's prospects for knowledge, and at the same time reach substantive metaphysical conclusions about the way the world is. (This broad idea, it seems to me, is taken up and worked out in extremely different ways by Locke, Berkeley, Hume, and Kant.) Descartes's own account of what the mind is and its origin in God has a definite normative dimension, explaining, for example, why when we assent to what we clearly perceive, we get to the truth (and why we should not assent to what we do not clearly see). It also plays an important role in his account of *scientia*, the highest form of cognition available to us. According to Descartes, in order to have *scientia*, I must first recognize that I have been created by a nondeceiving, supremely perfect being, who has made me in such a way that everything I perceive clearly is true. Descartes's way of looking at epistemology understands it to be more closely allied with philosophy of mind and general metaphysics than perhaps some philosophers would find natural. But it is a way of thinking about epistemology that dominated seventeenth- and eighteenth-century philosophy.[5]

But what then? Are we to suppose that the meditator enters the *Meditations* with a metaphysical/epistemological theory of cognition?[6] I think the answer to this question is both no and yes, depending on whether we think of the meditator as a naïf or as a more sophisticated Aristotelian scholastic. If we think of the meditator as a naïf, then it is not reasonable to suppose that she has a theory of cognition. But it is reasonable to suppose that she believes something along the following lines. Her ability to know anything about the world—to know truth or reality—runs essentially through her senses. She might put this thought to herself in this way: "If I had no senses, or if my senses did not (at least roughly) do what I think they do, then I would have no access to truth or reality; indeed, in such a situation, as far as I could tell, there might be no such thing as truth or reality." Thus, in the passage cited above from ¶12, the meditator, upon deciding to take the physical reality apparently presented to her through her senses to be merely the "delusions of dreams," is led to think that perhaps it might not be "in my power to know any truth [*siquidem non in potestate mea sit aliquid veri cognoscere*]." A similar line of thought recurs in the Second Meditation, where the meditator reflects:

> I will suppose then, that everything I see is false [*falsa*]. I will believe that my memory tells me lies, and that none of the things it reports ever happened. I have no senses. Body, shape, extension, movement and place are chimeras. So what remains true [*verum*]? Perhaps just this one thing [*unum*], that nothing is certain. (II.¶2; 7:24; 2:16)

So a naive meditator supposes that if there is no physical reality—if nothing she senses counts as real, as opposed to chimerical—then perhaps there is (practically) no truth at all ("Perhaps just this one thing, that nothing is certain").[7]

What I am attributing to the naive meditator is a primitive picture of how her cognition is related to the world. The thought that your access to truth or reality runs through the senses provides at least a rudimentary explanation of how you come to have true thoughts. It would also make quite unsettling the idea that your senses did not function more or less as you took them to, failing to connect you to reality. However, this thought, fundamental though it is, is sufficiently vague that it does not commit you to some family of evidential policies or some set of views about the justification of your beliefs. I do not think enough has been said yet to show that the idea of an epistemic principle or policy is in play. In fact, I find it easier to imagine someone naively entering the *Meditations* with this rudimentary explanation of how she comes to have true thoughts than someone naively entering the *Meditations* with a fairly sophisticated set of epistemic principles (e.g., "Believe such-and-such under optimal lighting conditions") that one sometimes sees attributed to the meditator in the secondary literature. I believe that it takes real philosophical work to elicit in someone the sense that she follows general "epistemic policies," or that she has at her disposal (or ought to have at her disposal) standing "justifications" for her beliefs. I won't try to say to what extent this philosophical work is a matter of bringing to consciousness something that is already there and to what extent it is the inculcation of something new. Whatever this work consists in, I do not find Descartes undertaking it in the *Meditations*.

The meditator's rudimentary picture of how her cognition is related to the world lacks the articulation and systematization of a theory. I think Descartes viewed the Thomistic account of cognition that we canvassed in the introduction as providing just that—as taking this naive picture and working it out systematically within an Aristotelian framework.[8] As we saw there, Aquinas develops a theory of cognition according to which all human cognition takes place through structure originally absorbed from the world by the senses. That structure is taken in from the world (as *sensible species*), stored and refined by the common sense/memory/imagination (as phantasms), and ultimately purified by the intellect through abstraction (as *intelligible species*). Thus the theory provides a thoroughgoing explanation of how human understanding of all subject matters—from natural philosophy (including the soul's understanding of itself), to arithmetic and geometry, to theology—works through what we have taken in from the world via the senses: "Nothing is in the intellect unless it was first in the senses." In this way, then, Aquinas systematically works out the naive idea that the mind's access to the world depends crucially on the senses, so much so that if one's senses were completely shut down, one's window to the world would be closed.

But is it reasonable to think that the foundation Descartes identifies in ¶3 is either the naive picture or its scholastic elaboration? An Aristotelian would be surprised, I think, to hear these doctrines described as foundational. They come rather late in an Aristotelian articulation of the world, after a good deal of other natural philosophy and metaphysics is in place. So, for a scholastic, philosophy does not (and could not) begin with these doctrines. If they are foundational, then, they do not provide, as Descartes seeks to provide in the *Meditations*, a foundation that philosophy can (or even ought to) begin with.

So in what sense are these doctrines foundational? Notice, to begin with, that the errors Descartes finds in the scholastic theory are of far-reaching significance. For example, the rejection of the scholastic picture of sensation is of considerable importance for mechanistic science. To think that one can read off of one's sensory experience that the world is populated by realities such as cold and hot emitting their forms into the mind is tantamount to rejecting a mechanistic ontology without a hearing. (Thus the first chapter of *Le Monde* is headed, "The difference between our sensations and the things that produce them," 11:3; 1:81.) The issues surrounding nativism are even more momentous. The incorrect view that our cognitive access to reality must run through the senses encourages the view that cognition is impossible without body, leading us to a flawed understanding of our nature as knowers; it also leads us to a faulty conception of what body is and—perhaps, for Descartes, most significant—a distorted picture of our cognitive relation to God. So it would be philosophically reasonable for Descartes to think of these doctrines as foundational in some general way.

But is this what is in view in ¶3? Well, the naive picture and its scholastic elaboration are at least consistent with the brief statement that Descartes gives there:

> Whatever I have up till now accepted as most true I have acquired either from the senses or through senses. (7:18; 2:12)

Moreover, while not decisive, the puzzling "most true" points in the direction of the foundations I am indicating. A naïf, who thinks that her primary contact with truth or reality is provided by the senses, might well believe that the closer she is to the senses, the greater her purchase on reality is, and register this thought by reporting that what she receives from the senses is what is "most true." A more sophisticated scholastic, who recognizes different modes of cognition (sense, imagination/memory, intellect), might think that since the proper object of the human intellect is the essence of material things, we understand these things best, and that as we move out from this base to our own intellects, to angels, and to God, our cognitive grip becomes more tenuous.

Further, the foundations I have identified have the sort of generality required by the strategy for doubt indicated by Descartes. In ¶2, after announcing his intention to call everything into doubt, he says that rather than run through all of his prior beliefs and criticize each one individually, he will look for something basic to attack such that if it were "undermined" everything else would be taken down with it:

> Once the foundations [fundamentis] of a building are undermined [suffosis], anything built on [superaedificatum] them collapses of its own accord; so I will go straight for the basic principles on which all my former beliefs rested. (7:18; 2:12)

So it is important that the meditator see all of her beliefs as depending on the foundations in question. But someone who thinks that all of her cognitive access to reality runs through the senses (either in the undifferentiated way that the naïf might hold this or in the more nuanced way that a Thomistic Aristotelian might hold this) would have to abandon her beliefs if this "foundation"—her sensory connection to reality—were undermined. So the naive picture and its Aristotelian elaboration fill this strategic role well.

Other interpretations, focusing more on evidence and justification, often seem to stumble over this last point. Consider, to begin with, mathematics. We saw in the introduction how Aquinas takes our cognition of mathematics to depend on the senses. The senses provide us with access to the subject matter of mathematics, namely, quantified matter. Without this access, the mathematician would have nothing to think about. However, once this access is secured, that is, once the form of quantified matter has been received through the senses, mathematical demonstration can take place in an *a priori* manner, in the old sense of *a priori*, that is, from causes to effects—in this case, from essences to their consequences (*propria*). So while demonstrations of mathematical theorems are not justified by appeal to sensory evidence, the whole discipline of mathematics presupposes that one has cognitively taken into the soul through the senses the structure of quantified matter. In this way, it is true, for the scholastics, that mathematics has a sensory foundation, even if this does not show up in the way that mathematical claims are demonstrated or justified. Other interpretations of the First Meditation either restrict its focus to knowledge of the external physical world—leaving mathematics out of the list of things the meditator is supposed to have previously counted as most true—or else attribute to the meditator an empiricism about the nature of mathematical knowledge.[9] With respect to the latter, I don't think it makes sense to attribute to the meditator the view that mathematical claims are justified by appeal to sensory evidence: this is to attribute to her a position that is in my view at once more crude and more sophisticated than anything found in the text.[10] And the idea that mathematics is not included among the meditator's most certain beliefs seems to conflict with a statement Descartes makes in the Fifth Meditation:

> I also remember that even before, when I was completely preoccupied with the objects of the senses, I always held that the most certain truths of all were the kind which I recognized clearly in connection with shapes, or numbers, or other items relating to arithmetic and geometry, or in general to pure and abstract mathematics. (V.¶6; 7:65; 2:45)

Here Descartes says he held "the most certain truths of all" to concern the things that arithmetic and geometry treat. I am not sure whether we want to attribute the "of all" part of this to the meditator, but this passage does make it surprising that arithmetic and geometry would not at least be included among the "most true" things.

Let's turn to self-knowledge and theology. Another important virtue of the candidate for the foundations that I have identified is that it has something to say about both our knowledge of ourselves as intellectual beings and our knowledge of God. Given the centrality of both these topics to the rest of the *Meditations*, it would be surprising if they were completely absent from view at the beginning. Even if the meditator's beliefs about herself and God are perhaps not (because of their remoteness from the senses) among her "most true" acceptances, they surely ought to be knocking about somewhere in the edifice soon to be overturned. In fact, when Descartes explains the value of withdrawing from the senses, what he highlights is its importance for correctly understanding the soul and

God. For example, in the Second Replies, Descartes explicitly associates the need for withdrawal from the senses with "our inability to understand with sufficient clarity the customary assertions about the soul and God":

> All our ideas of what belongs to the mind have up till now been very confused and mixed up with the ideas of things that can be perceived by the senses. This is the first and most important reason for our inability to understand with sufficient clarity the customary assertions about the soul and God. So I thought I would be doing something worthwhile if I explained how the properties or qualities of the mind are to be distinguished from the qualities of the body. Admittedly, many people had previously said that in order to understand metaphysical matters the mind must be drawn away [abducendam] from the senses; but no one, so far as I know, has shown how this could be done. (7:130–31; 2:94)

Further, he writes to a correspondent, "It is true that I have been too obscure in what I wrote about the existence of God in this treatise on Method, and I admit that although it is the most important, it is the least worked out section in the whole book." As Descartes explains a little later, "the principal reason for its obscurity" is that, since that work was intended for a wide audience, "I did not dare to go into everything that is necessary *to withdraw the mind from the senses* [ad abducendam mentem a sensibus]. The certainty and evidence of my kind of argument for the existence of God cannot really be known without distinctly recalling the arguments which display the uncertainty of all our knowledge of material things" (letter to Vatier, 22 February 1638; 1:560; 3:86).[11] It is hard to read these remarks without thinking of a (broadly) Thomistic philosopher who holds that all arguments for the existence of God must begin from sensory contact with reality, for example, the motion of the sun.[12] When one puts the targeted foundations in the context of Descartes's larger project, it seems quite unlikely that they concern primarily my knowledge of the external world and its properties, and touch upon my cognition of myself as a cognitive being and my cognition of God only tangentially, if at all.

¶¶4–5. OVERTURNING THE FOUNDATION: THE DREAMING DOUBT

In the remainder of the third paragraph and the next two paragraphs, Descartes undertakes to overthrow this sensory foundation through the dreaming doubt. The dreaming doubt has a significant burden to bear in this regard, serving to pry loose, at least *pro tem*, the grip of sensory ideology on the naive and scholastic meditator. If every time the meditator considers God, she subconsciously thinks to herself "the ultimate cause of everything I see around me" or "the unmoved mover," then she will fail to appreciate what is crucial to both of Descartes's arguments for the existence of God—that we have some cognitive access to God's essence, an access that is not conditioned by our senses (that is, she will fail to appreciate that her ability to cognize God does not come from her purchase on the physical world and its causes). Similarly, if every time the meditator considers her own mind, she thinks of it as the faculty that enables her to operate on sensory images in such a manner that she (unlike the animals) is able to comprehend the world in an abstract, intellectual manner, then she will fail to appreciate that she has a conception of herself as a cognitive being that does not have her essentially working with sensory materials. (Here we might recall the sense of exhilaration and discovery about to come, early in the Second Meditation: "I am a mind, or intelligence [*animus*], or intellect, or reason—words whose meaning I have been ignorant of until now" [7:27; 2:18]: the meditator will find a new way to understand her nature as a cognitive being.) Descartes uses the dreaming doubt as a way to get the meditator to put aside, at least for the time being, the naive conviction that her cognitive access to reality (as we might put it, using a somewhat more sophisticated idiom than she would herself use) runs through her sensory grasp of bodies, along with the more sophisticated scholastic articulation and development of this conviction. When she takes up the dreaming doubt, she is to suppose that, for all she knows, her sensory cognition is no more useful than her dreaming cognition; that her sensory windows to the world are closed shut; that her senses provide her with no cognitive access to body or the world.

What Descartes is asking the meditator to do—to seriously entertain the suggestion that she has no sensory contact with a physical reality—is difficult. There are indications in the text that Descartes recognizes the magnitude of the task and expects the meditator to find the exercise both difficult and unsettling. For example, as we have seen, the dreaming doubt (along with the evil-genius doubt) quickly leads her to worry that it may not even be in her "power to know the truth" (I.¶12) or that, for all she knows, there may be almost no truth (II.¶3). Further, Descartes observes at the end of the First Meditation, the skeptical considerations notwithstanding, "My habitual opinions keep coming back, and, despite my wishes, they capture my belief, which is as it were bound over to them as a result of long occupation and the law of custom" (I.¶11) and indicates the need to "stubbornly persist in this meditation" (I.¶12).

Because what Descartes is asking the meditator to do is difficult and unsettling, one might expect a certain amount of drama in the request. In addition, one might expect that Descartes would in some way draw attention to the radicalness of what he is asking the meditator to do: the meditator is to assume, for example, not merely that the senses are limited in certain respects but also that they afford *no* cognitive access to body, to corporeal reality. It seems to me that both of these expectations are met in the text leading up to the dreaming doubt:

> But from time to time I have found that the senses deceive, and it is prudent never to trust completely those who have deceived us even once.
> Yet although the senses occasionally deceive us with respect to objects which are very small or in the distance, there are many other beliefs about which doubt is quite impossible, even though they are derived from the senses—for example, that I am here, sitting by the fire, wearing a winter dressing-gown, holding this piece of paper in my hands, and so on. Again, how could it be denied that these hands or this whole body are mine? Unless perhaps I were to liken myself to madmen, whose brains are so damaged by persistent vapours of melancholia that they firmly maintain they are kings when they are paupers, or say they are dressed in purple when they are naked, or that their heads are made of earthenware, or that they are pumpkins, or made of glass. But such people are insane, and I would be thought equally mad if I took anything from them as a model for myself. (¶¶3–4; 7:18–19; 2:12–13)

This text has been subjected to detailed philosophical analysis over the years, often, in my view, involving a certain amount of overreading (which is not to say that the overreading is without its philosophical interest).[13] I think the main thing the passage is supposed to accomplish is to emphasize the radicalness of what Descartes is about to ask the meditator to do: she will be asked to call the senses into question fundamentally, as one might put it. This involves more than supposing that her senses function in a limited (and sometimes misleading) way, so that it can be difficult, for example, to make out things that are very small or far away (leading her to mistake one kind of thing for another). Rather, by questioning the senses fundamentally I mean supposing that the senses do not function (and have never functioned) at all, do not provide (and have never provided) any information about corporeal reality. I am to suppose, for example, when I am sitting here, to all appearances typing and looking at my keyboard in good light, that there may be, for all that the senses achieve, no keyboard, no computer, no hands or eyes. But how can the meditator do this without supposing that she is mad?

Well, Descartes says in the next paragraph, there is a way:

> A brilliant piece of reasoning! As if I were not a man who sleeps at night, and undergoes/experiences [*pati*] all the same (or sometimes even less likely) things in sleep as those men while awake. (¶5; 7:19; 2:13)

This is meant to repudiate the thought that there is no way for the meditator to do what Descartes wants her to do—question her senses fundamentally—without supposing that she is mad: for she can suppose that she is dreaming.[14] Although doing so gives her another way to suppose that her senses do not provide her with any cognitive access to reality, Descartes clearly expects the meditator to continue to find what he is asking her to do odd or peculiar (e.g., he will soon ask her to seriously suppose that she does not even have a body). So, although the main claim of ¶4 (that I could deny that these are hands or this a keyboard only if I were mad) is repudiated at the beginning of ¶5, I believe that ¶4 is supposed to have the lasting effect of signaling to the meditator that Descartes is aware of the extraordinariness of what he is asking her to do. His remark at the end of the dreaming paragraph (¶5) that, as he begins to lose his sensory bearings, he begins to feel "dazed [*obstupescam*]" seems to me to function similarly.

There is, then, as was to be expected, a certain amount of drama in the run-up to the dreaming doubt. The drama continues through the presentation of the doubt itself:

> A brilliant piece of reasoning! As if I were not a man who sleeps at night, and frequently undergoes/experiences [*pati*] all the same (or sometimes even less likely) things in sleep as those men while awake. How often, asleep at night, am I convinced of just such familiar events—that I am here in my dressing-gown, sitting by the fire—when in fact I am lying undressed in bed! Yet at the moment my eyes are certainly wide awake when I look at this piece of paper; I shake my head and it is not asleep; as I stretch out and feel my hand I do so deliberately, and I know what I am doing. All of this would not happen with such distinctness to someone asleep. Indeed! As if I did not remember other occasions when I have been tricked by exactly similar thoughts while asleep! As I think about this more carefully, I see plainly that there are never any sure signs by means of which being awake can be distinguished from being asleep. The result is that I begin to feel dazed [*obstupescam*], and this feeling only reinforces the notion that I may be asleep. (¶5; 7:19; 2:13)

Although this passage is usually taken to provide a skeptical argument, it must be admitted, I think, that what we get is more in the line of a suggestive sketch than a worked-out argument. Faced with the absence of an explicitly laid out argument in the text, commentators have needed to rely on their own resources (and other of Descartes's texts) in order to tease out an argument. As they have done so, they have arrived at strikingly different conceptions of how the passage's argument works and what its point is. To mention but a few: that in order for me know anything at all about the world, I must first know that a certain condition for knowledge is met (e.g., "I am awake"), and it is hard to see how I could ever know that the condition is satisfied (e.g., "there are never any sure signs"); or that the senses alone do not provide me with the wherewithal to distinguish between veridical and nonveridical perception (for this I need reason); or, again, that waking experience seems on its face sufficiently like dreaming experience that it is uncritical to trust the one when I do not trust the other.[15] I do not deny that such interpretations have led to interesting philosophy (many have), but one gets the sense that what is doing most of the work is some background philosophical agenda or problematic, and that the passage serves mainly as a springboard from which to launch the agenda. To be clear, I am not claiming that my treatment of this text is free of a background agenda or problematic. Indeed, I have been drawing freely both on the Thomistic background that I take to be relevant to Descartes's project, and on my understanding of subsequent developments in the *Meditations*. I do think, though, that limiting ourselves to these sorts of materials increases the chance of Descartes's own concerns filtering through the interpretive lens.

It is important, I think, to find a way to see the doubt as functioning gradually, as it were. It would be too much to expect the meditator to make some startling philosophical discovery in ¶5—for example, that her sensory cognition, being "merely" cognition, does not reach the world— which discovery (rationally) compels her to doubt that body exists. To be sure, the meditator's epistemic condition vis-à-vis the existence of body is, in Descartes's view, much more precarious than she realizes as she enters the *Meditations*; but it is not clear that ¶5 forces (or is intended to force) a realization of the fragility of her position upon her (I'll say more about this in a moment). In this sense the meditator and the director of the meditation are not yet in the same place. We can see the doubt as working gradually if we understand the meditator, especially at the beginning, to be primarily following Descartes's instructions.

We might, then, taking our cue from that lack of an explicitly laid out argument in ¶5, focus instead on what the doubt is supposed to get the meditator to *do*. Descartes seems rather more explicit about this. Here is how he describes the result of the First Meditation's doubt (in some of these texts, the dreaming doubt and the character of the evil-genius doubt are somehow working in tandem):

> I shall think that the sky, the air, the earth, colours, shapes, sounds and all external things are merely the delusions of dreams which he [some malicious demon] has devised to ensnare my judgement. I shall consider myself as not having hands or eyes, or flesh, or blood or senses, but as falsely believing that I have all these things. I shall stubbornly and firmly persist in this meditation. (I.¶12; 7:22–23; 2:15)

> I will suppose then, that everything I see is false [*falsa*]. I will believe that my memory tells me lies, and that none of the things it reports ever

happened. I have no senses. Body, shape, extension, movement and place
are chimeras. So what remains true [*verum*]? Perhaps just this one thing
[*unum*], that nothing is certain. (II.¶2; 7:24; 2:16)[16]

And finally it is the same I who senses, or who observes corporeal things
as if [*tanquam*] through the senses [*Idem denique ego sum qui sentio, sive qui
res corporeas tanquam per sensus animadverto*]. For example, I am now seeing
light, hearing a noise, feeling heat. But I am asleep, so all this is false [*falsa*].
Yet I certainly seem to see, to hear, and to be warmed. This cannot be false
[*falsum*]; and this is properly [*proprie*] what is called sensing in me [*quod in
me sentire appellatur*]; and this, precisely so taken [*praecise sic sumptum*], is
nothing other than thinking. (II.¶9; 7:28–29; 2:19)

I will now shut my eyes, stop my ears, and withdraw all my senses. I will
eliminate from my thoughts all images of bodily things, or rather, since
this is hardly possible, I will regard all such images as vacuous, false and
worthless. . . . I am . . . a thing . . . which also imagines and senses; for as I
noted before, even though those things that I sense or imagine may perhaps be nothing outside of me, nevertheless I am certain that those modes
of cognition/thinking [*cogitandi*] which I call sense and imagination, in so
far as they are only modes of thought, are in me. (III.¶1; 7:34; 2:24)

At times (e.g., in the first two passages) the doubt is employed to ask the
meditator to assume that, for all she knows, bodies do not exist and corporeal nature is chimerical.[17] In other places (e.g., in the second two passages), the dreaming doubt is used to help develop and demarcate what
is (I will argue in the chapter on the Second Meditation) a partial view of
sensing—"as it were sensing" or "sensing insofar as it is me." This partial
view takes in as much as I might know about sensing, as an activity or
operation of myself as a cognitive being, while remaining in doubt about
the existence of body.

So Descartes is clear enough about the *effect* that the dreaming doubt
(perhaps with assistance from the evil-genius doubt) is intended to have
on the meditator. She is to suppose that physical reality or body is chimerical, and she is to view her sensory (and imaginative) modes of cognition in a way that is neutral with respect to what sensing (and imagining)
ultimately are. If the doubt succeeds in getting the meditator to do this,
it will have achieved its primary purpose. That is why I think it best to
view the dreaming doubt as something that Descartes is directing the
meditator to do.[18]

But isn't the doubt more than just this, a direction to the meditator?
Isn't it an *argument*, and doesn't it present the meditator with a *problem* to
be solved (say, the problem of the external world)? After all, even if the
argumentative structure of ¶5 is not transparent, surely there is some

sort of argumentative give-and-take: a sarcastic rejection of the claim that I would have to be mad in order to doubt that I have hands ("A brilliant piece of reasoning! [*Praeclare sane*: well done!]"), followed by some back-and-forth over whether the things that are currently happening to me are happening with such distinctness that it is impossible for me to be asleep ("All of this would not happen with such distinctness to someone asleep. Indeed! As if I did not remember other occasions when I have been tricked by exactly similar thoughts asleep!"). And later on in the First Meditation, immediately after the evil-genius doubt, Descartes writes:

> I have no answer to these sound arguments [*Quibus sane argumentis*], but am finally compelled to admit that there is not one of my former beliefs about which a doubt may not properly be raised; and this is not a flippant or ill-considered conclusion, but is based on powerful and well thought-out reasons. (¶10; 7:21–22; 2:14–15)

Well, it is certainly true that the meditator, in Descartes's view, has a lot to learn before she will be able to answer satisfactorily either the dreaming doubt or the evil-genius doubt. In that sense, both doubts pose serious and substantial challenges to be met. Specifically, with respect to the dreaming doubt, the meditator has yet to realize that she does not simply see that bodies exist with her senses, but that this belief (like all beliefs) involves a judgment, which like all judgments depends on her intellect (which affords her an idea of what a body is) and her will. This judgment, moreover, has, according to Descartes, a peculiar structure. It is based on a (very powerful, one supposes) natural propensity to think that sensory ideas are conveyed to her from bodies. And before she should go along with the propensity, and make the judgment to which it inclines her, she will need to know that the author of her natural propensities and inclinations is God. All of this is necessary in order for her to know that the senses generally function in the way she takes them to function. Further, in order to be able to make particular sensory judgments, she also will need to understand the scopes and limits of the human faculty of sensations, as laid out in VI.¶¶12–23. Finally, beyond that, in order to fill out her response to the dreaming doubt, she will need to learn how to distinguish waking from dreaming in the manner indicated in VI.¶24, namely, on the basis of the fact that what happens in dreams cannot be integrated with the rest of the occurrences of one's life in the way that the things that happen when one is awake can.

However, it is unclear to me how much of all this Descartes means to be in play in the First Meditation. The dreaming doubt does seem to presuppose that my tendency to believe that there is a keyboard in front of me is merely a tendency and does not count as a seeing of something's being so, for if I simply saw that there was a keyboard in front of me in

the same way that (when I focus) I see that I exist, it would be as impossible for me to deny this (that there is a keyboard in front of me right now)
as it is for me to deny that I exist while thinking the matter through in a
focused way. (Whether the ability to deny the former adds up to the ability to really doubt that there is a keyboard in front of me is obviously a
tricky matter. I do not know that Descartes needs anything as strong as
this, although I do think that he believes that the closer he can bring the
meditator to full-fledged doubt, the easier it will be for her to appreciate
the force of the subsequent argument. See I.¶11.) Still, it seems unlikely
that the meditator is supposed to be able yet to recognize that her sensory-based beliefs about body originate in some instinctual way. At any
rate, it would be difficult for her to do this without first having become
acquainted with the idea of seeing that something is so (or perceiving
clearly), which I take to be a burden of the cogito passage; having this in
place would then allow her reflectively to discriminate between something
that is revealed by the natural light and something that is (instinctually)
taught by nature. It seems to me that initially the meditator is supposed to
notice that she is able to doubt that body exists, but without fully understanding why (and she can do this much, Descartes makes clear, only with
great difficulty, because doing so runs deeply counter to her natural
makeup, now reinforced by years of habit). She feels the force of a worry
that she cannot yet articulate. Gradually she will come to realize why she
can doubt such things as the presence of the keyboard (namely, she does
not see that bodies exist in the way that she sees that the largest side of a
triangle is opposite its greatest angle). And as she articulates the difficulty,
she will come to see the need for a substantive argument concerning the
standing of her natural propensities and inclinations.[19]

It might be suggested that what's on the meditator's mind in the First
Meditation is another aspect of the dreaming doubt, the need for an explanation of how to distinguish between waking and dreaming (which
will be given in VI.¶24). This explanation, it must be admitted, ties in
more directly with the text of ¶5, inasmuch as Descartes says there that
"there are never any sure signs by means of which being awake can be
distinguished from being asleep." Still, it is not obvious to me how much
interest Descartes has in the problem of telling when one is awake. His
response to this doubt comes at the very end of the Sixth Meditation.
After providing an extended discussion of how, God's goodness and skill
notwithstanding, sensory miscues are bound to occur from time to time,
Descartes first tells us how to guard against these miscues, and then goes
on to offer a short response to the dreaming doubt, which begins:

> Accordingly, I should not have any further fears about the falsity of what
> my senses tell me every day; on the contrary, the exaggerated doubts of

the last few days should be dismissed as laughable. This applies especially to the principal reason for doubt, namely my inability to distinguish between being asleep and being awake. For I now notice that there is a vast difference between the two, in that dreams are never linked by memory with all the other actions of life as are the things that happen when I am awake. (VI.¶24; 7:89; 2:61)

Descartes goes on to explain that if someone were to suddenly appear to him and then disappear, as happens in sleep, "it would not be unreasonable for me to judge that he was a ghost, or a vision created in my brain, and not a real [*verum*] man." But if I can see where things come from, when they come to me, and where they are, and if, moreover, my perceptions of them fit "with the whole of the rest of my life without a break," then "it is quite certain that when I encounter these things I am not asleep but awake." Finally, if my senses, memory, and intellect all concur in the matter, "I ought not to have even the slightest doubt concerning their reality [*ad ipsarum veritate*]" (VI.¶24; 7:89–90; 2:61–62).

While Descartes's treatment of this topic strikes me as both careful and interesting, the brevity of the discussion gives one the impression that he is tying up a loose end rather than responding to an issue of central importance (unlike his theodicy of sensory miscue, which occupies the meditator's attention for several pages). One does not get the impression that he thinks there is a philosophically deep problem here.[20] And in any case it is difficult to see that whatever problem there is here (e.g., telling for sure that you are awake?) can be leveraged to get the meditator to suppose the things that Descartes needs her to suppose (e.g., that she has no body).

I don't think Descartes has an argument that is available to the meditator in the First Meditation that would (so to speak) rationally compel her to do what he is asking her to do. Rather, I think that Descartes expects that the meditator will only gradually come to find some of the considerations advanced there as (again, so to speak) rationally compelling—only gradually come to appreciate that her picture of her knowledge of the existence of body is, in fact, seriously incomplete (and to the extent that it involves the resemblance doctrine, seriously flawed). So, in my view, when Descartes claims in the First Meditation that the doubtfulness of all his former beliefs "is not a flippant or ill-considered conclusion, but is based on powerful and well thought-out reasons," he is issuing something of a promissory note, to be redeemed over the course of the *Meditations*. Initially, the doubt must work through enlisting the meditator's cooperation. If she as inquirer is to have a chance of getting on to God or the mind in the right way, it is all but necessary that she be willing to resist nature and habit and suppose that her senses do not function, bodies do not exist, and (with the help of the evil-genius doubt) body is chimerical. But she cannot be rationally compelled to do so, not because reasons are unavailable, but because she is not yet in a position to appreciate their force.

¶¶6–8. THINKING AND PAINTING

Now, even if we think of the dreaming doubt (at least initially) as encompassing instructions the meditator is to follow, rather than an argument to be answered, it is not clear what the meditator will make of them. How far is it possible to doubt the senses fundamentally? Is it really possible, for example, to assume not only that my senses are not functioning now, but also that they have never functioned at all? Descartes writes near the beginning of the Second Meditation:

> I will suppose then, that everything I see is false [*falsa*]. I will believe that my memory tells me lies, and that none of the things it reports ever happened. I have no senses. Body, shape, extension, movement and place are chimeras. So what remains true [*verum*]? Perhaps just this one thing [*unum*], that nothing is certain. (II.¶2; 7:24; 2:16)

This is a way of asking the meditator to suppose not only that her senses do not function, but also that they have never functioned. If everything I see is false or spurious, then the sensible phantasms stored in memory are also unreliable. But how would a meditator committed to the view that her entire cognitive access to reality runs through the senses receive this suggestion? Wouldn't she be inclined to reason as follows: My entire cognitive access to reality runs through the senses. Therefore, the fact that I am able to think about reality is proof that my senses are not dysfunctional in the manner that I am being asked to suppose here.

Descartes, it seems to me, is very much alive to the concern that it will not be obvious to the meditator how far she can coherently take the assumption that her senses do not work at all, that she has been (as good as) dreaming for her entire life. Thus he is faced with a rhetorical problem. The meditator will find it difficult to use the dreaming doubt to question the senses fundamentally because she will tend to believe that her ability to think about reality at all is a sign that she acquired something from the world through her senses. But to persuade her that this is not the case—that her cognitive access to reality is not primarily through the senses—is a main burden of *Meditations*. How can he get the meditator to understand the doubt in the manner he wants without working through the entire *Meditations* in advance? The strategy that he adopts is to offer a metaphorical treatment of the relevant issues. While this metaphorical treatment cannot settle anything, it does give the meditator enough of a sense of where things are headed to help her assume that she is (as good as) dreaming in the fundamental, sweeping manner that is required, if the meditator is to come to see that she has cognitive access to her nature as a cognitive being, to God, and to the nature of matter that does not run through the senses.[21] I think it is the function of the extended comparison between thought and painting that takes place in ¶¶6–8 to acknowledge the meditator's reservations about how far she may coherently doubt her senses, and to offer her a different way to think about her cognitive access to reality.

Let's turn to that text:

> Suppose then that I am dreaming, and that these particulars—that my eyes are open, that I am moving my head and stretching out my hands—are not true. Perhaps, indeed, I do not even have such hands or such a body at all. Nonetheless, it must surely be admitted that the visions which come in sleep are like paintings, which must have been fashioned in the likeness of things that are real [*quae non nisi ad similitudinem rerum verarum fingi potuerunt*], and hence that at least these general kinds of things—eyes, head, hands and the body as a whole—are things which are not imaginary but are real and exist [*veras existere*]. For even when painters try to create sirens and satyrs with the most extraordinary bodies, they cannot give them natures which are new in all respects; they simply jumble up the limbs of different animals.
> (¶6; 7:19–20; 2:13)

Initially, the meditator is inclined to believe that even if I doubt that my current experience epistemically ties me into the world, my being able to think of heads and hands at all testifies to my having imported "head structure" and "hand structure" from the world (at some time or other),[22] and so witnesses the existence of heads and hands (at some time or other). So even if the supposition that I am dreaming enables me to question the existence of this or that hand, it does not enable me to doubt the existence of hands. There are obviously delicate questions about the appropriate units to begin with here. Hands? Fingers? Flesh? This turns out not to matter, because Descartes is about to shift gears. What is important for the moment is the thought that since our dream visions/false representations are formed out of more basic real elements acquired from sensory experience, somewhere down the line there need to be existing corporeal things that we have sensed.

This way of thinking about the limits of the supposition that I am dreaming is congruent with a scholastic conception of cognition, according to which my ability to cognize things depends on the stockpile of sensory phantasms (which are supposed to be likenesses or *similitudines*) that I have acquired through the senses. Now, to be sure, I can operate on these phantasms so that I can think of things that I have never experienced. For example, I can mentally join the image of a human trunk with a horse's body to form the representation of a centaur without having experienced any centaurs; and I can do this even if there do not exist any centaurs to be experienced. But my ability to represent to myself a human trunk or a horse's body in the first place testifies to my having acquired *similitudines* of animal parts (or some more basic animal stuff), through my sensory experience, from animals existing in the world.

So far so good. However, at this juncture the meditator's reflection takes a surprising course:

> Or if perhaps they manage to think up something so new that nothing remotely similar has ever been seen before—something which is therefore completely fictitious and unreal [*falsum*]—at least the colours used in the composition must be true [*veri*]. By similar reasoning, although these general kinds of things—eyes, head, hands and so on—could be imaginary, it must at least be admitted that certain other even simpler and more universal things are true [*vera*]. These are as it were the true [*veris*] colours from which we form all the images of things, whether true [*verae*] or false [*falsae*], that occur in our thought. (¶6; 7:20; 2:13–14)

Now the meditator moves away from the idea that one's ability to think about something depends on encountering it (or its elements) through the senses. Perhaps one can "think up something so new that nothing remotely similar has ever been seen before." With the "nothing remotely similar has ever been seen before," Descartes is dropping the idea that the painter's ability to represent things depends on his having acquired structure from the world through sensory experience. The dropping of the sensory requirement seems connected with the move to more basic simples—as we progress from bodies to body parts to the "simpler and more universal things" "from which we form all the images of things," it becomes hard to see exactly what sort of sensory experience would be relevant to their acquisition. We are now thinking of the painter as simply starting out with the pigments on his palette, and of his ability to depict things on the canvas as limited only by what can be done with the pigments. Analogously, perhaps it is the case that the human mind is not limited in its ability to depict the world by what is available in its stockpile of likenesses or *similitudines*; perhaps, rather, our cognitive boundaries are set by certain simples, already found in our mind in the way that paint is found on the palette.[23]

But what might occupy a place in human thought comparable to that of color in painting? Descartes suggests:

> This class appears to include corporeal nature in general, and its extension; the shape of extended things; the quantity, or size and number of

these things; the place in which they may exist, the time through which they may endure, and so on. (¶7; 7:20; 2:14)

According to Descartes, these items have a simplicity and generality that confers upon them a role in human thought similar to that played by color in painting. This suggestion that extension, shape, and size are simples related to human thought as colors are related to painting, and as such do not depend on likenesses absorbed through experience with the world, is, of course, of a piece with Descartes's own view that these ideas belong naturally to human thought, forming (part of) the basic cognitive equipment that God has provided for our cognition of corporeal nature. So as we move from the first half of the painting passage to the second, we move from a conception of cognition in line with scholastic abstractionism to a conception of cognition in keeping with Descartes's own nativism. And it is through this movement that the passage performs an important strategic function. While we are thinking of cognition, as at the beginning of the passage, as dependent on *similitudines*, acquired through the senses, it is difficult to see how we can use the dreaming doubt to question the senses fundamentally. But when, at the end of the passage, we begin to think that there may be certain simples, including corporeal nature in general, extension, shape, and so forth, that are independent of our stockpile of *similitudines*, it becomes possible for us to doubt the senses fundamentally, as we must do if we are to use the doubt as a means to disengage from the abstractionist conception of knowledge. For most of the remainder of the *Meditations*—until the tenth paragraph of the Sixth Meditation—the dreaming doubt will be used to question the senses fundamentally.

Now, what does Descartes mean at the end of I.¶6 when he claims that these simple and universal things are "true [*vera*]"? Although Descartes holds that truth (and presumably falsity) apply properly to judgments, he frequently applies the label *verus* to "subjudgmental" items, ideas, or things (we will discuss this more fully when we get to Descartes's account of true and immutable natures in chapter 5). Indeed, we have already seen a text where he uses *falsus* in this way ("I will suppose then, that everything I see is spurious/false [*falsa*]" [II.¶2; 7:24; 2:16]). The contrast between something's being *verus* and its being *falsus* is the contrast between something's being a reality and its being fantasy or chimerical. Realities, according to Descartes, have a "determinate nature, or essence, or form" and are "not invented by me or dependent on my mind." Chimerical cognition, as Descartes understands it, involves my own invention, as when, for example, I put together the head of a lion, the body of a goat, and the tail of a serpent, or put together wings and a horse. (Traditionally,

chimeras were supposed to be impossible things, so that there is no essence or nature—no possible living organism—that goes with the characteristics head of a lion, body of a goat, and tail of a serpent. Sometimes
Descartes seems to use *chimerae* that way [see II.¶2].) Descartes does
think, however, that even invented cognition is ultimately made up of
noninvented elements, which do exhibit reality (whether clearly and distinctly, as in the case of intellectual ideas, or confusedly and obscurely, in
the case of sensory ideas). This is what makes it natural for him to suppose in I.¶6 that our most simple and general ideas—the ones with the
least room for fabrication or invention—ought to exhibit reality, ought to
be *verus*, in a way that invented cognition may not be.[24]

To expand on the preceding, I believe it is Descartes's view that, as things
stand, it is hard for us to tell without help from our senses whether the essences of individual systems of matter—patterns of matter in motion—are
real. This is hinted at in a remark that he makes in passing in the First
Replies—"I will not now include the lion or the horse, since their natures
are not transparently clear to us" (7:117; 2:84). What Descartes has in
mind is this: a lion or horse is, for him, a fabulously complex automaton.
Grasping its nature would amount to something like having its mechanical blueprint. We know that such a blueprint exists because we know
that lions and horses exist and are natural machines, but we are far from
understanding this blueprint. In the case of a complex corporeal structure that lies beyond our grasp, the only way for us to be assured that it
is real (in the sense of even possible, and not merely a figment of our
imagination) is to be assured that beings possessing that structure exist,
and, in order to do this, we must make use of sensory information. Unless we had sensed a horse or a lion, we would have no way of being sure
that such mechanical structures are real, even in the sense of being possible. The same concern does not arise in the case of a corporeal structure that, on account of its universality and simplicity, is transparently
clear to us. There it does seem reasonable to think that our grasp of this
structure—"corporeal nature in general, and its extension; the shape of
extended things; the quantity, or size and number of these things; the
place in which they may exist, the time through which they may endure,
and so on"—enables us to appreciate its reality.

In any case, it is vital to distinguish, as I have been doing, between
reality/truth (*verus*) and existence. Descartes says in the Fifth Meditation:

> But I think that what is most of all to be considered here is that I find
> within me countless ideas of things which even though they may not exist
> anywhere outside me still cannot be called nothing; for although in a sense
> they can be thought at will, they are not my invention but have their own
> true and immutable natures. When, for example, I imagine a triangle, even

if perhaps no such figure exists, or has ever existed, anywhere outside my thought, there is still a determinate nature, or essence, or form of the triangle which is immutable and eternal, and not invented by me or dependent on my mind. (V.¶5; 7:64; 2:44–45)

Here he draws a distinction between a thing's not being a "nothing" or its having a "determinate nature, or form," on the one hand, and its real existence, on the other. I think that that same distinction is at work in I.¶6.[25]

If we understand Descartes to be suggesting that the truth of the simple and universal things does not depend on their real existence, we can make ready sense of a point that Descartes immediately goes on to make concerning how the epistemic standing of mathematical disciplines differs from that of the physical disciplines:

So a reasonable conclusion from this might be that physics, astronomy, medicine, and all other disciplines which depend on the study of composite things, are doubtful; while arithmetic, geometry and other subjects of this kind, which deal only with the simplest and most general things, and care little [parum curant] whether they really exist in nature or not, contain something certain and indubitable. For whether I am awake or asleep, two and three added together are five, and a square has no more than four sides. It seems impossible that such transparent truths should incur any suspicion of being false. (¶8; 7:20; 2:14)

This passage is sometimes read so as to emphasize the second sentence: The strongest ground for doubt uncovered thus far comes from the consideration that one might be dreaming; however, geometrical propositions, such as "A square has four sides," appear to be true both to someone who is dreaming and to someone who is awake; therefore, the meditator does not yet have good reason to call into question arithmetic and geometry. However, as is often pointed out by commentators who understand the passage thus, this leaves Descartes with a disappointingly shallow position. First, it is not obvious that we have very settled ideas about oneiric geometry or, for that matter, oneiric physics. It is not obvious that one couldn't dream of oneself as taking careful measurements of the angles of a triangle, tallying up the results, and arriving at the result that they make three right angles, not two. Conversely, simply to dream that a chunk of lead rises rather than falls is not to dream that the laws of physics are false; one needs somehow to dream as well that there are no hidden explanations of this occurrence compatible with the laws of physics. But, further, granted that we did have settled intuitions about oneiric science, the purported difference between doing geometry while asleep and doing physics while asleep would not in itself show the existence of some interesting distinction between the epistemic statuses of the two disciplines. Before coming to such a conclusion, we would first want to know the ground of the difference: Why is it that geometrical propositions that seem true to someone who is awake also seem true to that person when he dreams, whereas the same does not hold true of physical propositions?

It makes better sense to put the weight of Descartes's argument on the first sentence, in which he suggests that the epistemic status of geometry may be superior to that of physics because (1) geometry treats of simple and universal things, whereas physics deals with composite things, and (2) it does not matter to geometry whether the objects it deals with are in nature or not, whereas it does so matter to physics.[26] Obviously, these two points are connected with the painting passage. In that passage, we saw that the simple and universal things are supposed to play a role in human cognition similar to that played by color in painting. We were encouraged to think of these simple and universal things not as extracted from the world through the senses but as belonging naturally to human cognition, as part of our basic equipment for representing a corporeal world to ourselves. And if the intellectual primitives themselves do not depend on the absorption of forms from the world through the senses, then neither do the sciences erected on the basis of these primitives.

The situation of the physical sciences is different. They involve studying the composite configurations of matter in motion that have been instantiated by God, and doing this depends on having encountered those configurations through our senses. For example, in Rule 12 of the *Regulae*, Descartes discusses the investigation of magnetism.[27] That investigation is to begin from "all the available observations concerning the stone in question"; we proceed from there to try to "deduce" the mixture of simple elements responsible for those observations (10:427; 1:49–50). These observations, made by means of the senses, help us to ascertain which mixtures—that is, composite configurations—really exist in nature. This being so, the dreaming doubt, by calling into question the initial observations, calls into question the subsequent deduction based on those observations.

Notice that this point about the respective status of mathematics and physics depends in some measure on the painting passage, as the text suggests ("So a reasonable conclusion from this might be that . . ."). I noted in the introduction that, on a medieval Aristotelian view, the mathematician, no less than the physicist, depends on abstraction from sensory experience for epistemic contact with the object of his science, "quantified" matter. On the Aristotelian view, doubting the senses fundamentally would have brought with it doubt about mathematics, since on an Aristotelian view we would then be doubting whether the soul has any contact with an independent order (including "quantified" matter). But the painting passage opens up a different way of looking at mathematics. Mathematics, as the science of the "as it were . . . real colours from which we form all the images of things, whether true or false, that occur in our thought," can be thought of as taking place through our primitive (and natural) cognitive endowment for knowing corporeality and not through species taken in through the senses. As such, mathematics might have a different status from the physical sciences, where our getting to the truth of the matter depends on the way that particular arrangements of matter in motion affect us through our senses. So the comparison between cognition and painting helps the meditator to see why doubting the senses fundamentally, while calling into question all of the physical sciences, might nevertheless leave mathematics untouched.[28]

I say the comparison "opens up" a way of looking at cognition, because there are other ways of thinking about painting and its limitations that would be more congenial to an Aristotelian outlook. A meditator who did not feel like cooperating would be within her rights to insist on that way of thinking about painting. In other words, I do not think of the painting passage as an argument against the Aristotelian theory of cognition. Rather, I think it is supposed to telegraph nativism sufficiently so as to allow a cooperative Aristotelian to take the dreaming doubt in the way Descartes intends it, namely as a vehicle to doubt the senses fundamentally. Descartes cannot really compel someone who refuses to doubt the senses fundamentally by claiming, "I can't doubt my senses fundamentally. Since nothing is in the intellect unless it was first in the senses, there would be nothing left to think with." He is counting on a certain amount of cooperation from the meditator. A cooperative meditator should, with the help of the painting passage, receive enough of an inkling of a different way of looking at cognition to be able to continue with the exercise of doubting her senses fundamentally.

¶¶9–10. THE ROAD TO THE NEW FOUNDATIONS:
THE IMPERFECT-NATURE DOUBT

Let's turn to the second main doubt, which is introduced as follows:

> And yet [*Verumtamen*] firmly rooted in my mind is the long-standing opinion that there is an omnipotent God who has made me the kind of creature that I am [*a quo talis, qualis existo, sum creatus*: by whom I have been created in the way that I exist]. How do I know that he has not brought it about that there is no earth, no sky, no extended thing, no shape, no size, no place, while at the same time ensuring that all these things appear to me

to exist just as they do now? What is more, since I sometimes believe that others go astray in cases where they judge they have the most perfect knowledge / *scientia* [*se perfectissime scire arbitrantur*], may I not similarly go wrong every time I add two and three or count the sides of a square, or in some even simpler matter, if this is imaginable? But perhaps God would not have allowed me to be deceived in this way, since he is said to be supremely good. But if it were inconsistent with his goodness to have created [*creasse*] me such that I am deceived all the time, it would seem equally foreign to his goodness to allow me to be deceived even occasionally; yet this last assertion cannot be made. (¶9; 7:21; 2:14)

Descartes introduces a new skeptical consideration here. The "And yet [*Verumtamen*]" suggests that this new consideration is intended to be in some way opposed to the upshot of the passage comparing painting and cognition, that there are certain simple and universal things, which include extension and attendant things (I.¶7), that are true and real.[29] The evil-genius doubt calls into question this claim about extension and the attendant things listed in I.¶7. I am now to wonder—despite what the comparison between painting and cognition suggests—whether it is in fact the case that my cognition of extension and related things is of something real, as opposed to chimerical or a sham—whether, to borrow the terminology that Descartes uses in the Fifth Meditation, my idea of extension is of some "determinate nature, or essence, or form," as opposed to something merely "invented by me or dependent on my mind." Here it helps to remember that an idea, for Descartes, is not simply some "representation" that floats through the mind. Our "base" intellectual ideas accomplish something. They make available to the mind some structure (some "truth or reality") for the mind's consideration and judgment.[30] My idea of extension, as Descartes emphasizes in the Fifth Meditation, enables me to make substantive judgments in geometry— to see, for example, that three angles of a triangle sum to two right angles. The evil-genius doubt questions this accomplishment: Does my idea of extension, in fact, make some reality—a "nature"—available to the mind, for its consideration and judgment?

We need to be careful about the precise extent to which this accomplishment is being questioned. I will argue in chapter 5 that when one perceives clearly, one grasps the truth and is aware of doing so. While one perceives clearly, one is certain that one is onto the truth; there is no room for doubt, either psychologically or normatively (if one wishes to employ vocabulary that Descartes himself does not use). Doubt arises only when one ceases to perceive clearly and steps back to raise a second-order question about the nature of one's faculties. Now, I believe Descartes's introduction of the evil-genius doubt is consistent with his subsequent handling of the doubt. In particular (as most commentators would agree), the meditator is not in a "cogito moment" with respect to adding two and three or counting the sides of a square; she is not actively "thinking through" the addition or counting (it may be significant that the meditator does not get as far as explicitly noting the result of the adding or the counting). Rather, she keeps these things at arm's length; they are simply things that in some general way she takes to be very well known to her. Further, Descartes's remark that sometimes others "judge they have the most perfect knowledge/*scientia* [*se perfectissime scire arbitrantur*]" seems significant in two respects. First, his phrasing helps to bring out the second-order character of this ground for doubt: the doubt has to do with judging (*arbitrantur*) oneself to be in a certain condition, judging oneself to know perfectly. Second, he characterizes the condition that one takes oneself to be in as *perfectissime scire*. But, as we will see when we come to the Fifth Meditation, when Descartes modifies *scio* with *perfecte*, he has in view something he terms *scientia*. The problem he is raising, then, is whether the meditator is right to judge herself to *perfectissime scire*, to have *scientia* (the problem he is raising is not whether something the meditator currently clearly perceives to be the case is true). (To be clear, I do not think that Descartes expects the meditator to be operating already with a firm distinction between *cognitio* and *scientia*; but I do think he is being careful to express himself in a way that is consistent with the position he eventually develops in the Fifth Meditation.)

Now, what exactly is the basis for the worry that my ideas of extension and the like may not be of something true and real? At first blush, I.¶9 seems to suggest different possible grounds for this doubt. One might think, for example, that the doubt is lodged in God's omnipotence: God has so much power that he could disrupt my cognitive processes in ways that are utterly unfathomable to me. Or, again, one might think that Descartes has primarily in view the narrower problem of cognitive theodicy sketched at the end of the paragraph: how does human error square with our origin in a supremely good being?

When we look at the text a little more closely, however, it becomes apparent that the source of the doubt lies specifically in how I have been created. Descartes twice appeals in this passage to God's role as my creator, framing the issue in terms of God's "allowing [*permittere*] me to be deceived" rather than God's using his power to disrupt my natural cognitive processes. Moreover, in the next paragraph, the meditator is told that, as far as the issue at hand goes, she is free even to dismiss the idea of God as a "fiction [*fictitium*]"; there still remains the underlying question about her origin:

> Perhaps there may be some who would prefer to deny the existence of so powerful a God rather than believe that everything else is uncertain. Let

us not argue with them, but grant them that everything said about God is a fiction. According to their supposition, then, I have arrived at my present state by fate or chance or a continuous chain of events, or by some other means; yet since deception and error seem to be imperfections, the less powerful they make my original cause, the more likely it is that I am so imperfect as to be deceived always [*semper*]. (¶10; 7:21; 2:14)

This emphasis on my creator and the origin of my nature is consistent throughout the *Meditations*. In the fourth paragraph of the Third Meditation, for example, Descartes writes:

> But what about when I was considering something very simple and straightforward in arithmetic or geometry, for example that two and three together make five, and so on? Did I not see at least these things clearly enough to affirm their truth? Indeed, the only reason for my later judgement that they were open to doubt was that it occurred to me that perhaps some God could have given me a nature [*naturam*] such that I was deceived even in matters which seemed to me most evident. (III.¶4; 7:35–36; 2:25)

Similarly, when Descartes explains in the Fifth Meditation why *scientia* is unavailable to the meditator while she is ignorant of God, he writes:

> For example, when I consider the nature of a triangle, it appears most evident to me, steeped as I am in the principles of geometry, that its three angles are equal to two right angles; and so long as I attend to the proof, I cannot but believe this to be true. But as soon as I turn my mind's eye away from the proof, then in spite of still remembering perceiving it very clearly, I can easily fall into doubt about its truth, if I am without knowledge [*ignorem*] of God. For I can convince myself that I have been made by nature [*a natura factum esse*] to go wrong from time to time in matters which I think I perceive as evidently as can be (V.¶14; 7:69–70; 2:48)

Because the doubt is lodged specifically in God's role as the author of our nature, as opposed to the power of some malignant being, it is more accurate to refer to this doubt as an *imperfect-nature doubt* than as an evil-genius doubt.[31] For this reason, I sometimes refer to this doubt using the former term, although, because the latter usage is so well established, I also sometimes follow custom.

Now, why should the meditator find salient at this juncture a doubt built around the thought that her nature might be imperfect? Well, consider the line of reasoning from which the truth and reality of the simples emerge. What was argued there is essentially this: because our ideas of simple and universal things do not seem to be extracted from the world through the senses, they are not brought into question by doubting the senses, even doubting them fundamentally. As independent of (and perhaps prior to) anything taken in through the senses, these ideas appear to have a status that should be unaffected by the dreaming doubt, by the overturning of the naive/Aristotelian foundations. But notice that nothing yet has been put forward in a positive vein as to why these ideas actually do what they are supposed to. Surely there must be more to their functioning successfully than their not having come into the mind through the senses, than their seeming to belong to mind innately in some way (these ideas are among those, I take it, that, as Descartes writes in the Third Meditation, "appear to be innate," III.¶7; 7:37–38; 2:26). To be sure, it seems natural to assume that ideas that form, as it were, the substance of the mind's natural equipment for thinking about things would function as they are supposed to. But as Descartes emphasizes later in the *Meditations*, what is natural to suppose is one thing, and seeing that something is so is another thing. And in Descartes's view we will not be able to see that these ideas do what they are supposed to do until we know something about the author of our nature. Does our nature originate in such a way that the mind's innate ideas, its basic equipment for cognition, function so as to make real structure available to the mind, or is it consistent with the origin of our nature that our cognition be fundamentally chimerical, that what these ideas make available is only a sham (or the ideas themselves are a sham—at this point it becomes hard to distinguish)? Thus, a doubt located in the question of whether my nature is perfect (an "imperfect nature" doubt) is thematically called for at this juncture, and is better philosophically motivated than a doubt located in the question of what sort of powers might be lying in wait out there in the universe to thwart my cognitive faculties (an "evil genius" doubt).

It is worth bearing in mind that Descartes's way of thinking about this issue is unabashedly "realistic." This comes out in the Fifth Meditation, in his treatment of the "truth" of true and immutable natures (V.¶6). Recall that Descartes writes there:

> For I can think up countless other shapes which there can be no suspicion of my ever having encountered through the senses, and yet I can demonstrate various properties of these shapes, just as I can with the triangle. All these things [*omnes*] are firmly [*sane*] true [*verae*], inasmuch as they are clearly cognized by me [*quandoquidem a me clare cognoscuntur*], and therefore they are something, and not merely nothing [*aliquid . . . non merum nihil*]; for it is obvious that anything that is true is something [*illud omne quod verum est esse aliquid*]; and I have already amply demonstrated all those things that I clearly cognize are true [*demonstravi illa omnia quae clare cognosco esse vera*]. (V.¶6; 7:64–65; 2:45)

Notice that Descartes bases his argument for these things' being *verae* and "something, and not merely nothing" on the "truth rule," and so on a substantive metaphysical account of the origin of my nature in God. This is significant if only because one can perhaps imagine other strategies, in which Descartes would in some way try to "dissolve" the question, Does my idea of extension "work" as it should? without staking himself to any substantive metaphysics, by arguing, for example, that there is not enough distance between the representations and what is represented for us to intelligibly raise the question, Do the representations work? and see (perhaps) the structure instead as falling out of the character of the mind's representations themselves (a triangle just is whatever my idea of a triangle says it is, and so there is no need to appeal to the truth rule, and God's veracity, to establish that there is a structure that goes with the idea).³² I do wish to point out that Descartes sees enough distance between the nature and the idea of the nature to raise a question, the answer to which he thinks requires a certain amount of substantive metaphysics (the idea is doing what it is supposed to be doing, because it came from God, and God is not a deceiver). Now, to be sure, the sense of "reality" or "something" or "not merely nothing"—"structure," to use the word that I think covers what Descartes means by "nature, or essence, or form" (V.¶5; 7:64; 2:45)³³—that Descartes is working with is difficult and alien enough that it can be hard for us to hear the issue that he is trying to frame. But I think it is plain that he takes himself to be raising a substantive metaphysical question that is to be addressed by a substantive metaphysical theory.

It is important to distinguish between the imperfect-nature doubt that helps the meditator to articulate the worry that perhaps her mind's basic ideas do not function as they should from the character of the evil genius. Descartes often invokes the specter of the evil genius as a way to help the meditator refrain from giving her assent to anything that she does not see clearly to be so. One such use is found toward the end of the First Meditation:

> I will suppose therefore that not God, who is supremely good and the source of truth, but rather some malicious demon of the utmost power and cunning has employed all his energies in order to deceive me. I shall think that the sky, the air, the earth, colours, shapes, sounds, and all external things are merely the delusions [*ludificationes*] of dreams which he has devised to ensnare my judgement. I shall consider myself as not having hands or eyes, or flesh, or blood or senses, but merely falsely believing that I have all these things. I shall stubbornly and firmly persist in this meditation; and, even if it is not in my power to know any truth, I shall at least do what is in my power, that is, resolutely guard against assenting to anything

false, so that the deceiver, however powerful and cunning he may be, will be unable to impose on me in the slightest degree. (¶12; 7:22–23; 2:15)

It seems to me that Descartes is more interested here in telling the meditator what to do than in presenting her with a problem to think about. He is using the character of the evil genius in a way similar to the way in which he uses the dreaming doubt. The dreaming doubt, I have suggested, functions primarily to get the meditator to do something, namely, to get her to stop interpreting the world in terms of a sensory ideology—in particular, to stop, at least for the time being, trying to understand God, herself as a cognitive being, and the physical world in terms of what she receives through the senses (to stop thinking, for example, that her fundamental conception of God is of a being that is the first mover unmoved of observed change in the natural world). The dreaming doubt tries to get her to stop doing this by asking her to suppose that her senses fail fundamentally. Now, the character of the evil genius is being used, I think, essentially to the same effect here, to help the meditator withdraw from the sensory ideology. It gets her to do this by having her withhold her assent from anything that she does not clearly perceive to be the case. Since the sensory ideology is based on some false commitments (for example, the resemblance thesis) as well as on some true commitments that the meditator does not yet see to be so (for example, that sensory ideas are emitted from bodies), getting the meditator to withhold her assent from anything she does not see to be the case has the same effect as asking her to suppose that her senses fail fundamentally, in terms of working against the sensory ideology. I think of the character of the evil genius as primarily a rhetorical device, intended to help the meditator do something that Descartes clearly regards as very difficult (the passage cited above continues: "But this is an arduous undertaking, and a kind of laziness brings me back to normal life").

How are the dreaming doubt and the imperfect-nature doubt (as opposed to what I have called the character of the evil genius) related? The two doubts have rather different functions in the *Meditations*. The role of the dreaming doubt is to overturn the naive/Aristotelian foundations of knowledge by having the meditator question the senses fundamentally. The doubt suffices of itself to get the meditator to withhold commitment from the naive/Aristotelian foundations of knowledge (even though Descartes sometimes also employs the character of the evil genius to reinforce the dreaming doubt). Once these foundations have been brought into question, they stay there. By way of contrast, the imperfect-nature doubt gets its foothold only after some of the constructive work of the *Meditations* has been adumbrated in the comparison between cognition and painting. As Descartes sketches an account of human cognition in which relatively more weight is placed on the mind's original resources for knowledge and less on what arises out of the mind's interaction with the world, the question of the perfection of the mind's nature becomes inescapable. As Descartes addresses this question, his distinctive conception of knowledge or *scientia*—according to which having *scientia*, or knowing in the fullest sense, requires having an account of one's position as a knower—takes shape. The imperfect-nature doubt is a way of making clear to the meditator that she still lacks an account of her position as a knower and the consequences of this deficiency. So the dreaming doubt (along with the rhetorical device of the character of the evil genius) and the imperfect-nature doubt have very different functions: the one is backward-looking, helping to begin to undo a picture of human cognition that leads to a sensory ideology that poses a major obstacle, perhaps the major obstacle, in Descartes's view, to seeing the world aright; the other is forward-looking and deeply intertwined with Descartes's own positive conception of knowledge and its foundations.

¶¶10–12. STRUGGLING WITH DOUBT

The concluding section of the First Meditation is marked by a sense of struggle. Descartes spends about the last quarter of the meditation emphasizing the difficulty of what he is asking the meditator to do, and stiffening the meditator's resolve to do it. He plainly expects the meditator to have great difficulty in complying with his instructions, which is why he says, "I must withhold my assent from these former beliefs just as carefully as I would from what was openly false" and prescribes the extreme measure of "pretending for a time that these former opinions are utterly false and imaginary." In this, we hear again the drama that was present in the introduction of the dreaming doubt. Why this drama?

This stage of the discussion begins with the following pronouncement toward the end of ¶10:

> I have no answer to these arguments, but am finally compelled to admit that there is not one of my former beliefs about which a doubt may not properly be raised; and this is not a flippant or ill-considered conclusion, but is based on powerful and well thought-out reasons. So in the future I must withhold my assent from these former beliefs just as carefully as I would from what was openly false, if I want to discover any certainty. (7:21–22; 2:14–15)

As I indicated earlier, it is not clear that the meditator is yet able to appreciate the force of the "powerful and well thought-out reasons."

I suspect that initially she will have to take this on faith, only gradually coming to appreciate the deficiencies in her cognitive position that sustain the dreaming doubt (namely, she does not simply see that bodies exist, but comes to this judgment via a sort of instinct) and the imperfect-nature doubt (namely, she does not see why her natural cognitive equipment should do what it is supposed to). I am encouraged in this suspicion in part because of the difficulty that Descartes expects her to experience with staying with the doubt: if she really did see how her current cognitive situation was wanting, would she find it necessary to "withhold [her] assent from those former beliefs just as carefully as [she] would from what was openly false"?

Descartes comes back to this instruction in the middle of the next paragraph, where he prescribes the following strong medicine:

> In view of this, I think it will be a good plan to turn my will in completely the opposite direction and deceive myself, by pretending for a time that these former opinions are utterly false and imaginary. I shall do this until the weight of preconceived opinion is counter-balanced and the distorting influence of habit no longer prevents my judgement from perceiving things correctly. (¶11; 7:22; 2:15)

Again, the meditator does not feel so acutely the force of the arguments that show "that there is not one of my former beliefs about which a doubt may not properly raised" that she finds herself unable to continue believing those things in good epistemic conscience. Quite the contrary. She experiences difficulty *doubting* those beliefs. So part of what is going on here, in my view, is that the meditator does not yet fully appreciate the force of the reasons for doubt.

There is something else going on as well.[34] Descartes does not actually think that he has shown the meditator that it is unreasonable to hold on to her former beliefs:

> My habitual opinions keep coming back, and, despite my wishes, they capture my belief, which is as it were bound over to them as a result of long occupation and the law of custom, so long as I suppose them to be what they are, namely highly probable opinions—opinions which, despite the fact that they are in some sense doubtful, as has just been shown, it is still more reasonable to believe than to deny. (¶11; 7:22; 2:15)

We might fill out the reasonableness of her former beliefs as follows. Many of the things that the meditator is being asked to doubt (e.g., that she has body) are things that she is strongly inclined to believe by nature, and, as things turn out, nature *is* a generally reliable guide to the truth. Other things that she is being asked to doubt (e.g., that she gets things right when she adds two and three) require that she keep herself at arm's length from the underlying item of putative knowledge (two and three sum to five). There are still other beliefs that appear to the meditator to be probable and reasonable, which turn out, when more closely examined, to be false and unreasonable. The beliefs required for the sensory foundations of knowledge, one supposes, would count among them (after all, Descartes has yet to substantively criticize the sensory foundations: he only claims to show that they can be doubted).

One might appeal to the fact that the meditator is being asked to doubt probable and reasonable beliefs to support the following overall conception of Descartes's use of doubt. The meditator is to seek certainty. After all, Descartes writes, "I must withhold my assent from these former beliefs just as carefully as I would from what was openly false, *if I want to discover any certainty*" (¶10; 7:21–22; 2:14–15; emphasis added). By insisting on certainty, the meditator will discover that there are some things that are absolutely certain and conflict with some of the beliefs that she (heretofore) regarded as probable and reasonable; those beliefs will be, so to speak, overruled by absolutely certain things that she discovers.[35] So Descartes's methodology requires that the meditator forgo many "highly probable opinions" that "it is still more reasonable to believe than to deny" (many of which, as it turns out, are true) in order to arrive at some absolutely certain touchstones for belief. And this, again, might help us see why the meditator finds it hard to do what Descartes is asking her to.

The preceding explanation may tell us something about why the meditator finds the doubt difficult. What it does not really address, however, is why Descartes regards it as important that the meditator actually struggle with the doubt, actually enter the doubt, rather than take it up in a hypothetical frame of mind (the way it is often taken up nowadays in epistemology classes). It is not obvious, for example, how much by way of actual doubt is required to get someone to appreciate that p is more certain than some very likely q, with which p conflicts. A sort of hypothetical suspension of belief in q might suffice: "Although q is dubitable in the following way, p, which conflicts with q, cannot be doubted." And from the sound of things at the end of the First Meditation, Descartes really does want something more here—a stronger sense of supposing or "pretending for a time" (¶11; 7:22) than is involved in merely thinking to yourself, "What if . . . ?"

Descartes wants the meditator to try, as far as she can, to really put herself in a frame of mind where she supposes that her senses are fundamentally flawed, that she has no body, that there is no body, and so on, because he is trying to undo a deeply entrenched ideology—a whole way of looking at the world. I think he regards this way of looking at the world as pervasively coloring the meditator's basic conception of things—even her conception of herself and God. Its influence is as subtle as it is perverse. To undo this ideology—for example, to stop thinking of God as simply the being that is the ultimate cause of change in the physical world—it is important for the meditator to really believe (as far as she can) that her senses are so fundamentally flawed as to be worthless.

There is something more unsettling about this exercise than just the apparent bizarreness of trying to bring yourself to disbelieve something that seems much more likely than not. Stripping away the ideology will have the effect of depriving the meditator of her basic framework for negotiating the world cognitively. It is not an exercise from which she can count on emerging more or less intact. At least in the short term, she will find herself at sea. This sense of becoming unmoored is perhaps evident when she countenances the prospect that she will have to withdraw from a world that may prove not to be in her power to negotiate cognitively:

> I shall stubbornly and firmly persist in this meditation; and, even if it is not in my power to know any truth [*siquidem non in potestate mea sit aliquid veri cognoscere*], I shall at least do what is in my power, that is, resolutely guard against assenting to any falsehoods, so that the deceiver, however powerful and cunning he may be, will be unable to impose on me in the slightest degree. (¶12; 7:23; 2:15)

It is the prospect of such cognitive impotence, I take it, that leads her to prefer, in the immediate continuation of this passage, the blandishments of a fool's paradise to what is, for all she can tell, a forbidding and unyielding reality:

> But this is an arduous undertaking, and a kind of laziness brings me back to normal life [*consuetudinem vitae*]. I am like a prisoner who is enjoying an imaginary freedom while he is asleep; as he begins to suspect he is asleep, he dreads being woken up and goes along with the pleasant illusion [*blandisque illusionibus*] as long as he can. In the same way, I happily slide back into my old opinions and dread being shaken out of them, for fear my peaceful sleep may be followed by hard labor when I awake, and that I shall have to toil not in the light, but amid the inextricable darkness of the problems I have now raised. (¶12; 7:23; 2:15)

For Descartes, the exercise is marked by a happy ending. As things turn out, there is a light—the light of nature, originating in God—that will illuminate the meditator's basic metaphysical situation. At the end of the Third Meditation, the meditator will be encouraged to "pause . . . and spend some time in the contemplation of God; to reflect on his attributes, and to gaze with wonder and adoration on the beauty of this immense light, so far as the eye of [her] darkened intellect can bear it"

(III.¶39; 7:52; 2:35–36). But the stakes are high, and back here in the First Meditation it is not clear how things will turn out. Indeed, writing less than a century later, Hume, working with what seem to me not wholly dissimilar materials, will come to the conclusion that there is no such light illuminating our basic metaphysical situation. We labor in a darkness that makes it hard to understand our basic metaphysical situation; the more deeply we try to peer into that darkness, the less clearly we see what it is that holds the world or ourselves together; when closely scrutinized, both seem to dissolve into pieces. This is a condition Hume reports as demoralizing, producing a "philosophical melancholy and delirium" that can be cured, it seems, only by returning to normal life.[36]

⇥2⇤

The Second Meditation

THE CONSTRUCTIVE work of the *Meditations* begins with an account of the mind in the Second Meditation, entitled "The nature of the human mind, and how it is better known than body."[1] The first thing Descartes does is to demonstrate the existence of the mind through the famous cogito reflection. He shows the meditator that even while doubting the senses fundamentally, she knows at least this much: that she exists. But Descartes does not stop there. As the title suggests, he goes on to provide an understanding of *what* this thing that exists is, an account of the mind's essence or nature. Showing what the mind is is considerably more ambitious than showing that it exists. In ¶¶4–6 he provides an initial specification of its essence, and then fleshes out that specification in ¶¶7–9. In the remaining third of the meditation, ¶¶10–16, he undertakes the second task described in the title, namely, showing that the mind is better known than body, using a piece of wax as an example of a known body. (This discussion also contributes to a better understanding of what the mind is.) As becomes clear in ¶15, showing that mind is better known than body has two parts. The first part involves showing that I know that mind exists better than I know that body exists; the second, that I have a more distinct conception of what my mind is than of what body is, that is, I have a better grasp of the nature of the mind than I have of the nature of body.

Perhaps because Descartes's contribution to the history of philosophy seems bound up with his novel conception of mind and knowledge, I find the Second Meditation the most exciting of the six. I also find it the most difficult. It is hard to put one's finger on just what is novel or important about the conception of mind that Descartes advances there. I will attempt to do so by leaning on differences between Descartes's way of thinking about the nature of the mind and cognition and Aquinas's way, but I do not believe that this exhausts the topic. Another (related) difficulty with reading the Second Meditation is that it can be hard to discern a path through the text. It is difficult to see how the various points Descartes is making in the meditation fit together as a whole and, in particular, add up to an account of the nature of the mind, an account of what the mind is. Faced with this difficulty, commentators have tended to focus on certain highlights, for example, the cogito in ¶3, the claim that I am a thinking thing in ¶6, and the discussion of the piece of wax that occupies the final third, without looking for underlying unity in the discussion. I hope to show that there is a reasonably continuous and coherent plan underlying the text.

Trying to find a plan for the discussion is important not just for arriving at a satisfying overall picture of the meditation. It is also important for understanding individual passages in their appropriate context. For example, readers have sometimes attached greater weight to a few lines of text than the overall argumentative context suggests they can bear; and, conversely, readers have shied away from other admittedly difficult passages that that context suggests are important (and to which Descartes seems to be calling attention). Let me give some examples of what I have in mind.

Over the years, the last part of ¶9 has been treated as especially momentous:

> Lastly, it is also the same I who senses, or notices [animadverto: turn my soul toward] bodily things as it were [tanquam] through the senses. For example, I am now seeing light, hearing a noise, feeling heat. But I am asleep, so all this is false. Yet I certainly seem to see, to hear, and to be warmed. This cannot be false; what is called sensing in me is properly [proprie] just this, and this, precisely so taken [praecise sic sumptum], is nothing other than thinking. (7:29; 2:19)

It has seemed to many (perhaps encouraged by the "properly [proprie]" and by not paying sufficient attention to the qualifications "in me" and "precisely so taken") that Descartes is doing something quite striking with this remark, namely, ushering in a radical new conception of sensation as essentially mental. He has used methodological skepticism to pry off the cognitive or mental aspect of sensation from its (now, mere) bodily accompaniments. (What exactly this new conception of sensation involves is open to various further elaborations: according to one view, the new conception has sensation terminating at ideas as opposed to bodies or their qualities.)

I agree that a correct understanding of this difficult passage is important for understanding Descartes's theory of sensation; and we shall consider it carefully below. To anticipate, I disagree with any reading of the remark that commits Descartes to a robust metaphysics of sensation, that has Descartes telling us what the (so to speak) essence of sensation is. It is philosophically much too early in the game for that, and, in any event, it is clear, as a textual matter, that explaining what imagination is and what sensation is are tasks left for the Sixth Meditation. The point I want to make now, however, is that whatever its import, the passage does not have the marks of something that is supposed to be momentous or seminal. In terms of the larger argument, it is simply the last item in a list of things that belong to the mind. Although Descartes expresses himself carefully here—and we will want to understand why—this remark has the feel of a subsidiary observation and not of one of the crowning moments of the Second Meditation.

By way of contrast, there are other moments in the Second Meditation where Descartes does want to get the meditator's attention. One comes early on, in ¶6:

> I am, then, precisely [*praecise*] only a thing that thinks; that is, I am a mind, or intelligence [*animus*], or intellect, or reason—words whose meaning I have been ignorant of until now. (7:27; 2:18)

This is obviously a bold claim. Descartes is suggesting not only that the meditator did not know at the beginning of the *Meditations* what a mind is, but that he was able to teach her what one is within the space of a few paragraphs (presumably, ¶¶4–6). To be sure, it is not clear what Descartes means when he says he had not previously understood what a mind is but now does.[2] All the same, the claim is not something that should be passed over as incautious hyperbole.

There is another place in the Second Meditation where Descartes takes himself to be making an important and striking point. At the end of ¶12 he writes:

> And yet, and what is to be noted here [*quod notandum est*], the perception of it [the wax] is not vision, or touch, or imagination, nor was it ever, although it seemed so earlier, but the inspection of the mind alone [*solius mentis inspectio*], which can be imperfect and confused, as it was earlier, or clear and distinct, as it now is, according to whether I attend more or I attend less to what it consists in. (7:31; 2:21)

"What is to be noted here"—Descartes is telling the meditator to pay careful attention. As before, the underlying claim is difficult: why isn't our perception of the wax a case of vision? After all, as Descartes points out in the next paragraph, we commonly say that "we see the wax itself, if the wax is present" (¶13; 7:32; 2:21). But difficult as it may be, it is a point of some importance to Descartes, inasmuch as he emphasizes it in ¶12, elaborates it in ¶13, and returns to it in the final paragraph:

> And since it is now known to me that even bodies are not strictly [*proprie*] perceived by the senses or the faculty of the imagination [*imaginandi facultate*] but by the intellect alone, and that they are not perceived from their

being touched or seen but from their being understood, I plainly apprehend [*cognosco*] that nothing can be perceived more easily and more evidently by me than my mind. (¶16; 7:33–34; 2:22–23)

It is important to try to read the text in a way that accords with these indications, to attend to what Descartes would have us attend to, and to try to understand their importance within the larger scheme of the meditation.

THE NATURE OF THE MIND: OVERVIEW

The title of Second Meditation—"The nature of the human mind, and how it is better known than body"—indicates that it includes a treatment of the nature³ or essence of the mind; it seems to be the place in the *Meditations* where Descartes lays out his account of the mind. Early in the meditation (¶3), the meditator sees, even while working under the skeptical assumptions that the First Meditation left her with, that it must be the case that she exists. The overt topic of the next several paragraphs is to find out what this thing is whose existence was shown in the cogito passage (¶¶4–6, ¶7), and, after we have learned that it is a thinking thing, to find out what a thinking thing is (¶¶8–9). Along the way, Descartes asks a series of "What is it?" questions. I believe we should hear these questions in the spirit of an Aristotelian "What is it?" question—that is, as a request for the specification of a being's essence or nature. There is also, I will suggest, an important way in which the discussion of the wax, which, along with its fallout, makes up the last third of the Second Meditation (¶¶10–15), contributes significantly to Descartes's account of the nature of the mind.

Descartes's claim in ¶6 that he was previously ignorant of what a mind is indicates that he sees his conception of mind as importantly novel. What makes his conception of the mind distinctive?

To a certain extent, Descartes's conception of mind can be understood as a reaction to Aquinas's. According to Aquinas, all human understanding takes place through the abstraction of universals from sensible phantasms (themselves located in the body). As we saw in the introduction, Aquinas applies this doctrine even to the way the intellectual soul understands itself: it understands itself by employing species abstracted from phantasms, so sensible phantasms, stored in the (corporeal) imagination, are used in the intellectual soul's understanding of itself.

Now, Descartes holds that the mind possesses a certain amount of substantive knowledge that could not possibly have been abstracted from sensible phantasms. This understanding includes our basic grasp of what the mind is, what God is, and what body is. The case of our understanding of our own mind, Descartes believes, provides him with a strong foothold for making his case against Aquinas. He remarks in ¶7 that the imagination is *prima facie* an unsuitable faculty for cognizing the being that was shown to exist in the cogito passage; and, as things play out over the course of the Second Meditation, the lower cognitive faculties (sense, imagination) play no role in our understanding of the being that was shown to exist in the cogito passage (other than perhaps providing some of the data that must be accounted for).

Even if one agrees that when we are trying to understand our minds we ought not to turn to the phantasms, one might think that it is necessary to do so in order to understand body. I think a primary function of the wax discussion is to combat this impression. In that discussion, Descartes attempts to show that even when we are pursuing the nature of body, there is something that he refers to as "mind alone" [*solius mentis*] that operates independently of our lower cognitive faculties. This "mind alone" does not require materials from the lower faculties for its operation; rather, our lower cognitive faculties depend on and presuppose it.

This much is a mainly negative characterization of Descartes's conception of mind: that is, it does not operate in the way that Aquinas took the human intellect to; in particular, it does not depend on phantasms, and so (plausibly, given assumptions that many would have made in the period) does not depend on body. These negative points do not really show us what the mind *is*, do not help us see what is involved in Descartes's showing us what words like "mind, or intelligence, or intellect, or reason" really mean. For this, it helps to draw a second contrast with Aquinas. Aquinas held that the highest form of human cognition, understanding, characteristically involved universality. What we can do and the animals cannot is to cognize universally. The theory of abstraction is an account of what we do when we cognize universally. For Descartes, this puts the focus in very much the wrong place. On his telling, what is most fundamental to us as cognitive beings is our ability to see that things are so. Here it helps to think in terms of a practicing mathematician, who observes or sees the relationships within a particular geometrical figure or among certain numbers. What she notices may or may not be generalizable along various dimensions, but that does not lie at the heart of what she is doing, namely, discerning various relationships. It is this discerning or observing—a certain sort of seeing that something is so—that, in Descartes's view, sets us apart from the animals, places our cognition on a higher plane from theirs.

The word that Descartes eventually uses in the Second Meditation for this observing or seeing is *judgment*—judgment vocabulary abounds toward the end of the Second Meditation (see ¶¶12, 13, 14, and 15).[4] For Descartes, a human mind is something that actively engages with reality by trying to figure out what's what, trying to see what is so, an activity that involves understanding, doubting, affirming, and denying (and therefore, according to Descartes, willing). Absent this active engagement, there would be in the mind only some flow of images such as we might imagine takes place in the animals. This is how I understand a striking remark that Descartes makes toward the end of the wax discussion, in which he contrasts his sensory and imaginative cognition of the wax with his intellectual cognition of it, a form of cognition that seems intimately bound up with discrimination and judgment:

> What was there that it [the sensory and imaginative cognition of the wax] seems an animal could not possess? But when I distinguish the wax from its outward forms and, as it were, strip it and consider it naked, even if my judgement may still contain errors [*error in judicio me esse possit*], I cannot in any case perceive it thus without a human mind. (¶14; 7:32; 2:22)

What motivates this shift? Part of the answer has to do with Descartes's mathematical orientation. Reflecting on a Euclidean diagram and discerning various relationships within it is not naturally thought of as involving or resting on the extraction of universals from particulars. Beyond that, Descartes thinks (putting aside where exactly the mind-body union fits) that there are three main things that we understand—the mind, God, and body. The first two subject matters do not encourage the idea that understanding involves abstracting some common essential element of members of a kind: there is, after all, only one God, and in the *Meditations* I observe the operation of only one mind. And, perhaps most surprising, according to Descartes, our understanding of the third subject matter does not work through the abstraction of common essential elements from experience with individual members of a species (e.g., does not work through the pursuit of questions like, What do all these pieces of wax have in common?). For Descartes, the investigation of the natural world takes place within the single all-embracing framework of *res extensa*, wherein the individual systems of matter in motion find their place. The laws of motion, determined by principles of conservation, are general, but one can study the internal workings of a given mechanistic system without giving much, if any, thought to whether that system is replicated anywhere else in *res extensa*. Indeed, natural philosophy is about to enter a sort of "kind free" era, where leading philosophers will doubt that kinds play a fundamental role in our understanding of the natural world. Here it helps to recall Locke's distinction between real and nominal essence, according to which the kinds come as much from us as from the world; my impression is that other early modern thinkers, for example, Spinoza and Leibniz, would have agreed.

For all these reasons, then, Descartes took a characterization of human understanding drawn in terms of our ability to abstract universals to be very much on the wrong track. For him, what is distinctive of us as cognitive beings is the ability to see that something has to be true, in the way that a geometer sees that three angles of a triangle sum to two right angles. This ability to see that something has to be so is not exercised only in the case of eternal truths. In the appropriate circumstances, I can see that it has to be the case that I exist. This sort of ability is absent in the animals. The carnival horse may clop five times when asked what is two plus three, but it does not see that two and three together make five. (In fact, Descartes does not think that animals are cognitive at all, but at one point in the Second Meditation, in ¶14, he tries to bring out the distinctive character of our being creatures who judge and engage in closely related activities, by contrasting these activities with the sorts of things that we might take an animal to be able to do. I take him to be "speaking with the vulgar" there.)

For Descartes, the intellectual (the "pure" mind) comprises this ability to see that something is so and forms of cognition directly implicated in this ability, which include affirming, denying, doubting, and so forth. He understands lower forms of cognition, sensing and imagining, as auxiliary forms, which can assist the pure mind as it goes about its business (or the business of the composite of mind and body) but are not needed in order for it to carry out its core function. As the main focus shifts to the ability to see that things are so and closely related abilities, universality falls away as the primary defining characteristic of the intellectual, distinguishing it from the sensory and from imagination.

¶¶1–3. THE ARCHIMEDEAN POINT AND THE DISCOVERY OF MY EXISTENCE

In ¶1, after recounting the doubt and announcing his intention to continue on the path begun in the First Meditation "until I recognize something certain, or, if nothing else, I at least recognize for certain that there is no certainty," Descartes uses the metaphor of an Archimedean point:

> Archimedes used to demand just one firm and immovable point in order to shift the entire earth; so I too can hope for great things if I manage to find just one thing, however slight, that is certain and unshakeable. (7:24; 2:16)

Looking ahead, one wonders exactly what this Archimedean point is. A natural suggestion is that it is the knowledge the meditator is about to receive in the third paragraph, namely, that she exists. That suggestion may be correct as far as it goes, but it is difficult to see how the simple knowledge that the meditator exists can serve as a pivotal point from which great things are to be levered. If the meditator knew only that she existed and in the process learned nothing further about herself, it is hard to see how this might count as the Archimedean point.

In ¶2 Descartes reviews the epistemic conditions under which the meditator is currently operating:

> I will suppose then, that everything I see is false [*falsa*]. I will believe that my memory tells me lies, and that none of the things it reports ever happened. I have no senses. Body, shape, extension, movement and place are chimeras. So what remains true [*verum*]? Perhaps just this one thing [*unum*], that nothing is certain. (7:24; 2:16)

I am to suppose that nothing real enters my mind via vision (or by means of any of the other senses). I am to believe "that my memory tells me lies, and that none of the things that it reports ever happened": nothing real has ever entered my mind by means of the senses. In other words, not only are there no sensible species—that is, forms extracted from the world—but also there are no sensible phantasms—stored sensible species. This, at least at the present moment, seems as good as supposing that I have no senses. And as I suppose this, I suppose that body, shape, movement, and place are all chimerical or unreal.

At the end of the passage Descartes asks, "So what remains true [*verum*]?" and gives the answer, "Perhaps just this one thing [*unum*], that nothing is certain." This answer is puzzling in that there seem to be many things that are true in the envisaged situation, for example, that I have no senses and that bodies are chimeras. It may also be the case that in such a situation nothing would be certain. One natural way in which to smooth things out here would be to take Descartes as asking not, What would remain true in the envisioned situation? but rather, What I could know in such a situation? His answer to that: I could know nothing, except that nothing is certain.

I would like to suggest a different way of understanding this passage. Descartes often links the idea of truth with reality and the idea of falsity with unreality. Something like that seems to be going on here. He suggests that everything I see is "false," which I take to mean "unreal" in this context (CSM translate *falsa* as "spurious"), and that body is a "chimera." In other words, we are to suppose a world in which all corporeal things are unreal. So situated, the meditator might, somewhat inchoately, voice the following worry. In a world with no bodies, there would be no reality, and in a world with no reality there would be no basis (someone further along philosophically might say, no metaphysical or ontological basis) for truth. There might perhaps be propositions, for example, "I have no senses" or "There are no bodies" or "Bodies are unreal," that describe such a world truly. Such propositions would be negative in character. One might feel that a world exclusively characterized by negative propositions—"There is no Santa Claus," "There is no Vulcan," "Cold fusion is an illusion," "Astrology is fantasy," and so on—supported only notional truth, as opposed to what might be termed substantial or real truth. After all, there is nothing in the world that gives rise to the truths. In other words, the meditator's train of thought might run that a world in which body was illusory could not serve as a suitable object for either truth or knowledge. In such a world there is nothing to ground genuine truth, nothing for a faculty of cognition to latch on to or to grasp, and hence no certainty.

We can easily imagine the line of thought I just sketched taking hold with a meditator who is a materialist of some stripe or another. I do not think that Descartes's primary intended audience was materialists, however. Rather, I believe he takes his main audience to comprise naive thinkers, who lack robust metaphysical commitments (such as "to be is to be a body"), and scholastic Aristotelian philosophers, who recognize immaterial beings (for example, God, angels, the human intellect). But a close variation of this line of thought speaks to this larger audience. For although scholastic philosophers acknowledge the existence of immaterial things, they think our cognitive access to truth and reality runs through the senses and body (so that, for example, what we know about God arises from his relation to body, for example, in his capacity as the first mover unmoved of motion in bodies): in other words, they hold *nihil est in intellectu nisi prius fuerit in sensu*. Further, Descartes sees this particular Aristotelian commitment as arising out of naive experience (in the Sixth Meditation, ¶6, he traces the comment to the hold the senses have over us in early life; see also I.¶3), so he supposes naive meditators, too, to believe that access to truth and reality runs through the senses and body (though of course they would not put the point in terms of the vocabulary "cognitive access"). But scholastic and naive meditators would worry that if there were no bodies, then, for all they could know (for all their cognitive faculties could achieve), there might be no truth or reality: in such a situation, if there were truth or reality, they would not have cognitive access to it.

The passage becomes murkier on the reading I'm suggesting, and I am not claiming that the position that the meditator is left in would be (or is supposed by Descartes to be) stable. I am attracted to the reading because it helps us to keep in view an important aspect of Descartes's thought, namely, the connection he draws between truth and reality. It also helps us to understand the subsequent flow of the text. So when Descartes goes on to ask, "Yet apart from everything I have just listed, how do I know that there is not something else which does not allow even the slightest occasion for doubt?" the answers that he canvasses do not involve putative truths such as "A is A" or "Either I have senses or I do not have senses," because, while good candidates for certainties, they do not obviously involve reality.[5] Rather, what the meditator goes on to consider is whether there might be any real beings who inhabit this world. The meditator asks, first, after the evil genius's existence and then, when that does not lead anywhere, after her own existence. This focus on what might exist, given the working hypothesis that there are no bodies, accords with the idea that the train of thought at the end of ¶2 runs: no reality, no truth; no truth, no certainty.

Let's turn to ¶3. Here's how the discussion proceeds:

> Yet apart from everything I have just listed, how do I know that there is not something else which does not allow even the slightest occasion for doubt? Is there not a God, or whatever I may call him, who puts into [*immittet*] me the thoughts I am now having? But why do I think this, since I myself may perhaps be the author of these thoughts? In that case am not I, at least, something? But I have just said that I have no senses and no body. This is the sticking point: what follows from this? Am I not so bound up with a body and with senses that I cannot exist without them? But I have convinced myself that there is absolutely nothing in the world, no sky, no earth, no minds, no bodies. Does it now follow that I too do not exist? No: if I convinced myself of something then I certainly existed. But there is a deceiver of supreme power and cunning who is deliberately and constantly deceiving me. In that case too I undoubtedly exist, if he is deceiving me; and let him deceive me as much as he can, he will never bring it about that I am nothing so long as I think that I am something. So after considering everything very thoroughly, I must finally conclude that this proposition, *I am, I exist*, is necessarily true whenever it is put forward by me or conceived in my mind. (7:24–25; 2:16–17)

Let me try to summarize. The meditator is interested in whether or not there is something that does not allow for "the slightest occasion for doubt," and considers first God's existence. Indeed, I am currently assuming that there is a God-like being that is deceiving me; and it is not clear—is it?—that when I supposed there were no bodies, I supposed at the same time that there was no God. But then again, it is possible, for all I know, that I am in fact the author of my thoughts. This gives me pause. For, it is not obvious where a doubt about the senses and my body leaves my own existence. Perhaps my own nonexistence follows from such a doubt ("But I have convinced myself that there is absolutely nothing in the world, no sky, no earth, no minds, no bodies. Does it now follow that I too do not exist?"). Well, to be sure, there are a number of issues that will eventually need to be sorted out here, not the least of which is what a mind is, and how minds are related to the senses and bodies. But, in any event, however these questions about my existence, senses, and body are ultimately resolved,[6] this much at least is clear: if I persuaded myself of anything—if I am the author of my thoughts—then I exist. The same conclusion holds good if it should turn out that I am not the author of my thoughts, but that an evil genius is: "In that case I too undoubtedly exist, if he is deceiving me; and let him deceive me as much as he can, he will never bring it about that I am something so long as I think I am nothing." This leads me to recognize that it must be the case that I exist.[7] The line of thought leading up to my recognition of my existence has a certain amount of complexity, and is embedded within the context of an ongoing internal argument with the skeptic. I come to realize that if I am even so much as to participate in the activity in which I am now engaged, I must exist. The line of thought presented here seems to belong to the tradition of Augustine's refutation of skepticism in *De Civitate Dei*, when he argues: If I am mistaken, I am (*si enim fallor, sum*).[8]

A rather different picture of the cogito reasoning is suggested by the famous slogan *Cogito, ergo sum*, which does not appear in the *Meditations*. This suggests something much broader, not particularly tied to the give-and-take with the skeptic, to the effect that one's own thoughts make one's existence evident to oneself. On this broader picture, my give-and-take with the skeptic does show me I exist, but that is not so much because of the specific content of that give-and-take, but rather because this give-and-take is an instance of thinking on my part, and my thoughts make my existence evident to me. This broader picture fits well with a natural reading of a remark he makes to Gassendi in the Fifth Replies: "from the fact that I think I am walking I can very well infer [*inferam*] the existence of a mind which has this thought" (7:352; 2:244), which suggests I can "infer" my existence from any of my thoughts. (It is harder to find direct evidence for this broader picture in the Second Meditation, although it does seem reasonably clear that Descartes's ultimate position is that any of my thoughts enable me to see that I exist. Perhaps one finds signs of the broader view in the last clause of the remark, "let [an evil genius] deceive me as much as he can, he will never bring it about that I am something so long as I think I am nothing," but the remark is complicated. Perhaps one sees indications of the broader view in Descartes's comment in ¶6, "I am, I exist—that is certain. But for how long? For as long as I am thinking," but again the text is complicated.) The broader idea that one can infer one's existence from one's thoughts is of a piece with a brief argument that Aquinas makes in DV Q. 10, A. 12, ad 7, "No one can assent to the thought that he does not exist. For in thinking something he sees that he exists."

Somewhat frustratingly for his readers, Descartes never explicitly distinguishes the narrower idea that I cannot engage in give-and-take with the skeptic unless I exist, suggested by ¶3, from the broader idea, suggested by his response to Gassendi, that any of my thoughts proves my existence, or explain how they are related or why they amount to the same thing in the end, if that is indeed his view. The fact that he never distinguishes them may itself tell us something. Perhaps he thinks of these arguments as different ways of helping the meditator to see the same truth. Under the conditions of doubt in the Second Meditation, one way to make your existence obvious to yourself is to notice that you cannot be deceived (or doubt) without existing. Another way to make your existence obvious to yourself is to notice that you are thinking and that you cannot be engaged in the activity of thinking (as you presently are) without existing. Both lines of reasoning can be persuasive. Problems set in, if they do, only when one worries, for example, that some important question has been begged against the skeptic or, again, when one becomes concerned that the conclusion might illegitimately smuggle in a certain amount of metaphysics about the nature of the thinking subject. We will need to be sensitive to both worries, but for the moment I want to focus on what seems plain, namely, that either technique can enable me to see a truth (arguably the same truth), that is, that I exist.

Now, we might compare these two ways of seeing the same truth, I exist, to the way in which two different geometrical diagrams might help us see the same truth, say, that of the Pythagorean theorem. Consider, for example, these two diagrams:[9]

If one considers either diagram long enough, one eventually "gets it"— one comes to see that the square of the hypotenuse is equal to the sum of the squares on the legs. (That is something that we can do that presumably an animal cannot.) Each of the diagrams affords a different path to the same truth. For Descartes, it is the "getting it" or "seeing" that counts; the diagrams are merely vehicles to help us see the truth. I think it is much the same with the cogito. What is important to Descartes is to get the meditator to the point where she has indisputably seen some truth (namely, the truth that she exists). How exactly she gets there is not important. That, I think, is why Descartes does not show more interest in the apparently different argumentative structures presented in ¶3 and the more familiar *Cogito, ergo sum*.[10]

This way of viewing things is of a piece with Descartes's antiformal cast of mind. As early as the *Rules* he worried that focusing on the formal characteristics of an argument ran the danger of keeping the mind from penetrating to the subject matter underneath (see Rule 10; 10:405–6; 1:36). If arguments are instruments that one employs to help someone (either oneself or another) see a truth (and not an instantiation of some argument-form that conforms to a truth-preserving system of rules, which formal system of rules, Descartes worries, could encourage us to go on automatic pilot and not really think through to the underlying subject matter), then it is not so surprising that he should be as hard to pin down as he is on the question of whether the cogito is supposed to be an argument, and, if so, what exactly its logical form is.

So, I have suggested, what is crucial here for Descartes's purposes is to bring the meditator to a point where she sees that something must be so, that something is true "beyond all doubt," we might say. What is this "seeing that something must be so" that Descartes is trying to produce in the meditator? I have been employing the locution "seeing that something must be so" rather than "seeing that something is so" to capture an epistemic sense of "has to be the case" (as in "So, the butler must have done it!"). One feels that Descartes is trying to evoke something like this when he writes, "So after considering everything very thoroughly, I must finally conclude [*denique statuendum sit*] that this proposition, *I am, I exist*, is necessarily true [*necessario esse verum*]." As I reflect, I see that it cannot fail to be true that I exist (not, of course, that I cannot fail to exist). In what follows I will use "seeing that something must be so" in this epistemic sense exclusively; sometimes I will use the expression "seeing that something is so," where it is understood that "seeing that something is so" precludes doubt, and so brings with it an epistemic sense of "has to be the case."

By "seeing that something must be so" I have in mind what happens when, as Descartes will put it in the Third Meditation (¶9), something's "truth has been revealed to me by some natural light." Although having the truth revealed to you by natural light sounds rather mysterious,

I think the experience Descartes has in mind is quite ordinary and familiar (which is not to say that Descartes does not find it remarkable). It's what happens when you notice that, as you're thinking or as you're engaged in skeptical argument, you exist. It is also what happens when, staring at the diagrams, you "get" the Pythagorean theorem, or, to use an example that Descartes uses in the *Meditations*, when you realize that the longest side of a triangle subtends its greatest angle. In III.¶9 Descartes contrasts having a truth revealed to you by natural light with being led to believe something by what he calls "spontaneous impulse." According to him, we are initially led to almost all of our beliefs about body and our physical welfare through such impulses and propensities.[11] Having such a belief is a matter of going along with these impulses and propensities (perhaps unreflectively or perhaps because one has some further view about such propensities ultimately coming from God). So, according to Descartes, my believing that I exist or that the longest side of a triangle subtends its greatest angle, which is a matter of my response to the plainly seen truth, turns out to be structured quite differently from my believing that there is a keyboard beneath my hands, which is my responding to (going along with) something instinctual.

Descartes also tells us in III.¶9 that when something has been revealed to me by the light of nature, it "cannot in any way be open to doubt." I take this to be familiar as well. As I work through the cogito reflection, I am unable to doubt that I exist; or, again when I consider a triangle, I am unable not to judge that the longest side subtends the greatest angle. Moreover, I do not see an important distinction for Descartes between something's being revealed by some natural light and my perceiving clearly and distinctly that thing's being the case. And Descartes indicates in several places that when I clearly and distinctly perceive that something is so, I am unable to doubt that it is so.

One may worry that by relating the experience of seeing that something is so to the case of geometry, as I believe Descartes himself does, I may be undercutting the specialness of the cogito as an Archimedean point. If I am correct, why couldn't Descartes just as well have employed a mathematical example to puncture radical skepticism? Well, while I agree that the cogito is special, I do not think its specialness comes out in a singular invulnerability to radical skepticism. I will argue in chapter 5 that while I am having a clear perception, I am getting to truth (and know that I am getting to truth). My perception that I am is on the same footing, as far as skepticism and certainty go, as my perception that the longest side of a triangle subtends its greatest angle. That is, I am not more certain that I exist than that the longest side of a triangle subtends its greatest angle; the latter is not more vulnerable to doubt than the former.

A mathematical example, however, would not have served Descartes's purposes in the Second Meditation. For one thing, it would not have been as obvious that when I have the perception, I am onto a thing, a reality. (There is, as a matter of fact, a true and immutable nature—a "something," "not a nothing"—at the other end of a mathematical perception, but this is something that we do not learn until the beginning of the Fifth Meditation.) More important, the discovery of the cogito being sets the stage for the ensuing meditations, which are about it and its metaphysical preconditions: its origin (who turns out to be God), its proper functioning, the structures it cognizes, and its relation to body. Indeed, this is how I understand Descartes's suggestion that the cogito provides him with an Archimedean point.

Through the cogito reflection, the meditator is brought to see that it must be the case that she exists; this truth has been revealed to her. This raises questions about how to understand this "seeing that something is so" against skeptical doubt, particularly the evil-genius doubt. Isn't the point of the evil-genius doubt precisely to raise a question about whether we ever (really) see that something is so? I think it is best to postpone full consideration of the question of how to understand the relation of the evil-genius doubt to the cogito until we have opportunity to consider, first, the difficult ¶4 of the Third Meditation, where Descartes himself juxtaposes the cogito and the evil genius, in some way playing them off against each other, and, second, the last four paragraphs of the Fifth Meditation, which drew the charge from his objectors that he was reasoning in a circle. For present purposes, I think it is enough that Descartes thinks that we do—and, one might add, enough that we in fact do—now and then see that things are so, and this is how things are going with the meditator as she works through (note "after considering everything very thoroughly") the cogito. When she engages in the cogito reflection, in addition to seeing that something is so—namely, that she exists—I believe she is also supposed to recognize that she is doing this, that is, that she has succeeded in seeing that something is so. This is suggested by the *verum* in "I must finally conclude [*denique statuendum sit*] that this proposition [*pronuntiatum*], I am, I exist, is necessarily true [*necessario est verum*]." In particular, as she reflects on what she is doing, she does not see herself as merely having entertained a particularly compelling line of thought—she sees herself as also having got on to the truth, on to reality.

Descartes seems to move freely from the meditator's first-order seeing that something is so, to the meditator's being reflectively aware that she is seeing that something is so, getting to the truth. (That the meditator does see herself as getting to the truth is important for something that happens in the Third Meditation. There Descartes hypothesizes, on the basis of what took place in the Second Meditation, that everything I clearly and distinctly perceive is true. This procedure makes sense, however, only if the meditator saw herself as getting on to truth, on to reality, in the Second Meditation.) Descartes does not explain how one makes the transition from one's first-order seeing that one exists to one's higher-order, reflective cognition that one has seen that something is so. This transition seems natural enough. It is difficult, I think, to envision a being who has the first-order ability (who can see that it has to be the case that it exists) but who does not also have a higher-order, reflective knowledge of its being able to do this, or who is unable to tell when it has successfully exercised the first-order ability. Perhaps there is some deep explanation for why the two sorts of abilities go together. But Descartes does not offer one, and I will not try to offer one on his behalf.[12]

Let me try to clarify where we are. Although I want to leave open for now how exactly the evil-genius/imperfect-creator doubt ultimately interacts with the cogito experience, I do want to insist that it would be very unnatural for the meditator, while in the middle of the cogito reflection, to view the certainty that she has about her existence as merely subjective, or to view her inability to doubt her existence as based on some quirk of her psychology, or to view the judgment she is making that she exists as somehow arbitrary. Moreover, Descartes does not give any indication here that we should take the experience of seeing that something must be so other than at face value. Indeed, I believe that it is one of his primary purposes in the cogito passage to lead the meditator to a situation where her judgment is manifestly determined by her appreciation of what is the case, because this will say something important about the sort of being she is. Perhaps we could put it this way: When I, thinking or engaged in internal dialogue with the skeptic, see that I must exist, I take my inability to doubt to come from my seeing that I must exist. (The same is true, I believe, of my inability to doubt, in the appropriate frame of mind, that the longest side of a triangle subtends the greatest angle.) I also have some understanding of what's making it impossible to doubt this: as I reflect, I see that it must be so—I cannot make intelligible to myself how it might not be so. What pressure there is toward not taking this seeing that something must be so at face value, comes from trying to make sense of the radical skepticism posed by the evil genius. One might think that taking the evil genius on board precludes me from taking the cogito experience at face value: maybe, I begin to wonder, my unshakable conviction comes not from my seeing the truth but rather from some other source. Perhaps. However, Descartes does not explain in the Second Meditation how the evil-genius doubt interacts with seeing that something must be so. Pending a fuller consideration of III.¶4 and the issues connected with the Cartesian circle suggested in the text of the end of the Fifth Meditation and explicitly raised by the Second Objectors, we need to leave open what Descartes would have us make of this possibly inherently unstable situation.

¶¶4–6. THE ESSENCE OF THE BEING WHO IS CERTAIN THAT IT EXISTS

The next step is to try to figure out what this I is, the I that has seen that it must exist: "I do not yet have a sufficient understanding of what this I is, which necessarily exists [quisnam sim ego ille, qui jam necessario sum]."[13] The necessario goes back to the "is necessarily true [necessario esse verum]" in the previous paragraph, so that the force of Descartes's remark is this: I do not yet understand what this I is who has just seen that it must exist. In the next few paragraphs Descartes will try to clarify what the essence of this being is. This discussion has the flavor of taking us from an Aristotelian nominal definition (featherless biped) to an Aristotelian real definition (rational animal). We begin with the superficial characterization "being who has seen that it has to be the case that it exists" and advance to the more perspicuous formulation "thinking being." (A closer analogy would be moving from the characterization risible animal to rational animal, since risibility is related to rationality more closely than the way that my ability to see that I am is related to my being a thinking thing.) The nominal characterization here, being who has seen that it must exist, helps us to lock on to the target entity to be studied; the real definition, thinking being, displays what it is to be that being, exhibits that being's essence.

Let's refer to the entity whose existence was demonstrated in the cogito passage as the cogito being. This locution is intended to leave open whether it is a substance or an accident (e.g., perhaps a power of a substance). But the locution does prejudice the inquiry this much: it suggests that the thing we are concerned with is a being, that is, is something real. In this regard, we may benefit by thinking of the starting point of our investigation as the "being who has seen that it has to be the case that it exists" rather than simply the "being whose existence has been established," because the former characterization makes explicit the fact that the being whose essence we are attempting to discover has accomplished something, is able to do something.[14] (As the meditator will learn in the Fourth Meditation, this accomplishment involves judgment, and judgment involves both will, which Descartes regards as an active power, and perception, which Descartes regards as a passive power: so what we witnessed in the cogito is successful coordination of an active power with a passive power.) That the being accomplishes something or does something contributes to the sense that, in the cogito reflection, we have locked on to something real and not some ephemeral flash in the pan: real beings operate, do things, and undergo things in characteristic ways.[15] And this also fits in with the fact that, in the Aristotelian tradition, an account of the essence of a real being is often structured around that being's powers: explaining what a natural being is is closely tied to saying what it characteristically *does*. (This is a point we will return to in a moment.)

Janet Broughton has suggested that Descartes is not making a claim about the essence of the mind in ¶¶4–6; rather, he is articulating a special conception of himself.[16] I agree that a large part of the work in Descartes's discussion is to teach the meditator how to think of herself in a certain way. But I think it is clear that when Descartes seeks to understand what this I that has seen that it has to exist is, we are supposed to hear this as a request for an answer to the Aristotelian "What is it?" question. To answer the "What is it?" question concerning a thing is to do more than provide a special concept of it; it is to explain its core or central features—those features that make it be the thing that it is. Thus, when Descartes canvasses his former beliefs about himself in ¶5, what he puts forward are the two principal Aristotelian ways of specifying the essence of a human being (i.e., a rational animal, a composite of a human soul and body).

Now, one might agree that somewhere in the Second Meditation (or perhaps in the *Meditations*) Descartes comes to the conclusion that the essence of the cogito being is to think, while denying that this happens in ¶¶4–6.[17] I think this is incorrect. There is a specific methodology that Aristotelians followed when treating the essence of soul. That methodology makes plain the division of labor in the Second Meditation's account of the mind's essence. Let me explain.

In his *Commentary on Aristotle's De Anima*, Aquinas makes the following methodological remark:

> We proceed from objects to acts, from acts to faculties, and from faculties to the essence of the soul. (*In II De Anima*, Lect. 6, n. 308)

The soul, in the Aristotelian tradition, is the first principle of life (see, e.g., ST I, Q. 75, A. 1). The soul is what is ultimately responsible for a living thing's vital functions. In order to understand the soul's essence, we need to understand what powers or faculties are associated with life (the standard list of such powers comprises the faculties of nutrition and reproduction; sensation, imagination, and locomotion; and, finally, understanding). In order to understand these powers, we must understand their operation or "acts" (e.g., digestion or seeing), and in order to understand the operations or acts of these powers, we must understand their objects (e.g., nourishment or light and colors).

Descartes follows this rough pattern in the *Meditations*. The target of his investigation is not, of course, the soul (the first principle of life), but rather the cogito being, a cognitive being that is able to see that it exists. That investigation unfolds as follows. To begin with, Descartes writes at the end of ¶6 of the Second Meditation:

> I am, then, precisely only [*praecise tantum*] a thing that thinks; that is, I am mind, or intelligence, or intellect, or reason—words whose meaning I have been ignorant of until now. But for all of that I am a thing which is real [*res vera*] and really exists [*vere existens*]; but what sort of thing? I have said [*dixi*], thinking. (7:27; 2:18)

We may summarize: What the cogito being is is a thinking thing. The formulation "thinking thing" holds the same place in Descartes's characterization of the cogito being that the formulation "first principle of life in those things that live" (ST I, Q. 75, A. 1) holds for an Aristotelian thinker's characterization of the soul. And just as an Aristotelian proceeds from this basic characterization of a soul as the first principle of life to a consideration of the powers associated with living and their exercise ("acts"), so Descartes proceeds from his basic specification of the cogito being as a thinking thing to a consideration of the powers and acts associated with thinking (¶¶8–9). Subsequently, Descartes tells us what these various powers are (that is, explains their nature or essence): in the remainder of the Second Meditation, through the wax discussion, we learn what understanding is (and how it differs from sensing or imagining); in the Fourth Meditation we find out what judging and willing are; and in the Sixth Meditation we learn what imagining and sensing are.

So the characterization of the cogito being as a thinking thing is supposed to provide more than a special concept of me: it is intended to provide a specification of the core or constituting feature of the cogito being—what makes the cogito being the thing that it is. Still, there are ways in which this specification accomplishes less than is sometimes thought. It is sometimes assumed that when we learn in ¶6 that the cogito being's essence is to think, we know enough to conclude that it is a self-sufficient thing (a "substance"), capable of existing independently from body. I don't think that is correct. In order to reach these conclusions, we must move from this initial stage of the investigation—formulating the essence—to the subsequent stages. In particular, we need to know more about what thinking is, that is, about the powers and acts associated with thinking. In fact, I believe that Descartes holds that certain forms of think-ing are impossible without body (sensing, imagining): if it turned out that all forms of thinking were like this, then it would not be possible for the mind to exist without body. So, it seems to me, by the end of ¶6, Des-cartes has made an important claim about the metaphysical structure of the cogito being (its essence is to think), but significant issues remain.

Although I disagree with Broughton's assessment that Descartes is not making a claim about his essence in ¶¶4–6, I think there is something importantly right about her suggestion that much of the work in ¶¶4–6 lies with teaching the meditator how to think of herself, or at least of a certain aspect of herself, in a new way, and I agree further that the skep-tical doubt, especially the dreaming doubt, is an especially useful device for this project. In particular, I think Descartes is concerned to address a tendency he anticipates on the part of the meditator, to answer the ques-tion "What just happened in the cogito exercise?" with something like "I witnessed an exercise of my intellectual soul, that is, an example of one of the highest functions of a living being." (One can imagine other an-swers: "I just experienced some brain activity, or the rustling of my ani-mal spirits, that tenuous ether within me." Perhaps the details do not matter so much here.) That Descartes anticipates some such tendency is suggested by the meditator's initial hesitation in affirming her existence in the face of doubt about body:

> In that case am not I, at least, something? But I have just said that I have no senses and no body. This is the sticking point: what follows from this? Am I not so bound up with a body and with senses that I cannot exist without them? But I have convinced myself that there is absolutely nothing in the world, no sky, no earth, no minds, no bodies. Does it now follow that I too do not exist? No: if I convinced myself of something then I certainly ex-isted. (¶3; 7:24–25; 2:16)

That Descartes expects the meditator to have some difficulty in divorcing her conception of herself as a cognitive being from her more general conception of herself as a living being is also suggested, as we shall see, by the account the meditator gives of her former beliefs in ¶5, which ties the power of thought to a soul that is responsible for all her vital activi-ties (nutrition, locomotion, sensation), and so involves a view of think-ing as an (especially impressive) manifestation of living.

The meditator is going to need considerable help if she is not to bring all of this baggage to her account of the nature of the newly discovered cogito being. Descartes instructs the meditator to continue with the doubt, especially the dreaming doubt, as far as she can: "Do not suppose anything more concerning the cogito being than you absolutely must. Don't affirm anything of it other than what has to be the case. Continue in your skeptical assumption that there are no bodies, as far as you can. Don't, for example, suppose that it is a (high-end) power of an animal (or that your thought is the rustle of the animal spirits)."

Let's turn to the text. In ¶4, Descartes indicates the procedure that he will use to determine the essence of the being who sees that it has to exist. He'll consider his old beliefs about himself ("meditate on what I originally believed myself to be") and then "subtract anything capable of being weakened, even minimally, by the arguments now introduced." So, after reviewing his previous beliefs about himself, Descartes writes, "What shall I say that I am, when I am supposing that there is some supremely powerful and, if it is permissible to say so, malicious deceiver, who is deliberately trying to trick me in every way he can?" (¶6; 7:26; 2:18). I think we need to be careful about the force of the invocation of the deceiver here. Descartes is not using the deceiver, as he did in the First Meditation and will again in the Third Meditation, to raise a general issue of the relation of my cognition to the truth, to reality. Rather, I think, the meditator has, in the cogito, seen that something has to be so, and a mark of seeing that something has to be so is that one is unable to doubt what one sees has to be so—much in the same way that when you stare at one of the Pythagorean diagrams and you "get it," doubting the theorem becomes impossible. Descartes is enjoining the meditator not to settle for anything less as she sifts through her old views.

Here's how his account of his old beliefs begins:

> What then did I formerly think I was? A man. But what is a man? Shall I say a rational animal? No; for then I should have to inquire what an animal is, what rational is, and in this way one question would lead me down the slope to other harder ones, and I do not now have the time to waste on subtleties of this kind. Instead I propose to concentrate on what came into my thoughts spontaneously and quite naturally whenever I used to consider what I was. (¶5; 7:25–26; 2:17)

Descartes's lack of interest in the answer "rational animal" reflects his unhappiness with Aristotelian genus-species definition. He seems to regard such definitions, including the Aristotelian definition of man as a rational animal, as artificial and unilluminating. (There is also a problem, of course, that we will briefly explore in chapter 6, with exactly what a rational animal would look like from the point of view of Descartes's own metaphysics: a thinking automaton?)

Aristotelians thought that natural beings could be defined in two ways. One was in terms of genus and species, which definitions were termed logical or metaphysical. They could also be defined physically, in terms of form (soul, in the case of living beings) and matter, that is, as a composite of such-and-such a soul and such-and-such a body.[18] Something very close to the Aristotelian physical definition of a human being emerges from Descartes's recollection of what came to him "spontaneously and quite naturally when I used to consider what I was":

> [a] Well, the first thought to come to mind was that I had a face, hands, arms, and the whole mechanical structure of limbs which can be seen in a corpse, and which I called the body. [b] The next thought was that I was nourished, that I moved about, that I sensed, and that I thought; and these actions I attributed to the soul. [b'] But as to the nature of this soul [Sed quid esset haec anima], either I did not think about this or else I imagined it as some I know not what tenuous thing, like a wind or fire or ether, that permeated my coarser parts. [a'] As to body, however, I had no doubts about it, but thought I knew its nature distinctly. If I had tried to describe how I conceived it in my mind, I would have explained it thus: by a body I understand whatever has a determinable shape and a definable location and can occupy space in such a way as to exclude any other body; it can be perceived by touch, sight, hearing, taste, or smell, and can be moved in various ways, not by itself but by whatever else comes into contact with it. For, I judged that the power of moving itself, like the power of sensing or thinking, pertained not at all to the nature of body; indeed, I marveled that such faculties were found in certain bodies. (¶5; 7:26; 2:17–18)[19]

I have labeled the text so that the *a* segments concern body and the *b* segments concern mind; the "primed" segments concern the meditator's prior views about what the relevant item (body, mind) is—that is, its essence or nature. Rearranging slightly, I would summarize as follows: My old view of myself involves my having a body and a soul. The body is what remains of me after I die ("which can be seen in a corpse"). The key marks of body, as best I can tell, are (1) shape, location, and the ability to occupy space to the exclusion of other bodies, (2) the capacity to be sensed, (3) the capacity to be moved, but not to initiate movement.

Turning to the soul, I had some views about what it does. I took it to be responsible for my abilities to be nourished, to move, to sense, and to think. I did not have any real conception of what it is, though. To the extent that I gave any thought to this question, I pictured it as some sort of ethereal stuff.

It may seem surprising to see the suggestion that the soul is some kind of subtle matter in what is otherwise a recitation of an Aristotelian conception of the soul. But Descartes is trying to survey the naive ground view that gives rise to more sophisticated metaphysics; from that inchoate perspective, "some sort of ethereal stuff" does not seem such a bad answer to "What is the soul?" An attempt to record more faithfully the Aristotelian position threatens to become bogged down in scholastic hylomorphism—for example, when Aquinas treats of the essence of the soul in Q. 75 of Part I of the *Summa Theologiae*, he says, for example, that the soul "is not a body, but an act of body" (A. 1) and is form ("it belongs to the notion of soul to be the form of the body") rather than composed of form and matter (A. 5)—something that Descartes has little interest in delving into.

Now, how do these old views fare when subjected to the new cogito-like standard?

> [a] Can I now affirm [*affirmare*] that I have [*me habere*] even the most insignificant of all the attributes which I have just said belong to the nature of a body? I scrutinize them, think about them, go over them again and again, but nothing suggests itself; it is tiresome and pointless to go through the list once more. [b] But what about the attributes I assigned to the soul? Nutrition or movement? Since now I do not have a body, these are nothing but figments [*nihil sunt nisi figmenta*]. Sense [*Sentire*]? This surely does not occur without a body, and besides, when asleep I have appeared to perceive through the senses many things which I afterwards realized I did not perceive through the senses at all. [c] Thinking [*Cogitare*]? At last I have discovered it: It is thought [*cogitatio*]; this alone is inseparable from me. I am, I exist; this is certain. But for how long? For as long as I am thinking. For it could perhaps also happen that if I were to cease from all thinking [*ab omni cogitatio*: from all cogitation or cognition], I should totally cease to exist. At present I am not admitting anything except what is necessarily true. I am, then, precisely only [*praecise tantum*] a thing that thinks; that is, I am mind, or intelligence [*animus*], or intellect, or reason—words whose meaning I have been ignorant of until now. But for all of that I am a thing which is real [*res vera*] and really exists [*vere existens*]; but what sort of thing? I have said [*dixi*], thinking. (¶5; 7:26–27; 2:18)

There are both negative and positive stages to Descartes's account of the cogito being's essence. In the negative stage, which takes place in [a] and [b], Descartes attempts to keep the meditator from simply pushing through her previous beliefs about her essence into her account of the essence of the newly uncovered cogito being. The main problem here lies in appreciating that there is a new entity under consideration, not her entire self; in other words, Descartes must isolate that aspect or part of the meditator which currently is under examination from the rest of her (as Descartes puts it in the Third Meditation, "I am now concerned only and precisely with that part of me which is a thinking thing," 7:49; 2:34; in the Second he writes, "So far, remember, I am not admitting that there is anything else in me except a mind," 7:32; 2:22). The skeptical doubt is a valuable device for helping her to fix on the exact target. In the positive stage, [c], Descartes offers a characterization of the essence of the target entity.

Let's look more closely at the negative stage, beginning with [a]. There is an argument in [a] that is somewhat compressed. The meditator takes herself to have a reasonably good picture of what a body is, which was fleshed out in ¶5: bodies have (1) a determinable shape, a location, and the ability to occupy space to the exclusion of other bodies, (2) the capacity to be sensed, (3) the capacity to be moved, but not to initiate movement. In [a], Descartes asks whether she can find some compelling reason for thinking that the cogito being has a shape or a location or occupies space in such a way so as to exclude other bodies; that it can be sensed; that it can be moved. (Descartes's question to the meditator is, does she *really see* that it has any of these features or capacities?) But "nothing suggests itself"—in other words, she does not see that this being has a shape, a location, and so forth. (Part of the puzzle here lies, I think, in trying to figure out, for example, if it did have a shape, what that shape would be; and if it does not have a shape, how it acquires location.)

This conclusion is provisional. As I learn more about the cogito being, I might come to think otherwise; also, as I learn more about body, I might come to think otherwise (I might come to think, for example, that extension is a property of every being). But in order for me to make the judgment that the cogito being is a body (or, for that matter, that the cogito being has a body), I would need to see that this is so, in the way that I see that I exist, or I see that the three angles of a triangle sum to two right angles: but this, I find, I cannot do.

There is a question about exactly what Descartes is claiming in [a]. Is he claiming, for example, that he can find no basis for the judgment that the cogito being *is* a body? Or is he claiming that he can find no basis for the judgment that the cogito being *has* a body? Or both? This question is important because it bears on how the meditator's views develop over the course of the *Meditations*. In the Sixth Meditation, I will learn that "there is nothing that my own nature teaches me more vividly than that I have a body [*habeam corpus*]." How does this fit with [a]? For example, have I discovered in the Sixth Meditation some new consideration for making a judgment that I was unable to make in the Second?

It is hard to be sure, but I think that the claim Descartes makes in [a] is rather strong and yet is consistent with what is said in the Sixth Meditation. In particular, in [a] the meditator is not reporting merely that she can find no grounds for affirming that the cogito being is a body; rather, she is reporting that she can find no basis for affirming that the cogito being has a body. What leads me to think this is [b], where Descartes writes, "Since now I do not have a body [*corpus non habeo*] . . ." It is natural to think that this emerged from [a]. How, then, does this fit with the Sixth Meditation, when I learn that I have a body after all? Here we get an important clue from the end of the passage, [c], where Descartes indicates that he is considering himself "precisely," which I take to mean considering himself in a restricted manner, namely, insofar as he is the cogito being (that is, insofar as he is capable of seeing that he exists). The fullest elaboration of this restriction is found in a comment in the Third Meditation:

> For since I am nothing but a thinking thing—or at least since I am now concerned only and precisely with that part of me which is a thinking thing . . . [nam, cum nihil aliud sim quam res cogitans, vel saltem cum de ea tantum mei parte praecise nunc agam quae est res cogitans . . .] (III.¶32, 7:49; 2:34)

And it does not seem that we ever learn that *that* being (whatever it is) *has* a body; from Descartes's point of view, it is better to say that that being is *united* to a body. If we should perchance say that that being has a body, what we would mean is that the being is united to a body, which is different from what we would mean if we said I (unrestricted) have a body, which would mean that one of my two components—composite entity that I am—is a body. A corollary of this last point, I believe, has to do with how predication works for Descartes. Insofar as I am the cogito being (that is, the mind), I do not acquire a shape, location, color, or odor through being united to a body. And although Descartes is not explicit about this, I take it that the "logic" of the full human being—the "logic" of what Descartes sometimes calls the man—is supposed to work differently: through having a body as a component, the human being comes to have a shape, location, color, and odor. So I (unrestricted), that is, the human being, have shape and color, whereas I (qua cogito being) do not.

Now, there is an issue raised here by the fact that the characterization of the cogito being involves the first-person pronoun. This might give the impression that when I suggest that the first-person pronoun refers primarily to the composite (the whole person, as we might put it) and not the mind, my point is that the mind is not of itself a suitable candidate for personhood, or only becomes so through its membership in the composite—that of itself the mind is an "it," not an "I." The point I am making is rather different. It is that when Descartes says, "I am, then, precisely only [praecise tantum] a thing that thinks," the "precisely" does not carry the force of "fundamentally" or "essentially," which would imply that I am not fundamentally something else, or that my essence contains nothing else but thought. (Gassendi may have read Descartes along these lines when he addresses him derisively as "O Mind . . . ," 7:265; 2:185.) Further, there seems implicit in this manner of expression (although I have not emphasized this) a certain precedence of the whole package over its components. It is not clear that the point I am making requires the first-person pronoun. I think it could probably made be as follows: There is René Descartes, and there is René Descartes insofar as he is a thinking thing. The essence of the latter is to think, and the essence of the former involves thought but also something else. When Descartes writes that his essence is precisely to think, he is not saying that the essence of René Descartes is only to think; rather, he is saying that the essence of René Descartes insofar as he is a thinking thing is to think.

So I am not denying that the first-person pronoun has application to the cogito being of itself. Indeed, I would think that Descartes believes that it does, that the cogito being has, of itself, the marks of personality. I would conjecture further that Descartes thinks that the composite gets to be a person only through having the cogito being as a component. After all, animals are mere automata on his telling, and would not be suitable candidates for persons. It would make no more sense, on his view, for someone to use "you" to address a dog than to address a computer. What makes us different is the presence of mind. For that reason, I would think that Descartes thinks the expression "I am insofar as I am a thinking thing" makes sense in a way in which "I am insofar as I am an extended thing" does not (and I am not aware of his using expressions of the latter form—see, e.g., VI.¶9 and ¶15).

All the same, I believe that when Descartes does use the expression "I" to refer to the mind, this expression is elliptical for a longer one, along the lines of "I insofar as I am merely a thinking thing." For example, in the Sixth Meditation, he writes, "I have a clear and distinct idea of myself, in so far as I am simply a thinking, non-extended thing," where he is referring to the mind (¶9; 7:78; 2:54), and "when I consider the mind, or myself in so far as I am merely a thinking thing" (¶19; 7:86; 2:59). To be sure, in the *Meditations* the qualification often gets dropped (e.g., II.¶¶8–9), but this is understandable in light of the fact that the other, corporeal aspects of me are out of view until the Sixth Meditation, and it would be extremely tedious to keep on repeating it. Descartes could hold that these uses are shorthand for the more cumbersome "I insofar as I am a thinking thing" and still hold (as I think he does) that the cogito being is a suitable locus of personality, even the ultimate source of the composite's personality (which is perhaps why we find the shorthand uses so readily intelligible).[20]

To return then to [a]. When I find that I can discover no basis for judging that I am pale, or I am almost six feet tall, I find that I can discover not only no basis for thinking that I—or more precisely the part of me with which I am concerned—am a body, but also no basis for thinking that I—or the part of me with which I am concerned—am related to a body in such a way that I might "inherit" such properties; in other words, no basis for thinking that the I who can see that it exists is related to a body in the way, say, that the entire human being or man is related to a body. So there is no basis for me qua cogito being to think that I *have* a body (the question of whether I might be united to a body has yet to come up). And thus the meditator is ready to think to herself in [b], "Since now I do not have a body [corpus non habeo] . . . ," which should be taken in the spirit of [a]: given that she can find no basis for judging that she has a size or shape—given that she does not see that she must have such-and-such a size or color—she has no basis for judging that she has a body. This is true, from Descartes's point of view, so long as the I is restricted, as it is for most of the Meditations, to me insofar as I am able to do things like judge that I exist, or as he puts it in the Third Meditation, to "that part of me which is a thinking thing." This restriction is lifted only in the Sixth Meditation as I incorporate the discovery that my mind is united to a body. At that point the I begins to refer to something more, all of me, the combination of mind and body, and, in this new unrestricted sense of "I," it is true I have a body.

Let's turn to [b]. I have it from [a] that, as far as I can see, I, insofar as I am the cogito being, neither am a body nor have a body. As far as I can see, I (taken that way) lack all the marks I previously associated with being a body. But if, in my best judgment, I do not have a body, then, in my best judgment, I do not have the faculties of nutrition or movement. I do not have a faculty of sensation either, if this is understood as it is normally understood, that is, as a power to cognize ("represent") the world through physically interacting with it in various ways. Well, isn't it as obvious that I sense as that I judge that I exist? No. As a matter of fact, I have sometimes taken myself to sense when I haven't: "when asleep I have appeared to perceive through the senses many things which I afterwards realized I did not perceive through the senses at all" (¶6).

On then to the positive stage, [c]: "Thinking [Cogitare]? At last I have discovered it: It is thought [cogitatio]; this alone is inseparable from me." Let's regroup. We are trying to characterize the cogito being, which is some part or aspect (it is not clear which is the better way to put it) of me. I have supposed (how firmly is not clear to me) that its essential characteristics would be found among what I had previously regarded as my essential characteristics. The only one of what I previously took to be my essential characteristics that I can see beyond doubt must belong to this being is thought: it "alone is inseparable from me." That this is meant as a characterization of the cogito being's essence is indicated, I think, by the continuation of the passage:

I am, I exist; this is certain. But for how long? For as long as I am thinking. For it could perhaps also happen that if I were to cease from all thinking [ab omni cogitatio: from all cogitation or cognition], I should totally cease to exist. At present I am not admitting anything except what is necessarily true. I am, then, precisely only [praecise tantum] a thing that thinks; that is,

I am mind, or intelligence, or intellect, or reason—words whose meaning I
have been ignorant of until now. But for all of that I am a thing which is
real [*res vera*] and really exists [*vere existens*]; but what sort of thing? I have
said [*dixi*], thinking. (¶6; 7:26–27; 2:18)

I take the remark about the continuation of its existence as apparently
depending on its thinking to be a sign that we are concerned with its essence; in addition, the last two sentences read as a statement of a thing's
essence.

But how well does [*c*] do as an account of a thing's essence? It must be
admitted, I think, that the claim that what it is to be the cogito being, the
cogito being's essence, is to think, does not have the aura of indubitability or undeniability that the fact that I exist or that the greatest side of a
triangle subtends its greatest angle does: that the cogito being's core feature is thinking (or even, perhaps weaker, that thinking is inseparable
from the cogito being) is not transparent in the same way that I see that I
exist is. Moreover, the fact that, of all the things that I used to think were
essential to me, only thought (*cogitare*) belongs to the cogito being, while
in a certain way suggestive, and perhaps even to some degree probative,
hardly shows me that thought belongs to essence (for one thing, it seems
now to make pressing the question, Why did I formerly take my essence
to be what I did?). It does not exhibit an "internal connection" between
the cogito being and thinking.

Even so, I think the idea that there is some such internal connection
has something to be said for it. What we initially know about the cogito
being is that it can see that (at least some) things have to be so. But seeing that something has to be so is centrally connected, for Descartes,
with what thinking, what *cogitans*, is. Here it is important to take note of
an anomaly in Descartes's characterization of his prior views about what
he was. His account of those things assigned to the soul follows a standard Aristotelian pattern (nutrition, sensation) with this conspicuous exception: where one would have expected to find understanding, *intelle-
gens*, Descartes gives thinking, *cogitans*. Now, why the alteration? Well, if
the focal power of the cogito being is to see that things are so, to judge
(and, at least at times, correctly), then Descartes needs a term that covers
both aspects of judging, which for him involves both willing and understanding. In other words, *cogitans* is broad enough to cover the cogito
being's primary operation, judging.

Conversely, I believe that, for Descartes, the central abilities associated
with thinking are especially connected with judging: "But what then am
I? A thinking thing? What is that? A doubting, understanding, affirming,
willing, unwilling, and also imagining and sensing [*imaginans quoque, &
sentiens*] thing" (¶8; 7:28; 2:19). To be sure, something will need to be

said about the part of the list attached through the postpositive conjunction *quoque*, namely, imagining and sensing, but on its face this is a very judgment-oriented account of what a thinking thing is. So how Descartes views the cogito being and how Descartes views thinking lend support to the idea that there is the right sort of connection between the being and thinking to draw the conclusion that what the cogito being is is fundamentally a thinking thing.

One might worry here, of course, that the reason it seems natural to characterize the cogito being as a "thinking thing" is that we have taken such a narrow view of it: if all we know about it is that it has the power to see that something is, then how else to characterize it except as thinking, especially given how Descartes is viewing thinking? Whether there is a serious problem here depends in large part, it seems to me, on how satisfied we are with the rest of Descartes's theory. For example, I don't believe it is supposed to be clear yet whether the being is an autonomous substance in its own right, or merely a power of some more basic thing, although, to be sure, we seem to be headed in the direction of the former view. To the extent that we become eventually persuaded that the cogito being is an autonomous substance in its own right, we won't think we have been misled by our initial impression of it into an arbitrary or artificial account of it. Conversely, to the extent that we believe that it is inextricably connected to some larger entity, we will worry that our narrow focus has skewed our understanding of it.

Let's suppose, then, that what Descartes finds most remarkable about the cogito being (or about himself insofar as he is the cogito being) is that it can see that things are so, that it can think. This is what separates us from rocks and plants. In fact, according to Descartes, this is what separates us from animals (see ¶14). We can see that some things are so, and they cannot; we can doubt, affirm, and deny, and they cannot. One might imagine other ways of understanding the difference between us and them: for example, one might think that the most basic difference is that we can understand universal truth and universal good, whereas they can grasp only particular truths and go after particular goods. If one goes that way, one will emphasize, as Aquinas does, our ability to grasp universals, and what comes with this difference (immateriality and immortality, on our side). Or again, one might emphasize, as Augustine does, our ability to guide and control animals—to train them in a way that they cannot train us—and again try to work out what this difference involves (a certain position in the hierarchy of being). Or again, one might emphasize our ability to make tools. And so on. Descartes's account, as we have seen, of what is distinctive about a human mind is that it can think, where thinking, in the first instance, concerns what is involved in seeing that something has to be so. That Descartes's conception of mind is distinctive in this way helps us understand what is behind his puzzling remark: "I am, then, precisely only [*praecise tantum*] a thing that thinks; that is, I am mind, or intelligence, or intellect, or reason—words whose meaning I have been ignorant of until now."

Descartes introduces the word *mind* here, and so it would seem natural to replace the somewhat awkward phrase that I have been employing, *cogito being*, with the word *mind*, from here on out. However, the word *mind*, as it has been handed down by the philosophical tradition, especially when used in connection with Descartes, tends to carry with it a focus on consciousness that is not found in the text. For that reason I will continue to employ the less familiar and more neutral *cogito being*. Sometimes, in order to emphasize that we are supposed to think of this being as the seat of a set of (active and passive) powers and abilities, I will use the expression *cognitive agent* (even though the being undergoes things as well as does things): the being "which is real [*res vera*] and really exists [*vere existens*]" (¶6) uncovered in the cogito exercise is a genuine actor, complete with things it wants to do (to judge truly, with certainty) and things it wants to avoid (error, doubt).

A COMMENT ON *PRAECISE*

I want to amplify my discussion of *praecise*, because Descartes uses the word elsewhere in the *Meditations* and it is easy, I think, to misunderstand its force. When Descartes says X is precisely Y, it can sound as if he is saying that X is really just Y or X is essentially Y and Y only. Now, there are places where Descartes makes a claim of the latter sort. For example, when he writes in the Sixth Meditation, "when I give more consideration to what imagination is, it seems to be nothing else but an application of the cognitive faculty to a body, which is intimately present to it" (VI.¶1; 7:71–72; 2:50), I take the "nothing else" to have the force that imagination is by its very nature or essence an application of the cognitive faculty to a body, which is intimately present to it. However, *praecise*, which means cutting away from, tends to run in the other direction, that is, taking us away from a thing's complete metaphysical structure to merely some part of or aspect of it. So, as noted above, we cannot conclude from Descartes saying X is *praecise* Y that he holds that X is fundamentally just Y or really just Y; rather, to say X is *praecise* Y means that on a certain partial or incomplete view of X, it is Y. In particular, when he says in [c], "I am, then, precisely only [*sum igitur praecise tantum*] a thing that thinks," the force of *praecise* is not to limit my essence to thinking; rather, it is to signal that we are concerned with a certain partial or incomplete consideration of me (namely, me insofar as I am a being who can see that it exists), and the essence of what's picked out by that partial or incomplete consideration is thinking.

This way of understanding *praecise* fits with an established medieval usage, where to understand something *praecise* involves understanding it in an incomplete way, so as to exclude further properties. When we consider the body of a cat *praecise*, we are simply considering the body insofar as it is a body, in precision from—cutting away from—what other perfections the body may happen to possess. So, for example, the body of a cat, taken *praecise*, has three dimensions; the body of a cat, taken *praecise*, does not have life; living is one of the further properties of the body that we leave out when we consider the cat's body *praecise*. For a scholastic, the body of a cat, considered *praecise*, is an integral part of the cat (the other part is the soul). By way of contrast, when we consider the body of a cat normally, we consider its body in a way that includes whatever further perfections accrue to it. Since body, so understood, includes living, body considered in this way is not an integral *part* of a cat; the living feline body *is* the cat.

Descartes uses *praecise* eight times in the *Meditations*. Some of these uses seem to me to have the modern sense of "exact" (although usually the exactness involves cutting away something extraneous). Several of the uses, however, have the flavor of the medieval use of considering something in a way that abstracts from certain of its features, so as to exclude those features. Usually, these are marked in the text by a phrase to the effect of "considered," as in "considered precisely." Here are four such uses; we will consider a fifth when we get to the wax:[21]

> At present I am not admitting anything except what is necessarily true. I am, then, precisely only [*praecise tantum*] a thing that thinks; that is, I am a mind, or intelligence, or intellect, or reason—words whose meaning I have been ignorant of until now. (II.¶6; 7:27; 2:18)

> I know [*Novi*] that I exist. I ask what am I who knows this [*quis sim ego ille quem novi*]. It is certain that my cognition [*notitiam*] of myself taken in exactly this way [*sic praecise sumpti*] does not depend on things that I do not yet know exist. (II.¶7; 7:27–28; 2:18–19)

> But I am asleep, so all this is false [*falsa*]. Yet I certainly seem to see, to hear, and to be warmed. This cannot be false [*falsum*]; and this is properly [*proprie*] what is called sensing in me [*quod in me sentire appellatur*]; and this, precisely so taken, is nothing other than thinking [*atque hoc praecise sic sumptum nihil aliud est quam cogitare*]. (II.¶9; 7:29; 2:19)

> . . . or at least since I am now concerned only and precisely with that part of me which is a thinking thing [*vel saltem cum de ea tantum mei parte praecise nunc agam quae est res cogitans*]. (III.¶32; 7:49; 2:33–34)

The first instance does not make as explicit as the other three that my consideration of myself is restricted, but I think there is an implied "insofar as I am the cogito being, that is, a being who can see that it must exist," so that the sentence means that I, insofar as I am a being capable of seeing that I must exist, am simply a thinking thing. That we are restricting our attention only to this aspect of me, to the exclusion of whatever else may be the case about me, has been clear throughout ¶¶4–6; further, I think the precision that Descartes employs in III.¶32 ("I am now concerned only and precisely with that part of me which is a thinking thing") obviously applies here as well.

Noticing how *praecise* functions in ¶6 serves to bring out more clearly some of the philosophical work that Descartes must do. It is not so odd to begin with me, and ask of it, "What is the essence of that thing?" *Prima facie* there is something odd, however, about beginning with me qua this or that and asking after *that* thing's essence—as if I were to try to figure out what I am qua flesh colored or qua unable to read Chinese or qua taller than Napoleon. There is no guarantee ahead of time that the locution "me qua F" locks on to a thing, a something to be defined; and if it does, no guarantee that it locks on to something with at least the standing of what Descartes terms in the Third Meditation a "part" (e.g., my foot) of me rather than an aspect of me (e.g., my being flesh colored). (Descartes will ultimately claim in the Sixth Meditation that what we have locked on to through the locution "myself, in so far as I am simply a thinking, non-extended thing" [VI.¶9; 7:78; 2:54], that is, the cognitive agent or the mind, is sufficiently independent to be able to exist without the rest of me.)[22] Descartes will need to persuade us, then, that the thing we have been talking about since the cogito passage and whose essence we have been exploring has a certain metaphysical robustness or reality.

I think that Descartes is aware of this concern. The concern may surface explicitly in [c], "But for all of that I am a thing which is true / real [*res vera*] and truly / really exists [*vere existens*]" (I think it would be hard to read the *vera* and the *vere* as having to do with propositional truth). It is important, in this regard, as has already been noted, that Descartes is starting from the exercise of certain abilities, namely, those involved in seeing that something must be the case. It is natural to think that there must be some real being underlying these abilities; and it is also natural to think that the best way to explore this real being is through the exercise of these abilities and its relation to other exercises (e.g., affirming, denying, doubting— and later, in the wax passage, sensing and imagining). As we understand these exercises better, we will understand the ontological status of the agent who acts and undergoes here. It could, in principle, turn out that as I learn more about what is involved in my seeing that something must be so, I might conclude, as Aquinas thought, that this could not take place without intelligible species, and that I could not have any intelligible species unless I had phantasms, and that I could not have any phantasms unless I had a body. Before we can tell whether things do, in fact, turn out this way, we need a clearer view of what seeing that something is so is—which, I have claimed, lies at the heart of thinking for Descartes—and the place of imagining (the repository of the phantasms) and sensing in thinking.

I do not deny that instead of arguing from a power or an ability to reality and then exploring the nature of the real agent doing something by considering what it characteristically does and how these doings are interrelated, one could instead, at least in principle (as Descartes is sometimes read as doing), begin with a state—that of being conscious—and then reason to a bearer of consciousness and explore the relation of such a bearer to other beings. It is, however, difficult to see how such a story might go; moreover, the approach I am pursuing resonates better with the text of the Second Meditation, taken as a whole.

¶7. The (Apparent) Uselessness of Imagination for the Exploration of the Cognitive Agent

The seventh paragraph breaks off for the moment the substantive exploration of the cognitive agent in order to make a methodological point. The meditator attempts to understand herself further by using her imagination. Descartes argues that the imagination is an inappropriate faculty for attempting to understand the cognitive agent. The imagination is a faculty for cognizing the corporeal: imagining is "simply contemplating the shape or image of a corporeal thing" (7:28; 2:19), but, as far as we can tell, the cognitive agent is incorporeal, lacking all of the attributes associated with body. Now, Descartes believes that a good deal of bad philosophizing about the cognitive self comes from trying to read cognitive activity through the lens of an Aristotelian sensory ideology, an ideology that ultimately derives from the extent to which we rely on our senses when we are young (see VI.¶6; 7:75; 2:52). So he firmly enjoins:

> I thus realize that none of the things that the imagination enables me to grasp is at all relevant to this knowledge of myself which I possess, and that the mind must therefore be most carefully diverted from such things if it is to perceive its own nature as distinctly as possible. (¶7; 7:28; 2:19)

In terms of the larger conversation between Descartes and Thomistic Aristotelians, Descartes is claiming that he is developing an understanding of what he is that is thus far free from the involvement of sensible phantasms. Aquinas, as we saw earlier, did not think it was possible for the human intellect to understand anything, including the intellectual soul itself, without turning to those phantasms. Descartes is pointing out that the understanding of the cogito being as a thinking thing which he has developed has not involved turning to the phantasms at all: sensible phantasms simply do not seem to help us understand what it is to be a being that sees that things are so.

Beyond that, this paragraph is interesting for what it shows about Descartes's attitude toward the manner in which the meditator's current epistemic situation—which involves "supposing" that bodies do not exist—affects the current investigation. Here's how the passage begins:

> What else am I [*Quid praeterea*]? I will use my imagination. I am not that structure of limbs which is called a human body. I am not even some thin vapour which permeates the limbs—a wind, fire, breath, or whatever I depict in my imagination; for these are things which I have supposed [*supposui*] to be nothing [*nihil*]. Let this supposition [*positio*] stand; for all that I am still something [*aliquid sum*]. (¶7; 7:27; 2:18)²³

Consonant with the interpretation of the First Meditation, doubt about body works by asking the meditator to make certain assumptions. In particular, I am to suppose body to be nothing. Even as I make this supposition, I can still affirm my own reality—that "I am something." But this way of proceeding raises a question for the meditator. I am, after all, only supposing that bodies do not exist. Perhaps it will turn out that bodies do exist. Perhaps it will even turn out that I am one of these bodies. If things turn out this way, the imagination may, after all, have a role to play in my cognition of myself:

> But may it not perhaps happen that these very things which I am supposing to be nothing, nevertheless in reality [*in rei veritate*] do not differ from the me whom I know [*non differant ab eo me quem novi*]? (¶7; 7:27; 2:18)

How exactly might it turn out that "the me whom I know" does not differ from body? Descartes does not work this out, but at one end of the spectrum, I suppose, the cognitive agent might turn out to be a body—a brain, a thin vapor, or whatever. Somewhere in the middle of the spectrum, I suppose, the cognitive agent might turn out to be merely a mode or aspect of a corporeal substance. In this case, it is not obvious whether the meditator would want to say that the cognitive agent does not differ from a body. Perhaps at this point she would need to specify further what "not different from" means and become more explicit about what sort of distinction she envisions. At other end of the spectrum, if it turns out (as Descartes thinks it does) that the cognitive agent is "really distinct" from the human body, then that would create enough space between the cognitive agent and the body that the agent would differ from that body. This would be so, even if it should also turn out (as Descartes thinks it does) that the cognitive agent—I insofar as I am a thinking thing—is united to a body, so that the unrestricted I has a body and in this way "does not differ" from body.

The meditator's point is that it is too early to tell where things will end up, and this being so, the imagination may well play a role in my cognition of "the me whom I know." Descartes responds:

> I do not know, and for the moment I shall not argue the point, since I can make judgements [*judicium ferre possum*] only about things which are known to me [*mihi nota sunt*]. I know [*Novi*] that I exist. I ask what am I who knows this [*quis sim ego ille quem novi*]. It is certain that my cognition [*notitiam*] of myself taken in precisely this way [*huius sic praecise*] does not depend on things that I do not yet know exist. (¶7; 7:27–28; 2:18–19)

This is a difficult passage. I think what Descartes is saying may be paraphrased as follows. We are in the process of providing a *notitiam*—let's say some understanding or theory—of something. The theory's target is me insofar as I see that I must exist, me insofar as I am a cognitive agent. If we keep in mind that *that* is the target of the theory, and not some more generic me—say, me the human being—then it will become clear that the theory does not involve elements whose existence I am not sure of. Why? Well, I am certain of the existence of whatever is found in my current understanding of myself as the cogito being—as the being that sees that it must exist. For example, if having gray matter (or not being different from gray matter) were found in my current understanding of myself as the cogito being, I would now know that gray matter exists. If assimilating nourishment were one of the activities found in my current understanding of myself as the cogito being, I would now know that a digestive system exists as well as perhaps some sort of nourishment. If operating on corporeal phantasms were included in my current *notitiam* of myself as the cogito being, then I would now know that corporeal phantasms exist. But none of these things has shown up thus far.

What *has* shown up? Seeing that something must be so has characterized my current conception of myself as the cogito being, and as I notice that seeing that something must be so is bound up with doubting, affirming, denying, understanding, and willing, I realize that there exists in me the wherewithal to doubt, affirm, deny, understand, and will. All of this concerns my current understanding of myself insofar as I see that I must exist. My understanding of myself as the cogito being may evolve. It is in principle possible (though by now highly unlikely) that I will discover that I cannot see that anything is so unless I turn toward corporeal phantasms: getting clearer on this point awaits the wax discussion. But I have at least begun to understand this target self; and there is no role for the imagination in this initial understanding.

¶¶8–9. THE COGNITIVE AGENT'S POWERS

In ¶¶8–9 Descartes, in a manner reminiscent of Aristotelian treatments of powers and acts associated with being a living thing in their account of the soul, proceeds to consider the powers and abilities associated with being a thinking thing. Here is Descartes's list of powers:

> But what then am I? A thinking thing? What is that? A doubting, understanding, affirming, denying, willing, unwilling, and also imagining and sensing [*imaginans quoque, & sentiens*] thing. (¶8; 7:28; 2:19)

The postpositive *quoque* segregates the *imaginans* and *sentiens* from the rest of the list. There is some hesitation over whether these last two items—imagining and sensing—belong on the list. I believe there are two reasons for this hesitation.

First, and most obvious, the meditator has just eliminated the senses from the list of things that she could attribute to herself in ¶6, because of their apparent involvement with corporeality. Similar considerations apply to the imagination: it is, on its face, a faculty that is bound up with corporeality. (For example, Descartes will conclude—in the opening paragraphs of the Sixth Meditation—that his best account of what imagining is depends on assuming that he is joined to a body.)

Second, the place of the sensing and the imagining in the cognitive life of the cognitive being is less clear. They are less integral to, less bound up with, the focal operation of judging—of seeing that something is so—than the first items on the list: doubting, understanding, affirming, denying, willing, and unwilling. Indeed, Descartes will claim in the Sixth Meditation that "this power of imagining which is in me, differing as it does from the power of understanding, is not a necessary constituent of my own essence, that is, the essence of my mind" (VI.¶3; 7:73; 2:51); and "I can clearly and distinctly understand myself as a whole without these faculties [imagination and sensation]" (VI.¶10; 7:78; 2:54). Part of the idea here is that sensing and imagining are not as integral to seeing that something is so as the other things on the list: it would seem that the cognitive agent could not function—see that things are so—without these sorts of abilities, but, to all appearances, could function without sensation and imagination. It is also not clear exactly what sensation and imagination do in fact contribute to its ability to function (especially in view of the skeptical doubt now in effect). In short, the place these faculties hold in the economy of the cognitive agent is as yet obscure.

In ¶9, Descartes seeks to establish that all of these things do indeed belong to him.

> Is it not I myself [ego ipse] who understands, who now doubts almost everything, who understands some things, who affirms this one thing, denies everything else, who wants to know many things, does not want to be deceived, imagines many things even unwillingly, and also observes [animadverto] many things coming to it as if through the senses? (7:28; 2:19)

These are all things that I, the cognitive agent, am doing.[24] I see that I am doing all of these things, that I am doubting, affirming, denying, and so forth. Their truth, their reality, is as apparent to me as the truth and reality that I exist. When Descartes asks, "Which of these can be distinguished from my cognition/thought [cogitatione]? Which can be said to be separate from me myself?" he answers with respect to the core activities—the ones most intimately bound up with judging—that they so transparently cannot be separate that he sees no way of making this point plainer: "That it is I who doubts, who understands, who wills, is so manifest, that nothing occurs through which it may be explained more clearly."

Imagining and sensing raise, however, special issues.

Imagining. The meditator is currently supposing the realm of the corporeal to be a sham. Yet, as was observed in ¶7, imagination is a faculty whose point seems to be to cognize the corporeal: "for to imagine is nothing other than to contemplate the shape or image of a corporeal thing." If it should turn out that there is no such thing as the corporeal—if it should turn out that bodies are "nothing"—it will be unclear what to make of such a power or ability. (It would be a little like trying to figure out what a cold-fusion-contemplating power would be.) Descartes's response to this incipient worry is, Let all of this be so; it still remains the case that imagining—whatever it turns out to be—is something that the cognitive agent does, and so the power of imagining is real:

> But indeed I am the very same thing who imagines: for although perhaps, as I have supposed, no imagined thing at all is true/real [vera], the power itself of imagining nevertheless exists in reality [revera], and makes up a part of my cognition/thought [cogitationis]. (¶9; 7:29; 2:19)

Sensing. What Descartes has to say about sensing at this stage strikes me as both careful and delicate. Sensing raises issues similar to the ones raised by imagining—What would we think about sensing if some of the things that we are currently supposing should turn out to be the case?—but the issues are more difficult than in the case of imagining. There is arguably enough latitude in what counts as imagining that my

identification of a given form of cognition as imagining might survive an
unexpected turn of events. Maybe there is something that we would be
happy to call imagining even if it turned out that we had no bodies, even
if it turned out that there were no bodies, perhaps even if it turned out
that there was no such thing as corporeal nature. By way of contrast, it
would be less comfortable to identify a given form of cognition as sensing
if it turned out that I was always dreaming or did not even have a body.

How, then, while I am supposing that I am dreaming, while I am supposing that I do not have a body, should I think about sensing and how it
differs from imagining? How am I to think about the tactile experience
of the keyboard and visual experience of the computer screen (or the
tactile and visual experience that I appear to be having of the keyboard
and screen)? Descartes suggests I should think of myself as "noticing as
it were through the senses a corporeal thing." The point of the "as it
were," as I understand it, is to table these larger issues about what sensing is. So when I look at the screen in front of me and think to myself,
maybe I am not really sensing, maybe I am only dreaming there's a
screen or doing something else, I call this thing I'm doing (whatever it
turns out to be) "as it were observing the screen through the senses."
The point that Descartes wants to make now, the point that is thematically required, in fact, is that this thing I'm doing that seems so different
from imagining, the "as it were" sensing, whatever it turns out to be, is
something I, the cognitive agent, do.[25] And so Descartes writes:

> And finally it is the same I who senses, or who notices corporeal things as
> if through the senses [*Idem denique ego sum qui sentio, sive qui res corporeas
> tanquam per sensus animadverto*]. (¶9; 7:29; 2:19)

A little earlier, he had said that it is I myself who "also . . . notice many
things as if coming from the senses [*multa etiam tanquam a sensibus venientia animadverto*]." The way I understand this is that the meditator is, at
least for the time being, supposed to identify sensing, as opposed to
imagining or remembering, in terms of what seems to be going on.

All of this strikes me as straightforward and innocuous. Things become
more difficult when one considers the continuation of the passage; for
here, it has seemed to many, Descartes takes a momentous further step:

> And finally it is the same I who senses, or who observes corporeal things
> as if through the senses. For example, I am now seeing light, hearing a
> noise, feeling heat [*calorem sentio*]. But I am asleep, so all this is false [*falsa*].
> Yet I certainly seem to see, to hear, and to become warm [*calescere*].[26] This
> cannot be false [*falsum*]; and this is properly [*proprie*] what is called sensing
> in me [*quod in me sentire appellatur*]; and this, precisely so taken [*praecise sic
> sumptum*], is nothing other than thinking. (7:29; 2:19)

What Descartes writes here is carefully qualified (*proprie, praecise sic sumptum*), which gives the sense that he is trying to make a delicate point. I believe the delicacy arises from his wanting to claim that sensing clearly belongs to me, the cognitive agent, while wanting to remain noncommittal about what sensing actually is. If we delve too deeply into what sensing—a special mode of cognition that arises from the union of mind and body—is, we will not be able to continue in our assumption that there are no bodies.

Here, then, is how I would read this passage: It is true that I am supposing that I am dreaming, so I cannot take my apparent seeing of the light, hearing of the noise, feeling of the heat as I normally would. I must withdraw the commitment to there being light, noise, and heat, and describe what I am doing as just seeming to see light, hear a noise, and feel heat; it is clear that I, the cognitive agent, am (at least) doing that much, that is, that I am "as it were" seeing light, hearing noise, and feeling heat. So the force of "This cannot be false/unreal" as applied to "Yet I certainly seem to see, to hear, and to become warm" is not that I cannot be wrong about the content of what I seem to see, hear, or feel; rather, it is that what is going on in me as I look at the screen that I take to be in front of me is something that is really happening and is *my* doing (or *my* undergoing). In the most difficult part of the passage, Descartes goes on to say that doing that much—seeming to see, hear, and become warm—is properly what is termed sensing in me (the "in me" is important here), the cognitive agent. (We might say, doing that much is sensing insofar as sensing is something that the cognitive agent does.) And sensing taken in this way, that is, cutting away (*praecise*) from whatever else happens when the cognitive agent senses, is nothing other than thinking. From here on out (see III.¶1) Descartes will be comfortable speaking of sensing in me, the cognitive agent, as a mode of thought. The upshot: seeing—or to remain neutral, "as it were seeing," "seeming to see"—is something I am indisputably currently doing (it cannot be false/unreal); to seem to see, or to "as it were" see, is all that I mean by "sensing in me"; and to do this is nothing other than to think; in other words, "as it were" sensing is a mode of thought.

To expand, "*tanquam*/as it were" (7:28, line 28, and 7:29, line 12) functions similarly to the "*videor*/I seem" (7:29, line 15). Descartes uses them as devices to withdraw various commitments concerning the senses: "You say what you are doing right now is sensing, but how can you be sure? Sensing may involve body and you might not, for all you know, have a body. So maybe you are not really sensing." Descartes's response: "Fair enough. But I need some way, for the time being, to mark the difference between my current (visual) cognition of the fire that I take to be in front of me (or would take to be in front of me, were it not for the skeptical assumptions I am now making), and, for example, my current (visual) cognition of Paris (memory) and, for example again, my current (visual) cognition of the lost continent of Atlantis (imagination). So let me call what I am doing when I see a light or hear a noise 'as it were sensing' or 'seeming to sense.' The point I am now making is that these goings-on, whatever I call them, clearly belong to me, the cognitive agent. It is the exercise of one of *my* abilities. It is something that *I* do." In other words, the "as it were sensing" and "seeming to sense" function as tags to identify a certain sort of activity or passivity, an activity or passivity that belongs to the cognitive agent.

As I read this passage, then, Descartes is conceding that, for all I know, it may turn out that all I ever do by way of sensing is "as it were sensing" or "seeming to sense," and that I never actually sense. That is, for all I know, it might turn out that genuine sensing essentially involves bodies and there are no bodies. Sometimes the last sentence of ¶9 is taken to be incompatible with this concession, that is, as affirming that it is beyond doubt that I sense because there is nothing more to sensing than mentality. In my view, such readings do not give sufficient weight to the restrictions implicit in *in me* and *praecise sic sumptum*, which indicate that there may be, if not imply outright that there is, something more to sensing than what goes on in the cognitive agent. And, again, if this something more is not in place—if, for example, there are no bodies for me to look at, or there are but I have no eyes with which to look at them—then perhaps it will be the case that I do not really see but only seem to see. The possibility that I may not in fact be seeing when I think I am is also suggested by Descartes's comment a couple of pages later, at II.¶15: "But when I see, or think I see (I am not here distinguishing the two), it is simply not possible that I who am now thinking am not something" (7:33; 2:22). This would be a peculiar thing for him to say if he took himself to establish at the end of ¶9 that "properly" all that seeing really is is seeming to see. In other words, there remains, for all that has been claimed at the end of ¶9, a distinction between seeing and thinking that I see. Descartes's point is that we may neglect this distinction for present purposes. For now, it does not matter whether I actually see or merely think I see: either way, I am able to identify the phenomenon Descartes wishes to draw my attention to and determine that it is mine.

Descartes is sometimes understood to be advancing at the end of ¶9 a metaphysically ambitious claim to the effect that sensation is an exclusively mental going-on or that the nature of sensation is exhausted by consciousness, so that any bodily activities associated with sensation are mere "accompaniments." (The idea that there is nothing more to sensation than consciousness is encouraged by CSM's translation of *qui res corporeas tanquam per sensus animadverto* as "am aware of bodily things as it were through the senses." *Animadverto*—literally, I turn my soul toward—suggests more than simply awareness; it has a connotation of noticing or attending to.) Or, again, Descartes is sometimes understood to be advancing at the end of ¶9 an epistemologically ambitious thesis that it follows from what sensing "really is" that there is no difference between seeing a light or hearing a noise and seeming to see a light or seeming to hear a noise, and so I cannot be wrong about *what* I am sensing.

The epistemological thesis seems to assume that the only way I could go wrong in the vicinity of sensation is by taking myself to be sensing when I am only "as it were" sensing (because, say, I am dreaming or hallucinating): in any case, I could not be mistaken about the "content" of my experience. I do not see any reason to attribute such a view to Descartes. *Prima facie*, his remarks about the clarity and obscurity of sensory ideas and the attendant threat of their material falsity point in a different direction. With respect to the metaphysical thesis, it seems odd that the meditator should view herself as already in a position to know enough about what sensing is (or, for that matter, what imagining is) to make the judgment that she could sense even if no bodies existed to be sensed (or even if she had no body). The meditator, as it turns out, brings to the *Meditations* fairly well developed views about sensation, which are not canvassed and criticized until III.¶¶8–12, and refined in certain ways in the Sixth Meditation. This gives us reason to be cautious about how much we read into the end of ¶9. Again, thematically what is required by ¶9 is simply that the meditator determine that this occurrence (whatever it turns out to be), or at least some aspect of it, is in fact hers; and if there is a way of reading the passage that enables her to see this without staking her to a controversial and unargued theory of sensation, so much the better philosophically.

¶¶10–16. THE WAX

The discussion of the wax does three things. It gets the meditator started on thinking about what a body is, it introduces the meditator to what clear and distinct cognition (especially clear and distinct understanding) is, and, most important, it unearths the presence of what Descartes calls the "mind alone," which he distinguishes from the mind working with the assistance of the senses and the imagination.

Although I can see that imagining and sensing (or as it were sensing) belong to the cognitive agent, it is hard to see exactly where they fit in. What do they have to do with the being who can see that it must exist? We won't get the full story until the Sixth Meditation, but Descartes has some important, mainly negative and contrastive points to make now, which he does through the consideration of the wax. In the course of this discussion, the relationship of the cognitive agent to these two forms of cognition comes into sharper view.

In ¶10, Descartes takes stock. The meditator is coming to a better understanding of what she, the cognitive agent, is. Yet she cannot shake the sense that she understands the corporeal things whose images flood her senses and imagination "with much more distinctness" (or so she thinks) than she understands the cognitive agent, which does not fall within the scope of the sense or the imagination. In particular, she is persuaded that because she can imagine and sense body, she understands body better than she understands herself insofar as she is a thinking thing. The immediate background for the meditator's outlook here is the scholastic view that the human intellect is best suited for—best proportioned to—corporeal things, because the characteristic manner of human understanding is to turn to phantasms, acquired from the senses, and to abstract universals from them. To dispel the meditator's lingering sense that bodies are better understood by us than the mind is, and that the reason this is so is that they fall under the senses and imagination while the mind does not, Descartes has her reflect both on what it is that she really understands concerning body and on the contribution of the senses and imagination to this understanding. This general purpose frames the wax discussion, as is clear from the end, when Descartes comes back to consider, in the light of the meditator's reflection on her cognition of the piece of wax, whether the senses and imagination really do make the sort of difference to our ability to cognize the wax that the meditator had assumed (¶14) and whether body is really better known than mind (¶15).

In ¶11, the meditator considers a piece of wax as it undergoes a certain transformation. I think the text works better if we take the meditator to suspend temporarily skeptical doubt about body, and consider an actual piece of a wax, so that she is really seeing, smelling, tasting, feeling, and hearing the wax (and not, for example, supposing that she may, for all she knows, be only "as it were" sensing the wax). This is indicated by Descartes's remark in ¶10, "Very well then; just this once let us give it a completely free rein, so that after a while, when it is time to tighten the reins, it may more readily submit to being curbed." I think the "free rein" here is the freedom to drop temporally the skeptical doubt; merely giving the meditator permission to think about a possible body does not seem to account for the sense of exception. Descartes is going to claim that senses and imagination are limited in what they achieve; the limitations he is going to call attention to do not depend on an assumption that the meditator might for all she knows be only as it were sensing and not really sensing. "Assume you are awake, and your senses are working properly. Even so, they do not make the sort of contribution to your distinct grasp of body that you think they do."

Here's the report of the meditator's experience:

> Let us take, for example, this piece of wax [*hanc ceram*]. It has just been taken from the honeycomb; it has not yet quite lost the taste of the honey; it retains some of the scent of the flowers from which it was gathered; its colour, shape and size are plain to see; it is hard, cold and can be handled without difficulty; if you rap it with your knuckle it makes a sound. In short, it has everything which appears necessary to enable a body to be known as distinctly as possible. But even as I speak, I put the wax by the fire, and look: the residual taste is eliminated, the smell goes away, the colour changes, the shape is lost, the size increases; it becomes liquid and hot; you can hardly touch it, and if you strike it, it no longer makes a sound. But does the same wax remain? It must be admitted that it does; no one denies it, no one thinks otherwise. (¶11; 7:30; 2:20)

As the wax is heated, all of its proper sensible qualities (taste, odor, color, tactile qualities, sound) have either disappeared or been altered; the same is true of the wax's common sensible qualities (size, shape). But even though all of the qualities of the wax that the senses make available to me have been altered, it is still the same wax, and, more to the point, I can recognize that it is still the same wax. But what is it that I recognize as the same? The passage continues:

> So what was it in the wax that I comprehended with such distinctness? Evidently none of those things that are reached through the senses; for whatever came under taste, smell, sight, touch, or hearing has now altered—and the wax remains. (7:30; 2:20)

We need to treat this with some care. Descartes is not claiming that senses play no role in my ability to recognize the wax as the same wax, as if I could trace out its history over time without their assistance. We are to assume that the senses play some role in the story; indeed, one of the reasons, I take it, that the meditator needs to suspend the skeptical doubt is to reach cognitively *this* wax (*hanc ceram*). The question that Descartes asks is whether those aspects or things that the sense makes available to me are what I "comprehend with such distinctness." This goes back to the meditator's belief that she comprehends corporeal things more distinctly than she comprehends herself as a cognitive agent, because she can sense and imagine the former but not the latter.

Now, "comprehend with such distinctness," for Descartes, has to do with one's cognition of *what* something is. This is suggested by the beginning of ¶10: "From all this I am beginning to know [*nosse*] somewhat better *what* I am [*quisnam sim*]" (emphasis added). The thought that then

occurs to the meditator is that body is comprehended with more distinctness than mind, that is, I know more about *what* body is than *what* I
am (echoing the meditator's original assessment of her views about the
respective condition of her knowledge of body and soul in ¶5: whereas
she had no doubt about the "nature [*naturam*]" of body and thought she
knew it "distinctly," she took herself to have only very hazy ideas about
"what this soul [*quid esset haec anima*]" is). Linking comprehending something distinctly with understanding what it is, that is, understanding its
essence or nature, also explains the relevance of the wax's remaining the
same: for with my grasp of what something is comes a sense of what is
required for that thing to remain in existence. Finally, that our cognition
of the wax's essence or nature should be under consideration here fits
with the idea that what motivates the entire discussion is the scholastic
thesis that the proper object of the human intellect is body: for that thesis concerns human *understanding*, which involves a grasp of essences or
natures (i.e., of what things are).

It would be natural to say that "comprehend with such distinctness"
simply means to *understand* what something is, but Descartes appears to
deliberately delay using terminology related to *intellego* until the very
last paragraph of the Second Meditation, preferring in the meantime locutions such as "perceive distinctly" or "comprehend distinctly."[27] I think
that this may be because Descartes is self-consciously trying to give a new
account of understanding, one less connected to the idea of abstraction
or universality and more connected to the idea of judgment. So although
Descartes observes a consistent line between knowing that something is
(which for him is often a matter of the clarity of one's perception) and
knowing what something is (which for him is often a matter of the distinctness of one's perception),[28] and although knowing what something
is is traditionally a matter of understanding, he does not use *intellego* and
cognates until late in the discussion.[29]

When Descartes asks about his distinct comprehension of the wax,
the "What is it?" question that hovers in the background is not "What
makes the wax, wax?" As the passage unfolds, it becomes clear that the
question is "What makes this body, the body that it is?" and the wax has
been chosen as an example of a particular body; a piece of putty, molten
glass, or lead would have done as well.

Let's return to Descartes's question "So what was it in the wax that I
comprehended with such distinctness?" Is it what falls under the senses?
Well, the aspects of (or things belonging to) the wax manifested in sensory cognition, taken either singly or in aggregate, do not make perspicuous what the wax is. Descartes supposes, perhaps oversimplifying, that
if they did, those aspects (or things) would track the wax's identity in a

straightforward way; if cognition of those aspects showed us what the wax is, then those aspects, or at least some of them, would remain the same thing so long as the wax remained the same thing. It is possible, of course, to imagine more sophisticated proposals relating what the wax is to those aspects of it that fall under the senses. But the more complexity we introduce into the picture of the relation between what the wax is and those aspects of it that come under the senses, the harder it will be to think of the aspects (or things) coming under the senses as themselves making perspicuous what the wax is, as opposed to the further elements in the picture that add the additional structure to the sensory aspects.

All of this forces the meditator to think harder about what the wax is and, in particular, how the wax is related to its sensible qualities:

> Perhaps the answer lies in the thought which now comes to my mind; namely, the wax was not after all the sweetness of the honey, or the fragrance of the flowers, or the whiteness, or the shape, or the sound, but rather a body which has appeared to me, coming into view [conspicuum] in these ways [modis] a little while ago, and now those. (¶12; 7:30; 2:20)

This is meant as an answer to the question "What was it in the wax that I comprehended with such distinctness?" which, I am supposing, is the question "What do I take the wax to be: that is, how do I answer the 'What is it?' question, when asked of this wax?" The meditator's answer introduces some complexity into her account of what the wax is, creating some distance between what the wax is and the qualities of wax the senses make available to us (i.e., the aspects of the wax that fall under the senses): the wax is not any of these qualities, but rather something, a body; the qualities are (I take it, but Descartes could be clearer) the sources of the various ways this body appears to me. As this distance is created, it reinforces the thought that I do not grasp "what this wax is" with the senses, and so the qualities of the wax that are made available by the senses are not what I comprehend most distinctly in it.

The introduction of body into the more refined account of the wax raises a new question—"What is it, this body that underlies the qualities?" Here's the meditator's answer:

> But what precisely [praecise] is it that I am now imagining? Let us concentrate, take away everything which does not belong to the wax, and see what is left: merely something extended, flexible, and changeable. (7:30–31; 2:20)

It is easy to misunderstand what Descartes means when he says he is going to take away everything "which does not belong to the wax": it can sound as if he is denying that the sensible qualities listed above belong to the wax at all. Such a claim would not only be counterintuitive, but is unprepared for in the text: how does showing that I could lose a quality and remain the same thing show that the quality did not belong to me? However, paying heed to the *praecise* can help us understand the point Descartes is making. Here the force of *praecise* seems to be to narrow the focus of the discussion to what belongs to the wax simply insofar as it is a body, cutting away from everything else that belongs to it. He is asking what belongs to body qua body, and his point about the colors, sounds, and so forth is that they do not belong to this body simply insofar as it is a body—they do not constitute the essence or nature of this body, but rather are something extra.

One can see why, given Descartes's description of the scenario, that the yellowness, the savor of honey, and the fragrance of flowers do not belong to the wax simply insofar as it is a body; the body can continue to be without these particular qualities. It is perhaps appropriate to raise a question about sensibility in general. Does being sensible belong to body considered precisely as such? After all, in ¶5, the meditator had reported as part of her previous understanding of body that "it can be perceived by touch, sight, hearing, taste or smell." But when Descartes says that after we take away everything that does not belong to the wax—does not belong to body qua body, as I am interpreting him—all that's left is "something extended, flexible, and changeable," he is implicitly denying that being sensible belongs to body qua body, is a part of what it is to be a body. As a matter of fact, in the experiment the body lost many of its sensible qualities—it lost its taste, odor, and ability to make sounds. It is hard to see what would prevent a body, at least under certain circumstances, from losing its color and tactile qualities as well (imagine an ether).[30] To push a little beyond anything that Descartes says here, in his view the capacity of a body to be sensed seems dependent on what sort of beings there are (or, depending on how we unpack the modality inherent in capacity, could be) around to do the sensing, and how they are set up: so being sensible intuitively does not seem to be the right sort of feature to figure in an account of body.[31] (This is not to deny that body's being sensible will necessarily follow, in the right circumstances, from body's being what it is and a human being's being what it is; but this is not enough to make body's being sensible a part of what body is.)

Having refined my conception of what body is as something that is extended, flexible, and changeable—that is, having arrived at a better sense of what it is that I "distinctly comprehend" in body—Descartes pursues this conception further:

> But what is this being flexible, mutable? Is it this, that I imagine that the wax can change from a round shape into a square, and from that into a triangular one? (¶12; 7:31; 2:20)

Descartes is really asking two questions here: one concerns what flexibility and mutability are; the other concerns how I comprehend this (by my imagination?). He seeks an alignment between what is being comprehended and the agency that is doing the comprehending. So does the flexibility of the wax, Descartes asks, consist in something that I might imagine to myself, say, through a series of visualizations that I might run through in my imagination, of the wax's changing shape in various ways? Descartes's immediate response is no—there is, in fact, misalignment here. The wax's flexibility and mutability involve more than what might be captured through a series of visualizations:

> In no way [nullo modo]; for I comprehend it to be capable of changing in innumerable such ways, and I cannot run through innumerable things in my imagination; and so this comprehension is not achieved [perficitur] by the imagination. (¶12; 7:31; 2:21)

The fact that one cannot run through in one's imagination all of the changes that one comprehends that wax can undergo indicates, according to Descartes, that more is involved in our cognition of the wax than what the imagination could be responsible for. The idea that the sort of comprehension we have of the wax outstrips what can be depicted through imagination is clearly important to Descartes. One suspects, however, that it does not go to the heart of the matter. Even if I had a sort of "superimagination" that was able to run through infinitely many scenarios at once, there would still be something odd about thinking of such an exercise as counting as my comprehension of the wax's flexibility or mutability. This is because, I think, the most fundamental difference between my higher forms of cognition and my lower forms (such as I might readily think of as taking place in animals) is not really a matter of quantity.

Descartes continues the discussion by making a similar point about my grasp of the wax's extension:

> What is being extended? Is it, too, unknown? [Quid extensum? Nunquid etiam ipsa ejus extensio est ignota?] For it increases when the wax melts, increases more when the wax boils, and is greater still if the heat is increased; nor would I judge [judicarem] correctly what the wax is [quid sit cera], if I did not deem that it admitted more variation in its extension than I would ever be able to hold together [complexus] in my imagination. (¶12; 7:31; 2:21)

The second sentence is puzzling, because nothing so far seems "unknown." I think the easiest way to make sense of the passage is to supply an implicit "by the imagination," so that the sentence's sense is, "Is it, too, unknown by the imagination?" That is: We have just seen that the imagination does not comprehend what being flexible and mutable is.

What may be more surprising to the meditator (in light of traditional views about shape being the proper object of the common sense or imagination) is that the imagination does not even comprehend what being extended is, for the same considerations apply with respect to being extended that apply to being flexible and mutable. As before, one suspects that my inability to depict in my imagination all of the variations through time that the wax's extension admits of, while significant, cannot be the whole story about the limits of the imagination's contribution to my ability to cognize the wax distinctly.

Having observed that my distinct perception of the wax differs from my sensory and imaginative perception of the wax, Descartes draws the following moral:

> It remains therefore that I must concede that I do not imagine what this wax is [*quid sit haec cera*], but perceive it with my mind alone [*sola mente*]; I say this about this wax in particular; for concerning wax in general the point is clearer. (¶12; 7:31; 2:21)

This moral appears odd and seems somewhat abruptly drawn. It appears odd because when Descartes claims that I could perceive what a particular body—namely, this piece of wax—is with my mind alone, it sounds as if he is implying that I could somehow perceive what *this* piece of wax is without *any* help from the senses; but it is not clear that I could so much as think about *this* piece of wax (and so could not perceive what *it* is) unless I had senses. And the conclusion seems somewhat abruptly drawn because, granted I do not sense or imagine what the wax is, it is not clear what entitles Descartes to the further conclusion that my distinct perception of the wax is an exercise of "my mind alone [*sola mente*]."

Now, when Descartes claims that I perceive what this piece of wax is, not with my senses or with my imagination, but with my "mind alone," he is not implying that I could perceive what this piece of wax is without any help from the senses. Rather, his point is that distinct perception of what the wax is is an exercise of what he calls the mind alone (whatever that turns out to mean), as opposed to an exercise of our senses or imagination. And this point is compatible with the idea that the exercise of mind through which I perceive what the piece of wax is could not take place without *some* help from the senses, perhaps in order to lock on to, as it were, *this* piece of wax. (Indeed, that the senses are necessary for this much is why, I take it, the skeptical doubt concerning the senses was suspended for the discussion of wax.)

Let's turn to the apparent abruptness of Descartes's move from the fact that the distinct perception of what the wax is is not an exercise of the senses or the imagination, to the conclusion that it "remains" that the distinct perception is an exercise of the "mind alone." This raises more interesting issues. How Descartes is reasoning here depends to a certain extent on how he is thinking about the "mind alone." For example, he could be identifying the mind alone with its highest cognitive faculty, the intellect or understanding. Then, starting from the standard Aristotelian tripartite division of the human cognitive faculties into the senses, the imagination, and the intellect, he might infer by a process of elimination that, in view of the failure of the senses and imagination to distinctly perceive what the wax is, it "remains" that the intellect, that is, the mind alone, is the faculty that accomplishes this. Such an argument might be helped along by the further consideration that distinct perception of the wax does not seem to be an imagistic affair in the way that the goings-on in the senses or imagination are.

While I think that there is something to the preceding account, it would be disappointing to leave matters there. Such a "process of elimination" argument would do little to illuminate the, so to speak, positive relationship between the "mind alone" and this distinct perception. To pursue this positive relationship, we need to ask, What does Descartes mean by the locution "mind alone"? The meditator has been thinking of the cogito being as fundamentally characterized through an interrelated set of core abilities—doubting, understanding, affirming, denying, willing, unwilling—and as possessing a set of auxiliary abilities—imagining and sensing (*imaginans quoque, & sentiens*). We might, then, think of the line between what belongs to the "mind alone" and what does not in terms of what is bound up with these core abilities and what is not. I think his remark "nor would I judge [*judicarem*] correctly what the wax is [*quid sit cera*], if I did not deem that it admitted more variation in its extension than I would ever be able to hold together [*complexus*] in my imagination" is suggestive in this direction. As I look down upon and, as it were, survey the goings-on in the senses and imagination, measuring them against what the wax is—that is, as I make judgments about what the wax is—I realize that my distinct perception of the wax, my cognition of what the wax is, belongs to the agency that is doing the surveying, that is, is bound up with my core judging powers, that is, with the "mind alone." Distinctly cognizing (perceiving) takes place at a different level from sensing and imagining, a plane that involves discrimination and judgment.

The idea that our distinct perception of the wax is bound up with our judging abilities in a special way is a difficult one, which Descartes develops over the ensuing discussion. What emerges from this discussion, I think, is that judgment occupies for him a place similar to the one that abstraction holds for Aquinas. For Aquinas, abstraction takes us from our initial cognition of a thing to a grasp of its essence, to a grasp of what it is. According to him, we come to understand what something is by abstracting, from sensory experience of it and others of its kind, what that thing has in common with other members of its kind or species: we separate out what is common to Fido, Spot, and Rover ("caninehood"), distinguishing this from that which belongs to the dogs as individuals ("this brown," "that black").

For Descartes, by way of contrast, understanding involves penetrating beneath the surface to some underlying structure. Aquinas, of course, would claim that, on his view, too, one is getting at something underlying and deep as one reaches the commonalities, but Descartes would disagree. For him, Aquinas's commonalities are merely classificatory. What counts is the underlying microstructure, and to get to that, you do not abstract but judge. A sign of this is that one can get to the sort of underlying structure he has in view while focused on a single individual, without looking for some commonality. The process that takes me from my initial consideration of an individual to a more distinct perception of what it is to be that individual is not abstraction of the universal from the particular, but rather judgment.

At the end of ¶12 Descartes makes a delicate point about the place of "mind alone" in my cognition of what the wax is. It can seem from the tenor of the discussion thus far that each of my three main cognitive faculties has entered its own cognition of what the wax is, and that, in particular, the two lower cognitive faculties, sense and imagination, do so independently of the core abilities of discrimination and judgment found in the "mind alone." What, I think, contributes to this impression is the fact that Descartes does not want to distinguish the intellect (the "mind alone") from the lower cognitive powers in the traditional Aristotelian way, namely, through the respective "objects" of those powers; rather, he is committed to the view that the same thing—this piece of wax—falls under the senses, the imagination, and the intellect, and the differences between the various modes of cognition arise from how this thing is cognized. And that can, in turn, encourage the thought that vision or touch, imagination, and the mind alone all provide different perceptions of what the wax is, with the difference being that the former do so poorly and the latter does so well. This is a misunderstanding that Descartes seems especially anxious to combat. He writes at the end of ¶12 that *any* cognition of what the piece of wax is, be it adequate or inadequate, is a function of the judging/discriminating power of the mind, the mind alone:

> For what wax is this [*Quaenam vero est haec cera*], which is not perceived except by the mind? For it is the same thing [*eadem*] which I see, which I touch, which I imagine, in short the same wax that I have thought [*arbitrabar:* "judged" would also be a fair translation] it to be from the beginning.

And, what is to be noted here [*quod notandum est*], its perception is not vision, not touch, not imagination, nor was it ever, although it seemed so at first, but the inspection of the mind alone [*solius mentis inspectio*], which can be either imperfect [incomplete?] and confused, as it was before, or clear and distinct, as it is now, according as I attend more or less to those things from which it is constituted. (7:31; 2:21)

(The formulation *Quaenam ... est haec cera*, which I have translated as "What wax is this," seems to me importantly different from the formulation *Quid est haec cera* that Descartes has been using. The latter is a request for the essence or nature of the wax; the former, I think, is not. After all, I do not see, touch, and imagine the wax's *nature*; rather, I see, touch, and imagine the *wax*.)

Descartes evidently anticipates that the meditator will have some difficulty with this point. We are, after all, accustomed to saying things like "We see the wax." Taken incautiously, this might suggest that the seeing brings with it some (at least rudimentary, but perhaps flawed) view about what it is that we are seeing. But, as we have just seen, Descartes insists that any view about what the thing that we are seeing is, is a matter for judgment and discernment. He underscores this point in the next paragraph:

> But meanwhile I wonder at how prone my mind is to errors. For although I consider this within myself quietly, voicelessly, I trip over the very words and am almost taken in by customary ways of speaking. For we say we see the wax itself, if it is present, not that we judge [*judicare*] it to be present from its colour or shape.[32] Whence I might immediately conclude: the wax is cognized [*cognosci*] with the vision of the eyes, not the inspection of the mind alone; unless I should look out the window, as now happened by chance, at men crossing the square, whom I also customarily say that I see, no less than the wax. But what do I see besides hats and coats, under which could be concealed automata? But I judge [*judico*] them to be men. And so that which I thought I saw with my eyes, I comprehend only with my faculty of judging [*judicandi facultate*], which is in my mind. (¶13; 7:31–32; 2:21)

It is important not to get off on the wrong foot in reading this passage. Many readers have found it attractive to locate the passage in a context of skeptical worry, inspired by some form of indirect realism: they take, How do I really know that there are men out there when all I see are hats and coats? as a way of asking, How do I really know that there are bodies out there when all I perceive are my own ideas? To be sure, such a reading is encouraged by Descartes's remark, "For we say we see the wax itself, if it is present, not that we judge it to be present from its colour or shape," which makes it sound as if he is asking how we know that the wax exists. Nevertheless, I think such a reading is off

the mark. So far, the discussion has focused on my most distinct perception of the piece of wax, which is more a matter of what the wax is than
of whether the wax exists (indeed, we have practically stipulated that for
the purposes of this discussion the wax exists). It would be odd for Descartes to shift gears here and make an unannounced change in topic from
issues about understanding what something is to issues about knowledge
of a thing's existence.

There is, however, another way of taking Descartes's remark, "For
we say we see the wax itself, if it is present, not that we judge it to be
present from its colour or shape," that gives it greater continuity with
the preceding discussion. I know that something is present, but now the
question is, *What* is it that is present? Similarly with the things across the
square—I see that there are things in the square, but the question is,
What are those things? My eyes take me only as far as the coats; they do
not penetrate beneath the surface to the beings underneath the coats.
For this, judgment is required. If we understand the passage this way, it
lines up nicely with a metaphor that Descartes will employ a little later
in the Second Meditation: "But when I distinguish the wax from its outward forms and, as it were, strip it and consider it naked, even if my
judgement may still contain errors, I cannot in any case perceive it thus
without a human mind" (¶14; 7:32; 2:22). This "stripping it" is a matter
of discerning what something is, not that it exists.

Now, ¶13 is meant to elucidate the difficult remark that Descartes
makes at the end of ¶12:

> And, what is to be noted here [*quod notandum est*], its perception is not vi-
> sion, not touch, not imagination, nor was it ever, although it seemed so at
> first, but the inspection of the mind alone [*solius mentis inspectio*], which
> can be either imperfect [incomplete?] and confused, as it was before, or
> clear and distinct, as it is now, according as I attend more or less to those
> things from which it is constituted. (7:31; 2:21)

Although I say "I see the wax," which can make it seem as if what the
wax is is something that I simply take in through the senses—thereby
eclipsing the primary role that judgment or "inspection of the mind
alone" plays in any view about what the wax is—*what* I am seeing is no
more given to me in the case of the wax than it is in the case of those
things across the square: figuring out *what* those things are (i.e., understanding) is a matter for judgment or the inspection of the mind alone.
Notice that, as Descartes restates the point in ¶13, "that which I thought
I saw with my eyes," namely, what the wax is or what those things are, is
in fact the sort of thing that can be "comprehend[ed] with only my faculty of judging, which is in my mind."[33] So in ¶13 Descartes uses the expression "comprehend with only my faculty of judging" where he had

used the "inspection of the mind alone" in ¶12, marking a close relationship between the inspection and the core abilities belonging to the "mind
alone." The role of judging in one's distinct perception of a thing (coming to have a view about what it is, its essence) helps us to see why he
would treat these as more or less the same thing.

This may lead one to wonder what is given to us by the senses, according to Descartes, if the perception of wax and the mind alone are both a
matter of judgment and the inspection of the mind alone. How far do
exercises of vision, touch, and imagination take us by themselves, before
the judgmental activities connected with distinct perception—without
our knowing what it is that we are seeing, touching, and imagining—kick
in? We get some help with how Descartes is thinking about the senses
from a well-known passage in the Sixth Replies, in which Descartes discusses three grades of senses:

> The first [grade of sense] is limited to the immediate stimulation of the
> bodily organs by external objects; this can consist in nothing but the mo-
> tion of the particles of the organs, and any change of shape and position
> resulting from this motion. The second grade comprises all the immedi-
> ate effects produced in the mind as a result of its being united with a
> bodily organ which is affected in this way. Such effects include the percep-
> tions of pain, pleasure, thirst, hunger, colours, sound, taste, smell, heat,
> cold and the like, which arise from the union and as it were intermingling
> of mind and body, as explained in the Sixth Meditation. The third grade
> includes all the judgements [judicia] that we have been accustomed to
> make from our earliest years, concerning things outside of us, on the oc-
> casion of the impressions, or movements, which are in the organs of our
> senses. (7:436–37; 2:295)

If we are interested in what an act of vision is, the second grade is the
most relevant. The first grade does not get as far as perception, and Descartes thinks it is incorrect to attribute what happens in the third grade
to sense, and explains that he calls this a grade of sense only because of a
prevalent but inaccurate usage:

> [T]he first grade of sensing consists in this motion of the brain, which we
> have in common with the brutes. From this follows the second, which ex-
> tends only to the perception of colour and light reflected from the stick, and
> arises out of the mind's being so intimately joined with the brain that the
> mind is affected by motions that happen in the brain; and nothing other
> should be referred to sense [sensum], if we wish to accurately distinguish it
> from intellect [intellectu]. For, it is obvious that my judging [judicem] the stick,
> positioned outside me, is coloured, from this sensation [sensu] of colour, by
> which I am affected; and likewise my rationally determining [ratiociner]

the stick's extension, shape, and distance from this colour's extension and boundary, and the relation of the colour's situation to parts of the brain [*ac situs relatione ad partes cerebri*]—even if this is commonly attributed to sense, and which is the reason I have here referred to it as the third grade of sense—nevertheless depends on the intellect alone [*solo intellectu*]. (7:437–38; 2:295)

So when Descartes says at the end of ¶12 that my perception of the wax "is not vision, not touch, not imagination, nor was it ever, although it seemed so at first, but the inspection of the mind alone," I think we may paraphrase him thus: My perception of what the wax is does not belong—nor has it ever, despite what might have initially seemed to be the case, belonged—to the second grade of sense, but always requires judgment, and rests on the inspection of the mind alone.

In ¶14, Descartes sums up the import of the wax discussion. He begins by making the point that the perception of what the wax is that he arrives at is superior to his initial attempts, when he was trying to base a perception of what it is on the senses or the imagination:

> So let us proceed, and consider on which occasion my perception of what the wax is was more perfect and evident. Was it when I first looked at it, and believed I knew it by my external senses, or at least by what they call the common sense—that is, the power of imagination? Or is my knowledge more perfect now, after a more careful investigation of both what it is and how it is known? Any doubt on this issue would clearly be foolish; for what distinctness was there in my earlier perception? What was there that it does not seem an animal could not possess? (7:32; 2:21–22)

Although (I take it) Descartes's own view is that animals are nonthinking mechanisms, I think he is counting on the meditator to believe that animals have lower forms of cognition, namely, sense and imagination. And when he asks, "Was there anything in it which an animal could not possess?" we need to be careful. I think Descartes's point is that the content, so to speak, of the earlier perception, that is, images of sensory qualities, is something that (we naively think) an animal could possess. He is not suggesting that (we naively think) an animal could possess even a poor (e.g., confused and incomplete) perception of what the wax is.[34] For Descartes has just told us that this is a matter for the inspection of the mind alone, and I doubt he thinks that we (even naively) attribute this to animals. So his point must be something like this: Initially the meditator thought she could cognize what the wax is with her senses and imagination, which cognition involved some sort of identification of what the wax is with those of its aspects or qualities that can be sensed or imagined.

Now, to be sure, there is something incoherent in this attempt, because the "identifying" already points to the primary role of the "mind alone," unacknowledged by meditator, in this attempt to cognize what the wax is with the senses or the imagination. Let's put that point aside for the moment, and focus on the content of the resulting cognition of the wax: it would seem to be some flow or mix of corporeal images—some collection of colors, tactile qualities, shapes, and so forth. And we can readily imagine this flow or mix of images occurring in an animal. By way of contrast, we cannot imagine an animal having the distinct cognition of what the wax is that we have. For this involves (among other things) a recognition of the unbounded character of the ways in which the wax can alter in shape and size, implicit in our perception of its being a mutable, flexible, and extended thing.

In the last sentence of ¶14, Descartes turns to the point that we just put to the side: as I reflect on my different cognitions (Descartes would say perceptions) of what the wax is—the one drawn in terms of the flow or mix of images or the one drawn in terms of changeability, flexibility, and extension—measuring which is better, the place of the mind alone, with its powers of judgment and discrimination, comes into view:

> But when I distinguish the wax from its outward forms and, as it were, strip it and consider it naked, even if my judgement may still contain errors [*error in judicio me esse possit*], I cannot in any case perceive it thus without a human mind. (7:32; 2:22)

The project of even trying to distinctly perceive the wax, of even trying to figure out what the wax is, is a project that involves judgment and so is distinctive of a human mind. (Notice that this point Descartes is making derives its plausibility from the fact that distinctly perceiving and figuring out what something is, that is, giving an account of its essence, seem to be on their face high-end cognitive activities. It would be less plausible for Descartes to claim that—as we might put it—simply perceiving the wax as a body requires a human mind. Since Descartes thinks all cognition requires a mind, he presumably would endorse this second claim as well, but it would harder for him to defend it by directly appealing to intuitive differences between us and the animals.)

In ¶15 Descartes returns to the theme that prompted the wax discussion in ¶10, namely, the meditator's sense that she comprehends the things that she imagines and senses more distinctly than she comprehends the recently discovered cognitive being that cannot be imagined. He responds that, as a matter of fact, the meditator knows (*cognosco*) herself, the cognitive agent, not only (1) much more certainly and truly but also (2) much more distinctly and evidently. The claim in (1) concerns her knowledge

of her existence as a cognitive being; the claim in (2) concerns her grasp
of her nature.

Here's how he argues for (1):

> For if I judge [*judico*] that wax exists from the fact that I see it, surely it is
> made much more evident that I myself exist from this very fact that I see
> it. For it could happen that what I see is not really wax; it could happen
> that I do not even have eyes with which to see anything; but it could not
> happen, when I see, or when I think that I see (for I am not distinguishing
> here), that I myself who am thinking [*ego ipse cogitans*], am not something.
> By similar reasoning, if I judge [*judico*] there is wax, from the fact that I
> touch this, the same thing follows again, namely, that I exist. If [I judge
> that there is wax] from the fact that I imagine, or some other such cause,
> the same thing follows. But this that I observe concerning the wax applies
> to everything else located outside of me. (7:33; 2:22)

Descartes's explanation of the sense in which my own existence is more
evident than that of the wax is interesting. There is more room for error,
at least in principle, in the case of my perception of the wax. I might, for
example, think I am seeing wax when I am really seeing some clay or
metal (perhaps worked up to look like wax), a sort of misinterpretation
of my perception. Or matters might perhaps be worse than that—I might
not be seeing any body at all (as presumably would be the case if it
turned out "that I do not even have eyes with which to see anything"); I
might only be "as it were" seeing. There is no room for similar error
when I take myself to exist in view of the fact that "I see, or think that I
see." I believe this is because—Descartes does not explain—there cannot
be a seeing or a seeming to see without a seer or an apparent seer, that is,
without a being (a "something") that sees or appears to see. So I am not
faced with the same issues of judgment or interpretation in the case of
my own existence as I am in the case of the wax.

(One might wonder whether by describing this being merely as a seer
or apparent seer, we have characterized it too narrowly to tell whether it
counts as the me insofar as I am a thinking thing, that is, the cogito being,
whose core abilities are connected with judgment and understanding
(and not with sensory experience). Perhaps this is why Descartes makes
explicit elsewhere in this passage (broadly, in line with ¶13) that the see-
ing/appearing to see and similar exercises do not take place in a vacuum.
I can employ them to make judgments, so that, for example, "I judge
[*judico*] that wax exists from the fact that I see it" and "I judge [*judico*]
there is wax, from the fact that I touch it." So I think the main idea here is
that as soon as I raise the question of whether the wax exists (as might be
suggested by the word "imagine" toward the end of the passage), I can

see that a cognitive agent, capable of judging (and raising questions), exists; by way of contrast, determining whether a body exists is a more complicated affair of judgment and interpretation, with, in principle (if not always in practice), greater latitude for error.)

Ultimately, of course, for Descartes, determining whether any body exists requires having in place an account of what the senses accomplish, something that he provides in the Sixth Meditation. As the argument that he gives there runs through claims about the mind and its origin (for example, that its author is not a deceiver), the knowledge of the existence of body depends on knowledge about the mind and its origin. However, it is not obvious to me to what extent, if at all, Descartes is sounding that theme here, in ¶15.

Let's turn to Descartes's treatment of (2):

> Moreover, if my perception of the wax seemed more distinct after it became known to me not from vision or touch alone, but from many sources [*pluribus ex causis*], it must be admitted how much more distinctly am I myself known by me, inasmuch as no consideration [*rationes*] can assist the perception of the wax or any other body without showing [*probent*] me better the nature [*naturam*] of my mind. But in addition, there is so much else besides in the mind itself, from which its notion [*notitia*] can be rendered more distinct, that those things that emanate to it from body seem hardly worth calling to account. (¶15; 7:33; 2:22)

This passage concerns the relative merits of what is gleaned from sensory and imaginative cognition in a substantive account of mind (see "the nature [*naturam*] of my mind"). To be sure, we do learn something about the mind by reflecting on the limits of sensory and imaginative cognition of the piece of wax; we come to have a better appreciation of what the mind alone is and its relation to these modes of cognition. Descartes remarks that this is negligible and that the mind contains other, more important resources for its self-knowledge. What does he have in view here? Perhaps, looking backward, he's thinking of the cognitive agent's core operations—doubting, affirming, denying, willing, and refusing— operations that, as we have seen, are more intimately connected with the cognitive agent than sensing or imagining is, and will be explored more fully later in the course of the *Meditations*. Perhaps, looking forward, he's thinking of our idea of God; he will say in the Third Meditation (¶24) that our perception of God is in a sense prior to our perception of ourselves. Or perhaps both.

In the final paragraph of the Second Meditation, ¶16, Descartes explicitly links the important thesis entered at the end of ¶12, and developed in ¶13, (a) that the wax is perceived not by sense or imagination but only by the mind alone, to the claim (b) that I perceive my mind more easily and evidently than anything else:

> Since [Cum] I now know that even bodies are not strictly [proprie] perceived by the senses or the faculty of imagination but by the intellect alone [solo intellectu], and are not perceived from that they are touched or seen, but only from that they are understood [intelligantur], I clearly know [aperte cognosco] nothing more easily or evidently that can be perceived by me than my own mind. (¶16; 7:34; 2:22–23)

The text is not explicit on the connection Descartes is drawing between (a) and (b). I think it probably goes back to the worry evoked in ¶10 that framed the wax discussion, namely, the suspicion that my ability to sense and imagine body made it better known to me than the cogito being, or, as the scholastics would have put it, since the proper object of the human intellect is material things, we understand bodies better than immaterial things such as the soul or God. When one focuses on how complex my sensory cognition of wax is, and that senses do not reach all the way to this wax but only to color, and that it takes a judgment to traverse the rest of the way, the temptation to think that I know the wax better than my mind subsides. On the one hand, knowing the wax turns out to be a trickier affair than I had fully appreciated; on the other hand, since every act of seeing or touching this wax involves a judgment, each such act reveals the cognitive agent at work.

Finally, in this passage Descartes replaces the expression "mind alone" with "intellect alone."[35] One may conjecture that he feels he has characterized the mind alone fully enough by now that the reader will not think of an intellect as fundamentally a power to grasp universals, but will instead think of it in terms of the core abilities of a cognitive agent focally organized around judgment, a cognitive agent who, in particular, is able to make judgments both about what this body is and about what body in general is.

DESCARTES VERSUS SCHOLASTIC ARISTOTELIANS ON THE INTELLECT

The subtext of the wax discussion, as I have interpreted it, is the Aristotelian thesis that body is the proper object of the human intellect; this is what lies underneath the difficulty the meditator reports in ¶10 in shaking the feeling that, because body falls under the senses and the mind does not, she knows body better than mind. As Descartes attempts to assuage this worry, some of the most important work gets done in the articulation of his novel conception of mind.

It is possible to overlook this because superficially the overall tenor of the discussion seems congenial enough to a Thomistic Aristotelian outlook. If we draw a rough approximation, as I believe Descartes intends,[36] between his "mind alone" and Aquinas's intellect, then it would seem, at least at first glance, that Descartes's main point is that neither the senses nor the imagination is capable of grasping a body's essence; only the intellect is. An Aristotelian would have agreed, however, that it is the intellect and not the senses or the imagination that grasps essences. Further, Descartes's suggestion that the senses do not cognize what the wax is (e.g., we misleadingly say that "we see the wax itself, if it is present," when we should say instead that "we judge [judicare] it to be present from its colour and its shape"), resonates with the Aristotelian doctrine that the proper objects of the senses are colors, tastes, and so forth, and individual substances, trees, dogs, human beings, and pieces of wax fall under the senses only "incidentally." There might perhaps be something tendentious in Descartes's saying that the "mind alone" or, later, "intellect alone" grasps what this wax is, if this means, for example, that the intellect can grasp this wax's essence without any help from the lower, corporeal faculties (and so without the body). However, it is not obvious that Descartes denies that the senses play any role in my comprehension of what is to be this body: as I have interpreted him, he is claiming only that the intellect is principally responsible for the grasp of the wax's essence, and not that I could think of this piece of wax without the senses.

We need to look more closely, however. In fact, the conception of the "mind alone" that Descartes unfolds in the wax discussion encompasses a series of related fundamental departures from an Aristotelian, especially Aquinas's, way of thinking about cognition generally, and his understanding of the relation of intellectual function to lower forms of cognitive function in particular. Indeed, this is one of the places in the Meditations where Descartes's differences with his scholastic predecessors are put into sharpest relief.

I have already signaled what I take to be the fundamental difference between Descartes and Aquinas over abstraction. Aquinas views understanding as a matter of cognizing universally, of abstracting from particulars: that is how our intellects get on to the "what is it" (quiddity) of dogs or cows (caninehood or bovinehood). According to Aquinas, understanding is fundamentally a process in which we abstract what is common to Spot, Fido, and Rover so as to grasp what is universal respecting them. As he puts it in ST I, Q. 86, A. 1, "our intellect knows directly [directe] the universal only." This made it difficult for Aquinas to explain how individuals, say Peter or Paul, fall under the intellect, and his theory of how this happens—through a sort of reflection backward from the species to the

phantasm from which it was abstracted (ST I, Q. 86, A. 1)—was a subject
of considerable controversy in later medieval philosophy.

In any case, as we have just seen, Descartes has quite explicitly focused
the "What is it?" question on *this* piece of wax. His question is, What is
this piece of wax? (or, What is this particular body?), and not, What is
wax? (or, What are bodies?):

> It remains therefore that I must concede that I do not imagine what this
> wax is [*quid sit haec cera*], but perceive it with my mind alone [*sola mente*]; I
> say this about this wax in particular [*hanc in particulari*]; for concerning
> wax in general [*in communi*] the point is clearer. (¶12; 7:31; 2:21)

For him, understanding is not fundamentally a matter of finding the
general in the particular. (It is probably true, I think, that, for Descartes,
understanding a physical structure involves locating it within an all-embracing *res extensa*; but the relation of individual mechanical systems to
the overarching structure is not that of particular to universal.) One can
understand, it seems, even an individual piece of wax. In Descartes's
characterization, understanding, as we have seen, is a matter of using
judgment to penetrate from outward forms into inner constitution,
rather than a matter of abstracting the commonalities shared by members of a species.

Descartes's suggestion that we can directly understand a particular
body, that is, understand a particular body as the body it is, is bound up, I
believe, with Descartes's rejection of a hylomorphic account of a physical
being as a composite of form and matter in favor of a mechanistic account. On a hylomorphic account, all of the individual's important properties derive from a (substantial) form that it is supposed to share with
other members of its species. This makes it natural to think that to understand Fido is to understand Fido as a dog. The "What is it?" question,
when asked of Fido, seems to point to features he shares with other members of his species. This makes the import of a "What is it?" question
along the lines of the one Descartes is asking, "What is *this* dog?" quite
puzzling. By way of contrast, if one thinks of physical beings as complex
patterns of extension in motion, as Descartes does, it does not seem at all
unnatural that one might focus one's intellectual attention on *this* system
and try to understand it, without regard to other similar systems.[37]

So, for Descartes, when one progresses from sensing something to
imagining it and, finally, to understanding it, one does not move through a
series of objects—proper sensibles, common sensibles, universal natures.
It is not the case for Descartes that senses perceive the substance of the
wax only "incidentally." Rather, the same structure that is given to us (perhaps confusedly) when we sense is what we also understand. And the reason that material provided by the senses does not count as understanding

is not that the senses are limited to the particular (and so pre-abstracted) objects, but rather that sensory cognition is prejudgmental. That is, the difference between merely sensing and understanding is marked, as we have seen, by judgment: Any view about what a thing is involves judgment. But, for Descartes, the senses (and the imagination) do not make judgments; this is instead the office of the "mind alone."

Two other differences flow from Descartes's disagreement with Aquinas over abstraction. A first concerns whether or not the mind is independent of the body. This point will assume special importance in the Sixth Meditation, because it is a significant part of the basis for Descartes's argument, as I interpret it, that the mind cannot exist without body. On Aquinas's theory, the human intellect is unable to function, according to its natural mode of cognition, without its lower faculties, sense and imagination. It cannot operate without turning to the phantasms in order to abstract from them. It is important to recognize that Aquinas is claiming more than that all of our intellectual thought happens to be accompanied by images. The images are doing important *work* for us: they provide the material from which intellect abstracts universals; without them, the intellect would have no cognitive access to intelligible natures. The intellect's cognitive contact with the universal runs through the images. Descartes would allow, I think, that most of our thought is accompanied by images. He would also allow, I think, that we need something analogous to a sensible species in order to get a particular body like the piece of wax placed on the radar screen (so to speak) of the intellect or the "mind alone." But what the images do not supply is the basis for the piece of wax's intelligibility, for its coming to be understood. Rather, the "mind alone" already seems to have some grasp of what this piece of wax is, as manifested in the judgments that it takes itself to be able to correctly make concerning the body, and that it, in fact, could use this grasp of the body's nature to measure the adequacy of the imagination's comprehension of it.

Now, further, for Aquinas, sensory and imaginative cognition are strongly corporeal in the sense that their operations take place in corporeal organs. The idea that our lower, imagistic cognitive powers are bound up with body continues to exercise considerable pull for Descartes. He does not think the powers are bound up with body to the same degree that Aquinas does—in particular, part of the force of the claim that sensory and imaginative cognition are modes of mind is that the operation of these powers takes place in the mind and not in the body—but even for Descartes the "what it is" of these powers suggests that we could not possess them unless the mind is conjoined to a body (imagination) or united to a body. (This is to anticipate material that will be taken up in chapter 6.) So when Descartes frees the intellect from dependence on the lower faculties, sense and imagination, for its natural function, he at the same time frees it from dependence on the body.

The second difference that flows from Descartes's break with Aquinas over abstraction has to do with the architecture of the mind. For Aquinas, our cognitive abilities are "stacked" in a certain way. Imagination is a higher form of cognition than sensation, and understanding is a higher form of cognition than imagination. Moreover, the higher forms of cognition depend on the lower forms in certain ways. At the bottom are the senses. They must discharge their function—make available proper sensible qualities to the soul—in order for the imagination to discharge its various functions (assimilation of the common sensible qualities, memory, and, at least in our case, sometimes the creative rearrangement of these materials). And the imagination must discharge its function in order for the intellect to have material from which to abstract in order to understand. The lower faculties carry out their operations in relative independence of the higher ones. The reason for the qualification "relative" is that the fact that human beings have reason makes a difference to the lower faculties: reason exercises a "reflected influence [*refluentiam*]" on the lower faculties;[38] and, one supposes, the intellect directs the lower faculties, for example, directs the attention of the senses. But even so, the operation of the intellect, in general, depends on the senses and imagination having already operated. In an Aristotelian framework, because lower cognitive abilities have a sort of independence from the higher, it is coherent to think that there are beings, for example, that possess some of the lower cognitive abilities (sense, imagination) but not the higher one (understanding).

In a way, Descartes inverts this picture: rather than see understanding as Aquinas does—as built on sensation and imagination (even if understanding, on account of its connection with universality and immateriality, transcends these powers in certain respects)—he views sensation and imagination as dependent on understanding. Thus his curious claim in the Sixth Meditation that sensation and imagination contain an intellectual act in their formal concept and must inhere in an intellectual substance:

> Besides this, I find in myself faculties for certain special modes of thinking, namely faculties of sensing and of imagining. Now I can clearly and distinctly understand myself as a whole without these faculties; but I cannot, conversely, understand these faculties without me, that is, without an intellectual substance [*substantia intelligente*] to inhere in. This is because there is an intellectual act [*intellectionem*] included in their formal concept [*formali conceptu*]. (VI.¶10; 7:78; 2:54)

The senses and imagination are no longer fundamental powers for and of a living being, the manifestation of a certain degree of life; rather, they are fundamentally the powers of a cognitive being, a being that judges. They no longer serve as the platform upon which understanding (even if understanding involves transcending them in certain respects) is built. Rather, now they are powers for the cognitive being: they help it make judgments about what is in the world. The imagination, as we will learn in the Sixth Meditation, helps the cogito being know elementary geometrical truths. The senses, we have seen in the wax discussion, help the cogito being know about things that exist in the corporeal world. In addition, as we will learn in the Sixth Meditation, the senses help the cogito being preserve the body to which it is united (so there is a way in which, even for Descartes, sensation is connected with life, but he would disagree with the Aristotelian idea that sensation represents a certain grade or stage of life). Thus, for Descartes, the idea of a being with a faculty of sensation or imagination but without the core abilities of a cogito being is incoherent. In Descartes's world, there is no room for animals that sense and imagine but do not understand or judge. Finally, because neither sensing nor imagining is required for the cogito being's exercise of its core functions, sensing and imagining are now viewed as merely "special modes of thinking."

And so, in Descartes's hands, sensation and imagination become transformed from basic levels along the progression of the life forms, required in order for a subsequent form of understanding to appear on the scene, into appendages of a cognitive agent, a being that understands and judges. The senses and imagination are now for and of the cogito being. Every exercise of sensation and imagination is now an exercise of the cogito being, that is, now involves an intellectual act, whether it assists the cogito being in its intellectual pursuits or in its preservation of its union with its body.

I

The Third Meditation: The Truth Rule and the "Chief and Most Common Mistake"

THE THIRD Meditation contains two of Descartes's demonstrations of God's existence. These two demonstrations comprise the last two-thirds of the meditation. The first third is taken up with certain preliminary matters. These preliminary matters, which include the introduction of the "truth rule" and touch on Descartes's attitude toward how we know that bodies exist, are of considerable interest in their own right. I discuss the preliminary matters in this chapter, 3 (I); in the next chapter, 3 (II), I focus on Descartes's philosophical theology.

¶¶1–4. The "Truth Rule" and Skeptical Doubt

The meditator enters the Third Meditation having enjoyed a dual cognitive success in the Second Meditation. On the one side, she has found her way to truth and certainty, at least with respect to some matters, and, on the other side, she has learned how to use her cognitive faculties well, namely, by perceiving clearly and distinctly. Now she begins to wonder about the relationship between these two things:

> I am certain that I am a thinking thing. Do I not therefore also know what is required for my being certain about anything? In this first item of knowledge there is simply a clear and distinct perception of what I am asserting; this would not be enough to make me certain of the truth of the matter [*certum de rei veritate*] if it could ever turn out that something which I perceived with such clarity and distinctness was false. So I now seem to be able to lay it down as a general rule [*pro regula generali*] that whatever I perceive very clearly and distinctly is true. (¶2; 7:35; 2:24)

Certainty requires truth, the meditator reflects, so if clear and distinct perception is (as it appears to be) responsible for certainty, then everything she clearly and distinctly perceives must be true. She is plainly assuming here that certainty brings in its wake truth; that is, she is not thinking of certainty as some merely "subjective" state.

Now, I believe furthermore that Descartes understands truth itself in a robust way, that is, not as some internal or formal property of our thought, but rather as a substantive relation between the mind and reality, along the lines of the well-known scholastic definition of truth as the "adequation" of the mind with a thing: *veritas est adaequatio rei et intellectus*. In this tradition truth does not come on the cheap, as it were, without the *res* (without the thing or reality). So the hypothesis broached here is substantive: every time I perceive clearly and distinctly, I am in a truth relation with reality.

This train of thought tells us something about how the meditator views what took place in the Second Meditation. Evidently, she took herself to have reached the truth when she perceived clearly and distinctly, for if she had not taken herself to arrive at the truth there, it would not make sense for her to generalize now to the hypothesis that everything she clearly and distinctly perceives is true. For example, if she had taken herself there to be only in some rationally compelling epistemic state—some state in which everything was, so to speak, "internally" in order, but about whose relation to reality she had no particular view—it would not make sense for her to hypothesize now that everything she perceives clearly and distinctly is true. Rather, she would be primed to form some other hypothesis, perhaps that everything she perceives clearly and distinctly is rationally compelling and "internally" in order.

Moreover, since the truth rule is only a hypothesis at this point ("So I now *seem* [*videor*] to be able to lay it down . . ." [emphasis added]),[1] it follows that the establishment of the truth rule plays no role in the cognitive success she takes herself to have enjoyed in the Second Meditation, robust though that success may have been. But how is this possible? After all, the truth rule is in some sense foundational for Descartes. Indeed, he will claim toward the end of the Fifth Meditation that all *scientia*—the highest form of human knowledge—depends on the recognition of God's existence, and he claims this, it seems, mainly because recognition of God's existence is required for the establishment of the truth rule. So how was the meditator able to realize that success (or even to think that she had realized that success) when the truth rule was either completely out of view or at most only a hypothesis for her?

This is a version—in fact, a version rather close to the one raised by the authors of the Second Objections (7:124–25; 2:89)—of what is sometimes called the Cartesian Circle. We will take this issue up when we get to the end of the Fifth Meditation, where Descartes lays out his explanation of how all *scientia* depends on the recognition of God's existence. For the moment, I want to note simply that the way the Third Meditation opens suggests that, in the Second Meditation, the meditator took her cognition to get her to certainty and, with that, to truth and reality, and that that occurred before she knew that the truth rule itself is true.

Now, what needs to be done in order to establish the hypothesis that everything that I clearly and distinctly perceive is true? Since the argument thus far has the feel of generalizing from a single case of successful cognition to all cases, one thing we need to do is to check for counterinstances. And Descartes's initial discussion of the hypothesis, in ¶3, has that shape. He advances the following consideration against the truth rule: "Yet I previously accepted as wholly certain many things which I afterwards realized were doubtful," such as the mind-independent existence of the earth, sky, and stars. However, he says, I did not clearly perceive these things but only thought I did, so these experiences do not count against the hypothesis. Descartes also brings forward something else that he thought he perceived clearly but did not: namely, that external things are the source of my ideas and "resemble them in all respects." But this, too, was not a case of clear and distinct perception.

Neither of these putative counterexamples is intended to provide a case of clear and distinct false perception. Rather, they are meant to (but fail to) provide cases of clear and distinct doubtful perception. This suggests that the "truth rule" is a little more involved than the concluding sentence of ¶2 indicates, and that it has the force that when I cognize clearly and distinctly, I cognize certainly, where cognizing certainly involves cognizing truly (this fits well with the second half of the penultimate sentence of ¶2, "this [i.e., clear and distinct perception] would not be enough to make me certain of the truth of the matter if it could ever turn out that something which I perceived with such clarity and distinctness was false").

The truth rule has an air of plausibility about it, and there are no apparent counterexamples to it (at least ready at hand), but this hardly shows that it is so. Cognizing well, or clearly and distinctly, seems to be one thing, and being certain that you have arrived at truth or reality seems to be another. Why should the two be connected? Importantly, Descartes does not rest the case for the truth rule on the considerations raised in ¶3—the absence of counterexamples to the rule—but goes on to a consideration of a different order in ¶4:

> But what about when I was considering something very simple and straightforward in arithmetic or geometry, for example that two and three added together make five, and so on? Did I not see [*intuebar*] at least these

things clearly enough to affirm their truth? Indeed, the only reason for my later judgement that they were open to doubt was that it occurred to me that perhaps some God could have given me a nature such that I was deceived even in matters which seemed most evident. (7:35–36; 2:25)

Descartes is not recalling a putative failure of the truth rule here—a time when he clearly and distinctly perceived that 2 + 3 = 5 and he was either incorrect or doubtful that 2 + 3 = 5. Rather, I take him to be raising the issue just alluded to: why should cognizing truly follow from cognizing well? Cognizing well has to do with my nature—the appropriate use of my natural faculties; cognizing certainly (and therefore truly) involves something more—getting on to the truth, getting to reality. To be sure, as far as I can see, every time I clearly and distinctly perceive, I do manage to get on to the truth, but why should this be so?

Now Descartes does, of course, have an answer—the author of my nature is God, who is not a deceiver and therefore would not have given me a nature that would let me go wrong when I use my cognitive faculties well. But the meditator is not yet in possession of that answer. Her epistemic position is this: when she is clearly and distinctly perceiving, it seems obvious to her that she *is* getting on to the truth, but she would be hard pressed to say why there should be any connection between the two. After all, couldn't she have been so constructed that cognizing well and cognizing truly come apart? Couldn't God have made her so that perceiving clearly and distinctly comes apart from grasping the truth?

And whenever my preconceived belief [*praeconcepta opinio*] in the supreme power of God comes to mind, I cannot but admit that it would be easy for him, if he so desired, to bring it about that I go wrong even in those matters which I think [*puto*: deem, believe] I see [*intueri*] utterly clearly with my mind's eye. Yet when I turn to the things themselves [*ipsas res*] which I think [*arbitror*: I judge] I perceive very clearly, I am so convinced by them that I spontaneously declare [*sponte erumpam*]: let whoever can do so deceive me, he will never bring it about that I am nothing, so long as I continue to think I am something; or make it true at some future time that I have never existed, since it is now true that I exist; or bring it about that two and three added together are more or less than five, or anything of this kind in which I see a manifest contradiction. (¶4; 7:36; 2:25)

As I read this passage, there is meant to be some puzzlement on the part of the meditator here. On the one hand, she has to acknowledge a gap in principle between using her cognitive faculties well and getting to truth or reality. On the other hand, when she turns to "the things themselves," she does not see how she can doubt that she is getting on to the truth. If one were to ask her, "Well, which is it—are you certain of the truth that

two and three is five or aren't you?" there would be no easy answer.[2] All
there is is the uneasy back-and-forth experience of entering clear and distinct perception, with its attendant certainty and truth, and exiting it,
with the attendant room for doubt. The obvious way for her to smooth
out her cognitive situation is for her to examine more closely God and
his relation to her cognitive abilities. After all, it seems highly improbable
that God would have structured her in such a way that cognizing well did
not go hand in hand with cognizing truly. But until she has discovered
the truth about this, there is something missing in her current epistemic
situation—something that Descartes thinks of as depriving her of a special form of certainty, which he calls being "fully certain [*plane certus*]":

> And since I have no cause to think that there is a deceiving God, and I do
> not yet even know for sure whether there is a God at all, any reason for
> doubt which depends simply on this supposition is a very slight and, so to
> speak, metaphysical one. But in order to remove even this slight reason for
> doubt, as soon as the opportunity arises I must examine whether there is a
> God, and, if there is, whether he can be a deceiver. For if I do not know
> this, it seems that I can never be fully certain [*plane certus*] about anything
> else. (¶4; 7:36; 2:25)[3]

¶¶5–7. General Considerations concerning Thoughts

One might have expected that Descartes would have immediately proceeded to produce his two arguments for the existence of God. Instead,
he prefixes his arguments with two preliminary discussions (¶¶5–7 and
¶¶8–12), neither of which seems strictly necessary for the development
of the arguments for God's existence. There are signs that Descartes's
readers found this stretch of the *Meditations* a little bumpy. For one thing,
the topic sentence of ¶5 is significantly expanded in the French version;
for another, his correspondent Clerselier asked him about his aims at this
juncture in the *Meditations*. We will want to consider Descartes's reason
for this detour; but this topic is best postponed until after we have first
looked at the material covered in this stretch.

In ¶¶5–7, Descartes does a number of things rather briskly. In ¶5, he
attempts to isolate a purely representative function of ideas, which involves cutting away from ideas any extra (usually affective) elements of
cognition, yielding thoughts that are "as it were the images of things
[*tanquam rerum imagines*]" and to which "the term idea is strictly appropriate"; and says that judgment is one such extra element.[4] In ¶6, he indicates that ideas in this representative function cannot be false or involve
error: falsity or error enters the picture only when judgment is added.

Finally, in ¶7, Descartes divides ideas (taken representatively) into three basic categories:

> Among my ideas, some appear to be innate, some to be adventitious, and others to have been invented by me. My understanding of what a thing is, what truth is, and what thought is, seems to derive simply from my own nature. But my hearing a noise, as I do now, or seeing the sun, or feeling the fire, comes from things which are located outside me, or so I have hitherto judged. Lastly, sirens, hippogriffs and the like are my own invention. But perhaps all my ideas may be thought of as adventitious, or they may all be innate, or all made up; for as yet I have not clearly perceived their true origin. (¶7; 7:37–38; 2:26)

What is expressed tentatively here (consonant with the stage of the meditator's progress at this point in the *Meditations*) is expressed definitively in a 16 June 1641 letter to Mersenne:

> I use the word idea to mean everything which can be in our thought, and I distinguish three kinds. Some are adventitious, such as the idea we commonly have of the sun; others are constructed or made up, in which class we can put the idea which the astronomers construct of the sun by their reasoning; and others are innate, such as the idea of God, mind, body, triangle, and in general all those which represent true, immutable and eternal essences. (3:383; 3:183)

The letter to Mersenne supplies the significant detail that Descartes takes innate ideas to represent true and immutable natures, something that he does not discuss in the *Meditations* until the Fifth Meditation.

This basic categorization of ideas is of standing interest for Descartes. For example, part of the point of the comparison between thought and painting in the First Meditation was to distinguish cognitive materials that are simply given to us from those that involve some work on our part, and the distinction between "innate" and "invented" ideas will figure prominently in the Fifth Meditation (and related material in the Objections and Replies). The categorization is of particular use to Descartes in constructing his alternative to the scholastic theory of cognition. According to the scholastic theory of cognition, our cognition of the universe is about the world to the extent that cognition is formed out of structure borrowed from the world. This is a primary way in which the world exercises control over our cognition. It also provides a dimension along which our cognition can be assessed: if the material I have taken into the soul through the senses is deficient in some way, then the sensible species or likenesses may be good or bad, accurate or inaccurate, exact or inexact.[5] Similar evaluations are in principle possible further down the cognitive stream: depending on the materials I have begun with and how well the common sense has done its job, my sensible phantasms will include more or less accurate likenesses of common sensibles, and, again, depending on the material provided by the sensible phantasms and on how well I have abstracted, my intelligible species will be better or worse likenesses of the natures of things. These evaluations take place before the question of truth or falsity arises—before the "composing and dividing function" of the intellect comes into play—although one can imagine how working from sufficiently corrupt materials would lead one to embrace false conclusions or even make it unclear whether one had cognized anything at all.

Descartes's threefold division of ideas provides him with the basis for an alternative account of the evaluation of materials with which we cognize. According to him, there are two original categories of ideas, adventitious ideas and innate ideas; there is also a third category, invented, constructed, or fictive ideas, which are composed out of one or both of the original categories. The dimension along which ideas are evaluated is not that of truth and falsity ("Now as far as ideas are concerned, provided they are considered solely in themselves and I do not refer them to anything else, they cannot strictly speaking be false"),[6] although certain especially deficient ideas may lead us to make false judgments.[7] Descartes holds that innate ideas unproblematically make available to the mind true and immutable natures. In contrast, the situation of adventitious ideas turns out to be more complicated. As I understand Descartes, such ideas import reality or structure from the world, but do so only confusedly (the reason for this limitation has to do with certain exigencies of the mind-body union—it is best for the human composite that it receive this information about its environment in a shorthand way, and that involves the idea's "blurring" much of the detail). Invented ideas can be either good representations—as is the case presumably with the astronomical idea of the sun—or defective ones—as is the case, according to Descartes, with the idea of a real quality of gravity, which is, in his view, an unholy mixture of the ideas of substance, quality, thought, and body (7:441–42).

Descartes's classification of ideas raises a number of questions. For one thing, one might ask about the asymmetrical treatment of the adventitious and innate ideas: if both are equally independent of anything I do—if both are equally not the product of my work—why do they receive such different assessments? We can put this question in the context of Descartes's theological worldview: it seems that the adventitious ideas are as much God's responsibility as are my innate ideas, so if I am to trust my innate ideas on the strength of the fact that God isn't a deceiver, why shouldn't I also trust my adventitious ideas? For another thing, how do I tell whether a given idea is in some way my own work, that is, invented, or whether it is innate, in which case it displays a true and immutable nature? (For example, does the idea of a triangle inscribed in a square count as innate or invented?) When we consider an exchange between Caterus and Descartes, we will see that maintaining the line between an innate idea and an invented idea is more difficult than it first appears.

¶¶8–12. THE "CHIEF AND MOST COMMON MISTAKE"

Paragraphs 8–12 continue a discussion that is not necessary for the argument for God's existence that Descartes wishes to offer. The discussion is important. This is the place in the *Meditations* where Descartes begins to present his account of how I know that bodies exist. Here we should distinguish carefully between a response to skeptical argument—say, the dreaming doubt—and an argument for the existence of body. Descartes thinks that we need some sort of positive basis for our belief that body exists; and he separates this need from the need to respond to what skeptical challenges might be raised to undermine the belief. So, in the First Meditation, he raised a challenge to some knowledge that I took myself to possess but does not press the question of how I might have acquired such knowledge; and, in the Sixth Meditation, he first offers an argument for the existence of body—he shows me how to acquire the knowledge that body exists—in VI.¶10, well in advance of responding to the dreaming doubt (VI.¶24). In ¶¶8–12 the issue arises of what leads me to believe that bodies exist. It is also in ¶¶8–12 that the *Meditations* takes up for the first time the thesis that sensory ideas resemble qualities in body, a thesis that Descartes associates both with a naive, commonsense worldview and with the scholastic theory of sensible species. The Third Meditation discussion of both issues is difficult to understand without considering Descartes's subsequent treatment of these issues in the Sixth Meditation, where he offers a demonstration of the existence of body (VI.¶10) as well as his final account of sensory representation (VI.¶¶14–15), so in what follows I will draw freely on the relevant parts of the Sixth Meditation.

In the opening paragraphs of the Third Meditation, Descartes several times calls the meditator's attention to a "mistake" that he takes himself to have frequently made:

> But there was something else which I used to assert, and which through habitual belief I thought I perceived clearly, although I did not in fact do so. This was that there were things outside me from which these ideas proceeded and which resembled them in all respects [*omnino similes*]. Here was my mistake; or at any rate, if I judged truly, it was not thanks to the force of my perception. (¶3; 7:35; 2:25)

Thus the only remaining thoughts where I must be on my guard against making a mistake are judgements. And the chief and most common mistake which is to be found here consists in this, that I judge that the ideas which are in me resemble [*similes*], or conform to [*conformes*], certain things located outside of me. (¶6; 7:37; 2:26)

But the chief question at this point concerns the ideas which I take to be derived from things existing outside me: what is my reason for thinking that they resemble [*similes*] these things? (¶7; 7:38; 2:26)

What is this mistake? Why is it so important?

Descartes is describing his old conception of the senses, the conception of the senses that he takes the meditator to have held when she entered the *Meditations*. It is worth trying to get as clear a view as possible of this precritical conception of sensation. This will provide us the yardstick by which to measure the meditator's subsequent progress. We will see, I think, that the break the meditator makes with her earlier views is not as radical as might be thought.

Let's look more closely at how Descartes first characterizes his "chief mistake":

[T]here were things outside me from which these ideas proceeded [*a quibus ideae istae procedebant*] and which resembled them in all respects. Here was my mistake; or at any rate, if I judged truly, it was not thanks to the force of my perception. (III.¶3; 7:35; 2:25)

A little later he characterizes the mistake in this way:

Thus the only remaining thoughts where I must be on my guard against making a mistake are judgements [*judicia*]. And the chief and most common mistake which is to be found here consists in this, that I judge [*judicem*] that the ideas which are in me resemble, or conform to, certain things located outside of me. (III.¶6; 7:37; 2:26)

Still a little later, when he explains what an "adventitious" idea is, he says:

But my hearing a noise, as I now do, or seeing the sun, or feeling the fire, comes from things located outside me, or so I have hitherto judged [*judicavi*]. (III.¶7; 7:38; 2:26)

There seem to be three main elements to the picture of sensation under consideration: sensory ideas are (1) caused by bodies, which (2) exist and (3) resemble those sensory ideas. What should we make of the conception of sensation that is under examination here?

Let's begin with (3), the thought that sensory ideas resemble things located outside of me. The terminology of resemblance falls out of the general picture of Aristotelian thinking about cognition sketched in the introduction. Recall that the Aristotelians thought of cognition as a sort of assimilation of the known by the knower, which results from the cognizer's acquiring a form of the thing cognized. The new form is an image or replica—a resemblance—of the original form: through his possession of the form, a cognizer comes to be formally identical with thing cognized. Although the acquired form (or *sensible species*, to use the scholastic technical term) is of the same nature as the form of the thing cognized, it has a special "spiritual" manner of being in the cognizer, different from its "material" manner of being in the thing cognized.[8] So, for example, when I sense the red of a referee's card, the form red comes to exist in me "spiritually," and I become "in a way" identical with the red. One thing to be careful about here is the following. When the sensible species comes to exist in me, I do not need to inspect it with some set of interior eyes in order for my sensory cognition of red—my seeing of the red—to occur.[9] There is nothing more to my seeing red than my power of sensation being "actualized" by the species, and so there is no need for some interior act of vision directed at the species. For the card's red to exist in me, or for me to be formally identical in this way with the card, is what it is for me to sense the red. We might, then, think of my seeing red as a matter of my having my sensory cognition or sensory thought (or perhaps sensory experience) shaped up or molded or formed in a certain way by the redness of the card.

Does this Aristotelian account, which can appear rather technical and alien, have anything to do with how we ordinarily think about sensation? It seems to me that the Aristotelian picture of cognition, at least in its broad outlines, is not so remote from how we naively think of what goes on with the senses. We think of the senses as providing us with information about the world, and we often think of this as happening through the senses' making features (colors, sounds, and so forth) of the world present to us more or less without distortion. We take there to be (a more or less approximate) qualitative match between our sensory thought or cognition of a thing and the thing. We do not, to be sure, expect the match to be perfect; perhaps when the referee holds up his red card I find myself presented with something orange. We might put it thus: I see the card's color as orange, or I experience it as orange. (We would not say, of course, that my sensory cognition or that my sensory experience got "formed" or structured orange-wise, but, all the same, I am not sure that we would find that these are unintelligible or otherwise objectionable modes of expression.) When I see the red as orange, there is still some match or similarity—still some resemblance—between my sensation or experience and the card's color, even if there is also some failure of match, some dissimilarity. And, it seems, there are boundaries to how much dissimilarity—how much lack of resemblance—our ordinary picture of sensation will tolerate. If, for example, the referee blows his whistle without holding up a card, yet I wind up seeing red (red flashes before my mind, red comes to exist in my thought, my cognition becomes shaped red-wise), it is hard to think of this transaction as the sensing, even the very poor sensing, of the sound of the whistle. Something rather different seems to have happened.

Perhaps contemporary readers will find the notion of resemblance too general and vague, or the notion of shared formal structure too opaque and metaphorical, to be very helpful. Well, we might contrast a picture of sensation drawn in terms of resemblance with a picture of sensation draw in terms of the brute, arbitrary effects of the world on us. Perhaps if the effects are systematic enough and tractable enough, they provide us with the means to get information about the world. (This might happen through some quasi-inference that we are hardwired to make, along the lines of "same sort of effect in the mind, same sort of cause in the world.") This would be a picture of sensation that does not involve notions like resemblance, formal identity, or commonality of structure at the ground level (perhaps they can be bootstrapped somehow). It is also a picture that does not easily support the thought that when we sense things, the things that we sense come to exist in us, or in our mind (or, to use Descartes's favored idiom, that when we sense, the reality that we sense comes to exist "objectively" in us): given the absence of the shared structure between the mind and the world on the brute-causation picture, what would be this "something" that exists in the world in one way and in the mind in another way? So it strikes me that a resemblance picture of sensation, then, has enough content to be different from a brute-causation picture, and I think it is, in this respect, closer to a naive, everyday conception of sensation than the latter. Perhaps as we become more sophisticated we will accord a greater role to causal mechanisms in our thinking about perception (without going all the way over to a pure causation picture of sensory cognition). Still, it seems we start out with something more like the resemblance picture.

As is well known, Descartes is very critical of the view that sensory ideas resemble things in bodies (this is part and parcel of his criticism of the scholastic notion of the sensible species).[10] But, we will want to ask, how radically does he mean to depart from a naive commitment to resemblance? Does he mean to overthrow the resemblance framework completely in favor of, say, a more brutely causal picture? Or, does he, staying within a broad resemblance picture, mean simply to rework certain important elements having to do with the fine structure of the picture (e.g., the sort of, or level of, resemblance involved between our sensory ideas and structure found in bodies)? To anticipate, I think that it is the latter. Descartes, like the Aristotelians, thinks of cognition as broadly a matter of reality coming to exist in us ("the soul becomes all things"), and more than brute causation (or uniform brute causation) is required for this to happen: the mind needs to be given forms or ideas. I also think that it is harder than might be thought to break completely with a resemblance picture of sensation and still be left with a coherent view (one could see Berkeley's criticism of Locke as pointing in this direction).[11]

There were two other components besides resemblance in the picture of sensation that Descartes thinks we are naively led to. We assume that these resemblances (sensible species, sensory ideas, sensory experience, sensory cognition, etc.) are (1) caused by bodies that (2) exist. Descartes puts this idea variously: he says that sensory ideas "proceed [*procedere*]" from bodies, and later, in the Sixth Meditation, he speaks of bodies as "emitting [*emittere*: to send out]" ideas or "immitting [*immittere*: to place in]" ideas. The basic thought here seems familiar enough. When the referee holds up the red card, we think of the card as somehow producing my sensory cognition of it. The card or something in the card determines my cognition (so that my cognition becomes similar in some respect to the card). Because information about the card seems to flow from the card to me, let me put it that the card is the "source" of my cognition. Of course, the card gets a lot of help from the medium and my physiology, but we tend to think of these other factors as helping along the flow of information and not as the cognition's source. Descartes describes this source as something from which my sensory ideas "proceed," or as something that sends out or "emits" sensory ideas or places sensory ideas in me. Although we would not put matters that way, I do think there's an affinity between the sort of thing that Descartes seems to have in mind and the rudimentary thought I have been trying to tease out that bodies are the source of our sensory cognition. I will not pause, however, to consider exactly what these locutions ("proceed from," "emit," "immit") add (if anything) to that rudimentary thought, or how far (if at all) these locutions take us away from a naive picture of sensation.

The way we think about sensing the red card differs from the way we think about imagining the red card. When I imagine a red card, we do not think of the card as the source of what I imagine: either I myself am the source, or (perhaps better) there is no source in the relevant sense, that is, my imaginative ideas do not "proceed from" anything (which is not to deny that my imaginative ideas may be the result of creatively working with ideas that did proceed from something).[12] In addition, when I see the card, because of the way in which the card is the source of my sensory cognition, it has to exist while I see it.[13] Here we might contrast seeing the card with visually recalling it: in the case of visually recalling it, the card may be the source of the memory—the ideas that make up the remembered experience may originate with the card and proceed from it—but not in such a way that the card need now exist (as opposed to having once existed).

I should note that my description of the picture of perception that Descartes is working with as something that we are all "naively" led to at some point in our lives may court misunderstanding. Nowadays what is called the "naive theory of perception" is often a philosophical position to the effect that perception is to be analyzed in terms of a perceiver and the thing perceived without any further substantive commitments (in particular, without a substantive commitment to "ideas" or "representations," which would mark a loss of philosophical innocence).

Now, part of the motivation behind such an account, I take it, is not to complicate unduly the mind's relation to the world. And, in this regard, it is important that neither an Aristotelian sensible species nor a sensory idea for Descartes is something that we direct attention to or otherwise observe (with some interior set of eyes perhaps?), when we see; so in at least one sense of intermediary, neither is an intermediary, and in at least one sense of standing between mind and the world, neither does.

But, for all of that, a sensible species or a sensory idea is a *reality*. Ideas and *species* are connected in the tradition with *form*. Form in the Aristotelian tradition is a principle of actuality as opposed to potentiality, a principle of perfection or reality: privations (e.g., blindness) and negations (e.g., not seeing) do not have forms. It is not obvious that one can, strictly, have an idea (or species) of nothing or nonbeing (this seems to be a way in which the modern usage of *idea* differs from the early modern usage; it is also one of the sources of trouble for Descartes's suggestion in the course of his discussion of "material falsity," that there could be an idea of cold, even if cold itself turned out to be a privation, i.e., a nonbeing). Forms, even when existing only cognitively, are still realities: more precisely, ideas are modes that exist in the mind (just as sensible species for a scholastic are accidents that exist either in some medium or the soul); they add perfection or reality to the mind. So, I believe that Descartes's position is incompatible with any view that makes an idea out to be a mere *façon de parler* (so that, for example, to say that S has an idea of X is just another way of saying that S is thinking of X), as perhaps Thomas Reid holds, along with some modern theorists of perception.[14] Whether this commitment to the reality of the structure existing cognitively in the mind tends to move the theories away from what people naively think about perception, is hard to say.

Finally, I want to consider a passage from the Sixth Meditation that could be taken to present an account of the meditator's precritical picture of sensation different from the one I have offered here. The passage, which is a part of a survey of things I used to think about the senses before entering the *Meditations*, runs:

> I also sensed in bodies hardness and heat, and other tactile qualities; and in addition light, colours, smells, tastes, and sounds, the variety of which enabled me to distinguish the sky, the earth, the seas, and all other bodies, one from another. Nor was it without sound reason that, on account of the ideas of all these qualities which presented themselves to my thought, and which alone I properly and immediately sensed, I took myself to sense certain things fully distinct from my thought, namely bodies from which these ideas proceeded [*Nec sane absque ratione, ob ideas istarum omnium qualitatum quae cognitationi mea se offerebant, & quas solas proprie & immediate sentiebam, putabam me sentire res quasdam a mea cogitatione plane diversas, nempe corpora a quibus ideae istae procederent*]: For it was my experience [*experiebar*] that these ideas came to me without any consent of mine, so that I couldn't sense any object, however much I wanted, unless it was present to my sense organ, nor could I not sense it when it was present. (VI.¶6; 7:75; 2:52)

The key issue here is what the antecedent of the "which" in "which alone I properly and immediately sensed" is. Some translators decide the issue by inserting the word *ideas* at this point, so that Descartes comes out saying, "which ideas alone I properly and immediately sensed." That would, I think, be inconsistent with both the Aristotelian theory and a naive picture of sensation. According to those views, what we properly and immediately sense is some structure in the world, by having that structure come to exist in our mind.

But I don't think that's the right way to take this passage. As a matter of grammar, the word *qualities* is a more natural candidate for the antecedent. If we take the passage this way, so that qualities count as what we properly and immediately sense, then it is in line with a traditional Aristotelian conception of sensation, according to which the proper object of vision is color, the proper object of hearing is sound, and so forth.[15] Further, the main thrust of the passage is to suggest that there is something about our everyday experience with our senses that makes it reasonable for us to think that when we sense colors and sounds, we are sensing bodies "fully distinct" from our thought. Consider again the soccer referee who is sending off a player. I sense redness only while the referee holds out the card and not when the card is in the wallet. And when he holds it out and I am looking in that direction, I cannot avoid sensing redness. It is reasonable for me to read what is going on as that the card is at the other end of my visual experience, as its source.

In fairness, while the passage tells us that it was not without reason that I took myself to be seeing a body, the red card, the passage does not make clear whether I took the redness itself to be "fully distinct" from my thought, and so it leaves unclear the precise place of the sensible *quality*. I think the account runs more smoothly, however, and keeps us closer to something recognizable and familiar, if we think of the quality as belonging to the body rather than the mind. If I thought of the quality as belonging to the mind, it is hard to see how I would get from there to the conclusion that the bodies that I sense are "fully distinct" from my thought. Moreover, it seems more in keeping with the passage's being a review of what I previously took to be the case about the senses, before working through the *Meditations*, that the qualities that I sense, as well as the bodies, should be in the world.[16]

CRITICISM OF THE PRECRITICAL VIEW AND A SKETCH OF
A NEW POSITION

Taken together, these texts provide a baseline that tells us where we start out. Of course, Descartes criticizes our initial conception of perception, and it is possible that our final conception will be very different. After all, he terms his initial view his "chief mistake."

Descartes's main critical discussion of the initial view comes near the beginning of the Third Meditation, in ¶¶8–12. Although he is especially concerned about resemblance, it seems clear that the entire view is under consideration, as his rather harsh-sounding conclusion indicates:

> All these considerations are enough to establish that it is not reliable judgement [*ex certo judicio*] but merely some blind impulse [*caeco aliquo impulsu*] that has made me believe up till now that there exist things distinct from myself which transmit [*immittent*] ideas or images of themselves through the sense organs or in some other way. (III.¶12; 7:39–40; 2:27)

Does this assessment signal a radical departure from our initial view of sensation? Well, possibly. But let's keep in mind that in the Third Meditation, Descartes is not arguing that this familiar picture of perception is false, just that he cannot (yet, at least) find any reason to embrace it. A sketch of that discussion will serve to fix ideas. In ¶8, Descartes asks himself for his reasons for his initial, precritical beliefs about the senses. He finds he is able to muster two sets of considerations. The first is simply that (1) nature seems to teach him these things. Perhaps this means that, when I look at the referee's red card, I find it natural to think that the card (i) exists, (ii) is the source of my experience, and (iii) is more or less as I experience it to be. The second argument is a little more complex. (2a) Sensory ideas (or experience) come to me independently of my will. If I look at the red card, I see it whether I want to or not. This suggests that sensory ideas come to me from things distinct from me. (2b) But—and notice the thinness of the argument at this point—if this is so, "the most obvious judgement for me to make is that the thing in question sends in [*immittere*] to me its own likeness rather than something else" (7:38; 2:26).

In the next three paragraphs, Descartes examines the first argument— (1) in ¶9, (2a) in ¶10, (2b) in ¶11. The fact that we find ourselves naturally inclined to believe various things about the senses does not show that what we are thus inclined to think is true (¶9). The fact that sensory ideas come to us against our will does not show that they come from external things (¶10). And, even if they do, that doesn't show that the ideas resemble the things that produce them (¶11).

Now, while Descartes is critical of the meditator's grounds for holding the initial view, it is striking that each of them, suitably reshaped, finds its way into the final view. To see this, recall the argument that Descartes eventually offers for the existence of body in VI.¶10. It has two stages. In the first, he establishes that there's an active power for producing sensory ideas, corresponding to my passive ability to receive sensory ideas, and that this active power is in a substance that is distinct from me. At this point, it is left open what that power might be. We have it, on general metaphysical principles, that the power has at least as much reality as the ideas contain objectively, but this requirement is compatible with the possibility that God or an angel places the ideas in me. In the second stage, Descartes eliminates this possibility by appealing to my "great propensity to believe" that the source of my sensory ideas has the same reality as is found objectively in the ideas.

Notice, then, the following similarities between my initial and final beliefs about the senses:

(1) Initially, I thought nature taught me what the senses do. This is explicated as follows: "When I say 'Nature taught me to think this,' all I mean is that a spontaneous impulse leads me to believe it" (¶9; 7:38; 2:26–27). A teaching of nature is something we simply find ourselves naturally inclined to believe or do—for example, when we are thirsty, we find ourselves inclined to seek drink and to think that drink would be good for us. Now, in the Sixth Meditation argument for the existence of body, in order to eliminate the possibility that my sensory ideas are sent to me by God or an angel, Descartes appeals to the great propensity I have to "believe that [sensory ideas] are emitted [*emitti*] by corporeal things" (7:80; 2:55). And so my final theory of what the senses do rests on, as I had originally thought, what I find myself naturally inclined to believe that they do.

(2a) In both my initial and final view, the fact that sensory ideas come to me willy-nilly is part of an argument for their proceeding from something distinct from me.

(2b) Descartes rejects the resemblance thesis. More precisely, he rejects the Aristotelian thesis, that when we sense, what happens is that a form (a sensible species), resembling a (sensible) form in the thing that we sense, comes to exist cognitively or spiritually in us (so that we are thereby made "formally identical" "in a way" with the thing that we sense). But Descartes makes another assumption about the relationship between what sensory ideas represent and their source that seems to cover similar ground, namely, that their source contains in the same form (i.e., contains "formally" as opposed to "eminently") whatever reality is found objectively in the ideas. Because it is cloaked in scholastic jargon, "reality," "found objectively," and "contains formally," it is a little hard to know exactly what to make of this shift, and we will look at it in detail toward the end of this part of the chapter. For now, let's simply note that it is not clear how completely Descartes intends to be breaking with the Aristotelian resemblance picture.

So the final view, I think, is not all that far from the view we started with: initially I thought that when I sense, an existing body emits a sensory idea that resembles something in the body; subsequently, I believed that when I sense, a sensory idea is emitted by an existing body that contains formally the reality that the idea exhibits objectively.[17] Moreover, there is a similarity in the general shape of what I take to be the basis for my conception of sensation: in both cases, the fact that sensation happens independently of my will contributes to my reasons for thinking that it is fixed by something else, a source, and the fact that I find myself naturally inclined to believe various things about this source forms part of my basis for those beliefs.

This gives us a working picture of how the meditator's thinking about what the senses do develops over the course of the *Meditations*. In the remainder of this chapter, I want to look more closely, first, at the suggestion that our beliefs about what the senses do are somehow rooted in our natural inclinations or propensities; and second, at Descartes's rejection of the Aristotelian resemblance thesis and his replacement of it with a view about formal and objective reality.

The Difference between a "Teaching of Nature"
(Natural Inclination) and What Is Revealed by
the Natural Light

As we have just seen, both my initial and final beliefs about what happens when I sense depend on my natural tendencies. In the Third Meditation, I take my beliefs about the senses to be teachings of nature; in the

Sixth Meditation, my belief that sensory ideas proceed from bodies rests on my "great propensity to believe that [sensory ideas] are emitted by corporeal things."

This has the consequence that my beliefs about the senses and the external world have a character different from my beliefs about myself, God, or geometry. This difference in character is something of a discovery that the meditator is supposed to make, and this discovery is integral to my coming to realize that she does not yet have (in the Third Meditation) a successful argument for the existence of body. The pivotal text here is ¶9, where she learns what is meant by nature's teaching her something:

> When I say "Nature taught me to think this," all I mean is that a sponta-
> neous impulse leads me to believe it, not that it has been shown to be true
> by some natural light. There is a big difference here. Whatever is revealed
> to me by the natural light—for example from the fact that I am doubting it
> follows that I exist, and so on—cannot in any way be open to doubt. This
> is because there cannot be another faculty both as trustworthy as the natu-
> ral light and also capable of showing me that such things are not true. But
> as for my natural impulses, I have often judged in the past that they were
> pushing me in the wrong direction when it was a question of choosing the
> good, and I do not see why I should place any greater confidence in them
> than in other matters. (7:38–39; 2:27)

This is an intriguing passage. At the risk of overstructuring, let me lean on the idea of truth being revealed to me in the one case and not the other, and mark the contrast that Descartes draws here as the difference between what I believe because I can see that it is so (according to Descartes: from the fact that I am doubting, it follows that I exist, God exists, and, possibly, two and three added together make five) and what I find myself spontaneously inclined to believe without actually seeing that it is so (according to Descartes: that sensory ideas come from bodies, that I have a body that has various needs). So understood, the natural light works through insight or understanding, and teachings of nature or natural inclinations don't. When I recognize that I cannot doubt unless I exist, I see why this is so. By way of contrast, when I am thirsty and form a desire to drink water (or find myself with an inclination to think that water would be good for me), I do not thereby see why water would be good for me; my thirst may point me in the right direction, but it does not give me any insight into the matter.

Now, Descartes also says in this passage that what's revealed to me by the natural light is not open to doubt, whereas teachings of nature are. But the idea of something's either being open to doubt or not being open to doubt is not what is primary here; rather, this difference seems rooted in a more basic difference. When I perceive something through

the natural light, I see why it has to be the case and *that's* why I cannot
doubt it. Consider the cogito argument: as I work through it, I see that if
I doubt, I must exist, and it is this seeing that makes it impossible for me
to hold back, to doubt. It is this insight or understanding into the truth
that determines my judgment. The case of natural inclination is different. When I am thirsty I find myself desiring water or thinking that
water would be good for me without a sense of why water would be
good. I do not "see" a connection between thirst and water's being good.
This makes it possible for me even when very thirsty to wonder whether
water would in fact be good. In the case of something's being shown to
me by the natural light, my understanding of what is the case or what is
good leads me to believe or to act in a certain way and makes doubt
impossible; in the case of a natural inclination, there is a tendency to believe or act that urges me on independently of any insight or understanding I may have, and it is this lack of insight or understanding that leaves
room for doubt.

How We Are in a Better Position in the Sixth Meditation

I will come back in a moment to Descartes's idea that my belief about
what the senses do rests on my natural inclinations, but first it will prove
valuable to have a look at how my natural tendencies—that is, my great
propensity—enter into his Sixth Meditation argument for the existence
of body.

An obvious question to begin with is this. In the Third Meditation our
natural tendencies were not be trusted: they were regarded as mere
"blind impulses." Yet the Sixth Meditation argument is based on my natural tendency to believe something. Why the difference in attitude? Well,
in the Third Meditation I did not know that the author of my nature was
God, and so I did not know where natural tendencies ultimately came
from. In the Sixth Meditation, I know that they come from God, and that
tells me that they (generally) point me in the right direction. By placing
my natural inclinations and impulses within the larger structure that has
been developed over the intervening part of the *Meditations*, I am able to
achieve an understanding of my position that I previously lacked.

It is worth reflecting on exactly how my understanding of my position
has improved. What I acquire is a reason to go along with a constellation
of natural tendencies and cues that I was previously unsure just what to
make of. In particular, my natural inclination to believe that when I sense,
the source of my sensory ideas is (existing) bodies, receives both explanation and endorsement: this inclination comes from God, who will have
set things up so that, *ceteris paribus*, I will be led to the true and the good.

The Sixth Meditation argument is sometimes thought of as harboring a commitment to an infelicitous veil of ideas. On such a theory, what the mind properly and immediately senses are its own ideas, and the mind must make an inference on their basis to the existence of the physical structures that cause the ideas. The point of the Sixth Meditation argument on this reading is to build a bridge from our sensory ideas, of whose existence we are certain, to bodies, of whose existence we are in doubt. Descartes seems to have been read by Kant this way, who, in his "Refutation of Idealism," classified Descartes as an idealist and explained idealism as the position "that the only immediate experience is inner experience, and that from it we can only *infer* outer things."[18]

To be sure, it is true that Descartes holds that my knowledge of my mind is prior to my knowledge of the existence of body. In the Second Meditation he explains how the mind is better known than body. The argument that he gives for the existence of body runs through facts about my mind (that it has certain natural propensities, that God is the author of its nature). Still, it is unclear to me that a Kantian picture of what Descartes is doing here is apt, because of the way in which Descartes sees my knowledge of the existence of body as running through what I find myself naturally inclined to believe about the affair. In particular, I don't read Descartes as maintaining that my "only immediate" experience is of sensory ideas and that I get to bodies and their qualities only subsequently through inference. Rather, Descartes holds that what the senses do is to make the redness in the red card "immediately" present to the mind. We might look at the progress I make between the Third and Sixth Meditations this way: there is this thing that I do that I call "seeing a red card," and I am trying to work out for myself what this activity is. Of course, I find myself with strong views about what's going on when I sense—I am naturally inclined to think that when I see a red card, or when I have a sensory idea of a red card, this body is informing or shaping my thought, and so is noninferentially present to ("exists objectively in") my mind. Eventually, in the Sixth Meditation, I come to see why what I am inclined to believe in this regard has to be so (otherwise God would be a deceiver).

Further, if instead we take the Sixth Meditation project to be to construct a bridge from immediately perceived ideas to a world of bodies, we would have to think that the great propensity works along these lines: I find myself in a situation where I have learned that what I immediately perceive are my ideas, and yet I still feel an urge to hypothesize or postulate a realm of bodies from where these ideas come. It is, I think, harder to recognize ourselves in such a story; it is easier to locate ourselves in a story where what we have is an inclination to believe that the senses present us (directly, immediately) with a physical world. Here Descartes's wording of the propensity may matter: it is, he says, a propensity to "be-lieve that [sensory ideas] are emitted [*emitti*] by corporeal things" (7:80; 2:55). The language of emission recalls the scholastic tradition, in which the item emitted, the species, is not the thing we see but rather that by which we see: for Socrates to receive a sensible species of red emitted by the red card is what it is for him to sense the red card. So I believe that Descartes's position has the overall effect of God's instructing me, through my nature, that the window that all along I have suspected the senses afford me onto the world is, in fact, there. It is as if God tells me through my nature that there is no veil of ideas.

Finally, some might wonder whether this interpretation is consistent with Descartes's employment of the dreaming doubt. It might be sug-gested that a major function of the doubt is to cut back the content of sensory experience to that which we would be certain of under the as-sumption of a dreaming skepticism, so whatever else (if anything) is in the picture turns out to be, strictly speaking, extrinsic to our sensory cognition itself; and that this important result colors both Descartes's handling of our initial conception of sensation in the Third Meditation and his final account of what the senses do in the Sixth. The problem with this suggestion is that it assumes that the dreaming doubt com-mits one to a certain theory of sensory cognition. Here, it is important to separate, as I believe Descartes does, questions about what the senses actually do from questions about what one believes or judges that they do. It is easy to see how one might come out of the dreaming doubt (indeed ought to come out of the dreaming doubt) unsure about what the senses do, about what our sensory ideas actually achieve. Maybe sensory ideas proceed from bodies in such a way as to make them immediately present to my mind; maybe they do not. While it is easy to see how the dreaming doubt might help to raise and frame such issues, it is much harder to see how it might be supposed to settle them.

NATURAL INCLINATIONS

Let me set the veil of ideas aside. An overemphasis on this problem threatens to distract us from something more interesting in Descartes's treatment of our cognition of body, namely, his suggestion that my be-lief about what the senses do rests on my natural inclinations or propen-sities. (Indeed, since all beliefs about what particular bodies there are and how they are structured depend on what I take my senses to do, those beliefs, too, ultimately rest on my natural inclinations and propensities.)

We might wonder why Descartes thinks that my beliefs about the senses have this structure and whether he has correctly charted this region of my cognitive life: Don't I just *see* that there are bodies and that there are people in this room? Why should I think I must invoke my natural tendencies here?

Let me approach this question gradually. An important clue comes, I believe, toward the end of the wax discussion. There, Descartes discusses certain limitations in the ability of the senses or imagination in providing a perception of what the piece of wax is. He worries that language might mislead us into thinking that senses do more than they actually do:

> For we say we see the wax itself, if it is present, not that we judge [*judicare*] it to be present from its colour or shape. Whence I might immediately conclude: the wax is cognized [*cognosci*] with the vision of the eyes, not the inspection of the mind alone; unless I should look out the window, as now happened by chance, at men crossing the square, whom I also customarily say that I see, no less than the wax. But what do I see besides hats and coats, under which could be concealed automata? But I judge [*judico*] them to be men. And so that which I thought I saw with my eyes, I comprehend only with my faculty of judging [*judicandi facultate*], which is in my mind. (II.¶13; 7:32; 2:21)

Now, I argued in chapter 2 that the principal focus here is not the question, How do I know that bodies exist? but rather, What is it that I am seeing? Even so, I think what Descartes is saying here bears on the issue, and indicates that one sort of answer to the question is off base. While we might be tempted to think we know that bodies exist because the senses simply present them to us, this is wrong, because it eclipses the role that judgment plays in such cognition. We don't know that bodies exist simply by opening our eyes and looking, or holding out our hands and feeling, because there is always, at least in principle, an issue about what it is I am seeing or touching—a shape, a color, a piece of wax, a body? Or, hats and coats, men, automata? The senses cannot settle the question of what it is that they make available to us or how this is to be understood or interpreted. The latter involves judgment and, according to Descartes, requires the "mind alone."

Now, this passage comes toward the end of the Second Meditation, and so is fairly close to the material that we have been considering from the beginning of the Third. Moreover, there is an emphasis on judgment in his discussion of the senses in the first part of the Third Meditation: judgment terms occur frequently in this section (see III.¶3, III.¶6, and III.¶7, excerpted above). My initial view is not that I believe that bodies exist because it is the case that the senses just work this way; Descartes is careful to say that I judge that the senses work this way.[19]

The role that Descartes assigns judgment and the mind alone in these texts raises difficult and interesting questions about how to position what he is saying in the *Meditations* vis-à-vis modern perceptual psychology. It sounds as if Descartes is denying that beings who lack faculties of judgment see bodies as bodies, because seeing a body as a body requires a faculty of judgment. This conflicts with modern perceptual science, which attributes primitive categories, like body, to perceptual systems, that is, without any help from the higher faculties an organism may have. According to it, even some creatures that lack a capacity for judgment nevertheless are able to see bodies as bodies.

It is difficult to know what Descartes's reaction to modern perceptual psychology would be, but my guess is that he would be rather more sympathetic than the layer of his thought that we are currently examining might seem to suggest. Let me sketch a route to this conclusion by way of considering his views on animals, which cut both ways on this question. To be sure, animals, for Descartes, lack minds, and so they lack thought (cognition). He writes in a letter to Gibieuf:

> We observe in animals movements similar to those which result from our imaginations and sensations; but that does not mean we observe imaginations and sensations in them. On the contrary, these same movements can take place without imagination, and we have arguments to prove that they do so take place, as I hope to show clearly by describing in detail the structure of their limbs and the causes of their movements. (3:479; 3:203–4)

This might make it seem as if Descartes would be hostile to modern perceptual psychology, inasmuch as it tries to offer a theory of cognition in a domain where he believes there is no cognition. But the science of animal behavior he gestures toward involves more than their limbs; it involves their nervous systems and brains. We see signs of what might be called mechanistic animal psychology in Descartes's response to a question that Arnauld had asked him about a sheep's reaction to a wolf:

> When people take a fall, and stick out their hands so as to protect their head, it is not reason that instructs them to do this; it is simply that the sight of the impending fall reaches the brain and sends the animal spirits into the nerves in the manner necessary to produce this movement even with the mind being unwilling [*vel mente invita*], just as it would be produced in a machine. And since we experience this for certain in our own selves, why should we be so amazed that the "light reflected from the

body of a wolf onto the eyes of a sheep" should equally be capable of arousing the movements of flight in the sheep? (7:230; 2:161)

Notice there is a certain amount of complexity here. The (purely mechanistic) sheep responds, it seems, if not to wolf as wolf, then to the wolf as dangerous. In *The Passions of the Soul*, Descartes holds out the promise of mechanistic explanations of such things as a dog's chasing partridges and running away from gunfire, and of how, with training, the dog's animal spirits may reprogrammed so that the dog will halt at the sight of a partridge and approach the bird when someone fires:

> And the same may be observed in animals. For although they lack reason, and perhaps even thought, all the movements of the spirits and of the gland which produce passions in us are nevertheless present in them too, though in them they serve to maintain and strengthen only the movements of the nerves and the muscles which usually accompany the passions and not, as in us, the passions themselves. So when a dog sees a partridge, it is naturally disposed to run toward it; and when it hears a gun fired, the noise naturally impels it to run away. Nevertheless, setters are commonly trained so that the sight of a partridge makes them stop, and the noise they hear afterwards, when someone fires at the bird, makes them run towards it. These things are worth noting in order to encourage each of us to make a point of controlling our passions. For since we are able, with a little effort, to change the movements of the brain in animals devoid of reason, it is evident that we can do so still more effectively in the case of men. (A. 50; 11:369–70; 1:348)

So, even though animals lack minds, reason, thought, it is not too hard to detect a reasonably rich picture of mechanistic animal psychology underneath these remarks. No doubt Descartes underestimated the complexity involved (as he underestimated the complexity of much of empirical science), but it is not as if he is closed off to the idea of such a thing. We might perhaps put it that for Descartes there seem to be two kinds of sensing: a purely mechanistic sensing—the sensing a dog does when it "hears" a gun or stops at the "sight" of a partridge—and a cognitive sensing that we human beings with minds do.

Descartes does not go into enough detail for us to know how he would carve up what belongs to the various mechanistic animal systems—for example, what belongs to the mechanistic sensory system as opposed to what happens further downstream at the level of the flow of the spirits in the corporeal imagination or elsewhere in the brain. Still, I don't see anything preventing him from holding, for example, that the dog is responsive to body qua body at the level of a mechanistic sensory system, and responsive to the partridge qua partridge or qua prey only when the corporeal imagination (or some other mechanistic system downstream) is brought into play. I think it is also reasonable to suppose that Descartes would expect something like mechanistic beliefs to show up in mechanistic animal psychology, so that, for example, the dog has the mechanistic belief that the partridge that was just shot is lying somewhere on the other side of the hill.

Now, as I said, animals do not think, according to Descartes. The reason he believes this is that, in his view, thinking requires reflective judgment—the ability to see that something is so, in the way that I see that it has to be so that I exist, or that I see that the three angles of a triangle sum to two right angles. According to him, animals lack all of that. Still, I suspect that (what I am terming) mechanistic animal psychology is relevant to his theory of cognition, and that mechanistic animal psychology tells us something about the structure of our own natural inclinations. I think Descartes's view is that many of our own natural inclinations track, in some reasonably straightforward way, our mechanistic physiology, and our physiology is not all that different from those of the higher animals. So if a dog's mechanistic sensory system is geared toward body in some special way, so that, for example, the system mechanistically tends to represent certain things as bodies, the same will be generally true of our bodies, too, and this will show up in the mind through our natural inclinations. That is, we might, for example, be naturally inclined to judge, on the basis of our (now, cognitive) sensory perception, that certain things we are perceiving are bodies.

I don't think Descartes means to be denying that this sort of thing happens in the *Meditations*, when he raises scruples about our saying we see the people across the square. I think the point he is concerned to make there is that our beliefs are different in some basic way from the mechanistic beliefs of animals (if "mechanistic belief" is the right way, for Descartes, to think about a dog and its relation to the content *dead bird lying over the hill*). However much structure and sophistication is found in my natural inclinations, it is still up to me, rational and reflective creature that I am, to decide whether to give my endorsement to the direction in which they are prompting me or to withhold it. (By way of contrast, if I were a cognitive dog, there would be only the inclinations, and no further factor: I would always do or believe whenever my inclinations pointed me toward doing or believing.) Perhaps more controversially, Descartes seems to hold that none of my inclinations count as my beliefs without my mind's (at least tacit) endorsement. Unless I make a judgment, I do not believe. (I take this to be suggested by the texts we have been just considering from the Second Meditation and the beginning of the Third.) In any case, the fact that I, unlike the dog, do have a choice about whether to endorse my natural inclinations is something that my ability to entertain the dreaming doubt might be supposed to bring out in an especially com-pelling way: I can withhold judgment not just from there being a par-tridge over the hill, but from there being a partridge and a hill, indeed from there being a physical world at all.[20]

All of this helps explain why the meditator does not react with incompre-hension when Descartes asks her for her reasons for believing that sensory ideas come from bodies that exist and resemble those ideas. She cannot, for example, simply reject the request with "See for yourself," if this is sup-posed to mean that seeing is believing, because she has by now recognized that there is some distance between, on the one hand, what the senses provide us with and, on the other hand, the beliefs we have about, or the judgments that we make about, what it is that the senses provide us with.

Descartes tells us very little in the Second Meditation about what goes into the judgment that it is wax I am seeing, or that the things I am look-ing at out the window are human beings. It is not obvious to me that he's working with a model, for example, whereby the senses provide me with evidence for my beliefs. I think it is more likely that, when I judge the wax to be there from its shape, he supposes me to do something along the lines of understanding or interpreting what the senses provide. This seems to fit, for example, with what we do when we see the hats and coats: we locate that information within the context of general be-liefs about how things usually go and arrive at the conclusion that what I am looking at are, not automata. In another setting, we might reach a different conclusion.

Be that as it may, I think this much is obvious: any judgment I make about what the senses do in general should traverse at least the ground covered by the argument for the existence of body given in the Sixth Meditation. And if that is so, when I judge that the senses make bodies present to me, I am relying on my natural tendency—sanctioned, of course, by God, the author of my nature—to believe that sensory ideas are emitted by bodies.

Now, one might agree with Descartes that a judgment is involved in my beliefs about what the senses do and still wonder about his claim that the judgment in question is rooted in certain of my natural tendencies, in something instinctual, we might say. This is not a point that receives very much argument in the *Meditations*. We have already examined how Descartes motivates it in ¶9 of the Third Meditation, where he distin-guishes between what we are brought to by way of spontaneous impulse and what is revealed to us by the light of nature. It is there that Descartes first suggests that a certain constellation of beliefs that we have about the senses are not shown to be so on the basis of the natural light, but are simply things we find it natural to believe.

I think there is something right in Descartes's suggestion that my judgments about what my senses are doing are on a different footing from
my judgments about my own existence or about triangles. I can (it seems)
hold back, on reflection, from "I am seeing wax" or "I am seeing men" or
"When I sense, I sense bodies or features of bodies, fully different from
my thought" in a way that I cannot (it seems) hold back, on reflection,
from "If I think, I exist" or "The longest side of a triangle subtends its
greatest angle." Or I can "clearly perceive" that I exist or that the longest
side of a triangle subtends its greatest angle in a way that I cannot "clearly
perceive" that I am seeing wax or that when I sense, I sense bodies or
features of bodies, fully different from my thought. (Descartes does, of
course, think I can clearly perceive the latter via his demonstration invoking my propensities and God's not being a deceiver. But I cannot clearly
perceive this directly, as it were.) In the one case, there is room in principle for further consideration—room, one might say (as Descartes does
say in ¶9), for doubt; in the other case, if I have thought through the
claim, there is no room—not even in principle—for doubt: doubt, on its
face, is unintelligible.

Still, there seems some distance between this point and the idea that
my judgment that "there are bodies" represents the endorsement of a
natural inclination (or "great propensity"), which, in a peculiar way, seems
to divorce how I make the judgment from the content of the judgment. I
believe that there are bodies not because it is obvious to me that there are
bodies, but rather because I find myself with an inclination to believe
such a thing and decide to go along with it, perhaps because it is easier to
go along than to resist, or perhaps because I have learned that such inclinations come from God and so can be trusted.

To bring out what seems to me odd here, consider the way Descartes
thinks about hunger. In the Sixth Meditation, he reports being puzzled
about the connection between hunger and being directed to food:

> Again, why should that curious [nescio] tugging in the stomach which I call
> hunger tell me that I should eat . . . ? I was not able to give any explanation
> of all this, except that nature taught me so. For there is absolutely no con-
> nection (at least that I can understand) between this tugging and the voli-
> tion [voluntatem] to take food. (VI.¶6; 7:76; 2:53)

Since he can understand "absolutely no connection" between the tugging and the volition, from his point of view the volition seems to come
from nowhere. I take it that something is supposed to hold of my great
propensity to believe that bodies cause my sensory ideas. That, too, is an
inclination that, as far I can tell, I simply find myself with. But can my
belief that there are bodies be understood as my going along with (for
whatever reason) a propensity that, in a similar way, seems to me to come

from nowhere? When I see clearly that I exist or that the three angles of a triangle sum to two right angles, my clear view of the subject matter determines my judgment. In marked contrast, the propensity pointing me more toward a belief in body does not seem determined by the matter of the belief; it seems to be moving me along blindly toward the belief, somewhat as hunger moves me along blindly toward food. I could have had, it seems, a great propensity to believe just about anything, in the way that the curious stomach tugging I call hunger could have been followed, it seems, by a desire for just about anything. As it turns out, by the goodness of God, things are set up so that stomach tugging and the desire for food (generally) come at a time when food would be good for me; by the goodness of God also, the things I am primitively inclined to believe (generally) turn out to be true.

One wonders, then, granted that there is a difference between my belief that there are bodies and my belief that I exist or that the three angles of a triangle sum to two right angles, in that I can hold back from the former one in a way in which I cannot hold back from the latter two, isn't my belief in bodies closer to my belief that I exist than to my (blind) response to hunger? Might there not be, one wants to ask, two kinds of seeing that things are so—two different ways in which one's perception of a subject matter might determine or influence one's judgment? Perhaps when one sees that things are so in the one way, things are so rationally transparent that doubt is impossible, and when one sees that things are so in the other way, there is always, at least in principle, room for doubt.[21]

As we noticed earlier, doubt makes an appearance in Descartes's explication of the difference between natural impulses and the light of nature, so perhaps a brief comment is in order about the role that specifically skeptical doubt, especially the dreaming doubt, might be playing here. Descartes does not detail in ¶9 how natural impulses (or teaching of natures) may be doubted, and the example that he offers at the end of the paragraph concerns a practical case, as when, for example, my natural inclinations point me toward drink when drink would be bad for me. Still, it is reasonable to think that the dreaming doubt is playing some role in helping the meditator feel the difference between, on the one hand, "This is wax" and "Those are men" and, on the other hand, "I exist" or "Two plus three equals five." That is, dreams or hallucinations or whatnot might help us see that there is a place for the thought "Is this wax? Maybe it isn't" in a way in which there is not for "Do I exist? Maybe I don't" or "Does two plus three equal five? Maybe not." That said, I think we need to be cautious here. Dreams and hallucinations may help us see that there is a difference, but they cannot, as it were, create the difference.

If Descartes is correct that my judgment that "This is wax" runs through what I find it natural to believe, whereas the judgment that "I exist" is something I can see straight off must be so, this difference would remain even if I found it easy to tell whether or not I was dreaming or hallucinating (even if there should happen to be "sure signs by means of which being awake can be distinguished from being asleep" (I.¶5; 7:19; 2:13]).[22]

SAMENESS OF REALITY AS OPPOSED TO RESEMBLANCE

Thus far we have examined ¶¶8–12 with an eye toward what this discussion shows about how Descartes saw the project of demonstrating that the external world exists. I have suggested that the argument he advances and criticizes, while not itself successful, incorporates all the main ingredients but one—God—of the ultimately successful argument that is presented in the Sixth Meditation. The precritical view turns out to be in this way continuous with the final view.

There is another issue that is being addressed in this discussion, namely, whether sensory ideas resemble things found in bodies, or, more precisely, whether we have any good reason for thinking that this is the case. This contains the beginning of Descartes's critique of the commonsense idea that the world is more or less as it appears to be, or, as it is captured in scholastic Aristotelianism, that sensation involves the acquisition of a sensible species that makes the sensor similar to what is sensed. Here we might expect quite a bit of discontinuity. His treatment of the senses is avowedly revisionary. Like other new scientists, Descartes has serious misgivings about the resemblance thesis. One might think that the revisions he is calling for here are quite momentous, amounting to the overthrow of a commonsense worldview in favor of a more scientific worldview. I would like to leave open for now just how abrupt he sees the transition from the one worldview to the other as being. He may regard it as less jolting than is sometimes thought.

Our estrangement from the resemblance thesis might also be thought to lead us toward an infelicitous veil of ideas. If the resemblance thesis stands in for, as I believe it does, the scholastic notion of formal identity, then its abandonment involves the abandonment of formal identity. But I take the notion of formal identity to be part and parcel of Aristotelian direct realism: when Socrates receives the sensible species of the redness in the card, he becomes formally identical with a quality of the card and thereby senses the card. One might think that as we move away from resemblance (and formal identity) we will find ourselves drifting toward a "veil of ideas." This suspicion is heightened if we replace resemblance or formal identity with some relation of brute causal correspondence. One might worry that bare correspondence is not enough to allow the world to get in through the ideas.

Although Descartes rejects an Aristotelian account of sensory representation drawn in terms of resemblance, he is not as far from them as might be imagined. In particular, I don't think he is replacing resemblance with pure causal correspondence. How, then, does representation work for Descartes?

Descartes writes in the Sixth Meditation:

> But since God is not a deceiver, it is quite clear that he does not put the ideas in me [*immittere*] either immediately [*immediate*] from himself, nor by some mediating creature [*mediante aliqua creatura*], in which their objective reality is contained not formally but eminently. For, since God has given me no faculty at all for recognizing this, but rather on the contrary has given me a great propensity to believe that they are emitted from corporeal things [*a rebus corporeas emitti*], I do not see on what grounds [*qua ratione*] he could be understood not to be a deceiver, if they were emitted otherwise than from corporeal things [*a rebus corporeas emitterentur*]. (VI.¶10; 7:79–80; 2:55)

It is not quite clear from this text how my inclination ("great propensity") to believe that my sensory ideas are immitted/emitted by corporeal things, recorded in the second sentence, lines up with the claim, in the first sentence, that whatever immits/emits these ideas contains formally the reality found in those ideas objectively. I think Descartes holds that to possess corporeal reality formally is to be corporeal. So when he claims that the immitting/emitting causes of my sensory ideas contain formally the reality that those ideas contain objectively (namely, corporeal reality, since sensory ideas present bodies to me), this seems practically equivalent to the claim that those ideas are immitted/emitted by corporeal things.[23] It seems to me, then, that Descartes is thinking of sensation as a matter of the transfer of corporeal reality or structure from a corporeal source to the mind. Let's call it the sameness-of-reality assumption. We are naturally inclined—have a great propensity—to think that this is what is happening when we sense, and God would be a deceiver if this were not the case.

I should say that I think Descartes would be amenable to its being the case that our natural inclinations should lead us astray in all sorts of comparatively minor ways about, for example, the nature of color. He writes in *Principles*, I, 69, that we recognize much more evidently what it is for a body to have shape than what it is for a body to be colored. I think he does expect that it would be possible to provide a theodical explanation for these missteps, along the lines of the one he provides later in the Sixth Meditation for the occurrence of dropsy (which he construes as a misdirection of natural inclination). What Descartes thinks we cannot make out is that God should give us inclinations that mislead us in some very fundamental way about what is going on when we sense (as would be the case if my sensory ideas were transmitted to us by God or an angel) without somehow cluing us in to this being the case.

According to Descartes, when we sense bodies, their reality comes to exist in the mind. In general the way ideas function for Descartes is that they make reality available to the mind. That is, all ideas—whether purely intellectual (such as my idea of myself or of God) or imaginative (such as my idea of a chimera or my visualization of a triangle) or sensory (such as my idea of greenness)—exhibit or present reality to the mind: the reality contained in the thing that is being thought of exists objectively in the idea.[24] What seems special about sensory ideas is that they come to us via a process of emission/immission from the objects of those ideas to the ideas.[25] Again, this is something that we are naturally inclined to believe and can, upon reflection, see must be the case, in large part because our natural inclination comes from a nondeceiving God.

In certain respects, this sameness-of-reality assumption functions the way that formal identity or the resemblance thesis does for the Aristotelians. Both understand cognition as a matter of sameness of structure in the cognizer and the cognized, and both understand sensation as a process whereby structure makes its way from the cognized thing to the cognizer. In this sense, Descartes is operating in what might be called a resemblance framework, since what matters for sensory representation is sameness of something: if the same structure exists formally in the world and objectively in the idea, then there is a similarity or resemblance between the idea and the thing. Where Descartes and the Aristotelians part company is over whether we should understand this sameness of structure in terms of a shared (sensible) form. According to Descartes, there is no sensible form in the red card; there is only a microphysical texture, a pattern of matter in motion. So when I have an idea of red, I am not made formally identical with the microphysical texture. Moreover, when Descartes criticizes the Aristotelian resemblance thesis, he is thinking of resemblance principally in terms of this putative formal identity. Another way of putting Descartes's denial of sameness of form in idea and thing, then, is that my sensory idea of red does not resemble the red.

Descartes makes room for this lack of resemblance through the claim that the presentation of corporeal reality in our sensory ideas is obscure and confused. He writes toward the end of the demonstration of body in the Sixth Meditation:

> Perhaps, however, they [bodies] do not exist exactly [omnino] as I comprehend them by sense, for the comprehension of the senses is in many ways confused and obscure. (VI.¶10; 7:80; 2:55)

Corporeal reality is presented in our sensory ideas, but certain of its aspects are presented obscurely and confusedly. This makes it hard for us to say what is owed to the confusion and obscurity of the presentation and what belongs to the bodies that are being presented. It is difficult for us to determine what in corporeal reality as it exists in the world (i.e., formally) corresponds to the obscure and confused aspects of the objective presentation of that reality in our ideas. How Descartes thinks of the difference between the obscure and confused way corporeal reality exists in my sensory ideas and the way it exists in the world, formally, is hard to say. Is it simply an extreme version of my sensation of the shape of the table leaving out a vast amount of microdetail, or is there supposed to be a pronounced "in kind" or "qualitative" difference between the two? I lean toward the former view, but I know of nothing in the *Meditations* that would settle the question either way. It seems that Descartes thinks he can make the point he cares about without getting into such questions.

Descartes's claim that sensory ideas are obscure and confused is not easy, and we will examine it more closely later. For the moment, however, it is important to note his deep allegiance to an Aristotelian way of thinking about sensory cognition as a matter of structure (reality) making its way from the world (where it exists formally) into the mind (where it exists objectively) as well as his important departure from the way in which Aristotelians worked out this basic idea. In Descartes's view, the structure that exists in the mind and the world is not sensible form, there is no formal identity between the sensory idea and the thing sensed, and sensory ideas do not resemble sensible forms, but rather, in certain respects, present corporeal reality obscurely and confusedly.

No Natural Tendency toward Resemblance Thesis

This raises a question about Descartes's attitude toward the thesis that sensory ideas *resemble* their sources. One might think we also have a natural inclination to believe this—that is, a natural inclination to believe not only that the source of a sensory idea possesses the same reality that the idea exhibits, but also that the source resembles the idea. And if we do not, if we have only a natural inclination toward the sameness-in-reality assumption and not toward the resemblance thesis, can anything be said that helps explain the difference?

I think there is a fairly widespread view that, in effect, Descartes does hold that we have some sort of natural inclination toward the resemblance thesis.[26] A common view of the matter seems to be the following. Initially, our natures lead us to place in the world all manner of entities that do not belong there: a redness in the red card that is like my idea of it, a heat that is like my perception of a fire, and so forth. It is as if, in Hume's memorable phrase, "the mind has a great propensity to spread itself on external objects" (*A Treatise of Human Nature*, 1.3.14; p. 167). Subsequently reason corrects this mistake, pulling the objectionable entities out of the world and perhaps placing them in the mind. This correction may partly take place as the result of scientific investigation: science may teach us that there is nothing in the red card similar to my idea of it, only a surface texture.

There are places in the *Meditations* that might be taken to support this interpretation. Descartes does say that natural propensities are the sort of thing that can be overruled by reason, and he offers an extended discussion of how it is possible that a natural tendency might on occasion lead us astray. And in any case it is hard to see why we would make this error—why we would think that sensory ideas are like their corporeal sources, or why we would place sensible qualities in the world in some objectionable way—unless we had some sort of instinctual leaning in that direction.

But this is *not* Descartes's view. As a purely philosophical matter, it would be very hard to explain why God would give us a natural inclination that would lead us to make the sort of very systematic mistake at issue, and Descartes never attempts such an explanation.[27] This would, I grant, not be quite as hard to understand as why God would allow me to be fundamentally mistaken about the origin of my sensory ideas (as would be the case if they were produced in me immediately by God), but we would be heading in that direction.

As an exegetical matter, ¶15 of the Sixth Meditation ought, I believe, to settle decisively the question of whether Descartes holds that we have a natural inclination toward believing the resemblance thesis.[28] The resemblance thesis is found in a list of things "which I may *appear to* have been taught by nature, but which in reality I acquired not from nature but from a habit of making ill-considered judgements" (7:82; 2:56; emphasis added). Further, ¶15 is constructed so as to link the origin of our commitment to resemblance to the origin of two other dubious beliefs, namely, "the belief that any space in which nothing is occurring to stimulate my senses must be empty" and the belief "that stars and towers and other distant bodies have the same size and shape which they present to my senses." With respect to this last belief, Descartes writes that there is no "real or positive propensity in me to believe [*realis sive positiva propensio ad credendum*] that the star is no bigger than the flame of a small light; I have simply made this judgement from childhood onward without any rational basis" (7:83; 2:57). I do not think this remark applies only to the mistake about size; I think Descartes would say the same thing about the other two items on his list of things that we mistake for teachings of nature—in particular, that we have no real or positive propensity to believe that there is something in the fire resembling the heat as it is presented by my idea of heat, or in the red card resembling the redness as it is presented by my idea of red.

If we do not come to the resemblance thesis by way of natural inclination, how do we come to it? Descartes tells us at the beginning of ¶15 that although we confuse the resemblance thesis with a teaching of nature, it is acquired "not from nature but from a *habit* of making ill-considered *judgements*" (emphases added). We may usefully distinguish two elements here, judgment and habit. We noticed earlier that in his Third Meditation reconstruction of his initial view, Descartes presents the basis of our judgment that sensory ideas resemble their sources as rather thin. He simply says that after having arrived at the conclusion that sensory ideas are caused by bodies, "the most obvious judgement [*judicem*] for me to make is that the thing in question transmits to me its own likeness rather than something else" (III.¶8; 7:38; 2:26). The picture is filled out a bit in the Sixth Meditation, where he explains that this judgment is first made early in life, while I am heavily dependent on the senses and before I have the use of reason. Descartes writes of that time, "Since I had no notion [*notitiam*: knowledge, information] of these things [viz., the things from which sensory ideas proceed] from anywhere else besides the ideas themselves, nothing else could enter my mind but [*non poterat aliud mihi venire in mentem quam*] that the things resembled the ideas" (VI.¶6; 7:75; 2:52).

If this were all there was to the account, it would be hard to see why we confuse our belief in resemblance with a teaching or nature,[29] or why, given the judgment's shaky character, it can prove hard to get rid of, as Descartes seems to think it is. This is where habit comes in. Over time, through a kind of repetition, our belief in resemblance becomes entrenched. The belief comes to exercise a nonrational hold over us—a hold that is independent of our seeing that something is the case. This is what, I imagine, makes it easy for us to mistake the resemblance thesis for a teaching of nature. From Descartes's point of view it is important not to make this confusion: at the root of my belief in the resemblance thesis is a faulty judgment; at the root of a teaching of nature is my unadulterated nature. What results directly from my nature is God's responsibility; what results from my judging activity is my own.[30]

RESEMBLANCE AND REALITY

So Descartes is claiming that we have no primitive natural tendency toward the resemblance thesis. But isn't this simply to misdescribe human psychology? Wherever philosophical reflection and scientific theorizing might lead us, isn't Hume simply right that our starting point is one where the "mind has a great propensity to spread itself out on external objects"? And isn't Descartes's claim that we have a primitive tendency toward the sameness-in-reality assumption but not the resemblance thesis arbitrary?

Before we can think about the merits of Descartes's account of human psychology, we need to look more closely at the error connected with the resemblance thesis. It turns out that the thesis, as Descartes understands and criticizes it, brings with it a certain amount of metaphysics. It is this metaphysics that he's claiming we come to by way of "a habit of making ill-considered judgements" rather than through an original natural inclination. And this does not seem so implausible to me.

Let's look at how Descartes describes what we ought not to believe concerning resemblance. This comes in VI.¶15. I used to think

> that the heat in a body is something exactly resembling [*plane simile*] the idea of heat which is in me; or that in a white or green thing, there is the selfsame whiteness or greenness which I sense [*eadem albedo aut viriditas quam sentio*]; or that in a bitter or sweet thing there is the selfsame taste [*in amaro aut dulci idem sapor*], and so on. (¶15; 7:82; 2:56–57)

And here is what I now think:

> Similarly, although I feel heat when I go near a fire and feel pain when I go too near, there is no convincing argument [*nulla profecto ratio est quae suadeat*] for supposing that there is something in the fire which resembles the heat, any more than for supposing that there is something which resembles the pain. There is simply reason to suppose that there is something in the fire, whatever it may eventually turn out to be, which produces in us the feelings of heat or pain [*sensus caloris vel doloris efficiat*]. (¶15; 7:83; 2:57)

What seems targeted for discussion is whether there is in the white thing (presumably, a body) the "selfsame" whiteness as I sense. Now, there is something about the way Descartes frames the issue that, I believe, may court misunderstanding. When he implies that I ought not believe that there is a whiteness in the white body that is the same as whiteness that I sense, I don't think his point is that I ought to leave open the possibility that there might be two whitenesses, one in the world, which I do not sense, and another one in the mind, which I do sense. Rather, I think his point is that we ought not believe that the white in the body is the same as it appears to be, or that the obscure image of it that ends up in the mind, that is, the sensory idea of the white, resembles the white in the thing. An analogy may be helpful here. I look at a tree in my backyard through uneven glass. Because of the unevenness of the glass, information about the shape is lost to me. We might say that the shape of the tree's trunk is not the same shape that I see, in that the trunk is straight and what I see is wavy. But this need not be taken to mean there are two shapes, the shape that I see and the tree's. Another way to describe the situation is that there is just one shape, the tree's, and that because I am onto it poorly, the shape is not the same as it appears to me.

So I take Descartes to be claiming here that I do not have a natural tendency to think that my sensory idea presents the whiteness the way it is, or, in other words, that I ought to leave open the possibility that my sensory idea of whiteness might present whiteness to me in a way that somehow distorts the whiteness present in the body. But that may sound odd. Why don't I have a natural tendency to think that the whiteness is exactly the way it is presented by my sensory idea?

The reason I have no such tendency is that I find my sensory idea of whiteness obscure and confused. At the end of the argument for the existence of body, Descartes explains that the bodies "may perhaps [*forte*] not all exist completely such as they are comprehended by the senses [*omnes tales omnino existunt, quales illas sensu comprehendo*], for in many cases the comprehension of the senses is very obscure and confused." In contrast, "at least all those things are in [bodies] that I clearly and distinctly understand." This difference in attitude is to be traced back to my basic natural inclinations concerning the senses. I have a great propensity to think corporeal reality is being presented to me when I sense. In addition, or perhaps more specifically, to the extent that I find intelligible what is being presented to me—to the extent that I find what's being presented clear and distinct—I am inclined to believe that bodies are as they are presented; and, to the extent that I find what's being presented to me obscure and confused, I am not inclined to believe that bodies are as they are presented.

This relocates our problem. We wanted to know why Descartes thinks we are not naturally inclined to believe that our idea of whiteness resembles the whiteness in the white body, and now we are told this is because the idea of whiteness is obscure and confused. But, as Locke will later point out,[31] this is not how we normally use terminology like obscure and confused, in connection with senses: if I am looking at, say, the inside of a watch in good light and can make out the relevant detail, I see the machinery both clearly and distinctly. What does Descartes mean when he says my sensory comprehension of whiteness is obscure and confused?

Descartes's employment of this terminology is self-consciously technical. His main explanation of it as it applies to individual ideas occurs in ¶19 of the Third Meditation. He says there that, although all ideas, including sensory ideas, "are as it were of things" (III.¶19; 7:44; 2:30), sensory ideas present what they present in a way that leaves open whether what is being presented is a reality or an absence of reality. One cannot tell, for example, from the way in which my sensory ideas of hot and cold present hot and cold to me, whether heat is a reality or perfection, and cold is simply the absence of the heat, in which case, first appearances notwithstanding, what the idea of cold presents is a nothing, not a something. Similarly, for all that the ideas make available to me, cold may be a reality and heat its absence, or both may be realities or both may be absences. To the extent that we find an idea obscure and confused, we find opaque precisely what structure or reality the idea presents, even down to the point of being unsure whether the aspect of corporeal reality that the idea presents is a reality (say, motion in a certain setting) as opposed to a nonreality (say, the absence of motion in that setting).

This helps us to understand what Descartes is and is not denying when he says we do not have a natural tendency to the resemblance thesis. He is not denying that when I have a sensory idea of redness I have a tendency to believe that something corporeal is being presented to me. *Of course*, when I have a sensory idea of red, I am naturally inclined to believe that some feature of body is being presented to me, as opposed to, for example, some feature of my psychology. What I do not have, Descartes says, is a tendency to think that the corporeal structure being presented by my idea of red is being presented in such a way that I find myself inclined to very definite views about what is being presented, especially the ontological status of what is being presented. So if, for example, I wind up thinking that each sensory idea presents me with a determinate, positive reality, so that, for example, I imagine that hot and cold must each be realities, that is my own doing, not my nature's. This is, from Descartes's point of view, I believe, the fundamental difficulty with the scholastic theory of sensation: since the theory requires formal identity on both sides, it requires for each quality I sense that there be a specific form in the world answering to that quality, that is, a specific perfection or reality answering to that quality.

I think that, on Descartes's telling, coming to rethink my views about the underlying reality that is presented to me through my sensory ideas is supposed to be of a piece with, and as familiar and unsurprising as, my coming to rethink my views about the size of the sun or the stars, or coming to believe that there is (or may be) a body where I fail to sense anything. (That's why, I think, the list in ¶15 reads the way it does.) In each case, what I do is correct hastily made (but by now firmly entrenched) judgments rather than check my deep-seated natural tendencies. In this respect, he regards the path from the worldview I initially start out with to something more amenable to the new science, as smoother than he is sometimes read as maintaining.

There still remains the question of why Descartes chooses to begin his more substantive treatment of sensory representation at this point, early in the Third Meditation, as he is about to offer a pair of demonstrations for the existence of God. One of his correspondents, Clerselier, apparently asked him about this. Descartes writes in a letter to him with respect to the beginning of the Third Meditation:

> [a] I insisted on how little certainty we have concerning what we are persuaded of by all the ideas we think come from outside [i'ay insisté sur le peu de certitude que nous avons de ce que nous persuadent toutes les idées que nous pensons venir d'ailleurs], in order to show that there is no single idea which gives such certain knowledge as [qui fasse rien connoistre de si certain que] the one we have of God. [b] Finally, I could not have said "there is another way" if I had not first rejected all the others and thus prepared my readers to understand what I was about to write. (5:354–55; 3:376–77)

Let's begin with [b]. When Descartes writes, "I could not have said 'there is another way' if I had not first rejected all the others," he is referring to the transitional paragraph (¶13) that comes immediately after the discussion of the resemblance thesis; this "other way" involves considering ideas in terms of what they represent, their objective reality. Why did he feel he needed to prepare his readers by criticizing his precritical theory of sensation? Well, in ¶4 he announces that in order to establish the truth rule he needs to find out whether God exists. I think at this point he anticipates the following sort of reaction from at least the more educated of his readers: "Prove that God exists? Sure, no problem. We can employ one of the usual arguments, taken from Aquinas, for example, the one that begins with the motion of the sun, and demonstrate the existence of a first mover." Now, Descartes could point out that such a line of reasoning is off limits, in that the dreaming doubt is in effect, and so we do not know, for example, that the sun moves. But there has to be the concern that some of his readers will find this way of proceeding artificial: for them, the most natural way of demonstrating that God exists—indeed, the most natural way of establishing that *anything* exists—is by using the senses, and if methodological doubt is going to take this way of proceeding away from us, that only goes to show the bizarreness of trying to address such questions while laboring under methodological doubt.

The discussion in ¶¶8–12 serves to bring out that, from Descartes's point of view, the meditator is actually in a much worse cognitive position than this reaction acknowledges. It is not as if, for example, she would possess a satisfactory argument for the existence of God, if only she could find a reply to that annoying dreaming doubt—if only she would notice, say, that "dreams are never connected by memory with all the other events of my life, like the things that happen when I am awake" (7:89; Anscombe and Geach translation). Even if she did notice this, she would still not be ready to mount an argument for, say, the existence of an unmoved mover. For, in order to do this, she would need to defend the premise that there is motion, and what is the basis for that judgment? It cannot simply be that she knows that she is awake and she is watching the sun rise. One needs to connect the watching with judging somehow.

Asked to do so, she may reply that this is something that she does instinctually, believe what her senses seem to be telling her—"It is a teaching of nature." But, according to Descartes, this is not satisfactory. The only way to get from the watching to the judgment—the only way to prove that body exists—is by noticing that our various natural inclinations and propensities come from a supremely perfect creator, that is, God. By suggesting the ungroundedness of the meditator's conception of the senses and what they accomplish (until God is brought into the picture), ¶¶8–12 implicitly help to motivate a different, non-Thomistic approach to demonstrating the existence of God.[32] One reason, then, for Descartes to place a discussion of his precritical conception of the senses before his argument for the existence of God is to motivate his undertaking to address questions concerning the real existence of other things without using the senses.

There is another, in some ways deeper, reason that ¶¶8–12 are an appropriate preamble to Descartes's discussion of God, connected with Descartes's view that sensory ideas are obscure and confused. It is perhaps gestured at in [a], from Descartes's letter to Clerselier: "the reason why I insisted on our lack of certainty concerning the convictions that arise from all the ideas which we think come from outside was in order to show that there is no single idea which gives such certain knowledge as the one we have of God."[33] We are about to see in chapter 3 (II) that the fundamental issue separating Descartes and Aquinas concerning our knowledge of God is their different conceptions of how we cognize God. According to Aquinas, our representation of God is built out of sensory materials and oblique in that it is based on God's effects and falls short of God's essence. Descartes holds that our cognition of God is not constructed from sensory materials: we cognize God immediately, and our cognition of God reaches even to God's essence.

Now, the quality of sensory representation is of obvious relevance to the plausibility of Thomas's way of thinking about our cognition of God. In particular, if we do not think of sensory representation as straightforwardly making structure or reality available from the world for the mind's cogitation, but instead adopt the view that the senses make available what structure or reality they do only obscurely and confusedly, then the project of attempting to build one's conception of God out of sensory materials becomes less attractive. The question that Descartes is implicitly pressing in the Third Meditation is, Why would anyone want to construct a representation of God out of such obscure and confused materials when we have available an innate idea of God that is clear and distinct?

Both of these points about the senses—that the meditator is unable to defend her judgment about what the senses do and that the senses make reality available to mind only confusedly and obscurely—move the discussion beyond what sorts of hypothetical doubts are possible concerning the senses, into Descartes's substantive theory of the senses. The shift that Descartes is trying to effect concerning our cognition of God, from Aquinas's perspective to his own, is radical. In order to motivate that transition, it helps to begin to indicate what he takes to be problematic about the meditator's precritical worldview; it would be less effective for him to rely on skeptical scenarios, which, for all we know, once responded to might leave everything in place more or less as before. The meditator's inability to defend her judgment about the senses marks a lacuna in her view, eventually to be filled in by God; there is, if you will, a hidden reliance of her views about the senses on the thesis that our natural appetites, inclinations, and propensities come from God. Moreover, Descartes's discussion of the resemblance doctrine, which is soon followed up in the Third Meditation (¶¶19–20) by his claim that his sensory ideas are obscure and confused and that some of them may be "materially false," indicate to the meditator that the problems with her precritical worldview may go beyond a lack of certainty and reach to the correctness of the view.

II

The Third Meditation:
Two Demonstrations of God's Existence

A SIGNIFICANT CHANGE in philosophical theology took place with Descartes's work. Whereas philosophers working at the time Descartes was writing the *Meditations* tended to argue for the existence of God along the lines that Aquinas did, that is, via so-called cosmological arguments, philosophers writing after Descartes, including Spinoza and Leibniz, became much more friendly toward the ontological argument. This way of thinking about proofs of God's existence was so influential that by the time Kant undertook his important critique of rational theology, he maintained that cosmological arguments were really disguised ontological arguments.[1]

Why did this happen? One answer, which I believe has some hold on the truth, is that changes in thinking about causation occasioned by the new science undermined traditional Aristotelian cosmological arguments for God's existence, which, after all, were structured around the four Aristotelian causes. For instance, one might doubt whether the Aristotelian thesis that "everything that is in motion is being moved by another," essential to the argument for a first mover, would survive the acceptance of a principle of inertia. Or, again, one might wonder how the proscriptions against certain sorts of infinite causal regresses fared in the light of the new-science thinking about causation. In this context, it was only natural that philosophers and theologians, when faced with the loss of cosmological arguments for God's existence, would begin to look elsewhere and revisit other styles of argumentation for God's existence, such as Anselm's. So one thing that happened here was that Descartes—not surprisingly, in view of his role in the new science—recognized early on that traditional cosmological arguments were coming under pressure, as the new science displaced Aristotelian ways of thinking about causation.

However, it seems to me that there is something more fundamental lying beneath the question of how one proves that God exists. Before one gets to the question of whether we can prove that God exists, there is the question of how and to what extent human beings can have cognition of God at all. Indeed, I believe that it is Aquinas's and Descartes's differing stance on this prior issue that drives their differing position on the sort of demonstration of God's existence that is appropriate for human beings.

The basic question dividing Descartes and Aquinas is, I think, How do human beings come to cognize God? By that I mean, How do human beings come to be cognitively related to God? How and to what extent do human beings get to think about God at all (how do they get to be cognizers of God)? What sorts of representations[2] of God do human beings possess? How do they come by these representations? These questions are to be distinguished from questions concerning how human beings get to know, if they do get to know, that God exists.[3] According to Aquinas, our cognition (in this life) of God is a highly mediated affair, taking place at arm's length and falling short of God's essence, whereas for Descartes our cognition is much more direct, reaching even to God's essence.

In order to understand this disagreement, we need to review Aquinas's theory of human cognition of God. Recall that Aquinas holds that all of the soul's cognitive structure is absorbed from the world through the senses: *nihil est in intellectu nisi prius fuerit in sensu*. When I sense a dog, Fido, a sensible form—a sensible species—of the dog makes its way into my sensitive soul, thereby making me in a way identical (i.e., "formally identical") with the dog, which is to make me (immediately, so to speak) a cognizer of one of Fido's sensible qualities. Sensible species are further processed and stored as sensible phantasms in the common sense/imagination/memory. When I have accumulated a sufficient stock of canine phantasms, my intellect is able to abstract or draw out forms having to do with the essence or nature of dogs: that is to say, an intelligible species comes to exist in the soul, thereby making me formally identical with something—this time not with any particular dog, for example, Fido or Spot, but with caninehood.

This doctrine is not, in the first instance, a theory about how human cognition is justified, although it may have consequences for the "justification" of "knowledge claims." For example, in the case of mathematical cognition, the doctrine does not imply that all mathematical claims are justified through inductive generalization. Rather, this is a theory about where human cognitive structure originates that explains how our thought gets to be about the world. The basic idea is that our thought gets to be about the world because the structure through which that thought takes place is borrowed from the world. I get to think about dogs because when I interact with them they leave a mark upon my cognitive faculties. Higher cognitive faculties subsequently refine and purify this mark, but they do not introduce new content; rather, they work on and make manifest content that was already imported into the soul by the senses.[4]

The scholastic doctrine presents a picture of how the world, a mind-independent order of reality, exercises control over human thought. In forming our cognition, we are limited to materials imported from the world. It may seem that this view makes it impossible for us to think of nonexistent beings, because such beings cannot contribute the forms needed for us to think of them. However, the imagination has a creative aspect: we can use material acquired from the senses to form a conception of a one-eyed monster. What we cannot do, I take it, is grasp the *nature* of a Cyclops. In order to do *that*, we would have had to encounter Cyclopses in sensory experience, so as to have acquired, by interacting with them, a stock of sensible phantasms that contain immanently the essential structure of a Cyclops. This position seems philosophically plausible.[5] To be able to form the thought of a one-eye humanoid is not enough to enable us to lock on to some nature: Does it have one optic nerve or two? How big is the heart of such an animal? And so on. In other words, things being as they are, we are unable to form an intelligible species of a (the?) Cyclops's nature.[6]

For Aquinas, the most interesting fallout of the restriction of human cognition to materials acquired from sensory interaction with the world concerns our prospects not for cognition of chimeras and other monsters but rather for cognition of God. Although Aquinas thinks that human beings have cognition of God, he doesn't think God's essence is to be found immanently in our sensible phantasms, awaiting disentanglement by the intellect: we can no more abstract God's essence from our stockpile of experiences than we can abstract the nature of a Cyclops. So how do we form cognition of God? And how is the cognition thus formed any less imaginary or chimerical than cognition of a Cyclops?

To answer these questions, we need to consider the methodology that Aquinas follows in his arguments for the existence of God. When Aquinas argues for the existence of God, the conclusions of four of his arguments make explicit reference to language: "to which everyone gives the name God," "This all men speak of as God," "and this we call God," and "and this being we call God."[7] This is a matter of doctrine, not style. For Aquinas holds that we begin with various nominal characterizations of "God"—"first mover," "first efficient cause," "*per se* necessary being which is the source of the necessity of all other necessary beings," "source of being, goodness, and perfection," "governor of the universe"—and reason concerning whatever satisfies these nominal characterizations. And so, when he considers the objection that we cannot prove God exists because a demonstration ought to be based on *what* something is, that is, on a thing's essence, and "we cannot know in what God's essence consists, but solely in what it does not consist [*de Deo non possumus scire quid est, sed solum quid non est*]" (ST I, Q. 2, A. 2, ad 2), he responds:

> When the existence of a cause is demonstrated from an effect, this effect takes the place of the definition of the cause in the proof of the cause's existence. This is especially the case in regard to God, because, in order to prove the existence of anything, *it is necessary to accept as a middle term the meaning of the word*, and not its essence [*non autem quod quid est*], for the question of its essence [*quid est*] follows on the question of its existence [*an est*]. Now the names given to God are derived from His effects; consequently, in demonstrating the existence of God from His effects, we may take for the middle term the meaning of the word "God." (Emphasis added)

Our cognition of God is better grounded than that of Cyclops in that we are able to show that God exists. We can argue along these lines, for example: By "God" is meant whatever is the first cause of motion; there is, in fact, a first cause of motion; hence, God exists. The various demonstrations for the existence of God secure what might be thought of as the reality of our various representations of God, as those representations are recorded in the various divine names. They show that these representations are not mere chimerical fabrications of our own invention, but rather answer to something real in the world.[8]

Even so, for Aquinas, our cognition of God is limited in that we are unable to move from various nominal characterizations of God to God's essence. (When I say that Aquinas holds that our cognition of God is oblique, what I mainly have in mind is this aspect of his view, that our cognition does not reach God's essence; and when I say Descartes holds that our cognition of God is direct, what I have in mind is that he holds that it does reach God's essence.) This is not to say that all nominal characterizations of God are on the same footing—Aquinas argues in ST I, Q. 13, A. 11, that "He who is" is the most appropriate name of God.[9] But it does mean our cognition in this life of God is oblique or mediated in this particular way. Conversely, none of the cognition that we do have of God counts as abstracting an intelligible species of God's essence. When I acquire an intelligible species of caninehood, a form that exists in dogs comes to exist in me spiritually. However, Aquinas holds that there can be no created image or species of the divine essence (ST I, Q. 12, A. 2), and so long as I am confined to knowing things through species, as I am in this life, I will be unable to cognize God's essence.[10]

Descartes has a very different conception of our cognition of God. Aquinas, as we have just seen, attributes two distinct roles to the senses in our cognition of God. First, the representations that we form of God are constructed of materials acquired through sensory experience—for example, cause, motion, generation, and corruption.[11] Second, the senses are also required for establishing the reality of our representation of God. They are needed in order for us to ascertain facts—such as "there is motion" or "there is generation and corruption"—which are used as premises in the arguments that show that something described by our nominal representations of God actually exists. Descartes opposes Aquinas on both of these points. He does not think that the senses play any role in our knowledge that God exists. (Moreover, as we will see in chapter 5, Descartes thinks the "reality" of our representation of God—i.e., that my idea of God exhibits a true and immutable nature—is shown through my ability to make certain sorts of substantive judgments concerning God.) He also denies that the senses play any role in our ability to cognize God. In particular, he does not think that we use the senses to form various oblique representations of God (as, for example, the first mover unmoved). Further, in what may well be Descartes's most profound departure from Aquinas, he denies that our representation of God is oblique at all: according to Descartes, my idea of God makes available to me God's essence in more or less the same way that my idea of a triangle makes available to me its essence. Much of my discussion of his Third Meditation arguments for God's existence will revolve about these points of departure, especially the last two. It will be useful to lay them out in a preliminary way now.

Descartes's disagreement with Thomas over whether we need the senses in order to establish that God exists is part of his larger disagreement about the role that senses play in our knowledge of real existence. One might think, for example, that any knowledge of real existence depends on the senses. Against this Descartes maintains that neither our knowledge of God's existence nor our knowledge of our own existence depends on the senses. He does allow, of course, that the senses play a role in knowing that *some* things exist, namely bodies, but even this is rather delicate, as is suggested by his remark that he regards "the existence of God as more evident than the existence of anything that can be perceived by the senses" (First Replies, 7:106; 2:77). As we saw in chapter 3 (I), Descartes holds that my belief in the existence of bodies depends on a sort of natural instinct I have to take what is going on in my senses in a certain way. Before I can trust my natural instincts, I need to know something about the author of my nature, God. This being so, there would be something perverse, from Descartes's point of view, about basing an argument for God's existence on the fact that I see (or otherwise sense) motion in the world. Descartes seems to have wanted to juxtapose the problematic character of our knowledge of the existence of body with the relatively unproblematic character of our knowledge of the existence of God: that is why, I surmise, we get our first inkling of Descartes's own positive account of our knowledge that body exists in III.¶¶8–12.

Descartes's second disagreement with Aquinas, over whether the senses play any role in enabling us to cognize God, involves two commitments: first, we do not build our cognition of God out of sensory materials, and second, our cognition of God is not oblique but reaches even to some cognition of God's essence. Although these commitments are in principle distinct, the second seems to presuppose the first. It is difficult to see how the sort of cognition of God supported by sensory materials could make available to us God's essence, and, as a matter of fact, one of the reasons that Aquinas gives for our not being able to "see the essence of God" in this life is our cognitive dependence on the senses (ST I, Q. 12, A. 12).

Descartes does not replace Aquinas's sensory-based, oblique representation of God with another oblique representation of God (say, one based on my cognition of myself), but rather maintains that my (innate) idea of God reveals to me something of God's very essence. He writes to Mersenne on 16 June 1641, concerning the ontological argument:

> Thus I can draw out from the idea of a triangle that its three angles equal two right angles, and from the idea of God that he exists, etc. So far from being a begging of the question, this method of demonstration is even according to Aristotle the most perfect of all, for in it the true definition of a thing occurs as the middle term. (3:383; 3:184)

A "true definition" in the Aristotelian tradition is one that reveals a thing's essence, and Descartes implies here that our idea of God functions in the way that a true definition does in Aristotelian thought. Understood in this way, Descartes is maintaining against Aquinas that we have cognition not only that God is, but also of what God is. A passage from the First Replies, concerning the second of Descartes's two Third Meditation arguments for God's existence, is even more explicit:

> The whole force of my proof depends on this one fact [that there is within me the idea of a supremely perfect being]. For, firstly, this idea contains the essence of God [quid sit Deus], at least insofar as I am capable of understanding it; and according to the laws of true logic, we must never ask about the existence of anything [an est] until we first understand its essence [quid est]. (7:107–8; 2:78)

Descartes's suggestion that we should ask after existence (the Latin is an est: literally, whether something exists) until we understand its essence (quid est: what something is) is clearly directed against the methodology we previously saw Thomas defend in ST I, Q. 2, A. 2.

This difference over the sort of cognition of God we have affects how Descartes argues for God's existence. In particular, Descartes's claim that we start out with some cognition of what God is is necessary for each of his three arguments for God's existence.

Begin with the ontological argument. Suppose that Aquinas is correct and that all we start out with in our thinking about God are certain divine names. Then the ontological argument will look like an ill-starred attempt to argue from the definition of a name to the existence of its bearer. (In chapter 5, we will see Caterus, invoking Aquinas, make essentially the same objection against Descartes; however, because Descartes does not begin with mere nominal characterizations of God, but with some grasp of his very essence, it is not clear that the charge is fair.) By way of contrast, assume we begin with not some collection of nominal definitions but rather some access to God's very essence. Then an ontological argument looks very promising. Indeed, in view of the strong connection that there is supposed to be, in the tradition, between God's essence and God's existence, it is hard to see how this basic fact might escape our notice if our cognition of God began from God's essence.[12]

The nature of our cognition of God is crucial for the two Third Meditation arguments as well. This is fairly clear with respect to the first argument that Descartes offers (¶¶17–27), the one that focuses on the need for an explanation of the "objective reality" of my idea of God. If we really did have the sort of representation of God that Descartes thinks we have—one that makes immediately available to the mind something of God's essence—this would be a remarkable fact, calling for a very special explanation. Indeed, there is a way in which even Aquinas would have agreed that only God could bring about the sort of cognition of God that Descartes takes us to have. Conversely, if our representation of God works the way that Aquinas holds, then it looks as if one could account for our possession of it in a much more mundane way, without adverting to God's existence.

Admittedly, it is less obvious that the sort of cognition I have of God is playing a substantial role in the second argument that Descartes offers for the existence of God (¶¶28–39)—the one based on my needing a cause for my remaining in existence from one moment to the next. But when Caterus, in the First Objections, offers a reconstruction of this argument that, in effect, gives no role in the argument to my possession of the idea of God, Descartes protests:

> Moreover, in inquiring about what caused me I was not simply asking about myself as a thinking thing; principally and most importantly I was asking about myself insofar as I observe, amongst my other thoughts, that there is within me *the idea of a supremely perfect being. The whole force of my proof depends on this one fact.* (7:107; 2:78; emphasis added)

He expresses a similar position in a letter to Mesland of 2 May 1644:

> Just as it is an effect of God to have created me, so it is an effect of him to have put the idea of himself in me; and there is no effect coming from him from which one cannot prove his existence. Nevertheless, it seems to me that all these proofs based on his effects are reducible to a single one; and also that they are incomplete, if the effects are not evident to us (that is why I considered my own existence rather than that of heaven and earth, of which I am not equally certain) and *if we do not add to them the idea which we have of God.* (4:112; 3:232; emphasis added)

These texts do not make clear how or why having the sort of idea of God that Descartes takes us to have is important to his second argument for the existence of God; that is something that we will have to consider when we examine this argument in the final section of this chapter.

I. GOD'S EXISTENCE ADDRESSED FOR THE FIRST TIME

(¶¶ 13–27)

Descartes's first argument for the existence of God runs as follows: The cause of an idea must have as much reality as the reality found in the idea. My idea of God contains infinite reality; therefore, the cause of this idea contains infinite reality. But only God has infinite reality; therefore, only God can cause my idea of God. Hence God exists.

We can put the argument more technically, using vocabulary that Descartes borrows from Scholasticism. Let's say that when reality exists in the mind, it exists there objectively; let's say that when reality exists in the world, it exists formally. Suppose, further, that in order for an idea to exist that contains a given degree of reality objectively, that idea must have a cause that contains at least the same degree of reality formally (I will sometimes call this Descartes's cognitive causal principle). Then, since my idea of God contains infinite reality objectively, its cause must contain infinite reality formally. Therefore, a being that has infinite reality formally exists. But only God has infinite reality, so this existing being must be God.

This argument is bewildering. It is natural to lay the bewilderment at the door of the cognitive causal principle: why should we suppose that the cause of a representation of a thing requires as much reality as the thing being represented? That is, why should we imagine that the cause of an idea must possess formally the same level of reality as the idea possesses objectively?

I think that to a certain extent this emphasis on the causal principle is misplaced. It obscures the more fundamental disagreement (indicated above) between Aquinas and Descartes over our cognition of God, a disagreement that has much to do, I believe, with the philosophical attractiveness (or lack thereof) of the argument for God's existence along the general lines that Descartes is trying to pursue. Descartes thinks our cognition of God is much more robust than Aquinas does. As noted earlier, Descartes thinks that we have an idea of God that makes available to us something of what God is, that is, God's essence or nature. Aquinas does not think that our cognition in this life reaches to God's essence; rather, he takes cognition of God's essence to be something that is reserved for the blessed in the next. And this difference in starting place—in the, so to speak, *explanandum* of an account of our cognition of God—makes all the difference. For Aquinas would have agreed with Descartes that the sort of thing Descartes thinks we have—cognition of God's essence—is something that (however one works out the particular details) could be brought about only by God.

AQUINAS AND DESCARTES ON KNOWING WHAT GOD IS

Aquinas maintains that we have in this life only an oblique cognition of God, built out of the divine names, grounded in God's sensible effects, unlike Descartes, who holds that we have direct cognition of God's essence, which involves some purchase on unbounded perfection. But Aquinas holds that the blessed in the next life do have some cognition of God's essence or substance. I want to canvass the similarities between Descartes's account of our cognition of God in this life and Aquinas's account of our cognition of God in the next, with an eye toward the viability of an argument from the fact of such cognition to God's existence.

Let's begin with a point about how Descartes sees the *limits* of our cognition of God. Descartes remarks toward the end of ¶38:

> And the whole force of the argument lies in this, that I recognize that it could not happen that I should exist with the sort of nature that I am, namely, having the idea of God in me, unless God also were to exist—the very same God, I say, of whom the idea in me is, that is, who has all those perfections which I cannot comprehend [*comprehendere*], but which I can somehow touch in thought [*attingere cogitatione*], and is liable to no imperfections at all. (7:51–52; 2:35)[13]

This contrast between "comprehending" and "touching in thought" is stable in Descartes. In ¶25 Descartes writes:

> It does not matter that I do not grasp the infinite, or that there are innumerable other things in God which I cannot in any way grasp [*comprehendere*],

and perhaps cannot even reach in my thought [*attingere cogitatione*]; for it is in the nature of the infinite not to be grasped by a finite being like myself. (7:46; 2:32)

(In this passage, Descartes's point seems to be that having some purchase on the infinite does not require that we "touch" all of God's attributes "in thought.") The Latin terms seem to accord with the contrast between the French terms *comprendre* and *toucher de la pensée*. Descartes writes in a well-known letter to Mersenne:

> I say that I know this [that God is the author of the eternal truths], not that I conceive it or grasp it; because it is possible to know that God is infinite and all powerful although our soul, being finite, cannot grasp or conceive him [*comprendre ny concevoir*]. In the same way we can touch a mountain with our hands but we cannot put our arms around it as we could put them around a tree or something else not too large for them. To grasp [*comprendre*] something is to embrace it in one's thought; to know something, it is sufficient to touch it with one's thought [*toucher de la pensée*]. (1:152; 3:25)

This contrast between comprehending something and touching it with one's thought occurs in a closely related context in Aquinas concerning the cognition of the blessed. In Question 12 of Part I of the *Summa Theologiae*, Thomas takes up the topic "How God is cognized [*cognoscatur*] by us." Most of the question is devoted to defending the possibility of a created thing's "seeing the essence of God [*videre Deum per essentiam*]" and working out some of the more important details of the beatific vision. In Article 7, he raises the question "Whether those who see the essence of God comprehend [*comprehendant*] him?" Aquinas's basic answer is negative on account of God's infinity. Aquinas holds that to comprehend God would be to know or cognize him to the fullest extent that he is capable of being known or cognized and that no finite being, even the blessed, can do that. However, Aquinas does allow that there is a weaker sense of "comprehend," which he explains as follows:

> But in another sense comprehension is taken more largely as opposed to *non-attainment* [*insecutioni*: literally, pursuit]; for he who attains [*attingit*] to anyone is said to comprehend him when he attains [*tenet*] to him. (ST I, Q. 12, A. 12, ad 1)

Aquinas goes on to say that the created things, and in particular the blessed, can comprehend God in this second sense.

Descartes and Aquinas operate, then, with a similar contrast concerning our ability to cognize God: there is something that no created thing can do, which is to embrace God, which Descartes calls comprehending and Aquinas calls comprehending taken "strictly and properly [*stricte et proprie*]" (ST I, Q. 12, A. 7, ad 1). There is something else that created intellects can do, however, and that is in some way to make contact with God or his essence. Descartes describes this as "touching in thought," and Aquinas describes it as obtaining as opposed to pursuing (and one of the words that Aquinas uses here, *attingit*, is the same word that Descartes uses in ¶38 and ¶25). (Of course, it is difficult to say to what extent Descartes's thinking about this contrast was directly influenced by Aquinas, either directly or indirectly. In a letter he mentions that he has one of Thomas's *Summas* with him, and although there are reasons to believe that it is *Summa Theologiae*, this has not been definitively established.[14] In any case, the contrast between embracing the infinite and touching it in some way is natural enough to have suggested itself spontaneously.)

Why does Aquinas hold that this mode of cognition, in which we "see God in his essence [*videntes Deum per essentiam*]," is unavailable to us in this life? He traces this limitation back to our embodiment, which has the consequence that material things are the proper object of human knowledge:

> The reason is, because as was said above (A. 4), the mode of knowledge [*cognitionis*] follows the mode of the nature of the knower. But our soul, as long as we live in this life, has its being in corporeal matter; hence naturally it knows only what has a form in matter, or what can be known by such a form. Now it is evident that the divine essence cannot be known through the nature of material things. For it was shown above (AA. 2, 9) that the knowledge of God by means of any created similitude is not the vision of his essence. (ST I, Q. 12, A. 11)

In part this is a claim about proportion. The proper object of the human intellect is sensible reality, the material world. As such, there is a lack of fit between it and the divine essence. In the next article, where Thomas describes the sort of cognition of God that we are capable of achieving in this life, he emphasizes the disproportionateness between the sensible effects of God, which we can cognize, and God's essence, which we cannot cognize.[15]

In order for a created intellect to see God's essence, God must strengthen that intellect, giving it a new disposition, which Aquinas terms (following, I believe, an established tradition) the "light of glory." When he responds to the objection that owing to the great gulf between a created intellect and the divine substance, no additional light can make up that difference, he recalls a comparison that Aristotle makes between the relation of the human intellect to things that are most intelligible in themselves and the relation of an owl's eye to the sun. Just as the eye of the owl is too feeble to see the sun, so too the created intellect is too weak to reach "the divine substance," the "first intelligible."[16]

To return to Descartes, when he says in ¶37 that I can touch (if not comprehend) God in cognition, in ¶25 that I have a clear and distinct idea of God, and, even more explicitly, in the First Replies that my idea of God "contains the essence of God, at least insofar as I am capable of understanding it," he is attributing to us in this life something that is in certain respects similar to the sort of cognition of God that Aquinas thought was possible only in the next. My sense is that Descartes does so more or less self-consciously. It seems to be hovering about the surface of the last paragraph of the Third Meditation, in which he extols our idea of God, alluding to the joy of the next life and making use of a metaphor involving light:

> But before examining this point more carefully and investigating other truths which may be derived from it, I should like to pause here and spend some time in the contemplation of God; to reflect on his attributes and to gaze with wonder and adoration on the beauty of this immense light, so far as the eye of my darkened intellect can bear it. For just as we believe through faith that the supreme happiness of the next life consists solely in the contemplation of the divine majesty, so experience tells us that this same contemplation, albeit much less perfect, enables us to know the greatest joy of which we are capable in this life. (¶39; 7:52; 2:35–36)

Similarly, Descartes writes at the end of perhaps his most detailed defense of the thesis that God's infinity does not prevent us from having some understanding of him:

> But those who try to attend to God's individual perfections and try not so much to seize [capere] them as to be seized [capi] by them, using all the strength of their intellect to contemplate them, will certainly find that God provides much more ample and straightforward subject-matter for clear and distinct knowledge [cognitionis] than does any created thing. (7:114; 2:82)[17]

Aquinas adduces a variety of considerations in support of the thesis that a created being cannot by its own powers see God's essence. The two that strike me as closest to the sort of reasoning that Descartes employs in the Third Meditation are found near the beginning of III, 52, of the *Summa Contra Gentiles*:[18]

> [I]t is not possible for any created substance to attain, by its own power, this way of seeing God.
>
> For that which is proper to the higher nature cannot be acquired by a lower nature, except through the action of the higher nature to whom it properly belongs: thus water cannot become hot except through the action of heat. Now to see God in his essence is proper to the divine nature, since to operate through its own form is proper to the operator. Therefore

no intellectual substance can see God in the divine essence, unless God himself bring this about.

A little further in the same chapter:

Moreover. Whatever exceeds the limits of a nature, cannot be acquired by that nature except through the agency of another: thus water does not flow upwards unless it be moved by something else. Now it is beyond the limits of any created nature to see God's substance: because it is proper to every created intellectual nature to understand according to the mode of its substance: whereas the divine substance cannot be understood thus, as was proved above. Therefore no created intellect can possibly attain to a vision of the divine substance except by the agency of God who surpasses all creatures.

The reason Aquinas gives for thinking that the divine substance cannot be understood according to a mode of cognition natural to a created substance is that this mode involves cognizing God "as a cause is known from an effect," as when it sees God either in itself or in some other created being; but such effects fall short of the full extent of God's power, and so none of this cognition counts as seeing the divine essence (SCG III, 49).

The proximity between the mode of cognition that Descartes attributes to us in this life and the one that Aquinas attributes to creatures who are enjoying the *visio Dei* allows us to consider the relation of the first of the Third Meditation's arguments for God's existence to the scholastic tradition in a new way. The basic idea behind Descartes's argument is that the sort of cognition we have of God could not occur unless God brought it about. Now, it is striking that Aquinas holds something analogous about the *visio Dei*. In particular, he denies that any finite being could cognize God's essence without special assistance from God. So when he addresses the question "Whether any created intellect by its natural powers can see the divine essence?" (ST I, Q. 12, A. 4), he answers negatively, and SCG III, 52, is entitled "That No Created Substance Can by Its Natural Power Arrive at Seeing God in His Essence." This being so, it would seem to follow that if a finite being somehow found itself— as Descartes thinks we find ourselves—in possession of cognitive access to the divine essence, it would also have the wherewithal for a Third Meditation–style argument that God exists. That is, it would be able to argue that only God could bring about such cognition.

Strictly speaking, Descartes would deny what Aquinas is affirming here, namely, "That No Created Substance Can by Its Natural Power Arrive at Seeing God in His Essence," because, in Descartes's view, we are able to cognize God through an idea that belongs naturally to the human mind.

For Descartes the fact that I am able to cognize unbounded perfection testifies to the origin of my nature in an infinite being rather than to my receiving some subsequent help from an infinite being. All the same, this disagreement over how to draw the boundary between what can happen naturally and what can happen only supernaturally notwithstanding, both Aquinas and Descartes agree that the finite cannot cognize the infinite, unless the infinite helps to bring this about.

Descartes, on my telling, is launching an argument for the existence of God in the midst of a cognitive situation that he takes to resemble the beatific vision. But if he is sizing up our cognitive situation correctly, why is it necessary to argue backward to God's being the only possible cause of that situation? That is, given the proximity between God's essence and his existence, why wouldn't such a being immediately recognize that God exists? But while Descartes agrees that a being who has some cognition of God's essence ought to be able to tell that God exists—this is, after all, the ontological argument—he postpones presentation of this argument until the Fifth Meditation. Why?

Perhaps part of the explanation is as follows. Although we are natively capable of cognition of God's essence, our innate idea of God has been so obscured by bad habits that we have to work to uncover it, so to speak. Because of the distracting influence of the senses, we have a tendency to see our representation of God as something other than it is; that is, we tend to mistake it for some oblique construction out of sensory materials. So, in some sense, persuading the meditator that she has some cognition of God's essence goes hand in hand with persuading the meditator that her idea of God did not come from the senses. But this, in turn, makes the following question urgent: How do I come by this idea of God, if not through the senses? Do I just spontaneously generate it myself? It hardly seems likely that I could be responsible for such an achievement. I think that these obvious concerns help us understand why Descartes chose to advance the argument on several fronts at once as he did, and, in particular, in a manner that is intended to make clear the special (nonsensory) character of our idea of God along with showing that such an idea could ultimately originate only from God.[19]

While there is broad agreement between Aquinas and Descartes on this much—namely, that owing to discrepancies having to do with what is sometimes called the hierarchy of perfection or reality, a finite being is unable to cognize God's essence or substance without God's acting so as to bring this about—there is also significant disagreement on important details. Perhaps the most important is connected with Aquinas's claim that "to see God in his essence is proper to the divine nature, since to operate through its own form is proper to the operator." When the blessed see God in his essence, they use his essence, not some created facsimile. Aquinas argues that there could not, for example, be anything like an intelligible species of the divine essence. An intelligible species would be created, and as such finite, but nothing finite can comprehend the infinite:

> Every intelligible species through which the quiddity or essence of a thing is understood, comprehends that thing in representing it: wherefore words signifying what a thing is are called *terms* and *definitions*. But no created image [*similitudo*] can possibly represent God thus: since every created image belongs to some fixed genus, whereas God does not, as was proved in the First Book.[20] Therefore it is not possible to understand the divine substance through a created image. (SCG III, 49)

Rather, what happens is that God's essence itself comes to unite with the created intellect, playing the role of an intelligible species: "It is . . . clear that the divine essence can be compared to the created intellect as an intelligible species by which it understands" (SCG III, 51).

Descartes, in marked contrast, holds that we have an *idea* of God and regards the idea as an *effect* of God.[21] This disagreement with Aquinas over the mechanics of how we cognize the divine essence is closely related to the other disagreement that we noticed above. Aquinas holds, as we have seen, that cognition of God's essence or substance lies beyond the natural powers of any created thing. Descartes holds that my possession of the idea of God is part of my natural cognitive equipment, so the purchase it gives me on God's essence lies within my natural abilities. Descartes is able to maintain this position because he holds that a created intellect does not need to make use of God's essence in order to have cognitive access to God's essence: a created idea can perform this task.[22]

Descartes does not, to my knowledge, respond to the argument that Aquinas gives that no finite image (or species or idea) could allow us to cognize the divine essence, but I conjecture that one thing he might want to say is that the argument trades on a confusion between formal and objective reality: while it may be true that every created representation is finite in terms of its formal reality (determined, for example, to belong to the genus *human intellectual idea*), it does not follow that every created representation is finite in terms of its objective reality. Descartes, then, in some ways reduces the gap between creator and created in that he allows that a created image can make available the essence of God, and, consequently, that God can make creatures that are naturally capable of grasping his essence, while still maintaining that there is enough of a gap that a finite being's cognition of the infinite requires the efficient causal activity of the infinite.[23]

OBJECTIVE REALITY AND OBJECTIVE ARTIFICE

There are available in the tradition, then, the broad outlines of an argument from the character of cognition that Descartes takes us to have of God—cognition of what God is—to the conclusion that only God could have brought about such cognition. When we consider Descartes's cognitive causal principle linking the objective reality found in an idea with the formal reality found in the idea's cause, the nature of the "datum" to which the principle is applied, the sort of cognition that it is meant to explain, matters. That is, what is it for God (or infinite reality) to exist objectively in my mind? Is it merely to have my thought reach God in some manner or other, or is something more needed?

I take it that, in line with Descartes's claim that we know what God is, he thinks that our idea of God functions in a manner analogous to the way an intelligible species did for the scholastics. That is, in order for God's reality to exist objectively in me, my idea of God must make his very essence present to me; it is not enough that I form some remote or oblique thought about him. For example, suppose I think to myself "the ultimate cause of the universe whatever that may be," and suppose further that God is the ultimate cause of the universe. In some sense, I have formed a thought of God, but if the materials "ultimate," "cause," "universe," and so forth, are all that I have to work with in building that thought, then it is not obvious that infinite reality exists in me objectively via the resulting cognition. (This question is tricky because Descartes seems to hold that, as a matter of fact, when we form such thoughts we implicitly rely on our innate of idea of God, so that we never work only with limited materials like "ultimate," "cause," and "universe.")

Now, I don't think that the *Meditations* itself makes obvious how much is required in order for reality to exist objectively in our mind: one can easily get the impression that all that is required is that I be able to think of it, somehow or other. But something more is involved, as emerges reasonably clearly from Descartes's explication of the cognitive causal principle in the First Replies, in response to Caterus's objections. In that exchange, we learn more about exactly what the cause required by the cognitive principle is supposed to account for.

Caterus's basic complaint is that objective being is not really a thing at all, and so does not require an efficient cause. He reasons along the following lines: What has objective being is the thing as it exists in the intellect. If, for example, Socrates has an idea of Fido, Fido comes to exist objectively in Socrates' intellect. So if objective being were a perfection or reality, it would accrue to Fido, in virtue of the mode of existence that he enjoys by being in Socrates' intellect. But clearly Fido's being is not

enhanced through being thought of by Socrates; Fido was not augmented when Socrates began thinking about him, and he will not be diminished when Socrates stops thinking about him. "Being thought about
by Socrates" is a mere extrinsic denomination with respect to Fido. But if
objective being is not an actual thing, then it does not require an efficient
cause. This is how I interpret the following set of remarks by Caterus:

> My question is this: what sort of cause does an idea need? Indeed, what *is*
> an idea? It is the thing thought of, insofar as it has objective being in the
> intellect. But what is "objective being in the intellect"? According to what I
> was taught, this is simply the determination of the intellect by means of
> an object. And this is merely an extrinsic denomination which adds noth-
> ing to the thing itself. Just as being seen is nothing other than an act of vi-
> sion attributable to myself, so being thought of, or having objective being
> in the intellect, is simply a thought of the mind which stops and termi-
> nates in the mind. And this can occur without any movement or change in
> the thing itself, and indeed without the thing in question existing at all. So
> why should I look for a cause of something which is not actual, and which
> is simply a bare denomination, a nothing? (7:92; 2:66–67)

The exact details of Caterus's worry as he goes on to develop it are
hard to follow, but this much seems fairly clear: Caterus argues that there
are two senses of "nothing" and, correspondingly, two senses of "something" and accuses Descartes of equivocating on these different senses of
"nothing" (7:93; 2:67). Not to be a nothing in the first sense, and so to be
a something in the first sense, is to be an actual thing. (This is the sense of
nothing that is at issue, I take it, when Caterus writes that objective being
"is simply a bare denomination, a nothing.") A nothing in this sense does
not require a cause; a something in this sense does. Caterus does not
think that objective being is a something in this sense. Caterus's second
sense of something rests on a distinction between nothing and something
that arises within the context of things that have some sort of mental
standing. Among these things, there are, on the one hand, things that are
pure fictions, pure *entia rationis*,[24] and, on the other hand, real things
distinctly conceived. Pure fictions, I take it, would include things that are
incapable of really existing, such as contradictory entities, privations, negations, and relations, and perhaps mathematical points; real things distinctly conceived are things that can really exist. The former count as
nothings in the second sense; the latter count as somethings. But since
being a something in this second sense does not involve being actual, but
merely being conceived, being a something in this second sense is compatible with being a nothing in the first sense, and so is compatible with
not needing an efficient cause. Apparently, according to Caterus, the objective being of my idea of God may count as a something in the second

sense—my idea is not a pure fiction but a real thing distinctly conceived—
but it does not count as a something in the first sense, since objective
being (say, God as conceived by me) does not involve actual, but only
mental, existence. In other words, Caterus thinks that Descartes has taken
a causal principle (something cannot come from nothing) that applies
only to somethings in the first sense (i.e., to actual things) and illegitimately applied it to somethings in the second sense (e.g., to the sun as
conceived by me); but since a something in the second sense "is merely
conceived and is not actual, although it can be conceived, it cannot in any
way be caused" (7:94; 2:68).

Caterus's comments show how a reasonably sophisticated and well-
trained contemporary of Descartes found his handling of objective reality
perplexing. Part of Caterus's reaction might be explained by his evident
Thomistic leanings. Followers of Aquinas tended to treat objective being
as a nothing (in the first sense sketched above) and so as not the sort of
thing that required an efficient cause. By way of contrast, followers of
Duns Scotus tended to attribute some sort of a diminished ontological
status to objective being, so that objective being fell somewhere between
mere nothing and real existence. But, to my knowledge, the causal requirements are still a function of the ontological status (and not level of
reality of the thing that exists objectively) so that any thing existing objectively, any objective being, requires the same level of cause as any
other thing existing objectively, any other objective being.[25] One might
think that Descartes believes that he has found some resources within a
Scotist tradition in late Scholasticism that licenses a strong causal principle tying the causal requirements for an idea to the level of reality or
perfection of the thing that possesses intentional being rather than to the
merely intentional status of its existence. In his response, however, Descartes moves away from the quasi-technical details surrounding ontological status of existence in the mind to something less technical and more
intuitive.

Descartes interprets Caterus's charge thus:

> But he [Caterus] then adds "since it is merely conceived and is not actual"—
> i.e. since it is merely an idea, and not a thing located outside the intellect—
> "although it can be conceived it cannot in any way be caused." This is to
> say that it does not require a cause enabling it to exist outside the intellect.
> (7:103; 2:75)

Descartes takes Caterus to be making an obvious point—namely, that
something's existing objectively in the intellect does not generate a requirement for a cause of that thing's existing outside the intellect—which is
true but irrelevant to his argument. I think Descartes may have misunderstood the force of Caterus's objection, which seems to be that only actual

beings require causes, period (and so mental somethings do not require causes at all), and not, as Descartes suggests, that a mental something "does not require a cause enabling it to exist outside the intellect." But this may not matter. The continuation of Descartes's response is revealing:

> This [that something's existing objectively does not require a cause enabling that thing to exist extramentally] I accept; but it surely needs a cause enabling it to be conceived, which is the sole point at issue. Thus if someone possesses in his intellect the idea of a machine of a highly intricate design [*artificio*], it is perfectly fair to ask what is the cause of this idea. And it will not be an adequate reply to say that the idea is not anything outside the intellect and hence that it cannot be caused but can merely be conceived. For the precise question being raised is what is the cause of its being conceived. Nor will it suffice to say that the intellect itself is the cause of the idea, insofar as it is the cause of its own operations; for what is at issue is not this, but the cause of the objective artifice [*artificii*] which is in the idea. For in order for the idea of the machine to contain such and such objective artifice, it must derive it from some cause; and what applies to the objective reality belonging to this idea also applies to the objective reality belonging to the idea of God. Now admittedly there could be various causes of the artifice contained in the idea of the machine. Perhaps the cause was a real machine of this design which was seen on some previous occasion, thus producing an idea resembling the original. Or the cause might be an extensive knowledge of mechanics in the intellect of the person concerned, or perhaps a very subtle intelligence which enabled him to invent the idea without any previous knowledge. But notice that all the artifice which is to be found merely objectively in the idea must necessarily be found, either formally or eminently, in its cause, whatever this turns out to be. (7:103–4; 2:75–76)

Descartes was pleased with his example of the intricate machine. He refers to it in the Second Replies (7:134–35). It reappears in the *Principles'* version of the argument in article 17 of Part I. He also singles it out for attention in the Synopsis:

> In the Third Meditation I have explained quite fully enough, I think, my principal argument for proving the existence of God. But in order to draw my readers' minds away from the senses as far as possible, I was not willing to use any comparison taken from bodily things. So it may be that many obscurities remain; but I hope they will be completely removed later, in my Replies and Objections. One such problem, among others, is how the idea of a supremely perfect being, which is in us, possesses so much objective reality that it can come only from a cause which is supremely perfect. In the Replies this is illustrated by the comparison of a very perfect

machine, the idea of which is in the mind of some engineer. Just as the objective artifice belonging to the idea must have some cause, namely the scientific knowledge of the engineer, or of someone else who passed the idea on to him, so the idea of God which is in us must have God himself as its cause. (7:14–15; 2:10–11)

Spinoza, in his exposition of the *Principles*, offers a variant, having to do with a text written in the hand of a novice yet containing profound thoughts. We would suspect that the text did not originate with the novice but ultimately had some other origin.[26] (Indeed, suspicions of plagiarism work this way.)

With this explication, an important element in Descartes's thinking emerges clearly into view. As Descartes implicitly recognizes,[27] "objective artifice" and "objective reality" are different notions. For example, he writes in the Second Replies (7:134–35; 2:97) that "the objective perfection or reality of an idea . . . no less than the objective artifice [*artificium*] in the idea of a machine of very ingenious design, requires a cause," implying that the two notions are different. To judge from the examples, objective intricacy looks to be a sort of complexity or richness of structure contributing to overall perfection of an artifact (a machine, a painting, etc.). The appeal to objective intricacy suggests that at least part of what is triggering the need for a particular sort of cause of an idea is a certain richness of structure or content: in the case of a machine, this richness of structure in the idea might answer to the machine's impressive complexity. (Descartes is evidently assuming that as we go up the hierarchy of being or reality, there is a corresponding increase in the richness of structure; I will come back to this assumption presently.)

Descartes's comparison between objective reality and objective intricacy raises an interesting question. Consider my idea of a space shuttle and a NASA engineer's idea. She understands quite a bit about how the shuttle is put together and how it works, whereas I think of it as a big white thing that goes way up into the sky. Does her idea have more objective intricacy than my idea?

One might answer yes, it does, because more reality or perfection exists in her mind when she thinks of the space shuttle (she grasps some of the complex engineering that went into it) than exists in my mind (I do not): less of the shuttle made it into my mind than made it into hers. Perhaps the shuttle's surface structure made it into my mind, but none of its special complexity or intricacy. Since less of the shuttle's complexity or intricacy made it into my mind than into hers, not as much is required to account for my idea of the shuttle as for hers.

Or, one might answer no, it does not have more objective intricacy, because the same reality is in my mind as in hers. There is this difference: in her mind, the complexity of this reality—its objective intricacy—is displayed much more clearly and distinctly than it is in my mind; in my mind, the intricacy is present only obscurely and confusedly. But all the same, in order for something with that much (even implicit or latent) complexity to get into my mind, there had to be a cause actually possessed of that much complexity. To be sure, the fact that the artifice is not manifestly available to me—that I am unable to discern it in my rather foggy idea of it—means that I will not be able to argue directly from the idea alone to its having a cause of a certain sort, but that does not change the fact that the idea does require such a cause.

I am not positive which way Descartes would go here. I lean toward thinking he would give the second answer. That the two ideas contain the same intricacy, one manifestly, one confusedly, seems to fit better with his overall outlook on cognition: we get on to (perhaps with the help of the senses) the shuttle with all of its complexity, which awaits subsequent refinement by the intellect (penetration to its deep structure via judgment). I think this picture fits well with his employment of the vocabulary *clear*, *distinct*, *obscure*, and *confused*, which suggests that sometime there can be more structure in a cognition than meets the mind's eye. It also seems to fit with the general tenor of the wax discussion, where it sounds as if the entire wax (and not just some substructure of it) is supposed to fall under the senses, the imagination, and the intellect. But perhaps this is a too "Leibnizian" way of taking Descartes.

Be that as it may, taking to heart the point that Descartes is making about objective intricacy—that intuitively what triggers an idea's need for a certain sort of cause is the richness or complexity found in the idea—casts his argument for the existence of God in a different light. For now his point would be that our idea of God is too rich or complex for us to be able to conjure it up on our own.

Descartes seems to be assuming, then, that an idea with greater objective reality will have greater richness to its content (either greater objective intricacy or something closely analogous to that). This can be a difficult thought for us, for (I imagine) ideas of God often run thinner nowadays, which makes it hard to recover a sense that an idea of God can contain much food for thought, in a manner analogous to "a machine of a highly intricate design." However, it is not surprising that Descartes should have thought higher levels of reality are greater sources of intelligibility, so that to understand a higher level of reality is to understand more than to understand a lower level of reality. As we saw a little earlier, Descartes reports this about God:

> But those who try to attend to God's individual perfections and try not so much to seize [*capere*] them as to be seized [*capi*] by them, using all the

strength of their intellect to contemplate them, will certainly find that God provides much more ample and straightforward subject-matter for clear and distinct knowledge [*cognitionis*] than does any created thing. (7:114; 2:82)

And I take Descartes's view that our idea of God is thus rich in content to be obviously connected with his remark at the end of the Third Meditation that the idea of God gives us the joy in this life that comes closest to the joy that we hope for in the next:

But before examining this point more carefully and investigating other truths which may be derived from it, I should like to pause here and spend some time in the contemplation of God; to reflect on his attributes and to gaze with wonder and adoration on the beauty of this immense light, so far as the eye of my darkened intellect can bear it. For just as we believe through faith that the supreme happiness of the next life consists solely in the contemplation of the divine majesty, so experience tells us that this same contemplation, albeit much less perfect, enables us to know the greatest joy of which we are capable in this life. (7:52; 2:35–36)

It must be admitted, I think, that the various claims that Descartes makes about God in course of the *Meditations* and elsewhere, if taken at face value, add up to an impressive body of substantive knowledge.

So Descartes's reply to Caterus, through the introduction of the idea of objective intricacy, helps bring out an important aspect of the thinking surrounding the cognitive causal principle. What triggers the need for a certain level of a cause might be called the richness of the idea, the amount of intelligibility of reality it affords, and Descartes holds that the idea through which God exists in our intellect is rich in this way. It is important for his argument that we have some sense of the richness of this idea— that we be more like the NASA engineer and less like me with respect to the space shuttle. In this regard, Descartes claims in III.¶25 that our idea of God is not materially false but is "the truest and most distinct of all my ideas." I will not try to evaluate that claim here (some of the things I say in what follows will bear on it). In any case, the claim is important for the success of the sort of argument that Descartes is advancing.

When Descartes's argument for the existence of God based on the objective reality found in our idea of God is viewed in the manner I have been suggesting, to a certain extent the center of gravity of the argument shifts from the cognitive causal principle to the character of our cognition of God. I take it that the richness that Descartes finds in our idea of God makes available to us God's essence or nature, what God is. So the interest that Descartes shows in objective intricacy helps locate his argument in a general tradition that certain sorts of cognition of God could be brought about only by God.

THE ORIGINAL AND FUNDAMENTAL PLACE OF THE IDEA OF

GOD IN HUMAN COGNITION

Still, we do not have much of a sense—the supposed richness of the idea of God notwithstanding—of why Descartes thinks an account of acquisition of the idea of God along the lines suggested by Aquinas will not work. In this section, then, I want to examine Descartes's account of our idea of God with an eye toward understanding the basic role it plays in human cognition and why he thinks it cannot be, as it were, constructed from more modest materials.

Descartes maintains that our conception of God is quite special. The idea of God presents the human being (really, confronts the human mind)[28] with unbounded perfection or reality. We do not get access to this unbounded perfection by beginning with the cognition of a finite thing and operating on it in some way—for example, by extending it in some fashion or denying it limits. To be sure, if I begin with the cognition of a finite thing, say, myself, and remove its boundaries, I will be left with something unbounded. But, according to Descartes, this requires that I already see myself as limited, which requires in turn that I already have some conception of the unlimited. In one of the more striking paragraphs of the Third Meditation, ¶24, he writes:

> And I must not think that, just as my conceptions of rest and darkness are arrived at by negating movement and light, so my perception of the infinite is arrived at not by means of a true idea but merely by negating the finite. On the contrary, I manifestly understand that there is more reality in an infinite substance than in a finite one, and hence my perception of the infinite, that is God, is in some way prior to my perception of the finite, that is myself. For how could I understand that I doubted or desired—that is, lacked something—and that I was not wholly perfect, unless there were in me some idea of a more perfect being which enabled me to recognize my own defects by comparison? (7:45–46; 2:31)

This is a considered position, which Descartes elucidates somewhat in a late letter to Clerselier.

> I say that the notion I have of the infinite is in me before that of the finite because, by the mere fact that I conceive being, or that which is, without thinking whether it is finite or infinite, what I conceive is infinite being; but in order to conceive a finite being, I have to take away something from this general notion of being, which must accordingly be there first. (5:356; 3:377)

In these passages, Descartes advances the important, but difficult, thesis that the idea or perception of God or the infinite is prior to the idea of the finite: in the first, he says, somewhat cautiously, that "my perception of the infinite, that is God, is in some way prior to my perception of the finite, that is myself," and in the second, my conception of infinite being in general "must . . . be there first" in order for me "to conceive a finite being." It is not obvious how exactly to take this priority. If the perception of the infinite is prior to the perception of the finite, does that mean that no being could have a perception of the finite unless it also had perception of the infinite? If my idea of a finite being is simply some limited version of infinite being in general, would it be possible to have such an idea without having an idea of infinite being in general?

I am not sure. Perhaps Descartes holds that no being can have the idea of a finite thing unless that being also has the idea of God. I suspect, however, that these passages are best read as claims about how we, beings endowed with an idea of God, conceive finite things. There may be other possible beings who have no perception of the infinite, and so for whom it is not true that perception of the infinite is prior to the perception of the finite. Those beings, to judge from ¶24, would not be aware of themselves as limited, as lacking anything. That is, what they would be given to think about might still be (as Descartes says in the letter to Clerselier) the result of limiting unbounded being in various ways, but, without a perception of the unlimited, they would be unable to perceive those boundaries and so unable to negate them.

The claim that the idea of the infinite is prior to the idea of the finite does not mean that I must be aware of the infinite when I think of the finite, that is, does not mean that I am unable to think of myself without noticing that my idea of myself (finite being) is a limited version of my idea of God (infinite being). In fact, in the order of discovery, I can be led from my idea of myself to my idea of God. For example, Descartes writes at the beginning of the Fourth Meditation: "And when I consider the fact that I have doubts, or that I am a thing that is incomplete and dependent, there occurs to me [occurit mihi] a clear and distinct idea of a being who is independent and complete, that is, an idea of God" (IV.¶1; 7:53; 2:37). Burman reports Descartes's explanation of a closely related point as follows:

Explicitly, we are able to recognize [cognoscere] our own imperfection by recognizing the perfection of God. This is because we are able to direct our attention to ourselves before we direct our attention to God. Thus we can infer our own finiteness before we arrive at his infiniteness. Despite this, however, the knowledge of God and his perfection must implicitly always come before the knowledge of ourselves and our imperfections. For in reality the infinite perfection of God is prior to our imperfection, since our imperfection is a defect and negation of the perfection of God. And every defect and negation presupposes that of which it falls short and which it negates. (5:153; 3:338)

So Descartes does not think one can construct a conception of the unbounded by removing the boundaries of the finite: such a procedure presupposes that we already have the idea of the unbounded available.[29] Thus, we cannot arrive at the conception of God we have by way of negation; rather, our ability to negate presupposes that we already have the conception of God we have. I believe Descartes treats in the same manner the proposal that the way we come to have access to the idea of the unbounded is by "extending" or "amplifying" perfections we find either in ourselves or in the world, although his texts on this question are somewhat less clear. When such a proposal is put forward by his student Regius, Descartes responds:

In your first [objection] you say: "it is because we have in ourselves some wisdom, power and goodness that we form [*formare*] the idea of an infinite, or at least indefinite, wisdom, power, goodness and the other perfections which we attribute to God; just as it is because we have in ourselves some degree of quantity that we form the idea of an infinite quantity." I entirely agree, and am quite convinced that we have no idea of God except the one formed [*formatur*] in this manner. (3:64; 3:147)

Now, this makes it sound as if Descartes agrees that we can construct a representation of God from purely finite materials, for example, from the wisdom, power, and goodness we find in ourselves. That this is not what Descartes thinks becomes clear from his going on to say that my ability to extend these perfections draws on resources that testify to my involvement with the infinite:

But the whole point of my argument is this. These perfections are so slight that unless we derived our origin from a being in which they are actually infinite, my nature could not enable me to extend them in thought to an infinite degree. (3:64; 3:147)[30]

What Descartes may be saying here is that the way people discover the idea of God is by noticing the various perfections they find in themselves and "extending" them (so there is, on my interpretation, something misleading about Descartes's picking up of Regius's word *formare*). But, Descartes adds, this power to extend presupposes that I originate from a being in which these perfections are actually infinite.

There is room to wonder, in this exchange with Regius, whether it is specifically my possession of the idea of God that enables me to extend perfections, or if this ability is owed to some other trace that the infinite being from which I originate has left on me. In an exchange with Gassendi over more or less the same question, Descartes seems to make clear that it is the former. Gassendi attacks Descartes's thesis that our idea of God contains infinite objective reality on several grounds: (1) we do not have an idea of the infinite, (2) our idea of God is constructed out of finite resources and so does not have infinite objective reality, and (3) we do not have a "genuine idea of God, an idea which represents God as he is." He develops the second point thus:

> Next, although every supreme perfection is normally attributed to God, it seems that such perfections are all taken from things which we commonly admire in ourselves, such as longevity, power, knowledge, goodness, blessedness and so on. By amplifying these things as much as we can, we assert that God is eternal, omnipotent, omniscient, supremely good, supremely blessed and so on. Hence the idea representing all these things does not contain more objective reality than the finite things taken together; the idea in question is compounded and augmented from ideas of these finite things in the manner just described. (7:287; 2:200)

Descartes responds as follows:

> It is also false that the idea representing all the perfections which we attribute to God "does not contain more objective reality than do finite things." You yourself admit that these perfections must be amplified by our intellect if they are to be attributed to God. So do you think that the perfections which are amplified in this way are not, as a result, greater than they would be if they were not amplified? And how could we have a faculty for amplifying all created perfections (i.e. conceiving of something greater or more ample than they are) were it not for the fact that there is in us an idea of something greater, namely God? (7:365; 2:252)

Later in his response to Gassendi, Descartes makes it clear that, consonant with his remarks to Burman, he thinks of Gassendi's "amplification" of perfections as helping to make something that was already contained in our idea of God "distinct and explicit":

> [O]nce the idea of the true God has been conceived, although we may detect additional perfections in him which we had not yet noticed, this does not mean that we have augmented the idea of God; we have simply made it more distinct and explicit, since, so long as we suppose that our original idea was a true one, it must have contained all these perfections. Similarly, the idea of a triangle is not augmented when we notice various properties in the triangle of which we were previously ignorant. You must also realize that the idea of God is not gradually formed by us when we amplify

the perfections of his creatures; it is formed all at once and in its entirety as soon as our mind reaches an infinite being which is incapable of any amplification. (7:371; 2:256)

According to Descartes, then, our ability to amplify our way to cognition of God, like our ability to negate our way to cognition of God, depends on our already possessing the idea of God.

Descartes does not think alternative theories of the generation of our cognition are viable. Can we say more about why?

Perhaps. In the passage just cited from his reply to Gassendi, where Descartes compares our cognition of God to our cognition of a triangle, there is a hint of other considerations that might motivate his position. Descartes takes theological knowledge to be analogous to geometrical knowledge. That our theological knowledge is on a par with our geometrical knowledge is a particular emphasis of the Fifth Meditation.

Now, according to Descartes, we are able to do geometry because the idea of extension provides the mind with a content that allows the mind to make substantive discoveries about that content. The way in which Descartes puts the point there is that my geometrical ideas are of true and immutable natures. Thus, the fact that we can make substantive judgments in a given subject matter, that we have some insight or understanding with respect to a given subject matter, is a sign that we are onto a true and immutable nature, which serves as a sort of locus for this understanding or intelligibility. So, the fact that I can, for example, make substantive judgments concerning a triangle—for instance, that its three angles sum to two right angles—shows me that a triangle is not merely some fiction of my own invention, but has a true and immutable nature.

Consider, now, theology. Descartes sees here, too, a substantive body of knowledge. In fact, in his view, it is more fertile than other disciplines:

God provides much more ample and straightforward subject-matter for clear and distinct knowledge than does any created thing. (7:114; 2:82)

Moreover, it is marked by less disagreement than the nature of the physical:

If the idea [of God] were a mere figment, it would not be consistently conceived by everyone in the same manner. It is very striking that metaphysicians unanimously agree in their descriptions of the attributes of God (at least in the case of those which can be known solely by human reason). You will find that there is much more disagreement among philosophers about the nature of anything which is physical or perceivable by the senses, however firm or concrete our idea of it may be. (7:138; 2:99)

No doubt it is hard for us today to recover Descartes's confidence in theology as a branch of knowledge, alongside geometry. His first claim—that God provides the subject matter for much clear and distinct knowledge—is alien enough to contemporary sensibilities that it is hard to know what he has in mind. Here it helps to recognize that a fair amount of philosophical theology is developed in the *Meditations* itself, along with the Objections and Replies—for example, that God is the sort of being in which no potentiality is found (III.¶27), that God is simple (III.¶35), and that whereas God has the power to sustain himself in existence, everything else in the universe depends on God at each moment of its existence (III.¶¶32–33 and First Replies, 7:108–11). (In the next section we will look more closely at some of what is involved here.) Descartes's second claim—that there is a great deal of consensus among metaphysicians concerning God—can also seem surprising, but here it helps to distinguish, as Descartes suggests, between those aspects of theology that can be known by natural reason, where there was a fair degree of overlap among thinkers, and those things that are held only on the basis of faith or revelation, where there was much less consensus. As important, perhaps, is that when disputes arose over core commitments in natural theology, the discussion had the hallmarks of rational argument, with objections and replies and so forth. For example, even when Spinoza advances the unorthodox thesis that God is extended, he recognizes (*Ethics*, 1p15s) the need to reconcile it with the thesis that God, as a necessary being, is indivisible.

But if we think of rational theology as a stable body of substantive knowledge, like geometry, and if we take it naively, at face value, like geometry, then it is natural to think that we are able to have the insight we do because we have an idea that makes available to us the relevant true and immutable nature, in this case God's nature or essence. Our idea may not make available God's essence fully or completely, but all the same it is making available at least some of God's essence.

Of course, one can imagine arguments that we ought not take our apparent cognition of God's essence at face value. For example, one might think, with Kant, that the human idea of God is a sort of construct of human reason, and once one sees how it arises, one has reason to wonder about what sort of "objective reality" the idea has. (Kant, of course, will also have quite a bit to say about how we should view the other side of the comparison that impresses Descartes, geometry.) Or, as we have seen, Aquinas has various systematic reasons for thinking that human beings cannot (in this life) cognize God's essence, reasons that arise from his view that the proper object of human cognition is the sensible world. But unless one accepts a general theory of human cognition that sets limits to human knowledge, after the manner of Kant's or Aquinas's theory, it is not obvious why we shouldn't "read" the discipline of natural theology in the same way we do geometry.

In the case of Aquinas, there is, it seems, another issue, in addition to his general account of human cognition and its relation to the world. It is important to his outlook that we be available to view the content of philosophical theology as consisting entirely of negative (*via negativa*) and relational (the way of causality and the way of transcendence) claims. If Descartes is to work against this interpretation of philosophical theology, he will need to persuade us that we have some "inside out" cognition of God, that is, he will need to persuade us that working from some positive sense of *what* God is, we can see why certain things are true of God (e.g., that he exists). In the next section, I'll suggest that Descartes's insistence that we know God to be *a se* ("from itself") in some positive sense, which implies that we cognize God as a self-caused being rather than, as Aquinas thought, an uncaused being, is a step in this direction.

Finally, it is natural to wonder how Descartes's cognitive causal principle would apply to Aquinas's account of human cognition of God, which casts our cognition of God in terms of nominal definitions of God, based in sensory experience (so that we cognize God, for example, as a first mover unmoved). Here are two possibilities. Descartes might think that such representations do not bring infinite reality into the mind (perhaps they would not count as a "true idea" of God in the sense of III.¶24). (This would be analogous to holding that my primitive idea of the space shuttle does not contain the shuttle's intricacy objectively; something got lost in the translation from the world to my mind.) Or he might hold that such representations do have infinite objective reality, but do so only obscurely. (This would be analogous to holding that even my primitive idea of the space shuttle contains the shuttle's intricacy objectively, but that that intricacy is present only obscurely.) If so, Descartes might hold that figuring out that the thing that these representations present has infinite reality (and so the representations contain infinite reality objectively) requires connecting them in some appropriate way with my (innate) distinct idea of God.

Although it is hard to be sure, the general tenor of Descartes's remarks concerning the feasibility of getting to a cognition of God by negation or amplification seems to favor the second approach. Descartes does not deny that such approaches work—he does not deny that we can get to cognition of God in this way—but he wants to say that they do so only because we already have in place a rich and robust, distinct, innate idea of God.

II. *GOD'S EXISTENCE ADDRESSED FOR A SECOND TIME*

(¶¶28–39)

Descartes allows that the preceding argument is very difficult. Although he maintains that the argument is evident by the natural light, he finds that if he fails to concentrate, his sharpness of mind will become "blinded by the images of things perceived by the senses" and that it will not be "so easy for me to remember why the idea of a being more perfect than myself must necessarily proceed from some being which is in reality more perfect." This sets him off on another tack, inquiring "whether I myself, who have this idea, could exist if no such being existed."

Descartes's second argument can be summarized thus. Let's call a being that is causally responsible for its existing *self-sustained*.[31] (The Latin here is *a se*, which literally means "from itself." If A sustains B's existing, then A is responsible for B's existing rather than falling into nothingness, as opposed to B's originally coming into existence: if B exists in time, then its sustainer A is responsible for its currently existing, that is, is what "keeps" B in existence; moreover, if A does not withdraw its sustaining support, it is responsible for B's *ceteris paribus* continuing to exist.) If I were self-sustained, I would have given myself all of the perfections that I find in my idea of God and thus be God. (The thought here is that it is harder to cause something's existing *ex nihilo* than it is to add some further perfection to that thing; so if I had enough power to sustain my existing—to keep myself from falling back into nothingness—I would also have enough power to give myself all the perfections of which I am aware. Notice that this step makes clear that Descartes thinks of being self-sustained as involving more than the negative fact that one is not sustained by something else; this will become important later.) Since I am not God, something else must be responsible for my existing. Call this being my sustainer. We can now ask of my sustainer whether it is self-sustained. If it is not, it will have a sustainer. But a series of sustainers cannot go on forever. So we eventually reach a self-sustained sustainer. This self-sustainer will have ideas of the perfections found in my idea of God and the power to give itself those perfections, and will give itself those perfections, and so will be God.

Many problems might be raised for this argument. One might wonder about the idea that my existing requires sustaining (that is, why couldn't I simply exist unsustained, without any metaphysical propping up?). One might worry about the claim that there cannot be an infinite regress of sustainers. One might worry about the coherence of the idea of something's being self-sustained. And, finally, one might worry about the connection between being self-sustained and being God. (For example, when Spinoza expounds this argument, he complains that even if it is true that it requires more power to bring and keep something in existence *ex nihilo* than to add further perfections to that thing, it might be the case that the self-sustainer had to use up so much power in sustaining its existing that it did not have enough power left over to add the remaining perfections needed to be God; Spinoza goes on to suggest a way to fill in this perceived lacuna.)[32]

Of the three arguments that Descartes offers for God's existence in the *Meditations*—the two in the Third Meditation and the one in the Fifth—this is the argument that seems to resemble most the causal arguments for God's existence advanced in the scholastic Aristotelian tradition. Caterus, for example, thought that Descartes's second argument was similar to one of Aquinas's Five Ways. Such an appraisal makes one wonder about the relation between Descartes's first and second arguments: after all, the first argument, on account of its dependence on our possession of an idea of God that is much more robust than anything Aquinas thought possible, is, on its face, remote from Aquinas's arguments. So if Descartes's second argument were close to one of Aquinas's, it would seem to follow that Descartes's first and second arguments were fundamentally very different. Yet Descartes's own description, in the First Replies, of the relationship between the two arguments suggests that he sees them as basically the same argument:

> Hence I went on to inquire "whether I could exist if God did not exist." But my purpose here was not to produce a different proof from the preceding one, but rather to take the same proof and provide a more thorough explanation of it. (7:106; 2:77)

To be sure, this is not a point upon whose importance Descartes insists. He writes in a letter to Mesland on 2 May 1644, "It does not make much difference whether my second proof, the one based on our own existence, is regarded as different from the first proof, or merely as an explanation of it" (4:112; 3:231). In any case, it is difficult to see how Descartes's second argument could be regarded as a more thorough explanation of his first if the second argument is (as Caterus thought) simply a variation on Aquinas's Second Way.

My own view is that although Descartes's second argument is superficially similar to some of the Thomistic arguments for the existence of God, when one looks more closely, one sees profound differences: the *explananda* from which the arguments start are different (change for Aquinas, existence for Descartes), and the principles they employ are different (Aquinas's argument begins from a premise that denies self-causation, whereas Descartes's argument ends with the conclusion that there is a self-caused being, and they seem to think differently about the impossibility of the relevant causal regresses). At an even more fundamental level, Descartes and Aquinas have different attitudes toward the role of our conception of God in the argument: Descartes thinks that our ability to understand and appreciate such arguments—their intelligibility to us—depends on our having (already) in place a robust idea of God, whereas Aquinas's argument requires that we have at our disposal only a nominal characterization of God drawn in terms of materials acquired from our encounter with the natural world. The fact that our possession of the idea of God is, Descartes insists, prior to this second argument and required for its intelligibility marks an easily overlooked continuity between the first and second arguments; it also lends some support to my claim that the basic issue that separates Descartes and Aquinas is the nature of our cognition of God. Finally, when we take all these things into account, while it will admittedly remain unclear to what extent Descartes's second argument counts as an explanation of his first, it will, I think, become easier to see how both arguments are part of a unified perspective on our cognition of God.

As I just noted, Caterus was struck by the similarity between Descartes's second argument and Aquinas's causal arguments for the existence of God. He begins by summarizing Descartes's reasoning as follows:

> But he goes on: "I should like to go further and inquire whether I myself who have this idea could exist if no such being existed" (that is, as he says just before this, if there did not exist a being from whom my idea of a being more perfect than myself proceeds). He goes on: "From whom, in that case, would I derive my existence? From myself, presumably, or from my parents or from others etc. Yet if I derived my existence from myself, then I should neither doubt nor want, nor lack anything at all; for I should have given myself all the perfections of which I have any idea, and thus I should myself be God." But if I derive my existence from some other, then if I trace the series back I will eventually come to a being which derives its existence from itself; and so the argument here becomes the same as the argument based on the supposition that I derive my existence from myself. (7:94; 2:68)

Caterus goes on to argue that this line of thought is fundamentally the same as one employed by Aquinas. To be sure, Aquinas's argument is not based on my possession of the idea of God. But, Caterus thinks, this is not essential to the sort of reasoning that Descartes advances:

> This is exactly the same approach as that taken by St Thomas: he called this way "the way based on the causality of the efficient cause." He took the argument from Aristotle, although neither he nor Aristotle was bothered about the cause of ideas. And perhaps they had no need to be; for can I not take a much shorter and more direct line of argument? "I am thinking,

therefore I exist; indeed, I am thought itself, I am a mind. But this mind and thought derives its existence either from itself, or from another. If the latter, then we continue to repeat the question—where does this other being derive its existence from? And if the former, if it derives its existence from itself, it is God. For what derives existence from itself will without difficulty have endowed itself with all things." (7:94; 2:68)

The idea of God is not obviously playing a role in Caterus's summary of Descartes's argument (it could be suggested that the idea of God is alluded to implicitly in the sentence "Yet if I derived my existence from myself, then I should neither doubt nor want, nor lack anything at all; for I should have given myself all the perfections of which I have any idea, and thus I should myself be God"). And as is suggested by his remark that "neither he [Aquinas] nor Aristotle was bothered about the cause of ideas," it does not appear in the Thomistic argument that Caterus rehearses (where the corresponding ground is covered by the sentence "For what derives existence from itself will without difficulty have endowed itself with all things").

Now, Descartes appeals to my possession of the idea of God in order to argue that whatever sustains and is self-sustained will be God. Caterus objects to this part of Descartes's argument. So although Caterus believes that Descartes has taken "exactly the same approach as that taken by St Thomas," he also points out what is in fact a very striking difference between the two arguments:

> I beg and beseech our author not to hide his meaning from a reader who, though perhaps less intelligent, is eager to follow. The phrase "from itself [*a se*]" has two senses. In the first, positive sense, it means "from itself as from a cause." What derives existence from itself in this sense bestows its own existence on itself; so if by an act of premeditated choice it were to give itself what it desired, it would undoubtedly give itself all things, and so would be God. But in the second, negative sense, "from itself" simply means "not from another"; and this, as far as I remember, is the way in which everyone takes the phrase. (7:95; 2:68)

Caterus is unhappy with this part of Descartes's reasoning because it rests on the notion of something's producing itself in some fairly strong sense. That is, Descartes's argument concludes that there is something that is self-derived (*a se* in the Latin), where being *a se* here needs to be understood strongly enough to underwrite the notion that something that is *a se* would "give itself" at least all of the perfections of which it had an idea. And, as I think is implied by Caterus's remark that everyone takes the phrase *a se* simply to mean "not from another," Caterus finds the notion of something's being *a se* in this sense dubious.

The fact that Caterus thinks both that Descartes's approach is essentially the same as Thomas's and that Descartes has involved himself in a dubious positive sense of *a se* suggests that Caterus regards Descartes's commitment to the positive sense of *a se* as somehow inessential to the basic argument, as perhaps some unfortunate embellishment on Descartes's part. And, as a matter of fact, Caterus goes on to suggest (7:95; 2:68–69) an alternative way of getting from something's being *a se* to its being God, which does not depend on the dubious idea of self-causation (while he regards this second way as more promising, he is not entirely happy with it either). But we may wonder whether the point that Caterus has put his finger on is not some dispensable ornamentation but rather something that flows from the core of Descartes's argument, and reflects a basic difference between how he thinks about God and causality and how Thomas does.

To make further progress here, we will need to have in front of us an example of the sort of reasoning that Caterus is comparing to Descartes's. Although Caterus probably has in mind Aquinas's Second Way—Caterus terms the mode of argument in question "the way based on the causality of the efficient cause"—which leads to a first cause, I think it is more helpful to consider Aquinas's First Way, which leads to a first mover. Aquinas's first two proofs are commonly regarded as very similar. (One can see why, I think, if one keeps in mind that the First Way is not restricted to local motion. Motion in Aristotelian metaphysics is understood, to Descartes's chagrin, in a very wide sense, so as to encompass any gradual natural change. For example, the sun's warming of a rock counts as motion in Aristotelianism.) A motion in this context is a change, and a mover is an efficient, or agent, cause of that change. I think it is more illuminating to use Aquinas's First Way because certain points are worked out in more detail than in his Second Way.

Here's a schematic sketch of Aquinas's argument from motion:

1. Everything that is in motion is moved by another.
2. There is motion, for example, the motion of the sun.
3. By (1), the sun is moved by something M, not the sun.
4. Either M is in motion or not.
5. If not, M is a first mover, unmoved.
6. If so, there is an M' that moves M and is neither M nor the sun.
7. There cannot be an infinite regress of movers: M, M', M'' . . .
8. There is a first member of the series begun in step (6), that is, a first mover, unmoved.

Three of these—(1), (2), and (7)—function as premises in the argument. Aquinas regards (1) and (7) as unobvious enough to require further argument, but we will not pursue that further argument here. But

(1) and (7) raise interpretive issues that we do need to consider. As it is commonly understood, (1) requires not merely that there be a cause that initiates a motion (or change) but that there be a cause that acts throughout the motion or change: it requires that everything that is in motion or in a process of change *is being* moved or changed by another. (This commitment is connected with the notorious difficulties that Aristotelians faced in treating projectile motion: what is the mover after the arrow leaves the bow?) Gradually this principle becomes displaced in the new science by the principle of inertia, a natural interpretation of which is that things in uniform local motion do not require external movers—perhaps they move themselves or perhaps they do not require movers. The new science may well challenge (1) from another direction as well: in Descartes's case, it looks as if motion in the plenum often circles back on itself, so that there may be situations where M″ moves M′, which moves M′, which moves M, which circles back to move M‴; I believe that Aristotelians would have tended to regard that as a sort of self-movement in violation of (1).

Step (7)—that any given series of movers must terminate[33]—also requires careful handling. It is not a part of Aristotelian thinking about causation that any series of efficient causes must terminate in a first mover. As an example of series of causes that need *not* terminate, Aquinas offers a series of blacksmith hammers, where each hammer in the series is forged by the preceding hammer.[34] Such a series can extend backward forever. Another series that need not terminate, according to Aquinas, is that of progenitors: There can be a series of offspring and progenitors so that each member is the offspring of the preceding member; a series of offspring and progenitors can go on forever, so there is no first progenitor.

What sort of causal series must terminate? The series of movers established by (1), which Aquinas holds must terminate, involves the simultaneous operation of the members: M is moving the sun only because M′ is moving M, and M′ is moving M only because M″ is moving M′, and so on. (The example of a series of movers that Thomas gives is that of a ball, which is being moved by a stick, which is being moved by a hand.) It was a contested matter in scholastic Aristotelianism exactly how to characterize a causal series that must terminate in a first member, but, for our purposes, it is enough to say that the series that is started by (1) has the feature that the *exercise of the causality* of each member of the series depends on the exercise of the causality of the prior members.[35]

This sketch of Aquinas's argument puts us in a position to see that the feature of Descartes's argument that Caterus complains about—that Descartes is relying on the idea of something's being self-caused as opposed to being uncaused—reflects a basic difference between Descartes's Third Meditation argument and Aquinas's (efficient) causal arguments. Aquinas's causal arguments start from a premise that is restricted to things that are being moved (or being caused) and says that anything that is being moved (or being caused) is being moved (or being caused) by something *else*. The premise rules out from the start that anything is self-caused. The argument concludes to a first *unmoved* mover (or a first *uncaused* cause); since the causal principle is restricted to things in motion, this unmoved mover does not require a mover (or a cause). Descartes's argument, by way of contrast, begins from an unrestricted causal principle—absolutely everything that is existing requires something to sustain its existing—and concludes to something self-sustained and not unsustained. This difference is, in turn, traceable at least in part to the fact that the arguments apply their respective causal principles to different data: Aquinas's begins from change within the natural world, and Descartes's begins from a felt need to account for the metaphysical difference between staying in existence and falling out of existence.

Descartes has a lot to say in response to Caterus's comparison of the two arguments (7:106–8), as well as the point about God's being self-derived as opposed to underived (7:108–11). He begins by noting, "I did not base my argument on the fact that I observed there to be an order or succession of efficient causes among the objects perceived by the senses." Part of his reason for not proceeding this way is that he "regarded the existence of God as much more evident than anything that can be perceived by the senses." (Again, I take it that part of what backs up the "much more evident than" is Descartes's view that our natural instincts surrounding what we take the senses to do require the backing of a non-deceiving creator, so that our knowledge that there are bodies that send to us our sensory ideas runs through our cognition of God.) But this point about God's existence being more evident than the things perceived by the senses is not what Descartes concentrates on in his response. Rather, he focuses on three main points: (1) causal regresses (7:106–7), (2) the role of the idea of God in the argument (7:107–8), and (3) the positive sense of being *a se* (7:108–11).

Causal Regresses

Descartes's account of the difference between the sort of causal series that must terminate and the sort that can go on forever, while quite interesting, is rather puzzling. He says that we cannot know that a series of causes within the physical order ("an order or succession of efficient causes among the objects perceived by the senses") must terminate:

> I did not think that such a succession of causes could lead me anywhere except to a recognition of the imperfection of my intellect, since an infinite chain of such successive causes from eternity without any first cause is beyond my grasp. And my inability to grasp it certainly does not entail that there must be a first cause, any more than my inability to grasp the infinite number of divisions in a finite quantity entails that there is an ultimate division beyond which any further division is impossible. All that follows is that my intellect, which is finite, does not encompass the infinite. (7:106–7; 2:77)

Descartes indicates here that if I begin with the perceptible world—that is, if I begin with my cognition of the material world—and trace out various causal sequences, then I will not be led to a first cause but only to "a recognition of the imperfection of my intellect." Descartes expands somewhat on this passage in a letter to Mesland, written four years later, in a manner that suggests that, rather than being agnostic on the point, Descartes believed that such series could in fact go on without end. He comments that when writing the First Replies he did not wish

> to show contempt for the arguments of others, who commonly accept the principle that a series cannot go on for ever. I do not accept that principle; on the contrary, I think in the division of the parts of the matter there really is an endless series, as you will see in my treatise on philosophy. (4:112–13; 3:232)

The connection that Descartes sees between the causal regress principles and the infinite (or indefinite) divisibility of matter is obscure, but he may have something in mind like this: in *res extensa*, when something moves, it moves progressively smaller surrounding bodies, which move progressively smaller surrounding bodies, without end. So, in his view, there may well be throughout *res extensa* infinite series of bodies pushing on one another in a manner reminiscent of Aquinas's hand-ball-stick series.[36]

Now, Descartes's explication of the difference between those series that must have a terminus and those that need not, is in terms of whether the series is diachronic or synchronic. Series in which each member of the series acts before the next member may go forever; series where all members act simultaneously must have termini. Thus, in the First Replies, after explaining why he did not start his argument from "an order or succession of efficient causes among sensible things," he writes: "[T]he question I asked concerning myself was not what was the cause that originally produced me, but what is the cause that preserves me at present. In this way I aimed to escape the whole issue of the succession of causes" (7:106–7; 2:77). He comes back to this idea later in the First Replies, where he comments parenthetically concerning the causes that preserve his existing, "[T]here is no possibility of an infinite regress here, since the question concerns the present, not the past or the future" (7:111; 2:80). These remarks echo ¶34 of the Third Meditation, where Descartes explains as follows why an infinite regress of sustainers is impossible:

> It is clear enough that an infinite regress is impossible here, especially since I am dealing not just with the cause that produced me in the past, but also and most importantly with the cause that preserves me at the present moment. (7:50; 2:34)

Although Descartes does not say exactly why the fact that he is "dealing . . . with the cause that preserves me at the present moment" makes clear that an infinite series of causes is impossible, his comment suggests that he holds that while a temporally extended series of causes (so that each cause in the series makes its contribution after the prior causes and before the subsequent ones) is indeed possible, an infinite series of simultaneously acting causes is not.[37] This impression is encouraged by something that Descartes says in the First Replies:

> This is plainly a quite different approach from observing that my father begot me, inferring that my grandfather begot my father, and in view of the impossibility of going on *ad infinitum* in the search for parents of parents, bringing the inquiry to a close by deciding that there is a first cause. (7:107; 2:77–78)

It is hard to know exactly how to take the "quite different" approach, but if Descartes is implying that his approach is different from Aquinas's on this point, it looks as if he is being unfair. Aquinas explicitly allows that an infinite series of progenitors and offspring is possible (ST I, Q. 46, A. 2, ad 7). Gassendi makes a related point in the Fifth Objections:

> An infinite regress seems to be absurd only in the case of causes which are so linked and subordinated to each other that a cause which is lower in the chain cannot act without the motive power of one which is higher. This occurs when something is pushed by a stone, the stone by a stick, and the stick by a hand, or when the first link of a chain lifts a weight, and that link is pulled by the previous link and so on. In such cases we must eventually reach one link in the chain which is the first to move. But an infinite series does not seem to be absurd when we have causes which are arranged in such a way that if the earlier cause is destroyed the subsequent cause depending on it still survives and can still act. Hence when you say "It is clear enough that an infinite regress is impossible here," you must ask whether

this is equally evident to Aristotle, who was strongly convinced that there was never any first parent. (7:302–3; 2:210–11)

To which Descartes replies:

> Your further contention, that it is not absurd that there should be an infinite regress, is undermined by what you yourself say later on. For you admit that an infinite regress is absurd "in the case of causes which are so linked that a cause which is lower in the chain cannot act without one which is higher." But it is causes of this sort, and only of this sort, that are at issue here, since we are dealing with causes of being, not causes of coming into being, such as parents. Hence you cannot set the authority of Aristotle against me. (7:370; 2:255)

Descartes's response—that the causal series of sustainers in being that he is interested in has the feature of subordination that Gassendi says precludes an infinite regress—seems fair enough. But it does raise the question, as was pointed out by Étienne Gilson,[38] of what Descartes was doing in the First Replies. When asked by Caterus to compare his approach with that of Aquinas, he says that his own approach "is plainly quite a different approach from observing that my father begot me, inferring that my grandfather begot my father, and in view of the impossibility of going on *ad infinitum* in the search for parents of parents, bringing the inquiry to a close by deciding that there is a first cause" (7:107; 2:77–78). Gilson's hypothesis is that, pressed by Caterus to publicly disagree with Thomas, Descartes politely declines the invitation by instead contrasting his argument with one that neither he nor Thomas accepts.

I find it hard to be certain whether Descartes's use of the example of an infinite causal series of parents and offspring is a piece of diplomacy or whether it reflects some carelessness on his part. Descartes has fairly openly disagreed with Thomas a few paragraphs earlier when he says, "I did not base my argument on the fact that I observed there to be an order or succession of efficient causes among the objects perceived by the senses," and he is about to take aim at him again a couple of pages later when he writes pointedly that "according to the laws of the true logic, we must never ask about the existence [*an est*] of anything until we first understand its essence [*quid est*]" (7:107–8; 2:78), which makes one wonder whether diplomacy was uppermost in Descartes's mind when he wrote this section of the First Replies. It is possible that Descartes, persuaded at the outset that there is no path of the sort that Aquinas thought, which would take us from transactions within the physical order to God,[39] either overlooked some of the nuances of Aquinas's position or gave a misleading impression of where the differences lay. Be that as it may, I believe that there are fundamental differences, and it is worth trying to locate them as perspicuously as possible.

We noted above that Descartes and Thomas begin their arguments from quite different *explananda*. Aquinas argues for God's existence starting from change within the natural world on the basis of general views about causality. Descartes does not think such an approach is going to get us anywhere. His conviction may be informed by his conception of the natural world as *res extensa*; there is nothing special about the causal transactions that take place within *res extensa* that lends itself to the idea that they must be based in a special (transcendent?) first principle. I think this is the point that Descartes is trying to register in a passage that we considered above:

> I did not think that such a succession of causes [i.e., "an order or succession of efficient causes among the objects perceived by the senses"] could lead me anywhere except to a recognition of the imperfection of my intellect, since an infinite chain of such successive causes from eternity without any first cause is beyond my grasp. And my inability to grasp it certainly does not entail that there must be a first cause, any more than my inability to grasp the infinite number of divisions in a finite quantity entails that there is an ultimate division beyond which any further division is impossible. All that follows is that my intellect, which is finite, does not encompass the infinite. (7:106–7; 2:77)

From this point of view, it does not really matter whether the physical causal series are of the form of a ball-stick-hand (if we think of the hand as so much machinery) or parents and offspring (again, thinking of this, as Descartes does in the case of animals, as the production of certain mechanistic systems by others); neither causal series leads to something beyond the physical.

Descartes, as we have seen, bases his argument on a different, metaphysical *explanandum*—the need to account for staying in being, which relies on the meditator's sense that she does not have the wherewithal to keep herself in existence, that she is not metaphysically self-sufficient or independent. To be clear, Aquinas no less than Descartes thinks that we depend on God at each moment of our existence.[40] What they disagree about is the place of this tenet in a theory of God. For Aquinas, it is something that one comes to comparatively late in the discussion, after one has learned via reflection on the natural world a good deal about God, including that he exists;[41] for Descartes, it is one of the principal ways we have of knowing that God exists.

Although it is natural to present the question, as Descartes does, as one of whether I have what it takes to "keep" myself in existence from one moment to the next, what he is really asking, as he makes clear, is what holds me in being now. (If I need something to keep me from falling out of existence in the next instant, I am not the sort of thing whose current existence gets a free pass.) When Descartes connects the impossibility of an infinite regress of sustainers with the fact that he is asking about what keeps me in existence now, the point of those remarks is to move the meditator away from a question in natural philosophy, concerning her natural formation, where cause and effect are both located in space and time, to a nonphysical question of her metaphysical origin, which, as Descartes conceives it, involves a being outside of space and time exercising its power so as to instantaneously hold her in being at each moment of her existence. Moreover, while Descartes thinks that there cannot be an infinite regress in this order of dependence, his reasons for thinking so appear to be different from Aquinas's. Aquinas's reasons for thinking that certain sorts of series of movers must terminate have to do with the nature of causality and, in particular, the idea of instrumental cause (for example, the stick which is used to move the ball is an instrument of the hand); Descartes's reasons have to do rather with the nature of the metaphysical dependence involved and, in particular, the power required to support something in existence. In fact, as we shall see in the last subsection of this chapter, he holds that the series terminates immediately in a self-sustaining cause: whatever has the power to sustain something else will also have the power to sustain itself and so will be self-sustained.

THE IDEA OF GOD

Despite the similarities that Caterus points out between Descartes's second argument and certain of Thomas's arguments, there are important differences underneath the two arguments. Still, one thing that is not clear yet is whether or not Descartes's second argument lends itself to a theory of our cognition of God as constructed, of a sort that he resolutely eschewed in his First Argument and in exchanges with Regius and Gassendi concerning our cognition of God. The movement from the level of natural philosophy to metaphysics, while important, seems to be consistent with, perhaps even invites, a conception of our cognition of God as constructed. That is, granted that Descartes begins the second argument with a question about what sustains my existing rather than with what causes natural motion, and granted that he concludes with the existence of something self-caused rather than uncaused, and granted that his reasons for thinking that his causal series must terminate are different from the reasons that Aquinas has for thinking that there must be a first mover, why couldn't one construct a conception of God out of the materials employed in Descartes's second argument? Even if we accept Descartes's point that we will not arrive at cognition of God by working with characterizations of the form "first unmoved mover" or "first un-caused cause," why can't we generate cognition of God via the charac-terization "self-sustained sustainer of our existing"? To see how Descartes would respond to this question, we need to consider his contention that the meditator's antecedent possession of the idea of God is essential to the feasibility of the second argument.

We saw earlier that when Caterus compares Descartes's argument to Aquinas's, he suggests that our possession of the idea of God is not very important to Descartes's argument. In response, Descartes is emphatic that the idea of God does play a role in the argument, insisting that "the whole force of my argument depends on this one fact," namely, that "I was asking about myself in so far as I observe, amongst my other thoughts, that there is within me the idea of a supremely perfect being." Here is his explanation of the importance of the idea to the argument:

> For, firstly, this idea contains the essence of God [*quid sit Deus*], at least in so far as I am capable of understanding it; and according to the laws of true logic, we must never ask about the existence of anything until we first understand its essence [*de nulla unquam re quaeri debet* an est, *nisi prius* quid sit *intelligatur*]. Secondly, it is this idea which provides me with the oppor-tunity of inquiring whether I derive my existence from myself, or from another [*an sim a me, vel ab alio*], and of recognizing my defects. And, lastly, it is this same idea which shows me not just that I have a cause, but that this cause contains every perfection, and hence that it is God. (7:108; 2:78)

This passage seems difficult but important. I think Descartes's point is, broadly, that philosophical theological investigations presuppose that we already have some grasp of what God is; this is not the sort of thing we can bootstrap our way into. And I think Descartes is suggesting that the way this fact makes itself felt in practice is in our sensitivity to a constel-lation of considerations having to do with the need to be sustained in existence and the sorts of beings capable of sustaining things in existence (that is how I understand the remark that the idea "provides me with the opportunity of inquiring whether I derive my existence from myself, or from another [*an sim a me, vel ab alio*], and of recognizing my defects"). Beyond this, the idea of God plays a more specific role in the logic of the argument: it provides the basis for inferring that whatever sustains me will have (at least) all the perfections found in my idea of God (and so has to be God).

The first reason that Descartes enumerates in the passage is that the idea reveals to us God's essence and we need to know what God is (*quid est*) before we inquire whether God is (*an est*). Descartes's remark about true logic can be puzzling because it might be taken to suggest that he was simply following the standard methodology at the time. In fact, in an earlier draft of the First Replies, Descartes had written "my logic" instead of "true logic," but in a letter of 31 December 1640 he asked Mersenne to change it:

> In the place where I put "in accordance with the laws of my logic," please put "in accordance with the laws of the true logic"; it is near the middle of my Replies to Caterus, where he objects that I have borrowed my argument from St Thomas. The reason why I add "my" or "the true" to "logic" is that I have read theologians who follow the ordinary logic and inquire what God is before inquiring whether God exists. (3:272–73; 3:165)

(To judge from this passage, Descartes seems to have been reading theologians around the time he was working on the First Replies, and seems to have been reflecting on, at least in a general way, the sort of questions about the cognition of God that I have been drawing attention to. The remark does not indicate a very deep engagement with the people he happens to be reading. There is something casual about it. He does not, for example, bother to tell Mersenne who these theologians are or what their reasoning is; in order for him to change "my logic" to "true logic" it is enough that he has found some authorities who see things the same way.)[42]

Although this claim might sound like a piece of common sense—after all, I cannot ask whether something is, before I know what it is I am asking about—it is, in fact, as Descartes's original use of "my logic" instead of "true logic" implies, controversial. We noted earlier that this comment is directed against Aquinas's position in particular that our cognition that something exists precedes our cognition of its essence (ST I, Q. 2, A. 2, ad 2)—in fact, according to Aquinas, in the case of God, we are privy in this life only to cognition that he is, *an est*, and not of what he is, *quid est*. Moreover, while Descartes presents this as a piece of general methodology— that is, we must never ask about the existence of *anything*, he says, until we understand the essence of what we are looking for—it does not seem that he follows it consistently himself. In the Second Meditation, he establishes via the cogito reflection that something exists and then goes on to ask, What is this thing that I have discovered to exist?

Still, if the point that Descartes is making here is not as obvious and commonsensical as he makes it sound, it does helpfully record his sense that if I am going to know anything about God (including that he exists), I have to begin with some grasp of what God is. In particular, the remark suggests that, in Descartes's view, other accounts of our cognition of God, such as Aquinas's, which are supposed to allow us to have some cognition of God (short of knowing what he is) and which are supposed to be based on nominal characterizations built out of reflection on the world, underestimate how much we need to bring to the table in order to cognize God. We can get a better sense of why Descartes thinks this is so if we consider the remaining two reasons that Descartes gives for why "the whole force" of his second argument depends on our possession of an idea of God, which are as follows:

> Secondly, it is this idea which provides me with the opportunity of inquiring whether I derive my existence from myself, or from another [an sim a me, vel ab alio], and of recognizing my defects. And, lastly, it is this same idea which shows me not just that I have a cause, but that this cause contains every perfection, and hence that it is God. (7:107–8; 2:78)

It is helpful to consider this text in the light of the somewhat fuller explanation in a letter to Mesland that covers ground similar to the passage we have been considering from the First Replies:

> Just as it is an effect of God to have created me, so it is an effect of him to have put the idea of himself in me; and there is no effect coming from him from which one cannot prove his existence. Nevertheless, it seems to me that all these proofs based on his effects are reducible to a single one; and also that they are incomplete, if the effects are not evident to us (that is why I considered my own existence rather than that of heaven and earth, of which I am not equally certain) and if we do not add to them the idea which we have of God. For since my soul is finite, I cannot know that the order of causes is not infinite, except in so far as I have in myself that idea of the first cause; and even if there be admitted a first cause which keeps me in existence, I cannot say that it is God unless I truly have the idea of God. (4:112; 3:232)

The last sentence suggests that we might divide the work that the idea of God does into two pieces: (a) it is necessary in order to see that there is a first cause which sustains me and (b) it is necessary in order to see that this first cause must be God.

The more straightforward of the two is (b). Descartes's argument that my self-sustained sustainer is God runs through the thought that such a being has the wherewithal to give itself any perfection of which it has an idea, and has (at least) the ideas of all the perfections of which I have ideas. While it is true that as a matter of fact only God can sustain the existing of anything (I think this may be what lies behind Descartes's remark that "there is no effect coming from him from which one cannot prove his existence"), my recognition of this fact runs through my knowledge that this being has all the perfections found in my idea of God (since it has ideas of all perfections that I have ideas of, and it can give itself any perfection of which it has an idea) and so is God. In other words, if I did not know that my sustainer sustained something with an idea of God, I would not know what perfections it had and so I would not know whether it was God.

Descartes's claim (a)—that "since my soul is finite, I cannot know that the order of causes is not infinite, except in so far as I have in myself that idea of the first cause"—is more difficult to interpret. The corresponding claim from the First Replies appears to be that the idea of God "provides me with the opportunity of inquiring whether I derive my existence from myself, or from another [an sim a me, vel ab alio], and of recognizing my defects." We have already seen that Descartes's claim in ¶24 that my perception of myself as limited "in some way" is posterior to my perception of the unlimited, God. The thought contained in the second part of this sentence is that if I did not have the idea of God, I would not appreciate my own limitations and so (I take it) would not know, for example, whether or not I am self-sustained. But what about the first half of the sentence? What does Descartes mean when he says that the idea of God "provides me with the opportunity of inquiring whether I derive my existence from myself, or from another"? I think Descartes's thought here is that it is not, as it were, a basic fact about causation that causal series cannot be infinite. He immediately goes on to say that he does not accept the commonly held principle that "a series of causes cannot go on forever" and adverts to the infinite divisibility of matter. But if it is not a feature of causal series as such to terminate, how can I tell that the series of things sustaining me must terminate?

Descartes suggests, quite intriguingly, that our possession of the idea of a first cause plays an essential role in my awareness of this fact: "For since my soul is finite, I cannot know that the order of causes is not infinite, except in so far as I have in myself that idea of the first cause." What does this mean? Well, I doubt that it means that the idea functions as a sort of oracle, informing me that, as things turn out, the series of causes sustaining me happens to be finite. Rather, what an idea provides is understanding, an appreciation of why this is so. My possession of the idea of God is bound up with my recognition of a family of considerations concerning metaphysical dependence relations: for example, that my existence requires sustaining, that I do not sustain myself in existence, that sustaining something in existence involves enormous, unbounded power, and so forth. As I reflect on these considerations, I also notice that a series of sustainers cannot go on forever (as we shall see later, Descartes has more to say about this last point).

To get a better picture of the work I take the idea of God to be doing here, it may help to consider how the idea of extension functions for Descartes. Someone who has the idea of a triangle is thereby able to grasp the true and immutable nature of a triangle. In virtue of her grasp of the nature of a triangle, she is able to discover truths about triangles. She can see, for example, that the largest side must be opposite the largest angle. Compare her with someone who lacks the idea of extension, but who is given a stockpile of truths about triangles. Such a person would be able to do well for the "true-false" section of the test, but would founder on the "free response" section. She would even be able to manipulate her stockpile of geometry truths in various ways (conjoin truths and disjoin truths, and draw simple inferences such as from the fact that a triangle has three sides, it follows that a triangle has an odd number of sides, or fewer sides than a square). But still, lacking an idea of extension, she would be unable do geometry: she would not be connected with its subject matter in a way that would enable her to understand why various geometrical truths hold.

The idea of God works similarly. It does not confer upon its possessor a stockpile of truths about God so much as it confers access to a subject matter so that she may *recognize* its truths and understand *why* they hold. Her cognitive access to this subject matter enables her to recognize that she is not metaphysically self-sufficient, that the series of beings sustaining her terminates, and so forth. I find it helpful to think of the idea of God as accomplishing this in large part by providing me with the (interpreted, objectively real) categories *dependent* and *independent* in a manner that enables me to apply them to myself and see (1) that I fall on the dependent as opposed to the independent side of things and (2) that things that fall on the dependent side depend immediately on the thing that falls on the independent side.

With respect to (1), one thing that the idea of God contributes is the very intelligibility of the enterprise of philosophical theology (this is one way to take Descartes's remark that the idea of God "provides me with the opportunity of inquiring whether I derive my existence from myself, or from another [*an sim a me, vel ab alio*]"). Not everyone will react with comprehension to, for example, the thought, "For a lifespan can be divided into countless parts, each completely independent of the others, so that it does not follow from the fact I existed a little while ago that I must exist now, unless there is some cause which as it were creates me afresh at this moment—that is, which preserves me" (¶31, 7:48–49; 2:33). And to the extent that such considerations do register with us, we might think that it is because we possess what Descartes is calling the idea of the first cause, which makes us sensitive to certain considerations (in the way that possession of the idea of extension makes us appreciate certain considerations). In particular, the idea gives me the wherewithal to recognize that (at each moment of my being) I am metaphysically dependent, and that there must be something upon which I depend in this peculiarly metaphysical way, a metaphysical sustainer.

With respect to (2), according to Descartes, understanding what a first cause is shows me not only that I am dependent, but also that my existing is sustained by some one thing, rather than an infinite series of sustainers. Descartes writes to Mesland that "since my soul is finite, I cannot know that the order of causes is not infinite, except in so far as I have in myself that idea of the first cause." What does Descartes have in mind here? Perhaps we get some help on this point from a passage in the First Replies where Descartes defends his position that God is *a se* in a positive sense:

> [T]he fact that God derives his existence from himself, or has no cause apart from himself, depends not on nothing but on the real immensity of his power; hence, when we perceive this, we are quite entitled to think that in a sense he stands in the same relation to himself as an efficient cause to its effect, and hence derives his existence from himself in a positive sense. And each one may ask himself whether he derives his existence from himself in this sense. Since he will find no power which suffices to preserve him even for one moment of time, he will be right to conclude that he derives his existence from another being, and indeed that this other being derives his existence from itself (there is no possibility of an infinite regress here, since the question concerns the present, not the past or the future). Indeed, I will now add something which I have not put down in writing before, namely that the cause we arrive at cannot merely be a secondary cause; for a cause which possesses such great power that it can preserve something situated outside of itself must, a fortiori, preserve itself by its own power, and derive its existence from itself. (7:111; 2:80)

In the course of this passage, Descartes introduces that idea that whatever sustains me will be self-sustained. The reason he gives in parenthesis—that there cannot be infinite regress because the question concerns the present—does not explain, of course, why there could not be a finite series leading from me to a self-sustained sustainer. But a new consideration introduced at the end of the passage, having to do with the immensity of power involved in sustaining something's existing *ex nihilo*, does. It seems to me that this new claim also helps us flesh out his suggestion in the letter to Mesland that because our minds are finite we would have no way of knowing that the causal series of sustainers is infinite. If the idea of a first cause made available to a finite mind the idea of the infinite power involved in supporting *anything* in existence, then that same idea would make clear why something that supported, in particular, my own existence would itself be self-sustained. So, although Descartes presents this as a new thesis (something that he had "not put down in writing before"), it seems to me likely that this has been a crucial feature of his thinking about sustainers all along, and it may well be the clearest reason he has for thinking that there cannot be an infinite series of such beings.[43]

The idea of God (or the idea of the first cause) is necessary, then, in order to establish the following in the second argument for the existence of God: (*a*) it is involved in the recognition that my existing requires sustaining, (*b*) it is involved in my recognition that I do not have the power to sustain myself in existence, (*c*) it is involved in my recognition that whatever sustains my existing has enormous, unbounded power and so also sustains its own existing, and, finally, (*d*) it is involved in the argument that whatever sustains my existing must be God.

Need (*d*) (which answers in the text to Descartes's claim, "And, lastly, it is this same idea which shows me not just that I have a cause, but that this cause contains every perfection, and hence that it is God") differs from the first three. The first three needs all concern the intellectual equipment I must have if I am to pursue philosophical theology at all, if philosophical theology is to be intelligible to me. The last concerns the use of my possession of the idea as a premise in a causal argument: whatever causes me must also have the ideas of all the perfections that I attribute to God, and will give itself all the perfections of which it has ideas, from which I infer that that being is God. We might, encouraged by the letter to Mesland, put the point in this way: if I had the idea of the first cause but did not have the idea of God, I would be able to infer that my existence is sustained by a very powerful being, but I would not be able to infer that that being is God. The point here is not that I would lack the cognitive resources to grasp the conclusion of the argument (which is true enough, but irrelevant); rather, the point is that if all one knows about a given being X is that it sustains something (either itself or something else Y, or both), we do not know enough to conclude that X is God. In order to make this inference, we would need to know something more about X, such as that one of the beings that X sustains has the idea of God. It is here perhaps that the similarity between the second argument and the first argument is clearest: in both cases, my idea of God enters into the *explanandum* for which an explanation is sought (in the first argument it is the *explanandum*; in the second it is part of the *explanandum*).

The first three roles have a rather different character. They concern our sensitivity to the considerations in play in the Third Meditation, that is, they concern the condition that must obtain in order for me to find a certain line of reasoning meaningful. Hence, Descartes claims with respect to these uses of the idea of God that I cannot know certain things unless I have the idea of a first cause and the idea of the first cause "provides me with the opportunity of inquiring" into my cause. These first three roles have to do with how the idea of God makes available to the human mind the content (as we will learn in the Fifth Meditation, a true and immutable nature) that we need in order to reason about philosophical theology, analogously to the way in which the idea of extension makes available to the mind the content (a true and immutable nature) that we need in order to reason about geometrical matters.

Although (a)–(c) do not make for the same level of structural similarity that the other use of the idea of God does, they are as important for establishing Descartes's overall position, for they represent his thesis that the idea of God must be presupposed at the outset if we are to engage in philosophical theology; the idea does not somehow emerge out of our reflection on the goings-on in the natural world. As such, these roles are part and parcel of Descartes's fundamental disagreement with Aquinas over whether our idea of God is somehow constructed out of more basic materials, which I have claimed is of signal importance for Descartes's place in the history of philosophical theology. They make clear what Descartes's answer would be to the question raised at the end of the last section concerning the possibility of arriving at our cognition of God via a characterization like "the sustainer of my existing." In Descartes's view the deep intelligibility of such a characterization (as opposed to the merely nominal intelligibility), required in order for me to appreciate that I have a sustainer, rests on my possession of the idea of God. There is no getting from the characterization to the idea of God, we might say, because the characterization is too close to the idea of God.

Finally, it is worth observing that part of what the second argument accomplishes in terms of Descartes's overall purposes in the Third Meditation is to help persuade the meditator that we really do have the sort of idea of God claimed in the first argument. As was touched upon above, to the extent that I am moved by the question of what sustains me in existence at this very moment and to the extent that I find the moves in the subsequent dialectic well motivated (especially the thought that whatever sustains something in existence *ex nihilo* is enormously powerful), I may find myself knowing more about God—that is, more about the sort of thing that God is—than I had previously realized. If we assume, with Descartes, that our ability to make discoveries about things depends on our having an idea that makes available to a certain subject matter a "true and immutable nature," the second argument contributes to the meditator's sense that she really does possess an idea that makes available to the mind God's nature, which idea is the datum that is fed into the first argument's causal machinery.

THE TWO SENSES OF A SE

One of the aspects of Descartes's thinking about God that most raised the eyebrows of his scholastic critics was his claim that God is *a se* in a positive sense, so that God is, we might say, a self-sustained sustainer and not an unsustained sustainer. Descartes's argument that a self-sustained being will give itself every perfection of which it had an idea, made this aspect of his thinking about God hard to miss. This issue, we noted above, attracted the criticism of Caterus. It also elicited the following rather sternly worded warning from Arnauld in the Fourth Replies:

> I think the author's attention should be drawn to this point, so that he can give the matter his careful and attentive consideration. For I am sure that it will be scarcely possible to find a single theologian who will not object to the proposition that God derives his existence from himself in the positive sense, and as it were causally. (7:214; 2:150)

Something significant is afoot here, intimately connected with the change in the course of the history of philosophical theology that Descartes is bringing about. Spinoza, for example, will claim in the *Ethics* that God is *causa sui*, a claim that is important to the way he thinks about God.[44]

We noticed earlier that Descartes's novelty emerges before the point in the argument where he attempts to show that any self-sustainer must be God; it derives from a departure from the Aristotelian tradition at the very start of the argument. It is a premise of the Aristotelian arguments for a first mover that everything *that is moving* is moved by *another*, which is why those arguments deliver unmoved movers, not self-moved movers. Descartes begins from an unrestricted principle to the effect that anything that is existing requires something to keep it in existence. The fact that Aquinas's principle is restricted and Descartes's is not, is a function of a difference in the *explananda* to which these two thinkers apply their causal principles. Aquinas seeks a first cause for motion or change (and the causality of the movers or agents); Descartes seeks a first cause for something's existing rather than falling into nothingness. And while it makes sense to think, as Aquinas does, that there can be an unmoved move or an uncaused cause, that is, a cause that does not need a cause because it does not itself move or change, it is not clear what would be the analogue for Descartes's situation: if one starts from the idea that all existing requires sustaining (instead of the idea that all movement or change requires a mover or an efficient cause), then the most immediate analogue to a mover that is unmoved because it does not move or change would be a sustainer that is unsustained because it does not exist. But this seems incoherent.

Descartes's thinking of God as self-caused rather than uncaused is related, I think, to other aspects that we have been attending to, namely, his sense that philosophical theology begins with metaphysical questions (e.g., What sustains my existing from one moment to the next moment?), the appreciation of which is rooted in our possession of the idea of God. Let me explain by considering one way in which he might have kept his argument closer to Aquinas. We could imagine Descartes not starting from, as he does, the principle that all being requires sustaining, but some other, more restricted premise to the effect that anything whose existing is sustained (created, preserved) is sustained (created, preserved) by another and thus infer the existence of some first unsustained (uncreated, unpreserved) sustainer (creator, preserver). (As I understand it, some twentieth-century commentators have interpreted Aquinas's First Way along these lines.) But the reason why this approach will not work from Descartes's point of view is that unless one agrees that existing is the sort of thing that in general requires some power, some causal support, to sustain it, then it is hard to see why I should suppose that my existing, in particular, requires something to sustain it.[45] And so he is led not to the basically negative conception of God as a being without a sustainer but instead to the more positive conception of a being so powerful that it can sustain its own existing.

The idea of God as a being who is self-sustained runs deep in Descartes's philosophical theology. This is why Descartes holds his ground in his exchanges with Caterus and Arnauld with a resolve that might otherwise appear to be mere stubbornness. When Caterus criticizes him for apparently holding that God is *a se* in some positive sense and Arnauld presses him even harder, Descartes resists, conceding in effect certain points, but refusing to cede others. He recognizes that it is Arnauld's "principal complaint,"[46] but maintains that it is "the least well-taken of all of his objections" (7:235; 2:164). Even so, he spends some ten pages responding to it, concluding with an apology of sorts: "I have pursued this issue at somewhat greater length than perhaps the subject required, in order to show that I am extremely anxious to prevent anything at all being found in my writings which could justifiably give offence to the theologians" (7:245; 2:171). The exchange is instructive for what it reveals about what Descartes is and is not prepared to compromise on.

The main thing lying behind Arnauld's objection is a worry about the intelligibility of self-causation, more specifically, the intelligibility of something's being an efficient cause of its own existing.[47] In his reply to Caterus, Descartes had argued that efficient causes and their effects had to be distinct only in cases where the efficient cause is temporarily prior to the effect. Arnauld disputes this, maintaining that it is a general feature of causation that causes and effects be distinct. This is especially clear in cases of causation where we are thinking of something's coming into existence. To think of something as a cause of existence, we must think of it as already existing. To think of something as able to receive existence, we must think of it as not yet existing. How can we think of one thing in both of these ways?

> Now we cannot conceive of something under the concept of a cause as bestowing existence unless we conceive of it as possessing existence; for no one can give what he does not have. Hence we should be conceiving of a thing as having existence before conceiving of it as having received existence; yet in the case of any receiver, the receiving precedes the possessing. (7:210; 2:147–48)

Arnauld goes on to point out that since God, unlike us, is beyond time (appealing to Augustine, he notes that "in God there is no past or future but only eternally present existence"), the question that sets me off on a search for the cause of my existing (namely, What keeps me in existence from one moment to the next?) does not apply to God. Arnauld infers from this "that God cannot be conceived of as deriving existence from himself in a positive sense [*esse a seipso* positive]." Rather, God's essence is such that he does not need a cause:

> [I]f someone asks for an efficient cause of God, we should reply that he does not need an efficient cause. And if the questioner goes on to ask why he does not need an efficient cause, we should answer that this is because he is an infinite being, whose existence is his essence. For the only things that require an efficient cause, are those in which actual existence may be distinguished from essence. (7:213; 2:150)

Notice that Arnauld is trying to reintroduce a restricted causal principle, a principle that does not require that everything have a cause, but only those things whose existence is distinct from their essence; such a principle allows him to return to a conception of God as something that is uncaused (something that does not require a cause) rather than self-caused (*a se* in some positive sense).

Descartes does not quarrel with Arnauld's claim that God cannot be the efficient cause of himself, that God does not preserve himself in being in the same way that finite things are preserved in being, and Descartes is even willing to go along to a certain extent with Arnauld's formulation that God does not need an efficient cause. Referring back to the First Replies, he writes:

> And I never said that God preserves himself by some positive force, in the way in which created things are preserved by him; I simply said that the immensity of his power or essence, in virtue of which he does not need a preserver, is a *positive* thing. (7:236–37; 2:165)

The exact import of these remarks is unclear, however. They could be taken to suggest that God is simply uncaused, or they could be taken as acknowledgment of the fact that God's relation to himself in terms of his existence is very different from his relation to his creatures (so that what he does in his own case does not, for the reasons Arnauld appeals to, count as "preservation"). In any case, as the reply unfolds, it becomes clear that there are two closely related points that are, in Descartes's view, essential to a causal demonstration of God's existence. First, we have to be able to apply a causal principle universally, so as to apply even to God. Second, there is nothing that is simply uncaused.

To begin with the first, Descartes writes:

> But I think it is clear to everyone that a consideration of efficient causes is the primary and principal way, if not the only way, that we have of proving the existence of God. We cannot develop this proof with precision unless we grant our minds the freedom to inquire into the efficient causes of all things, even God himself. For what right do we have to make God an exception, if we have not yet proved that he exists? In every case, then, we must ask whether a thing derives its existence *from itself* or *from something else*; and by this means the existence of God can be inferred, even though we have not given an explicit account of what it is for something to be *from itself.* (7:238; 2:166)

In Descartes's view, we begin with a general, root notion of cause, which can be subsequently refined according to whether something is *ab alio*, in which case it is from another as from an efficient cause (*tanquam a causa efficiente*), or is *a se*, in which case it is from itself as from a formal cause (*tanquam a causa formali*), which Descartes glosses in this way: "that is, because it has the kind of essence which entails that it does not require an efficient cause." (Descartes goes on to compare the relationship between two sorts of causes to that between regular polygons and a circle. I think his idea is this: just as you might think of a circle as an infinite version of a regular polygon, you might think of the formal or essential cause of God's existence as the infinite version of an efficient cause.) What Descartes thinks must be rejected, if we are to have a causal demonstration of God's existence, is any version of a causal principle that has built into it exceptions (as Aquinas's principle, for example, does in that it applies only to things in motion). Descartes is willing to allow that there may be refinement down the road, but that refinement has to take the form of articulating some "common concept" of cause and not of allowing exceptions in through the back door. (Casting God's sustaining of himself as a species of "formal" causality makes the way God causes his existence like the way the essence of a triangle causes its properties, which was also regarded as formal causation.)

To turn to the second point, Descartes regards as crucial to the prospects of the demonstration that we not understand *a se* in a purely negative way, so as to mean simply "does not have a cause." He writes:

> Now some people are accustomed to judge that nothing can be the efficient cause of itself, and they carefully distinguish an efficient cause from a formal cause. Hence, when they see the question raised as to whether anything derives its existence from itself, it can easily happen that they think only of an efficient cause in the strict sense, and thus they suppose that *from itself* [*a se*] must not be understood as *from a cause* [*a causa*], but only in a *negative* way as *without a cause* [*sine causa*] (that is, as implying something such that we must not inquire why it exists). If we accept this interpretation of the words *a se*, then it will not be possible to produce any argument for the existence of God based on his effects, as was shown by the author of the First Set of Objections; hence this interpretation must be totally rejected. (7:239; 2:167)

What Descartes is referring to here is the movement from the claim that something is *a se* to the claim that that thing is God. The point he is making can fruitfully be viewed within the context of general rejection of a theology based on the *via negativa*. If we start with a merely negative characterization of a thing—say, a being that has no cause—we will not, in his view, have sufficient content to conclude that that being is God. However one parses in the end the first cause's being *a se*, there has to be enough of a positive characterization for us to be able to infer that an *a se* being has the further characteristics we associate with God; we have to perceive not simply that God does not have a cause, but something of the reason why God does not need a cause. It is fairly clear that Descartes takes this reason to be the power associated with existing *a se*. In the First Replies, after insisting that there is nothing of which we may not ask why it exists, he writes:

> However, I do readily admit that there can exist something which possesses such great and inexhaustible power that it never required the assistance of anything else in order to exist in the first place, and does not now require any assistance for its preservation, so that it is, in a sense, its own cause; and I understand God to be such a being. (7:109; 2:78)

In short, the intimation of self-causation that Caterus and Arnauld seize upon is not some unfortunate lapse on Descartes's part, to be corrected or excised with minimal effect on the rest of his thinking about how we cognize God. Rather, the contention that we cognize God immediately (and positively), as something *a se*, and not negatively (and obliquely), as something *sine causa*, is essential, Descartes holds, to our ability to advance causal demonstrations for God's existence. Near the end of his response to Arnauld on this topic, Descartes summarizes his position nicely:

> Thus, in refusing to allow us to say that God stands toward himself in a relation analogous to that of an efficient cause, M. Arnauld not only fails to clarify the proof of God's existence, but actually prevents the reader from understanding it. This is especially true at the end when he concludes that "if we thought we ought to look for the efficient cause, or quasi-efficient cause, of any given thing, then what we would be looking for would be a cause distinct from the thing in question." How would those who do not yet know God [*Deum nondum norunt*] be able to inquire into the efficient cause of other things, with the aim of eventually arriving at knowledge of God, unless they thought it possible to inquire into the efficient cause of anything whatsoever? And how could they reach the end of their inquiries by arriving at God as the first cause if they thought that for any given thing we must always look for a cause which is distinct from it? (7:244–45; 2:170)

⇥4⇤

The Fourth Meditation

THE FOURTH Meditation takes up a problem that came up in passing in the First Meditation. There, after considering a doubt based on the possibility that God might have made me so that I "go wrong every time I add two and three or count the sides of a square, or in some even simpler matter, if that is imaginable," the meditator anticipates the *Meditations'* response to this doubt: "But perhaps God would not have allowed me to be deceived in this way, for he is said to be supremely good." However, this response raises a further puzzle: "But if it were inconsistent with his goodness to have created me such that I am deceived all the time, it would seem equally foreign to his goodness to allow [*permittere*] me to be deceived even occasionally; yet this last assertion cannot be made" (I.¶9; 7:21; 2:14).

It is true that the First Meditation foreshadows the Fourth in this way, and that the Fourth Meditation is organized around the theodical project of explaining how error is compatible with the fact that the mind's author is a supremely perfect being, God. But I don't think that this explains fully the purpose of the meditation. For one thing, its title, "Truth and Falsity," suggests a different focus. For another, Descartes is explicit that the results of the earlier meditations are not hostage to finding a satisfying resolution of the theodical worry: he writes in IV.¶6 that we should not be surprised if, in view of God's infinite nature, we are unable to understand many things concerning God and what God has done; and, even if it should turn out that one of the things we cannot understand is why God allows error in the universe, "there is no call to doubt his existence" (IV.¶6; 7:55; 2:38). While, obviously, it would be good to have an explanation of why God allows error, Descartes's view seems to be that we do not have the right to expect to be able to understand such things, and our inability to do so would not threaten what we have learned so far.

If it is not strictly necessary to respond to the theodical worry raised in the First Meditation, how does the Fourth Meditation fit within Descartes's programmatic aims? In light of its title, I find it natural to think of the Fourth Meditation as a continuation of the discussion of the "truth rule" that was proposed in III.¶2: "So I now seem to be able to lay it down as a general rule that whatever I clearly and distinctly perceive is true." It was the consideration of this proposal that set the meditator upon the search for the author of her nature back in the Third Medita-tion. It is only to be expected, then, that after discovering who the author of her nature is, the meditator should return to the truth rule. And if re-sponding to theodical worry is not of itself clearly essential to Descartes's overall project, establishing the truth rule is.

But exactly what work is left to do concerning the truth rule? In the Third Meditation I learned that the author of my nature is a supremely perfect being, and Descartes regards it a short step from this to seeing that the author of my nature is not a deceiver (IV.¶2). Isn't this tanta-mount to establishing the truth rule? Why is there a meditation's worth of work left to do?

Well, what we have so far gets us something, but only so much. In particular, on the basis of what we have seen so far we could argue thus: God's not being a deceiver entails that when I am cognizing well and I make a judgment, my judgment is true. Put contrapositively, if I am in error, if I judge falsely, then I am not cognizing well. Moreover, I think that Descartes assumes that whether I am cognizing well or not is some-thing that is at least in principle available to me. This is not to say I never make mistakes about whether I am cognizing well or not—Descartes in-dicates, for example, that at times we think we have perceived something clearly when we haven't (III.¶3)—but that we have the ability to recog-nize, perhaps after reflection, when we have not cognized well. And if all this is right, then God's not being a deceiver has the interesting conse-quence that I am not subject to undetectable errors, that is, errors that I cannot in principle discover. When I err, I am cognizing poorly, and I can upon reflection determine that this is so.

This is a nontrivial result, even if we take the "upon reflection" very broadly. I note that it is not unnatural for someone who, like Descartes, is especially focused on mathematics to think that when I get something wrong, there will be a certain kind of explanation of my getting the thing wrong, so that it will possible for me to recognize that I am not seeing things with sufficient clarity. Such a view seems plausible with respect to the subject matters that Descartes is concerned with in the first five meditations—the nature of the mind, the nature and existence of God, the general nature of body—at least if we think that we have access to those subject matters in the purely intellectual way that Descartes believes we do. (Things become more complicated when we get to our knowledge of the existence of body in general and, especially, our knowledge of par-ticular bodies, because our cognition of these subject matters depends on the senses.)[1] But without the theological backing that Descartes provides, it is not obvious that he is correct. For example, to step outside the period for a moment, why couldn't it be a product of the way that evolutionary forces have shaped my cognitive faculties and that these faculties, while attuned to my immediate environment in the ways that are most relevant to my survival, are profoundly unsuited to the world in other ways, so that I am, through a sort of illusion, condemned to at least some undetectable errors? I don't have an answer, but there does seem to me to be enough to the question to bring out the nontriviality of the claim that I am not subject to undetectable error.

In any event, this much—that since God, the author of my nature, is not a deceiver, when I cognize well I am not subject to error—could be arrived at fairly quickly on the basis of what Descartes takes himself to have established so far. Although this result is nontrivial, it is very abstract; it still remains to work this result out more concretely. "Cognizing well," "judging," and "error" function as placeholders. What is left to do is to supply the next level of detail, to work out for the meditator what judging is (and what the will is), to explain, in the context of judging, what cognizing well and cognizing poorly are (in the context of judging), to detail how judging well and judging poorly interact with perceiving clearly and distinctly, and, along with that, to explain what counts as a misuse of my faculties (and so how error enters the picture). Cognizing well (in the context of judging) turns out to be affirming or denying where I have clearly and distinctly perceived and withholding judgment where I have not, and cognizing poorly turns out to be affirming or denying where I have not clearly and distinctly perceived. And since God is not a deceiver, the truth rule and an important corollary concerning falsity drop out: When I affirm (or deny) something that I clearly and distinctly perceive, I am using my faculties well, and so my judgment is true; when I affirm (or deny) something I do not clearly and distinctly perceive, I am not using my faculties well and judge culpably, risking falsity and error. So as Descartes goes about addressing the theodical issue signaled in the First Meditation (in perhaps more detail than is strictly required to disarm the theodical threat), a good deal of theory concerning the nature of judgment and the will is developed. Although the theodical worry provides Descartes with a convenient way to organize this material, it is my sense that Descartes would have needed to find a way of developing this theory, even if the worry had not been put on the table.

Truth and the Truth Rule

If the Fourth Meditation is about the truth rule, it makes sense to begin by considering how Descartes thinks about truth and true judgments. I believe that his general way of thinking about truth is indebted to the scholastic Thomistic tradition. For Aquinas, truth is the object of the intellect in the way that good is the object of the will:

> As good denotes that towards which the appetite tends, so the true denotes that towards which the intellect tends. (ST I, Q. 16, A. 1)

The relation between will and good or intellect and truth is supposed to be analogous to the relation between vision and color or hearing and sound. Nowadays it is tempting to think of such relations as formal (or perhaps "grammatical"), but my sense is that the medieval Aristotelians tended to think of such relations as substantive or structural (perhaps formal, where "form" is thought of as a real constituent). It is part of what it is to be, part of the makeup of, a faculty of vision that it is structured so as to track colors.

The objects of the faculties bring with them a certain normative dimension (in one sense of "normative"), standards of success and failure. Since seeking truth is built into what an intellect is, an intellect succeeds when it achieves truth and fails when it is in error, just as seeking good is built into what a will is, so that a will succeeds when it realizes good and fails when it does not, or cognizing color into what vision is, so that it succeeds when it does this and fails when it does not.

We might note that since, on this conception, the intellect has the same sort of internal relation to truth as the will does to good, there really isn't room for the question, Why judge in accordance with the truth? (Why not instead judge, e.g., so as to maximize some sort of psychic comfort?), any more than there is room for the question, Why want good? This is just what an intellect (or a faculty of judgment) is, a faculty oriented toward truth, in the way that a will is a faculty oriented toward good. Aquinas goes on to observe this difference between the properties *true* and *good*: the property *good* belongs primarily to the appetible thing (*re appetibili*), and is secondarily attributed to the appetite (so that a good desire is a desire for an appropriate object), whereas the property *true* is primarily a feature of an intellect conformed to reality in a certain way, and secondarily a feature of the reality to which the intellect is conformed (so that a true thing is simply a thing correctly judged by an intellect).[2]

Descartes makes both the true and the good objects of the will; what this means is that he considers judgment to be an operation of the will, not the intellect.[3] This reconfiguration is significant, but I think it is compatible with the point just noted that good primarily belongs to things, whereas true primarily belongs to the intellect. One might, for example, think of judging as a special species of volition, whose object is truth, in the way that the object of willing in general is the good; even so, one might continue to hold with Aquinas that truth is primarily a property of (now, volitional) judgments, and only secondarily, by extension, a property of things, and this makes for a contrast with good, which is primarily a property of the object of an appetite (the thing desired), and only secondarily a property of the appetite itself. At any rate, Descartes says in the *Rules for the Direction of Mind* that "there can be no truth or falsity in the strict sense except in the intellect alone" (10:396; 1:30), suggesting that truth "in the strict sense" belongs to the intellect and not things. It is true that this is an early text, coming before he articulates his doctrine that judgment is a species of volition, but I don't see a reason to think that he changed his view on this point. He writes, also in an early text, to a correspondent that when truth "is attributed to things outside thought, it signifies only that these things can be objects of true thoughts, be it our thoughts or those of God" (2:597; 3:139), indicating an allegiance to the traditional doctrine at this point in his career.

Since, in Aristotelian thought, the way one gets at what a faculty is is through its object, in order for Descartes's proposal that the true and good are both objects of the will to be coherent, one would have to think that there is the right sort of coherence in the objects true and good, so that judging truly could reasonably be seen as of a piece with some larger enterprise of pursuing good.[4] I don't find it implausible that Descartes, at least, should think there is a connection. His view that our highest good involves having the appropriate cognitive relation to a special locus of truth and reality, namely, God, encourages the thought that there is a close connection between practical good and cognitive good. As we saw in the last chapter, he remarks at the end of the Third Meditation that "just as we believe through faith that the supreme happiness of the next life consists solely in the contemplation of the divine majesty, so experience tells that this same contemplation, albeit much less perfect, enables us to know the greatest joy of which we are capable in this life" (7:52; 2:35–36).

What is this truth that the intellect aims at? If we turn to Aquinas, we see that he works to make room for a number of different (but related) accounts of truth. The one he privileges is that truth is the "adequation" of a thing and the intellect: *veritas est adaequatio rei et intellectus.*[5] I think Descartes has this in mind when he writes, in an early letter, that "the word *truth*, in its proper signification, denotes the conformity of the thought with the object, whereas when one attributes it to things which are outside thought, it signifies only that these things can be objects of true thoughts, be it our thoughts or those of God [*ce mot verité, en sa propre signification, denote la conformité de la pensée auec l'obiet, mais que, lors qu'on l'attribue aux choses qui sont hor de la pensée, il signifie seulement que ces choses peuuent seruir d'obiets a des pensées veritables, soit aux nostres, soit a celles de Dieu*]" (2:597; 3:139).[6] (The second piece of this, the part about things being true, picks up the traditional scholastic doctrine that *true* is a transcendental feature of being—all beings are such that they can be the objects of at least some cognizer's true thoughts—which we will consider later.)

There are different ways in which an intellect can be in conformity with things. For example, when an intellect possesses an intelligible species (when it grasps the essence or quiddity of a thing), it becomes formally identical with the thing that it understands. This conformity, however, is not the "adequation"—or alignment of intellect and thing—found in truth.[7] Rather, the "adequation" found in truth comes about when the intellect judges (or "composes and divides") and things are as it judges them to be:

> In forming the quiddities of things, the intellect merely has a likeness of a thing existing outside the soul, as a sense has a likeness when it receives the species of a sensible thing. But when the intellect begins to judge about the thing it has apprehended, then its judgment is something proper to itself—not something found outside in the thing. And the judgment is said to be true when it conforms to external reality. Moreover, the intellect judges about the thing it has apprehended at the moment when it says that something is or is not. This is the role of "the intellect composing and dividing." (DV Q. 1, A. 3)

Descartes seems to be thinking along similar lines in the *Meditations*. In the Third Meditation, in the course of considering "which of them [my thoughts] can properly be said to be the bearers of truth or falsity," Descartes arrives at this conclusion: "the only . . . thoughts where I must be on my guard against making a mistake are judgements" (III.¶6; 7:37; 2:26).

Further, if truth is the "adequation" of intellect and thing, falsity is the lack of such "adequation" ("Just as truth consists in an equation [*adaequatione*] of thing and intellect, so falsity consists in an inequality [*inequalitate*] between them" [DV Q. 1, A. 10]). But if falsity represents a lack of adequation in a judgment, then it is natural to identify falsity and error, since for one's judgment to lack "adequation" is for one to be in error. In this regard, Aquinas observes that the word *false* is derived from the Latin *fallere*, meaning to deceive. Descartes, too, links error and falsity. Although commentators have sometimes found this puzzling,[8] the linkage follows readily enough, as just noted, from a conception of truth as a property belonging to a judgment that is adequate to things.

The reason the identification of falsity and error sounds odd today is that we often think of truth and falsity as primarily attaching to propositions, thoughts, perceptions, or some other sort of representations. The idea of a proposition's (perception's, thought's) having a "truth value" comes first, and making a true judgment comes out to be something like the assigning of the correct "truth value" to a proposition. On this conception, to be in error is to assign an incorrect truth value to a proposition (perception, thought), either the value "false" to a true proposition or the value "true" to a false proposition, and so, on the contemporary conception, there is no special relation between being in error and false propositions. By way of contrast, on the Thomistic picture that Descartes inherits, truth is fundamentally a relation between the mind and reality, and propositions enter the picture only later.

One can imagine developing the Thomistic/Cartesian view in natural ways so as to introduce both true and false thoughts or perceptions. While Descartes rarely discusses true thoughts as opposed to true judgments,[9] he might think of a true thought or a true perception as an "adequating thought," a *cogitio* such that, when the will's affirmation is added, a true judgment ensues. Similarly, he might think of a false thought or a false perception as an "inadequating thought," a *cogitio* such that, when the will's affirmation is added, a false judgment ensues. Still, the underlying order of explanation would remain: truth is primarily what the mind attempts to achieve through its judgments, namely, a relation of "adequation" between an intellect and a thing; falsity (and error) is primarily an "inadequation," a certain sort of misalignment between the intellect and reality, that the mind attempts to avoid; and an account of true and false thoughts or perceptions is dependent on these more basic commitments.

I believe that Descartes, then, like Aquinas, thinks of truth as fundamentally a property of a judgment that brings about a relation of "adequation" between the mind and reality, and not as fundamentally a property of thoughts, perceptions, or propositions. This accords with Descartes's (early) citation of a version of the Thomistic definition of truth. It also accords, I believe, with the opening of the Second Meditation, where he seems to suggest that a world without things, a world without reality, would be a world practically without truth:

> I will suppose then, that everything I see is false [*falsa*]. I will believe that my memory tells me lies, and that none of the things it reports ever happened. I have no senses. Body, shape, extension, movement and place are chimeras. So what remains true [*verum*]? Perhaps just this one thing [*unum*], that nothing is certain. (II.¶2; 7:24; 2:16)

It also accords with, as we shall see, an important line of thought at the beginning of the Fifth Meditation, where he argues from my making a true (substantive) judgment, that is, from my "adequation," to there being a reality to which I am "adequated" in the judgment, namely, certain true and immutable natures, essences, or forms, which he describes as "somethings," "not . . . nothings."[10]

Descartes's commitment to truth being primarily a property of judgments has consequences for how we hear the truth rule: "So I now seem to be able to lay it down as a general rule that whatever I clearly and distinctly perceive is true." If we introduce a layer of propositions as primary, it becomes natural to think of judgment as the assignment of a truth value to a proposition. Then we might think that the point of the truth rule is to get us from a level of (clearly and distinctly understood) propositions down to the level of reality (the ultimate truth maker). That is, on this picture, what the truth rule says is that when we have clearly and distinctly understood a proposition, we can infallibly assign a truth value to it. I am not sure whether this picture can be coherently worked out: For example, what is it to clearly and distinctly perceive a proposition, on this picture? Perhaps to grasp some Fregean sense? But why should *that* be enough to enable me to assign (let alone infallibly assign) a truth value to the proposition?

We can avoid getting tangled up in such questions, I think, if we consider truth, as I believe Descartes and Thomas do, as fundamentally a relation between the mind and reality. If we go this route, the purpose of the truth rule is not to build a bridge from a level of propositions to a level of reality; rather, the rule says that when I am cognizing some reality clearly and distinctly, the judgments I am inclined to make "adequate" me with that reality. On this interpretation of the truth rule, clarity and distinctness come out to be a mark of my *thinking* well about some *thing*, that is, of my *understanding* some *thing*. So interpreted, the rule (as it concerns judgment) says that when I have done so, the judgments that I am inclined to make "adequate" me with things.

The reason that I introduce the qualification "as it concerns judgment" here is that, although this is not made obvious in the Fourth Meditation, Descartes also takes the truth rule to ensure that when I am cognizing clearly and distinctly, there *is* a reality—a something, not a nothing—that I am cognizing. That he holds this becomes clear from the way he argues for true and immutable natures (alluded to a couple of paragraphs above) in the Fifth Meditation (see, in particular, V.¶6).

There is one other point about truth that, although not directly relevant to the Fourth Meditation, is still worth keeping in mind. In the medieval tradition, *true* is a transcendental quality. This means that truth, like unity and good, is coextensive with being. Consider, for example, unity. Each being is one, that is, undivided. (Indeed, a principal way in which corporeal beings go out of existence is through division, i.e., the dissolution of parts.) Although being is coextensive with unity, to say of a being that it is one is not redundant. What the *one* expresses is the lack of internal division, which is not the same thing as what *being* expresses. Or consider again *good*. To be good is to be the object of an appetite, to be desirable. To hold that all beings are good, then, is to say that all beings have this

relation to an appetitive faculty. Again, although good and being are coextensive, to say of a being that it is good is not redundant, because what
good expresses, namely, a certain relation to an appetitive faculty, is not
the same as what *being* expresses. *True* is a transcendental property that
works more like *good* than *one*, in that it expresses a certain relation that
each being bears to something else rather than something about the being's internal structure. What *true* expresses, in particular, is a relation to
an intellect, namely, the tendency that things have to enter into a relation
of "adequation" with an intellect. Conversely, a false thing is something
that resists entering into such a relation. There are no false things, then,
in relation to God's intellect, but there are false things in relation to the
human intellect. Fool's gold, for example, has a tendency to mislead the
human intellect (although Thomas insists that even here the error itself
resides "principally in the soul's judgment"). From the fact that truth involves a relation to the intellect, Aquinas infers that "if, by impossible
supposition [since the existence of God's intellect is necessary], intellect
did not exist and things did continue to exist, then the essentials of truth
would in no way remain."

The natural challenge to the claim that *good* is a transcendental property of being is, of course, the worry that there seem to be beings that
are not good, that is, beings that are evil. The canonical response to this
challenge is to parse evil in such a way that it turns out to be an absence
of being, perfection, or reality, so that, for example, what is bad in disease is an absence of order in a living thing, or what is bad in a murder is
an absence of order in the murderer's practical system (a violent temper,
misplaced priorities, etc.). (Later we'll see Descartes make use of this response.) The natural challenge to the claim that *true* is a transcendental
property comes from the opposite direction. It is not that there are beings that are unable to enter in the "adequation" relation with the intellect; rather, it is that the "adequation" seems to extend even further, to
nonbeings. Aquinas responds to this objection by saying, "Being is, in
some way, predicated of non-being in so far as non-being is apprehended
by the intellect. For, as the Philosopher says, the negation or privation of
being may, in a sense, be called being" (DV Q. 1, A. 1, ad 7). I take this to
mean that, for Aquinas, when I judge that Homer is blind, the absence of
his sight that is apprehended by my intellect counts as a sort of being.

Although Aquinas does not make this point (at least, not here), even
when the intellect apprehends nonbeing, it does so by operating on various *beings* it has apprehended: so blindness, technically a privation in the
scholastic scheme of things, is apprehended as the absence of some being
(e.g., sight) in a being (e.g., a human) that by its nature is meant to see.
So in order to judge that Homer is blind, one has to have apprehended
Homer, sight, and human nature. It is fairly clear that Descartes has been

thinking along similar lines in the *Meditations*. It was suggested, for example, in the comparison between thought and painting in the First Meditation that our ability to form thoughts of things seems to depend on there being certain "true [*vera*]" things out of which all our thoughts (whether "true" or "false") are composed. I think this is also connected with Descartes's difficult suggestion in the Second Meditation that in a world in which nothing existed there would be almost no truth ("Perhaps just this one thing, that nothing is certain"). (Notice that part of the reason for the meditator's bleak assessment is that at that juncture she has yet to recognize that there might be the "true and immutable natures" already mentioned, those "somethings" and "not nothings" that do not depend on the existence of any material things.)

Let's turn to the text of the Fourth Meditation.

¶¶ 1–5. INTRODUCTION AND PRELIMINARY TREATMENT OF

THE PROBLEM

In ¶1, the meditator reports that she has made progress "leading my mind from the senses," so much so that she now has "no difficulty in turning my mind away from imaginable things and towards things which are objects of the intellect alone and are totally separate from matter." (What would be most surprising in this to a scholastic Aristotelian, of course, is not that she is able to think of immaterial beings such as the mind and God, but that, as Descartes is implying here, she has learned to do this in a way that does not require her to turn to phantasms.) Her newfound cognition of God brings with it new hope: "And now, from this contemplation of the true God, in whom all the treasures of wisdom the sciences lie hidden, I think I can see a way forward to the knowledge of other things."

In ¶2, Descartes begins his forward march toward the knowledge of other things by arguing that "it is impossible that God should ever deceive me" because deception is a sign of malice or weakness (and so, presumably, incompatible with God's benevolence or omnipotence). (To be clear, the claim here is not that it would be *wrong* for God to deceive us; rather, it is that deception would be inconsistent with certain aspects of God's nature. Although Descartes eventually conducts the discussion in terms of whether we have "cause for complaint [*causam conquerendi*]" against how God made us, I believe the problem of finding a metaphysics for error is what is fundamental here, as opposed to that of justifying the fairness of God's ways to us, to the extent that these can be separated.) The claim that deception is a sign of weakness or malice and so incompatible with God's benevolence or omnipotence was not obvious to all of Descartes's readers, and the authors of the Second and Sixth Objections pressed him on the point, basing their concern especially on what they took be scriptural indication that God does deceive from time to time. The philosophical issue is not perhaps as clear as Descartes takes it to be, depending in part on how broadly one construes deception. The main question here is, Would an omnipotent and benevolent being see fit, for whatever reason, to produce a universe that contained a creature who when using its cognitive faculties to the best of its abilities would err (and so, a creature who was subject to a sort of mistake that it could not even in principle detect)? Descartes's answer is no, an omnipotent and benevolent being would find a way of achieving whatever it wanted without resorting to this particular sort of disorder.

In ¶3, Descartes extracts the following consequence from God's not being a deceiver:

> Now, I experience [*experior*] in myself a faculty of judgement [*judicandi*] which, like everything else which is in me, I certainly received from God. And since God does not wish to deceive me, he surely did not give me the kind of faculty which would ever enable me to go wrong while using it correctly. (7:53–54; 2:37–38)

Although much remains to be filled in here—What is this faculty of judgment? What is it to use this faculty correctly?—Descartes regards the inference as sound. That is, it follows from God's not being a deceiver (which in turn follows from God's not being malevolent or weak) that my faculty of judgment cannot go wrong when I use it correctly.

The meditator does not yet understand what this conclusion means, as is evident from the following mistaken inference she is inclined to draw:

> There would be no further doubt on this issue were it not that what I have just said appears to imply that I am incapable of ever going wrong. For if everything that is in me comes from God, and he did not endow me with a faculty for making mistakes [*errandi facultatem*], it appears that I can never go wrong. (¶4; 7:54; 2:38)

The inference, as is signaled by the "appears to imply," is erroneous for two reasons: the meditator drops the "when I use it correctly" qualification from the conclusion in ¶3; at the same time she supposes that in order to go wrong God must have given her a faculty *for* making mistakes, an *errandi facultatem*. The two are closely related: a faculty for making mistakes would be a faculty that generates error when used "correctly," so if error requires a special "mistake-making power," it would be the case that in order for me to err I must have been endowed by God with a faculty that enables me to go wrong when used correctly.

The rest of ¶4 is devoted to sorting out the confusion in the meditator's position:

> And certainly, so long as I think only of God, and turn my whole attention to him, I can find no cause of error or falsity. But when I turn back to myself, I know by experience that I am prone to countless errors. On looking for the cause of these errors, I find that I possess not only a real and positive idea of God, or a being who is supremely perfect, but also what may be described[11] as a negative idea of nothingness, or of that which is farthest removed from perfection. I realize I am, as it were, something intermediate between God and nothingness, between supreme being and nonbeing: my nature is such that in so far as I was created by the supreme being, there is nothing in me through which I may be deceived or be led into error [per quod fallar aut in error inducar]; but in so far as I am not myself the supreme being I am lacking in countless respects, it is no wonder that I make mistakes. I understand, then [ita], that error as such is not something real [reale] which depends on God, but merely a defect [defectum]. Hence my going wrong does not require me to have a faculty specially bestowed on me by God; it simply happens as a result of the fact that the faculty of true judgement [verum judicandi] which I have from God is not infinite. (7:54; 2:38)

Here Descartes draws on a certain amount of traditional metaphysics. I fall somewhere in between "supreme being" and "nothingness." Moreover, everything I receive from God is positive, so "there is nothing in me" (which has the force here, I think, of "there is nothing in my nature") that is actively pointing me toward error. Still, I am not myself the supreme being, and there is much that it has that I don't have. One of the things that God has that I don't have is immunity from error. (Descartes is not saying here that God differs from *every* created thing in this way: he clearly indicates that God could have created me so that I would be immune from error [¶¶5, 15].) As I link my vulnerability to error with my not being the supreme being and so with my not having every reality or perfection, I notice that error itself is not a reality ("not something real") but an absence of reality ("a defect"). This resolves the problem raised at the outset of the paragraph: if error is not a reality, it does not require a special faculty dedicated to its production, a faculty, as the meditator put it at the beginning of the paragraph, "for" making errors. It does not require a faculty whose proper or correct use leads to error.

Notice that the position that Descartes develops here depends on a commitment to an Aristotelian, broadly speaking, "teleological" way of thinking about faculties. Faculties are not, as it were, metaphysically neutral. Perfection or reality is privileged with respect to faculties. When a new perfection or reality enters the universe, there has to be a faculty to account for its production, a faculty "for" making that perfection or reality. So, for example, since being able to see is a reality or a perfection (what an Aristotelian might call an "excellence") but blindness is not, there is a faculty of sight but no faculty of blindness or unsight. Notice also, then, that the way in which Descartes thinks about the mind and its faculties differs sharply from the way in which he thinks about body. The mind, for Descartes, is structured more or less along the lines of a traditional Aristotelian substance, with a constellation of related faculties or powers, organized around positive goals, reality, or ends that these faculties may on any given occasion realize or fail to realize. Bodies, by way of contrast, are simply patterns of matter in motion in *res extensa*, operating (if that's the right word) through the laws of motion. Descartes is much less comfortable with "faculty talk" in the context of corporeal goings-on (activities, passivities).

Having made this point about the metaphysics or ontology of error, Descartes now refocuses the inquiry:

> But this is still not entirely satisfactory. For error is not a pure negation, but rather a privation or lack of some cognition [*carentia cujusdam cognitionis*] which somehow should be in me. And when I concentrate on the nature of God, it seems impossible that he should have placed in me a faculty which is not perfect of its kind [*in suo genere perfecta*], or which is deprived of [*privata*] some perfection which it ought to have. The more skilled the craftsman the more perfect the work produced by him; if this is so, how can anything produced by the supreme creator of all things not be absolutely perfect [*omnibus numeris absolutum*: the French is *parfait & entierement acheué en toutes partes*]? There is, moreover, no doubt that God could have given me a nature such that I was never mistaken; again, there is no doubt that he always wills what is best. Is it then better that I should make mistakes than that I should not do so? (IV.¶5; 7:54–55; 2:38)

As the concerns voiced in this paragraph govern the remainder of the Fourth Meditation, it is worth considering carefully what is on the meditator's mind. I think she has basically two questions. First, is my vulnerability to error evidence that I was not created "perfect and complete in all respects"? Second, in view of the fact that God could have created me so that I would never be mistaken, why didn't God? The first question elicits a fuller characterization of my nature as a being capable of making judgments; it propels most of the remainder of the Fourth Meditation. The second, to the extent that it is distinct from the first, seems less central (it is perhaps touched upon in ¶7 and addressed, I think, in ¶15).

To understand the first concern, we need to be comfortable with the traditional distinction between a privation and a negation. In the

Aristotelian tradition, a negation was a simple absence of a reality, perfection, or being: a rock lacks the ability to see; blindness is a negation with respect to the rock. Privation tended to be used in two ways. First, it can mean a reality, perfection, or being that a thing ought by nature to possess but lacks, such as blindness in a dog. Second, it can mean a perfection that a thing is capable of taking on, and does not presently have, such as warmth in a cold rock: rocks are not by their nature supposed to be hot, but they can be hot. (In contrast, rocks neither ought by nature to see nor are able to see.) I think it is clear from Descartes's characterization of privation as the absence of some cognition "which somehow should [*deberet*] be in me" that he has in mind something closer to the first than the second meaning of privation.[12]

Now, privation, taken in the first way, is measured against a thing's nature or kind: blindness in a dog is a privation because a dog is something that by its nature, or by the kind of thing it is, ought to be able to see. It involves a sense of completeness or being perfected (i.e., being "made through"), which can be applied to the individual as a whole (the dog) or to some faculty of the dog (e.g., sensory faculty). We can discern this backdrop for privation in Descartes's remark that "it seems impossible that he [God] should have placed in me a faculty which is not perfect of its kind [*in suo genere perfecta*], or be deprived of [*privata*] some perfection which it ought [*debita*] to have." I believe the difficult Latin phrase toward the end of the passage, *omnibus numeris absolutum*, carries with it a sense of completion[13] (as Duc de Luynes's French translation, *parfait & entierement acheué en toutes partes*, "perfect and entirely achieved in all parts," suggests more strongly).

It may seem curious to see Descartes appeal to the idea of a kind or of being completed and perfected when there is only one individual around to supply the baseline, namely the meditator. One might think that the fact that a blind dog or a three-legged dog is not perfect or has a faculty that is not perfect of its kind, is witnessed mainly by the fact that there are other members of the species that see and have four legs. To be sure, this is one way to determine defect, but not the only one. The fact that a three-legged dog hobbles as it does provides another way of getting on to the fact that a three-legged dog has a faculty not perfect of its kind, without consulting other members of the kind. Similarly, the fact that a creature is possessed of a faculty of locomotion that it is unable to use effectively because it is unable to take in information about its environment might provide an indication that it is supposed to be able to take in such information and that therefore its senses are defective.

Privation, then, goes with an absolute or noncomparative sense of being perfect or being complete: the blind dog is, as it were, internally disordered, without reference to anything else.[14] So to claim that error is a privation is to claim that error involves such disorder. Although Descartes takes this as obvious, one could support the point as follows. Truth is the proper object of judgment. This is not to say that we are always able to discern the truth (it may prove too difficult for us), but that we always aim at truth. Therefore, when we judge falsely, something has gone wrong. We aimed at truth and got falsity (aimed at "adequation" and got "inadequation"). So judging falsely (unlike, for example, remaining in ignorance) is a privation. In any case, the meditator's worry is that, in view of error's being a privation, the fact that she sometimes errs is a mark of some imperfection in her natural endowments, in her nature as a thinking thing (in, as Descartes puts it at VI.¶15, the totality of things bestowed upon her by God insofar as she is a thinking thing).

So the problem raised by the question "[H]ow can anything produced by the supreme creator of all things not be absolutely perfect?" concerns the internal coherence or integrity of the structure of my mind and its faculties. As I reflect on error, does it seem that I have a nature like that of a three-legged dog (as understood by an Aristotelian), whose hobbling indicates that something is missing; or is error compatible with my nature being whole in all respects? In order to discern exactly what the disorder involved in error is and how it comes about, we must move from the general considerations about being and nonbeing put forward in ¶4 and consider the internal structure of judgment. When we have understood these things better, will error be revealed to be something that depends on a defect in the original equipment, given to us by God, or be shown instead to be something that arises postfactory, so to speak?

¶¶6–7. A PRELIMINARY OBSERVATION ABOUT
THE NATURE OF THE INQUIRY

After recognizing in ¶5 that error is a privation and not simply a negation, we are left with two questions: (1) How is it that error, a privation, enters the universe without its being the case that my nature is imperfect or defective? (2) Why does God allow error into the universe at all ("Is it . . . better that I should make mistakes than that I should not do so?")? In ¶6 Descartes begins his treatment of these questions by suggesting that in view of the incomprehensible nature of God we ought not expect to "understand the reasons for some of God's actions; and there is no call to doubt his existence if I happen to find that there are certain things which I do not comprehend why or how they were made by him" (IV.¶6; 7:55; 2:38–39). As noted at the beginning of this chapter, this comment indicates something important about the spirit in which the Fourth Meditation proceeds. Descartes is telling us that none of the results secured so far—in particular, my cognition that God, a supremely perfect being, exists and created me—are contingent on my ability to answer either of these questions. After all, I clearly saw in the Third Meditation that God exists and created me, and I have a general, if not very satisfying, explanation for why I might not be able to answer our two questions.

All the same, there would, from the point of view of the larger project of the *Meditations*, be a serious cost to my being unable to answer (1), which involves understanding how error interacts with nature. For without such an understanding, it is hard to see how I might defend the truth rule, that is, the "general rule that whatever I perceive clearly and distinctly is true" (III.¶2; 7:35; 2:24). In order to defend the rule, I need a better picture of exactly what happens when I err. The cost of not establishing the truth rule would be considerable for Descartes, because, as he will explain in the Fifth Meditation, the knowledge that everything that I clearly and distinctly perceive is true is an important ingredient in what he calls *scientia*. The advancement of Descartes's programmatic aims requires a substantive answer to (1).

Question (2) is less important from the point of view of Descartes's strategic objectives. And, as a matter of fact, what Descartes says about this problem remains at a fairly abstract level. In ¶7, he suggests that the perfection of the entire universe may require things that when taken by themselves would seem imperfect (e.g., things liable to err). His final answer to this question, which comes in ¶15, does not take us very much further:

> Had God made me this way [so that I should never err], then I can easily understand that, considered as a totality, I would have been more perfect than I am now. But I cannot therefore deny that there may in some way be more perfection in the universe as a whole because some of its parts are not immune from error, while others are immune, than there would be if all the parts were exactly alike. And I have no right to complain that the role God wished me to undertake in the world is not the principal one or the most perfect of all. (7:61; 2:42–43)

We might observe, finally, that in ¶6 Descartes makes in passing a frequently cited remark about final causality:

> For since I now know that my nature is very weak and limited, whereas the nature of God is immense, incomprehensible and infinite, I also know without more ado that he is capable of countless things whose causes are beyond my knowledge. And for this reason alone I consider the customary search for final causes to be totally useless in physics; there is considerable rashness in thinking myself capable of investigating the purposes of God. (7:55; 2:39)

It is a little odd to see this remark about final causality tucked away in a discussion of the problem of error. If I may speculate, the emphasis on the distinction between privation and negation in the previous paragraph may have elicited this comment. The notion of privation— an absence of a perfection that ought to be in a thing—is bound up with a conception of a thing's nature that sets the standards for how that thing ought to be. A dog ought to be able to see or to run on four legs; if it cannot, its sensitive faculties or locomotive faculties are defective. Descartes is quite at home with this way of thinking when it comes to the human mind: it has faculties that are supposed to cooperate in certain ways to achieve certain ends, which faculties may be used more or less well (less well, when I try to use the imagination to cognize God or the mind; more well, when I use the imagination to help me with a geometrical problem, or use the mind alone to cognize itself or God). In these respects, the mind, for Descartes, as noted earlier, is like a traditional, broadly speaking, teleologically ordered Aristotelian substance.

But Descartes does not, of course, view things found in *res extensa* in the same light. To anticipate a story that we will consider more fully later, Descartes lays out in VI.¶¶17–18 the position that when we say a purely corporeal system deviates from its nature (*a natura sua deflectere*) or has a disordered nature (*natura . . . corrupta*), we are using the term *nature* in an extended way, so that it refers to the system in virtue of extrinsic features (its relations to other things) rather than marking something in the system's internal constitution (i.e., "something which is in reality [*vera*] found in the things [*rebus*]"). In particular, this use of nature is extrinsic because its application requires that we compare the system with various notions we have about a "well made" or "healthy" system (which notions depend on comparing the system either with other systems that strike us as similar or with the intentions of its maker). These comparisons are neither here nor there as far as the internal natural operation of the system goes: everything that happens in the system happens strictly through the laws of motion. (So, as noted above, since Descartes thinks of a dog as such a system, he would be uncomfortable with my use of the example of a three-legged dog to illustrate the idea of a privation; attribution of a privation would rest on an idea of the dog's nature that is extrinsic to the mechanistic goings-on in the animal.) Now, in the Fourth Meditation, Descartes is not ready yet to explain why physical systems are not structured around final causes or ends, but he does not want to leave the impression that he thinks notions like privation and final cause have application throughout reality. It is for these reasons, I conjecture, that he decides to make a brief remark, more or less in passing, about final causality in physics.

As befits the occasional character of the remark, Descartes does not explain why it is rash to search for final causes in the case of physics but apparently all right to think in terms of faculties and privation when it comes to the mind (or, as we shall see later, when it comes to the composite of mind and body). It just seems that sometimes (e.g., when determining what a good judgment looks like or how the composite of mind and body ought to be set up) we have enough information to figure out how something should be, and sometimes (e.g., when determining the way a corporeal system ought to be) God's intentions prove to be unfathomable. One might also wonder whether Descartes's position does not distort his actual position on final causality and physics. I think his position is probably not that there are (or even may be) final causes in physics but that it would be foolhardy for us to try to figure out what they are; rather, I think he holds that there is nothing in a mechanical system that plays the same role as an end in an Aristotelian substance: in an Aristotelian substance, the end guides the exercise of the substance's faculties (as reflected in the slogan "No agent acts unless intending an end"), whereas everything that the Cartesian mechanical system does happens through its parts' obeying the laws of motion.

¶8. The Intellect and the Will

In ¶8, Descartes begins his account of error:

> Next, when I look more closely at myself and inquire into the nature of my errors (for these are the only evidence of some imperfection in me), I notice that they depend on two concurrent causes, namely on the faculty of cognizing [*cognoscendi*] which is in me, and on the faculty of choosing or freedom of the decision/judgment [*a facultate eligendi, sive arbitrii libertate*]; that is, they depend on both the intellect and at the same time the will [*ab intellectu & simul a voluntatem*]. (7:56; 2:39)

The rest of ¶8 falls into two parts, a shorter one concerning the intellect and a longer one on the will. The burden of each part is to show that in each case God has given us a faculty that is, as Descartes put it back in ¶5, "perfect in its kind."

Descartes begins his discussion of the intellect by explaining why error is not found in the intellect taken precisely (i.e., taken in abstraction from the will):

> For through the intellect alone I perceive only the ideas of things on which I can bring to bear judgment; and no error properly speaking [*proprie dictus*] is found in it looked at precisely [*praecise*] this way. (7:56; 2:39)[15]

Descartes elaborates by arguing that what limitations he does find in his intellect count as negations and not privations:

> For [Nam] although countless things may exist of which there are no ideas in me, it should not, strictly speaking, be said that I am deprived of these ideas, but merely that I lack them, in a negative sense. This is because I cannot produce any reason to prove that God ought to have given me a greater faculty of knowledge than he did; and no matter how skilled I understand a craftsman to be, this does not make me think he ought to have put into every one of his works all the perfections which he is able to put into some of them. (¶8; 7:56; 2:39)

The intellect lacks nothing that it ought to have, and so, to recall language that was used in ¶5, is "perfect in its kind." It may lack some perfections, but it is not imperfect.

So, according to Descartes, there is no internal demand coming from the character of my intellect that it ought to supply me with more ideas than it does (that is, that it ought to make more or different realities available for my consideration). Intellects by their nature do not lay claim to being omniscient. What may seem puzzling about our intellect, however, is not so much the quantity of my ideas (so to speak) as the quality of some of them. Some of my ideas are obscure and confused (and materially false); these ideas look, on their face, defective in the sense of privation (missing something that they should have) and not merely of negation. Descartes does have something to say about why God gave us such ideas, but he will not be ready to say it until the Sixth Meditation. There the meditator will learn that obscure and confused ideas play an important role in the preservation of the union between mind and body. For now, however, the question is left mainly to the side.[16]

Descartes's explanation of why error is not found in the intellect is brief. It leaves room for the impression that he is saying that the intellect supplies only ideas (as opposed to something ready to be judged), and ideas (as he points out in the Third Meditation) are not the sort of thing that, strictly speaking, can be false. If there is to be the possibility of falsity or error, I cannot be thinking about a triangle; rather, I have to be thinking about something like the longest side of a triangle's subtending its greatest angle. I am not sure how well this interpretation fits with the exact language of the text: after all, Descartes says that what the intellect contributes is "ideas of things on which I can bring to bear judgment [de quibus judicium ferre possum]," and it is natural to think that what I can bring judgment to bear on is not a triangle, but rather the longest side of a triangle's subtending its greatest angle. In any case, in ¶8, he describes the intellect as putting something forward "for affirmation or denial, pursuit or avoidance" and in ¶¶10–12 suggests again that the intellect presents the will with prejudgmental alternatives, for example, that the thinking nature in me is distinct from the corporeal nature or is identical with it, and that it is up to the will to embrace one or the other of these alternatives, or to refrain from judgment. His point about error not being found in the intellect does not revolve about the difference between an idea and something capable of being judged—let's say a possible judgment—but rather about the difference between merely entertaining a possible judgment and making the judgment.

The bulk of ¶8 concerns the will.[17] It falls into two parts. In the first, Descartes discusses the nature of the will; in the second, he develops a point about freedom of will and indifference.

What is a will for Descartes? Recall that Descartes wrote at the beginning of ¶8:

> Next, when I look more closely at myself and inquire into the nature of my errors (for these are the only evidence of some imperfection in me), I notice that they depend on two concurrent causes, namely the faculty of cognizing [*cognoscendi*] which is in me, and on the faculty of choosing or freedom of the decision/judgment [*a facultate eligendi, sive arbitrii libertate*]; that is, they depend on both the intellect and at the same time the will [*ab intellectu & simul a voluntatem*]. (7:56; 2:39)

In this passage Descartes refers to *voluntas* (will) and *arbitrii libertate* (freedom of decision/judgment) as if they were more or less the same thing. This is surprising. While Aquinas, for example, writes in ST I, Q. 83, A. 4, "the will [*voluntas*] and free decision/judgment [*liberum arbitrium*] are not two powers, but one," he also had fairly well developed views about how they differed, so that, roughly, *voluntas* is the basic faculty, and *liberum arbitrium*, freed decision/judgment, turns out to be an important aspect or perhaps subpower of that faculty.

We cannot get very far in understanding Descartes's thought here without first recovering some idea, in the tradition, of what a will *is* or what a faculty of free decision/judgment *is*. It is tempting to go past these questions and start with particular issues about the will, for example, whether the will, in Descartes's view, is necessitated in this or that way to do this or that, and, if it is, whether he thinks the form of necessitation in question is compatible with freedom. But Descartes's thought about the will takes place in a certain intellectual context where, for example, the idea that the will is a faculty is still taken seriously (as evidenced by his unhesitating reference to faculties in the passage already quoted). Often today the idea of a "faculty" is held in dispute. Many philosophers, I think, would prefer so far as possible to cut out faculties entirely as metaphysically suspect entities, and focus instead on individual eventlike acts, that is, individual decisions, choices, or volitions, with which they find themselves more comfortable philosophically. From the point of view of the Aristotelian this would look odd; trying to understand decisions, choices, and volitions without thinking about the will would be tantamount to trying to understand the exercise of faculty while ignoring the faculty.

AQUINAS ON WILL (*VOLUNTAS*) AND FREE DECISION/JUDGMENT
(*LIBERUM ARBITRIUM*)

For a sympathetic philosophical explication of *voluntas* and *liberum arbitrium*, I turn to Aquinas, whose writings contain an especially clear picture of what these faculties are. It is true that later thinkers departed from Aquinas in certain important ways—we will consider some of these toward the end of this section—but it seems to me that even these later discussions often began from a Thomistic framework and then proceeded to reject this or that (perhaps sometimes load-bearing) plank of that framework. (I also suspect that what Descartes learned at La Flèche would have been closer to Aquinas than to later theories, but it is hard to be sure.)

How does Aquinas view a will, a *voluntas*? A *voluntas* is a special form of appetite, a special sort of orientation toward good. According to Aquinas, running throughout all of reality is an aptitude toward good. This aptitude is expressed in different ways in different sorts of beings. For example, a tree is oriented toward the good of maintaining its own individual form and its species; its powers (e.g., nutrition and reproduction) are geared toward its seeking these goods and resting in them once possessed. Thus, the tree has "natural appetites" to assimilate nourishment and send out seed. Animals seek and possess their good in a different way from plants, because unlike plants they are able to cognize at least some of their ends; their orientation to good is through "animal appetite." Intellectual beings are related to the good in a still different way from animals, in that intellectual beings grasp their good intellectually. This distinctively intellectual orientation toward good is *voluntas* or will. Aquinas applies this framework even to God, arguing that since God is an intellectual being, God has a will:

> This aptitude to good in things without knowledge [*cognitione*] is called natural appetite. Whence also intellectual natures have a like aptitude as apprehended through its intelligible form; so as to rest therein when possessed, and when not possessed to seek to possess it, both of which pertain to the will. Hence in every intellectual being there is will, just as in every

sensible being there is animal appetite. And so there must be will in God, since there is intellect in him. (ST I, Q. 19, A. 1; see also DV Q. 23, A. 1)

A will, *voluntas*, for Aquinas, then, is simply the basic orientation toward good that is characteristic of an intellectual being.

Now, in the Aristotelian tradition, a faculty is understood through its proper object. Every will has an object, which is the good that is proper to the intellectual being in question. For example, according to Aquinas, God's will, like all wills, has an internal relation to its proper object, in this case, God's own goodness. God's will necessarily wills its proper object ("as any other faculty has a necessary relation to its proper and principal object, for instance sight to color," ST I, Q. 19, A. 3). The human will, too, has a proper object—happiness, a good characteristically suited to us—that it wills necessarily:

> Accordingly what the will necessarily wills, determined to it by a natural inclination, is the last end, happiness, and whatever is included in it: to be, knowledge of truth [*cognitio veritatis*], and the like. But it is determined to other things, not by a natural inclination, but by so disposing itself without any necessity. (DV Q. 22, A. 5)

I take the underlying philosophical idea here to have to do with what we might think of as the "constitution of the will": what it is to be a given (e.g., human) will is to seek the good appropriate to that given (e.g., human) intellectual being. It is a part of the will's nature or essence. Since an account of an essence or nature is a *ratio* or a *logos*, we might think of the connection between the will and its proper object as "logical" or "formal," so as long as we do not slip over into thinking of the relationship as empty or tautological or "merely" conceptual: in the Aristotelian tradition, it is a substantive fact about the will that it is a seeker of the good, determining the will's structure, just as it is a substantive fact about the faculty of vision that it takes in colors or the faculty of hearing that it takes in sounds.

This point about powers and their objects is worth noting because it marks something distinctive about an Aristotelian conception of a power or faculty. The primitive, quasi-logical relation between a faculty and its proper object gives an Aristotelian faculty a certain sort of metaphysical irreducibility or robustness. It is part of the reason why, I think, such faculties cannot be "reduced to" or "recovered from" their exercises: that is, we cannot begin with a collection of sequences of events, some of which are volitions, and extract out of them the will, as if the will were a logical product of volitions and circumstances. Later thinkers—for instance, Spinoza and Hume—had doubts about taking the relation of a faculty to its object as primitive in this Aristotelian way. They had doubts about the fundamental standing of the object (the good) and the idea that what is distinctive about us is the way in which we are oriented toward this object. Accordingly, they did not think of the will as a faculty. Spinoza, for example, holds that there is nothing more to the will than the totality of individual volitions (2P48S). For him, the will is merely a nominal entity (and therefore can be recovered from a being's motive tendencies), and what is distinctive of a rational being is that its motive tendencies fall into a certain pattern and not that it is attuned to the good in some special, distinctively rational, way.

According to Aquinas, a will wills its proper object necessarily.[18] This necessity is natural; it arises from the will's nature, its basic structure. Such natural necessity, the necessity of inclination, is compatible with the will's freedom. In his view, the only necessity incompatible with the will's freedom would be a necessity against its nature, a necessity of violence or force. But, according to Aquinas, it is impossible for the will to be necessitated in this way. The will, as rational appetite, works only through inclination, and so cannot will anything violently, by force:

> [I]t cannot happen that the will should will anything without having an inclination to it. Thus it is impossible for the will to will anything by force or violently even though it does will something by a natural inclination. It is therefore evident that the will does not will anything necessarily with the necessity of force, yet it does will something necessarily with the necessity of natural inclination. (DV Q. 22, A. 5)

For this reason, not even God can "force" the will (DV Q. 22, A. 8), let alone some creature (DV Q. 22, A. 9). Since only the necessity of force is incompatible with freedom, the will is always free. (This is not a point that Aquinas emphasizes; it tends to come up in objections and replies rather than in the main bodies of his responses to questions—see, e.g., DV Q. 22, A. 5, ad contra 3 and resp.)

So much for *voluntas*. How does *liberum arbitrium*, free decision/judgment, enter the picture? Our will's proper object, happiness, (as I will put it) *frames* everything that we will, but it does not *determine* everything that we do. This is because there are multiple specifications of what our happiness consists in, and there are various means by which we might attain happiness under any definite specification. Aquinas regards this indeterminacy as inherent in the condition of an intellectual being. Their relation to their will's proper object leaves much unsettled, and so they need some power for resolving this indeterminacy. This is what *liberum arbitrium* is.

We can better understand what it is by getting a better view of exactly how indeterminacy arises in the appetitive life of an intellectual being. In

DV Q. 22, A. 4, Aquinas explains how rational appetite, the appetite that is "called will [*voluntas*]," differs from sensitive appetite:

> A sensitive nature, however, being closer to God, has within itself some-thing which inclines [*inclinans*], i.e., the apprehended object of appetite. Yet this inclination is not within the control [*potestate*] of the animal which is inclined but is determined by something else. An animal is not able at the sight of something attractive not to crave it, because animals do not themselves have the mastery [*dominium*] over their own inclination. Hence "they do not act but rather are acted upon," as Damascene says. This is because the sensuous appetitive power has a bodily organ and so is nearly in the condition of matter and of corporeal things so as rather to be moved than to move.
>
> But a rational nature, being closest to God, not merely, like inanimate things, has an inclination to something, and, like a sentient nature, a mover of this inclination determined as it were extrinsically, but further so has its own inclination within its power [*potestate*] that it does not necessarily in-cline to anything appetible which is apprehended, but can incline or not incline. And so its inclination is not determined for it by anything else but by itself. This belongs to it inasmuch as it does not use a bodily organ; and so, getting farther away from the nature of what is moved, it approaches that of what moves and acts. It can come about that something deter-mines for itself its inclination to an end only if it knows the end and the bearing of the end upon the means to it. But this belongs to reason alone. Thus such an appetite, which is not determined of necessity by something else, follows the apprehension of reason. Hence, rational appetite, called will, is a power distinct from sense appetite.

On this picture, we have mastery or dominion (*dominium*) over our incli-nations in a way that the animals do not. They make judgments about what is to be done, but these judgments are instinctual and so are set for them by nature. By way of contrast, our judgments are our own, and so our activity is closer to God's than the activity of animals is.

How does Aquinas's claim about dominion and self-determination fit with his claim that we necessarily will our happiness? Well, although we necessarily will our happiness, and this basic fact about us shapes every-thing else we do, it is characteristic of a rational or intellectual orienta-tion toward the good that one must figure out for oneself in what one's happiness consists and choose the appropriate means to this end. (It might be thought that Aquinas holds that indeterminacy applies only to the selection of means, but I think it also applies to the specification of what happiness consists in. Aquinas writes in DV Q. 22, A. 7: "But man has implanted in him an appetite for the last end in general so that he naturally desires to be complete in goodness. But in just what that completeness consists, whether in virtue or knowledge or pleasure or anything else of the sort, has not been determined for him by nature.") Animals do not need to do this: when some good or some danger appears on the scene, it is as if the judgment is already made for them. For them, it is as if a judgment "Do this" or "Do that" simply pops up: when they make these judgments, they do not consider how the judgments fit into a larger scheme of things, as we do; to the extent that their judgments are coordinated, nature has done this for them.[19] Since self-determination takes place only in beings who practically reason in this reflective way—that is, who think about the specification of their ultimate end, and its relation to subsidiary ends and means—Aquinas takes there to be a deep connection between our being self-determiners and our being beings who reason: "It can come about that something determines for itself its inclination to an end only if it knows the end and the bearing of the end upon the means to it. But this belongs to reason alone."

Since judgments of an intellectual being, unlike the judgments of animals, are not determined by its nature, intellectual beings must have some power to decide some things for themselves. Unlike animals, they need the ability to get a general apprehension of the good, a cognition of the good which has a *universalem rationem* (a universal character or aspect) to "this" or "that" action. He terms this ability or power *liberum arbitrium*, free decision/judgment:

> Some things there are which act, not from any previous decision/judgment [*arbitrio*], but, as it were, [are] moved and made to act by others; just as the arrow is directed to the target by the archer. Others act from some kind of decision/judgment [*arbitrio*], but not from free decision/judgment, such as irrational animals; for the sheep flies from the wolf by a kind of judgment [*iudicio*] whereby it esteems it to be hurtful to itself: such a judgment [*iudicium*] is not a free one, but implanted by nature. Only an agent endowed with an intellect can act with a judgment [*iudicio*] that is free, in so far as it cognizes the universal character of good [*cognoscit universalem rationem boni*], from which it can judge [*judicare*] this or the other to be good. Consequently, wherever there is intellect, there is free decision/judgment [*liberum arbitrium*]. It is therefore manifest that just as there is intellect, so is there free decision/judgment [*liberum arbitrium*] in the angels, and in a higher degree than man. (ST I, Q. 59, A. 3)

I think of this *universalem rationem boni* along the lines of a general conception of good, and take Aquinas's point here to be that in order to act in light of a general conception of good (and so to aim to secure happiness), we must be able to make judgments about in what it consists (and act on those judgments). This, in turn, helps to spell out more clearly the place of *liberum arbitrium* in the self-determination characteristic of an intellectual or rational being: it must "adjudicate" among (exercise *liberum arbitrium* with respect to) various options, as it goes about resolving an indeterminate universal good into a more specific system of ends and means. And as it does this—that is, as it exercises *liberum arbitrium*—it fits its decisions/judgments into its larger conception of good, which requires that it have some understanding of ends and means, and how the latter relate to the former. Thus, *liberum arbitrium* is, at bottom, an aspect of the practical nature of an intellectual being who rationally orders its decisions and judgments in this reflective way, in the light of its understanding of the good appropriate to it:

> Unless there is something to prevent it, a motion or operation follows the appetite. Thus, if judgment of the cognitive faculty [*judicium cognitivae*] is not in a person's power but is determined for him extrinsically, neither will his appetite be in his power; and consequently neither will his motion or operation be in his power absolutely. Now judgment is in the power of the one judging in so far as he can judge about his own judgment [*potest de suo judico judicare*]; for concerning those things which are in our power, we are able to judge. But to judge about one's own judgment belongs only to reason, which reflects upon its own act [*quae super actum suum reflectitur*] and cognizes the relationships of the things which it judges and of the things through which it judges. Hence the whole root of freedom [*totius libertatis radix*] is located in reason. Consequently, a being is related to free decision/judgment [*liberum arbitrium*] in the same way as it is related to reason. (DV Q. 24, A. 2)[20]

Not surprisingly, then, Aquinas maintains that *voluntas* and *liberum arbitrium* represent different faces of the same power. The way Aquinas puts the point in DV Q. 24, A. 6, is:

> Free decision/judgment [*liberum arbitrium*] is the will itself [*ipsa voluntas*]. The term does not designate the will absolutely, however, but with reference to one of its acts, to choose [*eligere*].

And he concludes his discussion of the same question in ST I, Q. 83, A. 4, with:

> Wherefore it belongs also to the same power to will and to choose: and on this account the will [*voluntas*] and free decision/judgment [*liberum arbitrium*] are not two powers, but one.

The same power that provides an intellectual being with its orientation toward its good is also responsible for the being's ability to rationally specify its ends and means. Aquinas compares the relation of *liberum arbitrium* to *voluntas* to that of reasoning to understanding, both of which are rooted in the same power (ST I, Q. 83, A. 4; see also ST I, Q. 79, A. 8; DV Q. 24, A. 6).

According to Aquinas, we do not merit or incur blame by willing what we will necessarily. (This is true even though we freely will everything we will, including those things that we will necessarily.) That is, we do not deserve a reward or punishment for our necessary inclinations, for what we naturally desire (e.g., our ultimate end) or what belongs to the constitution of our will as such. Rather, we earn merit or incur demerit for the way we work out those general inclinations into a particular system of choices. After all, as we saw earlier, it is this that is in our power (*potestate*), under our mastery (*dominium*), in a way that the former are not. So Aquinas concludes his discussion of the question "Does a person earn merit by willing what he wills necessarily?" in this way:

> It is therefore clear that willing what anyone naturally wills is in itself neither meritorious nor blameworthy. But when it is specified to this or that, it can be either the one or the other. In this way the saints merit by desiring God and eternal life. (DV Q. 22, A. 7)

Thus, free decision/judgment plays a special role in our being meritorious or blameworthy. In fact, he argues that merit and demerit in us would not make sense without free decision/judgment (see ST I, Q. 83, A. 1 and DV Q. 24, A. 1). And we will see in what follows that Aquinas does think that under certain circumstances, namely, when fortified by divine grace, we do certain things by free decision/judgment necessarily. He does not say whether in such circumstances we will meritoriously, but since he is concerned with the condition of the blessed, after the Last Judgment, the question seems odd: it would seem that at that point the time for merit is over.

DESCARTES ON WILL (*VOLUNTAS*) AND FREE DECISION/JUDGMENT (*LIBERUM ARBITRIUM*)

I believe that, at least in broad outlines, Descartes inherited his way of thinking about powers and faculties from his Thomistic teachers. For him, the will is the power through which we, in a way that is characteristic of our nature as intellectual beings, pursue good and avoid evil. (Descartes would add, of course, that the will is the power through which we affirm truth and deny falsity.) It is a genuine power *for* doing something (pursuing good, avoiding evil; affirming truth, denying falsehood), unlike the pseudo-faculty *for* making mistakes considered briefly and dismissed in ¶4. But, of course, Descartes's views about what an intellectual being is (that is, what a mind is) differ from those of his teachers, as do his views about how intellectual beings are situated in the universe. We may expect these differences to show up in how Descartes thinks about the will and free decision/judgment.

Now, one might doubt this because Descartes's position on *God's* will is quite different from Aquinas's. Aquinas, as we have seen, holds that God's will necessarily wills its proper object ("as any other faculty has a necessary relation to its proper and principal object, for instance sight to color," ST I, Q. 19, A. 3). Descartes, by way of contrast, says in the Sixth Replies that God's will is prior to the good and the true, and so there is nothing God wills necessarily:

> It is self-contradictory to suppose that the will of God was not indiffer-
> ent from eternity with respect to everything which has happened or will
> ever happen; for it is impossible to imagine that anything is thought of in
> the divine intellect as good or true, or worthy of belief or action or omis-
> sion, prior to the decision of the divine will to make it so. (7:431–32; 2:291)

Since faculties are characterized through their proper objects, Aquinas would have found it hard to make sense of the idea that God's will is prior to the good; from his perspective, such a view makes it hard to understand just what God's will might *be*. But it is not surprising that Aquinas and Descartes part company on this point, since Descartes holds that God's power is beyond human comprehension—consider Descartes's view that God creates the eternal truths—in ways generally unrecognized by the tradition.[21]

Be that as it may, this important difference between Descartes and Aquinas over the logical relation between God's will and the good and the true is not reflected down into the realm of created intellects. For Descartes, after God has determined the good and the true, a created intellect is structured along lines similar to those envisioned by Aquinas. In particular, the created will is determined by the good and the true, along the lines that an Aristotelian-style faculty is determined by its proper object:

> But as for man, since he finds that the nature of all goodness and truth is
> already determined by God, and his will cannot tend towards anything
> else, it is evident that he will embrace what is good and true all the more
> willingly [*libentius*: gladly, agreeably], and hence more freely [*liberius*], in
> proportion as he sees more clearly. (7:432; 2:292)

For Descartes, there is a suitable object, the good (or the good and the true), which is prior to the faculty of the will and in terms of which it is defined (that is, which figures into the faculty's essence). This orientation to the good and the true belongs to a fundamental characterization of what the will is. It is not just an accident, as it were, that we embrace the good and the true; our wills are, by their very nature, good embracers and truth embracers.

One of the striking differences between the two treatments of the human will is that Descartes treats the terms *voluntas* and *liberum arbitrium* as interchangeable, whereas Aquinas does not. Near the beginning of ¶8, Descartes seems to equate a faculty of choosing (*facultate eligendi*), a faculty of freedom of decision/judgment (*facultate . . . arbitrii libertate*), and the will (*voluntatem*):

> Next, when I look more closely at myself and inquire into the nature of my errors (for these are the only evidence of some imperfection in me), I notice that they depend on two concurrent causes, namely the faculty of cognizing [*cognoscendi*] which is in me, and on the faculty of choosing or freedom of the will [*a facultate eligendi, sive arbitrii libertate*]; that is, they depend on both the intellect and at the same time the will [*ab intellectu & simul a voluntatem*]. (7:56; 2:39)

Twice more in ¶8, Descartes uses the phrase *voluntatem, sive arbitrii libertatem*, suggesting that there is no important distinction to be drawn between will and free decision/judgment. In one way, the departure from Aquinas might seem slight, because, as we noted earlier, he takes both to be the same power ("Free decision/judgment [*liberum arbitrium*] is the will itself [*ipsa voluntas*]"). But when one considers the different accounts that Aquinas gives of *voluntas* and free decision/judgment, as evidenced by the fact that in the *Summa Theologiae* and *De Veritate* each gets its own question, with different articles,[22] it would seem that there is for Aquinas, but not for Descartes, at least an important conceptual distinction (as we might put it today) between the faculty of will and free decision/judgment.

While it is possible that intervening developments in the tradition concerning *voluntas* and *liberum arbitrium* may have worked to encourage Descartes in this identification (I do not know that tradition well enough to have a view on the matter), there are in any event ways in which Descartes's general outlook makes Aquinas's way of thinking about the difference between *voluntas* and *liberum arbitrium* uncongenial. For one thing, Aquinas, as we have seen, saw the need for free decision/judgment as arising from indeterminacy in an intellectual being, who must find a means of getting from cognition of "the universal character of good [*cognoscit universalem rationem boni*]" to this or that good. As such, Aquinas's theorizing about free decision/judgment seems to reflect his basic association of the intellectual with universality, and the sensitive with particularity. Descartes does not seem to find the same metaphysical fault line running through the universe: the intellect understands the individual piece of wax, for example, no less than body in general. It is not clear that Descartes would want to cast our basic volitional condition in terms of getting from the universal to the particular. It would fit better with his general outlook to think that there are simply goods, and our job is to figure out which are more valuable than others, a task made difficult by the fact that we see some goods only obscurely. What indeterminacy there is results from our inability to see clearly.

Descartes's indeterminacy is often resolved not so much by decision or choice as by clear vision. Descartes holds that when I perceive something with sufficient clarity I cannot but embrace it (i.e., give my assent to a clearly perceived truth or pursue a clearly perceived good, and rest in it when secured). In such a situation, my will is necessarily determined to the true or the good. Now, this is a necessity that differs from either of the two sorts of necessity—necessity of force and necessity of inclination—that we encountered above in our survey of Aquinas's account of *voluntas*. It is not necessity of force, because, as Descartes emphasizes (see, e.g., IV.¶8), no external compulsion is involved. It is not necessity of inclination, because it is not part of the will's basic constitution to be inclined in this way. Rather, the inclination is contingent on the will's perceiving something clearly.

The necessity that Descartes finds in the will's determination through clear perception comes closest, I think, to a third kind of necessity that Aquinas discusses in connection with the will, in ST I, Q. 82, A. 2, where he draws an interesting comparison between necessity as it arises in theoretical reasoning and necessity as it arises in practical reasoning, that is, between the necessity of embracing certain theoretical conclusions and the necessity of embracing certain practical conclusions. In the case of theoretical reason, once we have recognized a necessary connection with first principles, our assent necessarily follows:

> Now there are some things intelligible which have not a necessary connection with the first principles; such as contingent propositions, the denial of which does not involve the denial of the first principles. And to such the intellect does not assent of necessity. But there are some propositions which have a necessary connection with the first principles: such as demonstrable conclusions, a denial of which involves the denial of the first principles. And to these the intellect assents of necessity, when once it is aware of the necessary connection of these conclusions with the principles; but it does not assent of necessity until through the demonstration it recognizes the necessity of such connection.

Something analogous happens in the case of will. Once we see that something is necessarily bound up with our final end, we necessarily will it:

> It is the same with the will. For there are certain individual goods which
> have not a necessary connection with happiness, because without them a
> man can be happy; and to such the will does not adhere of necessity. But
> there are some things which have a necessary connection with happiness,
> by means of which things man adheres to God, in Whom alone true hap-
> piness consists.

That our ultimate happiness is necessarily connected with God is something we recognize only through the certitude of the Divine Vision
(something given to the blessed in the next life through a special gift of
grace), Aquinas goes on to say:

> Nevertheless, until through the certitude of the Divine Vision the neces-
> sity of such connection be shown, the will does not adhere to God of ne-
> cessity, nor to those things which are of God. But the will of the man who
> sees God in His essence of necessity adheres to God, just as we now desire
> of necessity happiness.

Although Aquinas compares the necessity of the adherence of the will
of the blessed person to God, to the necessity with which someone
wills her own happiness, it seems to me different. The necessity by
which we will our own happiness is not the result of free choice/judg-
ment; it is in a certain sense prior to free choice/judgment, framing the
activity of that power. But the adherence to God that Aquinas has in
view here is, I think, the result of the exercise of our free choice/judg-
ment, that is, the result of the use of deliberative powers in the context
of its having been made plain to us—of its having been revealed to us
with certainty—that our true happiness lies in God. Thus Aquinas explains the condition of the blessed as a matter of *liberum arbitrium*'s
being "confirmed in good by a gift of grace" (DV Q. 24, A. 8), where
this involves reason's recognizing that "God Himself is the end to be
loved above all else" and one's not being distracted by lower appetitive
powers so as to be "drawn to something intensely." In Aquinas's famous
phrase, this special assistance—grace—does not destroy the nature of
free choice/judgment, but rather perfects it (see DV Q. 24, A. 8, objs.
1–3 and ad 1–3). We still employ free choice/judgment in specifying our
good (and the means to it), even if God, through the assistance of grace,
has made that specification so obvious to us that our decision necessarily follows.[23]

Now, Aquinas thought this sort of necessary determination of the will
could happen only with the assistance of grace; no creature can be naturally confirmed in the good (DV Q. 24, A. 7). This limitation arises from

the need of an intellectual or rational being to make its way from good in general to some particular good. Aquinas reasons as follows:

> A rational nature endowed with free choice, however, is different in its action from every other agent nature. Every other nature is ordained to some particular good, and its actions are determined in regard to that good. But a rational nature is ordained to good without further qualification. Good, taken absolutely, is the object of the will, just as truth, taken absolutely, is the object of the intellect. That is why the will reaches to the universal principle of good itself, to which no other appetite can obtain. And for this reason a rational creature does not have determined actions but is in a state of indifference in regard to innumerable actions. (DV Q. 24, A. 7)

Descartes, I take it, disagrees with this assessment of the basic condition of an intellectual being. Near the end of the Fourth Meditation, he suggests that "God could have easily brought it about that without losing my freedom and despite the limitations in my cognition [*cognitionis*], I should nevertheless never make a mistake" by, for example, having "endowed my intellect with a clear and distinct perception of everything about which I was ever likely to deliberate." If we suppose (as I think likely) that Descartes intends this endowment to be natural, then we would have a natural being who, as things turned out, was never indifferent in its use of free will, because its choice was always determined by clear perception. Beyond this, Descartes thinks that even as our nature is in fact constituted, we do from time to time perceive things so clearly that our will is necessarily determined to some truth or good, at least while we are so perceiving it.

The source of indetermination of the will for Descartes—lack of clarity—is different from the source of indetermination of the will for Aquinas—the basic metaphysical condition of the intellectual or rational being who needs to get from the general to the particular—which in turn colors their respective conceptions of *liberum arbitrium*. It helps explain why Descartes finds it easy to think that *liberum arbitrium* can be (momentarily) necessitated in this life by a clear grasp of the good (or truth) in a manner reminiscent of the way that, according to Aquinas, the *liberum arbitrium* of the blessed is determined in the next through the "certitude of the Divine Vision." Moreover, unless some special task is assigned to *liberum arbitrium*, such as getting us from a general conception to something more particular, the point of distinguishing sharply between *liberum arbitrium* and *voluntas* becomes less clear. This helps us understand why Descartes did not see the difference between them that Aquinas saw.

In the rest of ¶8, Descartes defends the claim that our wills are not defective (just as he earlier claimed that our intellects are not defective).

He does this by drawing a comparison between our will and God's will. He develops this comparison by giving a fuller account of what the will or free decision/judgment is, and explains why the form of necessitation that we have been recently considering, arising either from clear and distinct perception or through divine grace, does not interfere with freedom. Here's how that discussion begins:

> Besides, I cannot complain that the will or freedom of decision/judgment [*voluntatem, sive arbitrii libertatem*] which I received from God is not sufficiently extensive or perfect, for I, to be sure [*sane*], experience [*experior*] it to be bounded by no limits. Indeed, I think it is very noteworthy [*valde notandum*] that there is nothing else in me which is so perfect and so great that the possibility of a further increase in its perfection or greatness is beyond my understanding. If, for example, I consider the faculty of understanding, I immediately recognize that in my case it is extremely slight and very finite, and I at once form the idea of an understanding which is much greater—indeed supremely great and infinite; and from the very fact that I can form an idea of it, I perceive that it belongs to the nature of God. Similarly, if I examine the faculties of memory or imagination, or any others, I discover that in my case each one of these faculties is weak and limited, while in the case of God it is immeasurable. It is only the will, or freedom of decision/judgment [*voluntas, sive arbitrii libertatis*], which I experience in me to be so great that the idea of any greater faculty is beyond my grasp; so much so that it is above all in virtue of the will that I understand myself to bear in some way the very image and likeness of God. For although God's will is incomparably greater than mine, both in virtue of the knowledge [*cognitionis*] and power that accompany it and make it more efficacious, and also in virtue of its object, in that it ranges over a greater number of items, nevertheless it does not seem greater than mine when considered precisely and formally in itself [*in se formaliter & praecisa spectata*]. (7:56–57; 2:39–40)

Why does Descartes think our wills are unbounded in this way? Perhaps the "considered precisely and formally in itself" affords a clue. In the next sentence, we get what looks to be a definition of the will:

> This is because the will consists in this alone [*tantum in eo consistit*], that [a] we can either do or not do something (that is, to affirm or to deny, to pursue or to avoid); or better [*vel potius*] [b] it consists in this alone, that we are inclined [*feramur*] to a thing that the intellect puts forward for affirmation or denial or for pursuit or avoidance, in such a way that we experience [*sentiamus*] ourselves to be determined to it by no external force. (7:57; 2:40)

This is a difficult remark, in part on account of the *vel potius*, which suggests that [b] is something of a correction or refinement of [a]. How much of a shift is marked by this refinement?

Let's begin with [a]. This characterization of the will echoes some-thing Descartes says earlier in ¶8 when he describes the will as a faculty of choosing [facultate eligendi]. What I think Descartes has in view here is the idea that the will is what might be called a bidirectional power ("a real and positive power to determine oneself," as he puts it in a letter to Mesland [4:116; 3:234], picking up on language that Mesland had used in a previous letter), a power for doing or not doing something. Descartes does not say here that it is a power for doing or not doing in the light of an intellectual being's conception of the true or the good, but it is not unreasonable to see this as implied by what he does say elsewhere. An intellectual being's determination of its will does not take place in a vac-uum, but in the context of its reflectively seeking the true and the good, which is why our wills "cannot tend towards anything else" besides the "goodness and truth . . . determined by God" (7:432; 2:292) and why we cannot sin while clearly seeing that what we do is evil (4:117; 3:234). This bidirectional power, making us responsive to the true and the good, is very special, setting us apart, in particular, from everything in the purely physical world, where there are no bidirectional powers or powers that track (reflectively or otherwise) the true and the good.

Moreover, this bidirectional power is unbounded. The human will is like God's will in that it cannot be externally limited or circumscribed: my volitions are my volitions. The will has a certain integrity, inasmuch as nothing can be taken from it as such. Descartes argues in IV.¶14 that "since the will consists simply of one thing which is, as it were, indivisi-ble, it seems that its nature rules out the possibility of anything being taken away from it." (The claim about the will's being unbounded seems closely related to the one about its integrity: if there are two wills A and B, such that A is an "augmented" version of B, then B would be a "di-minished" version of A, i.e., A with something taken away from it, and that creates at least logical space for the possibility of something's being taken away from will A.) I think the main idea here is similar to Aquinas's idea that the will cannot be forced to will something, not even by God, because the will operates only through inclination (DV Q. 22, Aa. 5, 8, and 9). In this respect, there is no difference between my will and God's.

Now this raises a question. Perhaps it is true that my will, by its very nature, cannot be externally necessitated. But might not it be the case that my will is internally necessitated in a way that infringes on its free-dom, and shows that my will is less great than God's—perhaps even defective in some way? Descartes is concerned with addressing this ques-tion as he moves from [a] to [b]. What matters in a will's operation is that it not be externally determined; being internally determined is no defect in the will. Indeed, to think otherwise is to get matters upside down: the will functions at its best when it is determined by a clear view of the good and the true. (Notice that the internal necessitation that is up for consideration here is akin to the necessity Aquinas discusses in ST I, Q. 82, A. 3, which arises when someone appreciates the necessary connection between God and happiness through the "certitude of the Divine Vision.") Descartes explains:

> In order to be free, there is no need for me to be inclined [*ferri*] both ways; on the contrary, the more I incline [*propendeo*] in one direction—either because I clearly understand that reasons of truth and goodness point that way, or because of a divinely produced disposition of my inmost thoughts— the freer is my choice. Neither divine grace nor natural knowledge [*cognitio*] ever diminishes freedom; on the contrary, they increase and strengthen it. But the indifference I feel when there is no reason pushing me in one direction rather than another is the lowest grade of freedom; it is evidence not of any perfection of freedom, but rather a defect in knowledge or a kind of negation. For if I always saw clearly what was true and good, I should never have to deliberate about the right judgement or choice; in that case, although I should be wholly free, it would be impossible for me ever to be in a state of indifference. (IV.¶8; 7:57–58; 2:40)

So it would be wrong to view the will's determination by reasons of truth and goodness, as a pointing to some defect in the will, some lack of freedom or of some other good. Quite the contrary. It is when the will is least determined by a clear view of the true and the good that it is in its worst condition. (Notice that there is here an implicit rejection of Aquinas's idea that there is some indeterminacy endemic to our natural condition as intellectual beings oriented toward the "good without further qualification," DV Q. 24, A. 7; the only source of the indeterminacy is the lack of clear perception.)

Now, what happens to the bidirectionality here? As Descartes slides over to [b] from [a] via the *vel potius*, "or better," is he quietly taking back the bidirectionality in [a]?[24] I don't think so. At the beginning of ¶8 he characterizes the will as a faculty of choosing, and I think he means it. The point is that an internal determination does not eradicate the bidirectionality (as arguably a *per impossibile* external determination would by taking one of the options away from me). When something becomes very clear to me, it is not as if I somehow *lose* my ability to go in one of the two directions. For example, when, as I reflect on the cogito or some geometrical argument, the matter becomes so obvious that "I could not but judge [*non potui quidem non judicare*]" in a certain way (¶10), this does not *impair* my ability to choose—it is not, for example, as if my ability to go for one of the options becomes atrophied and withers away. I am still making a choice between the two options, and so my bidirectional power is preserved throughout the exercise. Far from eradicating the basic bidirectional power, clarity strengthens it, leading to its best possible operation. (Even for Aquinas, it is the *liberum arbitrium*, the power of free decision/judgment, of the creature that is determined through the certitude of the Divine Vision, and God's gift of grace does not destroy the power but perfect it.)

To be sure, we need to be careful about how we characterize the bidirectional ability. It is evidently not the ability to "do or not do something (that is, affirm or deny or pursue or avoid)" under any conditions. Since I cannot but judge that three angles of a triangle sum to two right angles when I am clearly and distinctly perceiving a demonstration of this fact, I do not have the ability to suspend judgment or deny that three angles of a triangle sum to two right angles in all circumstances.[25] But, I take it, for Descartes, the appropriate way to characterize the ability is not as the ability to affirm or deny *p* under any conditions C (or to pursue or avoid A under any conditions C), even where conditions C involve our denying a plain truth (or forgoing a manifest good). There is no such thing as an "ability" to deny the plain truth (or even not to respond to the plain truth), because denying (or failing to respond to) the truth is not an achievement, but a failure to achieve something. A power for denying the plain truth would be like a power for getting sick, or a power for making mistakes.[26]

Finally, as we have seen, in Descartes's view, as the operation of the will goes, so goes freedom. That is, when the will is running at its smoothest, perceiving clearly good and truth and unencumbered by doubt and uncertainty, it functions at its freest. This is emphasized in the continuation of ¶8, where Descartes writes that "the indifference I feel when there is no reason pushing me in one direction rather than another is the lowest grade of freedom; it is evidence not of any perfection of freedom, but rather a defect in knowledge or a kind of negation." He also writes in the Sixth Replies:

> But as for man, since he finds that the nature of all goodness and truth is already determined by God, and his will cannot tend towards anything else, it is evident that he will embrace what is good and true all the more willingly [*libentius*: gladly, agreeably], and hence more freely [*liberius*], in proportion as he sees more clearly. (7:432; 2:292)

The view I have just sketched is philosophically familiar, and most commentators would agree that it is the position that seems to predominate (at least on the surface) in Descartes's texts, especially those written around the time of the *Meditations*. I believe Descartes has special reason to be drawn toward this position, because he thinks of belief as a matter of willing and (I think) finds it unintelligible how one, in the midst of a cogito-like experience, could fail to give one's assent to what one so

clearly perceives. Even so, some commentators, philosophically dissatis-
fied with what be might called the "necessitarian" cast of this position,
have found another—what might be called more "voluntarist"—position
in Descartes's writings.

Lilli Alanen has developed what seems to me the most historically informed and philosophically sensitive interpretation along these lines. Alanen points out that the Thomistic background that I have been drawing
on was the subject of considerable controversy in the fourteenth and fif-
teenth centuries, and suggests that Descartes's position is in certain respects close to that of Duns Scotus. Scotus held that the will has an active
power of turning away from any good, that is, a power of not eliciting an
act no matter what good it is presented with, even happiness. He held
that each of us can experience this in ourselves; and that such a power is
required for our volitions to be contingent, which is required in turn for
them to be free.[27]

Alanen believes that Descartes held such a position (we will consider
the texts she draws on in a moment). In particular, she reads Descartes as
holding that when I am clearly perceiving a truth or a good, I have the
power to turn away from that truth or good, the power not to elicit a
volitional act with respect to that truth or good. This is not to say that I
can give my assent to something I clearly perceive to be false or pursue
something I clearly perceive to be bad (I cannot); it is to say that I can, if
I so choose, refuse to assent to something I clearly perceive to be true or
refuse to pursue something I clearly perceive to be good. This ability to
opt out is essential, as Alanen sees it, to my being free and morally worthy or unworthy with respect to some action: "Having the option, even
for a moment, to withhold assent to clear and distinct perceptions is all
that is required for moral agency and for making continued adherence to
those perceptions a possible ground for desert" (246).

To be sure, attributing to Descartes's picture of will this active ability
to hold back does have the benefit of doing something to satisfy the
sense of some philosophers that in order for something that one did to
be a fair subject for moral evaluation, one must have been able (in some
deep, all-things-considered way) to have done otherwise. I am not sure,
however, how closely, in the tradition, the movement of the will's being
free tracks its being subject to moral evaluation. In Aquinas, for example,
they seem to come apart. Aquinas seems to have thought that everything
the will does, including the things it does necessarily, it does freely, because only the necessitation of force impedes freedom, and the will cannot be forced (even by God).[28] But Aquinas also held that we incur merit
and demerit only for those things we do not necessarily will (DV Q. 22,
A. 7), thereby creating some distance between what we do freely and
what we do meritoriously or in a blameworthy manner. I think Descartes

may have held a similar view. In particular, we don't earn merit for responding to clear perception *per se*; what merit we have here derives from putting ourselves and keeping ourselves in a position where we clearly perceive. This seems to me the position he espouses in a letter to Mesland of 2 May 1644:

> And we may earn merit even though, seeing very clearly what we must do, we do it infallibly, and without any indifference, as Jesus Christ did during his earthly life. Since we cannot always attend perfectly to what we ought to do, it is good action to pay attention and thus to ensure that our will follows so promptly the light of our understanding that there is no longer any indifference at all. (4:117; 3:234)

It is hard to be sure whether the second sentence is meant to be a full explanation of the merit recorded in the first, but if it is, then Descartes's thought would be that what merit there is in doing what we see clearly should be done comes from our "paying attention," and (in this life) working so as to continue to pay attention. (I don't see signs, in Descartes's explanation of the merit involved in doing what one sees clearly, of the merit deriving from an ability to refuse to go along with something that one is currently perceiving clearly.)

In addition, I do not find the Scotus position philosophically attractive, especially when worked out within the Cartesian context. On a theoretical level, it is hard to understand how an active power to refuse to affirm a clearly perceived truth or pursue a clearly perceived good can be integrated with the rest of the will's principles of operation, that is, can be folded into the central framing concern for happiness. It seems to stand outside that project, and so has the appearance of something that has been grafted on, so that we can earn moral credit for what we do (in the relatively narrow range of cases) where we perceive clearly (perhaps this reaction simply reveals my Thomistic leanings). On a more concrete level, Scotus claims that we are familiar with this power from ordinary experience, but I find this dubious, especially given the sort of things Descartes has in mind. Since, for Descartes, one of the principal operations of the will is assent, this would mean that I am familiar from experience with an ability to refrain from believing that I exist while seeing clearly all of the considerations relevant to the cogito; or, again, that I am familiar from experience with an ability to refrain from believing the Pythagorean theorem as I work out its demonstration for myself, transparently noting all the relevant relationships in the constructions before my mind's eye. Perhaps we can do such things; I do not know, but I find it hard to think that Descartes thinks we are familiar with such an ability from experience, because what he seems to emphasize about those situations is their irresistibility.

There are texts that support Alanen's interpretation. One is found in *Principles* I, 37, where Descartes writes, "The supreme perfection of man is that he acts freely or voluntarily [*libere, sive per voluntatem*], and it is this which makes him deserve praise or blame [*laude vel vituperio*]":

> The extremely broad scope of the will is part of its very nature. And it is a supreme perfection in man that he acts voluntarily, that is, freely; this makes him in a special way the author of his actions and deserving of praise for what he does. We do not praise automata for accurately producing all the movements they were designed to perform, because the production of these movements occurs necessarily. It is the designer who is praised for constructing such carefully-made devices; for in constructing them he acted not out of necessity, but freely [*non necessario, sed libere*]. By the same principle, when we embrace the truth, our doing so voluntarily is much more to our credit than would be the case if we could not do otherwise [*quia voluntartie id agimus, quam si non possemus non amplecti*]. (8A:18–19; 1:205)

I agree that this passage has a much more voluntarist ring than what we find in the Fourth Meditation. Indeed, one might think that Descartes changed his views on freedom from a necessitarian, compatibilist conception to a more voluntarist, incompatibilist one between the *Meditations* and the *Principles*. I find this unlikely, however, because just a few articles later, we get a more "necessitarian" statement, toward the end of *Principles* I, 43:

> It is certain, however, that we will never mistake the false for the true provided we give our assent only to what we clearly and distinctly perceive. I say that this is certain, because God is not a deceiver, and so the faculty of perception which he has given us cannot incline to falsehood; and the same goes for the faculty of assent, provided its scope is limited to what is clearly perceived. And even if there were no way of proving this, the minds of all of us have been so moulded by nature that whenever we perceive something clearly, we spontaneously give our assent to it and cannot in any way doubt but that it is true [*nullo modo possimus dubitare quin sit verum*]. (8A:21; 1:207)

Is there a way to understand *Principles* I, 37 that is consistent with *Principles* I, 43? I think the simplest thing to do here is to read it along the lines of Descartes's explanation, in the May 1644 Mesland letter, of the merit in "infallibly" doing what one perceives clearly one ought to do as deriving from the difficulty of getting ourselves in a state of clear perception and keeping ourselves there. We deserve praise or earn merit when we do or assent to what we clearly perceive we should do or assent to, because we are not necessitated to "pay attention" and perceive clearly

what we should do or assent to, or, once we have done so, to continue to
do it. In fact, both are often difficult. And this is true even though while
we perceive clearly what to do or believe, we necessarily act or give our
assent.

The strongest support for Alanen's interpretation comes from a letter
of 9 February 1645 to Mesland that has attracted considerable scholarly
attention over the years. In that letter, Descartes appears to say that we
can deny a plainly seen truth or forgo a manifestly perceived good, albeit
with difficulty, provided we have sufficient reason to do so:

> But perhaps others mean by "indifference" a positive faculty of determin-
> ing oneself to one or other of two contraries, that is to say, to pursue or
> avoid, to affirm or deny. I do not deny that the will has this positive faculty.
> Indeed, I think it has it not only with respect to those actions to which it is
> not impelled by any evident reasons on one side or the other, but also with
> respect to all other actions; so that when a very evident reason moves us in
> one direction, although morally speaking we can hardly move in the con-
> trary direction, absolutely speaking we can. For it is always open to us to
> hold back from pursuing a clearly known good, or from admitting a clearly
> perceived truth, provided we consider it a good thing to demonstrate the
> freedom of our will by so doing. (4:173; 3:245)[29]

As Alanen points out, Descartes's talk of "holding back" here is reminiscent of Scotus's idea of an active power to not to elicit a volition.

However, there are other ways in which this passage might be read.
The letter admittedly suggests that I can hold back from pursuing a
clearly known good, or from admitting a clearly perceived truth, *while*
continuing to perceive clearly the thing in question to be a good or a
truth. But it does not explicitly say this, and, as Anthony Kenny has suggested, it is possible to think that holding back from a clearly known
good or a clearly perceived truth requires that one first *cease* perceiving
clearly the good or truth.[30] Understanding the letter this way accords
well with something that Descartes wrote in another letter to Mesland,
from 2 May 1644:

> And I agree with you when you say that we can suspend our judgment;
> but I tried to explain in what manner this can be done. For it seems to me
> certain that a great light in the intellect is followed by a great inclination in
> the will; so that if we see very clearly that a thing is good for us, it is very
> difficult—and, on my view, impossible, as long as one continues in the
> same thought—to stop the course of desire. But the nature of the soul is
> such that it hardly attends for more than a moment to a single thing;
> hence, as soon as our attention turns from the reasons which show us that
> the thing is good for us, and we merely keep in our memory the thought

that it appeared desirable to us, we can call up before our mind some other reason to make us doubt it, and so suspend our judgement, and perhaps even form a contrary judgement. (4:115–16; 3:233–34)

It is easy to feel that there is a little "bait and switch" going on here (as perhaps also in *Principles* I, 37, on my reading), occasioned by Descartes's wish to show that he is in basic agreement with his correspondent over the possibility of suspending judgment. But what Descartes is describing in this passage fits well with an important motif of the *Meditations*. While Descartes emphasizes the impossibility of doubting what one clearly and distinctly perceives, he also emphasizes that this impossibility lasts only as long as one is actually clearly and distinctly perceiving. So immediately after writing "my nature is such that so long as I perceive something very clearly and distinctly I cannot but believe [*credere*] it to be true," he continues:

> But my nature is also such that I cannot fix my mental vision continually on the same thing, so as to keep perceiving it clearly. . . . And so other arguments can now occur to me which might easily undermine my opinion. (V.¶14; 7:69; 2:48)

Indeed, I think an important example of the "holding back" from a clearly perceived truth described in the February 1645 letter to Mesland occurs in the fourth paragraph of the Third Meditation, where the meditator fluctuates between finding herself unable to doubt the cogito and stepping back and questioning it.[31] When she enters the cogito state, she is not able to doubt that she exists, and when she exits it, she can. It is, according to Descartes, very difficult to put oneself in a frame of mind where one holds back from such obvious truths; thus the meditator finds the exercise of the methodological doubt very difficult (see also I.¶¶11 and 12). But in order to pull oneself away from clearly perceived truth, one must first cease clearly perceiving it.

Now, if we read the remark in the February 1645 letter about its always being open to us to hold back from a clearly known good or a clearly perceived truth in the way I am suggesting, we might put it that what always remains in my power is to A or not to A—I always retain the ability to A or not to A—even if it is not possible for me to A or not to A in all circumstances. That I retain such an ability even when, as currently circumstanced, I can only A (because A is pursuing a clearly known good or admitting a clearly perceived truth) is evidenced by the fact that I can, if I decide to, subsequently not do A (which will involve ceasing to perceive clearly the good or truth in question); in other words, the *power* remains intact. So, in this sense, there is no thing A such that doing A (or not doing A) intrinsically lies beyond the scope of my will. Of course, one could imagine a different sort of bidirectional power to do A or not to do A, a power (mentioned earlier) to do A or not to do A however one is circumstanced (both internally and externally), but it is not obvious that Descartes would have found the idea of such a power coherent, and if it is coherent, why we would want to have such a power. In any case, seeing Descartes as holding that we have a basic bidirectional power, whose bidirectionality persists even through its internal determination by clear perception, accords well, I believe, with the immediately preceding part of the February 1645 letter:

> I would like you to notice that "indifference" in this context seems to me strictly to mean that state of the will when it is not impelled one way rather than another by any perception of truth or goodness. This is the sense in which I took it when I said that the lowest degree of freedom is that by which we determine ourselves to things to which we are indifferent. But perhaps others mean by "indifference" a positive faculty of determining oneself to one or other of two contraries, that is to say, to pursue or avoid, affirm or deny. I do not deny that the will has this positive faculty. Indeed, I think it has it not only with respect to those actions [actus] to which it is not impelled by any evident reasons on one side or the other, but also with respect to all other actions. (4:173; 3:244–45)

This "positive faculty of determining oneself to one or other of two contraries" (which is, I take it, just the will's bidirectional ability described in [a] above) extends to "all other actions," which, for Descartes, would have to include even my affirmation of my own existence while in the presence of the cogito, where my will is impelled by very evident reasons to one side rather than the other.

¶¶9–12. THE ORIGIN OF ERROR

In ¶8, Descartes makes three main claims: (1) error is not found in the intellect taken alone, that is, in abstraction from the will, but depends on "two concurrent causes," namely, on the "faculty or cognition" or "intellect" and the "faculty of choice" or "will"; (2) the intellect, although perhaps limited in certain ways, does not lack any perfection or reality that it ought to have; and (3) the will is not imperfect—indeed, it is in some sense my greatest faculty, the one "above all in virtue of which . . . I understand myself to bear in some way the image and likeness of God." Descartes has yet to explain, however, how error arises from these two concurrent causes. This he does in ¶9:

> So what then is the source of my mistakes? It must be simply this: the scope of the will is wider than that of the intellect; but instead of restricting

it within the same limits, I extend its use to matters which I do not understand. Since the will is indifferent in such cases, it easily turns aside from what is true and good, and this is the source of my error and sin. (7:58; 2:40–41)

In the next two paragraphs, he illustrates this account with instances taken from the *Meditations*. In ¶10, he contrasts (1) my taking a stand on my own existence "in light of my even raising the question" with (2) my taking a stand on whether the thinking nature which characterizes me (insofar as I am a thinking thing) is distinct from or identical with corporeal nature. Case (1) does not count as extending my will beyond what I understand. It is my grasp of the situation that compels me to judge that I exist: "a great light in the intellect was followed by a great inclination in the will" (IV.¶10; 7:59; 2:41). (Descartes adds, in line with what he said about indifference in ¶8, "and thus I believed something the more spontaneously and freely, the less indifferent I was to it." The situation with respect to (2) is different: since "my intellect has not yet come upon any persuasive reason in favour of one alternative rather than the other," I ought not to take up any position on it, but should instead "refrain from making any judgement on the matter." For me to make a judgment on the matter, under these circumstances, would be for me to extend my will to something that I do not understand. In ¶11, Descartes adds that this indifference that should prompt me to withhold judgment does not happen only "where the intellect is wholly ignorant," but in any situation where "the intellect does not have sufficiently clear knowledge at the time when the will deliberates" (7:59; 2:41). Again, he illustrates with the meditator's recent experience: "the mere fact that I found all my previous beliefs were in some sense open to doubt was enough to turn my absolutely confident belief in their truth into the supposition that they were wholly false."

That Descartes thinks the will is involved in our cognitive life in this way has struck many as odd. Margaret Wilson has presented some of the concerns that one might have here in an especially forceful way, arguing that Descartes seems unable to supply a credible account of my motivation for believing something I do not clearly and distinctly perceive. After all, if I am indifferent, why would I want to give the will's assent? She writes:

First, there is the question of *motivation*; why, one might ask, would the will do a thing like this? . . . A perhaps more warranted view is that Descartes supposes a sort of lust for knowledge leads us to affirm or deny things we are not justified in believing or disbelieving. This suggestion would fit in with a good deal of what is said in the *Discourse* and, especially, the *Rules* about the sources of human error and confusion. Or it is possible that, at least some of the time, Descartes thinks of the will as wandering among confused perceptions like a lost soul with no fixed purpose in life: embracing this or that for no definite reason.

This account of the will's role in our cognitive life still seems on the slightest reflection most implausible.[32]

In the continuation of this passage, building in part on work by E. M. Curley, Wilson worries, in particular, that "the assimilation of judging to 'pursuing or fleeing' suggests that accepting or rejecting a proposition is something we do on the basis of a *decision*" (145). She then (146–50) explores a partial line of defense, based on the thought that, for Descartes, what elicits our assent when we go wrong is that we mistake apparent or specious clarity and distinctness for genuine clarity and distinctness.

It is true that Descartes's account of judgment can make it sound as though believing is, or at least can be, an arbitrary affair, as if I can believe that it is raining outside by simply deciding to do so. That doesn't square well with the phenomenology of belief, and may well be, as Curley has argued, incoherent at some deeper level. And, as Wilson points out, even if I could do such a thing, it is hard to see why I would want to (except perhaps in very unusual circumstances, say, to display my dominion over my cognitive life, but this does not routinely go on when I err).

I do not think, however, that Descartes's account of error commits him to an objectionable picture of one's believing *ad libitum*. Here it helps to keep in mind that, as we have seen, Descartes does not think of the will primarily along the lines of a *liberum arbitrium* (as conceived by Aquinas), that is, as a faculty for making decisions, but rather along the lines of a *voluntas* (as conceived by Aquinas), that is, as a faculty through which we are oriented as intellectual beings toward the good and (according to Descartes) the true. For Descartes, the fact that my grasp of the good or the true completely determines my activity so that there is no room left for arbitrary decision (no room for *liberum arbitrium*, in Thomas's sense) does not prevent my will from being responsible for that activity. For example, the fact that "I could not but judge that something which I understood so clearly was true" does not prevent my affirming from being an operation of my will, that is, does not keep my affirmation from falling out of my basic orientation toward the true.

But what about situations in which I affirm something that is not clearly and distinctly understood, situations where Descartes says the will experiences "indifference" but affirms or denies anyway? Does it turn out, on his account, that in these situations I simply decide to believe something, in a way that seems either incoherent or false to the character of belief? Well, Descartes has a lot to say about what happens when I go wrong that seems helpful here.[33] In general, he seems to hold that the factors that lead us to affirm or deny where we shouldn't are carelessness and inattention, usually supported by habit; and it would not be very much of an extrapolation from what he says about the role of prejudice and preconceived opinion to add stubbornness and the lack of intellectual humility to the list. Doubt itself, on Descartes's telling, may well be an unsettling condition (see I.¶5, I.¶12, and III.¶30): its unpleasantness may either hasten the sense that we have understood something when we really have not, or lead us to settle for plausibility when we should wait until we have grasped the truth. One of the ways, Descartes tell us, in which God could have brought it about that I would never err is that "he could have simply impressed it unforgettably that I should never make a judgement about anything which I did not clearly and distinctly understand" (IV.¶15; 7:61; 2:42). So carelessness, prejudice, and the uncomfortableness of doubt (which is not quite, I think, the "lust for knowledge" that Wilson writes of) can move in to fill the void created by the indifference that results from my failing to clearly and distinctly perceive the truth concerning some matter.

Now, none of this adds up to deciding in a clear-eyed way to believe where one recognizes that one has not understood, or choosing to believe something in the face of the lack of "sufficient evidence" (let alone "evidence to the contrary"). That we do not do such things is of a piece, I think, with Descartes's apparent endorsement of the scholastic maxim that "the will does not tend towards evil except in so far as it is presented to it by the intellect under some aspect of goodness" (1:366; 3:56). In particular, since "it is clear by the natural light that the perception of the intellect should always precede the determination of the will," I don't think one can, on Descartes's view, reflectively assent while realizing that there has not been an appropriate perception of the intellect, any more than one can pursue an apparent good, whose goodness one recognizes is only specious.[34]

In the Sixth Meditation, Descartes discusses the genesis of a particularly significant false belief—namely, the belief that "I had nothing at all in the intellect which I had not previously had in the senses [*nullam plane me habere in intellectu, quam non prius habuissem in sensu*]"—in a way that fits well with this general picture of what happens when we assent improperly. It is worth considering that account carefully. According to Descartes, sensory qualities command our attention in our early life; presumably this has something to do with the fact that our survival depended on it. Ideas of sensory qualities were especially impressive. They were, Descartes tells us, "much more vivid [*vividae*] and definite [*expressae*] and even in their own way more distinct [*distinctae*] than any of those which I deliberately formed through meditating or which I found impressed on my memory." These aspects contributed to my thinking that what I was sensing was "certain things fully [*plane*] from my cognition," a tendency of thought that, interestingly, Descartes at least partially endorses. (He writes that it was not "without sound reason" that I believed this.)[35] However, we soon stray from this basically sound, if incomplete, start into more questionable views:

> [1] Since I had no other notion [*notitiam*] of these things other than these ideas, it could not but come into my mind that those things resembled [*similes esse*] these ideas. [2] In addition, I remembered that the use of my senses came first, while the use of my reason came only later; and I saw that the ideas which I formed myself were not as definite [*expressae*] as those which I perceived with the senses and were mostly composed of them as parts. [3] In this way I easily convinced myself that I had nothing at all in the intellect which I had not previously had in the senses [*nullam plane me habere in intellectu, quam non prius habuissem in sensu*]. (7:75; 2:52)

Descartes describes these missteps as understandable in a way—as brought about by a certain sort of carelessness or inattention, while our attention was focused elsewhere, on the business of staying alive. It is easy to see how someone who is not yet thinking very carefully or very critically, impressed by the vividness of her sensory experience, might come to think (1) that the world was more as less as presented by our senses and so, in particular, that qualities found in bodies are real in proportion to their effect on our senses; and it is easy to see, further, how such a person might be led to conclude (2) that all of her cognition is somehow made up of glimpses of reality afforded by the senses (i.e., we cannot have cognition of the world unless we "turn to the phantasms").

Now, it is compatible with everything Descartes says in these passages that the mistakes involved in (1) and (2) would have been easy to straighten out, had there been a way to get through to the meditator in very early childhood. However, Descartes supposes that by the time one reaches maturity these ways of thinking have become ingrained, and so it takes great effort to liberate oneself from them. Thus, Descartes complains to Gassendi:

> You here ask me to say briefly whether the will can extend to anything that escapes the intellect. The answer is that this occurs whenever we happen to go wrong. Thus when you judge that the mind is a kind of rarefied body, you can understand that the mind is itself, i.e. a thinking thing, and a rarefied body is an extended thing; but the proposition that it is one and the same thing that thinks and is extended is one which you certainly do not understand. You simply want [*vis*] to believe it, because you have believed it before and do not want [*libenter*] to change your view. (7:376–77; 2:259)

If the infant Gassendi could have avoided the errors inherent in steps (2) and (3) simply by being more careful, it is more difficult now for the adult Gassendi to extricate himself from his false beliefs; doing so will take him from the comfortable and familiar into uncharted waters. We might think of the condition that we all find ourselves in at some point fairly early in life as having the earmarks of a fallen cognitive state.[36]

None of what Descartes is describing here sounds like "the will as wandering among confused perceptions like a lost soul with no fixed purpose in life" and "embracing this or that for no definite reason." Rather, the vividness of ideas of sensory qualities, coupled with a certain sort of distraction and inattention, leads to hasty judgment, which is later reinforced by habit. Moreover, neither the role that Descartes assigns to inattention or lack of reflection in the acquisition of beliefs nor to habit in the persistence of beliefs, once acquired, is unfaithful to the surface feel of our cognitive lives. Even so, the account that Descartes offers in VI.¶6 seems compatible with the idea that the will is responsible for this error. After all, preoccupation, distraction, inattention, lack of reflection, and habit are factors that are not unknown in the practical sphere to lead to the sort of infelicity for which the will is (paradigmatically, we may suppose) responsible.

Beyond this, I think there is something else that makes it extremely natural from Descartes's point of view to regard affirming, denying, and suspending judgment as activities of the will. In the *Meditations*, Descartes is trying to bring about a fundamental reformation in the meditator's cognitive life. He takes the meditator to have entered the *Meditations* with what might be called a sensory ideology. All human cognition works through images, glimpses of reality, stored in the memory as phantasms. (The passage from VI.¶6 just considered is an account of how we arrive at this view, that is, that "I had nothing at all in the intellect which I had not previously had in the senses.") We read the world through the lens of this sensory prism.

Different readers will do this in different ways. Some readers, particularly naive readers, will find themselves attracted to some version of the view that all reality is sensible ("to be is to be a body"); they will think that the soul is "something tenuous, like a wind or fire or ether" (II.¶5) or that "it is one and the same thing that thinks and is extended" (7:376–77; 2:259). Other readers, those indoctrinated with scholastic Aristotelianism, will come to hold a more sophisticated, but, from Descartes's perspective, no less problematic, position. For him, Aristotelian philosophy is an uncritical development of the more naive worldview (a development that is, Descartes thinks, innocent of serious natural philosophy). So Aquinas maintains that all human cognition requires that we turn to phantasms (even in cases where our cognition does not "terminate" in them). According to Thomas, we use stored phantasms to achieve some cognition of essences (by abstraction from sensory images), and some cognition of our intellects (as a power to abstract universals from particulars), and even some cognition of God (as a being that is not a body, as a being that, unmoved, moves bodies, and as a being that transcends bodies); but reliance on sensory images essentially conditions all human cognition. We do not escape these limitations when we cognize, say, God; as we saw in chapter 3, in Thomas's view, whatever cognition of God is open to us is heavily shaped by our dependence on phantasms. For Descartes, the more sophisticated Thomistic Aristotelian view, far from rooting out the objectionable sensory ideology, serves only to entrench it, by codifying it and making it systematic.

By the Fourth Meditation, the meditator understands how false the sensory ideology is to human cognition. In the Second Meditation she achieved a grasp of her own nature as a cognizer that did not proceed through stored sensory images; and she saw that her cognition of even bodies owes much more to "the pure intellect" (and much less to the senses) than she initially realized. What is more striking still, in the Third Meditation she saw that she has a grasp of God's very essence that could not have possibly been afforded her through our (sensory) cognition of a corporeal order. Her cognitive life, and her sense of her cognitive life, has been radically transformed.

If we think of Descartes's aim as the reorientation of one's cognitive life, which requires undoing the effects of ideology, entrenched by years of custom, it becomes easier to see why he thinks that what he is doing involves the reformation of one's will.[37] Intuitively, the will has, at the very least, a significant role to play in such transformations. If the ideology that someone is caught up in is systematic enough, it will not be subject to easy internal refutation. The ideology's vocabulary and categories will fold back in on themselves, and it will not be possible to argue the person out of—to *force* the person out of—the ideology. To be sure, a false ideology has its problems. It will not connect appropriately with the way that things really are (let's suppose, with Descartes, that physical things are not composites of form and matter), and, because of this, some of its basic categories (form, matter, and so on) may not acquire enough traction to keep one from thinking (and speaking) a certain kind of nonsense; and all of this may keep one from recognizing important truths about the world. But, in part because the person is thinking a certain kind of nonsense, it will be hard to get someone in the throes of the ideology to see this. Descartes's pessimism about being able to reach readers "who refuse to meditate with [him]" and who would instead try to rely only on the geometrical-style arguments he appends to the Second Replies should,[38] I think, be understood in this vein. It indicates that *he* didn't think he could get through and accomplish his goal without a certain sort of cooperation on the part of the reader.

This cooperation is quite naturally thought of as involving the will. If Gassendi, for example, is to work his way out of his materialist commitments, he needs to find a way to open himself to a different way of looking at things, and this would seem to involve some effort of will on his part. If the meditator is to dig herself out of the view that she cannot think without images, she will have to follow the instructions that Descartes gives in the *Meditations*, which, Descartes supposes, if done seriously and not as an idle exercise, she will find difficult and unsettling. The work involved here as Gassendi and the meditator go about reshaping their cognitive lives does not seem so different from the effort involved when one goes about reorienting one's practical life. Indeed, on a natural understanding of the relation between the true and the good, properly aligning oneself cognitively with the truth is not a separate project from properly aligning oneself with the good (as is evidenced, perhaps, by the fact that both projects are subject to many of the same virtues and vices: laziness, complacency, carelessness, and stubbornness; humility, honesty, integrity, and reflectiveness). In fact, in Descartes's view, our highest good involves having the appropriate cognitive relation to a special locus of truth and reality, namely, God.

Now, one might agree that the will is at some level involved in the reformation of one's cognitive life but deny the specific connection that Descartes sees between the will and affirming, denying, and suspending judgment. One might, for example, draw a firm distinction between the activities involved in getting ready to judge well and the judging itself. Where the will plays its role (say, by cooperating in the exercise of methodological doubt so that one might consider certain things afresh) is in putting one in a position to affirm or deny, or withhold judgment, well— and, no doubt, getting into such a position takes work—but, once one is in such a position, "evidential considerations" take over and determine our judgment one way or the other, or not, according to the preponderance of the evidence.

From Descartes's point of view this proposal is artificial. For one thing, the metaphor of weighing up the evidence, which lends itself to a sort of natural division of labor between squaring the scales and the weighing itself, does not, I think, fit how Descartes is thinking about inquiry. It is true that he thinks that preconceived views can and do get in the way of thinking well; thus the need for the skeptical doubt. But even so, for Descartes rational inquiry does not, for the most part, consist of balancing and weighing considerations against one another: in his philosophy, the dominant metaphor is that of dissipating obscurity and confusion, which enables us to *understand* what is what, to *see* what is so. The preparatory activities involved in coming to perceive clearly and distinctly and the judgment that results are integrated for Descartes in a way that makes it unnatural to assign the preparatory activities to one faculty and judgment to another. Rather, these activities are all different facets of the fact that we are creatures, at some very basic level, who care about being appropriately related to the truth (being "adequated" to it), find doubt unsettling, and find the thought of embracing falsehood even more disturbing. Moreover, this basic orientation to the truth does not seem so different from our basic orientation toward other things that fundamentally matter to us, that is, from our basic orientation toward the good. This is one way to understand the genesis of Descartes's contention that the truth is just as much the object of our will as the good is, and that, in particular, the embrace of the truth in judgment is an operation of the will.

Descartes's focus in the *Meditations* is on foundational matters, the nature of mind, God, and body, as well as the character of our cognition thereof, and I believe his account of judgment is developed with an eye toward these basic matters. His goal is not merely to add to my stockpile of true beliefs, or even to make sure beyond all doubt that I have eliminated all the false ones, but rather to arrive at a correct understanding of what mind is, what God is, and what body is, as well as an understanding of what happens when we understand these things. His (to judge by what happens in the subsequent tradition) extremely optimistic assessment is that we can have clear and distinct perception of these fundamental matters. This, I believe, informs his view that clear and distinct perception is the appropriate standard to which to hold one's judgment.

But Descartes does not restrict this standard to fundamental matters: he does not hold that when it comes to these foundational issues we should insist on clear and distinct perception while we have to settle for less in other arenas (he does recognize, however, that there will be times when one will need to *act* quickly without clearly and distinctly perceiving what is best). In his response to Gassendi, he moves directly from a foundational belief about the nature of the mind to a more occasional belief about the nutritiousness of a piece of fruit:

> Thus when you judge that the mind is a kind of rarefied body, you can understand that the mind is itself, i.e. a thinking thing, and a rarefied body is an extended thing; but the proposition that it is one and the same thing that thinks and is extended is one which you certainly do not understand. You simply want [*vis*] to believe it, because you have believed it before and do not want [*libenter*] to change your view. It is the same when you judge that an apple, which may in fact be poisoned, is nutritious: you understand [*intelligis*] that its smell, colour and so on, are pleasant, but this does not

mean you understand this particular apple will be beneficial to eat; you judge that it will because you want [*vis*] to believe it. (7:376–77; 2:259)

Similarly, in the Sixth Meditation, Descartes discusses, in the context of God's not being a deceiver, the case of someone who "is tricked by the pleasant taste of some food into eating some poison concealed inside it" (¶16; 7:83; 2:58) briefly, and, in much more detail, the case of those who, suffering from dropsy, "may desire food or drink that will shortly afterwards turn out to be bad for them" (¶17; 7:84; 2:58).

Descartes does not, to my knowledge, offer a detailed account of how the injunction "assent only to what you do clearly and distinctly perceive" plays out in these cases, so we need to extrapolate a bit. It is clear that there is, for him, an important difference between those situations where, as he says to Gassendi, we understand (*intelligere*) something to be the case and those cases where we have a natural tendency or inclination to believe that something is so. Natural inclinations or tendencies (because they, unlike acquired habits, come from God) do in general point us toward the true and the good, but there are exceptions. At the end of the Sixth Meditation, Descartes traces these exceptions (at least in the case of misleading practical inclinations) to the ever-present possibility of some deviant causal mechanism in the body intervening between the prompting stimulus and the resulting effect in the pineal gland (which bears a special relation to the mind): so, although God united the mind with the body in the best possible manner, so that we are in general thirsty when drink would be good for us, it is in principle possible that in unusual circumstances the mechanism that causes thirst would be present when drink would be detrimental to health. I take it, then, that the (reflective) attitude we are to adopt toward such inclinations is something like wary respect: we ought to treat them, in the context of this general understanding of how they might mislead from time to time, as highly probable without giving them our full endorsement.

¶¶13–15. THE METAPHYSICS OF ERROR AND HOW TO AVOID ERROR

I have tried to present Descartes's account of error in a sympathetic manner, so as to keep it in contact with the reality of our cognitive lives. One might worry that, in doing so, we risk depriving of its significance either the general claim that God is not a deceiver or the more specific claim that I go wrong only when I affirm or deny something I do not clearly and distinctly understand. One might have thought, for example, that God's not being a deceiver entailed that it should have been practically possible from the beginning that I should have never erred; and one might think the discovery that I go wrong only when I affirm or deny something I do not clearly and distinctly understand is supposed to give me a way of never erring again.[39] I have argued that Descartes believes neither of these claims. Against the former, the account we examined earlier of how we are led to the view that there is nothing in the intellect that was not first in the senses seems to make it unavoidable that a human being will at some time in its life be in significant error about fundamental matters. Against the latter, human beings get tired and distracted, and are susceptible to intellectual stubbornness and worse; this being so, it seems in general likely that someone, even after coming to recognize that she goes wrong only when she affirms or denies what is not clearly and distinctly understood, will continue to make mistakes, either because she forgets to apply the standard (see ¶15) or misapplies it (i.e., thinks she has clearly and distinctly understood something when she hasn't).

But if the point of the claim that God is not a deceiver is *not* to show that a human cognitive life without error is practically possible, and if the point of the claim that we go wrong only when we affirm or deny what we do not clearly and distinctly understand is *not* to give us some foolproof device to prevent us from ever going wrong again, what is their purpose? Well, Descartes is telling us (*a*) something about what we might call the metaphysics of error and (*b*) something about how to avoid error. Intuitively, the two projects are connected, in that knowing what error is will show us something about how to avoid it. Let's look at how Descartes accomplishes each of these tasks.

In ¶12, Descartes explains what constitutes the "form" of error. This has a rather technical ring to it, and I take it that it represents Descartes's account of what error is (that is, what error is, not what the word *error* means—or at least as close as one can come to saying what the phenomenon of error is, given that error is in the end a privation, a form of nonbeing):

> Now when I do not perceive clearly and distinctly enough, then if I abstain from bringing my judgment to bear, it is clear that I act correctly and am not deceived. But if in such cases I either affirm or deny, then I am not using my free will [*libertate arbitrii*] correctly. If I go for the alternative which is false, then obviously I shall be in error; if I take the other side, then it is by pure chance that I arrive at the truth, and I shall still be at fault since it is clear by the natural light that the perception of the intellect should always precede the determination of the will. In this incorrect use of free will [*liberi arbitrii*] may be found the privation [*privatio*] which constitutes the form of error [*formam erroris constituit*]. The privation [*privatio*],

I say, lies in the operation of the will in so far as it proceeds from me, but not in the faculty of will which I received from God, nor even its operation, in so far as it depends on him. (7:59–60; 2:41)

According to this account, error involves a malfunction of the will. A properly functioning will assents only when there is an appropriate perception of the intellect; error occurs when the will does not operate correctly. This malfunction is metaphysically located in the operation of the will; it arises "postfactory," as it were, and not from the design or manufacture of the equipment. In other words, presence of error in the universe is compatible with what was implied in ¶5, namely, that the things "produced by the supreme creator" would be "complete and perfect in all respects."

Now, Descartes says that the privation is located in the operation insofar as it proceeds from me but not insofar as it depends on God. This qualification has to do with the fact that everything that is and happens in the world depends on God; in particular, nothing does anything without God's concurrence. Descartes develops the claim that privation is found at my end of the operation and not at God's in ¶15, where the technical formulation of what error is reappears:

> Finally, I must not complain that the forming of those acts of will or judgements in which I go wrong happens with God's concurrence. For in so far as these acts depend on God, they are wholly true and good; and my ability to perform them means that there is in a sense more perfection in me than would be the case if I lacked this ability. As for the privation involved—which is all that the formal nature of falsity and wrong consists in [*ratio formalis falsitatis & culpae consistit*]—this does not in any way require the concurrence of God, since it is not a thing; indeed, when it is referred to God as its cause, it should be called not a privation but simply a negation. (7:60–61; 2:42)

This is a more precise location of error vis-à-vis God. Error is a privation. A privation, as we have seen, is the absence of some perfection or reality that ought to be in the thing. Now, when something acts, perfection and reality are always involved. All beings and activities are sustained, moreover, by God: so to the extent that there is something positive involved in error, that positive thing is supported by God. We may, as it were, factor an error into two components, a "being" component and a "nonbeing" component. More "being" or reality is involved in erring than in doing nothing at all. The "nonbeing" component would be the failure involved in the determination of the will that was not preceded by the perception of the intellect (however this may have come about, perhaps through some lack of attentiveness to what I was giving my assent to or a failure to keep in mind that I ought to withhold judgment when I do not clearly and distinctly perceive). Descartes claims that this "nonbeing" component counts as a "privation" when referred to me, but only a "negation" when referred to God. God and I are positioned differently with respect to my going wrong: what *I* do is give my will's assent to something I do not clearly and distinctly perceive; what *God* does is create and sustain a certain being in existence and support its activities. To be sure, as Descartes goes on to explain in ¶15, God could have done more: he could have produced some better being instead of me or given me more assistance than he did, but the fact that he did not does not show, locally, that I was made in a defective manner (i.e., that my cognitive equipment itself is defective) or, globally, that the universe was made in a defective manner.

Descartes thinks understanding what error is shows us how to avoid it. The general shape of his cognitive theodicy, captured in the claim that God is not a deceiver, ensures this much, namely, that I have it in my power to avoid error. But, as we have seen, the sense in which this is true is compatible with our having different levels of difficulty in avoiding error. We can, compatible with God's not being a deceiver, find ourselves in circumstances in which it is practically impossible to avoid error; but we could, equally compatible with God's not being a deceiver, find ourselves in circumstances where it would be practically impossible for us to make a mistake. (Certainly, Descartes's accounts of how people come, in the normal course of events, to embrace the resemblance doctrine make it appear inevitable that we will find ourselves with false beliefs at some point during our lives.) Why we are circumstanced as we are is inscrutable, ultimately going back to God's design of the universe. What the general thesis that God is not a deceiver does imply, I think, is that any mistake I make is at least in principle detectable "from the inside," that is, is at least in principle discoverable by me, the cognizer.

Now that we have seen what error is—the incorrect use of free will involved in my affirming or denying when I do not perceive the truth with sufficient clarity and distinctness—I have a more concrete sense of how I am to govern my cognitive life. I now understand why the general rule, tentatively suggested back in the Third Meditation ("So I now seem to be able to lay it down as a general rule that whatever I perceive very clearly and distinctly is true"), is in fact correct. Realizing this is useful— at least to the extent that we are comfortable with notions of clear and distinct perception—but, as indicated in the preceding section, it is not supposed to be a panacea. For one thing, as Descartes allows (see III.¶3) but does not emphasize, we sometimes think we clearly perceive when we do not. For another thing, on account of factors considered earlier, such as the difficulty of keeping one's attention focused and the effects of habit (and, I suspect, the uncomfortableness of doubt—admitting that one does not know), Descartes suggests that it is not easy to govern one's cognitive life by this rule:

> What is more ... I can avoid error in the second way, which depends only on my remembering to withhold judgement on any occasion when the truth of the matter is not clear. Admittedly, I am aware of a certain weakness in me, in that I am unable to keep my attention fixed on one and the same cognition [*cognitioni*] at all times; but by attentive and repeated meditation I am nevertheless able to make myself remember it as often as the need arises, and thus get into the habit of avoiding error. (¶16; 7:61–62; 2:43)

In terms of its practical import, I think what the truth rule is supposed to give us is a project—it says that we should regulate our beliefs by clear and distinct perception, by cogito-like states, because by doing so we will avoid error. I do not think that it is supposed to be of much use for determining whether something I am currently perceiving is true: as if, finding myself in doubt about the truth of a geometrical position, I am supposed to gain some leverage by asking myself, "Well, do I perceive clearly and distinctly that the proposition is true?" This is not to deny that there may be occasions on which such self-examination is helpful—after all, Descartes does say we sometimes take ourselves to perceive something clearly when we do not—but in general the truth of something currently clearly and distinctly perceived speaks for itself. Rather, the practical import of the rule is mainly to get me to withhold judgment in those situations in which I internally recognize that I am not perceiving clearly and distinctly, and what's being recommended in ¶16 is that I reform my cognitive life in such a way that I withhold judgments in these situations automatically, by second nature.

This may make the practical import of the rule appear fairly uncontroversial, but really it reflects Descartes's considerable optimism concerning the ability of the human mind to grasp the fundamental structure of reality. He thinks that we have the same transparent grasp of what the mind is, of what God is and that God exists, and what body is, as we have of our existence in the cogito reflection. If one agreed that something like mathematical transparency was the appropriate standard to which to hold one's judgment, but disagreed about the transparent grasp, then it would seem that one would have to remain simply agnostic about these matters. To a large extent this seems to be the tack Locke took, at least with respect to metaphysics. But a different approach would be to continue doing metaphysics without expecting to find mathematical transparency.

¶17. Cognizing Well and Cognizing the Truth

So far the discussion has centered on what error is and how to avoid it. This is an artifact of the way the meditation is structured, as a cognitive theodicy, around the question, If I come from a supremely perfect being, how is it that I err? But as that question is answered, a link is implicitly put in place between cognizing clearly and distinctly and cognizing the truth: if I am not in error when I judge what is presented to me clearly and distinctly, then I judge truly when I judge what is presented to me clearly and distinctly.[40] Interestingly, Descartes seems to give an independent argument for the truth of what I clearly and distinctly perceive in the final paragraph of the Fourth Meditation:

> For, so long as I restrain my will in bringing to bear judgement so that it extends only to what is exhibited clearly and distinctly by the intellect, then it is quite impossible for me to go wrong. This is because every clear and distinct perception is undoubtedly something [*proculdubio est aliquid*], and hence cannot come from nothing, but must necessarily have God for its author. Its author, I say, is God, who is supremely perfect, and who cannot be a deceiver on pain of contradiction; hence the perception is undoubtedly true. (¶17; 7:62; 2:43)

In ¶12, Descartes told us what error is, that is, explaining its metaphysics: error is a privation, an absence of being or reality. Here Descartes gives us the metaphysics of truth: a clear and distinct perception is "something" (i.e., not a negation or privation), hence it is caused by God, hence it is true. The argument he now gives relating clear and distinct perception and truth may well cover more than judgment and truth: it can be read (and probably should be read) as affirming that anywhere there is clear and distinct perception, there is truth—a something, a reality—that is being perceived. This would fit with the use that Descartes makes of the truth rule in V.¶6, just six paragraphs ahead, where he appeals to it in order to argue for the truth of certain true and immutable *natures* (in particular, he appeals to the truth rule to argue for the truth of certain *properties* of a triangle).

In order to understand this argument, we need to understand why the same thing could not be said about an obscure and confused perception: Isn't it, too, a "something"? And doesn't it, too, come from God? Perhaps Descartes's claim that a clear and distinct perception "cannot come from nothing" provides a clue here. His point may be that obscure perceptions, insofar as they are obscure, lack reality (clarity, which we may suppose is a positive reality) and so *do* at least in part "come from nothing." That is, they may have a sort of mixed cause (in the way that, on

Descartes's view, error itself, being analyzable into being and nonbeing, has a sort of mixed cause—see ¶15). Thus, I cannot assume that obscure perception comes from God in the same way that clear and distinct perception does, and I risk error when I bring judgment to bear on what is perceived only obscurely. The basic idea would be, then, that it is one thing for me to be misled by a representation that is, as it were, internally defective, and it would be quite another for me to be misled by a representation that was, as it were, completely impeccable internally, because God is (ultimately) causally responsible for everything in the latter but not causally responsible for what is absent in the former.[41] Of course, Descartes will need to explain why we find ourselves weighed down with representations that are, in a certain respect, defective; I think he does this in the Sixth Meditation, when we learn that the function of sensory ideas is not primarily to help us understand the world.

⇥5⇤

The Fifth Meditation

THE FIFTH Meditation falls into three main parts. The first part, ¶¶1–6, is concerned with the nature of material things. Within this, ¶¶5 and 6, where Descartes presents his account of true and immutable natures, hold a special importance. This discussion tells the meditator something important about the truth to which she is related when she sees that something is so. It also helps her to see why a certain kind of argument for the existence of God, the ontological argument, should be possible. In the second part of the meditation, ¶¶7–12, Descartes presents this argument. In the final part, ¶¶13–16, Descartes carefully explains the sense in which the certainty of all other things depends on my recognition of God's existence, so that "without it nothing can ever be perfectly known [*perfecte sciri*]." (It is this discussion that draws a charge of circularity [and related objections] from Descartes's subsequent critics: If all knowledge depends on the knowledge of God, how can I know anything in advance of knowing that God exists [such as, in the Second Meditation, that I exist]? In particular, how can I know the truth of the various considerations used to show that God exists?) I see the end of the Fifth Meditation as the culmination of Descartes's account of the cogito being *per se* (his account of me insofar as I am a thinking thing). As we go to the Sixth Meditation, the discussion will turn to a new topic, the relation of the cogito being to something else, namely its body.

I. *TRUE AND IMMUTABLE NATURES* (¶¶1–6)

The opening third of the Fifth Meditation falls into two parts. The first part, which is somewhat obscure, apparently contains an account of the essence of material things (the meditation's title is "The essence of material things, and the existence of God considered a second time"). The second part, ¶¶5–6, contains Descartes's doctrine of true and immutable natures, which intersects in important ways with central themes that have been under development in the *Meditations*.

¶¶1–4. THE ESSENCE OF MATERIAL THINGS

Although the first half of the Fifth Meditation's heading reads "the essence of material things," the meditation contributes little to Descartes's substantive account of what is to be a body. In terms of its content, Descartes's account of body (as an "extended, flexible and changeable thing") is largely complete in the wax passage, perhaps supplemented somewhat by the Third Meditation's account of sensory qualities as "obscure and confused" and "materially false." Ultimately what Descartes wants to do in ¶¶1–6 is to defend a metaphysical thesis, and argue that there is a truth or reality corresponding to my grasp of body as an extended thing. He wants to show that my idea of extension exhibits to me a true and immutable nature, a nature that does not depend on the existence of any bodies.[1]

In this subsection, I try to get a better picture of the relation between Descartes's substantive views about body and the metaphysical work he is undertaking now. That he is now undertaking metaphysical work seems clear from his appeal in ¶6 to the truth rule. Why should the establishment of the essence of body involve a certain amount of metaphysics, ultimately the theses that our creator is not a deceiver and that our distinct cognition of body involves true and immutable natures?

I think it best to explore this issue in tandem with what seems to me a closely parallel moment in the Sixth Meditation, where Descartes appeals to certain facts about God in the course of trying to show that the mind and the body are two "really distinct" things, independent enough in their being that it is possible for the mind to exist without the body (see VI.¶9). In the Fourth Replies, Descartes makes a series of illuminating comments that tell us something important about how he sees the division of labor between what might be called the more substantive elements in a distinct conception of mind and body and the more metaphysical elements. He begins by explaining that he had already in place by the end of the Second Meditation much of what he needed—basically, his account of what the mind is and much of his account of what body is—in order to show that mind and body are distinct:

> Hence, had I not been looking for greater than ordinary certainty, I should have been content to have shown in the Second Meditation that the mind can be understood as a subsisting thing despite the fact that nothing belonging to the body is attributed to it, and that, conversely, the body can be understood as a subsisting thing despite the fact that nothing belonging

to the mind is attributed to it. I should have added nothing more in order
to demonstrate that the mind is really distinct from the body, since we
commonly judge that the order in which things are mutually related in our
perception of them corresponds to the order in which they are related according to truth itself [ad veritatem]. (7:226; 2:159)

Now, as the last clause of the passage indicates, what kept Descartes
from establishing the real distinction in the Second Meditation was that
he had not yet established the truth rule. He explains further:

But one of the exaggerated doubts which I put forward in the First Meditation went so far as to make it impossible for me to be certain of this very
point (namely whether things do according to truth [juxta veritatem] correspond to our perception of them), so long as I was supposing myself to
be ignorant of the author of my origin. And this is why everything I wrote
on the subject of God and truth in the Third, Fourth and Fifth Meditations
contributes to the conclusion that the mind is really distinct from the body,
which I finally established in the Sixth Meditation. (7:226; 2:159)

One might ask, what is the special relevance of the truth rule to showing that the mind is really distinct from the body? There are a couple of
related places in the Sixth Meditation's argument, where it seems that
the truth rule (or related doctrines) is being appealed to. First, the argument begins with a claim about clear and distinct perception and God's
power ("I know that everything which I clearly and distinctly understand
is capable of being created by God so as to be such as I understand it").
This links clear and distinct perception to possibility in the universe, to
some form of real possibility. Second, Descartes remarks in the course of
the argument, "Thus, from the fact that I know [sciam] that I exist and at
the same time I notice that nothing else at all belongs to my nature or
essence besides the one thing that I am a thinking thing, I can correctly
conclude that my essence consists solely in the fact that I am a thinking
thing" (VI.¶9; 7:78; 2:54). This is to say, roughly, that my essence corresponds to my grasp of it.

The second claim strikes me as more fundamental than the first. I believe that there is a background assumption to the effect that God can do
anything that the relevant essences admit of.[2] So if my clear and distinct
perception shows me that nothing more than thought is found in my essence, and my clear and distinct perception correctly tracks essences (the
truth rule), then my essence does not require anything besides thought;
but God can do anything that my essence admits of, so he can make me
without anything besides thought. In other words, modal views about
what God can do implicitly rest on views about what essences there are
and how they are structured.[3]

One thing that encourages me in thinking that, for Descartes, what we distinctly perceive is possible depends on the fact that distinct perception perspicuously presents essences, is the way the Sixth Meditation opens. There, Descartes appears to move directly from the Fifth Meditation's result that there is an essence or a true and immutable nature corresponding to my clear and distinct perception of body as extended, flexible, and changeable, to the claim that such bodies are capable of existing because God can make them: "I already know they [material things] are capable of existing, in so far as they are the subject matter of pure mathematics, since I perceive them clearly and distinctly. For there is no doubt that God is capable of creating everything I perceive in this manner" (VI.¶1; 7:71; 2:50). Although this opening sentence of the Sixth Meditation does not explicitly refer back to the Fifth Meditation, I think it is reasonable to suppose that Descartes believes he can draw this conclusion because he has established in the Fifth Meditation that his clear and distinct perception of body involves a true and immutable nature, an essence; without this much in place, it is not clear that there would be anything for God to create.[4]

Now, when Descartes suggests in the Fourth Replies that in order to show that the mind is really distinct from the body he needs first to establish that "the order in which things are mutually related in our perception of them corresponds to the order in which they are related according to truth itself [ad veritatem]" and thus settle "whether things do according to truth [juxta veritatem] correspond to our perception of them" (7:226; 2:159), I do not think he is raising the general issue of whether what I clearly and distinctly perceive to be the case is in fact so, but has something rather more specific in mind: how well (if at all) my distinct cognition of things tracks their *essences* or *natures*.

Moreover, it is worth noting that within the arena of my cognition of essence Descartes is concerned especially with what might be thought of as its completeness, that is, with whether my distinct cognition of a thing's essence leaves anything out. Consider again what Descartes says in the Sixth Meditation en route to the real distinction between the mind and the body: "Thus, from the fact that I know that I exist and at the same time I notice that nothing else at all belongs to my nature or essence besides the one thing that I am a thinking thing, I can correctly conclude that my essence consists solely in the fact that I am a thinking thing" (VI.¶9; 7:78; 2:54). The "nothing else" and "consists solely" here suggest that a large part of the force of this claim is to "close off" the account of my essence (the "I notice that nothing else at all belongs to my nature or essence" is, of course, important here; it is supposed to be stronger, I take it, than, say, my simply not noticing that there is anything else found in my essence).[5]

Indeed, I think that the need to "close off" my essence may well have been the primary reason Descartes thought in the Second Meditation that he was not in a position to demonstrate that the mind is really distinct from the body. Consider again Descartes's explanation in the Fourth Replies:

> I should have added nothing more in order to demonstrate that the mind is really distinct from the body, since we commonly judge that the order in which things are mutually related in our perception of them corresponds to the order in which they are related according to truth itself [ad veritatem].
>
> But one of the exaggerated doubts which I put forward in the First Meditation went so far as to make it impossible for me to be certain of this very point (namely whether things do according to truth [juxta veritatem] correspond to our perception of them), so long as I was supposing myself to be ignorant of the author of my origin. (7:226; 2:159)

One might read this as mainly a remark about metaphysical certainty—"I didn't demonstrate the real distinction in the Second Meditation because, given the skeptical assumptions I was then operating under, I would not have been metaphysically certain about what I have shown"—but this would make Descartes's comment puzzling, since there are plenty of things that Descartes *does* demonstrate in the Second Meditation, namely, I exist, I am a thinking thing, about which he shows no such reservation. I think it makes more sense to take Descartes's main point to be this: in order to close off the mind's essence or the body's essence we must know that our distinct perception of a thing does not *omit* anything fundamental to the thing. That our distinct perception of a thing does not do so is, I take it, the force of the natural (but, as of the Second Meditation, yet to be established) commonly made judgment "that the order in which things are mutually related in our perception of them corresponds to the order in which they are related according to truth itself [ad veritatem]." Until we see why this is so, we are not in a position to see that the mind is really distinct from the body. In other words, I think that Descartes holds that the truth rule is required specifically in order for me to conclude from the fact that I have a distinct perception of my mind as a thinking thing (and no more), that there is an essence or nature answering to my perception, that is, an essence or nature that involves thinking (and nothing else); and to conclude from the fact that I distinctly imagine body as an extended thing (and no more), that there is an essence that involves being extended (and nothing else).

So when Descartes says that "everything I wrote on the subject of God and truth in the Third, Fourth and Fifth Meditations contributes to the conclusion that there is a real distinction between the mind and the body, which I finally established in the Sixth Meditation," I think his point is that he needed to establish God's veracity and the truth rule in order to show the following: (1) there is an essence corresponding to my clear and distinct perception, (2) this essence contains everything I distinctly perceive to belong to it, and (3) my distinct perception does not omit anything fundamental.

Although it is not as clearly marked in the text, I take it that Descartes is doing something very similar with respect to body's essence in the opening paragraphs of the Fifth Meditation, namely, closing it off and limiting it to what we distinctly perceive (which may involve noticing that nothing else belongs to its essence, in the same way that limiting the mind's essence to thought involves noticing that "nothing else at all belongs to my nature or essence besides the one thing that I am a thinking thing").[6]

If this interpretation is on the right track, it is natural to ask, on a philosophical level, why Descartes sees the truth rule as especially relevant to our cognition of essences. That is, why should he feel the need to invoke the truth rule (and so God's not being a deceiver) in order to support claims such as that the essence of mind is (solely) thought and the essence of body is (solely) extension? A significant part of the answer, it seems to me, has to do with Descartes's rejection of an abstractionist account of understanding in favor of a nativist one. The abstractionist has a picture of how our grasp of the essences of things grows out of our sensory interaction with them, a picture that Descartes opposes (he is, for example, about to explicitly criticize a central tenet of the theory at the beginning of V.¶6: "It would be beside the point for me to say that since I have from time to time seen bodies of triangular shape, the idea of a triangle may have come to me from external things by means of the sense organs"). According to Descartes, God equips the mind with a basic understanding of what a mind is and what a body is. Since God is not a deceiver, everything that we clearly and distinctly perceive is true. Thus, there is a truth or reality involved in this basic understanding.

These different epistemologies of essence yield what might be called different methodologies for the discovery of essence. For an Aristotelian, the investigator begins by locking on to (usually with the help of the senses) some existing thing (or things) whose essence is to be sought. That is, one begins with some target individual (or individuals), for example, this animal (or those animals), and asks, What is it?, that is, What is its essence? Descartes does not follow such a procedure in the Fifth Meditation; indeed, he seems to have deliberately structured the discussion so as to have the meditator explore the essence of material things before she knows whether any material things exist; before she knows whether there are any target things in existence for her to lock on to and ask, What is it?[7] Since, for Descartes, my grasp of the essence of material things is in principle prior to my sensory encounter with them, there must be, in his view, a way for me to fix the object of investigation without presupposing the existence of material things.[8]

Some might infer from this that Descartes's theory of essence is not about things, is not *de re*, but about our representations of things and so, as it were, *de dicto*. In my view, this would be a serious mistake. I think the basic point of V.¶¶1–6 is to establish that the things whose natures we are exploring need not exist in the world in order for these natures, in some suitably broad sense, to determine our thought. This is quite different from saying that we can dispense with the natures or identify them with our ideas or representations, our own *dicta*, so to speak.[9] For Descartes, my distinct perception is *of* a thing, often an essence or nature, to which the perception is answerable. That is why I need to appeal to God in order to ensure that essences are as I perceive them. An exploration of the nature *extension* is not an exploration of my representations or ideas, even if I cognize that nature through my representations or ideas. The metaphysical robustness of natures for Descartes is, I think, hinted at in this parenthetical comment from the First Replies: "I will not include the lion or the horse, since their natures are not transparently clear to us." We know that there are such natures because such animals exist. But even so, we do not understand their natures, because that would be tantamount to having mechanical blueprints of these systems, something we manifestly do not have; Descartes's suggestion that these natures are opaque would be more surprising if he supposed that understanding the nature of a lion or horse were simply a matter of analyzing "our concept" of lion or of horse.

So how does the methodology of essence exploration, at least in the case of body, work, according to Descartes? Well, as a purely textual matter, in the *Meditations* he seems to characterize the sort of cognition that perspicuously presents an essence as distinct.[10] In the Second Meditation's discussion of the piece of wax, he places a conspicuous emphasis on what is distinct in my conception of the wax. For example, the question that sets the discussion in motion is "So what was it in the wax that I understood with such distinctness?" (II.¶11; 7:30; 2:20; *distinct* and its cognates occur in two other places in this paragraph).[11] I think it emerges from the discussion that what counts as my "distinct" understanding of the wax is what gives me my grasp of what the wax is (or, really, of what a body is). In addition, when toward the end of the Second Meditation, in II.¶15, Descartes compares his cognition of the mind and the wax in terms of which is "truer and more certain" and which is "more distinct and evident," it turns out that while the greater certainty of my cognition of my mind has to do with my greater certainty of its existence, the greater distinctness of my cognition has to do with my better purchase on its nature. I understand a thing distinctly to the extent that my grasp of its essence or nature is perspicuous; for Descartes, having distinct cognition of a thing is closely akin to having a logos of a thing for an Aristotelian.

Now, when we turn to the opening of the Fifth Meditation, we find a similar emphasis on distinct cognition. He begins in ¶2 by saying he is going to consider what is distinct in his conception of body:

> But before I inquire whether any such things [i.e., material things] exist outside me, I must consider their ideas [*illarum ideas*], in so far as they exist in my thought, and see which of them are distinct, and which are confused. (7:63; 2:44)

In ¶3 he goes on to report what he can distinctly imagine concerning body:

> Now, I distinctly imagine [*imaginor*][12] quantity (which philosophers commonly call continuous) or the extension in length, breadth and depth of this quantity or rather of the quantified thing; I number the various parts in it; I assign whatever magnitudes, figures, positions and local motions to these parts, and whatever duration to these motions. (7:63; 2:44)

We see here the methodological change alluded to earlier. Descartes is replacing here the more traditional way of locating an essence by locking on to some existing thing and asking, What is it? This is the procedure he himself followed more or less in the case of the mind in the Second Meditation,[13] with the thesis that a thing's essence is given through my distinct cognition of it.

This procedure works because when I distinctly cognize a thing, there is an essence (a "true and immutable nature") that I am cognizing. So Descartes's methodology depends on a substantive metaphysical claim about the nature of reality, which connects a fact about how I am cognizing (namely, distinctly) to a fact about the structure of reality (namely, there is a true and immutable nature, which I am cognizing). Further, if I stop to reflect on why this methodology works (as Descartes thinks I must do if I am to arrive at what he calls *scientia*), I will discover that it works because God is not a deceiver. This fact ensures that whenever I understand something distinctly, there is a true and immutable nature to which I am epistemically connected, and which I am tracking accurately.

In general, this higher-order reflection on the origin of my nature in God is not required for me to come to first-order conclusions about the way things are. (To be sure, as we shall see at the end of this chapter, there is a way in which all my clear cognition benefits from—is brought to a higher degree of certainty through—my knowing who the author of my nature is.) However, in line with what I said earlier about "closing off" essences, the higher-order reflection on the origin of my nature may, in Descartes's view, be necessary to see that my cognition of the essence of a thing does not leave out any fundamental feature of the thing (which has somewhat the ring of a second-order claim). That is, the knowledge that my distinct cognition of essence does not omit anything may be something that, in Descartes's view, we cannot arrive at in a first-order way, simply by examining the essence in question.

In ¶¶5 and 6, Descartes will develop the thesis that there *is* a true and immutable nature that I grasp when I cognize distinctly. However, before we take this up, it is worth pausing briefly to consider Descartes's substantive account of material things. (Readers not interested in this topic can skip to the following section without loss of continuity.)

MATTER AS EXTENSION

What is the substantive import of the claim that the essence of material things encompasses the things that I distinctly imagine and nothing else— that is, extension in three dimensions, parts, positions, shapes, sizes, and motions?

Notice, to begin with, that this account of what a material thing is does not commit us to any special view about the nature of what the Aristotelians call proper sensible qualities or what Locke calls secondary qualities. It is compatible with this account of body's nature that red should straightforwardly belong to body, in more or less the way that the Aristotelians thought. It is also compatible with this account of body's nature that red should be more ontologically complex, so to speak, so that red is, for example, a certain corporeal structure that is obscurely and confusedly presented to me in my idea of a red thing (which is what I think Descartes holds in the *Meditations*); or that red should be whatever it is in a body that produces red ideas in me; or, again, that red should be a mental entity not found in bodies in any manner whatsoever. To claim that what it is to be a body is to be an extended, flexible, mutable thing is not to take a stand on what it is to be a color, an odor, or a sound.

Descartes is claiming, to be sure, that sensory ideas do not belong to my distinct cognition of body, because they are confused. But this conclusion must be treated with care. In the *Principles*, Descartes remarks that "our knowledge of what it is for the body to have a shape is much more evident than our knowledge of what it is for it to be colored [*quid fit esse coloratum*]" (I, 69; 8A:34; 1:218).[14] We might, keying on this text, distinguish between our sensory idea of red and what it is for a body to be red (or, to use other terminology, between the idea *red* and the quality *red*). Now, the fact that my sensory idea of red is obscure and confused does not preclude a distinct conception of what it is for a body to be red from entering into a distinct conception of what a body is. I take it that, for Descartes, for a body to be red is for it to have a certain kind of surface texture (the kind that reflects light particles in a certain way). Possessing this determinate surface texture would have the same status as possessing some determinate shape, say, spherical. While it does not belong to the essence of body to have this or that determinate shape, body is the sort of thing that, by its nature, admits of being spherical; similarly, while it would not belong to the essence of body to have the determinate corporeal structure that is "what it is for it to be colored," body is the sort of thing that, by its nature, admits of having such a structure.[15]

If this is on the right track, then, given certain further plausible assumptions about the corporeal structure involved in a body's possession of sensible qualities, having sensible qualities will not be part of what it is to be a body. In particular, if we suppose that only certain determinate structures (e.g., textures, in the case of color, or sufficient bulk, in the case of tactile qualities) have any effect on our sensory organs, it seems possible that there should be bodies with no effect on our sense organs. Further, I don't think that even the *capacity* to assume such structure ought to be thought of as *part of* body's essence, that is, part of what it is to be a body, even if this capacity perhaps necessarily *flows from* body's essence or nature. So, although Descartes remarks in the Second Meditation, when detailing his pretheoretical conception of body, that body "can be perceived by touch, sight, hearing, taste or smell," I think that this remark should be taken as giving (what the Aristotelians would have called) a *proprium* of body, that is, as giving an important characteristic mark of body, that, strictly, lies outside its essence. It is unclear to me that this way of looking at the essence or nature of body would have been controversial from an Aristotelian point of view.

What is more clearly controversial here is Descartes's claim that with extension (and mobility) we have all that is required in order for something to be able to exist. Both his predecessors and successors would have disagreed. For a scholastic, bodies are essentially structured hylomorphically. A body is a composite of the form of corporeity and matter. Matter here is understood as potentiality; form as that which actualizes potentiality. This form of corporeity, moreover, bestows on the body various powers and abilities, including the capacity to receive additional forms, for example, quantity and quality (which allow bodies to possess sensible qualities). Descartes's predecessors would have thought that his account of body as extension neglected this metaphysically more basic level.[16] Descartes's successors will also argue that more is involved in body than extension and mobility, but for different reasons: force, too, belongs to the essence of matter. (Leibniz sees a connection between the two sorts of misgivings about Descartes's account of body.)[17] Some seemed to have found incoherent the idea that extension (and mobility) could be made real with no more; others thought the conception empirically inadequate (in that it seemed inconsistent with the observed laws of motion).

It is fairly easy to see why Descartes rejects the scholastic, hylomorphic conception of a body. He rejects the Aristotelians' account of change as the actualization of potentiality, and with that, their theory of mutable individuals as hylomorphic composites of formal elements (principles of actuality) and material elements (principles of potentiality). Substantial forms and prime matter are paradigmatic examples of entities that he claims cannot be distinctly understood (and so have no place in a perspicuous account of what something is, in a distinct understanding of an essence). It is harder to say how Descartes would have reacted to the conception of matter developed by his successors, Newton, Leibniz, and Kant, which involves a sophistication that was only beginning to become available in his day. On the one hand, such a conception involved notions that Descartes explicitly tried to reject as too obscure for a distinctly grasped science of matter. On the other hand, the mathematical manner in which dynamical notions were developed by later natural philosophers has more affinity with Descartes's conception than with that of his scholastic predecessors (although, as indicated above, the case of Leibniz is obviously complex). It is not obvious that Descartes would find Newtonian matter, or even Newtonian gravity, objectionable in the same way that he found the scholastic substantial forms or real qualities objectionable.

¶¶5–6. "I THINK WHAT IS MOST OF ALL TO BE CONSIDERED HERE . . ."

In ¶¶5–6, Descartes resumes the discussion of truth that has been occupying much of the Third and Fourth Meditations. Let me begin by supplying some context for that discussion.

As she worked through the cogito exercise, the meditator discovered that she had the remarkable ability to see that something is so, to, as Aquinas would put it, "adequate" her mind with reality. When, at the beginning of the Third Meditation, she reflected on this ability, the fact that she perceived clearly and distinctly seemed especially salient, and this brought her to formulate the so-called truth rule ("So I now seem to be able to lay it down as a general rule that whatever I perceive very

clearly and distinctly is true"). But before she could establish this rule—
see that this rule indeed held—she needed to find out whether the author of her nature is a deceiver (the rest of the Third Meditation) and
then, after determining that God, the author of her nature, is not a deceiver, she needed to detail how this fact played out within the context of
her cognitive architecture, especially as that architecture bears on judgment (Fourth Meditation).

The development of the truth rule has taken place thus far on the side
(so to speak) of the cognizing agent; but, in view of the fact that truth is,
to use Aquinas's word again, the "adequation" of mind and things (or
reality), to claim that certain of the cognitive agent's judgments are true
has implications for how things are (or how reality is). In the Fifth Meditation, Descartes develops one of these implications. He maintains that
certain of our judgments involve what he calls "true and immutable natures." These natures have some metaphysical standing—they are "somethings," not "mere nothings," and are "not invented by me or dependent
on my mind"—and, furthermore, their having this standing does not depend on there being any actual (really existing) thing exemplifying them.
There would be, for example, a true and immutable nature of a triangle,
even if it should turn out that the world, perhaps on account of its mess-
iness, does not contain any triangles.[18]

Now, Descartes's doctrine of true and immutable natures yields a special perspective on the ontological argument. (The precise relation between the doctrine and the argument is delicate; I take that up at the end
of the second part of this chapter.) For, as things turn out, one of the
mind-independent, true, and immutable natures to which the cognitive
agent has access belongs to God. Descartes's position on human cognition of God here is continuous with the position he develops in the Third
Meditation, where he implicitly rejects Thomas's theory, according to
which the human mind is limited to oblique, constructed representations
of God that fall short of God's essence. Descartes holds instead that the
mind finds itself endowed with an innate idea of God that makes available something of God's very essence or nature.

The prospects of the ontological argument are closely bound up with
this claim that human beings have some access to God's essence or nature. On the one hand, it is difficult to see how we can mount such an
argument if we start with considerably less than access to God's essence.
In particular, as we shall see, both Descartes and Aquinas agree that
some merely nominal characterization of God—some account of the
meaning of the word God—would not give us sufficient foothold to
mount an ontological argument. On the other hand, if we do have some
grasp of God's essence, it is hard to see why we would not possess the
sort of insight into God's existence that the ontological argument attests

to. A direct access to God's essence would provide us not simply with a set of the necessary and sufficient conditions for divinity, but with some purchase on God's core or constituting properties; and it is hard to see how we could have that without recognizing the necessity of his existence. As a matter of fact, I don't know of a theologian who holds that we have access to what God is (not just what "God" means) and who does not accept something like an ontological argument.

Since the prospects of the ontological argument are closely bound up with the claim that human beings have some access to God's essence or nature, it is natural to ask what persuades Descartes that we really do have this purchase on God. I believe that what persuades him of this is the way in which we operate with our idea of God. For him, philosophical theology is a substantive branch of knowledge, to be taken at face value, just like geometry. The judgments we make concerning God are, for him, on all fours with the judgments we make in geometry. So, if we read our geometrical judgments as showing us that we have access to mind-independent, real structure, namely, the essence or nature of extended being (and along with that, essence or nature of certain kinds of extended beings—for example, cubes, spheres, squares, circles, etc.), then we ought to read our theological judgments in the same way. We should take them, too, as witnessing our access to mind-independent, real structure, in this case, God's essence.

The idea that there is something going on in our ability to make certain sorts of geometrical judgments that calls out for special explanation is at least as old as Plato's *Meno*. Descartes makes allusion to Plato's doctrine of recollection in V.¶4. Moreover, he tells us, in his published letter to Voetius, that the situation with respect to our cognition of God is similar to the situation of the slave body, in the *Meno*, with respect to cognition of geometry:

> All geometrical truths are this sort [i.e., "such that we come to know them by the power of our native intelligence, without any sensory experience (*ullo sensuum experimento*)"]—not just the most obvious ones, but all the others, however abstruse they may appear. Hence, according to Plato, Socrates asks a slave boy about the elements of geometry and thereby makes the boy able to dig out certain truths from his own mind which he had not previously recognized were there, thus attempting to establish the doctrine of reminiscence. Our knowledge [*cognitio*] of God is of this sort. (8B:166–67; 3:222–23)

In fact, that my cognition of (the substantive truth of) God's existence is on all fours with my cognition of (substantive) geometrical truths is one of the leitmotifs of the Fifth Meditation (see, e.g., the end of ¶7).

There is in all of this, I think, an adumbration of Kant's question, How is synthetic *a priori* knowledge possible? For Kant, like Descartes, that question means, How it is possible for us to make a certain kind of judgment? Descartes thinks we can make substantive judgments concerning body and God because we have innate ideas, through which we grasp the essence or nature of body and of God.[19] Kant, of course, has a much more intricate theory of how our cognition of geometry works and argues that philosophical theology of the sort that lies so close to the heart of the *Meditations* is largely an illusion (which is not to say that Kant thinks it is somehow easy to see this, or that he lacks respect for the project). In any event, in the Fifth Meditation Descartes draws heavily on one's sense of being cognitively in touch with mind-independent structure (with truth or reality, as he puts it), and we will want to pay close attention to what goes into that sense.

In ¶¶5–6, Descartes seeks to move from the distinct cognition (reported in ¶3) to true and immutable natures, a movement that Descartes sees as depending on the truth rule. The basic direction of this argument involves a reorientation in the methodology of essence. As mentioned above, an Aristotelian comes into cognitive possession of the natures of things by abstracting them from her experience with things possessing those natures; Descartes thinks we are in cognitive possession of the nature of body before we experience any bodies, indeed, before we know whether any bodies exist to be experienced.

The reorientation is profound enough to raise important issues. A view like the one Descartes is advancing can create a sense that reality does not exercise control over our thought. It can make it hard to see how to distinguish between cognition of something real and mere flights of fancy, or, for that matter, why any of our cognition should be regarded as better than fictional cognition. Let me explain.

According to the abstractionist picture, when I understand a nature or essence, I work with something that originally existed in the world and was, so to speak, extracted from the world, through abstraction. This fact yields a certain picture of the difference between my cognition of, say, a cow and of, say, a griffin: There is a nature corresponding to my cognition of cowhood because that cognition originated in real things, in actually existing cows. We do not interact with griffins; our cognition of them is constructed out of more basic materials. (On the interpretation of I.¶6 presented in chapter 1, those materials would be, for the scholastics, parts of animals that we have interacted with—for example, the head of an eagle and the body of a lion—and for Descartes, certain simple and universal things.) Since our cognition of a griffin is constructed in this manner, there is, for all we know, no nature corresponding to it. As far as we can tell, our idea of a griffin (as opposed to the elements out of which it is constructed) is of an arbitrary invention. For the abstractionist, then,

the way the world exercises control over our cognition marks a line between our cognition of real essences and our cognition of what are, for
all we know, fictional beings.[20]

When Descartes rejects an abstractionist theory of human cognition
in favor of his own nativist account, he gives up that picture of how the
world exercises control over our cognition. As he does so, he loses that
means of distinguishing between cognition of the fictive or imaginary
and cognition of the real, and, more fundamentally, he loses that basis
for thinking that some of our cognition is indeed of something real. Descartes's new way of distinguishing between real and fictive cognition
trades heavily on the idea of substantive judgment: according to him,
our ability to make substantive judgments shows us the reality of our
cognition, shows us that our cognition involves what he terms true and
immutable natures. The emphasis that Descartes places on substantive
judgment here marks, I believe, a deep continuity with the primacy given
to judgment in the characterization of our nature as cognitive beings in
the Second Meditation: what we learn now is that the way to determine
whether our thought is real as opposed to fictive is not to consider
whether the cognition came from the world (via the senses), but instead
is to consider whether the cognition enables us to make substantive judgments. If it does, then we have it that (in part on the basis of the divine
guarantee) this cognition involves a real ("true and immutable") nature.

The place where Descartes takes these issues up is ¶¶5 and 6. I believe
that his break with abstractionism makes this discussion inevitable, because the departure requires him to provide his own account of real cognition. Commentators have often failed to understand the purpose of
this discussion; they tend to treat it as a sort of preamble to the ontological argument, which, I believe, is misleading on two counts. First, Descartes would have had to offer some account of the difference between
real and fictive cognition even if he were uninterested in the ontological
argument. Second, as I will argue at the end of the second part of this
chapter, the ontological argument is no more dependent on Descartes's
theory of true and immutable natures than any substantive judgment,
for example, the judgment that a triangle's angles sum to two right angles; in particular, Descartes recognizes a sense of ("objective") certainty
in which one can be certain of either without knowing the theory of
true and immutable natures.

Descartes signals the importance of his topic at the beginning of ¶5:

> I think that what is most of all to be considered here [*Quodque hic maxime
> considerandum puto*] is that I find within me countless ideas of things [*rerum*]
> which even though they may not exist [*fortassi nullibi existant*] anywhere

outside me still cannot be called nothing; for although in a sense they can be thought at will, they are not my invention but have their own true and immutable natures. (7:64; 2:44)

Although the two claims—that the natures in question (viz. the natures of certain *things* of which I have ideas)[21] are immutable and that they are true—are closely related, they have different emphases. The remainder of ¶5 focuses primarily on their immutability; ¶6, on their truth or reality.

Here is how Descartes develops, in ¶5, the thought that my geometrical ideas present me with "immutable and eternal" natures:

> When, for example, I imagine a triangle, even if perhaps no such figure exists, or has ever existed, anywhere outside my thought, there is still a determinate nature, or essence, or form of the triangle which is immutable and eternal, and not invented by me or dependent on my mind. This is clear from the fact that various properties can be demonstrated of the triangle, for example that its three angles equal two right angles, that its greatest side subtends its greatest angle, and the like; and since these properties are ones which I now clearly recognize [*agnosco*] whether I want to or not, even if I never thought of them at all when I previously imagined the triangle, it follows that they cannot have been invented by me. (7:64; 2:44–45)

Descartes is claiming here that my cognition of a triangle is of some structure—call it what you will, a "nature, or essence, or form"—which, on the one hand, does not depend on any existing triangles and, on the other hand, does not depend on my mind.

Let's begin by trying to understand better exactly what it is that is supposed to trigger the belief that, when I am doing geometry, I am onto a mind-independent structure, a mind-independent subject matter, some "eternal and immutable" "nature, or essence, or form" (whatever exactly these turn out to be). One line of interpretation runs as follows. If I ascribe properties truly to something, there must be some subject of my ascription. So if, for example, I think truly to myself that the longest side of a triangle subtends its greatest angle, there has to be a subject for this thought. This subject may not exist anywhere outside of my thought, but it has to have some manner of being, in order for me to be able to ascribe properties to it. (Descartes scholars have sometimes linked this interpretation with the theory of Alexius Meinong, who held that subjects of predication, even if they do not exist, must at least "subsist." These commentators have suggested that the position Descartes develops in the Fifth Meditation on true and immutable natures closely resembles the one Meinong holds on subsistence.)[22] On this line of interpretation, the need for true and immutable natures is generated by the need for there to be a subject of a true predication. Let's call this the true-predication-based interpretation.

Commentators who are drawn to this interpretation recognize that the situation is more complex. This is because there are subjects of apparent true predications that Descartes denies have true and immutable natures. These denials form the backbone of Descartes's response to certain obvious counterexamples to the ontological argument. For example, in the First Objections, Caterus offers the definition "existing lion." He argues that it follows from Descartes's principles that existence belongs to such a complex, from which we can infer that the existing lion exists. In his reply, Descartes denies that *existing lion* has a true and immutable nature. One requirement (more emphasized in the *Meditations*) is that true and immutable natures have nontrivial or unforeseen consequences (this is based in part on the clause "even if I never thought of them at all when I previously imagined the triangle" in the extract above). Another requirement (more emphasized in the First Replies) is that true and immutable natures do not admit of being "divided" "by a clear and distinct intellectual operation" (7:117; 2:83) in the way that *winged horse* can be divided into *winged* and *horse* (or *existing lion* into *existing* and *lion*).²³

It is not obvious how these new requirements sit with the initial idea that true predications require subjects. Perhaps the thought is that unless these additional requirements are met, there is no true predication after all; or perhaps, again, the thought is that, say, "a winged horse has wings" is a true predication, and so winged horse is a subject, but does not count as a true and immutable nature, because it fails to meet one of the additional requirements (that it have nontrivial consequences, that it be indivisible). (In the First Replies, Descartes says that it is divisible.) The secondary literature on this topic mainly struggles to locate a textually consistent position in Descartes, without asking after its larger philosophical coherence.²⁴

I find the true-predication-based interpretation unhelpful. To see why, it is useful to have an example of an impossible or dubiously possible thing. Let me take as an example a chimera. In the tradition, a chimera—a being with a lion's head, goat's body, and serpent's tail—was often taken to be impossible and not merely nonexistent. At some places Descartes seems to use the term *chimera* as a stand-in for an impossible thing (e.g., II.¶2 and III.¶5; on III.¶5, see 5:354; 3:376), a sense of the word that is in the same vein as the English adjective *chimerical*. At other places, Descartes's position sounds more nuanced. Chimeras come up in his conversation with Burman. According to Burman's notes, Descartes said:

> It must be stressed at this point that we are talking of clear perception, not
> of imagination. Even though we can with the utmost clarity imagine the

head of a lion joined to the body of a goat, or some such thing, it does not therefore follow that they exist [*existere*], since we do not clearly perceive the link [*nexus*], so to speak, between them. For example, I may clearly see Peter standing, but I do not clearly see that standing is contained in and conjoined [*contineri et connexum*] with Peter. (5:160; 3:343–44)[25]

Although what Descartes says (according to Burman's report) is that since we cannot perceive clearly the link between the parts, we cannot conclude that chimeras exist, I think it is likely that he also holds that unless we clearly perceive the link, we cannot conclude that chimeras are possible. Still, this is not as strong as to say that we know chimeras to be impossible. So I think we can detect a more cautious attitude in Descartes, to the effect that we can tell from the sort of perception we have of chimeras whether or not they are possible. (Hobbes seems to treat chimeras as of doubtful possibility in the Third Objections [7:179].)

Let's suppose, then, that chimeras are of dubious possibility (for most of what I say, it will not matter whether one makes this assumption or the stronger assumption that chimeras are impossible). Now consider the following two predications:

1. A chimera is a chimera.
2. A triangle is a triangle.

Both (1) and (2) are *prima facie* truths. Yet while there is a true and immutable nature of a triangle, we do not know that there is a true and immutable nature of a chimera. If (2) were enough to show us that a triangle has a true and immutable nature, why isn't (1) enough to show us that a chimera has a true and immutable nature? Let me try to sharpen the point. Consider:

3. A chimera has the head of a lion.
4. A triangle has three angles summing to two right angles.

Descartes indicates that (4) does show us that a triangle has a true and immutable nature. But he cannot think the same about (3), since he thinks we do not know that a chimera has a true and immutable nature.

Now, one can imagine two basic replies to these questions. The first reply is that if a chimera is an impossible thing, then (1) and (3) are not truths (any more than, many would argue, "A round square is round" is a truth). If so, then (1) and (3) cannot be known to be true so long as we do not know whether chimeras are possible. Although I do not find Descartes's texts explicit on this point, I am inclined to think this is his view, mainly because of the close connection he sees between truth and reality. In the Second Meditation, he seems to reason from there being no reality to there being no truth. This gives the impression: no chimera nature, no chimera truths. If this is right, then Descartes does indeed hold that a true predication requires a true and immutable nature for its subject, but (1) and (3) are not true predications (but only apparent true predications) and so do not require true and immutable natures for subjects.[26]

Notice, however, that if we go this route, whether we have in fact a true predication is not something that we can read off the surface structure of the predication. "A chimera is a chimera" looks a lot like "A triangle is a triangle," and "A chimera has the head of a lion" looks a lot like "A triangle has three angles summing to two right angles." The first member of each pair is not a true predication and the second is, because the first has no true and immutable nature underneath it and the second does. This suggests that there is something wrong with reading ¶5 in a way that would have us move from our antecedent sense of the truth of a given predication to there being a true and immutable nature underneath. It would seem rather that Descartes must be keying on something else besides truth, in getting us to see that a true and immutable nature is involved in our cognition of the triangle.[27]

The other reply—which seems less likely to me, but, as far as I know, consistent with the texts—is that (1) and (3) are bona fide truths. If this is so, then we cannot infer from our having cognized a truth that there must be a true and immutable nature underlying our cognition. Some truths—for example, a triangle has three angles summing to two right angles—involve truth and immutable natures, and some truths—for example, a chimera has the head of a lion—do not. One way to think about this second position is that some truths are "real," resting on mind-independent structure of some sort, and other truths are merely "nominal," arising, in effect, from a decision to group the features head of a lion, body of a goat, tail of serpent under the rubric *chimera*. On this reply, before we can conclude from a truth that there is a true and immutable nature involved, we need to figure out first whether the truth is real or nominal.

Whichever way we go here—whether we take "A chimera is a chimera" and "A chimera has a lion's head" not to be truths, or we take them to be truths—we seem to need to bring something else besides truth into the picture in order to determine whether the thing that we have cognized has a true and immutable nature. On the first view, this is because we need to figure out whether we have a true and immutable nature in play before we can tell whether we have a truth. On the second view, this is because we need to figure out whether the truth is real or nominal before we can tell whether the truth involves a true and immutable nature.

What else might Descartes be keying on? Well, notice that the two examples Descartes gives—"[the triangle's] three angles equal two right

angles" and "[the triangle's] greatest side subtends its greatest angle"—
are both cases of *substantive* judgments, the kind of judgments Kant will
later call synthetic. They do not have the form "A is A" or "A and B is A."
This fact contributes to the sense that my perception is not merely skim-
ming along a formal surface, but has penetrated to something real beneath
it. I believe that Descartes thinks that where we can make judgments that
are not merely formal, we can see that we have a sort of insight into a subject matter. But where we have insight, there must be a locus or source
of that intelligibility. In the tradition, essences or natures served as loci of
intelligibility: to understand what something is is to grasp its essence or
nature. This ability to make judgments that are not merely formal triggers
a sense that we are onto an essence or nature. (This is why, I take it, Descartes's reasoning leads to there being a true and immutable *nature* and
not just a *subject*.)

On this "understanding-based" interpretation, what is moving the meditator is the idea that where one has rational insight, where one has understood, there is an essence or nature that she has understood, serving as
the source of that intelligibility. It is this sense that we have such insight—
that our thought is being controlled by the mind-independent structure
into which we have insight—that shows us that our thought involves a
true and immutable nature. The importance that Descartes attaches to
our ability to make what I am calling nonformal judgments, in determining whether or not we are onto a true and immutable nature, is of a piece
with his reservations about purely formal thinking. When I think formally, as when I conclude from "A is A" that "Triangle is triangle," there is
no guarantee that I have understood anything—no guarantee, to paraphrase Descartes's well-known remark from Rule 10 of the *Regulae*, that
reason hasn't taken a holiday (10:406; 1:36). For example, when focusing
on surface structure, I conclude "Triangle is triangle," it is not obvious
from this that there is a nature underneath my cognition; for all I can tell
from that cognition, I might be in no better position than if I had con-
cluded "Chimera is chimera" (or "Winged horse is winged")—cases in
which we have no reason to think that there is a nature underlying our
thought. By way of contrast, when I make a substantive judgment, I can
see that I have penetrated down to the level of a nature or essence.

It is worth noticing that, when Descartes makes the point that these
natures are "somethings" and "not nothings," the distinction he is making is between a reality or a being and a nonreality or a nonbeing, and
that distinction is orthogonal to a distinction between existence and nonexistence. Sometimes Descartes is seen as carving out a special ontological status for these "somethings" and "not nothings." That is, sometimes
he is taken in ¶¶5–6 as attempting to answer the following question: if
we suppose that no triangles exist in the actual world, what sort of being

does the nature *triangle* have? (Thinking that Descartes is trying to answer this question is one of the things that has encouraged some commentators to see Descartes as reaching for something like Meinong's
theory of "subsistence" in ¶¶5–6.) However, I don't see Descartes as
much concerned here with the question of the ontological status. Rather,
he is interested in the structures that might have this or that ontological
status. This seems to me in keeping with a traditional medieval view,[28]
where reality or being (a "determinate nature, or essence, or form") is
viewed, in a way, as prior to existence. One begins with some reality
(some form or essence), say, triangle, and asks of it what mode of existence it has: for example, does it exist in the world (real existence) or in
the mind (objectively, as Descartes would say)? (If one recognizes subsistence as a relevant alternative, one could also ask: Does triangle subsist
or exist, and if it exists, does it exist in the world or exist in the mind?)[29]

What Descartes is concerned with here is *triangle*—that is, the structure of which we ask, Does it exist in the world or in the mind (or perhaps subsist)?—and not, as far as I can see, its mode of existence (or
subsistence, if this is added to the menu). (In other words, he is concerned with the being or reality that has the "ontological status," not
with the "ontological status" itself.) What is important to him is the idea
that such structures, for example, the triangle (the thing that may or may
not exist), can *determine* my cognition; and the point he is making is that
in order for them to do this, examples of such structures need not exist
anywhere outside my thought. This is the sense, I believe, of Descartes's
difficult remark that "even if perhaps no such figure exists, or has ever
existed, anywhere outside my thought, there is still a determinate nature,
or essence, or form of the triangle which is immutable and eternal, and
not invented by me or dependent on my mind" (¶5; 7:64; 2:45). (Another
way that my thought might be determined, of course, is by my decision
to use the word *chimera* to refer to something with a lion's head, a goat's
body, and a serpent's tail. But then my thought would be determined
only by my stipulation, not by a nature.)

Let me say a little more about the conception of nonformal or substantive judgment (or insight or understanding) that is supposed to clue us in
to when our thought is of a true and immutable nature. I believe *property*
in ¶¶5–6 carries with it something of the traditional medieval meaning
of a *proprium*, a necessary accident. Accidents are supposed to be a kind
of reality, as opposed to privations or negations, which are not. It is not
clear, for example, that Descartes would want to give the same treatment to a negation (e.g., the triangle's not having four sides) or a relation
(e.g., the triangle's having fewer sides than a square), because it is not
clear that negations or relations have natures. I think Descartes's basic

picture here is that in the case of the triangle, we begin with a reality, being a triangle, and notice that this reality involves a property, for example, having three angles that sum to two right angles. Usually, this property will be a further reality, over and above what is strictly contained in its nature; this is how Aristotelians viewed *propria*, that is, as accidents, and so as adding additional reality to a being, over and above what is contained in its essence. Since properties lie outside of the essences or nature they flow from, the judgment that, for example, a triangle has three angles summing to two right angles is not merely an elucidation of the essence of a triangle; it makes a substantive addition to our cognition of the triangle.[30] (I take it that much of what would later fall under the rubric of "necessary synthetic knowledge" would have in this period been seen as a matter of understanding how a property flows from an essence.)

Further, in the Aristotelian tradition, to see how a property flows from a thing is to understand something about the thing's nature. When I notice that a triangle must have three angles that sum to two right angles, I understand something about it; the nature of a triangle serves as a locus of understanding. And this fits with a traditional conception of essence, which connects essences or natures with understanding and intelligibility: as noted earlier, to understand what a thing is is to grasp its nature. That is why, I take it, Descartes thinks that there is a smooth path from my being able to demonstrate a property of a triangle to the triangle's possessing a nature.[31]

It is not clear to me that Descartes holds that every substantive judgment involves a nature.[32] I think that there are probably two requirements: first, that we are dealing with (putative) realities—that is, with things and properties—and second, that we have insight or understanding into how they are related. So very general eternal truths, those involving "common notions," for example, "Nothing comes from nothing" (see the list given in *Principles*, I, 49), are not, it seems to me, based in such natures, because *nothing*, I take it, does not have a nature (or properties). (It is also conceivable that Descartes regards these causal principles as somehow nonsubstantive or tautological, that is, as analytic rather than synthetic in Kant's sense, or formal in some other way. I doubt this, but I won't explore the issue here.)

I want to turn now specifically to Descartes's treatment of immutability in ¶5: what does Descartes mean when he says that a nature is immutable? What makes a subject mutable and what makes a subject immutable? I think the basic idea here falls out of what we discussed above. In the case of the chimera, what holds the subject together—what combines the lion's head, goat's body, and serpent's tail into one thing—is a more or less arbitrary decision on our part. In the case of the triangle, there is a nature that collects the various triangle *propria* (to which nature any attempt to define a triangle, on our part, must be faithful). The nature of a chimera is mutable, as far as we can tell, because it is arbitrary or invented, the product of our fictive activity: it does not, as far as we can tell, connect to any reality over and above that contained in the real elements in its composition, lion's head, goat's body, and serpent's tail (which may be in turn composed of even more basic real elements—see I.¶6). The nature of a triangle is immutable because it does not depend on anything we do—it is "already there," as we might put it. If we help ourselves to a bit of metaphysics that Descartes does not choose to share with the meditator, it is "already there" because God created it, and did so immutably. This is to provide a positive account of the essence or nature's "ontological status," something that Descartes conspicuously avoids doing in the Fifth Meditation. For the purposes of the Fifth Meditation, it is enough to make the point that true and immutable natures, whatever their ultimate ontological status is, determine our substantive judgments and so, for that reason and in that sense, do not depend on us.

But now, how do I tell when something is real (and hence immutable and "already there") and when something is merely the result of my fictive activity (and hence mutable and dependent on me)? It may seem a simple matter that one can determine just by asking oneself whether the entity in question resulted from one's own activity. But it turns out that the matter is rather more complicated than that. I "arbitrarily" put three lines together to form a triangle; I "arbitrarily" put a lion's head, a goat's body, and a serpent's tail together to form a chimera. What shows me that in the one case I have gotten on to reality while in the other case there is no reason to think I have done so? Descartes's idea, as we have seen, is that when I have combined elements together in a way that I can see yields new properties, I can tell that I have landed on a structure; so it is evident to me from the fact that I can extract new properties from the triangle—features that do not follow from linehood, threehood, and so on—that the thing of which I have formed my idea has a true and immutable nature. The reason the three-line structure resists division is that when it is divided, we lose the ground for these new properties. By way of contrast, I do not see any new properties issuing forth from the combination "chimera." Nothing similarly blocks its division into its original components. As far as I can tell, there are only the components (and whatever reality they contain) and my combining activity. Thus, I believe, although the nontrivial-consequences requirement and the indivisibility requirements initially appear to be two separate ideas (and are often treated that way in the secondary literature), they are very closely related in the end. I think this suggests that Descartes's thinking on this topic is more unified than might at first have been apparent.

This general outlook is confirmed, I think, by a well-known, difficult discussion from the First Replies. In that passage Descartes first claims that being a triangle inscribed in a square does not have a true and immutable nature and later claims that it does. The passage begins:

> [I]t should be noted that those ideas which do not contain true and immutable natures but only ones which are fictive and composed by the intellect, can be divided by that same intellect, not simply through abstraction but through a clear and distinct operation, so that those which cannot be divided in this way were without doubt not composed by it. When, for example, I think of a winged horse or an actually existing lion, or a triangle inscribed in a square, I readily understand that I am also able to think of a horse without wings, or a lion which does not exist, or a triangle apart from a square and so on; hence these things do not have true and immutable natures [*nec proinde illa veras & immutabiles naturas habere*]. (7:117; 2:83–84)

I should say that I believe that there is something misleading about what Descartes is saying here. It gives the impression that there is some fairly simple test to determine whether there is a true and immutable nature of a winged equine creature. However, as we saw earlier in connection with the chimera, whether there is such a nature depends on whether there exists some equinelike automaton structure with wings, and it is hard to see how the simple test that Descartes is proposing here is supposed to settle that question. I think the question that the test is designed to answer is subtly different: Does my cognition of a winged horse involve (contain) a true and immutable nature? We know that Descartes's answer is negative, because I can divide it into pieces: if my cognition had picked up some winged equine structure, it would resist such separation. So while there may in fact be, for all I know, a winged-horse nature, my cognition does not show me that this is so. (One way to put the point is that if there is a winged-horse essence, I cannot tell this, because I am working only with a nominal, and not a real, definition of it.)

In the continuation of the passage it emerges that divisibility of a thing is sensitive to its ability to generate new properties. As I reflect and notice that the combination of a triangle inscribed in a square does have special properties of its own (e.g., the area of the square component is at least double the area of the triangle component), I realize that the combination does have a true and immutable nature:

> But if I think of a triangle or square (I will not include the lion or the horse, since their natures are not transparently clear to us), then whatever

I apprehend as being contained in the idea of a triangle—for example that its three angles are equal to two right angles—I can with truth assert of the triangle. And the same applies to the square with respect to whatever I apprehend as being contained in the idea of a square. For even if I can understand what a triangle is if I abstract from the fact that its three angles are equal to two right angles, I cannot deny that this property applies to the triangle by a clear and distinct intellectual operation—that is, while understanding what I mean by my denial. Moreover, if I consider a triangle inscribed in a square, with a view not to attributing to the square properties that belong only to the triangle, or attributing to the triangle properties that belong to the square, but with a view to examining only the properties which arise out of the conjunction of the two, then the nature of the composite will be just as true and immutable as the nature of the triangle alone or the square alone. And hence it will be quite in order to maintain that the square is not less than double the area of the triangle inscribed in it, and to affirm other similar properties to the nature of this composite figure. (7:117–18; 2:84)

I think what Descartes is trying to say is this: I can see that a triangle has a true and immutable nature (even though I can think of one of its lines without the others by "a clear and distinct mental operation") because I can see that it has the further property of having three angles equal to two right angles, and, similarly, I can see that a triangle inscribed in a square has a true and immutable nature, even though I can think of the square without the triangle by "a clear and distinct mental operation," because I can see that it has the further property of the square's area not being less than double the triangle's. In other words, I think that subsequently noticing how new properties flow from a triangle inscribed in a square shows that such a figure has the same claim to having a true and immutable nature as does a triangle, canceling the earlier impression that such a figure lacks a true and immutable nature, as does a winged horse or existing lion (although I admit that the repudiation of the earlier impression is not explicitly marked in the text).

In order for this approach to work—and let me note that although I believe it fits well with the relevant texts, I concede that it is somewhat speculative—one has to be careful about what counts as a new property or perfection. Assume I put together golden, mountain, and conical, to form *golden conical mountain*. Then I can substantively conclude that its volume is one-third the area of its base times its height, and so I can substantively conclude that *golden conical mountain* has the property of both being metallic and having a volume that is one-third the area of its base times its height. I do not think Descartes would view this composite property as a new property or perfection. There are still just the two

realities, the property of having a volume related in a certain proportion
to its height and the area of its base (which already belongs to one of its
components, conical), and the property of being metallic (part of, let's
suppose, what it is to be golden): positing the complex subject does not
somehow combine these two realities into some new, third reality. So
one could not argue that a golden conical mountain has a true and immutable nature because it has the "new" property of both having a volume related in a certain proportion to its height and the area of its base
and being metallic. Noticing that the three angles of a triangle sum to
two right angles or that the longest side of a triangle subtends the greatest angle is, on Descartes's telling, very different. These properties cannot be "reduced" in the same way. That is why he thinks that in the case
of a triangle (or, later, of a supremely perfect being) we do have the
sense of charting out mind-independent structure, whereas in the case
of a golden conical mountain we do not. In the latter case, there is only
golden and whatever properties, if any, substantively flow from it, conical and whatever properties substantively flow from it, and mountain
and whatever properties substantively flow from it. We could also consider the "analytic summation" of these properties, that is, P and Q as
well as P and Q, but, again, to treat these as new perfections or realities
would be a form of double counting.[33]

Here is perhaps a more difficult case for the view. Consider the property "having the capacity to fly" (or maybe having the equipment to fly).
Might not this be a *proprium* that follows neither from winged nor from
horse, but rather only from the combination winged horse? The "distri-
bution" of this property across the original components is not as clear as
in the case of the golden conical mountain. I am not sure how much of a
problem this presents for Descartes's position (as I have tried to explain
it). Let's suppose, for the sake of argument, that the capacity to fly indeed follows from being a winged horse. I imagine that the first question
Descartes would want to ask is, Exactly how does it follow? Is it, for example, something we are assuming about the definition of winged (so
that everything winged "by definition" flies) or something we are assuming about a horse (so that horses are the kind of things which "by definition" fly, once they are given wings)? If so, then the "following" does not
encourage the thought that we have a true and immutable nature here.
Or, to go to the other extreme, if the reason it follows is that we can see
from our mechanical family of equine blueprints and our family of wing
blueprints how flying flows from being winged and equine (whereas the
same ability does not flow from, for example, being winged and ostrich-
like), then, of course, the ability to fly would be indicative of a true and
immutable nature. What Descartes seems to be supposing is that cases
will cleanly divide into the one situation or the other, an assumption that

does seem to me debatable. (Part of what is moving Descartes here, I think, is the thought that if I have not made my way to a new nature, I am functioning on a nominal plane; given his views about the sterility of traditional logic, he doesn't think that we could extract genuinely new properties from merely nominal definitions.) Still, the thought that we can tell the difference between when we are merely unfolding a series of consequences of (our own) definitions, our own *dicta*, and when we are tracking some nature or essence, *re*, found in the reality (independently of what we have done) seems powerful to me. Tracking the structure of a triangle does not seem like extracting the capacity to fly from being a winged horse, when no winged-horse structure (be it of the Cartesian mechanical variety I have been imagining here or of a more traditional Aristotelian teleological variety) is being appealed to.[34]

I want to turn now to ¶6, which concerns specifically the "truth" of these natures. This brings us face to face with what I take to be the central issue in this discussion, namely, how, having abandoned the doctrine of abstraction, Descartes intends to establish that, indeed, my cognition of a triangle is of something real.

Descartes begins ¶6 by explicitly rejecting the scholastic picture of how we get on to geometrical natures:

> It would be beside the point [*Neque ad rem attinet*] for me to say that since I have from time to time seen bodies of triangular shape, the idea of the triangle may have come to me from external things by means of the sense organs. For I can think up countless other shapes which there can be no suspicion of my ever having encountered through the senses, and yet I can demonstrate various properties of these shapes, just as I can with the triangle. (7:64–65; 2:45)

How might the claim that the idea of a triangle comes to me through the senses be construed as an objection to what has been said so far? And why does Descartes think this objection fails?

Well, in ¶5, Descartes claimed that there is "a determinate essence, nature, or form" that my idea of a triangle makes available to me, even if no triangle exists anywhere outside my thought. But someone might object: Since my access to the nature of a triangle depends on my having abstracted the species *triangle* from sensory experience of triangles (bodies shaped triangularly), I could not have access to a triangle's nature unless triangles exist, or at least unless triangles have existed at some time in the past. To this Descartes responds by rejecting the claim that our access to the nature *triangle* runs through the senses.

In support of this rejection, he makes an argument analogous to two others he makes concerning the imagination's role in our cognition of extension, one in the Second Meditation and one in the Sixth. Both of these other arguments concern what might be called the scope or extent of our cognition of the geometrical. In the wax discussion, he points out that what sequences we might run through in my imagination cannot capture the unbounded potential transformations implicit in our grasp of a body as an extended, flexible, changeable thing. In the Sixth Meditation, he argues that while we are able to operate cognitively with very large geometrical figures—we can see truths, note relationships, and so forth concerning them—the imagination's ability to depict such figures perspicuously is limited. Descartes takes this to show that geometrical cognition does not depend on the imagination. Here, in the Fifth Meditation, he argues that we encounter too few shapes through the senses for the senses to be plausibly considered the basis of our cognition of geometrical entities. So, in all three cases Descartes argues that because our cognitive grasp of geometry or extension outstrips the capacities of our lower cognitive faculties, sense and imagination, those lower cognitive faculties cannot be the source of that grasp.

It is unclear how much these sorts of considerations really show. In particular, they rest perhaps on an uncharitable construal of the scholastic position. According to that position, we do need our senses to grasp the object of geometry, quantified matter or matter considered as quantified, but whether it follows from this that one cannot successfully reason about shapes and volumes that one hasn't actually experienced is not obvious. Perhaps once we get on to the general subject matter through the senses, that is, matter qua quantified, we can subsequently operate on it, say, describe and delimit it in various ways. Exactly how much sensory input is required on this theory to put us into cognitive contact with the subject matter of geometry and, once we have grasped that subject matter, exactly what sorts of subsequent cognition (with the assistance of the imagination) become possible, seem open questions.

Descartes may be implicitly relying here on a different idea, namely, a sense of the relative unimportance of sensory input for our geometrical judgments—for seeing, for example, that the three angles of a triangle must sum to two right angles. In this context, it is natural to think of the sensory contribution to our judgments along the lines of what a diagram contributes to our ability to appreciate geometrical relationships. Diagrams can, to be sure, help us to see such relationships, but it is natural to think of them as merely heuristics, useful for suggesting various relationships that, if they are to be appreciated, must be intellectually apprehended (which is why, for example, the coarseness of the diagram seems largely irrelevant to its function). When I inspect a diagram, it is not as if the subject matter for a judgment is transmitted from the diagram through my inspection to the mind; rather, the diagram serves to highlight or to help bring out certain relationships in an antecedently available subject matter. So even if it should turn out, for some reason, that human beings were unable to appreciate certain geometrical relationships without the assistance of such props or pointers, that would not show that the senses are what makes this subject matter available to the mind (as the scholastics held). By keying on our ability to discern nontrivial relations between subjects and their properties as a guide to when we are (and when we are not) onto a real, mind-independent structure, Descartes may be quietly reorienting the discussion in a way that makes it harder to accept the scholastic thesis that the subject matter for our geometrical judgments is imported from the world by means of the senses.

But if the mind does not get on to what it thinks about through the senses in the way that the scholastics thought, what reason do we have for believing that reality is making a difference to our thought? Of course, it surely seems to me that there was a truth or reality that I grasped when I noticed that the longest side of a triangle subtends its greatest angle. But can I offer an argument that this is in fact the case, that is, that there is indeed something, a truth or reality, that I grasp when I notice that the longest side of a triangle subtends its greatest angle?

Descartes does provide an argument to this effect, one that is, significantly, based on the truth rule, and so on the main results of the Third and Fourth Meditations. In ¶6 he continues:

> For I can think up countless other shapes which there can be no suspicion of my ever having encountered through the senses, and yet I can demonstrate various properties of these shapes, just as I can with the triangle. All these things [omnes] are firmly [sane] true [verae], inasmuch as they are clearly cognized by me [quandoquidem a me clare cognoscuntur], and therefore they are something, and not merely nothing [aliquid . . . non merum nihil]; for it is obvious that anything that is true is something [illud omne quod verum est esse aliquid]; and I have already amply demonstrated all those things that I clearly cognize are true [demonstravi illa omnia quae clare cognosco esse vera]. (7:64–65; 2:45)

The general shape of Descartes's argument is clear enough—namely, that what has been established in the Third and Fourth Meditations shows me that I grasp something true and real (a "something") when I notice that the longest side of a triangle subtends its greatest angles—but precisely what is being claimed here is somewhat obscure.[35]

Part of the cause of the obscurity is that what Descartes calls "true" in the passage (i.e., the antecedent of omnes) seems to be properties, which properties are said to be "something, and not merely nothing." I take him to be advancing the same claim with respect to the natures in which the properties inhere, so that triangle or triangular shape (or, perhaps better, extension shaped in a triangular way) is also "true" and "something, and not merely nothing." So, the truth rule—here expressed as "all those things that I clearly cognize are true"—is supposed to get me from the clarity of my conception to the "truth" or "somethinghood" of the properties and natures that I cognize.

But Descartes's claim that a thing (a property or nature) is true sounds odd, and seems to conflict with his claim in the Third Meditation that "falsity in the strict sense, or formal falsity, can occur only in judgements" (III.¶19; 7:44; 2:30),[36] which presumably implies that truth also, "in the strict sense," can occur only in judgments. Moreover, in line with this statement from the Third Meditation, the Fourth Meditation focuses on truth as a property of judgment. This focus is, I suggested, of a piece with Thomas's account of truth as a matter of "adequation" between an intellect and a thing. But the relationship that Descartes has in view here, namely, the relationship between my idea of triangle and the nature *triangle*, seems close to the relationship that Aquinas sees between the "species" we acquire when our intellects form "the quiddities [essences] of things" and the quiddities themselves, a relation that Aquinas explicitly distinguishes from the "adequation" involved in truth (DV Q. 1, A. 3).

It helps to mitigate the sense of oddity here to realize that, although Descartes maintains that falsity in a strict sense, and so presumably truth as well, occurs only in judgments, he has been consistently applying the word *true* to things elsewhere in the *Meditations*. So, for example, in the First Meditation, in a paragraph comparing thought with painting, the meditator initially conjectures that certain general kinds of things—eyes, head, hands, and the whole body—are "things that exist not as imaginary but as true [*res . . . non imaginarias, sed veras existere*]"; and the eventual conclusion he reaches is that there are things that function in thought as the "as it were true colors [*tanquam coloribus veris*] from which we form all the images of things, whether true or false [*seu verae, seu falsae*]" (I.¶6; 7:19–20; 2:13–14).

In the Third Meditation, Descartes presents an account of material falsity, according to which an idea is materially false when it presents a nonthing as a thing, that is, when it presents an absence of reality as a reality, thereby inviting error. He also claims there that "the idea I have of God" is "the truest and most clear and distinct of all my ideas." This thesis is developed as follows:

> This idea of a supremely perfect and infinite being is, I say, true in the highest degree [*maxime vera*]; for although one perhaps may suppose that such a being does not exist, it cannot be supposed that the idea of such a being exhibits [*exhibere*] nothing real [*nihil reale*: no reality?], as I said before with regard to the idea of cold. The idea is, moreover, utterly clear and

distinct; for whatever I clearly and distinctly perceive as being real [*reale*] and true [*verum*], and implying any perfection, is wholly contained in it. (III.¶25; 7:46; 2:31–32)

Here the "truth" of the idea of God seems to be a function of the reality it exhibits. The point Descartes is making about the idea of God is parallel to the one he makes in the Fifth Meditation about the idea of the triangle. In the Fifth Meditation he claims that even if no triangles exist, the idea exhibits a something, not a nothing: a reality, we might say; in the Third he claims that even if we assume that God does not exist, it cannot be denied that the idea of God exhibits reality.

Although the passages are parallel in this way, there is an important difference. In the Third Meditation truth is predicated of the *idea*, whereas in the Fifth it is predicated of the *nature* that the idea exhibits or presents. In the Third Meditation the truth rule has yet to be established, so we are not in a position yet to say anything about the mind-independent status of what is exhibited, that is, about whether there is some "determinate nature, form, or essence" independent of my mind presented by the idea. For the purposes of the argument that Descartes is making there, it is enough for the *idea* not to be materially false, not to present "nonbeing" as "being"; and Descartes believes he can show this much without taking any stance on the extramental status of the "being," that is, the truth and reality, exhibited by the idea. That requires an additional step.

So, while falsity and truth strictly (*proprie*, 7:37) belong only to judgments, Descartes has been thinking also of truth all along as a property of things and ideas. One might imagine that Descartes is simply working with two different meanings of the word *true*, one as it applies to a judgment and another as it applies to a thing or an idea, and that these meanings have little to do with each other. However, that seems unlikely on its face, and the fact that Descartes understands the truth rule to apply to both judgments where we clearly and distinctly perceive (the Fourth Meditation) and our clear and distinct cognition of things (V.¶6) indicates that he sees these two uses of *true* as deeply connected.

I think we get an important clue as to how they are connected from an intriguing, if obscure, passage near the beginning of the Second Meditation. In ¶2, in the course of reviewing the epistemic conditions under which she is operating, the meditator reasons as follows:

I will suppose then, that everything I see is false [*falsa*]. I will believe that my memory tells me lies, and that none of the things it reports ever happened. I have no senses. Body, shape, extension, movement and place are chimeras [*chimerae*]. So what remains true [*verum*]? Perhaps just this one thing [*unum*], that nothing is certain. (II.¶2; 7:24; 2:16)

When the meditator asks, "So what remains true?" the answer she gives, "Perhaps just this one thing, that nothing is certain," seems puzzling. In the envisaged situation, there would seem to be many true judgments besides that nothing is certain, for example, that she has no senses and that bodies are mere chimeras. I think we should understand her reasoning in the following way. Since she supposes that her cognitive access to reality runs through her senses, she worries that in a world with no bodies, there is no reality or, if there is, she has no access to it. In the envisaged situation, there seems to be nothing to which she is able to "adequate" her intellect, and so it seems impossible for her to make a true judgment.[37]

The line of thought just sketched provides us with a picture of how true things are related to true judgments: unless there are true things, to which we have cognitive access, we won't be able to enter into a relation of "adequation" with them, and we won't be able form true judgments. Recall that, in the scholastic tradition, what the transcendental property *true*, which applies to things, expresses is the tendency of things to enter into a relation of "adequation" with an intellect. The meditator is worried that, in view of the skeptical assumptions that she is presently making, things might not have this tendency, with the result that she could not form true judgments about them. Since, in this tradition, truth is primarily a property of judgments (and not propositions), this would be tantamount to there being no truth.

This helps us understand why Descartes finds it natural to think of the truth rule as extending both to clear and distinct cognition found in judgments and to clear and distinct cognition of things. The judgment I make when I clearly and distinctly perceive a triangle as having the property of possessing three angles equal to two right angles is true inasmuch as I clearly and distinctly perceive the former to have the latter, but I couldn't do this unless the property of having three angles equal to two right angles is a true "something" and the nature *triangle* is a true "something."

Now, to be sure, there is a way of hearing this that would trivialize the claim that things are true. One might understand the claim that the thing T is true to be equivalent to the claim that there is a true (substantive) judgment, say, that T has P, which some cognitive being makes (or at least could make) about T. So, if I can form the true judgment that a triangle T has the property P of having a longest side subtending a greatest angle, then it would trivially follow that T and P are true, because to say this is to say no more than that they can figure in true judgments. I think it's obvious that this is not Descartes's position. The claim that the nature of a triangle is true does not reduce to the fact that we can make substantive judgments concerning the triangle; rather, the fact that there is such a nature is supposed to ground or make possible judgments about a triangle.

What, then, is the substance of the claim that the nature of a triangle and the property of having three angles that sum to two right angles are each true? In the Second Meditation, what sets the meditator on the path to worrying that there may be no truth is the thought that bodies might not exist. We might regard this as a first stab at saying what is necessary in order for there to be true judgments, namely, that the things that our judgments are about actually exist. However, by the time we get to the Fifth Meditation, it is no longer so obvious that the truth of the things our judgments are about requires their real existence—that is part of the force, I take it, of Descartes's suggestion that such things have true and immutable natures "even though they may not exist anywhere outside of me." What seems required instead is simply that these things have enough of a mind-independent standing that they can determine my cognition. This is what, I think, Descartes is trying to convey when he says that a triangle has "a determinate nature, or essence, or form . . . not invented by me or dependent on my mind" and that a property of a triangle is "something, and not merely nothing." This "determinate nature, or essence, or form," let's say *structure*, is prior to my cognition in that it is the true and immutable nature of a triangle that determines my clear and distinct perception of a triangle, and it is a triangle's possession of the property of having three angles summing to two right angles that determines my clear perception that a triangle has three angles summing to two right angles, which perception, in turn, determines my judgment. The sense of being determined by the thing is part of what Descartes was trying to capture in V.¶5 by the claim that the nature is "immutable" (i.e., not subject to my manipulation); it is evoked more directly later in a remark in V.¶10 about the relation of God's existence to my thought: "It is not that my thought makes it [viz., that God really exists] so, or imposes any necessity on any thing; on the contrary it is the necessity of the thing itself, namely, the existence of God, which determines my thinking in this respect" (7:67; 2:46).

Can we say more about the relevant notion of a "determining structure"? I take it that for Descartes it is closely linked to the notion of reality or perfection, so that, for example, blindness by itself would not count as such a structure. The language "nature, essence, or form" indicates this much. There is no form (or nature or essence) of blindness, for example, because blindness is a sort of nonbeing, an absence of reality or structure. What blindness is, more specifically, is the absence of reality or structure, usually set against some larger structure or reality, such as the absence of the ability to see in a rock (i.e., a negation) or in a dog (i.e., privation). We might say, then, that in order for there to be truth, our cognition must be determined by structures that are in this sense real (and as a matter of fact, translators sometimes render the Latin *verus* by the English *real* in these contexts, so that "true things" becomes "real things").

The thesis that when we make judgments our cognition has been determined by some real structure fits with Descartes's choice of the word *idea* to describe our basic mode of cognition of things. The word *idea* is etymologically connected with the notion of a Platonic form (it was Aristotle's word for Plato's theory), and I believe that there remains enough of this heritage in Descartes's usage so that having an idea is a way of having some real structure (a "something") in one's mind. For example, when Burman objects to Descartes's claim in the Third Meditation that "there can be no ideas which are not as it were of things," by saying, "But we have an idea of nothing, and this is not an idea of a thing," Descartes responds, "That idea is purely negative, and can hardly be called an idea" (5:153; 3:338).

That an idea should be a way for real structure (true things) to determine or exist in the mind also fits with Descartes's (to a large extent inherited) doctrine of objective reality. In the First Replies (7:102), he illustrates the doctrine with the remark that the idea of the sun is the sun existing in the intellect: in order for this model to make sense the sun has to be a being (as opposed to a nonbeing). More generally, objective reality is simply reality existing objectively, and the objective reality of an idea is simply the reality that exists objectively through that idea.[38]

I do not think it would be going too far to say that what an idea fundamentally is, for Descartes, is a way for reality to determine one's cognition, a vehicle through which a reality exists in one's mind. What ideas do is to make that structure available to the mind for its contemplation, reflection, and seeing that things are so (judgment). Ideas enable the cognitive agent to appreciate various connections or relationships: to understand. For me to have an idea of such a structure at all is an accomplishment; much has to go right in order for me even to be able to make a false judgment about triangles.[39] One might think that besides the ideas that serve as vehicles through which reality exists in one's mind, there are also ideas of nothing as well as negations and privations (a species of nonbeing). However, it is not clear to me to what extent Descartes recognizes an idea of "pure" nothing, and negations and privations are understood in terms of the realities that they are negations and privations of.[40]

I am not sure that there is a great deal more to be said about the truth of properties or natures; the notion of reality I have appealed to in explicating this seems to be fundamental in Descartes's philosophy and so in some sense primitive. One issue I have not taken up is what is sometimes called the "ontological status" of these properties and natures, that is, what sort of being they have, because Descartes, for whatever reason, refrains from taking this up in the Fifth Meditation. (As I noted above, he is, as I see it, more concerned with the thing that may or may not have this or that ontological status or mode of existence than with the ontological status or mode of existence itself.) What he says in the Fifth Meditation is compatible with a variety of positions on the matter. It seems to me compatible, for example, with Aquinas's position, following a well-established theological tradition, that essences or natures are grounded in God's essence: each finite essence is a different way of imitating God's unlimited essence. It is also compatible with Descartes's own position, to judge from other writings, that God creates these natures and is their efficient cause.

One account of the ontological status of true and immutable natures that has attracted interest does not seem to me compatible with the general outlook that Descartes provides in the Fifth Meditation. It has been suggested on certain so-called conceptualist interpretations of true and immutable natures that the natures are to be identified with the objective reality of (certain) ideas.[41] But if, as suggested above, a true and immutable nature is a real structure that determines the idea (the idea itself being simply that structure or reality existing objectively), there needs to be some metaphysical distance between the structure and the ideas that the structure determines. This makes it seem misguided to identify true and immutable natures with the objective reality of ideas. For Descartes, it is the case that my idea of triangle is what it is because the nature triangle is what it is, and not the case that the nature triangle is what it is because my idea of triangle is what it is.

Although Descartes leaves the ultimate ontological status of true and immutable natures open in the Fifth Meditation, one might wonder whether the account offered here in terms of the meditator's sense of being determined by a structure is compatible with the doctrine of the creation of eternal truths that he lays out in other texts.[42] On the interpretation offered here, the meditator's sense that she is onto a mind-independent structure depends on her seeing that it *has to be* the case (say) that three angles of a triangle sum to two right angles (hence my occasional comparison of Descartes's "data," our ability to make substantive judgments, to Kant's "data," our possession of synthetic *a priori*, i.e., necessary, knowledge or cognition). But according to Descartes's thesis that God created the eternal truths, and so presumably that he could have decided not to create them, it is not (absolutely?) necessary that the three angles of a triangle sum to two right angles. So on the interpretation developed here, the meditator is supposed to be moved by a necessity that may be, in view of certain considered commitments of Descartes, ultimately illusory.

A satisfactory treatment of this issue would require a better grasp of Descartes's doctrine of the creation of the eternal truths than I have, so I will simply confine myself to a sketch of a direction of response that I find promising. What may be moving the meditator is not her sense of the "absolute" or an "all things considered" necessity of her (say) geometrical judgments, but rather a sort of conditional necessity. She thinks something like this: triangles being what they are, their angles must sum to two right angles.[43] That is, what is required in order for Descartes's general line of thought to exercise pull may not be that the meditator think that the structures themselves are necessarily as they are—that she think that it is impossible for them to have been different from the way they are (perhaps simply because God could have ordained that there be no such structure)[44]—but rather that she think that given what structures there are, it is necessary that she think or judge a certain way. Perhaps this is why Descartes characterizes the natures as "immutable" rather than "necessary": they are not open to being changed—certainly not by me and, apparently, according to Descartes, not by God, whose will is immutable. But their being unchangeable now is not to deny that they could have been different from the beginning, so to speak. In other words, it may be my sense of being determined by an immutable, eternal structure that is supposed to persuade me that I am onto a nature, and not my sense of being determined by something that could not have been otherwise.

Descartes concludes ¶6 with a significant comment:

> And even if I had not demonstrated this [viz., I have already amply demonstrated all those things that I clearly cognize are true (*demonstravi illa omnia quae clare cognosco esse vera*)], the nature of my mind is such that I cannot but assent to these things, at least so long as I clearly perceive them. I also remember that even before, when I was completely preoccupied with the objects of the senses, I always held that the most certain truths of all were the kind which I recognized clearly in connection with shapes, or numbers, or other items relating to arithmetic and geometry, or in general to pure and abstract mathematics. (7:65; 2:45)

The point that Descartes is making here is both subtle and important. He is introducing a theme that will be picked up again briefly in the next paragraph and developed more thoroughly in ¶¶13–16, concerning how to position everyday mathematical knowledge vis-à-vis his current metaphysical investigation into the nature of human cognition and its involvement with true and immutable natures. Doing mathematics does not depend on my recognizing the metaphysical substructure that Descartes details in ¶¶5–6; even so, there is a way in which, as Descartes will explain in the concluding section of the Fifth Meditation (¶¶13–16), the standing of my mathematical cognition is enhanced by having a purchase on this metaphysical substructure.

Why, and in what sense, is doing mathematics independent of having "already amply demonstrated all those things that I clearly cognize are true"? Well, Descartes writes that "the nature of my mind is such that I cannot but assent to these things, at least so long as I clearly perceive them" and implies in the next sentence that this yields a kind of certainty concerning them. Often Descartes is understood to be claiming that what certainty is involved here is merely psychological, where this means something like that while my perception is rationally compelling, its truth is not guaranteed; for that, we have to have demonstrated that everything I clearly and distinctly perceive is true (and so we need to have established the metaphysical underpinnings of cognition).[45] I think this is a mistake: Descartes usually understands certainty in such a way that it involves truth (see III.¶2). I will consider psychological readings of this remark more fully later on, when we take up the Cartesian Circle. For now, I will content myself with providing a different, and what seems to me more natural, reading of the passage.

I suggest that Descartes's remark is occasioned by the following. The discussion in ¶5 and thus far in ¶6 might easily lead to the impression that before one can do any mathematics, one must have done considerable metaphysics. That seems odd. Can it really be the case that one needs to have mastered the doctrine of true and immutable natures before one does geometry? Why couldn't there be, for example, an atheistic geometer? (This puzzlement foreshadows a concern raised by the authors of the Second Objections.) Descartes, anticipating a reaction along these lines, wishes to say something at this point about what we *would* have going for us even if we did not know the metaphysical foundations of our cognition. Thus, he notes that even before taking up his foundational project he held mathematical truths to be the "most certain . . . of all." While one is doing mathematics one is certain that one is getting on to the truth, just as while one is in the middle of a cogito experience one is certain that one is getting on to the truth.

But, one may wonder, if she has so much going for even her without knowing the metaphysical foundations of cognition, does the geometer stand to gain anything from learning what these foundations are? Is it simply that geometry and metaphysics are two separate and independent domains of inquiry? As we shall see in the final part of this chapter, the answer is no. Descartes holds that for the geometer to come to an appreciation of the metaphysical underpinnings of her cognition does improve her cognitive situation, yielding what he implies in the next paragraph is another, in some way better, grade (*gradus*) or type of certainty. What exactly this means is not yet clear and is not explained until the end of the meditation (¶¶13–16), but I don't think the existence of this better type of certainty should be taken to imply that the certainty he reports originally finding in mathematics is not really certainty or is certainty only in some subjective sense of certainty, such that being certain is compatible with being wrong.

II. *THE ONTOLOGICAL ARGUMENT* (¶¶7–12)

Let's turn to the ontological argument. Here is how Descartes puts the argument:

> But if the mere fact that I can produce from my thought the idea of something entails that everything I clearly and distinctly perceive to belong to that thing really does belong to it, is this not a possible basis for another argument to prove the existence of God? Certainly, the idea of God, or a supremely perfect being, is one which I find within me just as surely as the idea of any shape or number. And I no less clearly and distinctly understand it to pertain to his nature that he always [*semper*] exists than I understand that which I demonstrate of a figure or number to pertain to the nature [*naturam*] of the figure or number. Hence, even if it turned out that not everything on which I have meditated in these past days is true, the existence of God ought to hold for me at least the same grade of certainty as the truths of mathematics have hitherto held. (¶7; 7:65–66; 2:45)

The heart of the argument is the claim that I clearly and distinctly understand that (eternal) existence pertains to God's nature. We'll want to look more closely at what goes into this claim: how exactly is this something we *understand* about God (and so grasped with a certain amount of insight into God's nature), as opposed to something that is tacked on or stipulated? Further, the general movement of thought here, from clear and distinct cognition of a thing to certain things being true of it in virtue of the structure of its nature, is of a piece with the discussion in ¶¶5–6. This is not to say that the success of the demonstration given in ¶7 depends on one's knowing what was established in ¶¶5–6: *prima facie*, the "even if it turned out that not everything on which I have meditated in these past days is true" points in the other direction. But, then, what is the relationship between the argument taken up in ¶7 and the position developed in ¶¶5–6? This is a matter we will take up at the end of this section.

I think it is fruitful to approach the argument by attempting to focus on Descartes's differences with Thomas over the viability of an ontological argument. As noted in chapter 3 (II), Descartes's development of the ontological argument seems to have been important for the history of philosophical theology. In particular, it seems to have been locally decisive for the rationalist tradition through Kant. At the time that Descartes was writing, cosmological arguments were the most common way to try to prove God's existence. This shifts with the *Meditations*. Descartes's two most prominent rationalist successors, Spinoza and Leibniz, each advance versions of the ontological argument, and Kant, in his critique of rationalist philosophical theology, accords it the preeminent place. It is worth trying to understand what happened here, to locate as precisely as possible how and why Descartes is breaking with the Thomistic Aristotelian tradition around this topic.

To begin with, it helps to notice that what is at issue between Descartes and the Thomistic Aristotelian tradition is not the question of whether God's essence involves his existence. For that tradition, divine simplicity firmly settles the issue in favor of God's being in some strong way identical with his essence. What is at issue is rather an epistemological question, namely, How do human beings come to be in a position to know things about God, such as, for example, that his essence is identical with his existence, or even simply that he exists? In this regard, we saw in chapter 3 (II) two dramatically opposed pictures of how human beings come to be able to think about God at all, that is, of how and to what extent human beings cognize God. These different outlooks strongly affect—one could say determine—the fortune of the ontological argument. Let me explain.

According to Aquinas, human beings, because of their creaturely remoteness from God, in general, and their dependence on the senses, in particular, know God only obliquely. They do not (in this life) have immediate access to God's essence or substance; rather, they work with something resembling an Aristotelian nominal definition of God, the so-called divine names. With the help of these names—for example, everyone gives "the first efficient cause" "the name God" (ST I, Q. 2, A. 3)—human beings build mediated representations of God. God is the (as can be argued, unique) first efficient cause, whatever that being turns out to be.

By way of contrast, Descartes thinks that we start out in our philosophical theological reflection with some access to God's very essence or nature. Descartes strongly suggests in ¶7 that my access to God's nature—in particular, seeing that certain things pertain to it—is on a par with my access to a triangle's nature. In the First Replies, Descartes is explicit that we have some understanding of *what God is*, that is, God's nature or essence, when he writes of our idea of God:

> For, firstly, this idea contains what is God [*quid sit Deus*: i.e., the essence of God], at least in so far as I am capable of understanding it; and according to the laws of true logic, we must never ask whether something is until we first understand what it is [*de nulla unquam re quaeri debet* an est, *nisi prius* quid sit *intelligatur*]. (7:107–8; 2:78)

He makes a similar comment to Mersenne in a letter of 16 June 1641:

> Thus I can draw out from the idea of a triangle that its three angles equal
> two right angles, and from the idea of God that he exists, etc. So far from
> being a begging of the question, this method of demonstration is even ac-
> cording to Aristotle the most perfect of all, for in it the true definition of a
> thing occurs as the middle term. (3:383; 3:184)

But in this context, a true definition of a thing, as opposed to a nominal
definition, is an account of what that thing is, an account of its essence,
so that what Descartes is saying to Mersenne is very close to the point he
makes in the First Replies.[46]

Now, both Descartes's comment about not asking *an est* (whether a
thing is) before we understand *quid est* (what it is) and his comment about
the most perfect sort of demonstration employing a true definition as its
middle term seem squarely directed at certain things Thomas has to say
surrounding the demonstrability of God's existence. In the *Summa Theologiae* I, Q. 2, A. 2, Obj. 2, Aquinas considers the feasibility of a demonstration of God's existence, in light of the fact that we are (in his view)
unable to cognize God's essence:

> Further, the middle term of demonstration is what a thing is. But con-
> cerning God we cannot know [*scire*] what he is, but only what he is not; as
> Damascene says. Therefore we cannot demonstrate that God exists.[47]

Consider an Aristotelian syllogism of the form "All A's are B's, all B's are
C's, therefore all A's are C's." The objection is based on a requirement
that the middle term, B, represent an account of what something is, its
essence. The reason for the requirement, I take it, is the expectation that
the demonstration will be explanatory. Consider, for example: All humans are animals, all animals are mortal, therefore all humans are mortal. Here, the fact that it is part of the human essence to be an animal
serves to explain and ground the fact that humans are mortal. The force
of the objection, then, is that since we do not have access to God's essence, do not grasp what God is, we are unable to provide this sort of
demonstration of God's existence, a demonstration that yields some insight into why God exists.

Aquinas responds to the objection thus:

> When a cause is demonstrated from an effect, this effect takes the place
> of a definition of the cause in a proof of the cause's existence. This is espe-
> cially the case in regard to God, because, in order to prove that something
> is [*esse*], it is necessary to take for the middle term what a name signifies,
> and not what the thing is, for the question of what it is [*quid est*] follows
> the question of whether it is [*an est*]. Now the names of God are derived

from his effects; consequently, in demonstrating the existence of God from his effects, we may take for the middle term the meaning of the word God.[48]

Aquinas begins by making the general point that when we demonstrate the existence of a cause from its effect, we use the effect where we would have otherwise used the definition of the cause. Evidently, Thomas has in view here some form of *a posteriori* reasoning—that is, reasoning from an effect to its cause—as opposed to *a priori* reasoning—that is, reasoning from a cause to its effect. Because *a posteriori* arguments are not based on the definition of the cause, that is, an account of the cause's essence, which would serve to make clear how the effect follows from the cause, they do not have the same explanatory value as *a priori* demonstrations that do work through definitions of essences.[49]

Now, Aquinas goes on to say that this structural feature of a demonstration, wherein an effect replaces a definition, is "especially true" in the case of demonstrations of God's existence. I think his point may simply be this. Since in the case of God, unlike the case of other causes, it is impossible for us (in this life) to have a definition, that is, to understand what God is, to grasp God's essence, we *must* proceed in this other way. In the last sentence of his reply, Aquinas elaborates this point by noting that in philosophical theology, as he understands it, we must work from nominal characterizations of God, the so-called divine names. Thus, as we noted in chapter 3 (II), all of Aquinas's arguments for the existence of God conclude with a step along the lines of "And this all people call God."

Now, the fact that we do not know what God is—do not, as I have sometimes been putting it, cognize God's essence—does not preclude us from making inferences about God's essence. For example, one of the divine names is "first efficient cause." Aquinas thinks we can show that such a being exists and is uncaused. Further, he thinks we can show that such a being is absolutely simple (otherwise, it would have required a cause of its components coming together). And from this, we can infer that its essence is identical with its existence (any difference between them would introduce complexity). But here we reason backward, in an *a posteriori* fashion, from certain consequences of God's essence (God is uncaused, God is simple) to a conclusion about how God's essence must be (identical with God's existence); we do not reason forward from a prior grasp of God's essence to its consequences. This sort of indirect, triangulated cognition concerning God's essence does not count as understanding what God is, does not count as cognizing God's essence. Perhaps we might capture the flavor of Thomas's position by saying that we do not know God's essence itself, but only that it must be such that it is identical with God's existence.

Aquinas's basic picture of how human beings cognize God shapes his attitude toward the ontological argument. As we saw in chapter 3 (II), for Aquinas the human intellect does not naturally have access to God's essence. Aquinas traces this limitation both to our dependence on the senses and to a more general idea that no created cognitive form is commensurate with the uncreated divine essence. Since he thinks we work from nominal characterizations of God rather than from God's essence, proving that God exists from our basic conception of God would be tantamount to proving that the bearer of a name exists from the meaning of the name. In ST I, Q. 2, A. 1, Obj. 2, he interprets an Anselmian argument for God's existence in this spirit. He takes the point of this argument to be that the proposition that God exists is self-evident from the meaning of its terms (in the way that every whole is greater than the part is self-evident from the meaning of its terms):

> Further, those things are said to be self-evident which are known to be true as soon as the terms are known [*quae statim, cognitis terminis, cognoscuntur*], which the Philosopher (1 *Poster.* iii) says is true of the first principles of demonstration. Thus, when what whole is and what part is is known, it is at once recognized that every whole is greater than its part. But as soon as the signification of the word God is understood [*quid significet hoc nomen Deus*], it is at once seen that God exists. For by this word is signified that thing than which nothing greater can be conceived. But that which exists in reality and in the intellect is greater than that which exists only in the intellect. Therefore, since as soon as the word God is understood it exists in the intellect, it also follows that it exists in reality. Therefore that God exists is self-evident.[50]

In his response to this argument, Aquinas makes two criticisms, the second of which is the more important for our purposes.[51] It is, roughly, that one cannot, working purely from the meaning of the term *God*, infer that the bearer of the term exists. If our argument starts only from the definition of a name, that is, let the name *God* stand for such-and-such, then the most we can hope to arrive at is some hypothetical conclusion of the form "If God exists, then he is such-and-such":

> Yet, granted that everyone understands that by this word God is signified something than which nothing greater can be thought, nevertheless, it does not therefore follow that he understands that what the word signifies exists in the real world [*in rerum natura*], but only in the apprehension of the intellect. Nor can it be argued that it exists in reality [*in re*], unless it be admitted that there exists in reality [*in re*] something than which nothing greater can be thought; and this precisely is not admitted by those who hold that God does not exist.[52]

It can seem here that all that Aquinas is doing is denying the validity of the inference, and not really criticizing the argument. That may be, but much of the critical work has already been done by casting the argument as an attempt to get from something nominal to something real. If he can get that far, many philosophers, including Descartes in the First Replies, will agree that this cannot be done.

To be exact, it cannot be right to say that Aquinas casts the argument as an attempt to get from a purely nominal plane of our representations (e.g., the signification of words or our ideas or concepts) to a plane of real existence. Even our nominal characterizations tie us into mind-independent reality (notice, for example, that Aquinas describes the self-evidence of the whole's being greater than the part as a matter of knowing what whole is and what part is, and not a matter of knowing what *whole* means and what *part* means). So what exactly is his point here?[53]

Consider, to begin with, how, according to Thomas, humans do arrive at knowledge of God. We start from some nominal characterization of God, say, first mover. In order to determine that there is a first mover, one needs to know first that there is motion and one needs to apprehend various basic principles about motion and its causes ("everything that is moved, is moved by another," "there cannot be an infinite regress of movers ordered in a *per se* manner"). We ascertain that there is motion through the senses, and then apply these principles to this empirically observed motion, in order to determine that something satisfying the nominal characterization actually exists. Here we reason in an *a posteriori* fashion, from motion, an effect, to a first mover, the ultimate cause of the motion.

Now, one might wonder whether we can do something similar with Anselm's characterization of God as "something than which nothing greater can be thought," that is, show that something satisfying that characterization actually exists. Well, evidently, it would not be in the spirit of Anselm's argument to show that something exists in an *a posteriori* way, that is, by reasoning from some effect to its cause. Rather, Anselm's argument is an attempt to reason to something's existence in an *a priori* way, along the lines of reasoning from an essence to one of its *propria*.

What exactly are the materials that we start with in the case of Anselm's argument? Well, we may suppose that the formula "that being than which nothing greater can be conceived" involves being, goodness or perfection (the occurrence of *greater* in the formula suggests this), and intellection. But—here I think is the source of Aquinas's misgivings concerning the argument—it is not yet clear whether there is any essence or reality corresponding to the constellation of these perfections in the way indicated by the formula.[54] That is, it is not clear whether this combination of entities designates something "real" or "true" in the sense of V.¶7.

It is an open matter whether the assemblage of realities indicated by the formula describes a chimera—something with the head of a lion, the body of a goat, and the tail of a serpent—that, for all we know, may not have a nature or essence. Or to take another example, with a somewhat different emphasis, closer to the relational character of Anselm's formula, consider the formulas "the right heart of a human being" or the "sixth finger on a human hand." Even though the pieces of these formulas signify realities and the formulas are, in a certain sense, well formed, they do not signify any thing or reality—any essence or nature.

Further, on this account of Aquinas's position, until we know that there is such an essence or nature, all our thought concerning the formula has a hypothetical character: if there is a right heart of a human being, it has two auricles and two ventricles (because all mammalian hearts are structured this way); or if there are chimeras, their tails have scales. That is, until we know there is such an essence or nature, we can only draw conclusions about how such (possibly fictional) things are "in the apprehension of the intellect [*in apprehensione intellectus tantum*]." Moreover, I think, Aquinas supposes that (in general) the only way for humans to find out that there are essences or natures is to locate one of them in existence. This seems to lie behind his somewhat cryptic remark, "Nor can it be argued that it [something than which nothing greater can be thought] exists in reality [*in re*], unless it be admitted that there exists in reality [*in re*] something than which nothing greater can be thought." Thus, he holds that our reasoning about that being than which nothing greater can be thought must remain purely hypothetical until we can (already, so to speak) show that a being satisfying that characterization exists.

Thomas's account of the Anselmian argument and his response make clear that he regards the argument as a failed attempt to get from a definition of a word to a truth about what exists in the world. The way we operate when forming nominal characterizations does not guarantee that what we characterize has an essence or nature going with it—has, to use a term that appears with different but related meanings in both Descartes and Kant, objective reality—even if the components of the characterization bottom out in something real. One can imagine a view according to which, if we begin with essences and build entities out of them according to certain prescribed rules, the results would also count as real essences or natures. That would be a fairly substantial metaphysical thesis. Moreover, I see little sympathy in either Aquinas or Descartes for the idea that construction alone can guarantee the objective reality of what is constructed. According to Aquinas, I have suggested, human beings in general need to determine that something satisfying the characterization exists, and according to Descartes, as we have seen, before we can determine whether a triangle inscribed in a square has a true and immutable nature we need first to see whether we can make a substantive judgment specifically of it, for example, that the area of the square is at least twice the area of the triangle (see 7:117–18; 2:83–84).

We do not need to speculate about how Descartes would have responded to Aquinas's criticism of Anselm's argument. Caterus, the author of the First Replies, takes Descartes's ontological argument to be essentially the same as the Anselmian one that Thomas criticizes.[55] In particular, after presenting a detailed comparison between Descartes's argument and the one Thomas criticizes, Caterus argues that Aquinas's criticism of the Anselmian argument has equal force against Descartes's argument:

> My own answer to M. Descartes, which is based on this passage [i.e., ST I, Q. 2, A. 1, ad 2], is briefly this. Even if it is granted that a supremely perfect being carries with it existence in virtue of its very name [*ens summe perfectum ipso nomine suo importare existentiam*], it still does not follow that the existence in question is anything actual in the real world [*in rerum natura actu*]; all that follows is that the concept of existence is inseparably linked to the concept of a supreme being. So you cannot infer that the existence of God is anything actual unless you suppose that the supreme being actually exists; for then it will actually contain all perfections, including the perfection of real existence. (7:99; 2:72)

Now, as one might imagine, Descartes does not recognize his argument in the one critiqued by Aquinas and Caterus. His argument was not an attempt to get from the signification of a word to its bearer; rather, he was arguing from our grasp of a true and immutable nature, namely, God's essence, to a property that pertains to that essence:

> In this form [the form that concerns the signification of the name *God*] the argument is manifestly invalid, for the only conclusion that should have been drawn is: *therefore, once what the name* God *signifies is understood, it is understood to signify God to exist in reality and in the understanding*; but because this is signified by a word, it does not appear for that reason to be true. My argument, however, was this: What we clearly and distinctly understand to pertain to the true and immutable nature or essence or form of something can be affirmed concerning that thing with truth; but after we have investigated with sufficient accuracy what God is [*quid sit Deus*], we clearly and distinctly understand that it pertains to his true and immutable nature that he should exist; therefore, we can thence affirm concerning God with truth, that he exists. (7:115–16; 2:82–83)

The exchange between Descartes and (through the mediation of Caterus) Aquinas serves to confirm the suggestion that what fundamentally separates Descartes and Aquinas is a prior issue concerning the character of our cognition of God.[56] It brings the disagreement back to the following questions: Is it the case, as Thomas suggests, that human beings work from nominal characterizations of God, characterizations that keep us at some distance from what God is, from his essence? Or is it the case, as Descartes maintains, that my idea of God makes available for my cognition something of his true and immutable nature itself?

It is philosophically natural to wonder, then, what might be said in support of Descartes's side on this fundamental question. As we saw in our discussion of ¶¶5 and 6, for Descartes, an important mark of an idea's making available a true and immutable nature is its enabling us to come to substantive judgments about a subject matter (roughly, judgments of the type that Kant would later call synthetic a priori).[57] So, from Descartes's point of view, the issue is this: Can we make the sort of judgments about God that we make about a triangle, substantive judgments such as that the longest side of a triangle is opposite its greatest angle; or are all of the judgments that we are able to make concerning God (prior to consulting empirical reality) simply elucidations of various significations that we attribute to the word God? In particular, with respect to existence, are we able to provide a demonstration of God's existence that goes from cause to effect, in a way that seems accompanied by insight and understanding?

Before I try to answer these questions, we need to take up a technical question in philosophical theology, if only to put it to the side. It may reasonably be wondered whether it is possible to make any substantive judgment concerning God. Since God is simple (and so, in particular, free of the composition of substance and accident), God does not have perfections that lie outside of his essence. This can make it seem as if all judgments of God should be trivial or tautological restatements of God's essence. As Aquinas puts such a worry:

> It seems that these names applied to God are synonymous names. For synonymous names are those which mean exactly the same. But these names applied to God mean entirely the same thing in God: for the goodness of God is His essence, and likewise it is His wisdom. Therefore these names are entirely synonymous. (ST I, Q. 13, A. 4, Obj. 1)

Aquinas responds to this concern by maintaining that although God is indeed simple in the way the objection supposes, the difference in names arises from the difference in the ways that creatures cognize God, the different "aspects [rationibus]" under which they conceptualize God. This is enough to prevent affirmations concerning God from collapsing into triviality.

Although Descartes does not, to my knowledge, explicitly discuss this matter, it seems clear that he follows the tradition in thinking that God's simplicity does not preclude the judgments we make concerning God from being substantive. This comes out, I think, in the richness he ascribes to our cognition of God. Although God is simple, God also has unbounded reality. And when Descartes says in the Third Meditation that my idea of God is "the truest and most clear and distinct" of all my ideas, I think this means that it expresses more reality, and expresses that reality more clearly and distinctly, than any of my other ideas. This unlimited reality or perfection becomes available to my finite mind in a fragmented way, and is grasped by me as different "individual perfections." So, God's simplicity notwithstanding, my idea of God is extremely rich, as Descartes suggests in the First Replies:

> But those who try to attend to God's individual perfections and try not so much to seize [*capere*] them as to be seized [*capi*] by them, using all the strength of their intellect to contemplate them, will certainly find that God provides much more ample and straightforward subject-matter for clear and distinct knowledge [*cognitionis*] than does any created thing. (7:114; 2:82)

It is because the idea of God I have is so rich that Descartes believes that the greatest joy I can have in this life consists in the contemplation of God:

> But before examining this point more carefully and investigating other truths which may be derived from it, I should like to pause here and spend some time in the contemplation of God; to reflect on his attributes and to gaze with wonder and adoration on the beauty of this immense light, so far as the eye of my darkened intellect can bear it. For just as we believe through faith that the supreme happiness of the next life consists solely in the contemplation of the divine majesty, so experience tells us that this same contemplation, albeit much less perfect, enables us to know the greatest joy of which we are capable in this life. (7:52; 2:35–36)

In any case, what is important for our present purposes is that although God is ontologically simple, God is cognized by us in a complex manner, so that the judgments we make concerning God are substantive. I think, moreover, that Descartes thinks of our substantive judgments concerning God's individual perfections on the traditional model of seeing how a property flows from an essence, even though, technically speaking, God's perfections are not properties (i.e., realities or perfections that are in God but lie outside of God's essence). This, of course, is not a question that arises for Aquinas, who does not think we could cognize God's essence (in this life) in the first place, and so does not think that judgments about God (in this life) could be a matter of seeing how God's perfections flow from God's essence; rather, for Aquinas, our cognition of God's essence is inferential: we use what we know about God to reach conclusions about how God's essence must be.[58]

Let's return to Descartes's treatment of our cognition of God. It must be said that in the Fifth Meditation Descartes does not do a particularly good job of making clear that when we reason about God's existence we are making a substantive judgment. For example, in ¶7 he simply asserts, "And my understanding that it belongs to his nature that he always exists is no less clear and distinct than is the case when I prove of any shape or number that some property belongs to its nature." To make matters worse, in ¶11 he can easily be misread (I think) as advancing a nonsubstantive argument for God's existence based on a stipulation to the effect that the term *God* means the being with all perfections:

> Now admittedly, it is not necessary that I ever light upon any thought of God; but whenever I do choose to think of the first and supreme being, and bring forth the idea of God from the treasure house of my mind as it were, it is necessary that I attribute all perfections to him, even if I do not at that time enumerate them or attend to them individually. And this necessity plainly guarantees that, when I later realize that existence is a perfection, I am correct in inferring that the first and supreme being exists. (7:67; 2:46–47)

It is easy to take Descartes to be reasoning along the following lines. Let God be the being with all perfections; existence is a perfection; hence, God exists. Such an argument has the feel of trafficking in tautology. Either there is no insight here or the discovery is in the wrong place, that is, that existence is a perfection ("I later realize that existence is a perfection"). I don't think that this is in fact what Descartes is doing in the passage. As is signaled perhaps by his suggestion that the idea of God comes from a "treasure house," I think he has in view a more substantive line of thought, which he, perhaps overly relying on the meditator's native sense of philosophical theology, only sketches here rather than works through. But the passage certainly does not make this clear.

Be that as it may, Descartes soon saw the need to offer a fuller explanation of why God must exist. In the First Replies, he presents as one of the premises of the ontological argument: "But once we have made a sufficiently careful investigation of what God is, we clearly and distinctly understand that existence belongs to his true and immutable nature" (7:116; 2:83). Descartes acknowledges, somewhat uncharacteristically for him, concerning this premise: "[H]ere I confess there is no small difficulty." In what follows, he offers a fuller (and perhaps somewhat different)[59] explanation of why God must exist. What this presentation brings out is the substantive metaphysics that informs Descartes's thinking on this topic; it would be a mistake to think of reasoning as merely formal.

Descartes begins with an explanation of why an ontological argument will not work for a supremely perfect body:

> But if I were to think that the idea of a supremely perfect body contained existence, on the grounds that it is a greater perfection to exist both in reality and in the intellect than it is to exist in the intellect alone, I could not infer from this that the supremely perfect body exists, but only that it is capable of existing. For I can see quite well that this idea has been put together by my own intellect which has linked together all bodily perfections; and existence does not arise out of the other bodily perfections because it can equally well be affirmed or denied of them. (7:118; 2:84)

Observe that Descartes does not claim that a supremely perfect body is impossible or contradictory, as one might have expected. (His conception of matter as indefinitely extended may encourage him in the thought that there is a supremely perfect corporeal structure; indeed, he may regard *res extensa* as a supremely perfect body.) What Descartes claims, rather, is that there is no integral connection between existence and being a supremely perfect body. That is, no corporeal perfection (or, apparently, combination of corporeal perfections) implies existence; no corporeal perfection (or combination of corporeal perfections) involves existence. Now, one might wonder, what makes Descartes confident of this? The continuation of the passage is meant to help here:

> Indeed, when I examine the idea of a body, I perceive that a body has no power to produce or conserve itself in existence; and I rightly conclude that necessary existence—and it is only necessary existence[60] that is at issue here—no more belongs to the nature of a body, however perfect, than it belongs to the nature of a mountain to be without a valley, or the nature of a triangle to have angles whose sum is greater than two right angles. (7:118; 2:84)

The claim that existence does not follow from corporeal perfection is bolstered by our sense that—we might say the necessary synthetic judgment that—no body has the "power to produce or conserve itself in existence."

We could develop this claim (somewhat) by recalling some of the thinking surrounding the second of the Third Meditation's arguments for the existence of God. There, I noticed that I am not responsible for keeping myself in existence from one moment to the next, which got me to see that at any given moment I am being sustained in existence. In the Third Meditation, Descartes argued that a series of sustaining beings (the being that sustains me, the being that sustains the being that sustains me, and so forth) could not go on forever but had to bottom out in a (unique) self-sustained being. Earlier, in the First Replies (7:111), Descartes took a further step and argued that sustaining something in existence requires infinite power, which could be possessed only by a self-sustainer. The power to sustain something in existence cannot, then, be delegated to some finite cause, and everything that exists is immediately sustained by the self-sustainer.

What Descartes thinks is obvious upon reflection is that no body has the infinite power involved in being self-sustained. If he felt further argument on this score were necessary, he might point out that self-sustained beings are simple, but bodies have parts. Whatever one makes of the merits of Descartes's position—whether one, too, finds it obvious upon reflection that nothing corporeal could be responsible for its staying in existence or falling back into nothingness, or if one finds talk of staying in existence or falling back into nothingness an unintelligible relic of an unfortunate philosophical past (as Hume, for example, describes Aristotelian philosophy in *Treatise*, 1.4.3)—it is important to recognize that there is a certain amount of substantive metaphysics at the heart of why one will not be able to base an ontological argument on a supremely perfect body.

Conversely, more or less the same metaphysics (our sense of how various dependence and power relationships sort themselves out in the universe) informs his thinking that existence is bound up with the nature of a supremely perfect being (as opposed to a supremely perfect corporeal being). The passage from the First Replies continues:

> Now, however, if we were to ask not concerning a body, but of a thing, regardless of kind [*non de corpore, sed de re, qualiscunque tandem illa fit*: not of a body, but of a thing of whatever sort it ultimately be], which has all perfections that can exist together, whether existence should be included among these perfections, we will admittedly be in some doubt at first. For our mind, which is finite, normally thinks of these perfections only separately, and hence may not immediately notice the necessity of their being joined together. (7:118–19; 2:85)

To fill this out a bit, I think Descartes is suggesting that if we start from the characterization "being with all compatible perfections," it is not obvious that we are onto a nature. This is because it is not obvious that the relevant perfections are integrally unified in some way, that is, that they are bound by anything more than the formula that we began with, "being with all compatible perfections."[61] It may be clear that each of the perfections is a nature or reality, but what is not yet clear is that there is some nature besides the nature of the various individual perfections; and if there is no such nature, then the combination of perfections would count as what Descartes calls a "fiction of the intellect," that is, something put together by the mind. Therefore, it is not obvious whether the perfection of existence, in particular, is integrally bound up with the other perfections, or something just "tacked on" to other perfections to form a conglomeration of some sort. This being so, even if existence belongs to whatever is characterized by the formula "supremely perfect being," it is not clear that such a being exists.

However, if we start our inquiry from a slightly different angle[62] and consider a supremely powerful being, we can, Descartes suggests, trace out a path, first, to its possible existence, then to its necessary existence, and then, finally, to its possession of all perfections:

> Yet if we attentively examine whether existence belongs to a supremely powerful being, and what sort of existence it is, we shall be able to perceive clearly and distinctly the following facts. First, possible existence, at the very least, belongs to such a being, just as it belongs to all the other things of which we have a distinct idea, even to those which are put together through a fiction of the intellect. (7:119; 2:85)

Notice that in order for us to know that something has possible existence, we do not have to know whether it has a true and immutable nature; we just have to be able to conceive it distinctly. That's supposed to be enough, I take it, to show that the entity in question—be it a true or immutable nature or something merely fictive—does not involve some hidden contradiction. This requirement may seem weak, but it can do some work. Descartes does not think, I believe, that we can distinctly conceive traditional natural kinds, for example, lion and horse, and so forth, which would involve something like the possession of their mechanistic blueprint; he hints at this in the First Replies: "I will not now include the lion or the horse, since their natures are not transparently clear to us" (7:117; 2:84). I take it, then, that in order to know that such beings are possible we need to consult experience; and for this reason we cannot definitively determine one way or the other whether a winged horse or a chimera is possible. By way of contrast, Descartes thinks that we do understand what a supremely powerful being is well enough (we have a "distinct idea" of such a being) for us to see that it is possible.[63]

Descartes moves, next, from the possibility of such a being to its necessary existence. Underneath this move is reasoning similar to that involved in our judgment that no body necessarily exists through its own power:

> Next, since we cannot think of its existence as possible unless we also at the same time, attending to its immense power, recognize that it can exist by its own power; and we will conclude from this that this being does really exist and has existed from eternity, since it is quite evident by the natural light that what can exist by its own power always exists. So we shall come to understand that necessary existence is contained in the idea

of a supremely powerful being, not by any fiction of the intellect, but because it belongs to the true and immutable nature of such a being that it
exists. (7:119; 2:85)

While it is somewhat unclear exactly how the argument is supposed to
flow, I hope the following is close enough: reflection on the relevant notion of power ("attending to its immense power") reveals at least, positively, that this being has the causal wherewithal to be responsible for its
existence. Descartes then adds the claim that "it is quite evident by the
natural light that what can exist by its own power always exists." What
he may have in mind—the claim is obviously difficult for us—is this.
Consider a being, A, of such a nature that it can exist through its own
power. Suppose A's essence or nature leaves open whether A exists or
not. Then (it would seem that) whether A exists depends on the real doings of some other being, call it D (for the "decider"). But if this is so,
then A exists through D's power and not its own power, contradicting
our original assumption that A is a being that can exist through its own
power. (I am assuming if A ever needs D's help in order to exist, it "must"
have D's help. This is because I am thinking of the need for D's help as
marking some lack in A's essence or nature.) In other words, there is
something incoherent about supposing that A can exist through its own
power but does not exist. My attempt to motivate this claim takes us past
anything that Descartes says here, but seems to me close in spirit to the
way others in the period reasoned about this sort of question.[64]
So, we have it that there is a real nature, or perhaps some constellation
of real natures, that possesses the power to be responsible for its own
existence. Descartes concludes from this, on the basis of a principle made
"evident by the natural light" that "what can exist by its own power always exists," that such a being really exists and has existed from all eternity. I take the principle here to be a substantive metaphysical principle,
which holds roughly the same status for Descartes that a synthetic *a priori* principle will hold later for Kant. As reflection on infinite power reveals in this way the consequence of necessary existence (and here one is
supposed to feel, I think, that the same sort of thing is going on as when
reflection on a triangle reveals that such a figure has three angles summing to two right angles), we can be confident that we have not simply
tacked the idea of existence onto the idea of a supremely powerful being
by way of some sort of stipulation. Moreover, since we can discover substantive consequences in a supremely powerful being, we can be confident that such a being does possess a true and immutable nature (which
Descartes implies now, as opposed to earlier in the passage).
Finally, because a supremely powerful being would also give itself
every perfection found in the idea of God, we can now see why a "being

which possesses all the perfections that can exist together" represents a true and immutable nature (and not a stipulated assemblage), something concerning which we were initially in doubt:

> And we shall also easily perceive that this supremely powerful being cannot but possess within it all the perfections of the idea of God; and hence these perfections exist in God and are joined together not by any fiction of the intellect but by their very nature. (7:119; 2:85)

This line of thought is first and foremost meant to convince us that we are able to reason substantively to God's existence. It is supposed to convey a sense of insight or illumination into why God, being the being that God is, must exist, and so has the sort of explanatory aspect that one expects of a "perfect demonstration," where the middle term is based on what a thing is, that is, on a "true definition." In order to provide such illumination, Descartes relies on our having a direct purchase on God's infinite power—something that Aquinas does not think we have. We have a native metaphysical sense that clues us in to our own dependence, the fact that what we depend on is infinitely powerful, and the fact that an infinitely powerful being is self-caused in some positive sense. (Aquinas would deny that the last claim is true: according to him, God is uncaused, not self-caused.) Another way of saying that we have this "native metaphysical sense" is that we possess innately an idea of God. It is worth noting that these considerations about dependence and power give us one avenue of approach to God's nature; they are not the only avenue, nor do they somehow exhaust the idea. Here it may help to think in terms of an analogy with the idea of extension: our possession of the idea enables us to carry out all kinds of geometrical constructions and reasoning. But we shouldn't think of the idea as somehow "recoverable" from those constructions and reasoning.

The preceding is based on a close reading of a discussion from the First Replies. There are internal signs that Descartes is working out his position more fully in the face of Caterus's objections, so it makes sense to consider that discussion carefully. Still, in fairness to the Fifth Meditation itself, it is not as if Descartes gives no attention to the issue of whether my idea of God presents me with a true and immutable nature as opposed to some fiction of my own invention (perhaps some combination of true and immutable natures that is not itself a true and immutable nature). At the end of ¶11 Descartes explicitly addresses this issue:

> There are many ways in which I understand that this idea is not something fictitious which is dependent on my thought, but is an image of a true and immutable nature. First of all, there is the fact that, apart from God, there is nothing else of which I am capable of thinking such that existence

belongs to its essence. Second, I cannot understand how there could be two or more Gods of this kind; and after supposing that one God exists at this time, I plainly see that it is necessary that he has existed from eternity and will abide for eternity. And finally, I perceive many other attributes of God, none of which I can remove or alter. (7:68; 2:47)

Descartes is reminding the meditator of some of the nontrivial judgments that she finds herself in a position to make concerning God—providing the theological analogue, as it were, of my judgment that the longest side of a triangle subtends its greatest angle or that the three angles of triangle are equal to two right angles. This is part of an effort to establish that the idea of God is not made up but has a certain unity or integrity. What Descartes does not do here, however, but attempts to do in the First Replies, is try to make clear how (necessary) existence flows from God's nature, so that our idea of God and (necessary) existence is not made up (a composite of the idea of God and the idea of existence) but has a certain unity or integrity.

For Descartes, then, the viability of the ontological argument rests on his conviction that our theological ideas, especially the idea of God, make available to the mind a subject matter for its consideration—for it to reason about, to make judgments about, to reflect on in various ways—in more or less the same way that our geometrical ideas, especially the idea of extension, do. He articulates this felt sense of being onto a subject matter as opposed to working with an entity that is merely constructed or fictional informally (e.g., the sense of making a discovery, the sense of a property's being found in a structure whether I want it to be there or not) and perhaps naively. It is not clear how much pressure the marks he relies on can bear: it may not be possible, for example, to draw a philosophically satisfying line between substantive and trivial judgment in the wake of developments in modern logic and the consequent pressure that the distinction between analytic and synthetic came under. It may also be possible that simply appealing to one's sense that one's judgment has (even substantively) been determined by some structure, is not enough to persuade us that that structure is a mind-independent reality, a true and immutable nature, because we no longer recognize Descartes's sense of "something" or "not nothing."

Still, I think that the general issue Descartes is concerned with here is less alien than it might first seem. Consider a (less momentous) analogy from contemporary mathematics. There are some outstanding problems in set theory that are not settled by current axiomizations. One reaction to this state of affairs is that set theory does not reach beyond the axioms, so there is no answer to these problems. Our concept of set is, one might say, open to different alternative specifications, and whether to

specify further and, if so, how, is a matter for more or less arbitrary stipulation. We might someday find a way of extending our current axioms
in such a way that a given problem becomes settled, and we might even
find a natural way of doing so, but this would be to create a new concept
of set (a new "fictive" thing, in Descartes's sense). Another reaction is
that there is, or at least may be, a structure, "a something and not nothing," that our axioms are meant to capture, and we may discover the answer to at least some of the questions not currently determined by our
current axioms. Which reaction, if either, is correct seems to be a very
difficult question and may itself be hostage to the future course of set
theory. But if one feels the difference between these two reactions, one
can at least begin to get a grip on the sort of question that Descartes is
raising when he asks whether his idea of God makes available a true and
immutable nature. And, for that matter, the phenomenon he appeals
to—our sense of discovery or our sense of when we are responsive to a
structure as opposed to when a structure is responsive to us—if naive
and informal, seems a reasonable enough place to start.

We noted earlier that Descartes's handling of the ontological argument seems to have been particularly influential in the rationalist tradition. (The situation with the empiricist tradition is, of course, different.
Locke is lukewarm about the argument, and Berkeley and Hume do not
address it.) Spinoza and Leibniz each offer versions of the ontological
arguments, and Kant accords the ontological argument a special place in
the project of the rational theology that he critiques. Correspondingly,
one does not find much evidence of a *via negativa* in their philosophies,
or the idea that human beings, in the words of Damascene, cited by
Aquinas above, cannot know what God is, but only what God is not. It is
hard to say whether this influence has to do with Descartes's articulation
in the Third Meditation, Fifth Meditation, and First Replies of the sense
that we are natively given a theological subject matter to cognize. Spinoza, for his part, shows some interest in God as *causa sui*; this plays a
role, as we have just seen, in Descartes's explanation of why God must
exist, so that we have some understanding here and not just an inference
that God must exist. But it may be rather that Spinoza and Leibniz
simply follow Descartes in his rejection of the doctrine of abstraction.
Aquinas works out the methodology of *via negativa* in the context of his
endorsement of the Aristotelian principle, *nihil est in intellectu nisi prius
fuerit in sensu*. Neither Spinoza nor Leibniz wants to go back to a picture
of human cognition where our ability to think about a subject matter
depends on our extracting it with the assistance of the senses from the
world. Descartes, by freeing his rationalist successors from the constraints of an Aristotelian conception of cognition, may have opened the
door to thinking our ability to cognize God is more straightforward and

less problematic than his Aristotelian, particularly Thomistic Aristotelian, predecessors thought.

I want to conclude this section by considering a remark that Descartes makes at the end of ¶7. After sketching the ontological argument, Descartes adds:

> Hence, even if it turned out that not everything on which I have meditated in these past days is true, the existence of God ought to hold for me at least the same grade of certainty as the truths of mathematics have hitherto held. (7:65–66; 2:45)

This remark, I take it, foreshadows the detailed discussion at the end of the Fifth Meditation of the place of the central tenets developed in the Third through Fifth Meditations in human knowledge generally, allowing that there is a grade or type of certainty that is available without cognizance of those tenets (and at the same time implying that there is another grade of certainty that does require cognizance of them). As such, the remark echoes a theme broached at the end of ¶6:

> And even if I had not demonstrated this [viz., I have already amply demonstrated all those things that I clearly cognize are true (*demonstravi illa omnia quae clare cognosco esse vera*)], the nature of my mind is such that I cannot but assent to these things, at least so long as I clearly perceive them. I also remember that even before, when I was completely preoccupied with the objects of the senses, I always held that the most certain truths of all were the kind which I recognized clearly in connection with shapes, or numbers, or other items relating to arithmetic and geometry, or in general to pure and abstract mathematics. (7:65; 2:45)

The point I take Descartes to be making in ¶7 about philosophical theology is the analogue to the point made at the end of ¶6 about geometry. Someone can pursue philosophical theology without having discovered that everything she clearly and distinctly perceives is true (without, say, having covered the ground taken in the Fourth Meditation) in the same frame of mind as an atheist pursues geometry. And in the same way that there is a certainty available to the geometer who has not reflected on the metaphysical substructure of her cognition, so, too, is there a certainty available to someone who grasps the ontological argument—someone who sees how and why existence is contained in God's essence—but has never reflected on the metaphysical substructure of her cognition. Neither certainty is merely subjective; in both cases I can see that my judgment is being determined by the truth (I will consider briefly below the idea that the certainty is merely a psychological rational conviction of some sort). Descartes implies that someone who does so forgoes some better type of certainty, a point that he will explain in the remainder of the Fifth Meditation.

Descartes's explicit statement that the meditator does not need to know the doctrine of true and immutable natures in order to be certain that God exists can make the layout of the Fifth Meditation puzzling. Surely the discussion of true and immutable natures in ¶¶5–6 is in some way preparatory for the ontological argument that is to follow. Yet Descartes says I can be certain that God exists without knowing this material.

The way the doctrine of true and immutable natures helps prepare the meditator for the ontological argument is this. The doctrine provides the meditator with a picture of how such an argument is possible. What makes such an argument possible is that I have some purchase on God's true and immutable nature. And if the question comes up, I can see that I have some purchase on God's nature, because every time I can make a substantive judgment it involves a true and immutable nature, and I can make substantive judgments involving God, in particular the (substantive) judgment that God exists. This gives me a fuller understanding of what is going on as I, say, work through a series of considerations that take me from *supremely powerful being,* to its possible existence, to its necessary existence, and, from there, to its having all perfections—namely, that what I am doing is exploring a true and immutable nature, that of a supremely powerful being and its perfections.

Although Descartes's treatment of true and immutable natures gives me an understanding of what is happening as I work through the ontological argument, it is no more necessary for an appreciation of the ontological argument than it is for the Pythagorean theorem. As I work through the Pythagorean theorem, I see that it must be the case that the square of the hypotenuse is equal to the sum of the squares on the other two sides; similarly, as I work through the ontological argument, I see that it must be the case that an omnipotent, supremely perfect being exists. If there is a difference between them, I would hazard that, in Descartes's view, this has to do, first, with the greater difficulty of getting someone to see that God's nature involves existence and, second, with what happens when one exits from a clear perception in the two cases. In particular, while the meditator would be happy to suppose even before the *Meditations* that our geometrical thought connects us with geometrical essences or natures (although, as things turn out, she had a very faulty conception of how this happens), she would have denied that her cognition (or, for that matter, any human cognition in this life) reaches God's essence. That will, I think, make it harder for her to take the ontological argument at face value, and, when she withdraws from her clear perception of the argument, easier for doubts to creep back in.[65]

In any case, the ontological argument taken by itself does give God's existence "the same grade of certainty as the truths of mathematics have hitherto held," that is, have held before taking up and resolving hyperbolic doubt, implying not only that the argument taken by itself does give us something by way of certainty, but also that we can achieve a new grade of certainty once we have resolved hyperbolic doubt. In ¶¶11–16, Descartes explains what this new grade of certainty is through developing the thesis that the certainty and truth of all that Descartes calls *scientia* depends uniquely on my cognizance of God, a thesis that draws the charge that Descartes's reasoning is inherently circular. We now turn to that discussion.

III. *COGNITIO, SCIENTIA, AND THE CARTESIAN CIRCLE*

(¶¶13–16)

At least since Arnauld, students of Descartes's *Meditations* have wondered whether he argues in a circle. The natural place to locate this issue with respect to the text of the *Meditations* is in these concluding paragraphs of the Fifth Meditation.

This perceived circularity arises from Descartes's suggestion that he is laying the foundations of knowledge. He writes that having been "struck by the large number of falsehoods that I had accepted as true in my childhood, and by the highly doubtful nature of the whole edifice that I had subsequently based on them[,] I realized that it was necessary, once in the course of my life, to overthrow everything completely and start again right from the foundations if I wanted to establish anything at all in the sciences that was stable and likely to last" (I.¶1; 7:17; 2:12). The envisioned foundations of knowledge are what I have been calling the metaphysical underpinnings of cognition. They include the truth rule, that everything that I clearly and distinctly perceive is true. The truth rule represents a fact about my nature: I have been so constructed by God that everything I clearly perceive is true. So establishing the truth rule involves a certain amount of quite substantive metaphysics about me, my place in the universe, and the universe itself.

Immediate questions arise about the coherence of Descartes's foundational enterprise. It is natural to think that knowing the foundations of knowledge should somehow bolster or reinforce all of human knowledge, so that until we know the foundations we cannot know anything else, at least not in the fullest sense of knowing. Descartes seems to hold something along these lines. He writes near the end of the Fifth Meditation, "Thus I see plainly that the certainty and truth of all knowledge [*omnis scientiae certitudinem & veritatem*] depends uniquely on my awareness [*cognitione*] of the true God, to such an extent that I was incapable of perfect knowledge [*perfecte scire*] about anything else until I became aware of [*nossem*] him" (¶16; 7:71; 2:49; as translated in CSM's more recent student editions). And this raises problems.

First, as Arnauld points out, if I can know anything only *through* knowing the foundations of knowledge, it is unclear how I come to know the foundations of knowledge themselves:

> I have one further worry, namely how the author avoids reasoning in a circle when he says that we are sure that what we clearly and distinctly perceive is true only because God exists.
>
> But we can be sure that God exists only because we clearly and distinctly perceive this. Hence, before we can be sure that God exists, we ought to be able to be sure that whatever we perceive clearly and evidently is true. (7:214; 2:150)

Arnauld takes Descartes to maintain that my certainty of God's existence rests on my certainty of the truth rule (thus: "before we can be sure that God exists, we ought to be able to be sure that whatever we perceive clearly and evidently is true"); in other words, that we know that God exists through knowing the metaphysical underpinnings of cognition. But since knowing the metaphysical underpinnings of cognition requires knowing that God exists, it looks as if we are caught in a circle.

Second, as the authors of the Second Objections point out, it seems false to claim that I cannot know anything *before* I know the foundations of knowledge. In the *Meditations* themselves, doesn't the meditator discover her own existence before she learns that God exists? For that matter, can't someone know geometry without ever learning that her creator made her such that her clear perception is always true?

These objections constitute at least one version of what is called the Cartesian Circle. I take the basic problem here to be, Can we make sense of the idea that knowing the metaphysical underpinnings of cognition somehow bolsters or reinforces all of human knowledge without courting the unwelcome consequence that we know everything *through* knowing the foundations (Arnauld) or that we can know nothing *until* we know the foundations (the Second Objectors)? There is a second version of the Circle, having specifically to do with whether Descartes can answer skeptical doubt (particularly the challenge posed by the so-called evil-genius doubt) in a non-question-begging way. I will briefly take that up at the end of this chapter. For the most part, however, I want to focus on the version of the Circle that worried Descartes's contemporaries, namely the relation between knowing and knowing the metaphysical underpinnings of cognition.

It seems clear that Descartes thought carefully about this relation and that he has philosophically interesting things to say about it. But the territory was new—since the idea that philosophy should begin by laying the foundations of knowledge was new—and it requires a certain amount of patience with his text to follow his thought on the matter. One thing that turns out to be very important but very easy to miss is that Descartes is not working with a single, uniform mode of cognition (or "knowledge") but actually with two rather different modes of cognition (or "knowledge"), clear perception and *scientia*. By paying careful attention to each of them, especially to what each is supposed to provide and how, we will, I believe, be able to make progress with understanding Descartes's thinking about this topic.

"PSYCHOLOGICAL" CERTAINTY AND CLEAR PERCEPTION

I want to begin by reviewing Descartes's notion of clear perception. It seems to me that certain pictures of the relation between clear perception and the truth rule seriously underestimate what clear and distinct perception accomplishes on its own, before one has learned why the truth rule holds.

Although Descartes does not use the word *clear* there, the meditator's first taste of clear perception comes in the cogito passage. There, from deep within methodological doubt, the meditator is brought to see that something is the case:

> Yet apart from everything I have just listed, how do I know that there is not something else which does not allow even the slightest occasion for doubt? Is there not a God, or whatever I may call him, who puts into me the thoughts I am now having? But why do I think this, since I myself may perhaps be the author of these thoughts? In that case am not I, at least, something? But I have just said that I have no senses and no body. This is the sticking point: what follows from this? Am I not so bound up with a body and with senses that I cannot exist without them? But I have convinced myself that there is absolutely nothing in the world, no sky, no earth, no minds, no bodies. Does it now follow that I too do not exist? No: if I convinced myself of something then I certainly existed. But there is a deceiver of supreme power and cunning who is deliberately and constantly deceiving me. In that case too I undoubtedly exist, if he is deceiving me; and let him deceive me as much as he can, he will never bring it about that I am nothing so long as I think that I am something. So after considering everything very thoroughly, I must finally conclude [*denique statuendum sit*] that this proposition, *I am, I exist*, is necessarily true [*necessario est verum*] whenever it is put forward by me or conceived in my mind. (II.¶3; 7:24–25; 2:16–17)

I argued in chapter 2 that what Descartes is trying to bring about through the series of considerations presented in the early part of the passage is the experience of seeing that something must be so, the experience of grasping the truth. Consider the concluding sentence of the passage, "I must finally conclude [*denique statuendum sit*] that this proposition, *I am, I exist*, is necessarily true [*necessario est verum*]." The implicit "must" in *statuendum sit* (literally: it is to be held) and the *necessario* are meant to capture the experience of seeing that something has to be the case (as in, "Aha—it must be, that I exist"); and the *verum* makes explicit that the meditator's seeing that something is so is a matter of her getting on to the truth. This experience of seeing that something must be so is surely very remarkable to the meditator, who only a moment ago, in thrall to skeptical doubt, worried aloud that there might be practically no truth ("So what remains true? Perhaps just this one thing, that nothing is certain"). It is a moment in which she recognizes that she has the ability to see that at least some things are true—the skeptical doubt notwithstanding—for example, that she exists.

In chapter 2, I connected "seeing that something must be so" with what happens, as Descartes describes it in the Third Meditation (¶9), when something's "truth has been revealed to me by some natural light." Recall that there he contrasts having the truth revealed to one by the natural light with what he calls a teaching of nature. When I am taught something by nature I am led to believe it by some "spontaneous impulse." I am initially brought to almost all of my beliefs about my body and its welfare through such impulses and propensities. For example, when I am thirsty, I just "find myself" inclined to believe that drink would good for me. In this case, my inclination to believe is not determined by any clear perception that drink would be good for me. However, when something is revealed to me by the natural light, I believe it because I can see that it must be so. We should take the experience of having something revealed to us by the light of nature as ordinary and familiar. It's what happens when you notice that, as you're thinking or as you engage in argument with the skeptic, you must exist; or, again, when you realize that the longest side of a triangle subtends its greatest angle. Descartes also tells us in III.¶9 that when something has been revealed to you by the light of nature it "cannot in any way be open to doubt." I take this to be familiar as well. As I work through the cogito reflection, I am unable to doubt that I exist; or, again when I consider carefully a triangle, I am unable not to judge that the longest side subtends the greatest angle. It is not simply, of course, that I find myself unable to doubt, as if under the influence of a posthypnotic suggestion. There is a reason I cannot doubt: namely, I see that (under the circumstances) it *must* be the case that I exist, or that the three angles of a triangle sum to two right angles.

In a moment I will want to consider carefully how this seeing that something is so interacts with the evil-genius doubt; for that we will look to the passage near the beginning of the Third Meditation where Descartes brings clear perception face to face with the evil genius. But I believe that even the little that we have seen so far makes it unlikely that Descartes holds a view that has often been attributed to him, an attribution that, in my opinion, has greatly obscured our understanding of how he sees human knowledge. This is the view that until I know the truth rule (and so until I know the metaphysical underpinnings of my cognition or until I am able to refute the evil-genius doubt), perceiving clearly affords me only what is sometimes termed "psychological certainty." Let me explain.

To my knowledge, "psychological certainty" in the context of Descartes exegesis first appears in an influential, classic 1941 article by Alan Gewirth (then spelled Gewirtz), "The Cartesian Circle." For Gewirth, psychological certainty is the state of a compulsory belief that you find yourself in when you clearly perceive something but have not refuted the evil genius. In that article, he characterizes psychological certainty as the sort of certainty you have when "the mind is compelled to assent to the truth of directly presented clear and distinct perceptions, but in which metaphysical doubt is still possible" (386). But I find it hard to understand this as *certainty*. If metaphysical doubt is still open to the meditator, then there is a doubt that she can take up (and perhaps should take up). If for whatever reason she is at the moment unable to take it up, I would think it more accurate to describe her condition as "almost" certain or "all but certain."

More important, it is hard to understand how the compulsion to assent is supposed to work in such a situation. On the one hand, as many commentators, including Gewirth, agree, the compulsion in clear and distinct perception is supposed to be rational; on the other hand, the meditator's inability to take up a pertinent doubt while clearly perceiving makes it seem as if clearly perceiving produces a temporary blind spot in her, as if the sheen from her clear perception makes her insensible to considerations whose relevance she would recognize under other conditions.

I do not think this can be right. It seems at odds with how Descartes structures the cogito experience. I am not all-but-certain that I exist; I am certain that I exist.[66] When I am working through the cogito, it is not that I am somehow failing to acknowledge a skeptical consideration (the evil genius) that in another mood would impress me (and should impress me); rather, the doubt does not faze me because I can *see* that I exist or, as Descartes puts it, "I must finally conclude [*denique statuendum sit*] that this proposition, *I am, I exist*, is necessarily true [*necessario est verum*] whenever it is put forward by me or conceived in my mind." It may be that the cogito is special in the *specific way* that it is immune to the evil-genius doubt, for my existence is directly implicated in the doubt itself (viz. that *I* have been created by an evil genius, or that an evil genius is deceiving *me*).[67] However, I think Descartes's position is that *any* clear perception is immune to doubt. As a textual matter, Descartes holds that it is impossible to doubt any clear perception while entertaining it. And, again, it does not make sense to view this inability as a sort of defect, as if my clear perception made me oblivious to a pertinent skeptical consideration, rendering me psychologically incapable of taking it up. Rather, the reason why I, in my current condition, (rightly) find the skeptical consideration impotent is that my current perception makes clear to me that something is so. Thus, for example, if I am perceiving clearly why the three angles of a triangle must sum to two right angles—working through my perception, noting various relationships, and so forth—Descartes's view is not simply that I *cannot* withhold my assent on the basis of the evil-genius doubt, it is also that I *should not* withhold my assent.

So, even if there are interesting philosophical differences between the relation of the cogito to the evil-genius doubt, on the one hand, and the relation of clearly perceived mathematics to the doubt, on the other, these differences do not show up, I think, in a difference in their general immunity to the doubt. Thus, in the passage where, it seems to me, Descartes is most explicitly concerned to position clear perception vis-à-vis the evil-genius doubt, namely, the fourth paragraph of the Third Meditation, he treats "something very simple and straightforward in arithmetic and geometry" as on an even footing with the cogito ("let whoever can do so deceive me, he will never bring it about that I am nothing") (7:35–36; 2:25).

CLEAR PERCEPTION AND THE TRUTH RULE

If we understand clear perception along the lines I have just suggested, so that someone who clearly perceives the truth is aware of her judgment's being determined by the truth, then it might seem that there is no need to establish the truth rule or to respond to the evil-genius doubt: someone who is perceiving clearly seems to be getting along perfectly fine without doing either.

To get a better picture of the point of knowing the truth rule and the interplay between clear and distinct perception and the evil-genius doubt, we should begin by carefully considering Descartes's introduction of the truth rule. This comes near the beginning of the Third Meditation:

> I am certain that I am a thinking thing. Do I not therefore also know what is required for my being certain about anything? In this first item of

knowledge [*cognitione*] there is simply a clear and distinct perception of what I am asserting; this would not be enough to make me certain of the truth of the matter [*certum de rei veritate*] if it could ever turn out that something which I perceived with such clarity and distinctness was false. So I now seem to be able to lay it down as a general rule that whatever I perceive very clearly and distinctly is true. (III.¶2; 7:35; 2:24)

Descartes introduces the rule as the product of reflection on what went well in the Second Meditation's exploration of the mind's existence and nature. Two things would seem to follow. First, the truth rule is a higher-order thesis, that is, a thesis about the nature of our cognition: it involves taking up a reflective position on our cognition. Second, the procedure Descartes follows here makes the best sense if, during the cogito experience itself, the meditator is really certain and not simply all-but-certain. That is, it makes the best sense if we view the meditator as saying to herself, "I recall being certain that I was getting on to the truth. That cognition was marked by special clarity and distinctness. Perhaps everything I clearly and distinctly perceive is true." In contrast, the flow of thought seems rather awkward if the meditator takes herself to be only all-but-certain: "I recall being psychologically compelled to believe that I exist on the basis of internal rational considerations that were so convincing that they made it impossible for me doubt this, even if there remains, I must admit, an outstanding worry about the evil genius. That cognition was marked by special clarity and distinctness. Perhaps everything I clearly and distinctly perceive is true." "True"? Wouldn't the natural outcome of this chain of reflection be "I'm ready to hypothesize that everything I clearly and distinctly perceive is in such internal rational order that it is assent-compelling"?

One might object, in terms of the text itself, that what Descartes emphasizes is certainty: "I am *certain* that I am a thinking thing. Do I not therefore also know what is required for my being *certain* of anything?" (emphasis added). And surely being certain of something is compatible with being wrong, as in "But I was certain that he had weapons of mass destruction." I don't know that the English word *certain* generally works this way, but in any case Descartes is plainly assuming here that I cannot be certain of something false, for he immediately goes on to remark that clear and distinct perception "would not be enough to make me certain of the truth of the matter [*certum de rei veritate*] if it could ever turn out that something which I perceived with such clarity and distinctness was false." As Descartes uses the term, certainty brings with it truth.

The truth rule is introduced, then, as a higher-order hypothesis about the nature of my cognition, arrived at by my reflecting on what seems to allow me, when I am in a cogito-like state, to get on to the truth. In the next paragraph he begins to assess the prospects of this hypothesis. Although there he "accepted [*admisi*] as wholly certain and evident" things that were not—consonant with the connection between certainty and truth just noted, I take "*accepting* as certain" (emphasis added) to be different from actually *being* certain, so that you can accept as certain things that are not really certain—these were things that "I thought I perceived clearly, although I did not in fact do so" (7:35; 2:24–25). (It is worth noting, if only to counter certain popular views about his position on the "transparency" of thought, that Descartes quite openly allows that one might, through carelessness or inattention, think that one has clearly perceived when one hasn't, or take oneself to have been in a cogito-like state when one wasn't.) So the hypothesis that everything I clearly and distinctly perceive is true is at least consistent with my past experience.

Now, although the hypothesis is plausible and appears to be consistent with past experience, this hardly counts as seeing that it is true. Descartes brings this out by adverting to the evil-genius doubt, in a remarkable paragraph where he brings the doubt face to face with clear and distinct perception. It is an important paragraph for understanding how Descartes sees the relation between perceiving clearly and knowing the foundations of knowledge. The paragraph begins:

> But what about when I was considering something very simple and straightforward in arithmetic or geometry, for example that two and three added together make five, and so on? Did I not see at least these things clearly enough to affirm their truth? Indeed, the only reason that I afterwards judged [*postea judicavi*] that they were open to doubt was that it occurred to me that perhaps some God could have given me a nature such that I was deceived even in matters which seemed most evident. And whenever my preconceived belief [*praeconcepta*] in the supreme power of God comes to mind, I cannot but admit that it would be easy for him, if he so desired, to bring it about that I go wrong even in those matters which I think [*puto*: deem, believe] I see utterly clearly with my mind's eye. (III.¶4; 7:35–36; 2:25)

In the first two sentences the meditator seems tempted to affirm the truth rule on the basis of her experience with very simple subject matters. It seems obvious to her in such situations that it is the clarity of her perception that is getting her on to the truth; it may even seem obvious to her that it is in the nature of perceiving clearly always to have this result. But, then again, stepping back and sizing up her cognitive situation, she has to allow that for all she knows, "perhaps some God could have given me a nature such that I was deceived even in matters which seemed most evident." The issue that is being raised here, I think, is really one about the absence of knowledge on her part; she does not know enough about her nature to say why what seems to be the case—that everything she clearly perceives is true—should in fact be the case. While her cogito-like experiences are suggestive in this direction, they hardly show her that this must be the case.

Notice that Descartes describes the doubtfulness of what is clearly perceived as a judgment that she makes "afterwards" (*postea*). One might think that his point is that raising this question about her nature is something that simply did not occur to the meditator earlier. I think there is another reason for the *postea*: when I am clearly and distinctly perceiving something, the truth is present to me and I know that it is; there is no room for doubt. Doubt becomes possible only afterward, when I stop clearly perceiving that something is so. Descartes carefully develops this point in the remainder of the paragraph, by having the meditator move into and out of a cogito-like state. While in such a state—while she is focused on the "things themselves"—it is obvious to her that she is getting on to the truth:

> Yet when I turn to the things themselves [*ipsas res*] which I think [*arbitror:* I judge] I perceive very clearly, I am so convinced by them that I spontaneously declare [*sponte erumpam*]: let whoever can do so deceive me, he will never bring it about that I am nothing, so long as I continue to think I am something; or make it true at some future time that I have never existed, since it is now true that I exist; or bring it about that two and three added together are more or less than five, or anything of this kind in which I see a manifest contradiction. (III.¶4; 7:36; 2:25)

But after she exits this cogito-like state, she returns to the higher-order question about the author of her nature broached earlier in the paragraph:

> And since I have no cause to think that there is a deceiving God, and I do not yet even know for sure whether there is a God at all, any reason for doubt which depends simply on this supposition is a very slight and, so to speak, metaphysical one. But in order to remove even this slight reason for doubt, as soon as the opportunity arises I must examine whether there is a God, and, if there is, whether he can be a deceiver. For if I do not know this, it seems that I can never be fully certain [*plane certus*] about anything else. (III.¶4; 7:36; 2:25)

We should pay attention to the "fully [*plane*]" in the "fully certain" in the last line: until I know the metaphysical underpinnings of cognition, I cannot be fully certain. Yet, earlier in the meditation, it was suggested that when I am in a cogito-like state, I am certain, where that goes beyond mere rational conviction, reaching all the way to the truth. Evidently, there are two types of certainty, both involving truth—plain certainty and full certainty. This is confirmed later in the Fifth Meditation, when Descartes implies that there are different "grades [*gradus*]" of certainty. Of course, how there can be more than one grade or type of certainty is not obvious; Descartes does not clear this up until the end of the Fifth Meditation.

Descartes's putting us into a cogito-like state and pulling us back out again is masterly. There is (and, I think, there is supposed to be) something unsettling about this now-you-see-it/now-you-don't experience. When I'm in the cogito-like state, it is plain to me that I am onto the truth. When I exit a cogito-like state, I am no longer seeing that something is so. If I experience a tendency to continue to give my assent to what I had just clearly perceived in the absence of clearly seeing that something is so, it would seem that this tendency is simply a sort of cognitive inertia brought on by the afterglow of the previous perception. I would have more than simply the afterglow to work with, however, if I saw why it should be the case that when I am in a cogito-like state I always get on to the truth. For, understanding this, coupled with the fact that I had been a cogito-like state, would give me, in effect, another way of seeing that what I had previously perceived is true. But absent such an understanding, I can now begin at least to wonder about—Descartes says doubt—the efficacy of the cogito-like state I was in just a moment ago: Was I really seeing the truth then, or did it only seem to me that I was seeing the truth?

Now, I don't deny that one might have qualms about how Descartes thinks about the difference between being in a cogito-like experience and being out of it. For one thing, there are obviously delicate issues about the temporal boundaries of a cogito-like experience and the role of memory both within it and between it and subsequent cognition. For another thing, there are issues about the meditator's cognitive unity or integrity: if one has sufficient distance on one's past cogito experience, it may not be difficult for one to adopt a higher-order perspective on it and treat it, as I believe Descartes is in effect doing, in a "third person" sort of way. It is harder to do this, however, while the experience is fresh in one's mind; it seems to induce a sort of epistemic schizophrenia. From one instant to the next, depending on whether she directs her attention to the "things themselves" or to God and the origin of her nature, the meditator finds herself either in a condition of being certain of at least some things (where this involves, I think, being onto the truth and knowing that one is onto the truth) or of doubting whether even her best perception gets her to the truth.

One of the things that may encourage Descartes in his way of thinking about the difference between being in a cogito-like experience and remembering having been in a cogito-like experience is that, once knowledge of the metaphysical underpinnings of cognition is in place, the difference becomes practically unimportant. Be that as it may, we might well agree with him that there is an important philosophical distinction to be drawn in the vicinity between one's first-order cognition and one's second-order reflection on one's nature as a knower, however exactly the details are worked out. And we might well agree, further, that doubts that arise at the second-order, reflective level about my being the sort of cognizer who gets on to the truth can have (let me be vague) a destabilizing effect on one's confidence in the deliverances of one's first-order cognition.

Let's return to the Fifth Meditation. Earlier in this chapter we considered Descartes's remark, at the end of ¶6, to the effect that there is a type of certainty available to a mathematician who has yet to discover the metaphysical foundations of cognition, and another remark, at the end of ¶7, to the effect that that same type of certainty is available to someone who is entertaining the ontological argument but has yet to discover the metaphysical foundations of cognition. Sometimes these remarks are read as concerned with a "merely psychological" certainty, but, as I have argued, to characterize clear and distinct perception as merely psychologically certain sells short what such perception achieves. Ultimately, I think "merely psychological" certainty is a construct invented by commentators, who have misunderstood how the evil-genius doubt interacts with clear and distinct perception. But if that's right, then there are two types of genuine certainty (i.e., certainty that involves truth)—and how can this be?

It seems to me that it is the burden of the last four paragraphs of the Fifth Meditation, in which Descartes develops his conception of *scientia*, to explain this very point. (Very roughly, having *scientia* is the condition the meditator is in after she has recognized the metaphysical underpinnings of her cognition.) That discussion culminates with a remark we considered earlier:

> Thus I see plainly that the certainty and truth of all knowledge [*omnis scientiae certitudinem & veritatem*] depends uniquely on my awareness [*cognitione*] of the true God, to such an extent that I was incapable of perfect knowledge [*perfecte scire*] about anything else until I became aware of [*nossem*] him. And now it is possible for me to achieve full and certain knowledge [*plane nota & certa*] of countless matters, both concerning God himself and other things whose nature is intellectual, and also concerning the whole of that corporeal nature which is the subject-matter of pure mathematics. (¶16; 7:71; 2:49)

One might take this passage to suggest (as the authors of the Second Objections apparently did) that we cannot know anything until we know the foundations of knowledge, thereby raising the specter of the Cartesian Circle. However, closer inspection of this passage indicates that Descartes has in view two different modes of cognition. There is *scientia* or

perfecte scire, the condition one has reached after recognizing the foundations of knowledge. And there is the means by which one recognizes
those foundations, which is, I take it, simply to perceive them clearly—
that is, simply to perceive clearly that the author of my nature is not a
deceiver and that this entails that everything I clearly and distinctly perceive is true. (Although Descartes mentions only God here, I take it that
this is a kind of shorthand, and that in order to have *scientia* I also need
to have perceived clearly the rest of the metaphysical underpinnings of
cognition.)

What should we make of these two modes of cognition? One senses
that Descartes is being careful with his terminology here, and perhaps
struggling with it a bit, as if (perhaps because of the originality of his
project of laying the foundations of knowledge) he has ready at hand no
off-the-shelf vocabulary that will answer his needs. Let's look briefly at
the vocabulary.

Clearly perceiving by itself, as we have seen, entails only the lower
grade of certainty, the one I've called plain certainty (certainty *simpliciter*
as opposed to metaphysical certainty). So cognition that Descartes characterizes as *certus* as opposed to *plane certus* belongs this mode. I think cognition (*cognitio*), especially clear cognition (see Second Replies, 7:141),
noscere (knowing in the sense of being acquainted with), and *scire*, when it
is not qualified by *perfecte*, all belong to this mode of cognition. In addition, *ignorare* (i.e., not-*noscere*; to be unacquainted with) marks the absence
of this mode of cognition. For the second mode of cognition Descartes
uses the phrases *scientia*, *plane certus*, *perfecte scire*, and *plane nota & certa*.
I will use the Latin *scientia* to mark it. The word was a well-established
term of art in the tradition, and I believe that Descartes consciously borrowed the word.

According to the tradition, what is *scientia*? *Scientia* was the term used
in the Latin tradition to translate the Greek *episteme*. *Episteme* is knowledge of reasoned fact—that is, the sort of knowledge one has of a thing
by seeing why it is true. For Aristotelians, syllogisms were supposed not
only to make the conclusion of the syllogism certain, but also to exhibit
relevant causes, and so provide an explanation of why the conclusion is
true. Many commentators have thought that it is better to translate the
Greek word *episteme* by the English word *understanding* than by *knowledge*
in order to mark this connection with explanation: to have *episteme* (or
scientia) of something is not just to be certain that it is so, but also to understand why it is so. Now, for Descartes, too, *scientia* or *episteme* involves
both certainty and explanation, although, as I will suggest, he alters the
notion in a fundamental way.

How, according to Descartes, is *scientia* connected with certainty? His
basic thought here is that without an understanding of my cognitive

faculties and why they lead me to the truth, I am continually subject to the now-you-see-it/now-you-don't experience presented in the Third Meditation. Here's how he puts the general point:

> Admittedly my nature is such that so long as I perceive something very clearly and distinctly I cannot but believe it to be true. But my nature is also such that I cannot fix my mental vision continually on the same thing, so as to keep perceiving it clearly; and often the memory of a previously made judgement may come back, when I am no longer attending to the arguments which led me to make it. And so other arguments can now occur to me which might easily undermine my opinion, if I did not possess knowledge [*ignorarem*] of God; and I should thus never have true and certain knowledge [*scientiam*] about anything, but only shifting and changeable opinions. (V.¶14; 7:69; 2:48)

In the remainder of the paragraph, he makes this somewhat more concrete by playing an example from geometry off against the worry that he might have a defective nature (only "somewhat more" concrete because he does not actually lead the meditator through a geometrical demonstration):

> For example, when I consider the nature of a triangle, it appears most evident to me, steeped as I am in the principles of geometry, that its three angles are equal to two right angles; and so long as I attend to the demonstration, I cannot but believe this to be true. (¶14; 7:69–70; 2:48)

We are asked to imagine someone attending a demonstration, which, I take it, puts someone in what I have been calling a cogito-like state. Here it helps to remember that Descartes thinks of a demonstration as a set of cues for helping one to see that something is or must be so, rather than as an abstract object relating premises and conclusions according to truth-preserving rules. Now, if the meditator could remain in such a condition her entire life—that is, if she continually "saw through" the subject matters she thinks about in the way that someone attending fully to a mathematical argument does—then there would be no room for "fuller" certainty; she would have as much certainty as possible. However, no one can continually remain in such a condition, where her judgment is constantly determined by clear perception; and when she exits the cogito-like condition there is room for doubt:

> But as soon as I turn my mind's eye away from the demonstration, then in spite of still remembering that I perceived it very clearly, I can easily fall into doubt about its truth, if I am without knowledge of God [*Deum ignorarem*]. For I can convince myself that I have a natural disposition to go wrong from time to time in matters which I think I perceive as evidently as can be. This will seem even more likely when I remember that there have been

frequent cases where I have regarded things as true and certain, but have later been led by other arguments to judge them as false. (¶14; 7:70; 2:48)

So: When I am not in a cogito-like condition, that is, not clearly perceiving, but instead only looking back on having previously been in such a condition, then my current judgment is not being determined by my clear apprehension of the truth. As Descartes sees it, my current reasons for believing that a triangle's three angles are equal to two right angles run through my having once clearly perceived *and* a belief about my nature, namely that it is reliable in such a way that things that I clearly perceive are in fact true. (Sometimes this is described as a doubt about the reliability of memory, but that is misleading.) When I am in a cogito-like condition my perception of the truth determines my judgment. But what is there to determine my judgment now that I am no longer in a cogito-like condition, when the salient considerations are no longer clearly before my mind's eye, so to speak? Well, there is the fact that the salient considerations were once clearly perceived. But how does this help me make my way to the truth now, unless I make some assumption to the effect that when I previously perceived clearly, I got things right so that my judgment was determined in accordance with truth? Until I have seen why this should be so, it seems that there will always be room to doubt things that I have previously clearly perceived but am not presently clearly perceiving: "Yes, I recall clearly perceiving it, but maybe I am so constituted that I often go wrong even when I perceive clearly." Someone who has perceived the metaphysical underpinnings of her cognition can fill in this missing piece of the puzzle: she understands that the author of her nature is not a deceiver, and so she can see why it is the case that she has been made in such a way that what she perceives clearly is true. Thus, when she exits a clear perception, the doubt that can arise for someone who lacks an understanding of such things does not arise for her. She is fully certain.[68]

Descartes covers similar ground in a well-known letter to Regius, writing:

> In your second objection you say: "the truths of axioms which are clearly and distinctly understood is self-evident [*manifestam per se*]." This too, I agree, is true, during the time they are clearly and distinctly understood; for our mind is of such a nature that it cannot help assenting to what it clearly understands. But because we often remember conclusions that we have deduced from such premises without actually attending to the premises themselves, I say that on such occasions, if we are ignorant [*ignoremus*] of God, we can imagine that the conclusions are uncertain even though we remember that they were deduced from clear principles: because perhaps our nature is such that we go wrong even in the most

evident matters. Consequently, even at the moment we deduced them from those principles, we did not have *scientia* of them, but only persuasion [*persuasionem*] of them. I distinguish the two as follows: there is persuasion [*persuasio*] when there remains some reason which might lead us to doubt, but *scientia* is persuasion [*persuasio*] based on a reason so strong that it can never be shaken by any stronger reason. Nobody can have the latter who is ignorant [*ignorant*] of God. But a man who has once clearly understood the reasons which persuade [*persuadent*] us that God exist and is not a deceiver, provided he remembers the conclusion that "God is no deceiver" whether or not he continues to attend to the reasons for it, will continue to possess not only the persuasion [*persuasio*], but real *scientia* [*vera scientia*] of this and all other conclusions the reasons for which he remembers he once clearly perceived. (3:64–65; 3:147)

The way Descartes puts the point here—in terms of "persuasion"—is one of the factors that have encouraged some readers to think of the determination of one's judgment by a clear perception as a subjective or psychological affair.[69] (Some translations render the Latin *persuado* and *persuasio* as "convince" and "conviction," respectively, but I think these have different connotations and it is worth trying to stay close to the original.) Although it is easy to see how this passage gives that impression, I believe the impression is misleading.

Persuasion here, I think, means a determination grounded in that special relation to the truth (and, hence, the world and reality) I enjoy from time to time. For Descartes, being persuaded (like being certain) is a matter of having one's views about a thing determined by a clear view of the truth of the matter. This would be in keeping with a natural way of thinking about self-evidence, which is, after all, what Descartes is overtly trying to explain in the passage: that is, it is the truth of the axioms' being open to view that "persuades" me. Moreover, I believe that the contrast he is drawing here between *persuasio* and *scientia* is between momentary glimpses of the truth determining my judgment—momentary "persuasions"—and the more enduring and more stable cognitive situation that results from one's having a worked-out understanding of one's place as a knower in the world that one knows. That increased stability, I take it, depends on the momentary *persuasio*'s getting me to truth and reality; without such mooring the perspective afforded to me by *scientia* would be a castle in the air. I allow that there may be some awkwardness in Descartes's choice of the terminology *persuasio*, but I think that this is because there is no ready, off-the-shelf vocabulary available for him to draw the contrast he wants, between clearly and distinctly perceiving/being persuaded, on the one hand, and *scientia*, on the other.

Persuasio, I should note, also figures prominently in another well-known passage, this one from the Second Replies:

> First of all, as soon as we think that we correctly perceive something, we are spontaneously persuaded that it is true [*persuademus illud esse verum*]. Now if this persuasion [*persuasio*] is so firm that it is impossible for us ever to have any reason for doubting what we are persuaded of [*persuademus*], then there are no further questions for us to ask: we have everything we could reasonably [*cum ratione*] wish for. What is it to us that someone imagines [*fingat*] that the thing, of whose truth we are so firmly persuaded [*persuasi*], appears false to God or an angel, so that it is, absolutely speaking, false. What do we care about this absolute falsity, when we in no way believe in it, nor have even the smallest suspicion of it? For the supposition which we are making here is of a persuasion [*persuasionem*] so firm that it is quite incapable of being removed; which persuasion [*persuasio*] therefore is fully the same thing as perfect certainty. (7:144–45; 2:103)

This difficult and intriguing passage has received a great deal of attention over the years. I believe that, taken alone, it is susceptible to different interpretations. For my part, I read it as simply the dismissal of an unfounded skeptical challenge. When I am thinking through the cogito or a geometrical argument, it is impossible for me not to believe the truth of what I see so clearly, because I see it so clearly. Say, for example, I am entertaining a "persuasive" geometrical argument, carrying out the relevant constructions, noting the appropriate relationships, and, voilà, I notice that the three angles of the triangle sum to two right angles. Suppose, as I am doing this, someone comes up to me and feigns (*fingat*), "Perhaps this truth that you are seeing so clearly appears false to God or an angel." I think that Descartes's point is that I shouldn't pay attention to such idle speculation. That I shouldn't comes out in my inability to take it seriously—not so much in the *fact* that I am unable to, but rather in *why* I am unable to: my sense of being determined by the truth not only makes it impossible to take the doubt seriously, but also makes it foolish for me to do so. And it seems to me Descartes is on strong ground here: I am not quite sure what it would mean for me, in the midst of a cogito-like experience, to say to myself something like, "Well, it certainly seems to me that I exist, but (scrupulous believer/critical thinker that I am) I have to admit that that is only my opinion, and allow that perhaps the absolute truth with regard to this matter, as seen by God and angels, runs differently." As Descartes says, my "persuasion" here, which comes from a clear vision of reality, gives me everything I could reasonably wish for (one might add: imagine). So, again, I don't think that the persuasion in question is aptly characterized as psychological (or subjective).

One might ask, of course, if Descartes is willing to dismiss a doubt about the truth appearing differently to God or an angel from how it appears to us as unfounded, how is the evil-genius/imperfect-creator doubt any better? Well, as he explains, the evil-genius/imperfect-creator doubt does not apply to my currently perceiving clearly—no kind of doubt could—but only to my past clear perceivings. As he sees it, my attitude toward them involves implicitly taking up a sort of reflective stance on myself as a cognizer. When no longer perceiving clearly the truth, I ask myself, "Granted, things went well on that past occasion, but why should that count for anything, unless I have the sort of nature that gets me to truth?" Moreover, this reflective doubt (that I am able to subsequently take up) is itself not lodged in some idle speculation, but rather in my ignorance of my situation as knower: Was I just parachuted into the universe and left to fend for myself, or is there some reason to think that I am in some deep cognitive attunement with it? When doubt is first raised, I find I cannot say.

To be fair, the thought that what Descartes may be aiming for is primarily a sort of psychological stability is motivated by philosophical as well as textual considerations. It arises, I think, in large part from a recognition that if we read the evil-genius doubt as cutting the mind off from reality completely and issuing the implicit challenge to construct a bridge back to reality, it is very difficult to see how we can make any progress with the doubt. This makes it natural to look for something else that Descartes might have been doing with the doubt, such as using it in a project to secure psychological stability. However, I don't see the evil-genius doubt as asking us to abandon the mooring to truth and reality that perceiving clearly evidently brings with it. Rather, I think the doubt challenges us to come up with an account of why it should be the case that clear perceivings relate us to truth and reality, so that we may achieve a reflective, systematic perspective on ourselves as knowers. As we attempt to achieve this perspective we are free to use individual moorings to truth and reality that our various clear perceivings afford.[70]

One thing that can make it hard for us to follow Descartes's thought is an almost unconscious tendency in modern readers to think of knowledge in more abstract terms, say, as a matter of having true beliefs that are justified in the right sort of way. If we think along these lines, then it is hard to make sense of the movement back and forth between "now you see it" and "now you don't" that seems essential to Descartes's way of thinking about epistemology. For—we would want to ask today—if in the midst of a cogito experience or while working through a geometrical demonstration, the meditator justifies a belief in the right sort of way to count as knowledge, how did the meditator subsequently *lose* that justification? Here it is important to recognize that although Descartes may be the father of modern epistemology, he does not think of clear perception as the possession of a standing "justification." For Descartes, clear perception is a way of seeing that something is so. What achieving *scientia* enables me to do is to understand (now) why if I have (sometime in the past) perceived clearly that something is so, it is so. (One might say that *scientia* converts past clear perception into a sort of justification, although I do not think Descartes himself puts the matter that way.)

Scientia, in the Aristotelian tradition, involves both certainty and systematic understanding. The same is true for Descartes. Even so, Descartes's handling of *scientia* is quite novel. To appreciate this, consider his suggestion, just explored, that there is a grade of certainty available to the geometer that involves extra-geometrical considerations. This marks a striking break with Aristotelian thinking about *scientia*. For Aristotelians, the certainty associated with *scientia* was supposed to flow from the first principles of a particular subject matter through to the conclusion. (These first principles, although better known in themselves, are not necessarily better known to us; particular geometrical propositions may be more obvious to us than the basic principles of geometry that account for them.) As the geometer sees how the theorem flows from principles that are, on reflection, self-evident, her knowledge becomes more certain. Here the certainty associated with *scientia* is acquired through a better command of one's discipline. Descartes claims, as we have seen, that there is a fuller grade of certainty available to the geometer than this, that comes from her understanding of her nature as a cognitive being and its place within the universe that she knows. This is, in effect, to require as a part of the systematicity involved in *scientia* that there be a chapter that explains one's position as a knower.

Indeed, if there is such a thing as a "Cartesian" conception of knowledge, or such a thing as Cartesian foundationalism, I would be tempted to locate it here, in the broad thought that human knowledge in the fullest sense (call it *scientia* or whatever) necessarily includes a special kind of (perhaps *a priori*) perspective on our position as knowers. This idea, I think, has proven more influential than many of the particular details in Descartes's account of knowledge, and may well have eventually led to the idea, not present I think in Descartes's own thought, that having knowledge in the fullest sense involves being able to justify oneself.

Let's return to the Cartesian Circle. Keeping firmly in view the difference between clearly perceiving and *scientia* helps us to see why Descartes does not hold that I know everything I know *through* knowing the foundations of my knowledge, and so why there is no foundational circle. Perceiving clearly works whether or not I have reached *scientia*. To be sure, once I have reached *scientia* (by perceiving clearly the metaphysical underpinnings of knowledge), I will view my clear perceivings differently. I will now take it that the things I clearly perceived in the past were perceived as they are, and so *scientia* will endow those things with a full certainty, that is, with a certainty that remains when I cease to perceive them clearly. But the fact that *scientia* extends the value of my clear perceivings in this way does not imply that the clear perceivings themselves, at the time I am having them, are in any way less than certain, or only "psychologically" certain or all-but-certain.

One gets the appearance of circularity only when one collapses these two forms of cognition, clear perception and *scientia*, into some relatively flat sense of knowing. Then it does begin to look as if instead of saying that all *scientia* depends on clear perception of God (the metaphysical underpinnings of cognition), Descartes is saying that all knowledge depends on knowledge of God. The Second Objectors seem to have read him as working with a single, flat conception of knowledge. They object that, on his view, it follows that nothing could be known in the Second Meditation before God's existence was demonstrated: "[Y]ou say that you are not certain of anything, and cannot know [*cognoscere*] anything clearly and distinctly until you have achieved clear and certain knowledge [*noveris*] of the existence of God," from which it follows that "you do not yet clearly and distinctly know [*clare & distincte scire*] that you are a thinking thing" (7:124–25; 2:89). They also object: "[A]n atheist is clearly and distinctly aware [*cognoscere*] that the three angles of a triangle are equal to two right angles; but so far is he from supposing the existence of God he completely denies it" (7:125; 2:89).

As might be imagined, Descartes responds indignantly. He complains that in the Fifth Meditation he said in "express words [*expressis verbis*]" that *cognitio* of God was required for the *subsequent* certainty of what is clearly and distinctly perceived (7:140; 2:100). Moreover, he protests that he never denied that an atheist could have clear and distinct *cognitio* of a geometrical theorem; he denied only that such cognition counts as *scientia* (7:141; 2:101). By ignoring Descartes's patient (even labored) explanation of how things currently clearly and distinctly perceived become subsequently subject to doubt (for someone who does not know the author of her nature), and by neglecting his distinction between clear perception and *scientia*, the Second Objectors manufacture a difficulty where there is none.

Toward the beginning of this section, I said that it is natural to think that knowing the foundations of knowledge should somehow bolster or reinforce all of human knowledge, so that until we know the foundations we cannot know anything else, at least not in the fullest sense of knowing. We are now in a position to appreciate the sense in which this is true for Descartes. To be sure, it is not true for Descartes that knowing the foundations is necessary for any cognitive success. Perceiving clearly works without my understanding the metaphysical underpinnings of cognition. When I perceive clearly, the truth is revealed to me and I am aware of its being so revealed. However, simply perceiving clearly does not yield knowledge in the fullest sense, full certainty or *scientia*. (Descartes works this idea out in terms of the episodic character of clear perception, but one could imagine, I think, other ways of working out what is unsatisfying about having only clear perception.) According to Descartes, in order to have knowledge in its fullest sense, full certainty or *scientia*, one must have understood the metaphysical underpinnings of one's cognition (through clearly perceiving those underpinnings) and so, in effect, must have in one's possession a reflective, worked-out account of one's nature as a knower.

There is a second version of the Cartesian Circle I would like to mention that has to do with Descartes's employment of skeptical arguments. In the First Meditation, Descartes worries that the author of his nature might have made him so that he goes wrong in the simplest and most obvious matters, or, as he puts it in the Fifth Meditation, that he might have "a natural disposition to go wrong from time to time in matters which I think I can perceive as evidently as can be" (7:70; 2:48). This doubt is quite far-reaching, taking within its ambit absolutely everything, no matter how evident (Descartes instances two and three added together are five, and counting the sides of a square and coming up with four as the answer, as examples of things that the doubt brings into question). This makes any attempt to refute it seem question-begging: any reasoning or argument that one might use while attempting to answer the doubt looks to require materials (premises, modes of inference, etc.) put at risk by the doubt.

How much difference there is between these two versions of the Circle is open to dispute. If one thinks, as I am inclined to, that the primary function of the evil-genius doubt is to bring to the meditator's attention her lack of a correct understanding of the foundations of her knowledge, then the versions of the Circle would be different ways of putting the same problem. That is, if what makes the evil-genius doubt salient is either that I lack an account of the foundations of knowledge (as perhaps Descartes thinks the common person does) or that I have a mistaken conception of the foundations of knowledge (as perhaps Descartes thinks the Aristotelian scholastic does, because she takes her basic cognitive relation to the universe to run through the senses), then to claim that I must refute the evil-genius doubt before I could know anything at all would be equivalent to claiming that I must have a correct understanding of the foundations of my knowledge before I can know anything. So, in my view, in the same way that I am certain that what I am clearly perceiving is true while I am clearly perceiving before I have discerned the foundations of knowledge, I am certain that what I am clearly perceiving is true before I have responded to the evil-genius doubt.

But by the same token, if one did not think that the force of the evil-genius doubt derives from the meditator's inadequate understanding of the foundations of her knowledge, then one might think that there is an important difference between the two versions of the Circle, and one might think, further, that even if Descartes is able to lay the foundations of knowledge in a noncircular way, he might be unable to answer the evil-genius challenge in a non-question-begging way. Let me sketch one way in which this might go. This is something of a caricature, but not so far off, I hope, as to be a straw person.

Human knowledge, it might be suggested, necessarily begins from *representations* or, in Descartes's terms, *ideas*. All we have to go on, all we have access to, are our own representations or ideas. This being so, how is it possible for us to know anything besides our own ideas—or even that there *is* a truth or reality lying beyond our ideas? Perhaps these ideas are simply implanted in us by some evil genius. If one starts down this path, it becomes hard not to view clarity as only a property that some of these (suspect) representations have that others lack, and so it is an open question whether clear representations, even if possessing an internal order and rational coherence, really get us to truth or reality. Some such idea, I think, is a source of the view that prior to our refuting the evil genius, even though our perceptions may be "rationally" in order and "internally" in order, they cannot be more than "psychologically" certain. In this setting, using my clear ideas to build up a case that my clear ideas get me through to the world is viciously circular. The thesis that representations with the property clarity also have the feature of linking me to truth or reality needs some support *independent* of what my clear ideas supposedly show me, if it is not to be blatantly question-begging.

I do not have enough space to argue the case fully here, so let me simply register my sense that this problematic, as fascinating as it may be, is not Descartes's. Interpreters who understand Descartes as engaged in this problematic often depict him as resolving the problem by pointing out some supposed deep incoherence in the skeptical hypothesis that our thought does not connect us with reality. This has the consequence, as Janet Broughton has insisted, that there would need to be two philosophical moments in Descartes's handling of the evil-genius doubt—a prior, negative one showing that the hypothesis that my thought does not connect me to reality is incoherent, and a subsequent, constructive one developing the metaphysical underpinnings of cognition. As Broughton points out, it is very difficult to discern an independent negative moment in the text, and to the extent that it is there at all, it would seem to come after rather than before the constructive moment.[71]

I think that the negative moment is a phantom, invented in order to give Descartes a solution to a problem that is alien to his thought. For one of the most important things we discover in the *Meditations* quite early on, in the cogito passage (Archimedean point that it is), is that our thought does connect us to the *truth*. Consider again the conclusion of the cogito passage: "So after considering everything very thoroughly, I must finally conclude [*denique statuendum sit*] that this proposition, *I am, I exist*, is necessarily true [*necessario est verum*] whenever it is put forward by me or conceived in my mind" (II.¶3; 7:25; 2:17). This is a pivotal moment for the meditator: she *sees* that she exists, and so discovers that she has the remarkable ability to see that things are so, to grasp the truth. While she perceives that she exists, she can tell that there must be something wrong with the evil-genius doubt, even if she cannot say what and even if once she exits her clear perception the doubt can recur in its full generality. Current clear perceivings are never mere representations, of doubtful relation to reality. To think otherwise—to understand the cogito experience as if there were room for a metaphysical doubt that is somehow not currently available to the meditator transfixed by the clarity of her perception—is to forget what perceiving clearly *is* for Descartes and to surreptitiously replace it with something like a two-dimensional Berkeleyan idea.

⇢6⇠

The Sixth Meditation

WHAT IS the Sixth Meditation about? Its heading reads, "The existence of material things, and the real distinction between mind and body," and Descartes's handling of these topics has drawn considerable attention over the years. However, these topics come fairly early in the meditation—in ¶¶10 and 9 respectively—and while they are relevant to the remaining twenty-two paragraphs, it is hard to see that larger discussion as structured around them. The headings serve not so much to orient the meditator as to signal important moments in the discussion. This fits with Descartes's own description of the individual meditation headings as simply "the things that I want people mainly to notice" (letter to Mersenne of 4 March 1641, 3:298; 3:172–73).

If the Sixth Meditation is not constructed around its two highlights, how is it organized? One idea that I find attractive is that the meditation's purpose is to provide accounts of the imagination and the senses, the two cognitive faculties whose nature remains to be explained. Descartes begins the meditation by announcing that "it remains for me to examine whether material things exist," and this examination immediately turns into an account of "what imagining is" (¶¶1–3). This account yields an argument for the existence of body, but only a probable one. As he casts about for a stronger argument, he notices things like "colours, sounds, tastes, pain and so on," which are better perceived by the senses than by the imagination. He decides that "in order to deal with them more fully, I must pay equal attention to the senses, and see whether the things which are perceived by means of that mode of thinking which I call sensing provide any sure argument for the existence of corporeal things" (¶4). Although the subsequent discussion contains various twists and turns, there is no sign that we are leaving the general topic of the nature of the senses. This yields a picture of the Sixth Meditation as composed of two unequal parts, a shorter discussion of the imagination (three paragraphs) and a longer discussion of the senses (twenty-one paragraphs).

Although I think there is something right about this picture, I believe that there is a still more illuminating way to look at the purpose of the Sixth Meditation. In the Second Meditation, when Descartes asks, "What then did I formerly think I was?" his first answer is, "A man." When he goes on to ask, "But what is a man?" he considers and rejects the following answer:

> Shall I say a rational animal? No; for then I should have to inquire what an animal is, what rational is, and in this way one question would lead me down the slope to other harder ones, and I do not now have the time to waste on subtleties of this kind. (II.¶5; 7:25; 2:17)

But Descartes did not pursue the question "What is a man?" or "What is a human being?" further at that juncture. It would have been inappropriate because at the time methodological doubt screened off the corporeal part of myself from view. So, in the Second Meditation, Descartes was concerned exclusively with the cognitive part of me, the cognitive agent.[1] The nature of the me who is a man, that is, a human being, was in effect left to the side. Descartes is picking up that question, "What is a human being?" now. I see it as the main topic of the Sixth Meditation.

Although Descartes dismisses *rational animal* as an answer to the question "What is a human being?" because it is the first step on a slippery slope of subtleties, he does, of course, have considered positions on both what an animal is and what a rational being is. His understanding of animals as machines and of rational beings as beings who are able to engage in the sort of activities that the cognitive agent participates in makes it hard to give the answer *rational animal* to the question "What is a human being?" If this answer is taken in the usual way, so as to mean that I am a certain kind of animal, namely, one that is rational, it would come out, when translated into Descartes's metaphysics, something like *an automaton that thinks*. It is true that I am, on Descartes's view, a composite entity, from which it follows, one might suppose, that I am both rational and animal, since one of my components thinks and one of my components is an automaton of the appropriate sort (though I am not sure that Descartes would be happy with the formulation *I am an animal*), but the characterization *rational animal* is not, given Descartes's theory of the metaphysics of the human being, a particularly happy or terribly illuminating way of explaining what a human being is. Clearly some other picture of the human being is called for by Cartesian metaphysics.

One might wonder how Descartes's treatment of the lower two cognitive faculties, sense and imagination, dovetails with his account of human nature.[2] Well, each of the lower cognitive faculties witnesses a different liaison that a cognitive agent might enjoy with body; and, of these two liaisons, it is the sensory one (as opposed to the imaginative one) that shows us what it is to be united to a body in a distinctively human way (and not as a sailor to his ship). That the senses witness a special relationship to a body is not so surprising when we note that Descartes takes the perception of hunger, thirst, and pain to fall under the senses (as so-called internal senses), and emphasizes them more in his account of the nature of a human being than the so-called external senses, which include our perception of color and sound.

Let me say a little more about what is involved, for Descartes, in giving an account of human nature. We enter the Sixth Meditation having become intimately familiar with the cognitive agent. We have observed it as it decided to undergo the exercise of methodological doubt and have observed how, by so doing, it was eventually able to achieve a thorough and deep understanding of itself and its cognitive position within the universe. We have seen it learn the difference between obscure and confused and clear and distinct cognition. We have seen how it cognizes itself, God, and the essence of matter.

Up to this point in the *Meditations* we have explored the cognitive agent while using the device of the dreaming doubt in order to screen off from view whatever corporeal order might exist. (To be sure, the corporeal has intruded into the discussion now and then: the wax, the sun, and the essence of body have all come up, but no commitments have yet been made to body's existence.) In the Sixth Meditation, Descartes removes this screen and positions the cognitive agent vis-à-vis the order that is revealed. The last point that he makes before he removes it is that the cognitive agent is in principle severable from body. His basic thought here, I think, is that none of the cognitive agent's core activities that we have explored over the course of the *Meditations*—doubting, affirming, denying, and cognizing self, God, and the essence of matter—witness any intrinsic connection to body. Indeed, I think he finds hard to fathom what it would mean to think of these activities as embodied, as somehow taking place on a corporeal platform, let alone insist that they are inseparable from such a platform. In ¶9, he confirms what has become increasingly obvious as the meditator has progressed through the *Meditations*, namely, that the cognitive agent counts as an independent being. In ¶10 Descartes argues for the existence of body in a way that entitles the meditator to conclude that body exists with all of its geometrical-kinetic properties but does not entitle her to conclude anything else about body. In other words, she is entitled to conclude that the subject matter of mechanistic natural philosophy exists. She learns shortly thereafter, in ¶12, that she has a body.

This way of proceeding—first by arguing that my mind is severable from my body (¶9), then that the subject matter of mechanism exists (¶10), then that I have a (mechanistic) body (¶12)—may suggest that Descartes sees his task as taking a disembodied mind and a (mechanistic) human body and then working from our accounts of what a mind is and what body is to explain how a mind may be united to a body to form a human being. If we look for such a project, we will be disappointed. Rather, in order to understand the union we must be given some new piece of information, certain "teachings of nature," which turn out to be closely connected to the fact that we are beings who sense, and sensing is not something that is, according to Descartes, essential to what we are as cognitive beings.

We get some help with understanding the nature of the project from a well-known letter Descartes wrote to Princess Elizabeth. In it, Descartes writes that he recognizes "three kinds of primitive ideas or notions, each of which is known in its own proper manner and not by comparison with any of the others; the notions we have of the soul, of body and of the union between the soul and the body" (3:691; 3:226). I think he is saying to Elizabeth that the notions of mind, body, and their union are primitive, in the sense that one cannot construct them out of more basic materials. The cognitive agent cannot be understood, for example, as simply the sum of its operations, body as simply the collection of properties and activities associated with matter, and the union as simply the sum of the interactions that take place between mind and body or, perhaps, as the sum of activities that involve both. Understanding what the mind is and what body is does not suffice for understanding what the union is. All three must somehow be given to us for our reflection. According to Descartes, they are given to us in different ways:

> The soul is conceived only by the pure intellect; body (i.e. extension, shapes and motions) can likewise be known by the intellect alone, but much better by the intellect aided by the imagination; and finally what belongs to the union of the soul and the body is known only obscurely by the intellect alone or even by the intellect aided by the imagination, but it is known very clearly by the senses. That is why people who never philosophize and use only their senses have no doubt that the soul moves the body and that the body acts on the soul. They regard both of them as a single thing, that is to say, they conceive their union; because to conceive the union between two things is to conceive them as one single thing. (3:691–92; 3:227)

That fact that our basic cognitive purchase on the union is given to us through the senses gives Descartes's discussion of the union an *a posteriori* flavor. He does not begin with accounts of what a mind is and what a body is and explain from there how to build a human composite from these materials. Sometimes, it seems to me, disappointment with Descartes's account of mind-body union is rooted in his failure to do this: to show how, given what the mind is and given what the body is, it is possible for them to interact. What this reaction misses is the fact that a sensory

liaison is supposed to represent, I think, a genuine expansion of possibility for both sides, which is why we need the senses in order to discover
that such possibility exists. One may still worry, of course, about how
well these new possibilities can be integrated with the old, but this seems
to me a worry different from one based on the idea that one ought to be
able to find the seeds of the union in a thorough understanding of the
body and of the mind.

In any case, the fact of sensation makes it clear that God has made a
human composite. That I experience pain, hunger, and thirst (coupled
with the fact that God would not systematically deceive me) makes plain
to me that I have a body, for which I have a special concern. And this
shows me that there is such a thing as a human being, that is, a mind
united to a body. The goal of the Sixth Meditation is to understand what
a human being is within the context of the rest of Descartes's metaphysics. Interpreting human nature within the context of Descartes's metaphysics brings with it certain constraints. They are roughly these: A
human being is a composite entity, a union of two relatively independent
things, a mind and a body. So the theory of what a human being is is to
be drawn in terms of the mind and the body, and the relationship between them. This is not to go back on Descartes's claim that the notion
of the union is primitive, because the relationship between mind and
body involves possibilities that are not intelligible in terms of our understanding of what a cognitive agent is or what a body is. The relationship
between them involves possibilities that are not given through the essence of the mind and the essence of the body alone.

Descartes begins with a set of pretheoretical beliefs about human nature, what a human being is, and tries to give a certain amount of theoretical structure to these beliefs by working them out within the context
of certain of his substantive metaphysical commitments. His task, even
thus circumscribed, turns out to be formidable. It is not clear that one
can provide a philosophically satisfying account of what it is to be a
human being in terms of the materials at his disposal, the mind, the
body, and the relationship between them.

Minds and Machines

When considering Descartes's conception of human nature, it is helpful
to have in the background his understanding of animals, because it tells
us something about how he thinks of the human body and because it
helps brings out more clearly the place of the mind in his account of
human nature.

As is well known (and as I have been assuming in the discussion thus far), the dominant view in Descartes's writings (allowing for some slight hedging in some of his later writings, which I shall touch on later) is that animals are purely corporeal beings and, in particular, do not have minds or souls: they are machines or automata. Descartes is very much aware that this runs against the grain of what people usually think: "There is no preconceived opinion to which we are all more accustomed from our earliest years than the belief that dumb animals think," he writes in a late letter to Henry More (5:275–76; 3:365). Although they are purely corporeal beings, some of them have physiologies quite similar to ours. For example, some of them have the physiological accompaniments to sensation and imagination. Descartes writes in a letter to Gibieuf:

> We observe in animals movements similar to those which result from our imaginations and sensations; but that does not mean we observe imaginations and sensations in them. On the contrary, these same movements can take place without imagination, and we have arguments to prove that they do so take place in animals, as I hope to show clearly by describing in detail the structure of their limbs and the causes of their movements. (3:479; 3:203–4)

When light bounces off the wolf automaton and strikes the eyes of the sheep automaton, images are formed on the pineal gland of the sheep that produce a stirring of the animal spirits (the corporeal side, if you will, of the passion of fear), which subsequently causes a release of those spirits to the legs (the corporeal side of flight).[3] So animal automata have not only the physiological side of sensation and imagination, but also the physiological side of the passions. It is, in principle, possible, Descartes explains in *The Passions of the Soul*, to provide mechanistic accounts of why a dog chases partridges and runs away from loud noises and how this wiring may be reconnected through training, so that the dog stops when it sees a partridge and runs when a gun is fired:

> And the same may be observed in animals. For although they lack reason, and perhaps even thought, all the movements of the spirits and of the gland which produce passions in us are nevertheless present in them too, though in them they serve to maintain and strengthen only the movements of the nerves and the muscles which usually accompany the passions and not, as in us, the passions themselves. So when a dog sees a partridge, it is naturally disposed to run towards it; and when it hears a gun fired, the noise naturally impels it to run away. Nevertheless, setters are commonly trained so that the sight of a partridge makes them stop, and the noise they hear afterwards, when someone fires at the bird, makes them run towards it. These things are worth noting in order to encourage each of us to make a point of controlling our passions. For since we are

able, with a little effort, to change the movements of the brain in animals devoid of reason, it is evident that we can do so still more effectively in the case of men. (A. 50; 11:369–70; 1:348)

Although in the letter to Gibieuf Descartes refuses to attribute to animals sensation and imagination (on the grounds that sensing and imagining are modes of cognition and animals do not have cognition), he seems happy here to describe the setter as "seeing" the partridge and "hearing" the noise of the gun. I take this to show that seeing and hearing and so forth are, for Descartes, systematically ambiguous between merely physiological seeing, which can take place in automata, and seeing that is a form of cognition, which takes place, according to Descartes, only in human beings.

Let me also mention in passing, mainly to place to the side, a worry about what it means to provide a "mechanistic account" of partridge chasing and the like, to the effect that a mechanistic theory of such phenomena must borrow nonmechanistic vocabulary and concepts. Perhaps the idea of "chasing" is ineliminable from a description of the *explananda*; perhaps, even, functional idioms cannot be eliminated from the *explanans*. Descartes has a reasonably clear picture of the success conditions for a "mechanistic account." He holds that if we can construct machines that pass for dogs, he will have proven his point. The automata that he describes are fairly coarse approximations of the animals they imitate, but we can imagine constructing finer approximations. If we could put together from our fantastically fine mechanistic Erector Set something that no one could tell apart from a dog, no matter what examinations were carried out (abstracting away, let's suppose, from information about the origin of the entity being examined), then there is a sense of "mechanistic" in which a mechanistic account of a dog has been provided. I take this to be the case, even if functional idioms turn up in the blueprints. This is not to deny that there are interesting and difficult questions here. For our purposes, however, I think the best strategy is to take the functional language as equivocal, somewhat in the sense that *eyes* is used equivocally in the case of the eyes of a human being and the eyes of a statue. In the same vein, we could take Descartes's characterization of the sheep as "fleeing" the wolf as a convenient shorthand for summarizing some rather elaborate, but all the same mechanistic, goings-on (such as: if the wolf system moves this way, the sheep system goes that way).[4]

The sort of complex interactions with the environment that Descartes envisions between an animal and its environment through sensory (sensory-like?) apparatus and the subsequent processing of the traces of those interactions in imaginative and affective systems would provide sufficient grounds for many theorists today to attribute some level of cognition or thought to animals. Why does Descartes deny cognition to animals? Well, one might have thought that he would reason along these lines: cognition involves consciousness, but animals are not conscious (this claim would, of course, require some sort of support), and so animals do not have cognition.

However, as is widely recognized, Descartes's reasoning takes a different course: cognition involves rationality, but animals are not rational, and so animals do not have cognition. The most fundamental difference between us and the animals is not that we are conscious and they are not, but rather that we are rational and they are not (it is possible, of course, that the former difference might be thought to follow from the latter one). In other words, Descartes's refusal to attribute cognition (or thought) to animals rests on a more "intellectualist" conception of cognition (or thought) than many people today would embrace. This emphasis on higher-order cognitive ability comes out in the two main criteria Descartes offers for determining whether animals have minds or souls, one having to do with linguistic ability and the other having to do with a generalized problem-solving ability, and, in his view, animals satisfy neither. These criteria are not aimed at testing for some low-level cognitive abilities—say, determining whether an organism is able to acquire and process information from its environment—nor are they considerations especially geared toward revealing the presence of consciousness (whatever such criteria might look like). Rather, they are tests for higher-level cognition.

Notice that there are two assumptions implicit in Descartes's thinking about what sorts of abilities demonstrate the presence of a mind.

First, he is assuming that no mere machine could embody rationality: I believe he takes it as obvious both that (1) our rationality enables us to negotiate an indefinite variety of unforeseen problems, projects, and new circumstances, and that (2) no mechanical structure, no matter how intricate and complex, is able to do the same. I think the first assumption amounts to the thought that there is in principle an unlimited way for the cognitive agent to pursue its goals and surmount what obstacles it might discover in its way. Descartes finds support for the claim that animals, unlike rational beings, cannot negotiate indefinitely many novel situations in the fact that it is easy to trick animals ("we see that animals are often deceived by lures, and in seeking to avoid small evils they throw themselves into greater evils").[5]

Second, he is assuming that when our rationality does make a difference to the world, it does so via redirecting the flow of animal spirits about the pineal gland, so that the pineal gland and its immediate physical environment do not form a closed system but rather can be influenced by something extraphysical. The way he puts this in a letter to More is that there are in us "two different principles causing our movements," one of which "is purely mechanical and corporeal, and depends solely on the force of the spirits and the structure of our organs" and the other of which, "an incorporeal principle," "is the mind or soul I have defined as a thinking substance" (5:276; 3:365).[6] In this manner, our rationality makes itself manifest in the corporeal world; if it did not make a difference to the flow of the spirits in this way, there would be no more reason to think that other human bodies had minds than to think that animals had minds. Descartes does not, for example, suggest that the fact that we are rational and that animals are not shows up in anatomical differences (say, in terms of the size and number of folds in the cerebral cortex).

Where does this leave consciousness in Descartes's understanding of how we differ from animals? Well, he seems to hold that rational beings—what I have been calling cognitive agents—are (or perhaps at least can be made) conscious of their cognitive activities. But he is willing to consider other ways of viewing cognition, so as to allow for some form of nonrational cognition. There is a hint of this in A. 50 of *The Passions of the Soul*, where, as we have seen, he writes of animals that "they lack reason, and perhaps even thought [*pensée*]." If we assume—and I find it hard to be sure here because the texts are not very explicit on the point—that Descartes supposes that all forms of cognition are accompanied by consciousness, then these thoughts in beings without reason would afford a means of separating consciousness from rationality.

Descartes's fullest discussion of this sort of thing comes in a letter of 23 November 1646 to the Marquess of Newcastle. He begins by maintaining that the actions of animals do not argue for the presence in them of anything nonmechanical:

> I know that animals do many things better than we do, but this does not surprise me. It can even be used to prove that they act naturally and mechanically, like a clock which tells the time better than our judgement does. Doubtless when the swallows come in spring, they operate like clocks. The actions of honeybees are of the same nature; so also is the discipline of cranes in flight, and of apes in fighting, if it is true that they keep discipline. Their instinct to bury their dead is no stranger than that of dogs and cats which scratch the earth for the purpose of burying their excrement; they hardly ever actually bury it, which shows that they act only by instinct and without thinking [*penser*]. (4:575–76; 3:304)

Descartes goes on to allow that one might argue from the similarity of structure of the organs in their bodies to ours that there is a form of thought in animals:

> The most that one can say is that though the animals do not perform any action which shows us that they think [*pensent*], still, since the organs of

their bodies are not very different from ours, it may be conjectured that there is attached to these organs some thought [*pensée*] such as we experience [*experimentons*] in ourselves, but of a very much less perfect kind. (4:576; 3:304)

He regards this as unlikely:

To this I have nothing to reply except that if they thought as we do, they would have an immortal soul like us. This is unlikely, because there is no reason to believe it of some animals without believing it of all, and many of them such as oysters and sponges are too imperfect for this to be credible. But I am afraid of boring you with this discussion. (4:576; 3:304)

It is hard to know how to read his suggestion that animals might have "attached to these organs some thought [*pensée*] such as we experience [*experimentons*] in ourselves, but of a very much less perfect kind." The word *experimentons* encourages the supposition that this conjectured animal thought involves some sort of minimal consciousness. Would this be (conscious) cognition without rationality, or cognition with diminished rationality? The former looks more likely. First, Descartes finds it intelligible to attribute such *pensée* to oysters and sponges. Second, the point of commonality between our *pensée* and the conjectured animal *pensée* is that it is something we both *experimentons*. Finally, the line of thought leading Descartes to countenance the possibility is not based on some relatively sophisticated (possibly nonmechanical?) activity of the animals (perhaps some "information processing" of some sort) but rather the similarity between their organs and ours, a sort of argument from analogy.

Be that as it may, what I find most striking here is just how uninterested Descartes seems to be in the question ("But I am afraid of boring you"). I think that this is because full-fledged rational activity, of the sort that we have been witnesses to throughout the *Meditations*, lies at the heart of his conception of mind, his theory of what a cognitive agent is.

Keeping this last point in view—the limited interest Descartes shows in consciousness—will help keep us from getting off on the wrong foot in our understanding of the overall project of the Sixth Meditation. He will attempt, I have indicated, to make clear the place of the mind, the body, and their relationship in an account of what a human being is. One might have thought that what we are trying to understand here is what it is for a locus of consciousness or a subjective center of awareness to be united with a nonconscious machine; rather, we are focused on explaining what it is for a specifically *rational* being to be united with a mechanistic being. His problem is how there can be a rational animal, not how there can be a conscious animal. A sign that, in explaining human nature,

Descartes's interest lies more in the interface between rationality and mechanism than in the interface between consciousness and matter, comes in his ¶6 review of precritical views about himself. There he seems to find it unexceptionable that he is (as we might put it) aware of various goings-on in his body; rather, what he singles out for remark is that certain *desires* should result from this awareness (for example, a desire for food results from the sensation of a tugging in the stomach). This is, I take it, to signal an issue about the relationship between the desires of a rational being and the state of a machine.[7]

We have then, on the one hand, the data (to be laid out in ¶¶6–7), my pretheoretical views about myself, and, on the other hand, the following materials to work with: the cognitive agent, the automaton, and whatever relationship holds between the two. It is not obvious what it means for a cognitive being, which has a fundamentally rational and, for Descartes, a basically teleological logos or essence (ordered to the good and the true), to be in union with an automaton, which has a mechanistic, pattern-like logos or essence. And it is not obvious whether the resulting configuration can capture the data about myself that I began with. Is there a plausible reconstruction of the data (perhaps involving some revision of it or even throwing out of it) in terms of the cognitive agent, the automaton, and their relationship? *Prima facie*, such a reconstruction would seem to involve more than there being some systematic, perhaps causal, correlation between what goes on in my pineal gland and what ideas appear in my mind, but what more?

Let's turn to the text. In what follows I will take the passages slightly out of order. I will consider ¶¶6–7, where Descartes reviews various old beliefs about the senses, immediately before I discuss his account of union between the mind and body in ¶¶11–13, and since the argument for the existence of body was extensively discussed in chapter 3 (I), I won't take it up again now.

I. *WHAT IS THE IMAGINATION?*

¶¶1–3. IMAGINATION

The Sixth Meditation begins, "It remains for me to examine whether material things exist." However, this search for the existence of body quickly turns into an account of imagining.[8] The connection between the two is this: he takes imagining to be an activity of the cognitive agent that seems impossible to make sense of unless it has a body present to it. So in the first paragraph he takes up the question, What is imagining?

(*quidnam sit imaginatio*),[9] and proposes the answer that it "seems to be nothing else but [*nihil aliud . . . quam*] an application of the cognitive faculty [*facultatis cognoscitivae*] to a body which is intimately present to it, and which therefore exists" (¶1). Although the subsequent discussion affirms this definition of imagining, Descartes does not have enough confidence in the account to provide him with more than a probable argument for the existence of body:

> I can, as I say, easily understand that this is how imagination comes about, if the body exists; and since there is no other equally suitable way of explaining imagination that comes to mind, I can make a probable conjecture that the body exists. But this is only a probability; and despite a careful and comprehensive investigation, I do not yet see how the distinct idea of corporeal nature which I find in my imagination can provide any basis for a necessary inference that some body exists. (¶3; 7:73; 2:51)[10]

Although Descartes's account of imagining comes up in the context of an attempt to prove the existence of body, it is clear enough, I think, that he is interested in the topic for its own sake. After all, it is not necessary to provide a probable (but not fully satisfactory) argument en route to providing an argument that Descartes regards as more successful, and the successful argument does not build on or develop the probable one. Rather, the *Meditations'* account of the mind and its attendant cognitive abilities would be incomplete without a treatment of the imagination. Descartes begins his account of imagination thus:

> To make this clear, I will first examine the difference between imagination and pure understanding [*puram intellectionem*]. When I imagine a triangle, for example, I do not merely understand that it is a figure bounded by three lines, but at the same time I also see the three lines with my mind's eye as if they were present before me; and this is what I call imagining. (¶2; 7:72; 2:50)

He goes on to note that the imagination cannot perspicuously depict large figures. If I were to try to depict a chiliagon to myself, the confused figure that would result from my efforts would be more or less the same as the figure I would depict if I were to try to imagine a myriagon. In particular, the depicted figure would be "useless for recognizing the properties which distinguish a chiliagon from other polygons." Descartes continues:

> But suppose I am dealing with a pentagon: I can of course understand the figure of a pentagon, just as I can the figure of a chiliagon, without the help of the imagination; but I can also imagine a pentagon, by applying my mind's eye to its five sides and the area contained within them. And in doing this I notice quite clearly that imagination requires a peculiar effort

of mind which is not required for understanding; this additional effort of mind clearly shows the difference between imagination and pure understanding [*intellectionem puram*]. (¶2; 7:72–73; 2:50–51)

Descartes is attempting to isolate for the meditator the phenomenon of imagining from that of pure understanding. Imagining, we are told, is a kind of cognitive activity that requires a "peculiar" effort. We might think of the "peculiar effort of mind" as what's involved in following someone's command, "Picture a triangle to yourself" (or "Picture a bright red triangle to yourself"). This effort is something extra; it is not integral to thinking about triangles. Sometimes we simply think about triangles, using our pure understanding and not our imaginations. This is clear from the way in which we think about (and reason about) very large figures. Even if such reasoning is accompanied by blurry images, the blurry images seem irrelevant to the distinctions we draw between large polygons, and so seem incidental to that form of cognition.

Having located for the meditator the difference between pure understanding and imagining, Descartes proceeds to present a theory of what the power of imagining[11] is. One thing suggested by what has been observed so far is that we do not really need the imagination in order to do geometry; it can help us when we are concerned with small figures, but it is not of use when it comes to understanding a chiliagon and how it differs from other polygons. This helps us to understand the first point Descartes makes in ¶3, where he attempts to explain what imagining is:

> Besides this, I consider that this power of imagining [*vim imaginandi*] which is in me, differing as it does from the power of understanding [*vi intelligendi*], is not required for my essence, that is, the essence of my mind. For if I lacked it, I should undoubtedly remain the same thing that I am now [*ille idem qui nunc sum*] . . . (7:73; 2:51)

I take the force of this remark to be that the imagination does not belong to my essence as a cognitive being: I would be able to function cognitively (doubt, affirm, deny, understand, etc.) without my imagination, and so it is "not required for . . . the essence of my mind." On an abstractionist theory of the intellect this would be controversial. For according to that theory, understanding requires the use of phantasms stored in the imagination. The intellectual faculty cannot function without applying itself to body, and this would seem to involve body in its essence at least in some oblique way. We will come back to this point presently.

Descartes's next move is harder to follow. From the fact that my mind does not depend on my power of imagination, he wishes to infer that my power of imagination depends on something distinct from myself (in this context, distinct from my mind). The passage continues simply,

> ... from which it seems to follow that it [my power of imagination] depends on something distinct from myself. (7:73; 2:51)

It is not obvious how this inference works. After all, there seem to be powers one has that are not part of one's essence but which do not seem to depend on something else. For example, suppose I cultivated by myself an ability to do algebra. I would be the same individual without this ability, and this ability does not seem to be a necessary constituent of me (as opposed to, arguably, the ability to cultivate such an ability). Yet it does not seem to follow that it depends on something distinct from myself. Part of Descartes's point here, I take it, is that what imagining adds to pure understanding does not feel like the refinement of or development of an already existing ability—does not seem to be, we might put it using Aristotelian vocabulary, a subsequent or second actualization (e.g., the ability to speak Latin) of a prior or first actuality (e.g., a basic linguistic ability). When we imagine (as opposed to simply understand), something new seems to happen, something not fully explicable in terms of my simply being a cognitive agent. It is some such consideration that brings Descartes to introduce a new element, beyond the cognitive agent, into his account of imagination:

> And I can easily understand that, if there does exist some body to which the mind is so joined that it can apply itself to contemplate it, as it were, whenever it pleases, then it can happen that this very body enables me to imagine corporeal things. So the difference between this mode of thinking and pure understanding may simply be this: when the mind understands, it in some way turns towards itself and inspects one of the ideas which are within it; but when it imagines, it turns towards the body and looks at something in the body which conforms to an idea understood by the mind or perceived by the senses. (¶3; 7:73; 2:51)

Descartes's treatment of imagination is interesting in several respects. Let me begin with a small point. Descartes's discussion of the imagination does not, it seems to me, run very smoothly on the assumption that he is concerned with some dualism revolving about some problem of consciousness, some felt chasm between thought and matter. It is true that his language concerning the nexus between thought and matter is delicate and metaphorical—the mind "contemplate[s] . . . as it were" and "turns toward the body" that is present to it—but, even so, he seems to advance the metaphors readily enough, without a sign of the worry that they run some risk of an incoherent mixing of the mental and the physical.[12] Moreover, Descartes's discussion is surprising in that he seems to regard imagination as a form of cognition that witnesses an intimate relationship between the cognitive agent and a body, a form of cognition that by its essence or nature involves body. The idea that there might be some forms of cognition that essentially involve body is also suggested by the language that Descartes uses to describe imagination-free geometry, namely, "pure understanding [*intellectionem puram*]," which picks up a locution that he employs in the Second Meditation to describe our nonsensory, nonimaginative cognition of the wax—namely, that our best cognition of the wax was provided by *sola mente*, that is, the mind alone, or *solius mentis inspectio*, that is, the examination of the mind alone. Taken at face value, this language implies a contrast between cognition that takes place free of body and cognition that involves body in some fundamental way.[13]

To get as far as suggesting that imagining is a form of cognition that involves body in some fundamental way is still to leave a great deal unsettled. Could we (if only by the power of God) imagine without body? Is the involvement of body in imaginative cognition exhausted by the efficient causal contribution that body makes to the occurrence of imaginative cognition, or is the relation of body to imagining somehow more "internal" than this? Finally, does Descartes hold that imagining is embodied, in the sense that it occurs in a corporeal organ (perhaps somewhere on the surface of the pineal gland)?

To the extent that we get answers to these questions from the *Meditations*, they come through Descartes's characterization of "what imagining is"—*quidnam sit imaginatio*—as "nothing else but an application of the cognitive faculty to a body which is intimately present to it." As noted earlier, this sounds like the posing of an Aristotelian "What is it?" question with respect to the imagination, and a proposed answer has the force of a real definition of the nature or essence of imagining. In other words, the question signals that we are engaged in substantive metaphysics about what imagining might be. If we read the text in this way, then in order for me to imagine, I must apply my cognitive faculty to a body that is intimately present to me.[14]

Descartes's account of imagining as the application of the cognitive faculty to body is helpfully understood in analogy with Aquinas's account of understanding as abstraction from corporeal phantasms. According to Aquinas, abstraction by its very nature involves the use of a body; I take Descartes to be making a similar claim about imagination.[15] And if that is correct, it would be impossible for me to imagine if I did not have a body intimately present to me, much as Aquinas held it to be impossible for me to cognize through abstraction between death and bodily resurrection.

It is natural to ask at this point whether God, at least, could bring it about that I might imagine without my body. After all, since God can do anything a body can do, one might suppose that God could miraculously supply the contribution to the process that the body normally supplies. There are two possible ways to go here. One is to maintain that, if this were to happen, it would not feel different to me from how it feels when I imagine—I could not tell the difference from the inside, as it were—but even so there would be no imagining, that is, there would be no application of the cognitive faculty to a body intimately present to it. The other is to maintain that Descartes's characterization applies only to the natural order and that the modalities implicit in the characterization (viz., imagination is impossible without body) are natural modalities, and do not include what is possible when the supernatural is also taken into account. Which side one takes here, however, may be more sensitive to one's commitments in philosophical theology than to one's philosophy of mind; in any case, I do not see any evidence in this discussion for thinking that Descartes would go one way rather than the other.

Since Descartes is, on my interpretation, providing a piece of substantive metaphysics when he gives his account of what imagination is, it would be in order to object that his account does not carve reality at its joints but rather bundles together two distinct things—a mental item, the imaginative idea itself, and a physical item, the idea's cause. But this objection rests on the assumption that the imaginative idea metaphysically floats free from the cognitive faculty's application to a body intimately present to it, and grounds would need to be offered for thinking that Descartes is (or should be) committed to this assumption. If we were to judge simply from the discussion of the imagination at the beginning of the Sixth Meditation, the text gives no indication that imaginative ideas are metaphysically detachable from my possession of a body, and some reason for thinking that they are not.[16]

If we expand our horizons a bit and consider other aspects of the *Meditations*, is there any reason for thinking that Descartes holds that imaginative thought floats free from my possession of a body? Two things give the impression that he does. The first is that for the greater part of the *Meditations* the meditator is certain that she imagines while she doubts that she has a body. But that occurs before she has tried to figure out what imagining is, and once she does so she finds she has a probable argument at her command for the existence of body. The second is that he plainly holds that I am able to distinguish between, on the one hand, imaginative cognition from sensory cognition and, on the other, (purely) intellectual cognition, prior to making any claims about corporeal aspects of imagination. However, the fact that we are able to get on to imaginative cognition without taking into account its corporeal dimension is no more revelatory of the nature of imagination than the fact that we are able to get on to human beings by rough superficial features (say, as featherless bipeds) without taking into account their rational character.

A final set of considerations that may carry weight for some readers is their general sense of the way consciousness or awareness figures into Descartes's conception of mind. In view of how Descartes is thinking about the mind, it makes sense for him to make a metaphysical cut in the vicinity of imagination at conscious experience, so that any form of conscious experience ought to be in principle ontologically independent from everything else in the universe. I do not know of a line of thought that Descartes presents in the *Meditations* that either explicitly advances or presupposes such a position. There is some reason to suppose that he assumes that the mind is more or less coextensive with consciousness, so that what I am (or can become) conscious of belongs to the mind and vice versa (although I am not sure how strictly he would be inclined to take even this). However, such a view is obviously very different from the thesis that any activity of which I am conscious is ontologically or metaphysically independent of body. I see no reason to suppose that Descartes adopted this metaphysical thesis.[17]

I am going to take it, then, that when Descartes presents an account that implies that imagining requires a body, part of what it is to be an imaginative idea is to come from a body, and so he is not failing to carve nature at its joints. We do not cobble imagining together from an idea and a particular sort of causal genesis; rather, imagining and the power of imagination come first, and we understand what an imaginative idea is in terms of imagining and the power of imagining. Part of my reason for reading Descartes in this way is that he is clearly trying to make out the idea that there is such a thing as human nature, which has to do with the sorts of relationship that are open to the two components of the human being, the cognitive agent and the humanoid machine. If there are activities—such as imagining is, for Descartes—that essentially involve both components, the prospects of carrying out such a project look better. Conversely, if we attribute to Descartes the assumption that none of the mind's activities by their essence or nature involve body or that every mental activity is ontologically separable from body (because of the mind's intimate involvement with consciousness?), then it starts to seem that what connections there are between what happens in my mind and what goes on in my body must be extrinsic and accidental to the happenings in question. This would make it harder to see how he could have thought there is such a thing as a human nature.

If Descartes holds that imagination essentially and necessarily involves body, does he take a further step and hold that the activity of imagining is embodied, taking place in a corporeal organ, as the Aristotelians did? Descartes's characterization seems carefully crafted so as to avoid such an implication. All he says is that imagination is the application of the cognitive faculty to a body that is intimately present to it; there is no reason to think that the application takes place in the body (any more than the application of my visual faculty to a tree takes place in the tree). A parallel with scholastic views on abstraction may again be helpful. Human understanding is an activity that by its nature requires the use of a body, but it does not take place in the body.

Descartes's account of imagination as a faculty differs from standard Aristotelian accounts in other ways. Aristotelian scholastics understood the imagination or phantasy to be the power to retain sensible species as phantasms (and so closely related to memory) and grouped this power with "the interior senses," which were decidedly practical in character (the interior senses included, for example, the "estimative power," which enabled birds to see straw as useful for nest building and sheep to see wolves as dangerous). By way of contrast, Descartes presents the imagination in the Sixth Meditation as primarily a cognitive faculty that assists the intellect.[18] Perhaps this is misleading.[19] This may be an artifact of the theoretical focus of the *Meditations* or of the fact that Descartes chose to discuss the imagination before he took up the mind-body union later in the Sixth Meditation. In any case, Descartes's presentation of imagining as a cognitive activity, as a sort of "impure" intellectual activity, of some value to the cognitive agent as it geometrically deals with elementary figures, does seem to help pave the way for his claim in ¶10 that "intellection" (*intellectionem*) is included in the "formal concept" of imagination (which I take to mean that imagination is a species of intellection, i.e., a special kind of activity of the cognitive faculty).

We might add that Descartes is thinking about imaginative activity differently from how the scholastics did. The scholastics thought of our ability to do something creative, such as imagining a pentagon, as dependent on having stored images to work with.[20] Descartes does not present the imagination as working with materials stored in the mind. When we imagine the pentagon we do not, for example, rearrange remembered lines into a new configuration; we seem to follow the pure understanding's lead so as to generate an image of a figure. He makes only oblique reference (if at all)[21] to the imagination's function as a repository of images received from the senses, which images are made available for subsequent processing in various ways. (In fact, of all the functions associated with imagination, this repository function is the one Aquinas entitles "imagination" or "phantasy.")[22]

This emphasis suits Descartes's strategic objectives. He wishes to underscore the point that the imagination is not a faculty that the mind needs or upon which the mind relies; so the picture of the imagination he presents is that of a faculty at the beck and call of the mind. In particular, there is no suspicion that the mind relies on the imagination for the material it thinks about when it does geometry. Although this theme has been sounded at other places in the *Meditations*, it is appropriately emphasized now, for the next substantive claim that Descartes will make is that the mind can exist independently of the body. Even when the mind cognizes geometry—let alone when it cognizes itself or God—it does not need to make use of the imagination, a faculty whose activity Descartes's audience would have thought (at least prior to the *Meditations*) takes place in a corporeal organ, and which Descartes himself, as I have interpreted him, thinks requires the presence of a body.

As Descartes breaks with Aquinas over the intellect's need for the body in order to function, he implicitly rejects his account of how the various aspects of a human being hang together, that is, his account of the nature of a human being. Aquinas holds that the individual human soul can exist apart from the body, and does so between death and bodily resurrection. (Aquinas, in fact, devotes much effort to arguing that such a possibility is compatible with Aristotle's metaphysics. Aristotle was often interpreted as holding that, while there is a separate soul for all of humankind, there is not a separate soul for each individual because of the close connection between embodiment and individuation within a species.) Now, if the human intellectual soul can exist without a body, what is it that makes each of us—body and soul together—essentially one thing? Aquinas's answer runs through the idea of our nature. The human intellect is the sort of faculty that by its nature cognizes by abstraction from sensory experience. Deprived of our senses, we are unable to carry out the highest cognitive function naturally. This is the point, according to Thomas, of God's uniting the intellectual soul with the body. Indeed, in order for the human intellect to cognize during the gap between death and bodily resurrection, it requires special assistance from God so that it may operate *praeter naturam*, that is, beyond its nature. Indeed, Aquinas reverses his view over the course of his career, first believing that the mode of human cognition between death and resurrection is better than the mode in this life because it is more like that which the angels enjoy, and later believing it is worse because in the absence of a body we operate in a way unnatural to us.[23] In any case, the separate soul, on Thomas's view, comes to be somewhat like a detached body part, subsistent but essentially incomplete, inasmuch as it by nature requires attachment to a body to perform its characteristic functions.

The account of the imagination in ¶¶1–3—the last substantive discussion on the road to Descartes's claim in ¶9 that mind and body are really distinct—serves, then, to make clear that the functioning of the pure mind does not depend on the imagination. From the perspective of

Thomistic Scholasticism, this removes the principal reason for thinking that the cognitive agent requires a body for its natural functioning. Consequently, Descartes will not be able to account for the mind's relationship to the body as Thomas did, namely, through the idea that the intellect could only operate (naturally) within the larger economy of the human being, with her senses and phantasms.

II. *THE REAL DISTINCTION BETWEEN MIND AND BODY*

After Descartes presents his account of the imagination, he says in ¶4 that he will turn to the senses in order to understand those things that he can imagine which do not belong to the "pure subject-matter of mathematics," that is, "colours, sounds, tastes, pain and so on." He indicates in ¶5 that he is going to review the course of his progress through the *Meditations* as it concerns the senses, undertakes that review in ¶¶6–7, and signals a new attitude toward the senses in ¶8, announcing that "although I do not think I should heedlessly accept everything I seem to have acquired from the senses, neither do I think that everything should be called into doubt." This announcement leads to the accounts of sensation and mind-body union that Descartes provides in ¶11 and the following paragraphs. However, before he proceeds to these accounts, he establishes two important framing commitments—the real distinction between mind and body (¶9) and the argument for the existence of body (¶10). In this section, I take up the real distinction between mind and body. I discussed the argument for existence of body in some detail in chapter 3 (I); I will consider Descartes's review (¶¶6–7) of what he used to think about the senses later in connection with his account of the mind-body union, since these are so closely related. There are, however, two points from ¶¶6–7 that are worth noting now.

First, Descartes says that one of the main things the senses taught him (and so one of the things he has been strongly inclined to believe all along) was that he had a body: "First of all then, I perceived by my senses that I had a head, hands, feet and other limbs making up the body which I regarded as part of myself, or perhaps even as my whole self" (7:74; 2:51–52). Our strong natural inclination to take ourselves to have bodies provides, I think, an important part of the background of the argument that mind and body are really distinct. If we did not have the inclination to believe that mind and body are intimately connected, Descartes would not feel the same need to argue that whatever this intimate relation of my mind to my body turns out to be, it is not the case that my body belongs to the essence of my mind.

Second, Descartes's most explicit statement in the *Meditations* of his belief in the doctrine of abstraction comes in ¶6. He describes there how the importance of the senses in his early life led him to think that sensory ideas had external causes, which the ideas resembled. At that time the senses were more important than reason to him and, in part because of the vividness of his sensory ideas, came to dominate his thinking about reality generally: "In this way I easily convinced myself that I had nothing at all in the intellect which I had not previously had in sensation" (7:75; 2:52). This belief's genesis is explained in such a way as to make the belief suspect. It is significant that Descartes explicitly describes the shaky origins of the doctrine of abstraction here before heading into the argument he offers in ¶9 that body does not belong to the essence of mind, because that argument, as I understand it, ultimately rests on the rejection of the idea that in order to understand, the intellect must turn to phantasms stored in the corporeal imagination, from which it abstracts.

¶9. The Real Distinction between Mind and Body

In ¶9, Descartes argues that the mind is really distinct from the body and can exist without it. Descartes's own explication in the *Principles of Philosophy* of what it is to be really distinct is in terms of the ontological categories substance and mode. I find it more helpful, however, to think in terms of essence or nature: Body does not belong to the essence or nature of the mind, and mind does not belong to the essence or nature of body. Since there is no essential dependence of mind on body, and no essential dependence of body on mind, mind and body are two independent realities, and since this is so, God has the power to create the one without the other.

At the bottom of Descartes's thinking about the real distinction is what I shall call a ground fact, namely, "the fact that I know that I exist and at the same time I notice that nothing else at all belongs to my nature or essence besides the one thing that I am a thinking thing" (7:78; 2:54). Descartes is not very explicit about what sort of reflection on his nature or essence goes into the establishment of this ground fact; how one sees the route to the ground fact depends to a large extent on one's sense of the flow of the discussion in the *Meditations*. In addition to getting clearer on what the ground fact involves, there is the further question of what exactly the argument in ¶9 adds to it. My own view is that most of the important substantive philosophical work surrounding the claim that mind and body are really distinct lies in the prior development of the ground fact. In ¶9, Descartes translates what should be more or less obvious to the meditator by now (namely, that the cognitive agent is an independent being) into a more technical metaphysical vocabulary, involving nature or essence, possibility, and real distinction.

Let me begin with an account of the ground fact. To begin with, it has to do with my nature or essence as a thinking thing, that is, the nature or the essence of the cognitive agent. In the surrounding text, Descartes makes some telling claims about the cognitive agent's essence or nature:

> Besides this, I consider that this power of imagining which is in me, differing as it does from the power of understanding, is not required for my essence, that is, the essence of my mind. (¶3; 7:73; 2:51)

> Besides this, I find in myself faculties for certain special modes of thinking, namely the faculties of imagining and sensing. Now I can clearly and distinctly understand myself as a whole without these faculties; but I cannot, conversely, understand these faculties without me, that is, without an intellectual substance to inhere in. (¶10; 7:78; 2:54)

These passages are significant because they indicate the sort of control that Descartes takes the meditator to have by this point over what is in her nature or essence. She has enough confidence to see in ¶3, before the argument for the real distinction, that imagination does not figure centrally in what it is to be a cognitive agent; this confidence surfaces again in ¶10, immediately subsequent to the argument, this time with respect to both the senses and imagination.

The nature or essence that the meditator is concerned with is that of a specifically intellectual being. Descartes writes in ¶10 that imagination and sensation cannot be understood "without an intellectual substance to inhere in" and that "this is because there is an intellectual act [*intellectionem*] included in their [imagination's and sensation's] essential definition [*formali conceptu*]." Our discussion of imagination, which presented it as a faculty that can, when called on, illustrate the pure intellect's geometrical thought, yields some idea of why Descartes thinks this way about the imagination; and the account of the relation between the senses and the "mind alone" in the discussion of wax in the Second Meditation (especially ¶¶12–13) yields some idea of why Descartes would make a similar claim about sensation (as does the subsequent theory of the senses developed in ¶¶11–15 of the Sixth Meditation).

Allow me a brief digression. Notice that Descartes is assuming that if a faculty inheres in a subject, that dependence will show up in the faculty's "formal concept." As one tries to characterize what a faculty is, any subject that the faculty depends on will show up in that characterization. This is related to Descartes's well-known claim that modes are conceived through the principal attributes in which they inhere (*Principles of Philosophy*, I, 53 and 61) and ultimately, I believe, goes back to Aristotelian views about the definition of an accident's making reference to the subject in which the accident inheres, so that, for example, the definition of snubness ("curvature of a nose") makes reference to nose, in which snubness inheres.[24] It is important to keep in view that just as, for an Aristotelian, what is being defined or characterized is an essence, and the definition or characterization is answerable to the essence (so that, for example, one might define an essence incorrectly), so too, for Descartes, the metaphysical structure of the mode and the various dependence relations it enters into are prior, and the way in which the mode is appropriately conceived—its "formal concept"— is posterior. Since the mode is prior and the formal concept posterior, it would be misleading to think of the claim that sensation and imagination involve intellection as merely "conceptual truths," if one takes the "concepts" in question to be understood as epistemically "free floating," that is, as prior to and independent of the things falling under them. It is not as if I consult my concept of imagination in order to figure out what imagination is; rather, I reflect on what imagination is (for example, by observing myself imagine) in order to produce an appropriate characterization, essential definition, or "formal concept" of imagination.

The establishment of the ground fact, then, comes through my purchase on the essence of the cognitive agent, where a cognitive agent is a being that engages in specifically intellectual activities. As we have observed this being at work—as we have watched it doubt, discover, affirm, deny, cognize itself, cognize God, cognize geometry intellectually—and tried to characterize it and its activities, nothing else besides cognition has shown up in our characterization. My distinct understanding of it does not involve more than cognition.

As I try to draw the boundary of the cognitive agent's essence, that is, my essence as a thinking thing, it is of special interest to determine where body falls with respect to the boundary. Does it lie wholly outside my essence, or is it somehow included in it? Descartes's account of imagining provides one picture of how body might turn up in an account of a specific kind of cognitive activity. If *all* of my cognitive activity turned out to be the application of the cognitive faculty to a body intimately present to it, then it is not clear that it would make sense to demarcate my essence or nature in a way that excluded body—it is not clear that I would be inclined to affirm that "absolutely nothing else belongs to my nature or essence except that I am a thinking thing." And, of course, Aquinas holds a view about intellectual cognition that is not all that far in this respect from the view Descartes holds about imaginative cognition: understanding is an activity that essentially involves turning toward the phantasms, which reside in corporeal organs. So, in order to defend the correctness of drawing the boundary of my—the cognitive agent's—essence, in such a way as to put body outside my essence, Descartes needs to articulate and defend a conception of higher-order cognitive activity that is significantly different from Aquinas's.

So the ground fact involves the idea that my higher-level cognitive activities take place independently of matter. We can get some insight into Descartes's thinking on this point by considering something he writes in the Fifth Replies.[25] Gassendi, impressed by the fact that our ability to exercise our higher cognitive functions seems to vary with the condition of our bodies, asks Descartes "to produce some operation which is of a quite different kind from those which brutes perform—one which takes place outside the brain, or at least independently of the brain." Descartes replies:

> I also distinctly showed on many occasions that the mind can operate independently of the brain; for the brain cannot in any way be employed [usus esse] in pure understanding, but only in imagining or sensing. (7:358; 2:248)

The remark to Gassendi is helpful because it suggests that if the only thinking I did required the use of imagination and the senses, then there wouldn't be any operations of the mind that took place independently of the brain. The reply allows that the brain is "employed" in imagining and sensing; it denies that it can "be employed in pure understanding." We might wonder where and how it was "distinctly show[n] on many occasions" that the brain is not employed in pure understanding. Well, it has been a recurring theme throughout the entire *Meditations* thus far. In the Second Meditation, I saw that imagination is irrelevant to the cognitive agent's cognition of itself (¶7), and I learned that the nature of the piece of wax is perceived by the "mind alone [*sola mente*]" (¶12), which involved the discovery that there *is* such a thing as the "mind alone." In the Third Meditation, I found out that my ability to cognize God does not, as Aquinas thought, run through our cognition of the natural world, but rests on a form or idea of God's essence intellectually given to me. In the Fifth Meditation, I saw that the senses do not play an essential role in a cognitive agent's geometrical cognition (¶6) and, finally, just now, in the Sixth, I noticed that imagination plays only an auxiliary role in that activity. And, I take it, it is not only these primary cognitive activities that to all appearances take place independently of body; the same seems true of other related activities that I have noticed along the way—doubting, willing, and its species, affirming and denying—they, too, to all appearances, can take place independently of matter.

If we understand what I have been calling the ground fact in the manner I have been suggesting, then what stands at the bottom of Descartes's argument that mind and body are distinct is his sense that we cannot find a *role* for body to play—a "use" for body—in our cognitive activities. That is why he finds perplexing the suggestion that the cognitive activities he draws attention to should take place on a corporeal platform, let alone essentially depend on such platform. What would it even mean, he would want to ask, for my cognition of myself or God, or an activity such as doubting, to make use of a body?[26]

If we keep in view how Descartes thinks about the activities of the mind and their requirements, we can understand better why he does not take more seriously certain sorts of materialist positions. Consider, for example, someone who is committed to a form of materialism ("to be is to be a body"), or who holds that the mind supervenes on the brain. Descartes's first reaction would be to ask for specification of the mind's essence. We could imagine the materialist or supervenience theorist responding that mind is a physical entity (after all, only physical entities exist) that does such and such. But Descartes, I speculate, would first want to divorce the "physical entity" from "that does such and such," and claim that the latter characterization is the sort of thing that defines an essence; he would then go on to suggest that unless the dependence on matter shows up in the doing of such and such, God, at least, could make a doer of such and such without making a body. That is to say, unless the supervenience theorist is willing to spell out how the doing of such and such (cognizing the mind, God, abstract geometry) requires a physical platform (in the way that, for Descartes, imagining and sensing require physical platforms), the theorist will not have given us reason to think that the mind could not exist without the body. This seems to be a tall order. Naively at least, it is difficult to see what on the corporeal side "fits" our higher-level intellectual activities in the way Descartes supposes that the formation of an image on the pineal gland "fits" what goes on in the mind when I imagine the pentagon.

If keeping in view how Descartes's thinking is informed by a conception of the mind's operations and their natures helps us see why certain considerations that would weigh with some today do not move Descartes, it also, conversely, helps us understand why some of the considerations that weigh with Descartes carry less weight with some contemporary thinkers. It is quite a bit more controversial today to think of an essence or nature as given, quasi-teleologically, through activities and operations. Our stock example of an essence is that water is H_2O, and we do not think of the "activities" and "operations" associated with water as themselves having their own standing, as if a chemical reaction were something over and above the underlying physics it results from. Therefore, it is less natural for us to begin with some higher-level cognition, say rumination over a chess puzzle, and ask, Could such activity take place ("in principle"?) without a physical platform, or must such *activity*, by its very nature, "employ" a brain or some material analogue?

In addition, nowadays at least some theorists are inclined to think in terms of different levels of explanation (physics, chemistry, biology, cognitive psychology) and, at least in some instances, separate an activity that is taking place at a higher level of explanation from how that activity is "realized" at some lower level of explanation. This arguably makes it easier to think that one and the same activity such as chess playing might be "realized" in different manners, perhaps one of which involves a physical platform. I don't see a tendency in Descartes to understand an activity through different levels of explanation, or to separate an activity from its various possible "realizations."

And, finally, the considerations that drive thinkers toward some form of physicalism from which it follows that the mental necessarily supervenes on the physical tend to be global and do not fall out of characterizations of activities and their natures, and steer clear of senses of possibility that invoke divine omnipotence. So, even if we somehow arrived at the conclusion that rumination over a chess puzzle was not the sort of activity that by its nature required a physical platform, many would be much more hesitant about making the inference that it is really possible for there to be a disembodied chess enthusiast.

All of this has been by way of getting a clear view of the ground fact on which Descartes bases his argument for the real distinction between mind and body. How does ¶9 build on the ground fact? It begins:

> First, I know that everything [omnia] which I clearly and distinctly understand is capable of being created by God to be such as I understand it. Hence the fact that I can clearly and distinctly understand one thing apart from another is enough to make me certain that the two things are diverse [diversam], since they are capable of being separated, at least by God. The question of what kind of power is required to bring about such a separation does not affect the judgement that the two things are diverse [diversa]. (7:78; 2:54)

The beginning of this paragraph echoes the opening of the Sixth Meditation. There Descartes claimed that material things are capable of existing because they can be clearly and distinctly understood:

> I already know they [material things] are capable of existing, in so far as they are the subject matter of pure mathematics, since I perceive them clearly and distinctly. For there is no doubt that God is capable of creating everything I perceive in this manner. (¶1; 7:71; 2:50).

I argued in chapter 5 that the divine guarantee, and not just divine omnipotence, is involved in these claims. When I clearly and distinctly perceive something, I am assured that there *is* a true and immutable nature that I am clearly and distinctly perceiving and that my perception does not *omit* anything fundamental to that nature. I think a similar line of thought is operative in the general principle laid out at the beginning of ¶9. My clear and distinct understanding of A—my grasp of A's essence—does not omit anything fundamental to it, nor does my clear and distinct understanding of B omit anything fundamental to it. If I can clearly understand A and B apart from each other, then the essence or nature of neither involves the other, and, since God can do whatever the relevant essences admit of, God has the power to separate A and B. But if A and B can be separated, then A and B are distinct realities (for example, neither is a part, a mode or property, or an aspect of the other).

I have explained the general principle on which the argument for real distinction rests through the idea of essence, even though the term does not appear in the first two sentences of ¶9. I take it that the things falling under the "everything [*omnia*]" in the first sentence do have essences and that these essences determine their relations of distinctness or diversity from other things, as well as their relations of dependence on other things, and, through this, the sort of possibilities that are open for them. (I also think that, for Descartes, "distinct perception" of a thing is perception that makes perspicuous the thing's essence or nature.) In any case, when Descartes applies his general principle to the case of the mind and the body, he does employ essence terminology:

> Thus, from the fact that I know [*sciam*] that I exist and at the same time I notice that nothing else at all belongs to my nature or essence besides the one thing that I am a thinking thing, I can correctly conclude that my essence consists solely in the fact that I am a thinking thing. It is true that I may have (or, to anticipate, that I certainly have) a body that is very closely joined to me. But nevertheless, on the one hand I have a clear and distinct idea of myself, in so far as [*quatenus*] I am simply a thinking, non-extended thing; and on the other hand I have a distinct idea of body, in so far as [*quatenus*] this is simply an extended, non-thinking thing. And accordingly, it is certain that I am really distinct [*distinctum*] from my body, and can exist without it. (¶9; 7:78; 2:54)

I think this is meant as an instantiation of the general principle presented at the beginning of the paragraph. There is a concern here to move from one's cognition of one's essence (as a cognitive agent) to what one's essence really is, so as specifically to establish the closure of that essence. That is, the meditator moves from the fact that (after, I take it, careful examination) nothing else but cognition has shown up in her distinct perception of what she is, to the conclusion that nothing else but cognition is involved in her essence. This movement from her cognition of her essence to the way it is, is in line with the movement we saw in the Fifth

Meditation, where Descartes, buttressed by the Fourth Meditation result that his creator is not a deceiver, argued that the things he could make genuine discoveries about "cannot be called nothing" but "have their own true and immutable natures." Our distinct cognition of a true and immutable nature, I take it, does not leave out anything fundamental to that nature.

Prima facie, there is something odd about feeling a need to argue from the fact that one does not find anything else in one's essence to there actually being nothing else in it. It would be a little like an Aristotelian, having reflected on the matter carefully and done his best, and having reached the conclusion that the essence of a human being is *rational animal*, starting to worry that something has been left out. Perhaps triangles or cheeseburgers figure somehow into what it is to be a human being. One way in which to understand the need that Descartes seems to feel for specific argument on this point is to view the meditator's current situation against the backdrop of ¶6, where it has already come up that I seem to enjoy some sort of intimate relationship with corporeality. If I did not suspect that there is such a relationship—a suspicion that Descartes raises again in ¶9 itself, when he writes, "It is true that I may have (or, to anticipate, that I certainly have) a body that is very closely joined to me"—the need to make explicit that the essence of my mind does not include body might not arise, or at least not with such urgency.

In any case, if, after carefully examining the cognitive agent and its activities, nothing but cognition has shown up in its nature, I can conclude that its nature does, in fact, involve nothing else but cognition, then whatever relations (especially of distinctness or diversity) the cognitive agent happens to enjoy with other beings, God at least could make it without any other being. (Notice that we are concerned only with the cognitive agent's essence, i.e., what it needs in order to exist: in particular, Descartes explicitly says that when the human mind exists without its body, as a separate soul, it lacks sensation; one supposes that he holds the same with respect to imagination as well.)[27] Moreover, that God could make the cognitive agent exist, with its nature intact, without any other being is enough to show that it is a substance (while Descartes does not say this explicitly in ¶9, he writes in the next paragraph that he can understand the cognitive agent "as a whole without" the senses and the imagination, and refers to it as an "intellectual substance"). Finally, returning specifically to the question of the cognitive agent to its body, we can now see that whatever relationship the cognitive agent turns out to bear to its body (and we have reason to think that this relationship is quite intimate), it will not be the case that the cognitive agent depends on the body for its existence or exercise of its essential abilities. Thus, it makes sense to draw the boundary of the cognitive agent's essence in a way that leaves its body on the other side of that boundary.

III. *THE UNION BETWEEN MIND AND BODY*

¶¶6–8. Review of Previous Beliefs and of Criticism of Them

After arguing for the real distinction between mind and body, and the existence of body, Descartes goes on to develop his theory of human nature. When, in the Second Meditation, he presented his account of what he (the thinking thing) is, he did so against the background of previous beliefs he had about himself. Something similar takes place in the Sixth Meditation. In ¶6 he presents a series of things he used to believe about himself—now about the entire human being and not just the cognitive agent—acquired through the senses, which will be subjected to a certain amount of criticism and restructuring. The paragraph provides a good sense of how Descartes organizes the topic, as well as some clues to his attitude toward prominent features of this landscape. It consists of three parts, one concerning certain basic, foundational beliefs about my body, the so-called internal senses (e.g., pain, hunger, and certain emotions), and the external senses, a second part concerning certain views that we come to hold about the external senses, and a third part concerning some things Descartes finds puzzling about his body and the internal senses.[28] Roughly, the first part foreshadows ¶¶9 and 11–13 of the subsequent discussion; the second, ¶¶10 and 14–15; and the third, ¶¶16–23.

The first part consists of certain fundamental beliefs I acquire from the senses:

> First of all then, [1] I perceived by my senses that I had a head, hands, feet, and other limbs making up the body which I regarded as part of myself, or perhaps even as my whole self. [2] I also perceived by my senses that this body was situated among many other bodies which could affect it in various favourable and unfavourable ways; and I gauged the favourable effects by a sensation [*sensu*] of pleasure, and the unfavourable ones by a sensation of pain. [3] In addition to pain and pleasure, I also had sensations within me of hunger, thirst, and other such appetites, and likewise corporeal propensities towards cheerfulness, sadness, anger and similar emotions. [4] And outside me, besides extension, shapes and movements of bodies, I also had sensations of [*a*] their hardness and heat, other tactile qualities. In addition, I had sensations of [*b*] light, colours, [*c*] smells, [*d*] tastes and [*e*] sounds, the variety of which enabled me to distinguish the sky, the earth, the seas, and all other bodies, one from another. (7:74–75; 2:51–52)

Descartes divides the senses into internal and external: the internal senses include pain, hunger, and certain emotions (*Principles*, IV, 190; 8A:316;

1:280); the external senses include the five proper senses. The first part of this passage reads as a review of some of the main features of his primitive affective life. There is a movement of thought here from (1) the fact of my having a body to (2) that body's being helped and hurt by other bodies, which helping registers as pleasure and which hurting registers as pain, to (3) appetites and emotions that seem to be bound up with corporeality in various ways. Hunger seems to have something to do with both my stomach and food. Tendencies toward cheerfulness and sadness have a connection with the health of the body.[29] Only after reviewing these basic aspects of his affective life does he come to (4) the external senses, that is, various forms of tactile perception, sight, smell, taste, and hearing (what would nowadays be thought of as the focal cases of sensation).

In the second part of ¶6, Descartes lists some conclusions he drew connected with the external senses:

> [1] Nor was it without sound reason [*nec sane absque ratione*] that, with respect to the ideas of all these qualities which presented themselves to my thought, and which alone I properly and immediately sense, I took myself to sense certain things fully [*plane*] distinct from my cognition, namely bodies from which those ideas proceeded. For my experience was that these ideas came to me quite without my consent, so that I could not sense any object, even if I wanted to unless it was present to a sense organ, nor could I not sense it when it was present. And since the ideas perceived by the senses were much more vivid [*vividae*] and express [*expressae*: clear, prominent] and even in their own way more distinct [*distinctae*] than any of those which I deliberately formed through meditating or which I found impressed on my memory, it seemed impossible that they should have proceeded from myself; so the only alternative was that they came from other things. [2] Since I had no other notion [*notitiam*] of these things than from these ideas, it could not but come into my mind that those things resembled [*similes esse*] these ideas. [3] In addition, I remembered that the use of my senses came first, while the use of my reason came only later; and I saw that the ideas which I formed myself were not as express [*expressae*] as those which I perceived with the senses and were mostly composed of them as parts. In this way I easily convinced myself that I had nothing at all in the intellect which I had not previously had in the senses [*nullam plane me habere in intellectu, quam non prius habuissem in sensu*]. (7:75; 2:52)

It is worth trying to keep track here (to the extent that we can) of what nature teaches us, that is, what we find ourselves primitively inclined to believe, as opposed to conclusions that we come to on the basis of our own reasoning and judgment. This is because God bears a special responsibility for what we are primitively inclined to believe; there can be misfires, but these misfires, as we shall see when we get to the final third of the meditation, are in a special way God's responsibility and so require a special justification. By way of contrast, beliefs that we arrive at as a result of our own reasoning are our own responsibility. It seems to me that the beliefs that Descartes presents in this part of ¶6 fall into the second category. They are not teachings of nature, but involve some (perhaps very rudimentary and elementary) work on my part.

The first conclusion, which receives a qualified endorsement—Descartes says it was reached *nec sane absque ratione*, that is, "not without sound reason"—is not explained in enough detail for us to be able to determine exactly what it means. I take the gist of the belief to be that when I am sensing I am thereby made aware of various structures in bodies (I came to believe that corporeal qualities, Descartes appears to say,[30] are presented to my thought in sensation). Although this conclusion receives a qualified endorsement, the argument that Descartes eventually gives for the existence of body in ¶10 has a somewhat different emphasis (for example, while the fact that sensory ideas are independent of my will is cited, their vividness and expressness is not). After reaching this first conclusion, I draw two other conclusions, the resemblance thesis and the thesis, closely connected to the doctrine of abstraction, that *nihil est in intellectu nisi prius fuerit in sensu*. These two conclusions do not receive same *nec sane absque ratione* endorsement that the first received.

In the third part of ¶6, Descartes returns to the internal senses and his body. He begins by fleshing out the character of his special relationship to body in terms of appetites, emotions, and pain and pleasure:

> Also, I judged [*arbitrabar*] not without reason [*sine ratione*] that this body which by some special right I called mine belonged to me more than any other. For [a] I could never be separated from it, as I could from other bodies; and [b] I felt all my appetites and emotions in it and on account of it; and [c] finally, I was aware of pain and pleasurable ticklings in parts of this body, but not in other bodies external to it. (7:75–76; 2:52)

The claim that "I judged [*arbitrabar*] not without reason [*sine ratione*]" suggests that we are not concerned with a natural belief, but with something that is the product of reasoning. This seems to be in tension with the impression that the first part of ¶6 gives, that I more or less take myself to simply perceive that I have a body, and so that the belief I have a body is something that I come to instinctually or naturally, without any special ratiocination on my part. Perhaps that impression is misleading. Or perhaps Descartes's thought is that the belief that there *is* a body "which by some special right I call mine," namely, the one mentioned at the beginning of ¶6, is something that I seem to simply perceive by the senses, and he is explaining here how we arrive at the judgment that this body belongs to me *more* than any other, on the basis of (*a*)–(*c*), themselves beliefs that I arrive at in a quasi-instinctual manner.

Descartes does not report finding anything very remarkable in the fact that he should be aware of the goings-on in his body. In the continuation of ¶6, however, he does find occasion for wonder:

> But why should that curious [*nescio*] sensation of pain give rise to a particular distress of mind; or why should a certain kind of delight follow on a tickling sensation? Again, why should that curious [*nescio*] tugging in the stomach which I call hunger tell me that I should eat, or dryness of the throat tell me to drink, and so on? I was not able to give any explanation of all this, except that nature taught me so. For there is absolutely no connection (at least that I can understand) between this tugging and the volition [*voluntatem*] to take food, or between the sensing of the thing inflicting [*inferentis*] pain and the cognition of distress [*tristitiae*] which arises from this sensing [*sensu*]. These and other judgements that I made concerning sensory objects, I was apparently taught to make by nature; for I had already been persuaded that things were so before I laid out any reasons by which this might be shown. (7:76; 2:52–53)

Notice exactly what Descartes reports to find puzzling here. Hunger, thirst, and pain each involve three elements: stomach tugging, sensation of stomach tugging (hunger), and desire for food; dryness of the throat, sensation of throat dryness (thirst), and desire for drink; and the cause of pain, sensation of cause (pain), and the upset or distress that the pain gives rise to. What Descartes finds hard to understand is not the connection between the first (physical) and second (cognitive) items in each of the three lists, but rather between the second and third items, that is, between a cognitive item and the cognitive agent's reaction to that item. This relation lies at the center of what it is for a rational cognitive being to be united to a machine.

Some commentators appeal to this passage as evidence that Descartes holds that there is something ultimately unintelligible about the relation of the cognitive agent to its body.[31] I think it is more likely that Descartes, in this review of his premeditative beliefs, is pointing to something that he does not yet understand but will understand better by the end of the Sixth Meditation. In particular, what he does not yet recognize is that the stomach usually tugs when the body *needs* food, and that hunger, the sensation of this stomach tugging, registers in the mind as a confused cognition of the body's *need* for food, and this is *why* the cognitive agent forms a subsequent desire to get the body food; and that the throat is usually dry when the body *needs* drink, and that thirst, the sensation of throat dryness, is a confused cognition of the body's *need* for drink, and this is *why* it subsequently forms a desire to get the body drink that it needs;

and that the sensation of pain is a confused cognition of bodily *damage*, which is *why* the cognitive agent reacts to the sensation with distress.[32]

In ¶7, Descartes turns to criticism of his earlier views. He begins by reviewing his reasons for losing confidence in the senses, beginning with a list of experiences where "the judgements of the external senses were mistaken." He now extends this point to the internal senses so prominent in ¶6, instancing phantom pain as a case where the internal senses are mistaken. To this he adds the more general considerations raised by the dreaming doubt and the imperfect-creator doubt, which he expresses as "since I was then ignorant of the author of my origin, or at least I was pretending to be ignorant, I saw nothing to preclude that I am so constituted by nature so that I am deceived, even in those things which appear to me to be truest." Descartes also criticizes (in effect, reviewing some of what came up in III.¶8–12) the reasons that persuaded him of, as he puts it now, "the truth of sensible things [*rerum sensibilium veritatem*]," on the grounds that natural impulses sometimes lead us astray and that sensory ideas, although coming to me against my will, might proceed from "a faculty not yet known to me" rather than body.[33]

Finally, in ¶8 he signals a new attitude toward what "I seem [*videor*] to have acquired from the senses," citing the fact that he now knows both himself and the author of his nature better: "[A]lthough I do not think I should heedlessly accept everything I seem to have acquired from the senses, neither do I think that everything should be called into doubt" (7:77–78; 2:54). The "seem" is significant here, because, as noted a little earlier, God bears responsibility for what I have actually acquired from the senses. There can be misfires, but the misfires receive a special sort of justification as the inevitable by-product of a well-designed system. By way of contrast, if I only "seem" to have acquired something from the senses, through some hasty or otherwise ill-considered judgment on my part, then God bears no special responsibility.

¶¶11–13. TEACHINGS OF NATURE AND THE "TRUE MODE OF UNION" BETWEEN MIND AND BODY

In ¶¶9 and 10, Descartes set the parameters for the subsequent account of what it is to be a human being. In ¶9, we found out that the cognitive agent was an independent being, a substance. In ¶10, we found out that bodies exist, but that we are only entitled to conclude that "those things are in them that I clearly and distinctly understand, that is, all those things, generally considered, which are comprehended within the object of pure Mathematics." The account of what a human being is is to be based on these two items and their relationship to each other.

In ¶11 Descartes signals a new attitude toward teachings of nature by announcing "there is no doubt that everything that I am taught by nature contains some truth." He first developed the idea of a teaching of nature in III.¶9, in connection with his account of his belief in the existence of body. There he explained that a teaching of nature is something that we are inclined to believe on a quasi-instinctual basis, and, as such, it is to be carefully distinguished from something revealed to him by the natural light (something, as I have been putting it from time to time, that he sees is so). In the Third Meditation, while it was noted that teachings of nature can on occasion lead us astray, their ultimate status was left undetermined. Now, Descartes begins to explain that status. Since I now know that nature comes from a nondeceiving God, I now know that they must contain "some truth." This affirmation must, however, be tempered by an account of how and why some teachings of nature misfire; Descartes supplies this in the final third of the Sixth Meditation.

Descartes develops the claim about teachings of nature containing "some truth" in the context of a more general conception of nature as "God himself, or the ordered system of created things established by God," and, within that context, a more specific conception of human nature as "nothing other than the complex of things bestowed upon me by God." Later, in ¶15, he divides this totality into three groups:

> But to make sure that perceptions in this matter are sufficiently distinct, I must more accurately define exactly what I mean when I say that I am taught something by nature. In this context, I am taking nature to be something more limited than the complex of things bestowed on me by God. For this includes [1] many things that belong to the mind alone—for example my perception that what is done cannot be undone, and all other things that are known by the natural light; but at this stage I am not speaking of these matters. It also includes [2] much that relates to the body alone, like the tendency to move in a downward direction, and so on; but I am not speaking of these matters either. My sole concern here is [3] with what God has bestowed on me as something composed out of a mind and a body [ut composito ex mente & corpore]. And therefore this nature [Ideoque haec natura] does indeed teach me to avoid what brings on [inferunt] a sensation of pain and to seek out what brings on a sensation of pleasure, and so on. (7:82; 2:57)

This passage can create the impression that what is primary are the various things that God has bestowed on me, and the mind, the body, and the combination of the mind and body represent convenient ways of sorting those things. I don't think that this is right, however. In particular, we have seen that the complex of things that God has bestowed on me that belong to the mind hang together in a certain way, as do the totality of things that belong to body alone.[34] The same holds good, I believe, of my nature as a composite being. I think that Descartes is indicating here that all the things that God has bestowed upon me—all of my real properties—are traceable to one of these three sources: my nature as a mind, my nature as a being with a body, or my nature as a being that is something composed out of a mind and a body. Each of these natures has its own integrity. (It is less clear how Descartes views my nature as a whole, that is, my nature in the sense of the "complex of things bestowed on me by God": it may be that this is exhausted by these three natures, my nature as a cognitive agent, my nature as a being united to a body, and the nature of the body to which I am united.)

If we agree that, for Descartes, human nature is not simply a *façon de parler*, that is, if we agree that there is such a thing as human nature, then the next question is, What is this nature? What licenses my taking the complex of things bestowed on me as something composed out of a mind and a body as constituting *a* nature?[35] I think Descartes believes that my nature as a composite being is something that is made manifest to me through the teachings of nature that I find myself subject to. These teachings of nature have a certain coherence about them. That is, the promptings and urgings (including, among other things, pain and pleasure, hunger and thirst) that occur naturally in me fit together in a certain way; they are not a miscellaneous or arbitrary collection of messages from God that mysteriously appear from time to time in me. That is why it makes sense to think of them as reflecting a nature. But how, exactly, does the collection of promptings and urgings that make up what nature "teaches us" hang together? What unifies them?

In ¶¶12–13, Descartes appeals to certain basic teachings of nature in order to lay the foundation for his account of the human being. In ¶12, he writes:

> There is nothing that my own nature teaches me more expressly than
> that I have a body that is badly off [*cui male est*] when I sense pain, that
> needs food or drink, when I suffer hunger or thirst, and so on; hence I
> should not doubt but that there is some truth in this. (7:80; 2:56)

I think it is best not to view this passage as making two independent, if related, claims, (*a*) that I have a body and (*b*) that the body is badly off when I sense pain and so on. Rather, that I have a body and the sense in which I have a body is made apparent to me through the fact that the body is badly off when I sense pain, needs food or drink when I suffer hunger or thirst, and so on. This first teaching of nature concerns how we instinctually read low-level affective phenomena such as pain, hunger, and thirst. We take pain to be something that happens when the body is damaged, thirst to be something we undergo when the body stands in need of water, and so on. We do this naturally and unreflectively.

In the next paragraph, ¶13, Descartes moves beyond the claim that he has a body to say something about how it is that he is united to this body:

> Nature also teaches me, through these sensations [*sensus*] of pain, hunger, thirst, etc., that I am not merely present to my body as a sailor is present to a ship, but most closely [*arctissime*] joined to it, and as if intermingled [*permixtum*] with it, and on that account I with it compose some one thing. For otherwise, when the body is hurt [*laeditur*], I, who am nothing other than a thinking thing, would not on that account sense pain, but would perceive this injury [*laesionem*] with the pure intellect, as a sailor perceives by sight whether something is broken in his boat; and when the body needs food or drink, I would expressly understand this thing itself, and I would not have the confused sensations [*sensus*] of hunger and thirst. For surely these sensations of thirst, hunger, pain, and so on are nothing other than certain confused modes of cognition, arising from the union of, and the as if intermingling of, the mind with the body. (7:81; 2:56)

In order to understand how the cognitive agent is united to its body—to understand how "I, who am nothing other than *res cogitans*" am united to my body—Descartes asks us to continue to focus on primitive affective phenomena: pain, hunger, thirst, and so on. These phenomena witness the natural interest I have in how things go for my body, my natural concern[36] for my body.

Now, one might think that all that has happened is that God has so arranged things that when things are not well with the body, I, the cognitive agent, find myself bombarded with troublesome pain, hunger, and thirst messages. I have no concern for the body for its own sake, but I do have an interest in shutting off the unpleasant messages (and perhaps increasing the production of the pleasant ones). I think that it is unlikely that this is what Descartes has in mind. If that were the character of the connection of the cognitive agent to its body, then what God would have done is to set things up so that the cognitive agent is pulled and tugged by the needs of an entity that is fundamentally alien to its own concerns. In order for human nature to be something genuine, I think, there needs to be a deeper connection between the mind and the body than just this.

I think it much more likely that what pain, hunger, and thirst do, in Descartes's view, is to witness the fact that the condition of my body *matters* to me (the cognitive agent). This fits with his thinking of pain, hunger, and thirst as confused modes of cognition, which suggests that it is a species of the same genus that distinct cognition belongs to, and so in important ways is like distinct cognition. The sailor's distinct cognition of the broken rudder is upsetting to him because he understands that it is bad for the ship; my painful cognition of my hurt foot is supposed to be a confused analogue of the sailor's understanding of the boat's damage. But this structure makes most sense if one thinks that the cognitive agent has a concern for its body analogous to the concern that the sailor has for his ship.[37] The sailor's distinct cognition of the broken rudder is upsetting because he cares about the ship; if the rudder belonged to a ship that he did not care about, say, his enemy's ship that he is trying at present to sink, he would not be upset by it. Similarly, God's setting things up so that the cognitive agent's confused cognition of its hurt foot registers as unpleasant works best against a background where it cares about its body, so that the body's bads, goods, and needs are its bads, goods, and needs. If we go this way, so that the messages that the cognitive agent receives reflect a genuine interest it has in its body, then the "glue" for human nature is teleological (as it was so often in Aristotelian theory about natural beings).

I am going to work, then, with the following picture of the union, suggested by ¶¶12 and 13. The body, of itself, has certain goods, bads, and needs. The cognitive agent has a basic interest in the condition of the body. Finally, the body's goods, bads, and needs are reflected in the cognitive agent.

Two rather delicate questions arise here. One is whether the cognitive agent's interest lies so much in the body itself as with preserving a union with the body; a second is whether the body possesses goods, bads, and needs of its own, or only inherits them through the union. Both of these questions arise from a certain queasiness about thinking of the body—a mere piece of res extensa, after all—in (broadly speaking) teleological terms, as a suitable object in which something could have a basic interest or something which could have of itself good, bads, and needs.

The issues are complex, and which way one goes will not matter for much of my account of the union, so let me simply indicate my point of view on the issue. I don't think Descartes was uncomfortable with the idea that a purely mechanistic being can be harmed, benefited, and have needs.[38] He does not give any sign that the fact that human bodies can be harmed or benefited—possess goods, bad, and needs—depends on the fact that they are human bodies, on the fact that they are united to the mind.[39] It is a difficult question, as mentioned above, whether we can really think of the rabbit automaton as a sort of complex inanimate being, like a hurricane, as Descartes seems to want to do, within the context of his mechanical philosophy. But I think he would hold that we are to view the human body in the same way that we view a rabbit automaton, and that we are to view the latter in more or less the same way that we view a hurricane or tornado or a solar system. All can be enhanced or diminished. For example, there might be goings-on in the hurricane or tornado or solar system that contribute to its well-being (where this well-being is made out in terms of ideas like structural stability of the relevant patterns of motion), and there might be other goings-on that contribute to its demise.

What Descartes would object to is the idea that there is a way a mechanistic individual ought to be, so that when it is not this way it suffers a "privation." In traditional Aristotelianism, the idea of privation was understood through the kind to which it belongs, and in Descartes's mechanistic physics, kinds no longer have the same fundamental standing they had in Aristotelian metaphysics. But one might think that the healthy rabbit automaton has a higher state of perfection than a diseased rabbit automaton, without taking the further step of maintaining that the diseased rabbit automaton is undergoing a privation and is not as it "should" be (where the standards of what it "should" be are given not by its simply being a mechanistic system, but its being a certain *kind* of mechanistic system, i.e., a rabbit machine). This is something we will look more closely at in the last section of this chapter, in connection with ¶¶17 and 18.

Sensory versus Intellectual Linkages between Minds and Bodies

We have considered certain ways in which the cognitive agent's relation to its body is *like* that of the sailor's to his ship. Descartes, taking for granted the similarities in ¶13, draws our attention to the differences. This contrast concerns how the body's needs are expressed in my psyche. The relationship of a sailor to his ship is a metaphor for an intellectual liaison between a cognitive agent and its body; it appears to be closely related to a liaison between an angelic being and a human body that Descartes describes in a letter to Regius:

> You must say that they [the mind and the body] are united ... by a true mode of union, as everyone agrees, though nobody explains what this amounts to, and so you need not do so either. You could do so, however, as I did in my *Metaphysics*, by saying that we perceive that sensations [*sensus*] such as pain are not pure thoughts of a mind distinct from a body, but confused perceptions of a mind really [*realiter*] united to a body. For if an angel were in a human body [*corpori humano inesset*], it would not sense [*sentiret*] as we do, but would simply perceive the motions which are caused

by external objects, and in this way would differ from a true man [*vero homine*]. (3:493; 3:206)

(Notice, incidentally, that in this passage Descartes indicates that he has explained the "true mode of union" in the *Metaphysics*, which is sometimes how he refers to the *Meditations*. I think it is obvious that he has the Sixth Meditation in mind, especially ¶¶12–13.)

How does the "true mode of union" found in a "true man" differ from the relation of a sailor to his ship or of an angel to a human body in which it is? Where there is a true union, the cognitive agent experiences (some of) the goings-on in its body as needs of the body, confusedly through sensations. So when I, a human being, am hungry, I find myself with a desire for food. Initially, I cannot say why I want the food—what the point of wanting food is—I just want food. I go to the refrigerator (or, as an infant, scream in distress) in one sense without knowing why I am doing what I am doing (and in another sense, I suppose, knowing exactly why I am doing what I am doing: I am hungry). The lack of transparency here is, I think, the primary idea behind Descartes's claim that hunger involves a confused mode of cognition.[40]

By way of contrast, things work differently for the sailor and his ship or the angelic being in a body. Let's continue to assume that the sailor's concern for his ship is already in place. Since the sailor cares for his ship, the perception of the broken rudder matters to the sailor, but this is because he "expressly understands" what is good for his ship, and so, in particular, he understands that broken rudders are bad for the ship and require repair. Similarly, if we assume that the angel cares for the body in which it found itself and wished to preserve it so that it might remain joined to it, it would take whatever appropriate steps it could in order to preserve its body. Although such a being would be distressed at the bodily damage, it would not feel pain when its body was damaged. There would be no need for it to. It would simply notice the damage and respond appropriately to it in the light of its general understanding of the body's nature, in somewhat the same way that a collector might feel distress at the pages becoming brittle on a prized rare book. Or, again, when an angelic being registers that the body which is present to it stands in need of food (in somewhat the same way I register that my car is low on fuel), it too may take similar steps (e.g., rechannel the flow of spirits through its pineal gland and so forth so as to obtain nourishment), but it does this in light of its understanding of how the body works, what promotes its well-being, and perhaps what is necessary in order for it to continue to be present in it (assuming that that presence counts as a sort of good), and not because it feels hunger.[41]

The inherent practical difference between these two sorts of corporeal liaison, angelic and human, is parallel to the difference, in the theoretical

sphere, between clear and distinct perception of the truth leading us to believe something and our simply finding ourselves with a natural propensity
to believe something. In the case of the angelic liaison, an understanding
of what is good or bad for the body brings about certain motive tendencies
(desires) and affects (distress); in the case of the human mind-body union,
confused perception inclines us in certain ways, independently of whether
we understand the appropriateness of those inclinations.

PAIN AS CONFUSED COGNITION OF BODILY DAMAGE

Something that seems counterintuitive on Descartes's theory is the way
pain is embedded in one's concern for one's body. One might think I
want to get rid of pain not because of some concern I have for my body,
but simply because it is pain, and pain is something that is inherently unpleasant. And, for that matter, isn't phantom pain, which does not register bodily damage, just as obnoxious as ordinary pain?

Now, Descartes, I take it, agrees that we want to get rid of pain because
it is unpleasant. He is presenting a theory of what this unpleasantness is.
He would disagree that I avoid pain "simply" because it is unpleasant, if
this means that the unpleasantness is supposed to be detachable from
pain's being a confused mode of cognition of bodily damage. (For that
reason, I think, he will have a difficult time making sense of the thought
that it is this property I am concerned about, as opposed to the bodily
damage.) Phantom pain, too, is unpleasant because it, too, is a confused
mode of cognition of bodily damage; it just happens to be a false or inaccurate cognition.

We can develop the point by considering what we think of as "phantom thirst," where we are thirsty when the body does not need drink (as
in the case of dropsy that Descartes discusses at the end of the Sixth
Meditation). Phantom thirst is an apparent need, and apparent needs can
register with the same urgency as true ones. That is, thirst is the way the
body's need for drink registers in the cognitive agent, and that need is felt
the same way whether the registering is accurate or inaccurate. Here is a
dis-analogy, then, with the sailor: once he finds out his perception of the
broken rudder is inaccurate, he settles down. This goes back to the basic
function of the senses, which is to prompt us to act appropriately independently of what we *understand* to be the case: to get me to move my
hand away from the fire before I understand why that would be good for
my hand. My clear and distinct perception of what is to be done does
not cancel the prompting.

Now, if I were thirsty even when my body didn't need water, I would
have some reason to remove this internal sensation that goes beyond not

wanting to be saddled with an inaccurate sensation, namely, the prompting of the report of the unmet need is distracting and unpleasant. But as I come to understand that I am suffering from phantom thirst and that the report is inaccurate, what I want subtly shifts: before, I wanted drink—I wanted the need to be satisfied—and now I simply want for the thirst to subside, for the distraction and unpleasantness to go away.

One could view phantom pain similarly. Pain is the registering of bodily damage, and its unpleasantness derives from this. While we might consider the unpleasantness apart from the rest of the pain, we cannot coherently separate out the one from the other. (To borrow terminology that Descartes employs in a different context, we can form a conception of the unpleasantness that *abstracts from* bodily damage, but not a conception of the unpleasantness that *excludes* bodily damage.)[42] On this view of pain, phantom pain would turn out to be a false registering of bodily damage, which, for all of its inaccuracy, is just as unpleasant as a true registering of bodily damage. As I come to realize that it is merely phantom pain and its report is inaccurate, my desires shift from wanting to fix the bodily damage to just wanting the distracting and unpleasant message to go away. I don't know how far the view I have attributed to Descartes can be defended in the end, but it does have the virtue of taking note of complexity in thirst and bodily pain (both real and apparent) that is easy to overlook.

The Role of the Senses in the Union

In ¶¶12 and 13 Descartes provides his basic understanding of human nature, of what it is to be a human being, or what he refers in his letter to Regius as the "true mode of union" between the mind and the body. We might see his theory as his interpretation of certain basic natural beliefs ("teachings of nature")—that I have a body and am subject to bodily needs—within the context of his metaphysical commitment to an understanding of my cognitive abilities as residing in a freestanding cognitive agent and a conception of a body as more or less a machine. To be a human being is to be so joined to a body that bodily needs register in the way they do for us, as pain, as hunger, as thirst, and therefore as confused modes of cognition, in contrast to, say, the way such needs register for an angel. And so when Descartes writes in the letter to Elizabeth (considered toward the beginning of this chapter) that the "notion of the union between the soul and the body" is one of "three kinds of primitive ideas or notions, each of which is known in its own proper manner and not by comparison with any of the others," and explains that "what belongs to the union of the soul and body is known only obscurely by the intellect

alone or even by the intellect aided by the imagination, but is known
very clearly by the senses" (3:691–92; 3:226–27), I think he means that the
senses make it obvious to us that the body's needs, bads, and goods are
the cognitive agent's needs, bads, and goods, and that we can tell that
they do this in a nonintellectual way. That my body's needs, bads, and
goods matter to me (the cognitive agent) is not something that is understood, but rather something that is naturally registered through the
senses.[43] (That there should be this kind of connection helps underwrite
the idea that there *is* a composite nature, as opposed to two entities related only by some frequent and peculiar causal interaction.)

One might wonder about the exact place of the senses in the union.
Are they conduits by which the goods, bads, and needs of a body in
which the cognitive agent has a prior interest are transmitted to the cognitive agent? Or do they perhaps constitute the very bond through which
the goods, bads, and needs of the body come to matter to the cognitive
agent in the first place? I find this a difficult question. Although Descartes
tends to emphasize the epistemological point that the senses show me
both that I am united to body and how I am united to it, he does not say
that the union consists in or is brought about through my having senses.
To be sure, since it is characteristic of a "true human being" that the cognitive agent be attuned to the needs of its body via a specifically sensory
mode of cognition (as opposed to an intellectual mode of cognition), it
does not seem possible for there to be a human being without senses.
But this is not quite to say that the union consists in the possession of
senses; rather, it is compatible with the position that the senses are (what
the Aristotelians would have termed) a necessary accident (a *proprium*) of
a true human being.

I find it more natural to think of the senses as making plain a prior interest that the cognitive agent has in its body—of a general sort that an
angel might have in a body—rather than constituting that interest. Exeget-
ically, this better fits the places in the text where Descartes describes pain,
hunger, and thirst as confused modes of cognition "arising from [*ab . . .
exorti*]" the union (7:81).[44] On a more philosophical level, if we can make
sense of the idea that the cognitive agent has a prior interest in the well-
being of its body (and I allow that this is not easy), we can make out more
sharply the difference between welcoming the senses because they help us
look after something that we care about and viewing them as intrusively
making apparent the needs of some alien entity.

On Descartes's account, the welfare of the human body turns out to
depend on the teachings of nature that the cognitive agent receives. Were
it not for these teachings, the human body would quickly perish. This,
too, can seem puzzling. After all, according to Descartes, horses and rabbits are merely automata. They get around in the world automatically,

without any help from a mind to redirect the flow of animal spirits through their pineal glands. Why do we, then, need teachings of nature in order to survive? Descartes never, to my knowledge, addresses this question, so the answer that I offer will have to be speculative. I think his view must be that a union such as ours requires giving the cognitive agent some way of caring for the body, some way of directing the flow of the animal spirits. But that creates the possibility of directing the spirits in nonproductive or even destructive ways (the toddler near the fire), which creates the need for teachings of nature. The difference here is akin to that between an aircraft that is controlled by an automatic pilot and one that is not: horses and rabbits are controlled by automatic pilots; human bodies, too, may have an automatic pilot,[45] but they also have unskilled pilots—the minds that are united to them—who threaten to constantly override the mechanism; these unskilled pilots require a lot of assistance from the control tower not to cause damage. This means that as things stand, the human body is dependent on the cognitive agent for its persistence.[46]

The Coherence of Human Nature Examined from the Point of View of Theodicy

Why has God structured our natures so that our minds are really (*realiter*) united to our bodies, as opposed to the way in which an angelic being might be in a human body (3:493; 3:206)? Taken in one way, this is just to ask why God made a created order with both human beings (*veri homines*) and angels instead of a created order with only angelic beings. To this question, Descartes would, I take it, give the same answer that he gives in ¶7 of the Fourth Meditation, namely, that the overall perfection of the universe may well be enhanced by such variety.

But Descartes also recognizes constraints on what God may do that arise from an essence's or nature's coherence, and so one might ask: Doesn't it involve a defect in my very nature that I should be united to my body instead of merely present to it, so that I am saddled with confused thoughts, instead of clear and distinct perceptions, of what is going on in my body? And if my very nature involves a defect, then don't we have a violation of the principle tacitly endorsed in ¶5 of the Fourth Meditation, that "it seems impossible that he [God] should have placed in me a faculty which is not perfect of its kind, or which is deprived of some perfection which it ought to have"?

The question I am trying to raise about God's rationale for uniting the mind with the body is, to a large extent, a consequence of Descartes's thinking about the mind's independence from the body. According to Aquinas, the intellect needs the body in order to cognize in the manner natural to it; so although the intellect is subsistent and can cognize without it, with some special assistance from God between death and bodily resurrection, it needs the body for its natural mode of cognition. Its union with the body is of great benefit to it.[47] By way of contrast, it is not clear how, on Descartes's view of the union, the mind is supposed to benefit from it. This makes God's decision to unite the mind with the body—to make, in some deep way, the goods, bads, and needs of the body, also those of the mind—look capricious, when considered from the point of view of the mind.

Descartes does not have a lot to say that directly bears on this question. He does imply in one place that the mind has a "natural aptitude" for union with the body (7:585), although it is hard to know how to fill this idea out. I think he also probably holds that the only way an intellect as weak as ours could be united to a body requires confused and obscure cognition. If the senses provided us with only clear and distinct cognition, we would be overwhelmed by detail and would not be able to make timely use of that information (like a young child with a physiology textbook). In the general context of the project of joining a human mind to a body, in such a way that the mind has important responsibility for the welfare of the body, a certain degree of confusion and obscurity in our perception seems a virtue. Finally, Descartes writes in the last article of the *Passions*:

> For the rest, the soul can have pleasures of its own. But the pleasures common to it and the body depend entirely on the passions, so that persons whom the passions can move most deeply are capable of enjoying the sweetest pleasures of this life. (A. 212; 11:488; 1:404)

Although a human mind could function without its body, in such a condition it would be deprived of a kind of satisfaction of which it is capable and which seems to be appropriate to it. Further, I take it that for Descartes "the sweetest pleasure" and "source of joy" work in a way analogous to the way bodily pain and pleasure work. That is, the pleasure and joy are not to be thought of as mere feelings, but rather as a kind of well-founded satisfaction taken in some aspect of the order of things. Here what one would be taking satisfaction in is apparently a well-functioning mind-body system. There may, then, be for Descartes—although this is admittedly speculative—some special value accruing to the human mind through its participation in such a system. Perhaps it is the case that the human mind is set up, by its nature, for such intercourse with body, so that the mind is the richer for it when it has this relationship, and in some way impoverished or diminished when it lacks it.[48]

IV. *THE EXTERNAL SENSES AND ERRORS FOR WHICH*
I AM RESPONSIBLE

¶¶14–15. EXTERNAL SENSES

In ¶¶14–15 Descartes moves from the internal senses to the external senses. In ¶14, he explains a limitation of the external senses; in ¶15, he corrects three mistakes that we commonly make with respect to external senses. We covered some of this ground in chapter 3 (I), when we considered Descartes's own positive views concerning sensory representation and his criticism of related Aristotelian views. There I suggested that Descartes's position is both like and unlike the Aristotelian position. Descartes's theory was like the Aristotelian theory in that both theories understand cognition in general as a matter of sameness of structure in the cognizer and the cognized, and both understand sensation, in particular, as a process whereby structure makes its way from the cognized thing into the cognizer. Descartes differs from the Aristotelians, however, in that he does not understand this sameness of structure in terms of a shared (sensible) form. According to Descartes, there is no sensible form in a referee's red card; there is only a microphysical texture, a pattern of matter in motion. When Descartes raises doubt about sensory ideas resembling, or being similar to, their causes, I believe he primarily has in mind the Aristotelian doctrine that what happens when we sense is that a sensible form sends out a replica or copy through a medium until it ends up in our faculty of sensation. (The sensible form, when existing either in the medium or in a faculty of sensation, is called a sensible species.) I will interpret the remarks that Descartes makes in ¶¶14–15 about the external senses in the context of this general picture of his thinking about sensory cognition.

Descartes writes in ¶14:

> I am also taught by nature that various other bodies exist in the vicinity of my body, and that some of these are to be sought out and others avoided. And from the fact that I perceive by my senses [*sentiam*] a great variety of colours, sounds, smells and tastes, as well as differences in heat, hardness and the like, I correctly conclude that there is in bodies from which these various perceptions of the senses come [*perceptiones sensuum adveniunt*] a variety corresponding [*respondentes*] to, though perhaps not resembling [*similes*], them. Also, the fact that some of the perceptions are agreeable to me while others are disagreeable makes it quite certain that my body, or rather my whole self, in so far as I am a combination of body and mind, can be affected by the various beneficial or harmful bodies which surround it. (7:81; 2:56)

It is possible to take this passage as a freestanding account of sensation, so that Descartes is trying to build a theory of sensory representation from the ground up based on the practical role the senses play in preserving the body. However, I think these remarks are best read in the context of the account of sensory representation that seems implicit in ¶10, where Descartes treated sensation as a matter of transmission (the inmission/emission) of corporeal structure from bodies to the mind, so that corporeal structure originally existing formally in bodies comes to exist objectively in the mind. Descartes suggests that the raison d'être of the external senses is to preserve the body in an environment of friendly and hostile bodies. Accordingly, he indicates, we should not be surprised if our sensory cognition, while corresponding to the corporeal structure that originally gives rise to it, does not resemble that structure in certain of its aspects.

The aspects in question are those Descartes describes as obscure and confused, namely, our sensory cognition of the proper sensibles: "colours, sounds, smells and tastes, as well as differences in heat, hardness and the like." If our cognition of these things were clear and distinct, we would (and should) take them to straightforwardly present corporeal structure. Since they are not, we face the question of what to do with them. In ¶14, Descartes indicates that while we should assume that there is something in bodies which answers to (*respondentes*) our sensory ideas (otherwise this cognition would play no role in preserving the body), we have no reason to expect that there is a structure in bodies which is similar to them (or, as he writes in the next paragraph, "fully similar [*plane simile*]" to them). I think that, in this context, for an idea to be similar (or "fully similar") to a corporeal quality is for the idea to be structured as the quality. Descartes's point is that our sensory perception of proper sensibles (on account of its obscurity and confusion) leaves open the exact character of the structure that we are perceiving. Perhaps we perceive something along the lines of an Aristotelian sensible form, a thing in the world that is fully similar to our idea. Perhaps we perceive something quite a bit messier than that (a very complex microphysical texture, on Descartes's telling). In this case the relevant corporeal structure would still be present objectively in the idea, but only confusedly and obscurely, and so would exist in the idea in a different way from the way in which it is found formally in the world.

In ¶15 Descartes discusses our tendency to suppose otherwise, our tendency to assume, for example, that

> the heat in a body is something exactly resembling [*plane simile*] the idea of heat which is in me; or that in a white or green thing, there is the self-same whiteness or greenness which I sense [*eadem albedo aut viriditas quam*

sentio]; or that in a bitter or sweet thing there is the selfsame taste [*in amaro aut dulci idem sapor*], and so on. (7:82; 2:56–57)

It is, Descartes says, a mistake to assume this. I want to look at both the content of the mistake and the nature of the error involved.

Let me begin with the content. I believe that the controlling issue in the extract is the one broached in the previous paragraph, namely, whether a sensory idea (¶15) or a sensory perception (*perceptiones sensuum*) (¶14) is "similar" or "fully similar" to some corporeal structure found in bodies. On an Aristotelian theory of sensation, a sensible species existing in the sensitive soul was supposed to be a replica of a sensory form existing in a body, and this, I believe, helps us spell out what is meant by similarity in this context. On Descartes's own view of sensory perception, the microphysical texture as it exists objectively (and obscurely and confusedly) in a sensory idea is not similar to—is not a replica of—the microphysical texture as it exists in the body. In the part of the sentence before the first semicolon, Descartes says we are not taught by nature that the opposite is the case. That is, we are not taught by nature that the Aristotelian view is correct.

Descartes is making basically the same point after the first semicolon, but now he is putting it in terms of the relation of the way things are perceived to the way they are in the world (rather than in terms of the relation of an idea to its object). We might paraphrase this part of the extract thus: (It is a mistake to suppose that) the white or green in a body is the same as it appears to be. Understanding it this way keeps the claim equivalent to what came before the semicolon: (It is a mistake to suppose that) the confused and obscure image of these colors that ends up in my mind is similar to something in the colored body. In particular, I don't think that when Descartes denies the sameness of the white that I sense and the white in the colored thing, he is denying that there is some single structure that exists both in the body formally and in the idea objectively. Rather, what he is denying is that the way the structure exists in the idea resembles the way it is in the body (for the structure became obscure and confused when it was taken up into the idea). From Descartes's point of view, to insist otherwise, to insist that there must be in the world some entity resembling the idea (such as an Aristotelian sensible form or reality quality), runs the risk, depending on how things turn out (e.g., depending on whether mechanistic science turns out to be correct), of populating the world with unneeded entities (e.g., sensible forms, some "resembling entities," over and above microphysical textures).

I have tried to characterize the content of the mistake so as to make Descartes's adjustment to an Aristotelian picture of perception fairly modest and conservative. I think his primary goal was not the wholesale

rejection of their theory. Rather, it was merely to free things up enough
to leave the door open for a mechanistic account of secondary qualities.
Moreover, Descartes does not claim in ¶15 that there isn't an entity in
the white thing that is similar to our idea of it; he claims only that we
cannot assume that there is. For all we know, there is nothing in our ontology that is similar to our sensory idea of white. To assume otherwise
is, in effect, to think that we can read off from sensory experience what
sorts of structures are found in the world. Later in ¶15, Descartes coun-
sels that this is a misuse of the senses:

> I see that in very many cases I have been in the habit of perverting the
> order of nature, since I have been using the perceptions of the senses
> which have been properly given by nature only for indicating to the mind
> [*proprie tantum a natura datae sunt ad menti significandum*] what things are
> helpful or harmful to the composite of which the mind is a part as a cer-
> tain rule for the immediate discernment of what the essence [*essentia*] of
> bodies located outside of me is, although they indicate nothing concern-
> ing this save quite obscurely and confusedly. (7:83; 2:57)

Many commentators take the point Descartes is making at the end of
the paragraph to be the general and platitudinous one that figuring out
the essences of things is the office of the intellect rather than of the
senses. I think, however, the phrase "certain rule for the immediate discernment of what the essence [*essentia*] of bodies located outside of me
is" carries a somewhat different force. In this context, to infer from my
sensory idea of red that there must exist in the body a structure or entity
resembling it, would be a prime example of using the senses as a guide
for the immediate discernment of structures found in bodies. I think the
word *essence* here probably carries overtones of "being" or "entity" (as it
sometimes does in the tradition), and that Descartes's emphasis is not so
much on the inappropriateness of looking to the senses to understand
the essences of things (which is, after all, the office of the intellect), as on
the inappropriateness of using the senses as a guide to ontology, to tell
me what sorts of beings or entities are found in corporeal reality. (Of
course one's understanding of the world and one's account of its ontology are ultimately closely connected, but nevertheless Descartes's focus
here is more on the latter than the former.)

Let me turn from the content of the mistake to the nature of the
error. Three points are worth noting.

First, as I mentioned earlier, Descartes's point is not that there are not
these resembling entities, but only that we do not have good reason for
believing that there are.

Second, the specific form of the error is to take something for a teaching of nature that is not. The paragraph begins, "There are, however,

many other things which I may appear to have been taught by nature, but which in reality I acquired not from nature but from a habit of making ill-considered judgements; and it is therefore quite possible that these are false." He adds later in the paragraph that I have "no real or positive propensity [*nulla . . . realis siva positiva propensio*]" to believe that a star is no bigger than a flicker of light (the context makes it obvious that this applies to my belief in the resemblance thesis as well). According to Descartes, we do not have an original tendency, implanted in us by God, to use our senses as a guide to ontology in the way that he finds objectionable. Rather, our doing so is the result of a hasty judgment made when we were young (explained in VI.¶6), reinforced by years of habit.

Third, Descartes groups this error with two other things we mistake for teachings of nature, namely, "that any space in which nothing is occurring to stimulate my senses must be empty" and "that stars and towers and other distant bodies have the size and shape which they present to my senses" (¶15; 7:82; 2:56–57). (Notice that the former error also involves an attempt to read ontology off of sensory experience—this time, to conclude from the absence of sensory qualities to the absence of corporeal being.) It is significant that Descartes groups these three things together, I think, because it indicates that he sees withholding one's belief from the resemblance thesis as continuous with being open to revising one's views about the size of the stars or whether or not there might be, say, an insensible ether permeating space. I think this gives us some reason to understand Descartes's rejection of the Aristotelian resemblance thesis in the relatively modest or conservative way that I have been suggesting, as an openness to the idea that what answers to the idea of red in our ontology might be different from what one might have expected—might be unlike our idea of red, might not be a replica of it. In particular, Descartes's grouping of these three things together ought to give us some pause about reading too much into the rejection of the resemblance thesis. It makes it hard to think that his point is that I ought to be open to some much more metaphysically ambitious view, for example, that what is really going on when I am seeing a red thing is that I am made aware of some mental item that is related to the relevant physical item only by causal covariance. There is already, I think, some distance between the rejection of the Aristotelian resemblance thesis and the other two examples that Descartes gives. It would become distractingly disingenuous for Descartes to imply that being open to the radical, metaphysically ambitious revision in one's picture of perception is simply of a piece with allowing that the stars might be larger than they seem or with being open to the thought that an apparently empty space is really occupied by matter.

THE CONFUSION AND OBSCURITY OF PROPER SENSIBLES AND
THEIR MATERIAL FALSITY

A lot of work is being done here by the claim that our ideas of size and shape are clear and distinct whereas our ideas of proper sensibles are obscure and confused. Were it not for their obscurity and confusion, we would be entitled, I take it, on the basis of the great propensity cited in ¶10, to suppose that there are resembling structures in the world, in the way that we are apparently entitled to do in the case of shape and size. The reason that I am supposed to leave the ontology of proper sensible structures relatively open, Descartes explains, is that "they indicate nothing concerning this save quite obscurely and confusedly." The general interpretive outlook I have just sketched dovetails nicely, I think, with Descartes's development of the claim that sensory cognition of proper sensible qualities is obscure and confused in the Third Meditation, through his discussion of material falsity.

In ¶19 of the Third Meditation, Descartes surveys his ideas of corporeal things. He begins by claiming that "the things which I perceive clearly and distinctly in [bodies] are very few in number" and include "size, or extension in length, breadth and depth; shape, which is a function of the boundaries of this extension; position, which is a relation between various items possessing shape; and motion, or change in position; to these may be added substance, duration and number." Descartes goes on to say of the proper sensible qualities:

> But as for all the rest, including light and colours, sounds, smells, tastes, heat and cold and the other tactile qualities, I think of these only in a very confused and obscure way, to the extent that I do not even know whether they are true or false, that is, whether the ideas I have of them are ideas of real things or non-things [*verae, vel falsae, hoc est, an ideae, quas de illis habeo, sint rerum quarundum idea, an non rerum*]. For although, as I have noted before, falsity in the strict sense, or formal falsity, can occur only in judgements, there is another kind of falsity, material falsity, which occurs in ideas, when they represent non-things as things [*non rem tanquam rem repraesentant*]. For example, the ideas which I have of heat and cold contain so little clarity and distinctness that they do not enable me to tell whether cold is merely the absence of heat [*privatio caloris*] or vice versa, or whether both of them are real [*realis*] qualities, or neither is. And since there can be no ideas which are not as it were of things [*Et quia nullae idea nisi tanquam rerum esse possunt*], if it is true that cold is nothing but the absence of heat, the idea which represents it to me as something real and positive [*idea quae mihi tanquam reale quid & positivum repraesentat*]

deserves to be called false; and the same goes for other ideas of this kind. (III.¶19; 7:43–44; 2:30)

Descartes explains the confusion and obscurity of my cognition of proper sensible things in terms of my ideas of them being materially false. His explanation of their material falsity, which focuses on the contrast between a thing (*rem*) and a nonthing (*non rem*), is that I cannot tell from these ideas whether they represent a something's-being-there as opposed to an absence (privation) of something's-being-there.

Let's develop Descartes's example here, hot and cold. Suppose, for instance, that motion is a reality and rest an absence of reality.[49] Suppose, further, that heat is the motion of corporeal particles and cold is the absence of motion of corporeal particles. Then, I take it, my idea of heat is of a thing (a *rem*) and my idea of cold is of the absence of a thing (a *non rem*). Descartes's question is, Can I tell from my sensory cognition of heat whether heat is a reality and cold is the absence of that reality, or whether cold is a reality and heat is the absence of cold, or whether both are realities or neither? Descartes wants to make two points in response. First, he takes it as obvious that I cannot read the underlying metaphysical situation from the ideas. The sensory ideas do not make clear to me whether both heat and cold are realities, only one, or neither. Second, since all sensory ideas register as of something positive ("as something real and positive [*idea quae mihi tanquam reale quid & positivum repraesentat*]"), if it should turn out that cold, for example, is an absence of reality, then the idea of cold is misleading, because it suggests the presence of a thing instead of the absence of a thing. In this case, it would deserve to be thought of as "materially false."

I do not think that Descartes is suggesting that the idea of cold in such a case would be an idea of absolute or pure nonbeing, as it were; there are still the nonmoving particles that are affecting me, say, by slowing down the motion of the particles in my hand. I think all sensory ideas, including cold in the imagined case, involve the confused importation of corporeal structure from the world, so even if cold is an absence or privation, it involves corporeal structure. The point is rather that cold as opposed to heat is the absence of something. When Descartes suggests that cold might, as far as the clarity of sensory cognition goes, be a nonbeing, I think he means that, for all that cognition makes plain to me, the appearance of cold on the cognitive scene might be the cognition of the disappearance of some reality (motion) from the world. As far as one can tell from the idea, what the idea of cold presents obscurely is the absence of something (the reality: motion of particles) rather than the presence of something (the nonreality: absence of motion of particles).[50]

Now, if we understand the obscurity and confusion of sensory ideas in the manner I have been suggesting, then an idea's being obscure and confused comes down to my being unable to determine from the idea whether it is presenting being or nonbeing, that is, whether the specific aspect of the situation that the sensory idea of cold is making available to me counts as a reality or the absence of a reality. Notice that this brings Descartes's account of the confusion and obscurity of sensory ideas closely in line with the point that he makes in paragraphs VI.¶¶14–15 about the resemblance. There, Descartes is saying that my nature does not teach me that there are entities or structures in the corporeal world that are like my sensory ideas. In III.¶19, Descartes is claiming that my sensory ideas are obscure and confused, because I cannot determine whether they present being or nonbeing. Both claims are different ways of making the point that we should not try to read ontology off of one's sensory experience.

The general point that Descartes is making, about the inappropriateness of reading ontology off of one's sensory experience, seems clearly correct. It is not as easy as that to determine when one is confronted with a species of being as opposed to nonbeing. It is harder to say, however, whether this is something that is manifest from the character of sensory experience itself, so that I determine from a certain quality of my ideas themselves (where they lie on a dimension of clarity and distinctness versus obscurity and confusedness) that the proper sensibles (colors, sounds, odors, tastes, and tactile qualities) are on a footing different from the common sensibles (shapes, sizes, number).

At any rate, there does seem to be some plausibility to what Descartes wants to say about our ideas of proper sensibles. It is easy to imagine oneself reflecting on the character of our cognition of hot and cold and finding oneself puzzled about what their apparent contrariety comes to in the world, and this can suggest some distance between the corporeal structures themselves that are presented in the ideas and the way they are presented; this reflection might help one resist the temptation to think that there are corporeal structures "fully similar" to the ideas. The point that Descartes is making here seems to work better for hot and cold than it does as sensation gets more sophisticated, and we move from the tactile, gustatory, and olfactory toward the auditory and visual, notwithstanding his assertion at the end of the passage that "the same goes for other ideas of this kind."[51] But even with a form of sensation as advanced and complex as vision, it is not, I suppose, immediately apparent how various oppositions and contrarieties in our visual experience are reflected in oppositions and contrarieties in the world that our visual ideas present.

Finally, there is an issue that arises here with respect to the senses, similar to one that arose with respect to the imagination, which has to do with the metaphysical possibility of sensation without body. Descartes suggests in a number of places that if I were not united to a body, I would not have the faculty of sensation. God could, one might suppose, produce in the cognitive agent ideas that a cognitive agent could not tell apart from sensations or sensory perceptions. Would this count as a supernatural cause of sensing, or something else, say, simulacrum sensation? If we treat the account of the senses implicit in ¶¶12–14 in the way we treated the account of imagining in ¶¶1–3, we might think that in the same way that what imagining is is the application of the cognitive faculty to a body that is present to it, what sensing is is the transmission of information concerning bodily welfare to a cognitive agent united to it. And if that is correct, then there will not be any supernatural sensing, only supernatural simulacrum sensing. As before, whether it seems natural to think of sensation as essentially involving the body will depend on whether it seems reasonable to think of sensing as an activity that is prior to its components (e.g., bodily damage, sensory idea of pain) and through which the components are understood, or whether it seems more reasonable to think of sensing as built up out of prior components. To my mind, the clearer sense we have of the role that sensing plays in the overall nature of the composite makes it more natural to think along the former lines, but I concede that this is debatable.

V. ABERRANT TEACHINGS OF NATURE

In ¶¶16–23, Descartes takes up an issue that he has alluded to twice before in the *Meditations* (III.¶¶9 and 10, and VI.¶7), that of natural impulses that point us in the wrong direction. The discussion divides into two main subsections, ¶¶16–18, where he offers a statement and elaboration of the difficulty, and ¶¶19–23, where he presents a solution. Of the two sections, the first perhaps raises the more interesting issues; the second is comparatively straightforward.

¶¶16–18. THE PROBLEM

Although our natural impulses generally point us in the right direction, sometimes they do not. Why doesn't this reflect poorly on God, the author of my nature, as it would if he gave me a faulty faculty of understanding or a faulty will? Here is Descartes's initial statement of the difficulty:

> But a further problem now comes to mind regarding the things themselves [*circa illa ipsa*] which nature presents to me as to be pursued or

avoided, and also regarding the internal senses [*internos sensus*] in which I
seem to have noticed errors [*errores*], as happens, for example, when someone is tricked [*delusus*] by the pleasant taste of some food into eating the
poison concealed inside of it. (¶16; 7:83; 2:58)

Notice that Descartes puts the problem in specifically cognitive terms:
the problem is sometimes that errors (*errores*) seem to be found in the
internal senses, as when I am tricked (*delusus*) by the pleasantness of
something.[52]

Descartes does not think that the example he gives at the end of the
extract quite hits the mark. The case of poison concealed within some
food is a case of the senses failing to provide us with complete information about our environment. But there is no reason to think that our
senses are supposed to provide complete information:

> Yet in this case, what the man's nature impels him to seek is simply what
> gives the food its pleasant taste, and not the poison, which his nature is ig-
> norant of. All that can be concluded from this is that his nature is not om-
> niscient. And this is not surprising, since man is a limited thing, and so it is
> only fitting that his perfection should be limited. (¶16; 7:84; 2:58)

We might, borrowing some scholastic terminology that Descartes himself uses in the Fourth Meditation, say that the fact that our senses are
not "omniscient" counts as a negation, the simple absence of some perfection (as with the lack of sight in a rock).[53] It does not mark a privation,
the absence of some perfection that "should" be there (as with blindness
in a dog). Descartes thinks, however, that other situations arise in the internal senses that do have the character of privation:

> And yet it is not unusual for us to err [*erramus*] concerning those things
> toward which nature does impel us. Those who are ill, for example, may
> desire food or drink that will shortly afterwards turn out to be bad for
> them. (¶17; 7:84; 2:58)

We are now envisioning a case where the internal senses provide us with
incorrect as opposed to *incomplete* information. The example that Descartes
has in mind is dropsy, which, he takes it, involves having a sensation of
throat dryness—thirst—at a time when the body does not need drink,
even when drink would be bad for it. Since thirst is followed by a desire
for drink, the internal senses mislead in this situation. The sick person's
nature is telling him to drink when drink would not be good for him.

I (following a general suggestion of Guéroult's) find putting Descartes's problem in terms of the distinction between negation and privation useful because it helps us appreciate certain issues lying just below
the surface.[54] In particular, the distinction between a privation and a

negation is traditionally made out in terms of a thing's nature. For Aristotelian scholastics, a thing's nature was in turn worked out in terms of its kind. Its genus and species (which enter into the definition of its essence or nature) contribute the relevant standards for what something "ought" (by its "nature") to have. Now, Descartes thinks of natures—especially the natures of physical systems—in a very different way from his scholastic predecessors, which makes unclear what the "should" implicit in the notion of privation answers to in his case. To judge from what we have seen so far, it seems to arise (as it did in the Fourth Meditation) mainly from the fact that error (or incorrect information) involves things being not as they should be, rather than from a reference to kinds. (In addition, it may be that enough has been said about the internal senses, in ¶¶11–13, to convey the idea that the internal senses have an intrinsic purpose, a purpose that they are working against in the case of dropsy. It is less clear to me to what extent Descartes is drawing on this sort of consideration.)

Now, one reason it is important to mark the distinction that Descartes draws between the two cases (lack of omniscience, error) is that God bears different sorts of responsibility in the two cases. Which perfections God gives me and which perfections God does not give me is a function of God's overall plan for the universe.[55] Every being he creates has some perfections and lacks other perfections, so that it is limited in some ways; that is, every being has some negations. By way of contrast, that my nature is susceptible to privation raises special issues about whether I have been, as Descartes puts it in the Fourth Meditation, made "complete and perfect in all respects" (IV.¶5; 7:55; 2:38), that is, whether my nature is somehow internally flawed. In particular, we need to understand why God allows it to happen that my nature, on occasion, leads me in the wrong direction, because being led in the wrong direction is a privation and not merely a negation. This responsibility that God bears for privations surfaces explicitly in the continuation of VI.¶17, where Descartes imagines someone saying that there is no problem with the case of dropsy because the nature of a sick person is disordered (*corrupta*):

> Perhaps it may be said that they go wrong because their nature is disordered [*corrupta*], but this does not remove the difficulty. A sick man is no less one of God's creatures than a healthy one, and it seems no less repugnant to suppose that he has received a deceptive [*fallacem*] nature from God. (7:84; 2:58)

The force of the solution suggested by the first sentence seems to be this: There is nothing wrong with human nature in itself. Human nature is such that we are thirsty when drink would be good for us and hungry when food would be good for us and so forth. It is only when human

nature is disordered (*corrupta*) or deviant in some way that problems set
in. But, Descartes says in the second sentence, this response does not the
meet the problem, for God is responsible for both the corrupt nature and
the deception that comes with it.

With the introduction of the word *corrupta*, it becomes clear that we
are indeed in the territory of privation: a corrupted nature is a nature that
is not as it "should" be. *Prima facie*, the idea of a *corrupta* nature does not
sit well with mechanistic physics. If we think of a rabbit as a certain pattern of matter in motion, like a hurricane or the solar system, then it is
not obvious what we mean when we say that its nature is *corrupta*, or that
there is a way that the pattern should be, from which it might deviate. Is
there, for example, any way that a hurricane "should be"? Mechanistic
characterizations of physical systems—patterns of matter in motion, occurring according to the conservation laws—do not have the right sort of
"logical form" to support a notion of disorder or deviation from nature.
Aristotelian natures are structured teleologically, that is, around some
characteristic good that their possessors strive to realize. It is a feature of
the logical form of an Aristotelian nature (a feature of the sort of logos it
has) that an individual may exemplify it more or less well (as when a blind
dog exhibits the nature canine less well than a sighted dog). Natures of
this form support the possibility of intrinsic disorder and deviation. Mechanistic natures, by way of contrast, are structured in a way that does not
seem to leave room for intrinsic disorder or deviation.

Descartes takes up this set of issues in the next stretch of text. Although the discussion is brief, it is carefully enough worked out so as to
repay close attention. It will be convenient to have that discussion before
us in its entirety (the subscripting of the word *nature*, to be explained
later, is mine):[56]

[a] Now a clock constructed with wheels and weights observes all the laws
of its nature$_1$ just as closely when it is badly made and tells the wrong time
as when it completely fulfills the wishes of the clockmaker. In the same
way, I might consider the body of a man as a kind of machine equipped
with and made up of bones, nerves, muscles, veins, blood and skin in such
a way that, even if there were no mind in it, it would still perform all the
same movements as it now does in those cases where movement is not
under control of the will or, consequently, of the mind. I can easily see
that if such a body suffers from dropsy, for example, and is affected by the
dryness of the throat that usually [*solet*] produces in the mind the sensation of thirst, the resulting condition of the nerves and other parts will
dispose the body to take drink, with the result that the disease will be
aggravated. Yet this is just as natural$_1$ as the body's being stimulated by
a similar dryness of the throat to take drink when there is no such fault

[*vitium*] and drink is beneficial. [*b*] Admittedly, when I consider the envisioned [*praeconceptum*] use of a clock, I may say that it is departing from [*deflectere*] its nature₂ when it does not tell the right time; and similarly when I consider the mechanism of the human body, I may think that, in relation to the movements which usually [*solent*] take place there, it too is deviating from [*aberrare*] its nature₂ if the throat is dry at a time when drinking is not beneficial to its preservation [*conservationem*]. [*c*] But I am well aware that this last use of nature [i.e., nature₂] is very different from the other one [i.e., nature₁]. For this one [i.e., nature₂] is nothing but a denomination [*denominatio*] that depends on my thought [*cognitione*], comparing a sick man and a poorly made clock with the idea of a healthy man and a correctly made clock, and is extrinsic [*extrinseca*] to the things that it is said of. By the other use [i.e., nature₁] I understand something that is in fact [*vero*] found in things, and for that reason possesses some truth [*veritatis*]. (¶17; 7:84–85; 2:58–59)

Thematically, the point of this paragraph and the next is to sharpen the difficulty that is to be solved in ¶¶19–23. But Descartes is doing more than simply that. He is trying to explain something about how the notion of a disordered nature works in the context of his mechanistic science.

[*a*]: Here Descartes compares the body to a clock. Before we work out that comparison, we need to address a general interpretive question. Descartes invites the meditator to consider the body as a machine, abstracting away from the fact that the mind exercises a certain amount of control over it. He asks us to consider "the body of man as a kind of machine equipped with bones, nerves, muscles, veins, blood and skin in such a way that, even if there were no mind in it, it would still perform the same movements as it now does in those cases where movement is not under control of the will, or consequently, of the mind." I take it that when Descartes asks us to consider the human body in this particular way, in abstraction from its union with the mind, he is considering the human body in the same way that he would consider the body of a rabbit, which is on his telling an automaton. I think he is, in effect, telling us something about those things in my nature that relate to "body alone" (¶15).

An alternative reading might be based on the idea that the body's being united to the mind is supposed to cast its shadow over the discussion, so that much of what he is saying here would not apply to a rabbit. For example, our bodies, because they are united to minds, are susceptible to diseases, which can be aggravated, and so forth. But a rabbit—mere automaton that it is—cannot really become ill. I don't see any sign that Descartes is drawing this sort of distinction between a human body and a rabbit. I think that for Descartes a purely mechanistic body "can suffer dropsy [*hydrope laboret*]" and the "disease [*morbus*]" can be "aggravated [*augeatur*]"; it can also be "disposed to take drink [*disponi ut potum sumat*]" and (Descartes implies) undergo things that benefit its preservation (*conservationem . . . prodest*). I imagine that Descartes thinks he can make this out in terms of what contributes to the overall integrity of a mechanism, so that a diseased automaton comes out to be something like a rusting piece of iron. (Descartes's attitude here seems of a piece with his willingness to say that a purely mechanistic dog "sees" and "hears.")

Now, if Descartes is on board with using a notion of disease with a machine, what is his hesitation about the idea that some (mechanistic) bodies have *corrupta* natures? Well, *corrupta* introduces some notion as to the way a mechanical system ought to be, and, as I put it above, mechanical natures are of the wrong logical form to support such an "ought." This, I take it, is the point of the comparison between the sick body and the poorly made clock in [*a*]. The poorly made clock is following the laws of its nature when it tells the wrong time. Indeed, it would be something of a miracle—a suspension of the laws of nature—if the hands of a clock with uneven gears should move as if its gears were uniform. Similarly, an automaton whose internal mechanical structure primes it to imbibe drink when drink would be detrimental to it, would be doing what is natural to it when it heads toward drink, notwithstanding the fact that drink would be detrimental to it. The sense of nature here is given through a physical being's mechanical structure and the relevant laws of motion. I'm calling nature, taken in this way, nature$_1$. The general upshot of [*a*] is that nature$_1$ does not support an idea of a *corrupta* nature, some sense that a mechanism might behave otherwise than it "should." The only way for that to happen would be for the mechanism to violate the laws of motion.

[*b*]: Descartes allows that there is a second sense of nature, which I am calling nature$_2$, according to which a mechanism like a clock or a rabbit (or a human body) can either "depart from [*deflectere*]" its nature (what Descartes says about the poorly made clock) or "deviate from [*aberrare*]" its nature (what Descartes says about the sick body).

[*c*]: Here Descartes privileges nature$_1$ over nature$_2$. This is the trickiest part of the passage. It is important to get the exact sense of the privileging. What he says is that nature$_2$ "is nothing but a denomination [*denominatio*] that depends on my thought [*cognitione*], comparing a sick man and a poorly made clock with the idea of a healthy man and a correctly made clock, and is extrinsic [*extrinseca*] to the things that it is said of." By way of contrast, nature$_1$ "is in fact [*vero*] found in things, and for that reason possesses some truth [*veritatis*]."

The contrast that Descartes draws here, between what is found in things and what depends on comparisons with other things, and so counts as an "extrinsic denomination," depends on a traditional view of relations as in some way the product of the mind.[57] For example, Plato's being-taller-than-Socrates is an "extrinsic denomination," the result of the mind's comparison of Plato's stature with Socrates'. As far as the world goes, there is only Plato and his stature, and Socrates and his stature. The being-taller-than-Socrates is not some extra thing over and above the two individuals and their respective statures. When Socrates died, Plato's reality was not diminished by his losing his being-taller-than-Socrates. In this (rather special) sense, being-taller-than-Socrates is "not found in things." Notice, in particular, although the being-taller-than-Socrates is not found in things, there is nothing "subjective" or "arbitrary" about Plato's being taller than Socrates; it is not somehow imaginary or a fiction that Plato is taller than Socrates.

When Descartes says nature$_2$ is an extrinsic denomination, not found in the things, he is not saying that nature$_2$ is merely subjective or arbitrary or a piece of fancy. Rather, his point is that nature$_2$ is a relational notion that we arrive at through comparing a physical system with something else. We, for example, compare the poorly made clock to the intention of its maker to arrive at the clock's nature$_2$ (and, in particular, to work out the thought that the poorly made clock is deviating from its nature$_2$). We compare the sick man to the idea of the healthy man (*idea homines sani*) to arrive at the body's nature$_2$ (and, in particular, to work out the thought that the sick man is deviating from his nature$_2$). (Descartes does not say where we get the idea of the healthy man, given that we cannot consult its maker's intentions. The two occurrences of *soleo*—one in [a] and one in [b]—suggest that this has something to do with comparing that body to other human bodies.) Descartes is not denying that we make such comparisons for good reasons, or that such comparisons can be illuminating or useful. He is not saying we should (or could) stop making such comparisons. Rather, he is claiming that our nature$_2$ talk can easily mislead us. We tend to overlook the fact that nature$_2$ is not grounded in things in the way that nature$_1$ is.

In fact—although this is admittedly speculative—it seems to me Descartes's remarks here contain the seeds of a constructive account of what he thinks happens when we invent (again, possibly for very good reasons) a nature$_2$.[58] These remarks help to explain not only how "disordered nature" talk works when applied to purely mechanistic systems, but also how other sorts of (broadly speaking) functional idioms are supposed to work when applied to mechanical systems. For example, a heart valve that allows blood to slosh backward when an auricle contracts is disordered or defective because in an ideal body (as compared to "an idea of the body"), the valve allows the blood to flow in only one direction. The ideal body makes clear that the heart valve "should" allow the blood to flow through in only one direction; otherwise it is defective. It makes clear that the "function" of the heart valve is to allow the blood to flow in only one way. The point that Descartes is making in ¶17 is not that we should stop saying or thinking such things. It is simply that such judgments are not based in the mechanical structure of the valve itself, but rather in certain models of the valve we form to which it seems appropriate and illuminating to compare the actual valve.[59]

Thus far—that is, through the end of ¶17—Descartes's point is this. Since the idea of a corrupted/disordered nature rests on the nature$_2$ sense of nature, and since that sense results from the comparisons we make among things and is not found in things themselves, corruption/disorder does not raise any issues with respect to God's providence. It just turns out that some mechanical systems come out better than others when they are compared to certain ideas that we have about how such systems might work. There is no sense that when we stick to a given system itself—that is, independently of such comparisons—it is doing anything other than what it "should" be doing, and so nothing is going on which we might feel we need to reconcile with God's beneficence. In other words, God is responsible only for what is found in things (i.e., nature$_1$) and not how a system measures up to certain ideals we might form concerning it (i.e., its nature$_2$).

In ¶18, Descartes tells us that the situation is different if we consider the composite rather than simply the body (that is, the body taken in abstraction from its union with the mind):

> But certainly even if, with respect to the body suffering from dropsy [*hydrope laborans*], there is only an extrinsic denomination [*tantum denominatio extrinseca*] when we say that its nature [nature$_2$] is disordered [*corrupta*], on account of its having a dry throat and yet not needing drink; nevertheless with respect to the composite, or to the mind united to such a body, it is not a pure denomination [*pura denominatio*], but a true error of nature$_1$ [*verus error naturae*] that it thirsts when drink would be harmful for it; and thus it remains to be asked, how the goodness of God fails to prevent nature so taken [i.e., nature$_1$] from being deceptive [*fallax*]. (7:85; 2:59)

Evidently, then, the nature$_1$ of the composite is structured differently from the nature$_1$ of the body taken apart from its union with the mind. The nature$_1$ of the body (at least when considered in abstraction from its union with the mind) cannot be intrinsically corrupted/disordered, but the nature$_1$ of the composite can be intrinsically corrupted/disordered. Since nature$_1$ is God's responsibility in a way that nature$_2$ is not, the fact that the composite's nature$_1$ can become disordered raises special questions of theodicy. As Descartes puts it, how is it that "the goodness of God fails to prevent nature so taken [i.e., nature$_1$] from being deceptive [*fallax*]"? This is the problem that Descartes attempts to solve in ¶¶19–23.

Before we go on to consider his solution, I want to consider exactly how ¶18 adds to the picture developed in ¶17. It is easy to get the impression, on the basis of ¶18, that Descartes thinks that the human body is a teleological or functional being in a way that a rabbit is not on his telling; and that the human body derives this special teleological status through its union with the mind. The way Martial Guéroult puts the view that I vaguely have in mind here is, "It is the union with a soul *that transforms into a teleological relation*, with respect to the totality of the body, the purely mechanical relation in itself of the parts assembled in this totality, and it is thus that the corporeal mechanism acquires a true functional indivisibility," and "It [the union of soul with body] transforms the foundation in some manner from within, and one part at a time, in its most intimate details, by introducing a new relation between its parts and between the parts and the whole—the relation of internal finality."[60]

It is hard to know exactly what Guéroult intends by the characterizations "teleological relation," "true functional indivisibility," and "internal finality," but one thing I take him to be implying is that the functional idioms that Descartes grounds in nature$_2$ in part [c] of ¶17 somehow reach deeper into the nature of things in the case of the human body, on account of its union with the mind, than they do in the case of a rabbit.[61] I find this unlikely. I don't see any evidence in ¶18 that Descartes thinks that the body's union with the mind somehow either converts the body's nature$_1$ into a teleological structure or gives it a new, teleological, nature$_1$ so that the body is now subject to non-extrinsically grounded corruption, disorder, or privation. I don't think ¶¶17–18 support the idea, for example, that Descartes would count any condition of the human body tending toward the dissolution of the union, say, for example, arteriosclerosis, as a "disorder" of its nature, except in the nature$_2$ sense. Bad plumbing in the human body has the same status as bad plumbing in a rabbit. Both are understood in reference to some external ideal (generated by comparisons with other similar bodies) that yields a sense as to how things "ought" to go with such bodies. The human body's union with the mind does not, in my view, change the status of the "functionality" of the circulatory system, somehow giving it a deeper status than in the case of the rabbit.

Here is where it is important to keep in view that Descartes is focused on error and deception in ¶¶17–18. The reason that dropsy, I think, differs from arteriosclerosis is that dropsy (as Descartes is parsing it) involves *misinformation*—a message that prompts one to think that drink would be good for one's body when drink would in fact be bad for it.

Importantly, the defect in question belongs to the mind-body system (ultimately, to the union) and not to the body alone. The point that Descartes is making in ¶18 turns on the specific idea of misinformation, resulting from a cognitive being working in tandem with a mechanical being, and not some more general idea of malfunction.

In fairness to Guéroult, his thinking about this topic seems to be shaped not so much by ¶¶17 and 18 of the Sixth Meditation as by some of Descartes's correspondence, especially a letter to Mesland of 9 February 1645, where in the course of offering a theory of transubstantiation Descartes claims that the numerical identity of the human body depends on its being united to the mind. He writes that even though the matter of the body constantly changes over the course of our lives,

> we still believe that it is the same body, numerically the same body, so long as it remains joined and substantially united with the same soul; we think of this body as whole and entire so long as it has in itself all the dispositions required to preserve the union. (4:166; 3:243)

He adds a little further below:

> [O]ur body, qua human body, remains always numerically the same so long as it is united with the same soul. In that sense, it can even be called indivisible; because if an arm or a leg of a man is amputated, we think that it is only in the first sense of body [i.e., body as a determinate part of matter] that his body is divided—we do not think that a man who has lost an arm or a leg is less a man than any other. Altogether then, provided that a body is united with the same rational soul, we always take it as the body of the same man, whatever matter it may be and whatever quantity or shape it may have; and we count it as the whole and entire body, provided that it needs no additional matter in order to remain joined to this soul. (4:167; 3:243)

Although I agree that these are important texts for understanding Descartes's views on the unity of the human body, it is not clear to me how close they get us to Guéroult's claims, mentioned above, that "it is the union with a soul *that transforms into a teleological relation*, with respect to the totality of the body, the purely mechanical relation in itself of the parts assembled in this totality, and it is thus that the corporeal mechanism acquires a true functional indivisibility" or "it [the union of soul with body] transforms the foundation in some manner from within, and one part at a time, in its most intimate details, by introducing a new relation between its parts and between the parts and the whole—the relation of internal finality."[62] After all, the point that Descartes is making in the passage is simply that in the case of a human body its union with the mind is dispositive with respect to certain questions about its identity and individuation (this is what he needs to defend his account of how the matter in the sacred host becomes Christ's body). In addition, when Descartes writes of the "whole and entire body" in the letter, it does not seem to me that he is emphasizing some general issue of finality or functionality there. Finally, it is unclear where this discussion is supposed to leave the bodies of animals.[63] Is Descartes suggesting that the bodies of animals are not "numerically the same" over time because they lack a unity that is not metaphysically grounded in a union with some mind (and so lack what Guéroult terms "true functional indivisibility" and "the relation of internal finality")? Guéroult claims for Descartes that animal and other bodies "are without real unity and constitute only precarious unities without reality within extended substance," but it is not obvious to me that Descartes is drawing this sort of contrast between animal bodies and human bodies in the letters to Mesland.[64] He may, for example, simply be pointing out that there is an additional and overriding consideration that applies in our case, so that to be part of my body is to be united to my mind, which is what he needs to show that to be part of Christ's body is to be united to his mind, thereby paving the way for his theory of transubstantiation.[65]

¶¶19–23. The Solution

So human nature is liable to a certain kind of internal disorder. How is this possibility consistent with the fact that God is the author of human nature? Descartes makes four points en route to offering a solution to the problem of disordered natures. First, he claims that the mind is indivisible, whereas the body with which it is united is divisible (¶19); second, that the mind is immediately affected by the pineal gland and not by the entire body, in such a way that "whenever [the pineal gland] is disposed in the same way, the same thing is exhibited to the mind [*quotiescunque eodem modo est disposita, menti idem exhibet*]" independently of what is occurring in the rest of the body (¶20); third, that it is in the nature of causal paths in *res extensa* that different goings-on earlier in the path can lead to the same goings-on later in the path (so that there are different ways to vibrate a nerve so as to produce the same motion in the pineal gland) (¶21); and since there is (what amounts to) a type-type correspondence between pineal gland movements and the sensings/sensations (*sensus*) they bring on (*infert*), "there is nothing better that could be thought up in this affair than that it [the bodily movement] should bring on the one [sensing/sensation], out of all those which it could bring on, that is most greatly and most often conducive to the preservation of the health of a human being" (¶22).

The basic outline of Descartes's response to the difficulty is, I think, fairly clear. When one looks at the basic parameters of the engineering task that God set for himself, one can see that it is in the nature of that task that different goings-on in the world lead to the same information being presented to the cognitive agent. So even if (as Descartes thinks is the case) God designed human nature in the best possible way, so that movements in the pineal gland do in fact bring on in the indivisible cognitive agent the sensings/sensations that are maximally conducive to the health of the human being, it still remains the case that

> the nature of man as a combination of mind and body is such that it is bound to mislead him from time to time. For there may be some occurrence, not in the foot but in one of the other areas through which the nerves travel in their route from the foot to the brain, or even in the brain itself; and if this cause produces the same motion which is usually produced by the foot, then pain will be sensed [*sentietur*] as if [*tanquam*] it were in the foot. This deception of the senses is natural, because a given motion in the brain must always produce the same sensation in the mind; and the origin of the motion in question is much more often going to be something which is hurting the foot, rather than something existing elsewhere. So it agrees with reason [*rationi consentaneum*] that this motion should always exhibit [*exhibeat*] to the mind a pain in the foot rather than in any other part of the body. Again, dryness of the throat may sometimes arise not, as it usually does, from the fact that drink would be conducive to the health of the body, but from some quite opposite cause, as happens in the case of the man with dropsy. Yet it is much better that it should mislead on this occasion than that it should always mislead when the body is well constituted. And the same goes for the other cases. (¶23; 7:88–89; 2:61)

If we take the project that God set for himself to be very general—say, to unite an indivisible being to a divisible, extended order—then one might quarrel with some aspects of Descartes's defense of God. Leibniz, for example, does not seem to have agreed that the fact that a mind or soul is indivisible and the body divisible precludes God from setting things up so that all the information found in the body (indeed, in the entire created universe) was found—in varying degrees of perspicuity—in the soul.[66] Even here, however, it looks as if some choices have to be made in the case of finite beings in terms of what information becomes salient for them, and one might suppose that if this salience works in a systematic enough way, the sort of in-principle misfiring that Descartes is pointing to will become unavoidable. Perhaps in the end the problem has to do with how to make available information about an extremely complex entity to a cognitive being of limited capacities, so that the finiteness of the cognitive agent matters as much as its indivisibility.

Be that as it may, it may make better sense to attribute to God a more specific project and to view Descartes as working here in an *a posteriori* manner, more or less taking human nature as (he thinks) he finds it, and working backward to figure out the constraints that God was operating under when he designed it. So even if there might be other natures similar in some respects to ours—say, extremely powerful minds united to bodies—that are not liable to miscues or are not liable to miscues in the same way as ours, they are not human natures; rather, they represent others of God's possible projects.[67]

We should give ¶22 special attention because this passage has been thought to suggest a conception of the union between mind and body that is in some respects at odds with the one developed above. In that paragraph Descartes gives us a rough idea of how God went about joining certain sensory information to certain motions in the pineal gland:

> My final observation is that any given movement occurring in the part of the brain that immediately affects the mind produces just some one sensation [*unum aliquem sensum*]; and hence there is nothing better that could be thought up in this matter than that it [the movement] should bring on the one, out of all those which it could bring on, that is most greatly and most often conducive to the preservation of the health of a human being. And experience shows that the sensations which nature has given us are all of this kind; and so there is absolutely nothing to be found in them that does not bear witness to the power and goodness of God. For example, when the nerves in the foot are set in motion in a violent and unusual manner, this motion, by way of the spinal cord, reaches the inner parts of the brain, and there gives the mind a sign that something is to be sensed [*menti signum dat ad aliquid sentiendum*], namely pain as if [*tanquam*] existing in the foot, by which the mind is excited to remove the pain's cause as harmful to the foot, so far as it can. The nature of man could have indeed been so constituted by God that the same motion in the brain would exhibit whatever [*quidvis*] else to the mind: namely, either itself [i.e., the motion] insofar as it is in the brain, or insofar as it is in the foot, or insofar as it is in some intermediary place, or finally anything else you like [*quidlibet*]; but nothing else would be equally conducive to the preservation of the body. (VI.¶22; 7:87–88; 2:60–61)[68]

It is possible—keying on the passage's suggestion that God's annexing of messages and motions is "arbitrary" (the sense that the relation between messages and motions is arbitrary is expressed by the *quidvis* and *quidlibet*)—to think Descartes is providing us here with an account *ab initio* of the union, so that the union consists in God's linking of the annexing of sensory messages to the motions.[69] On this view, the construction of human nature seems to be a bottom-up affair that proceeds by arbitrary attachment of certain sensory ideas to certain bodily motions so that certain behaviors initiated by the mind result, and what the union is is simply the collection of these linkages, and what the composite entity— that is, the human being—is is a mind and a body connected by those linkages.

I don't think this is the best way to take ¶22. To be sure, there is, on Descartes's telling, more arbitrariness in how God put together a faculty of sensation than there was on an Aristotelian view. On the Aristotelian view a faculty of sensation is about getting qualities that exist materially in the world to exist spiritually in the soul. On Descartes's view the faculty of sensation provides the cognitive agent with information about the condition of the body and information about the bodies in its environment. There is more play—more degrees of freedom—as to what information is made available under what circumstances. This is perhaps easier to see in the case of the external senses. For an Aristotelian, the faculty of vision simply imports the sensible form red from the world into the soul. For Descartes, the sensory idea red contains objectively the reality of a given surface structure. There is then some choice about how the reality found in different surface structures becomes confused and obscure when that reality comes to exists objectively in human sensory ideas.

While there is, in this respect, more arbitrariness on Descartes's view in how God put together the sensory system of the human composite than there is on an Aristotelian view, I don't think we should take this arbitrariness as an invitation to think that union consists in God's attaching certain idea-types to certain pineal-gland-motion-types. Rather, it is better to view God as working out the problem of how corporeal structure is to be presented in sensation against the background of a certain project. What God is doing is devising a nature that involves one component, a mind, with a certain level of intellectual power, having a sort of concern for and responsibility for the other component, the body. The mind can take various steps to protect the body. But to do so it must receive information from the body, and in a form that the mind, at its level of ability, can use. The power of sensation is the power that the mind has to receive such information. What Descartes is telling us in ¶22 is that while there is some play in exactly how the senses convey this information, God has designed the power of sensation in the best possible way.

I think it might be more in tune with some contemporary sensibilities to cut both the power and the project out of the picture, and to try to get by with only the type-type correlations between sensory ideas and pineal gland motions. Those correlations yield as it were the solid data, and everything else is so much metaphysical fluff. Trying to restrict oneself to the correlation seems more "austere."

While I understand this attitude, I don't think it was Descartes's. From his point of view, this would be to try to understand the exercise of a power without understanding the power. When it comes to the union and the faculty of sensation, I don't think he's all that far from the spirit of Aquinas's methodological remark, in his *Commentary on Aristotle's De Anima*:

> We proceed from objects to acts, from acts to faculties, and from faculties to the essence of the soul. (*In II De Anima*, Lect. 6, n. 308)

To stop at the type-type correlations would be akin to stopping at the acts, without proceeding to the faculties. I don't think Descartes wanted to reduce the faculty of sensation to its acts any more than Aquinas did. That there is a power underneath our sensory activities, giving them their rhyme and reason, and that there is a union beneath the power, in turn giving the power its rhyme and reason, seems to be integral to how Descartes is thinking of the nature of the composite. Indeed, from his point of view, trying to limit oneself to the bare correlations runs the risk of losing the idea that there is such a thing as the nature of a human being.

Notes

➤◄

INTRODUCTION

1. A sign of the difference between the scholastic theory and contemporary views is that one finds the labels *empiricist* and *rationalist* both applied to scholastic Aristotelianism, but this may also have something to do with the fluidity of the labels.

2. Among the books that have tried to read that work from start to finish are Martial Guéroult's *Descartes selon l'ordre des raisons, l'âme et Dieu*; Gary C. Hatfield's *Routledge Philosophy Guidebook to Descartes and the "Meditations"*; and Catherine Wilson's *Descartes's "Meditations": An Introduction*. Denis Kambouchner's *Les Méditations métaphysiques de Descartes* will eventually provide a complete commentary on the *Meditations*, but to date only the first volume, which includes a general introduction and a treatment of the First Meditation, has appeared. Margaret Wilson's *Descartes*, a work I greatly admire, is organized around each of the six meditations. However, her individual chapters, with the exception of chapters on the first two meditations, take up philosophically significant topics in the meditation under discussion rather than attempt to work through the meditation in order.

Jorge Secada presents a stimulating interpretation of Descartes's thought against the background of (late) Thomistic Aristotelian philosophy in *Cartesian Metaphysics: The Late Scholastic Origins of Modern Philosophy*. Roger Ariew situates Descartes's thought within the context of late Scholasticism more generally in *Descartes and the Last Scholastics*.

3. One could take this as a point about the order of subjects in the scholastic Aristotelian curriculum. I do not mean to take issue here with Étienne Gilson's claim that we cannot "reconstruct St. Aquinas's teaching in the philosophical order proceeding from things to God rather than in the theological order proceeding from God to things" (*The Christian Philosophy of St. Thomas Aquinas*, 443–44).

4. See, for example, Caterus's treatment of the argument in the First Objections (7:94) and Étienne Gilson, *Études sur le rôle de la pensée médiévale dans la formation du système cartésien*, 207ff.

5. *De Anima* 431a20–21 and Aquinas's *Commentary* §§787–90, especially §789.

6. The sort of abstraction involved here is different from the sort of abstraction in the case of natural philosophy. Aquinas distinguishes the two sorts in *In Boetium de Trinitate* Q. 5, A. 3; Questions 5 and 6 of this work are found in Armand Maurer, trans., *The Division and Methods of the Sciences*. See also Vincent Edward Smith's Aquinas Lecture, *St. Thomas on the Object of Geometry*.

7. See Aquinas, *In Boetium de Trinitate* Q. 5, A. 3, Obj. 1 and Reply.

8. So, as Gilson points out on pp. 356–57 of his commentary on Descartes's *Discours de la Méthode*, the scholastics' commitment to *nihil est in intellectu nisi prius*

fuerit in sensu does not preclude them from agreeing with Descartes that "the ideas of God and of the soul have never been in the senses" (6:37; 1:129).

9. Aquinas writes in *In Boetium de Trinitate* Q. 6, A. 2, ad 5:

Clearly, we cannot know that God causes bodies, or transcends all bodies, or is not a body, if we do not form an image of bodies; but our judgment of what is divine is not made according to the imagination. Consequently, even though in our present state of life the imagination is necessary in all our knowledge of the divine, with regard to such matters we must never terminate in it. (Maurer, 71–72)

10. Aquinas writes:

An image is the starting point of our knowledge, for it is that from which the operation of the intellect begins; not that it passes away, but it remains as the foundation of intellectual activity, just as the principles of demonstration must remain throughout the whole process of science. This is because images are related to the intellect as objects in which it sees whatever it sees, either through a perfect representation or through a negation. Consequently, when our knowledge of images is impeded, we must be completely incapable of knowing anything with our intellect even about divine things. (Maurer, 71)

11. Translations of *De Veritate* have been taken from *Truth*, trans. Robert W. Mulligan, S.J., James V. McGlynn, S.J., and Robert W. Schmidt, S.J.

12. See Anton C. Pegis, "The Separated Soul and Its Nature in St. Thomas," 1:131–58.

13. It should be kept in mind here that for Descartes making a judgment is not bound up, as it will be for Kant, with bringing objects under general concepts.

14. This remains so even if, as Aquinas also held, the intellect could exist without a body, in some preternatural condition, such that it would require special assistance from God in order to function in a manner unnatural to it.

15. Paul Hoffman has argued in "The Unity of Descartes's Man" that Descartes understands the relationship of the human mind to its body on the model of form to matter. I agree with Hoffman that Descartes thought he could use this model (so we should take Descartes at his word when he invokes it), but as Hoffman allows (see 70–71), Descartes's understanding of this relation is different from that found in the classical Thomistic picture. Hoffman argues, intriguingly, that Descartes's account "is really the same as that of Ockham and Scotus" (74). While I think Descartes would have welcomed precursors with credible Aristotelian credentials, it is unclear to me that he thought the relationship had very much determinate content (for one thing, the Aristotelian form-matter distinction seems to be closely tied to the Aristotelian account of change as the actualization of something in potency insofar as it is in potency, and Descartes has little patience with this definition). That Descartes thought that the Aristotelian formulations, to the extent that one can make sense of them, were rather open and indeterminate is suggested by a remark Descartes makes on a related topic to his disciple Regius: "You must say that they [the mind and the body] are united not by position or disposition, as you say in your last paper—for this too is open to objection and, in my opinion, quite untrue—but by a true mode of union, as everyone agrees, though nobody explains what this means and so you need not do so either." (Descartes goes on to say that he himself

did explain the union in the *Meditations*. He seems to have in mind the Sixth Meditation. Nothing he says there, however, seems to bear on the appropriateness of the idea that the mind is the substantial form of the body.)

16. See DV Q. 3, A. 1, where Aquinas cites Augustine as an authority for this equivalence. See also ST I, Q. 15, A. 1.

17. In *Cartesian Metaphysics*, Jorge Secada argues that Descartes has "an *immanent* or *indirect* theory of ideas," by which Secada means that the objects of ideas are "mental entities which are the immediate and direct objects of mental acts" (84):

> It is in virtue of having these immediate or immanent realities as the immediate objects of its acts that the mind can reach external things mediately and extrinsically, not properly or directly by representation from these objects but through a true judgement that certain realities exist outside the mind. So contrary to the Scholastics, Descartes explains the intentional or representative character of ideas solely in terms of the existence within the mind of their objects. In so far as the mind succeeds in "apprehending" things outside it, it is through acts of judgement based on the fact that its immediate objects display objectively the essences or natures which are found actually in the substances that populate the world. (84–85)

One of Secada's main reasons for attributing this view to Descartes is that in the First Replies objective reality emerges (7:102–3; 2:75) as a genuine reality for Descartes and not, as it was for Suarez, a mere "extrinsic denomination."

I agree that the difference that Secada calls attention to between Suarez and Descartes is interesting, but I am not sure what to make of it. For one thing, I am not sure how exactly to locate the disagreement. From Descartes's side, I do not think he is denying that the sun's having a mode of existence in me is an extrinsic denomination with respect to the sun (that is, I do not think that Descartes holds that this mode of existence adds anything to the sun's reality). From the Thomistic Aristotelian side, I am not sure that the presence of new forms (species) in the mind, and so in the universe, does not add reality to the universe. The basic difference seems to be over what causal principles (if any) relate an idea's objective reality to the generation or causation of that idea. And I do not see how to get from this point that objective reality is in some sense more of a thing for Descartes than it was for Suarez, requiring a special level of efficient cause, to the thesis about the structure of cognition (i.e., the mind is only directly acquainted with immanent objects).

This may be because I do not understand very well what Secada means by an "immanent object." One thing I consider important here is the relation of the immanent object to the external object: are they the same thing with two modes of existence, or are they two different things standing in some other relation? It seems to me that Descartes wants the "one thing, two modes of existence" view: "By this [sc. objective being in the intellect] I mean that the idea of the sun is the sun itself existing in the intellect—not of course formally existing, as it does in the heavens, but objectively existing, i.e. in the way in which objects are normally in the intellect" (7:102–3; 2:75). If we posit a realm of distinct interior objects, what is the one thing that exists in the sky and also exists in (some) intellects?

I don't know whether there is a way of developing a theory of immanent objects so as to render it consistent with Descartes's claim that there is some single structure, say, triangle (or extension), that exists both in my mind and in the natural world.

18. I am grateful for discussion with Joe Hwang on this topic.

19. See Deborah J. Brown, "Descartes on True and False Ideas."

20. This is not the only reason people resist the view. There are other textual considerations that we need to consider in due course. One of these has to do with Descartes's treatment of "material falsity," which, on some interpretations, commits him to the existence of ideas lacking objective reality: how can an idea be some reality or structure existing objectively, if there are ideas that have no objective reality? To anticipate, my answer is that when Descartes suggests that the idea of cold, e.g., might be of nonbeing, he does not mean that it is an idea of pure nonbeing, but of relative nonbeing, e.g., the absence of motion in some body or bodies: there is plenty of structure—e.g., the particles—or reality to exist objectively in the idea.

21. I borrow this phrase from Tyler Burge, who used it in a different but related context.

22. See, e.g., Margaret Wilson, Descartes, chap. 6; John Carriero, Descartes and the Autonomy of the Human Understanding, part 2, sec. 9; Marleen Rozemond, Descartes's Dualism, 59–60; Lilli Alanen, Descartes's Concept of Mind, chap. 3; Hatfield, Descartes and the Meditations, 259.

23. For a helpful account of some of the positions that have been taken, see Margaret Dauler Wilson, "Descartes on Sense and 'Resemblance,'" especially 13–14.

24. So, for example, Richard Rorty, a commentator who I believe is generally sympathetic to the familiar view, has written that Descartes "allowed, I think, most of the work of changing the notion of 'mind' to be done under the table, not by any explicit argument but simply by verbal maneuvers which reshuffled the deck slightly, and slightly differently, at each passage in which the mind-body distinction came to the fore" (Philosophy and the Mirror of Nature, 57–58).

I think one can see something similar happening in Barry Stroud's account of the First Meditation in The Significance of Philosophical Scepticism. (It is not clear to me whether Stroud endorses the familiar view; his focus is on Descartes's external-world skepticism and not his conception of mind.) Stroud targets, as the key move in the First Meditation's skeptical dialectic, Descartes's claim that "he must know that he is not dreaming if he is to know something about the world around him" (14; see also 23) and presents a philosophically illuminating discussion of the legitimacy of this requirement, as a general condition of human knowledge about the external world (23–31). But Descartes himself signals neither the importance of this condition nor its controversial nature (as Stroud presents it, it is something that Descartes simply finds natural to assume). Thus, the most interesting philosophical work takes place offstage, away from the text, with the introduction of a controversial and crucial thesis that is not singled out for attention in Descartes's text (let alone developed and defended).

25. I believe both of these lines of interpretation, in effect, have Descartes uncritically extracting an ontological account of the structure of sensation from epistemological considerations—have Descartes moving from my ability to know that I am having a given experience while doubting whether bodies exist, to the conclusion that this experience does not essentially involve bodies. In fact, I think Descartes is rather careful about the relevant issues, and that when I am having a sensory experience but don't know whether I have a body, he thinks the proper way to describe my situation is as having an "as it were" sensory experience, leaving open whether I am having the genuine item or some simulacrum. See chapter 2.

26. It is worth observing that Descartes does not explicitly address the issue of whether one can have unconscious thoughts in the *Meditations*; the question simply does not come up. What does come up, more or less in passing, is the question of whether the mind can have *powers* of which it is not conscious (*conscius*) or that it does not experience (*experior*). The evidence for his position on this point is ambiguous. In the Third Meditation, he takes seriously, at least for the time being, the idea that I might have "some other faculty in me not yet fully known to me [*nondum mihi satis cognita*]" (7:39; 2:27) that produces sensory ideas in me; and when he ultimately rejects this suggestion in the Sixth Meditation (7:79; 2:55), it is not obvious that he is basing his rejection on the fact that we are not conscious of such a power. Later in the Third Meditation, however, he does argue that he does not have the power to sustain himself in existence, because if he did, he would be conscious of it, and he experiences no such power. But even here, it is not that this argument is supposed to rest on some general principle that the mind can become conscious of, in the sense of experience, each of its faculties. This is not to deny that Descartes would endorse some thesis making consciousness a requirement of mentality, perhaps something to the effect that mind is or at least can become aware of the exercise of each of its powers (but perhaps not each exercise of each power—consider the extremely rapid calculations that take place, according to Descartes, when I use the distance between my eyes to triangulate a three-dimensional visual field—let alone all of the "mental contents" involved in those exercises). In any case, whatever the exact relation is, Descartes does not develop it in the *Meditations* (let alone present it as a central commitment).

27. Notice that this is not to deny that I might have a nonsensory idea of the keyboard that I am unable to distinguish ("from the inside") from a sensory idea of the keyboard. It is one thing to ask, How can I tell whether or not I am sensing? and another thing to ask, What is the metaphysical structure of sensing?

28. The problematic that gives this family of terms their familiar meanings takes shape, in my view, only later in the early modern tradition. I offer an account of the evolution of the sense that we begin our epistemic life from behind a veil of ideas in "Berkeley, Resemblance, and Sensible Things."

Chapter One

1. This paragraph was prompted by Janet Broughton's stimulating discussion in *Descartes's Method of Doubt*, 28–32. I am trying to sketch a view of Descartes's project where less is asked of the skeptical doubt, and so some of the difficulties she raises (31) seem less pressing. See also Denis Kambouchner's *Méditations métaphysiques de Descartes*, sec. 15.

2. As we shall see below, I think the same thing holds of the dreaming doubt itself. There is a reason for the meditator to doubt that her senses make available a corporeal world (inasmuch as this belief is based on her natural inclinations and instincts—it is "a teaching of nature" and not something revealed by the natural light). But that this represents her actual cognitive/epistemic situation may be something that she only gradually comes to appreciate. For example, Descartes's discussion of the difference between a teaching of nature and what is revealed by the natural light, which does not take place until III.¶9, seems to be helpful to that end.

3. Another way to put this point is that God has made me so that these ideas are really ideas, that is, are forms of true and immutable natures or reality existing objectively, rather than pseudo-ideas, that is, specters of various kinds of nonentity.

4. See, e.g., Harry Frankfurt, *Demons, Dreamers, and Madmen*, 33ff.

5. Discussion with Roger Florka and Tyler Burge has helped to shape this paragraph.

6. I am grateful to Lilli Alanen for pressing these questions in conversation.

7. It might be suggested that the reason the meditator thinks this is that she is supposed to identify implicitly the real with the physical ("to be is to be a body"). Although some things that Descartes says encourage such a view (see, for example, 7:131; 2:94), I think we should resist attributing to the meditator a controversial metaphysical thesis. For example, Descartes supposes the meditator to be at least familiar with a reasonably sophisticated conception of God—see ¶¶9 and 12—and it is hard to believe that he is counting on her to assume that God is a corporeal being. I think the line of thought here is subtly but importantly different: the meditator is supposed to think that her entire *access* to reality (both material and immaterial, both physical and supernatural) is ultimately through her senses, so that if her senses did not accomplish at least roughly what she takes them to, then either she could not know any truth or, for all she would know, there might be no truth. In any case, what is most clear here is that the *root* of the problem, according to Descartes, is a tendency to try to understand the world through the senses and imagination, whether that leads to the outright identification of the real with the physical, or to the more complex position of the sort held by Aquinas. (In fact, I suspect that one thing that is going on in those places where Descartes associates the sensory/imaginative starting point with materialism is that he is trying to suggest that the scholastic dictum *nihil est in intellectu nisi prius fuerit in sensu* is only a step away from a materialism that Christian Aristotelianism would have found most unpalatable, a sort of guilt by association, if you will.)

8. Kambouchner also connects the naive view and the scholastic principle in *Méditations métaphysiques de Descartes*, 256.

9. The fact that my knowledge of arithmetic and geometry survives the dreaming doubt (¶¶8–9) can mislead one into thinking that the scope of the dreaming doubt is not supposed to be so extensive as to overthrow "everything." But they survive only on account of the work that is undertaken in ¶6.

10. I have in mind Frankfurt here, but I am not sure whether I am being fair to him. He argues in chap. 7 of *Demons, Dreamers, and Madmen*, "Mathematics in the First Meditation," that the meditator's naive empiricism affects his view of mathematics:

> It is somewhat imprecise to say, as I have just now and at other times said, that the First Meditation considers only material provided by the senses. It is more accurate to say that the First Meditation considers only material that the naïve empiricist, in behalf of whom its argument is conducted, *thinks* the senses provide. Now it is characteristic of such a person, as it is of those geometers who cannot free themselves of dependence on a drawn figure, that he is incapable of considering anything in decisive and unequivocal abstraction from a sensory context. He ascribes to the senses, therefore, many things that are not properly to be found in them. (61–62)

It is unclear to me where this treatment of the naive meditator's views of mathematics leaves her mathematical beliefs with respect to the epistemic principles Frankfurt develops in chap. 4 of *Demons, Dreamers, and Madmen*. Do her mathematical beliefs come under these policies? Is there a special set of policies in effect when one is studying geometrical diagrams? For further criticism of Frankfurt's interpretation, along what I take to be similar lines, see Margaret Wilson, *Descartes*, 38–40.

11. Descartes expresses a similar sentiment to Mersenne: "However, I am convinced that those who study my arguments [in the "Discourse on Method"] for the existence of God will find them the more probative the more they try to fault them. I claim that they are clearer in themselves than any of the demonstrations of geometers; in my view they are obscure only to those who cannot *withdraw their mind from the senses [abducere mentem a sensibus]* as I wrote on p. 38" (27 February 1637; 1:350–51; 3:53).

12. In the "Discourse on Method," Descartes links the scholastic doctrine *nihil est in intellectu nisi prius fuerit in sensu* to an inadequate picture of our knowledge of God and the soul:

> But many are convinced that there is some difficulty in knowing God, and even in knowing what their soul is. The reason for this is that they never raise their minds above things which can be perceived by the senses: they are so used to thinking of things only by imagining them (a way of thinking specially suited to material things) that whatever is unimaginable seems to them unintelligible. This is sufficiently obvious from the fact that even the scholastic philosophers take it as a maxim that there is nothing in the intellect which has not previously been in the senses. (6:37; 1:129)

13. For an example of what I mean, see Frankfurt, *Demons, Dreamers, and Madmen*, 36ff. For criticism of Frankfurt's view and a different account of the purpose of this passage, see Janet Broughton, "Dreamers and Madmen."

14. Perhaps only so long as I do not look too closely at what dreaming actually is (after all, as Descartes could be taken to suggest in the last paragraph of the Sixth Meditation, dreams have something to do with the brain). Perhaps it would be more accurate to say instead, I can suppose I am dreaming, or I am doing something near enough to dreaming.

15. Barry Stroud, *The Significance of Philosophical Scepticism*, chap. 1; Harry Frankfurt, *Demons, Dreamers, and Madmen*, part 1 (3–87); Margaret Wilson, *Descartes*, chap. 1 (1–49), especially sec. 6 (17–31), respectively. To this list, one might add the philosophically challenging account that Janet Broughton provides in *Descartes's Method of Doubt*, especially chaps. 3 through 5 (42–93). Broughton understands Descartes's employment of doubt to involve "high strategy," whereby the doubt is used to help show the absolute certainty of basic principles. The absolutely certain basic principles are subsequently used to trump various commonsense beliefs, which, although reasonable and likely, are nevertheless false.

16. What has happened here to mathematics, which, as Descartes tells us in the Fifth Meditation, he had previously regarded as the most certain truth of all? We are supposing that the subject matter of mathematics may be chimerical, which would threaten its truth and certainty.

17. There is a delicate issue here about whether the evil-genius doubt is required for the conclusion that body is chimerical, that is, to call into question the reality of corporeal nature (as opposed to the conclusion that bodies do not exist). I think that the answer to this depends on the meditator's perspective (which evolves in the *Meditations*). If one thinks, with a naive or scholastic meditator, that all our cognitive access to the world runs through the senses, then doubting the senses fundamentally should have this effect. On the other hand, if one thinks, with Descartes, and as I argue below is adumbrated in ¶¶6–7, that our nature gives us some cognitive access to the nature of extension ("corporeal nature in general"), then something more will be required to reach this conclusion, namely, the evil genius (I.¶9).

18. I take my interpretation to be in the spirit of Étienne Gilson's well-known remark in *Études*, 186, that "la première Méditation n'est plus une theorie à comprendre, c'est un exercice à pratique." See also Gary Hatfield, "The Senses and the Fleshless Eye."

19. I think the situation is similar with respect to the evil-genius doubt. The doubt embodies a genuine problem that needs to be addressed, but the force of the difficulty is something that, I believe, dawns only gradually upon the meditator.

20. That Descartes's primary interest in the dreaming doubt is not to point to the need for finding a way of distinguishing between dreaming and waking has been persuasively argued by Margaret Wilson, *Descartes*, 20ff.

21. Sarah Patterson has pointed out in an unpublished paper that Descartes does not explicitly give the dreaming doubt full rein until after I.¶6.

22. That the senses are (initially) thought to play some such role is indicated by the next sentence of the passage, which begins, "Or if perhaps they manage to think up something so new that nothing remotely similar has ever been seen before . . ."

23. But where did the pigment come from? Was it conjured up *ex nihilo*? Descartes would answer no, that our idea of extension is the form of a true and immutable nature, placed in our mind by God at its inception. Moreover, the idea comes from the world in this sense: true and immutable natures are prior to ideas of true and immutable natures, and a true and immutable nature is, Descartes says, a "something," not a "nothing" (V.¶6). But the idea did not come in through the senses, and no extended thing need really exist in order for God to give me an idea with such a structure.

There is, then, a way in which it is true for Descartes that cognition of true and immutable natures is embedded in the world, but we have to keep in mind that "world" includes more than what actually exists, and that the mechanism through which this embedding (nativism, backed up by our having a creator of a certain sort) is independent of the senses (and so is nonphysical). The comparison between thought and painting suggests both points. The limits of our cognition do not depend on what we have seen, and the structures we are related to in cognition do not presuppose real existence. I think he would have expected to encounter more resistance on the former point than the latter from the Aristotelian audience. They took the embedding of our cognition in the world to be thoroughly dependent on the senses; but many would have had no objection to unrealized essences or natures (which were sometimes understood as ideas in the mind of God).

24. The marks that Descartes keys on here, namely, the generality and simplicity of the things in question, are different from what he gives in the Fifth Meditation as

the mark of being a true and immutable nature, which involves my ability to make nontrivial judgments concerning something. The meditator is not yet ready for the second mark (which requires that she perceive clearly). Moreover, the generality and simplicity of the simple and universal things works, I think, against the plausibility of their having been taken in through the senses, which is the main point that Descartes wants to suggest now. There are true and immutable natures, e.g., God's, that do not seem to me to have these marks.

25. Marleen Rozemond has suggested to me in correspondence that this way of taking I.¶6 conflicts with Duc de Luynes's French translation (approved by Descartes), which runs:

> Et par la mesme raison, encore que ces chose generales, à sçavoir, des yeaux, une teste, des mains, & autres semblables, peussent estre imaginaires, il faut toutesfois avoüer qu'il y a des choses encore plus simples & plus universelles, qui sont vrayes & existantes, du mélange desquelles, ne plus ne moins que de celuy de quelques veritables couleurs, toutes ces images des choses qui resident en nostre pensée, soit vrayes & réelles, soit feintes & fantastiques, sont formées.

> [And by the same reason, while these general things, namely, eyes, a head, the hands, and other similar things, could be imaginary, it is nevertheless necessary to admit that there are things still more simple and more universal, which are true and existing, from the combination of which, no more or less than those from the true colors, all the images of the things which reside in our thought, be they true and real, be they imaginary and fantastic, are formed.]

According to Duc de Luynes's translation, the simple and universal things are "true/ real and existing." We might take this to mean that the simple and universal things, corporeal nature in general and attendant properties, have extramental existence; and we might understand this to mean that things possessing corporeal nature, i.e., bodies, have extramental existence, so that Descartes is claiming in the French version that reflection on the limits of intelligibility of the dreaming doubt suggests that at least some bodies must exist. (One might go on to argue that evil genius is required in order to question the existence of all bodies, and so the existence of an external, physical world.)

However, I think it must be admitted that it is not very clear what is being claimed for the simple and universal things in Duc de Luynes's French version. For example, it is not obvious that *existantes* refers to real existence as opposed to some other reality that these things may possess. For that matter, it is not obvious what it is for a universal thing, corporeal nature in general, to have real existence. One might think that corporeal nature in general has real existence only if some bodies exist, but such a line of thought is not explicit in the French version and seems to me to conflict with the tenor of Descartes's account of a true and immutable nature, where he emphasizes that there is something mind-independent about such a nature even if nothing exhibiting that nature should happen to exist outside my thought (see V.¶5; see also V.¶2). For these reasons, I am not inclined to allow the French version to override the impression that one gets from the Latin version that it would not follow from the way that the meditator is thinking about cognition in the second half of I.¶6 that any bodies exist.

26. "[W]hile arithmetic, geometry and other subjects of this kind, which deal only with the simplest and most general things, regardless of whether they really exist in nature or not" is CSM's rendering of *"atqui Arithmeticam, Geometriam aliasque ejusmodi, quae nonnisi de simplicissimis & maxime generalibus rebus tractan, atque utrum eae sint rerum natura necne, parum currant"* (French version: *mais que l'Arithmetique, la Geometrie, & les autres sciences de cette nature, qui ne traittent que de choses fort simples & fort generales, sans se mettre beaucoup en peine si elles sont dans la nature, ou si elles n'y sont pas*). A more literal rendering of the *parum currant* (or *sans se mettre beaucoup en peine*) might be that arithmetic and geometry *hardly care* (or *do not trouble themselves much as to*) whether the things they deal with exist in nature or not. The more literal rendering leaves open the possibility that these sciences do care, a little, about whether the things that they treat really exist. While others have wanted to take this suggestion seriously, I find it difficult to understand what it would mean for a science to care, but only a "little [*parum*]," about whether the things it is concerned with really exist or not.

27. For further discussion relating the *Rules* to the First Meditation, see my "Painting and Dreaming in the First Meditation," and sec. 26 of Denis Kambouchner's *Méditations métaphysiques de Descartes*.

28. In "Painting and Dreaming in the First Meditation," 29–32, I discuss Descartes's intriguing claim that the simple notions "form all the images of things . . . that occur in our thought." I argue there that this point is connected with the fact that, for Descartes, nativism does not lead him away from the physical world (to some realm of Platonic forms, for example) but rather to a deeper understanding of it (see note 32 of that essay).

29. It might be wondered whether the new consideration is being used to do something besides raising a question of the truth or reality of the simples that emerge from the discussion of painting. After all, he writes, "How do I know that he has not brought it about that there is no earth, no sky, no extended thing, no shape, no size, no place, while at the same time ensuring that all these things appear to me to exist [*existere*] just as they do now?" As I explain below, I think Descartes often uses the specter of the evil genius and dreaming doubt in tandem, using the evil genius to reinforce the dreaming doubt to the extent that they overlap. Further, I think that Descartes wants to make it explicit that the meditator is now (after the comparison between thought and painting) supposed to be doubting the senses fundamentally, and so doubting the existence of body. This, I think, was implied in the comparison between thought and painting, but not actually stated.

In other words, the evil-genius doubt is not required in order to doubt the senses fundamentally; this is the office of the dreaming doubt. A reasonably clear indication that Descartes does not think that the evil-genius doubt is required in order to doubt the senses fundamentally is that the meditator continues to be unsure whether body exists at the beginning of the Sixth Meditation, after she has worked through the response to the evil-genius doubt at the end of the Fifth.

30. The situation with imaginative and sensory ideas is more complex: imaginative ideas can fail to make reality available to the mind, but their components cannot; and sensory ideas make reality available to the mind, but do so only confusedly.

31. There is a deep connection between God's role as creator and his omnipotence: in Descartes's view, only an omnipotent being can create. Still, I find it helpful

to distinguish between a doubt that is located in my nature and a doubt that concerns factors external to my nature. Roughly, the former concerns whether when I am functioning well internally, I get on to the truth; the latter concerns what sort of external manipulation my cognitive processes might be subject to. As I explain in the text, it is philosophically significant that Descartes is focused on the former and not the latter.

32. Externalist or anti-individualist theories of cognition might offer a different approach for establishing a connection between the nature of a triangle and the idea of a triangle, not so much because the nature of the triangle is whatever my idea says it is, but rather because what the idea itself is is a reflection of a nature (and so, no nature, no idea).

33. I like the word *structure* in part because I find it natural to think of at least some mathematical structures as mind-independent (although that is not all there is, I take it, to being a "something" and "not merely nothing").

34. As Broughton has pointed out. See *Descartes's Method of Doubt*, 47.

35. See Broughton, *Descartes's Method of Doubt*, 49–54.

36. David Hume, *A Treatise of Human Nature*, edited by L. A. Selby-Bigge, with text revision and notes by P. H. Nidditch, 1.4.7, especially p. 269. I am grateful to Barbara Herman for helpful discussion surrounding the formulation of this point.

CHAPTER TWO

1. CSM's translation is "better known than the body," which is curious because it is natural to take "the body" to refer specifically to the human body, but the only body discussed in any detail in the Second Meditation is a piece of wax. The Latin is ambiguous, because there are no articles in Latin. I conjecture that CSM deferred to the French, which does have an article (*"le Corps"*). But in French it is very hard not to have an article, even where what one means to say is that the nature of the mind is better known than body. So I hear the French as ambiguous as well. (Descartes makes a remark about the heading at 3:297, but it does not seem to clear up the ambiguity.)

2. The point Descartes is making is not really a linguistic one. I think the reason the meditator did not know what the word *mind* means is simply that she was too confused about what a mind is, so one can shift, in this context, from not knowing what the words mean to not knowing what the underlying thing is.

3. Stephen Menn points out in *Descartes and Augustine*, 56 n. 37, that the word *nature* in the heading does not seem to be Descartes's, to judge by his instructions given in a letter to Mersenne (3:297). (The translators add the word *nature* at 3:172, but the Latin has simply *"de Mente humana."*)

4. This can be confusing to a modern reader because of an almost unconscious tendency after Kant to think of judgments in terms of the placement of an object under some general concept. It is not clear to me that Descartes's seeings or judgments must be articulated in this way; in any case, it is not something he emphasizes.

5. Two other examples that would be problematic in this setting: (1) "Two and three together make five," which does involve reality (what Descartes calls "true and immutable natures" in the Fifth Meditation), but seeing this takes work (ultimately,

I think, it rests on the so-called truth rule; see V.¶6). (2) "I am doubting," which also involves reality, but my doubting's being a real thing depends on my being a real thing, so it is more natural to begin, as Descartes does, with the cogito.

6. CSM translate this sentence—*Imo certe ego eram, si quid mihi persuasi*—as "No: if I convinced myself of something then I certainly existed." This makes it look as if Descartes is answering the question he just asked, "Am I not so bound up with a body and with senses that I cannot exist without them? But I have convinced myself that there is absolutely nothing in the world, no sky, no earth, no minds, no bodies. Does it now follow that I too do not exist?"—affirming, in effect, that I can exist without a body and senses. While it is possible that Descartes is doing that here— although I think it is too early for him to be claiming that he can exist without body—the Latin *imo* is compatible with a sharper break: i.e., however we answer these questions about whether I can exist without my body, this much is clear: if I convinced myself of something, I existed.

7. Strictly, she has considered only the possibilities that she deceives herself, in which case she must exist, and that an evil genius deceives her, in which case she must exist. But I think that whatever makes it true that if an evil genius deceives her she must exist, will also make it true that if anything else deceives her she must exist, and indeed that if deceived at all she must exist.

8. XI, 26, PL 41, 339–40, as cited by Étienne Gilson, *The Christian Philosophy of Saint Augustine*, 269 n. 22. See also Gilson's discussion (41–43) of Descartes's relation to Augustine.

9. These diagrams are adapted from Roger B. Nelson, *Proofs without Words*, 3–4. Nelson attributes the first to *Chou pei suan ching* (author unknown, ca. 200 B.C.) and the second to Bhāskara (twelfth century).

10. There are perhaps—as Descartes's objectors urged—other ways of seeing that I exist, for example from the fact that I breathe or from the fact that I walk, that will not work in the present context. They will not work because I am supposing that I do not have a body, and so that I am not breathing or walking. But part of what is at issue here is whether the context that Descartes has set up is arbitrary or not, so we might ask, are there other contexts in which one might come to see that one existed by noticing that one is walking or breathing? Descartes's general answer is this: that I breathe or that I walk is not as evident as that I exist. (In his view, my belief that I have a body is based on something like instinct—what he calls a "teach-ing of nature" [see VI.¶12]—and I must know that God is the author of nature be-fore I should embrace it.) In general, he thinks that there is something misguided in trying to argue from my breathing to my existing. To the extent that we share Des-cartes's sense of what is more evident than what, we will not find the context in which he is operating in the Second Meditation arbitrary.

11. For that matter, even after such impulses and natural propensities receive di-vine sanction in the Sixth Meditation, they continue to play an essential role in the structure of our beliefs.

12. If I were to speculate about how to connect the two, I would begin by focus-ing on the "must" and the "necessarily," which are conspicuous (almost awkwardly so) in the formulation "I must finally conclude [*denique statuendum sit*] that this prop-osition [*pronuntiatum*], I am, I exist, is necessarily true [*necessario est verum*]." They suggest at some level an awareness of being determined (an idea that comes up

again in a slightly different context in ¶¶5–6 in the Fifth Meditation). It may be that one cannot see that it has to be the case that I exist in the sense that Descartes intends without having the sense of one's being determined by something, or at least without one's being able, on reflection, to arrive at some sense of one's being so determined.

13. I am grateful to discussion with Paul Hoffman that significantly influenced this section.

14. I should say that I don't think everything that Descartes takes to be real operates. It seems to me, in particular, that part of the force of the claim advanced in the Fifth Meditation that there is a "true and immutable nature" of a triangle is that the nature is "real." I suspect that Descartes conceives of such structures as making a difference to the world and its possibilities (which difference I track through my judgments), but I don't think that a triangle (qua triangle) operates. Still, the fact that something does operate makes its status as a real thing more obvious.

15. E. M. Curley argues that the cogito involves a movement from action to agent (as opposed to some more general movement from property to bearer) in *Descartes against the Skeptics*, 92–93 and 155.

16. See Broughton, *Descartes's Method of Doubt*, 120–24; as Broughton points out (n. 19), Frankfurt, in *Demons, Dreamers, and Madmen*, 110, also denies that Descartes makes a claim about his essence in this passage. See also Norman Malcolm, "Descartes's Proof That His Essence Is Thinking."

17. I believe this is Broughton's view. See *Descartes's Method of Doubt*, 124 n. 19.

18. For an account of the relation between "logical" (i.e., genus-species) definitions and "physical" (i.e., form-matter) definitions in Aristotelian thought, see Aquinas, *De ente et essentia*.

19. I am not sure quite how to take Descartes's remark about his wonder at finding that "such faculties" were found in certain bodies. If we take "such faculties" to refer to the powers of moving, sensing, and thinking, then what he is saying seems odd on two counts. First, he has told us earlier in the paragraph that he attributes such powers to the soul and not the body, and such faculties are not really "found in certain bodies" except insofar as the soul is found in certain bodies. Second, it is unclear why we should be surprised at finding such faculties in bodies animated by the soul; this would be to express surprise at discovering that there were living things. (And I think it unlikely that Descartes is counting on the meditator's familiarity with his position that animals are machines, and so their vital functions can be explained mechanistically, without appeal to an animating principle or soul.)

Perhaps what is going on here is this: when Descartes writes "such faculties [*tales facultates*]," what he has specifically in view are faculties of self-motion, and what he is saying is that since such faculties (like the faculties of sensation and cognition) do not pertain to the nature of the body, he was surprised to find some inanimate bodies, e.g., magnets, with faculties of self-movement. If Descartes had in mind the self-motion of inanimate bodies, we could more easily make sense of his reported wonder. (On this reading, the plural *facultates* would be explained by Descartes's framing of the last part of the sentence in terms of "bodies" and not just a single "body"; its point would not be to refer back to the powers of sensation and of thinking along with the power of self-movement.)

20. I am grateful to Tyler Burge for raising this issue with me.

21. The other four uses occur at 7:25, l. 22; 7:29, l. 17 (to be considered later); 7:56, l. 16; and 7:57, l. 20.

22. Aristotelians would have denied that this is the case with physical parts of an animal—a hand that is severed from the rest of the animal's body is no longer really a hand; it is a hand in name only.

23. I think the *aliquid* is probably being used to contrast with the *nihil*, so that the force of the last clause is that I am a something as opposed to a nothing, i.e., something real. But it has to be admitted that *aliquid* by itself can be indefinite, as in "I am something or other."

24. *Animadverto* appears twice in the passage, in connection with the senses: at 7:28, ll. 28–29, Descartes writes *"multa etiam tanquam a sensibus venientia animadverto* [and also I notice many things as if coming from the senses]," which CSM translate as "and is aware of many things which apparently come from the senses," and at 7:29, ll. 11–12, *"Idem denique ego sum qui sentio, sive qui res corporeas tanquam per sensus animadverto* [And finally it is the same I who senses, or who notices corporeal things as if through the senses]," which CSM translate as "Lastly, it is also the same 'I' who has sensory perceptions, or is aware of bodily things as it were through the senses." *Animadverto*—literally, I turn my soul toward—on its face carries a sense of activity: it is something that the cognitive agent *does*. CSM's translation turns this activity into a state of being aware (something similar is going on with their translation of *sentio*—I sense—by "has sensory perceptions"). I think the more literal translation better captures Descartes's meaning. (A small point: the very first word of the First Meditation is *"Animadverti,"* and it seems to mean "observed" or "noticed.")

25. In two respects, it might be clearer to say that sensing is something that I undergo (rather than do). First, Descartes regards perception in general, as opposed to volition, as passive rather than active. He writes, for example, to Regius:

> Finally, where you say "Willing and understanding differ only as different ways of acting in regard to different objects" I would prefer "They differ only as the activity and passivity of one and the same substance." For properly, understanding is the passivity of the mind and willing is its activity; but because we cannot will anything without understanding what we will, and we scarcely ever understand something without at the same time willing something, we do not easily distinguish in this matter passivity [*passionem*] from activity [*actione*]. (3:372; 3:182)

In addition, we are (doubly, it seems) passive in sensation because of the role of the body. So in the Sixth Meditation Descartes writes:

> Now there is in me a passive faculty of sensing, that is, a faculty for receiving and recognizing the ideas of sensible objects; but I could not make use of it unless there was also an active faculty, either in me or in something else, which produced and brought about these ideas. (7:79; 2:55)

What it is important here for the outlook I am developing is that even if I am passive when I sense and therefore sensing is something I undergo, it still makes sense to think of sensation as a *power* or *ability* that I have that is related in certain (broadly speaking teleological) ways to my other powers and abilities.

26. Tyler Burge has pointed out to me that physical-world things/objects (the light, the noise, the heat) are conspicuously left out of the "seeming" formulations,

perhaps reflecting some sensitivity, on Descartes's part, to the difficulty of saying just *what* it is that one would be sensing if one were only "as it were" sensing. (One would be as-it-were seeing as-it-were the light, etc.)

27. Gary Hatfield helpfully points this out in *Descartes and the "Meditations,"* 132.

28. In II.¶15, Descartes links distinct perception to knowing what something is (in the sense of knowing its nature), implicitly contrasting this with knowing that something exists. There he claims that my cognition of myself is both (1) "truer and more certain" than my cognition of the wax and (2) "more distinct and evident." When Descartes develops these claims in the rest of the paragraph, it becomes clear that (1) has to do with my greater certainty of the mind's existence and (2) has to do with my greater purchase on my mind's nature. In addition, in the stretch of text in the Fifth Meditation that is addressed to "The essence of material things," Descartes begins by saying "I must consider the ideas of these things [viz., things that might exist outside me], in so far as they exist in my thought, and see which of them are distinct, and which confused" (V.¶2; 7:63; 2:44). He is doing the same thing in the wax discussion. I have not tried to figure out how this usage relates to the explanation of clarity and distinctness Descartes gives in *Principles* I, 45. For a helpful discussion, see Sarah Patterson, "Clear and Distinct Perception."

29. The word *nature* appears in both CSM's and Anscombe and Geach's translations of ¶12 (7:31 ll. 16–17). The underlying Latin here is *quid sit haec cera* (what is this wax) and not, for example, *natura*. Such a translation follows a well-established philosophical tradition; in the translations I supply, I stick to the more literal "What is it?" and make the connection between "What is X" and X's nature extratextually. My reason for doing so is not that I doubt that there is such a link, but rather to preserve the connection between this instance of a "What is it?" question and other instances in the *Meditations*, especially the Second Meditation.

30. See *Principles* II, 4.

31. Why not? Is it because the sensory properties are, on Descartes's telling, relational, and relational properties are not suitable candidates to characterize a thing's essence? That may be part of what is moving Descartes, but I doubt that it is the whole story. Mobility is an essential property of body, and it is not clear that it can be understood nonrelationally (or that Descartes thought it could). I think Descartes is probably thinking along the following lines. What a sensible property, say, a color, is is a particular configuration of matter in motion, say, a texture. What seems fundamental to a texture is its mechanical properties. (That the texture is able to reflect light particles so that they affect the nervous system of animals in a certain way does not seem fundamental.) It is important to note that to deny that sensibility belongs to the essence of body is not to deny that sensibility is a feature of body, either as a necessary concomitant of body in general (what the Aristotelians would have called a *proprium*) or else as an accident of some bodies (e.g., those that are so structured that they affect the nervous systems of animals). I see Descartes as concerned with the first claim in the wax passage, that sensibility is not a part of what it is to be body.

32. One might ask, in view of the fact that "It is the same wax that I see, touch, and imagine" (¶12), why does Descartes criticize "our ordinary ways of talking" when we say, for example, "we see the wax itself" (¶13)? The problem that Descartes sees with "we see the wax itself," it seems, is not that it is false to say this, but rather that it is misleading: someone might conclude from this that the way I know what

I am seeing is a piece of wax is that I see the thing (or the way I know that what I am touching is a piece of wax is that I touch it). Roughly, the problem is that by using the description *wax* to characterize what I am seeing or touching, I might conclude that part of the information I am receiving through the seeing or touching is that it is wax that I am seeing or touching. And, according to Descartes, that it is wax I am seeing or touching is not the sort of information I receive from the senses; knowing this requires the inspection of "mind alone" (or "the faculty of judgement which is in mind"). We would not be tempted to draw this (from Descartes's point of view, erroneous) conclusion if we used instead the more cumbersome "we judge [the wax] to be there from its colour or shape."

33. Can't one make the same point about coats that Descartes makes about the people? I think so, but I don't think it affects the point that Descartes is trying to make. He is drawing an analogy between getting from wax's sensible qualities and cognizing what the wax is, on the one hand, and getting from the coats to the human beings underneath, on the other. The movement from wax's sensible qualities to what the wax is is like the movement from the coats to the human beings underneath. Both involve judgment. One might then point out that on Descartes's view getting from the, say, black color of the coats to what the color is (say, the surface texture of a coat) also involves judgment. Be that as it may, Descartes's basic point here is that determining what something is is a matter of judgment.

34. It is easy to get the impression that when Descartes denies that the envisioned flow of images counts as a perception of what the wax is (or what body is), he is denying (something like) that the flow of images counts as a perception of the wax as wax, or the wax as a body (in the way that the notion of "perceiving as" is understood in modern perceptual psychology). In particular, in this passage, he would seem to be denying that animals, because they lack judgment, see the wax "as wax" or "as a body." (Descartes has other views about animals, which complicate the situation, but apparently they are not in play in ¶14.)

This may be correct, but I find the question difficult. It is hard to know how exactly Descartes's notion of what X is / the essence of X lines up with the notion of a perceptual category. What we seem to need judgment for, in Descartes's view, is (to speak metaphorically) to strip away from the surface so as to get at the bottom of things, to get at their essences or natures. The attribution of a perceptual category to a perceptual system or organism seems to be tracking a different ability—the ability to respond to a certain type (e.g., bodies as bodies). So it is not clear that when Descartes denies that he sees the people across the square, he is denying that he is set up so as to be responsive to the kind *people* (or at least the kind *body*). What he may be saying, in effect, is just don't mistake such responsiveness for some progress on the "what is it" front (i.e., don't mistake it for progress toward understanding what's at the other end of the seeing). I return briefly to this question in the next chapter.

35. See note 27 above.

36. Compare the use of "intellect" in the "three grades" passage where "mind alone" would have been called for at the end of ¶12 and presumably on into ¶13.

37. For further discussion of the interplay between Descartes's new conception of body and his new conception of mind, see Amy Schmitter, "The Wax and I: Perceptibility and Modality in the Second Meditation."

38. See ST I, Q. 78, A. 4, ad 5; this text concerns the cogitative and memorative

powers, associated with the interior senses; but there is no reason to think that the same would not hold good for the exterior senses. I owe the translation of *refluentiam* as "reflected influence" to Gilson, in *Christian Philosophy of Aquinas*, 471 n. 23.

Chapter Three (I)

1. In fact, he does not regard the rule as established until the Fourth Meditation. See IV.¶12, where Descartes affirms unqualifiedly, "If, however, I simply refrain from making a judgment in cases where I do not perceive the truth with sufficient clarity and distinctness, then it is clear that I am behaving correctly and avoiding error" (7:59; 2:41).

2. Later on, she will be able to describe her current condition as one of "certainty" but not "full certainty," as being able to have momentary *cognitio* of some truths but not enduring *scientia*.

3. Does this mean that the meditator is not, after all, "fully certain [*plane certus*]" that she exists or that two and three added together make five? Descartes tells us in the Synopsis that he explains in the Fifth Meditation the sense in which the "certainty even of geometrical demonstrations depends on the knowledge [*cognitione*] of God" (Synopsis, 7:15); it will be best to postpone discussion of this question until we get to the last four paragraphs of that meditation.

4. He does not say that judgment is an affective element, and he could easily be read as distinguishing judgment from volitions. "Some thoughts in this category [of thoughts that include more than the likeness of thing represented] are called volitions or emotions, while others are called judgements" (7:37; 2:26).

5. One can imagine problematic cases for the theory, e.g., afterimages or the colors of the back of the neck of a dove that appear in certain kinds of light (a standard example), in which case the object of the cognition does not exist. Thomas does not seem to have shown much interest in such cases, but some later scholastic philosophers did. For an instructive overview, see David Clemenson, *Seventeenth-Century Scholastic Philosophy of Cognition and Descartes' Causal Proof of God's Existence*, especially chaps. 1 and 2.

6. "By showing that not even chimeras contain falsehood in themselves, I hoped to forestall those who might reject my reasoning on the grounds that our idea of God belongs to the class of chimeras" (to Clerselier, 5:354; 2:376).

7. Could we say that the dimension in question is clarity and distinctness versus obscurity and confusion? This works for the adventitious ideas—these representations are obscure and confused—and the innate ideas, which are clear and distinct. I am not sure what to say, however, about the invented ideas.

8. Forms existing in various media, e.g., in light or in a mirror, also were supposed to have a spiritual manner of being.

9. I take Aquinas to be making the analogous point about intellectual cognition in a well-known article in the *Summa Theologiae* (ST I, Q. 85, A. 2), where he argues that the intelligible species is not what is (in the first instance) known, but rather that by which something external to the soul is known. I think it obvious that the same holds of the sensible species; i.e., the sensible species red is not what I see, but rather that by which I see some red thing in the world.

10. In formulating this issue and thinking about it, I have been helped by discussion with Joseph Hwang and his unpublished dissertation on Descartes on sensation. Hwang defends the intriguing proposal that perceiving a sensory idea for Descartes occupies roughly the same ground as receiving a sensible species did for Aristotelian scholastics.

11. See my "Berkeley, Resemblance, and Sensible Things."

12. It is possible that Descartes holds that when I imagine, I am doing something fairly close to looking at a disruption on my pineal gland. In ¶3 of the Sixth Meditation he writes that when the mind "imagines, it turns toward the body and looks at [*intueatur*] something in the body which conforms to an idea understood by the mind or perceived by the senses" (7:73; 2:51). Even so, I don't believe that Descartes thinks of me as using the imagination as a means to get information about the state of my pineal gland (if anything, the state of the gland is responsive to the exercise of imagination).

13. Modern sophistication about the speed of light calls for modification of this naive commitment: e.g., sometimes the source of what I see—the distant star—no longer exists, even if the light that it threw off does.

14. In *Essays on the Intellectual Powers of Man*, originally published in 1785, Reid writes, "In the popular meaning, to have an idea of anything, signifies nothing more than to think of it" (158). The modern position I have in mind goes by the name of *naive realism*. I am indebted to a seminar given by Tyler Burge and to Michael Thau's *Consciousness and Cognition* for exposure to some contemporary thought about perception. (While it seems to me that the view that Thau advocates in his book has some affinities with the view I have characterized as naive realism, there may be differences too.)

15. It is not very surprising for an Aristotelian position to show up in Descartes's account of his previous view. They often do, because Descartes often thinks of Aristotelianism as the outgrowth of an uncritical worldview that we all find ourselves burdened with at some point in our lives. In any case, the "properly and immediately" suggests that something quasi-technical is afoot.

16. As a matter of fact, I will suggest later, more in accord with Descartes's own view, according to which redness is some feature of body (e.g., some microphysical surface texture) and the idea of redness is that structure presented obscurely and confusedly to the mind.

I mention that there is a difference between this passage and the earlier ones in that Descartes suggests here that he did have some reason for embracing this much of his precritical view. (By "this much of the view," I mean the view without the resemblance component. Descartes does not think our belief in resemblance has anything to do with sound reason.) But, in the Third Meditation, he sees that entire precritical position as resting on blind impulse rather than reliable judgment. I don't think we should make very much of this discrepancy. "Blind impulses"—teachings of nature—turn out to have more going for them than it might first appear.

17. One might wonder whether the view of sensation I think is operative in the *Meditations* is consistent with the following well-known passage from *Comments on a Certain Broadsheet*, which suggests that even sensory ideas are innate:

[W]e must admit that in no case are the ideas of things exhibited [*exhibere*] to us by the senses just as [*quales*] we form them in our thinking. So much so that there is nothing in our ideas which is not innate to the mind or the faculty of thinking, with the sole exception of those circumstances which relate to experience: for example, that we judge that this or that idea which we now have present to our faculty of thinking is referred to a certain thing situated outside us. We make such a judgement not because the things transmit [*immiserunt*] the ideas to our mind through the sense organs, but because they transmit [*immiserunt*] something which gives the mind occasion to form these ideas, at that time rather than some other, by means of the faculty innate to it. Nothing reaches [*accedat*] our mind from external objects through the sense organs except certain corporeal motions, as our author [Regius] himself asserts in article nineteen, in accordance with my own principles. But neither the motions themselves nor the figures arising from them are conceived by us just as [*quales*] they occur in the sense organs, as I have explained at length in my *Optics*. Hence it follows that the very ideas of the motions themselves and of the figures are innate in us. The ideas of pain, colours, sound and the like must be all the more innate if, on the occasion of certain corporeal motions, our mind is to be capable of exhibiting [*exhibere*] them to itself, for there is no similarity between the ideas and the corporeal motions. (8B:358–59; 1:304)

This is a difficult passage. It is hard to know how to take the qualifications inherent in "there is nothing in our ideas which is not innate to the mind or the faculty of thinking, *with the sole exception* of those circumstances which relate to experience" (emphasis added) and "Nothing reaches [*accedat*] our mind from external objects through the sense organs *except* certain corporeal motions" (emphasis added). One way to understand this, which would be broadly congenial to the view that I take Descartes to be developing in the *Meditations*, is that there is some structure which is indeed "immitted" by the bodies that I sense, but much less is getting through than one might have thought, and the faculty of thought is correspondingly making a much larger contribution to the end product—so much so that we should view the end product as innate (more so in the case of proper sensible qualities than in the case of the common sensible qualities). But, I agree, other readings, less congenial to the view that I take Descartes to be developing in the *Meditations*, are reasonable. One might, for example, understand Descartes's talk of "occasion" to suggest that there is no content or structure—the medieval word for it would have been *form*—that is transferred from bodies into the mind: it is more a matter of one thing happening in the body giving the mind occasion to do another thing. My general sense is that Descartes wants to retain something of a basic picture in which the world does shape or form our thought, but also, principally on account of his scientific commitments, wants to emphasize that there is quite a bit of distortion (some at the level of the common sensible qualities and much more at the level of the proper sensible qualities), and when he makes this latter, dramatic (given the assumptions of the period) point, he sometimes does so in a way that makes it sound as if he is going back on the basic picture more than he means to.

18. Kant, *Critique of Pure Reason*, B276.

19. Whether it is better to think of this as part of the view of sensation I took into the *Meditations* or something that I learned in the wax passage is hard to say.

20. These past few paragraphs were prompted by some comments by Tyler Burge. While I am unhappy with the sketchiness of my remarks, I hope that they will at least help to bring out some of the complexity of the situation.

21. I must admit that early modern treatment of real existential judgments ("There is a man over there") in general strike me as odd. See Spinoza, *Ethics*, 2p17ff. (Gebhardt 2:104ff.; Curley 463ff.); Locke, *Essay*, IV.2.14 and IV.11; and Hume, *Treatise of Human Nature*, 1.3.7, especially n. 1, pp. 96–97.

22. Indeed, beings constituted similarly to us except that they could neither dream nor hallucinate would still face the question of how they come by their beliefs about sensory cognition and the beliefs about bodies they subsequently form on the basis of that cognition.

23. It can sound as if the only thing that Descartes has ruled out in the first sentence is the possibility that the cause of my sensory ideas should contain *more* reality formally than is found in those ideas, leaving open the possibility that there might be a noncorporeal cause at the *same* level of reality as corporeality that could be causing my sensory ideas; and then winnowing things down further in the second sentence, by appealing to my propensity to believe specifically that sensory ideas are produced by corporeal things. I think that this impression is misleading. Traditionally, the idea of eminent causation has to do with a cause containing the reality found in an effect in a higher form, so that God, for example, could cause fire without being hot, whereas causes that contain what is found in the effect formally, have what is found in the effect in the same form, as in procreation. So, in the tradition, to say that the cause of my sensory ideas contain corporeality formally, would be tantamount to saying that the cause of my sensory ideas is a corporeal thing, i.e., is a body.

24. To amplify, what ideas do, more or less well, is make available reality for us to think about, that is, to reason and make judgments about. So to have an idea is an accomplishment of sorts. The suggestion that what ideas do is to make available reality for us to think about is implicit in the many places in the *Meditations* where Descartes evaluates our various ideas of things, as in the First Meditation, where he does not quite say, but seems to imply, that my idea of corporeal nature in general is true and what the idea exhibits is real, or in the Second Meditation's discussion of the wax, where the question under discussion is how to make the structure presented to me by the perception of the wax clear and distinct. In the Third Meditation, Descartes suggests that sensory ideas are obscure and confused because of an issue having to do with the way in which they exhibit reality (we will come back to this in a moment); and says that because the idea of God exhibits so much perfection and reality, it is "the truest and most clear and distinct of all my ideas." In the Fifth Meditation, Descartes indicates that we can use the fact of our ability to make nontrivial judgments about a given subject matter as a sign of when an idea presents "a true and immutable nature," that is, a sign of when an idea is making available some mind-independent structure for us to think about, opposed to something fictive or made up.

25. It was Janet Broughton who brought to my attention the interest of the particular causal terminology that Descartes uses in connection with the production of sensory ideas.

26. For instance, Hatfield, in *Descartes and the "Meditations,"* 154–55 and 262, understands Descartes to hold that we have a natural impulse to believe the resemblance thesis.

27. Indeed, one of the things that emerge from his discussion of how our natures occasionally lead us astray is that such errors are an unfortunate by-product of the "best system that could be devised" (VI.¶22, 7:87–88; 2:60).

28. It is clear from III.¶8 that the meditator thinks of the resemblance thesis as something that nature teaches here:

> But the chief question at this point concerns the ideas which I take to be derived from things existing outside me: what is my reason for thinking that they resemble these things? Obviously, I seem to have been taught this by nature [*Nempe ita videor doctus a natura*]. (7:38; 2:26)

I think the point of the *videor* is to make room for, in line with VI.¶15, the thought that this may be something that she only thinks she has been taught by nature, but has not been really taught by nature. Admittedly, this sentence is difficult because the Latin *nempe* can mean either "namely" or something like "obviously" or "surely" or "evidently." If we take it as "surely," it can clash with *videor* (it appears to me that): this is surely something that I have been taught by nature, as opposed to this is something that I seem to have been taught by nature. I think the force of the sentence may be the following: surely one of my reasons for accepting the resemblance thesis is that this is something that I seem to have been taught by nature. I am grateful to Janet Broughton (who has expressed a preference for reading this passage in such a way that the *nempe* trumps the *videor*, so that it means "Surely nature has taught me this") for bringing this translation issue to my attention.

29. The meditator twice suggests that the belief appears to be a teaching of nature, at III.¶8 (7:38; 2:26) and VI.¶15 (7:82; 2:56).

30. There is, on Descartes's telling, a certain inevitability to our becoming attached to the resemblance thesis, which makes the process seem natural, in a sense of *natural* meaning "what transpires in the normal course of events." I am not sure to what extent Descartes himself recognizes this sense of natural, but the discussion of dropsy (which, as Descartes construes it, involves a misfiring of our natural instincts) suggests that he would agree that God bears some sort of responsibility here. I think two things might be said in response from the point of view of theodicy. First, it is not clear how blameworthy Descartes takes us to be for becoming attached to the resemblance thesis. What we may be blameworthy for is not reflecting and working our way out of it when the occasion arises (e.g., by insisting that red cannot possibly be a microphysical texture because red must resemble my idea). Second, I think there probably is, lying in the background, a general reason for why God set things up as he did (this is the strategy he follows in explaining why dropsy is allowed to happen). Descartes may hold, for example, that if God allowed our intellects to be bombarded with full information about our environment (that is, gave us clear and distinct sensory presentations of corporeal structure in all of its incredible detail instead of presentations that confused certain aspects of that structure), we would all perish before we figured out what to do with this information.

31. In his chapter from his *Essay* entitled "Of Clear and Obscure, Distinct and Confused Ideas" (II.29, especially 1–6).

32. Indeed, as the arbitrariness of the meditator's conception of the senses sinks in—at least as far as she is able to defend it at that point in the project—she begins to worry that she will never have reason to believe that anything else exists, except the entity shown to exist in the cogito argument. Although the topic called for at the end of ¶4 is specifically God's existence, the worry is voiced in the aftermath of the unhappiness with the resemblance doctrine that the course begun in the cogito will end

in solipsism. ¶13 frames the interest in the existence of other things quite generally—"But it now occurs to me that there is another way of investigating whether some of the things of which I possess ideas exist outside of me" (7:40; 2:27)—and, after developing the notion of objective reality, Descartes makes this remark in ¶16:

> If the objective reality of my ideas turns out to be so great that I am sure this same reality does not reside in me, either formally or eminently, and hence that I myself cannot be its cause, it will necessarily follow that I am not alone in this world, but that some other thing which is the cause of this idea also exists. But if no such idea is to be found in me, I shall have no argument to convince me of the existence of anything apart from myself. (7:42; 2:29)

33. A more literal translation would run: "Moreover, I have insisted on the small amount of certitude that we have concerning what those ideas that we take to come from without persuade us of, in order to show that not one of them allows us to have cognizance of anything as certain as the one we have of God."

CHAPTER THREE (II)

1. See Kant, *Critique of Pure Reason*, B630.

2. *Representation* is not a term that figures prominently in either Aquinas's or Descartes's treatment of these topics (although Descartes does use it at least occasionally in this context—see 7:136), and my use of it may seem to slant the discussion toward some sort of "representative" or "indirect" realism. That is not my intention. To have a representation of God, as I intend it here, is simply to have a way of thinking about God. I need a convenient term broad enough to cover two very different theories of our cognitive relation to God, and I mean to leave questions about the "directness" of these ways of cognizing God to the details of the underlying theories.

3. I am not claiming that Descartes is the first person in the history of Western theology to hold that we have direct cognition of God. One of the themes of Étienne Gilson's work is that there is a tradition of thought, to which Descartes belongs, along with Bonaventure, Anselm, and Augustine, which takes our cognition of God to be direct. Thinkers in that tradition tend to be friendly to the ontological argument and in the eyes of their critics confuse an effect of God with God. Gilson's conclusion seems accurate to me. Still, it is worth emphasizing this aspect of Descartes's thought, in part because it is a point on which he seems to have been especially influential locally: his work seems to mark the transition from a climate where Thomistic ways of thinking about our cognition of God dominate to a climate in which our cognition of God is taken to be unproblematically direct, albeit limited. (It is admittedly difficult to say how much of this change in thinking about our cognition of God is simply a consequence of the general demise of the doctrine of abstraction, as opposed to the influence of Descartes's work.) An even more important reason (for my purposes) for focusing on Descartes's thesis that we have direct cognition of God's essence is that, as I hope to show, this issue lies underneath much of what is going on in the Third Meditation and is important for understanding some of the more difficult (and interesting) aspects of that text and related passages in the

Replies and Objections and the correspondence. Keeping this issue front and center will be helpful for making sense of Descartes's thought on this topic.

4. In his stimulating article "Aquinas's Abstractionism," Houston Smit argues that, according to Aquinas, the agent intellect "produces [intelligible] forms by supplementing our sensible apprehension of the proper accidents of a thing with our innate cognitions of being and unity" (112), on the basis of certain passages where Aquinas says that there are certain "first principles whose cognition is innate is us" because of our intellect's relation to the uncreated truth (see p. 108 and the texts cited there). I am not sure that the texts that Smit discusses (which are admittedly very difficult) favor one of the following two pictures over the other: (1) Because of our intellect's relation to the uncreated truth, it has an innate tendency, given any sensory content, to immediately pull out being, unity, and so forth. (2) The content being and the content unity already exist in the intellect, and as soon as it receives sensory material, they are added to our conception of the sensory material. Smit, as I understand him, favors the second picture, but it seems to me that the texts he cites fit equally well with the first. The passage he cites on p. 109 from DV Q. 11, A. 1 (and discusses on p. 111) seems to me to square better with the first than the second picture; and the passages in which Aquinas relates the human intellect to the uncreated truth, it seems to me, are at least compatible with the view that what the relationship of our intellect to the uncreated intellect explains is why our intellect is primed to form immediately certain principles and conceptions upon being given sensory material, and not why it is able to arrive at that content without abstracting it from sensory material.

I am not sure to what extent this disagreement over how to interpret Aquinas on our cognition of the transcendental properties (being, unity, good, etc.) plays into the basic contrast I see between Descartes and Aquinas over their respective theories of human cognition of God.

5. Given a sufficiently different natural philosophy, it might be possible to specify the natures of at least some things in advance of encountering them. For example, once chemistry has gathered enough steam, it might be possible to specify in advance the nature of an element that has not been experimentally encountered. (Keith Donnellan made this observation during the discussion of a lecture given at UCLA.) This sort of thing seems to be possible in situations where one has certain primitive materials (electrons, protons, and neutrons) and a set of laws that determine their possibility of combination, as when scientists anticipate the discovery of an element in the periodic table. We noted in our discussion of the simple and universal things in the First Meditation (¶¶6 and 7) that Descartes's physics seems to have this feature, whereas scholastic natural philosophy does not.

6. I discuss Descartes's views on chimeras further in the first section of chapter 5.

7. The first way ends with "everyone understands to be God," but I take the force of that conclusion to be the same as the conclusion of the other four arguments.

8. My use of *real* and *chimerical* is borrowed from Locke's *Essay* II.30 (see, e.g., sec. 5).

9. I am grateful to discussion with Marilyn Adams here.

10. We will see in our subsequent discussion of Descartes's first argument for the existence of God that Aquinas does allow the blessed another mode of cognition in the next life, through which they are able to cognize God's essence. In this

mode of cognition, God's essence itself plays the role of an intelligible species (see SCG III, 51).

11. There are interesting questions here about how modal notions are supposed to be acquired from experience, which I leave to the side.

12. "Hard to see" but not impossible. After all, even Descartes allows that, because God is infinite and we are finite, we can only "understand" God but not "grasp" God (III.¶25). Descartes elaborates this point in various places (see, e.g., *Principles* I, 19, the letter to Mersenne of 17 May 1630 [1:152; 3:25], and the Fifth Replies [7:364–65; 2:252]), often metaphorically. It would be possible in principle, then, to hold that although we directly cognize God's essence, nevertheless owing to the fact that we are unable to grasp it fully or completely or adequately, we are unable to discern the relation of real existence to that essence. I am unaware, however, of any thinker who held such a position.

13. CSM's translation gives the impression, not supported by the Latin, that Descartes concerns himself with the meaning of the word *God* in the second half of this passage.

14. See the letter to Mersenne of 25 December 1639 (2:630; 3:142).

15. Aquinas writes:

Our natural knowledge begins from sense. Hence our natural knowledge can go as far as it can be led by sensible things. But our mind cannot be led by sense so far as to see the essence of God [*ex sensibilius autem non potest usque ad hoc intellectus noster pertingere quod divinam essentiam videat*: but from sensible things our intellect cannot stretch out to this, that it should see the divine essence]; because the sensible effects of God do not equal the power of God as their cause. Hence from the knowledge [*cognitionem*] of sensible things the whole power of God cannot be known [*cognosci*]; nor therefore can his essence be seen. But because they are effects and depend on their cause, we can be led from them so far as to know of God whether he exists, and to know of him what must necessarily belong to him, as the first cause of all things, exceeding all things caused by him.

Hence we know that his relationship with creatures so far as to be the cause of them all; also that creatures differ from him, inasmuch as he is not in any way part of what is caused by him; and that creatures are not removed from him by reason of any defect on his part, but because he superexceeds them all. (ST I, Q. 12, A. 12)

16. Aquinas writes:

[T]he divine substance is not so outside the range of the created intellect, as to be absolutely beyond its reach, as sound is to sight, or an immaterial substance to the senses: because the divine substance is the first intelligible, and the principle of all intellectual knowledge: yet it is outside the range of the created intellect, as exceeding its power, just as the highest sensibles are outside the range of the senses. Wherefore the Philosopher (2 *Metaph.*) says that *our intellect stands in relation to the most evident things, as the owl's eye does in relation to the sun.* Therefore the created intellect needs to be strengthened by some divine light in order to see the divine substance. (SCG III, 54)

17. Although Descartes does not explicitly advert to the idea of God in this passage, it seems clear that what makes present to the mind the perfections that one is

to be seized by and makes available the "ample and straightforward subject-matter" is the idea of God.

18. See also ST I, Q. 12, A. 4.

19. There seems to me a similar moment in Anselm's *Proslogion*. Toward the end of chapter 1, before presenting his ontological argument, Anselm writes, in M. J. Charlesworth, trans., *St. Anselm's Proslogion with A Reply on the Behalf of the Fool by Gaunilo and The Author's Reply to Gaunilo*:

> I acknowledge, Lord, and I give thanks that You have created Your image in me, so that I may remember You, think of You, love You. But this image is so effaced and worn away by vice, so darkened by the smoke of sin, that it cannot do what it was made to do unless You renew and reform it. (115)

For the ontological argument to make sense, I think, one needs to have at least in the background some view about how we come by materials we use in the argument—how God came to exist in the intellect (Anselm) or how his reality came to exist objectively in the mind (Descartes)—e.g., through God's creating his image in us (Anselm) or his endowing us with an innate idea (Descartes).

20. It is not clear that Descartes would endorse the claim that God does not belong to a genus. For Aquinas the claim that God does not belong to a genus is a reason for denying that God is a substance, as opposed to something subsistent, whereas Descartes holds that God is a substance *par excellence*.

21. Descartes's most explicit statement of this comes in a letter to Mesland of 2 May 1644:

> Just as it is an effect of God to have created me, so it is an effect of him to have put the idea of himself in me; and there is no effect coming from him from which one cannot prove his existence. Nevertheless, it seems to me that all these proofs based on his effects are incomplete, if the effects are not evident to us (that is why I considered my existence rather than that of heaven or earth, of which I am not equally certain) and if we do not add to them the idea which we have of God. (4:112; 3:232)

Although there is some room to wonder whether the addition of the idea of God is the addition of an "effect," the role of the Third Meditation's causal principle makes clear that Descartes is thinking of my idea of God as an effect (he also says in ¶13 that all my ideas, including my idea of God, are modes of thought).

I note that Descartes's viewing the idea of God as one of his effects may sit somewhat uneasily with his remark in the First Replies that the idea of the sun is simply the sun itself existing in the intellect: applied to God, this would suggest that the idea of God is simply God himself existing in the (e.g., human) intellect, i.e., the existence of something uncreated in the (e.g., created) intellect. Perhaps Descartes would claim that to infer from this that the idea of God is not an effect is to confuse the formal status of the idea of God (a mode of thought, caused by God) with its objective (or representative) status (an uncaused being).

22. To speculate, Descartes's doctrine of the creation of the eternal truths, if it takes within its scope the divine essence itself (this is a controversial matter, upon which there is little, if any, direct textual evidence), may be playing a role here. That is, it may be easier to maintain that there is a created idea that exhibits a created essence (even an infinite created essence) than a created idea that exhibits something uncreated.

23. Perhaps Descartes's creation of the eternal truths plays some role here. *Prima facie*, it makes for a chasm between God and all the essences, including perhaps his own, although this is contested. If God does create his own essence, then it is hard to see why God could not create an idea of that essence in a creature.

24. I suspect that Caterus has in mind an *ens rationis* without any foundation in reality. Descartes, for his part, thinks all *entia rationis* have some foundation in reality (see 4:349–50).

25. See Gilson, *Études*, 204, especially n. 3, and the Dalbiez essay cited there.

26. See also the letter to Regius of June 1642 (3:566–67) (paintings) and the response in the Second Replies to a suggestion in the Second Objections that we can reach an idea of God by a construction out of degrees of perfection (7:139).

27. See Second Replies (7:134–35; 2:97), where Descartes writes that "the objective perfection or reality of an idea . . . no less than the objective artifice [*artificium*] in the idea of a machine of very ingenious design, requires a cause," implying that the notions are different. See also the Third Definition in the appendix to the Second Replies, where Descartes, after defining "Objective reality of an idea" as "the being of the thing which is represented through [*per*] an idea, in so far as this exists in the idea," goes on to remark:

> In the same way it is possible to speak of objective perfection, and objective intricacy, and so on. For whatever we perceive as being in the objects of our ideas exists objectively in the ideas themselves. (7:161; 2:113–14)

I take Descartes to be expanding the scope of objective existence with this remark, so that it includes a thing's perfection and intricacy as well as its reality. But notice that something interesting happens with this expansion: it seems that I might have two ideas of the same thing, where one contained objective intricacy and the other did not. (Compare a NASA engineer's idea of the space shuttle to my idea.) So the objective intricacy of the idea is a function of more than the thing that is represented. (Perhaps it is the case that the engineer's idea and my idea have different "objects"; however, the wax discussion seems to suggest otherwise.)

28. The language "confront" is suggested by Descartes's comment in the First Replies that we should allow ourselves to be "seized [*capi*]" by God's perfections.

29. For related discussion, see Jean-Marie Beyssade's "The Idea of God and the Proofs of His Existence," especially 180–82.

30. The continuation of the passage is obscure: "Similarly, I could not conceive of an indefinite quantity by looking at a very small quantity or a finite body unless the size of the world was actually or at least possibly indefinite." I am inclined to take this to mean that in order for me to form a conception of an indefinite body, there has to be a nature with this property (something actually or possibly indefinite); a full explanation of my cognition of the indefinite would explain how I came to cognize such a nature; and while my looking at a finite body might be a step in this direction, it cannot be the full story.

31. CSM translate *a se* as "self-derived." I prefer "self-sustained" because this term better suggests, as Descartes seems concerned to emphasize, that the dependence involved is current.

32. See Spinoza's *Parts I and II of Descartes' "Principles of Philosophy,"* Part 1, Proposition 7, Scholium (Gebhardt 1:160–66; Curley 247–50).

33. I am going to use the thesis that there cannot be an infinite regress of movers interchangeably with the thesis that any series of movers must terminate (must have a first member), because I do not think Aquinas or Descartes had the conceptual resources necessary to distinguish between the two theses. I think the more important claim for them is that the series must terminate, so that there is a privileged (uncaused; self-caused) first member.

34. See ST I, Q. 46, A. 2, ad 7. I owe this reference to Anthony Kenny, *The Five Ways: St. Thomas Aquinas' Proofs of God's Existence*, 13, 41.

35. Some such idea, I think, is suggested by Caterus's description of Thomas's second argument as "the way based on the causality of the efficient cause." Caterus presents this as Thomas's description of the argument ("He [Thomas] called this way 'the way based on the causality [*causalitate*] of the efficient cause'"); Thomas's own description of it in ST I, Q. 2, A. 3 is "the way based on the nature [*rationem*] of the efficient cause."

36. See also Descartes's letter to Hyperaspistes, August 1641 (3:430, at "8") and the translators' explanation in n. 3 on p. 194.

37. It is not clear whether the infinite series of movers in *res extensa*, sketched previously, would be temporally extended or not, in Descartes's view. One might think that there is a time lag as motion is transferred through the various movers, or one might think that in some cases they push on one another instantaneously.

38. In Gilson, *Études*, 207–10.

39. Couldn't Descartes's attempt to ground the laws of motion in the immutability of God's will be viewed as a "path" from causal transactions within the realm of body to God? Well, the grounding depends on a heavy metaphysical commitment at the outset to the effect that God conserves the world in existence from one moment to the next. So Descartes's "path" does not arise out of reflection on the natural world and its causal order, but rather is the result of bringing a (prior) metaphysical apparatus to the natural world in order to interpret it.

40. See, e.g., ST I, Q. 104, A. 1 (see also ST I, Q. 44, A. 1).

41. So, for example, the articles in the previous note come after a lot of natural theology is in place. A. 104 depends on the claim that "God alone is Being by virtue of His own Essence, since His Essence is existence," which goes back to ST I, Q. 3, A. 4, which ultimately goes back to the Five Ways (see ST I, Q. 3, A. 1).

It is an interesting question to what extent Thomas thought it possible to organize our knowledge of God in a different way, less continuous with our knowledge of the natural order. Perhaps one could see the seeds of such a project in *De ente et essentia*, but, in any event, I take Aquinas's commitment to *nihil est in intellectu nisi prius fuerit in sensu* to be fundamental.

42. If I understand him, there is something tendentious about Descartes's comment that inquiring what something is before determining that it is, follows the "ordinary logic." As we saw above, Aquinas thinks that the methodology he uses to prove God's existence is one that is generally followed in showing existence. He writes in ST I, Q. 2, A. 2, "[I]n order to prove the existence of *anything*, it is necessary to accept as a middle term the meaning of the word, and not its essence, for the question of essence follows on the question of its existence" (emphasis added). In order to prove that a dog exists, I do not begin my demonstration from its essence, but rather a nominal definition, e.g., "Let's call a dog a four-legged, furry animal that wags its

tail and barks." Why? Aquinas is, I take it, working with the following picture of the usual progress of natural philosophy. One's earliest cognition of a thing proceeds in terms of nominal characterizations—"those furry, four-legged animals over there." After a certain amount of experience with the animals and reflection on that experience, we can begin to approach the question, What are those things, i.e., what is their essence or nature? (Although this is to go past the texts, I do not see anything in this procedure that would preclude us from revising our original nominal definition: we might decide on reflection that there are dogs that do not have fur after all but instead have hair.) It would be unusual then if we were in possession of the essence of a being before we were aware of its existence. So while it is true that "ordinary logic" requires that demonstrations of *finished* science move from causes to effects, from essences to the properties consequent on the essences, establishing that something exists is not a part of finished science but a preliminary step requisite in order to determine that something *exists*. (This picture concerns the relationship between our cognition of real existence and essence. It may well be the case that mathematics works differently so that we often possess a characterization of what we are looking for—say, the roots to such and such a polynomial—before we know that the roots exist.) And, as observed already, Descartes does not consistently follow a methodology whereby cognition of essence precedes cognition of existence. In the Second Meditation, the existence of the mind is established prior to, and used in the exploration of, what the mind is: the discussion continues by having the meditator ask, What is the thing whose existence was demonstrated through the cogito argument?

(Locke seems to be arguing, *Essay* III.6.19, that this general approach will fail, because we won't be able to determine the *propria* that are used in the nominal characterization of the thing unless we know its essence, but this criticism seems based on a mechanistic ontology, according to which kinds are not sufficiently independent for it to make sense for us to track them.)

43. I think Thomas would have agreed with this claim. He answers the question he asks in ST I, Q. 45, A. 5, "Whether it Belongs to God Alone to Create?" in the affirmative. There is a puzzle in that he later says, in ST I, Q. 104, A. 1, ad 4, that "The preservation of things by God is a continuation of that action whereby He gives existence, which action is without either motion or time" and goes on to answer the question raised in the next article, ST I, Q. 104, A. 2, "Whether God Preserves Every Creature Immediately?" negatively. Thomas attempts to reconcile this apparent tension in ST I, Q. 104, A. 2, ad 1. He appears to me to reconcile it in such a way that would leave him in basic agreement with Descartes's view that no secondary cause can sustain something in existence, but a full examination of this issue would take us too far afield.

44. For example, in 1p7 (Gebhardt 2:49; Curley 412), he argues from the fact that a substance cannot be caused by anything else, it must be self-caused, and so exists. If we tried to understand *causa sui* in Spinoza purely negatively, so that being *causa sui* amounted to being uncaused, this line of reasoning would not make sense. Moreover, in 1p25s Spinoza writes that "God must be called the cause of all things in the same sense in which he is called the cause of himself" (Gebhardt 2:68; Curley 431). See also 1p12, p24, and p34.

45. This point is related to the argument that Kenny offers on p. 10 of *The Five Ways* against interpreting Aquinas's first argument to take as its data "metaphysical

change," annihilation and creation, rather than ordinary natural change within the physical world. I agree with Kenny that Aquinas's arguments are based on natural change as opposed to metaphysical change and agree with his suggestion that Aquinas's "arguments would never have been interpreted in terms of metaphysical motions, one feels, had not the interpreters feared that the First Way, understood in terms of visible *changes*, had not been undermined by Newton's laws of motion" (10). Descartes was one of the first to feel the force of this issue: given the way the new science was developing, he realized that the arguments would have to be altered, although he also realized that the alterations would have to go farther than simply taking the old argument and applying to it metaphysical *explananda* rather than physical *explananda*. In my view, Descartes's importance for the subsequent tradition's handling of philosophical theology is bound up with these realizations.

46. It is unclear whether Descartes means that this is Arnauld's principal complaint in the Fourth Objections, or the principal complaint in the section of the Fourth Objections entitled "Concerning God."

47. Descartes's statements to the effect that anything that is *a se* will give itself all of the perfections of which it has any idea did not help matters here: they conjure up a picture of something deciding how it is going to make itself. Caterus and Arnauld both complain about this (7:95 and 207–8), and Descartes responds specifically to this point on 7:240–41.

Chapter Four

1. Part of the problem here is that our knowledge of body requires the interpretation of a constellation of natural cues and instincts, all of which are inherently confused, and some of which are, on occasion, misleading (see VI.¶¶16ff.). I discuss some of the relevant issues in chapter 3 (I), in connection with Descartes's treatment in III.¶¶8–11 of the resemblance thesis.

2. *ST* I, Q. 16, A. 1:

Now there is this difference between the appetite and the intellect, or any knowledge whatsoever, that knowledge is according as the thing known is in the knower, whilst appetite is according as the desirer tends toward the thing desired. Thus the term of the appetite, namely, good, is in the object desirable, and the term of the intellect, namely, true, is in the intellect itself. Now as good exists in a thing so far as that thing is related to the appetite—and hence the aspect of goodness passes on from the desirable thing to the appetite, in so far as the appetite is called good if its object is good; so, since the true is in the intellect in so far as it is conformed to the object understood, so that also the thing understood is said to be true in so far as it has some relation to the intellect.

3. This is true at least when the term *intellect* is being used in a narrow sense, so as to exclude will; sometimes *intellect* is used in a broader sense so as to be coextensive with mind. Thus Descartes writes at II.¶6, "I am a mind, or intelligence, or intellect, or reason" (7:27; 2:18). See note 15 below.

4. In *Descartes and Augustine*, Stephen Menn suggests: "The 'faculty of judgment' which the Meditator had originally claimed to perceive within himself (AT VII, 53),

consequently disappears. Since we judge freely or voluntarily, the only real faculty that might be called a faculty of judgment would be the faculty of *will* in its act of judging" (309). I agree with Menn that in some sense of "real faculty" there is only one real faculty here, but wonder whether we ought not think of judgment as a sort of subfaculty, in view of the fact that the true seems different (at least *in ratione*) from the good.

5. This formulation is rather well known. It figures prominently at one point in James Joyce's *Portrait of the Artist as a Young Man*.

6. In the letter, Descartes complains that this definition is only nominal (that is, only of the word *true*), "because no logical definition can be given which will help anyone to become acquainted with its nature [*ayde a connoistre sa nature*]." Descartes's point seems to be that truth is so basic and obvious that no one could be unfamiliar with it, and so the only thing that one could be doing when defining truth is explaining the meaning of a word. I find it more natural to think, with the Aristotelian tradition, of the definition of truth as a characterization of something in the world, not the meaning of a word, even if Descartes is correct that we all already must in some sense know what truth is to appreciate the definition. There are other sorts of characterizations of things besides those that, as it were, first acquaint one with the thing.

7. For one thing, truth involves a sort of conformity proper to the intellect, but the conformity brought about by the possession of an intelligible species is similar to that brought about in the senses by the possession of a sensible species.

8. Margaret Wilson writes on p. 141 of *Descartes*:

Descartes does not distinguish carefully enough the various *sorts* of mental representation (for example concepts and propositions), and he also tends to run together the notions of *falsity* and *error*. A mental image may fail to be true or false because it is a "mere image," not the sort of thing which has a truth value. A proposition cannot fail to be true or false (except in the special cases of vagueness or indeterminacy or failure of reference, etc.), but one may have a false proposition "in the understanding" without being in *error*, if he merely considers it, without taking it to be true. Descartes should say that the ideas "perceived by the understanding" may be (true or) false, but error arises not in the "perception," but in the affirmation.

9. One place in the *Meditations* where Descartes looks to invoke something propositional is at II.¶3: "this pronouncement [*pronuntiatum*], I am, I exist, is necessarily true whenever it is put forward by me or conceived in my mind" (7:25; 2:17). Descartes does sometimes say perceptions are true (see, e.g., IV.¶17; 7:62), but what this means, I think, is that the judgment that the perception inclines me to make is true.

10. It should be noted, to ward off a possible misunderstanding, that the *res* to which I am related in a true judgment need not be something that actually exists in nature: the "true and immutable natures" (e.g., the nature of a triangle) that Descartes discusses in the Fifth Meditation will do. Descartes writes of these natures that "even though they may not exist anywhere outside me [they] still cannot be called nothing," adding with respect to a triangle, "even if perhaps no such figure exists, or has ever existed, anywhere outside my thought, there is still a determinate nature, or essence, or form of the triangle which is immutable and eternal, and not invented by me or dependent on my mind" (V.¶5; 7:64; 2:44–45).

11. Descartes's hedge surrounding the idea of nothing is interesting. If we think of ideas as presenting objective reality and involving something like the traditional idea of a form, then there is strictly no idea of nothing: there is no reality being presented, and negations (for example, blindness) are not supposed to have forms (they are marked rather by the absence of form). What conception of nothing we form (!) is relative and does not strictly involve an idea of nothing (as opposed to ideas of various perfections, considered as absent). Descartes says in his conversation with Burman (5:153; 3:338) that strictly speaking there is no idea of nothing.

12. "Privation or lack of some cognition" (as translated by CSM; Anscombe and Geach translate it as "a privation—the lack of some knowledge") makes it sound as if Descartes has ignorance in mind, but this is misleading. As the Fourth Meditation unfolds, he makes clear that error is different from mere ignorance, and that ignorance (in the sense of absence of knowledge) is not (at least in general) a privation. If it is ignorance, it is the kind of ignorance that leads to false belief.

13. The meaning of *absolutum* in the passage is filled out by the *perfectiora* that occurred earlier, and *perfectio absoluta* involves a sense of perfection that is opposed to imperfection, according to Roy J. Deferrari's *A Latin-English Dictionary of St. Thomas Aquinas*. (See the entry under *absolvo* and the headings under *perfectio* to which this entry refers.)

14. To prevent confusion, we should note that Descartes uses *perfect* or *perfection* in senses other than the one that is correlative with privation. In ¶7, for example, we find this:

> [W]henever we are inquiring whether the works of God are perfect [*perfectum*], we ought to look at the whole universe, not just at one created thing on its own. For what would perhaps rightly appear very imperfect [*imperfectum*] on its own is quite perfect [*perfectissimum*] when its function [*rationem*] as a part of the universe is considered. (7:55–56; 2:39)

Imperfection here seems to involve a sort of internal disorder, but a disorder of the universe taken as a whole, and not of some individual part of the universe. In particular, I think the point that Descartes is making in the second sentence (perhaps somewhat awkwardly) is that whereas a universe consisting of, for example, only a slug might be internally disordered (for one thing, without air or water the slug would perish), a universe consisting of that same slug along with other things might be perfect. I don't think Descartes means to claim that whether or not a slug, taken as an individual, is perfect depends on what else is in the universe (after all, we could be working with an exemplary slug in both cases).

Perfection is also used by Descartes, as it was often used in this period, to mean being or reality. (Recall Spinoza's definition in the *Ethics*, "By perfection and reality I mean the same thing," 2d6.) This use of perfection is not contrastive with imperfection or incompleteness: the fact that I do not have the being, reality, or excellence of being able to speak fluent Finnish is not an incompleteness or imperfection in me; it is just an excellence that I happen to lack. Descartes uses perfection in this way in ¶8 of the Fourth Meditation:

> For although countless things may exist of which there are no corresponding ideas in me, it should not, strictly speaking, be said that I am deprived [*privatus*] of these

ideas, but merely that I lack them, negatively. This is because I cannot produce any reason to prove that God ought to have given me a greater faculty of cognizing [*cognoscendi*] than he did; and no matter how skilled I understand the craftsman to be, this does not make me think he ought to have put into every one of his works all the perfections [*perfectiones*] which he is able to put into some of them. (7:56; 2:39)

So sometimes the absence of a perfection (reality, being, excellence) renders something imperfect (and its craftsman culpable in a certain way), and in this case the absence will count as a privation; sometimes the absence of a perfection does not do this, and in this case the absence will count as a negation. Again, what determines whether the missing perfection counts as a privation or as a negation is whether the thing lacking the perfection is thereby internally disordered or only deficient in comparison with other, more impressive things.

15. Why the *praecise* here? I think that this may be because Descartes sometimes uses the word *intellect* to encompass either the entire mind or at least its core abilities. See, e.g., II.¶6: "I am, then, in the strict sense only a thing that thinks; that is, I am a mind, or intelligence [*animus*], or intellect, or reason—words whose meaning I have been ignorant of until now" (7:27; 2:18).

16. In a way, it comes up very obliquely in ¶15, when Descartes observes:

[God] could, for example, have endowed my intellect with a clear and distinct perception of everything about which I was ever likely to deliberate; or he could simply have impressed it unforgettably on my memory that I should never make a judgement about anything which I did not clearly and distinctly understand. Had God made me this way, then I easily understand that, considered as a totality, I would have been more perfect than I am now. But I cannot therefore deny that there may in some way be more perfection in the universe as a whole because some of its parts are not immune from error, while others are immune, than there would be if all the parts were exactly alike. (7:61; 2:42–43)

The point Descartes is making here is quite general, and would apply to fallible angelic beings as well as human beings. But the Sixth Meditation provides somewhat more detail as to why we do not have clear and distinct perception of everything about which we deliberate: this turns out to be a by-product of the specifically human way of being united to a body. Allowing beings who depend on confused and obscure ideas to get around in the world seems to be a cost of admitting human beings into the universe.

17. In thinking about Descartes's conception of the will, I have been helped by chap. 7 of Lilli Alanen's *Descartes's Concept of Mind* and by numerous conversations with Calvin Normore. In particular, my way of thinking about bidirectional powers is indebted to lectures and a seminar given by Normore.

18. As Lilli Alanen points out in *Descartes's Concept of Mind*, chap. 7, secs. 6–8, drawing on work of John Boler and Calvin Normore, later thinkers—in particular, Duns Scotus—disagreed on this point. I will consider this departure later.

19. Even if it were shown that the animals engage in some forms of primitive means-ends reasoning, I think the basic point may remain intact: the fact that we act in light of a conception of the good creates a certain indeterminacy in our practical life not found in the lives of animals. Perhaps the place to locate this indeterminacy

is more at the level of the specification of what one's happiness consists in than in the selection of means. But even our selection of means happens in a more reflective way than an animal's.

20. A natural question at this point is that if freedom is connected to reason in this way, then how is free will found in beings that do not cognize discursively, such as God and the angels? Aquinas discusses this in DV Q. 24, A. 3 (see especially Obj. 1 and Res. 1).

21. So although Descartes, unlike Aquinas, believes we can cognitively "touch" God's infinite essence in this life, there are aspects of God's being that seem even more remote from our comprehension on his view than on Aquinas's.

22. ST I, Q. 82 and Q. 83, and DV Q. 22 and Q. 24.

23. In "Descartes on the Will," Kenny writes, "According to most scholastics, the saints in heaven loved God voluntarily (because they did so willingly and not reluctantly) but not freely (since, seeing clearly the goodness of God, they could not do otherwise)" (24), and cites a text (n. 62), apparently from Gibieuf's *De Libertate Dei et Creaturae*, which contains an argument that will (*voluntatem*) is nothing but liberty (*libertatem*). As far as I can tell, Aquinas, at least, holds that free is coextensive with voluntary, even when the will is internally necessitated to something. This is because he holds that only external necessitation, i.e., force, is opposed to freedom. So, in DV Q. 22, A. 5, the third *ad contra* objection (in support of a negative answer to "Does the will will anything necessarily?") reads:

> Freedom is opposed to necessity. But the will is free. Therefore it does not will anything of necessity.

To which, after giving an affirmative answer in the main body of his response, Aquinas replies:

> Freedom is opposed to the necessity of force, according to Augustine, but not to the necessity of natural inclination.

(See also, e.g., ST I, Q. 82, A. 1, ad 1; DV Q. 24, A. 1, ad 20; *De Potentia* Q. 10, A. 2, ad 5. I owe these references to Paul Hoffman's "Aquinas on Threats and Temptations," 242 n. 30. Hoffman brought this point to my attention in commenting on an earlier version of this chapter.) Thus, I do not think that Aquinas would have accepted the argument that Kenny attributes to "the scholastics" that the blessed do not will freely because they cannot do otherwise. Further, in DV, confirmation of the blessed in the good is explained as a matter of strengthening specifically *liberum arbitrium*.

24. In her careful study "Descartes's Doctrine of Freedom: Differences between the French and Latin Texts of the Fourth Meditation," Michelle Beyssade argues that the *vel potius* does take back what came before, but the corresponding *ou plutôt* in the French version does not (206), because Descartes changed the [*b*] clause and the next sentence from the Latin version to the French version. Based on Beyssade's argument, the Latin version would be translated as follows:

> [*b*: Latin] it consists in this alone, that to a thing that the intellect puts forward for affirmation or denial or for pursuit or avoidance, we move (go) [*ita feramur ut a nulla vi externa nos ad id determinari*] in such a manner that we do not feel we are

determined by any external force. Nor is it necessary that I can move (go) [*me in utramque partem ferri posse*] both ways in order that I am free.

The French would be translated:

[*b*: French] it consists in this alone, that to a thing that the intellect puts forward for affirmation or denial or for pursuit or avoidance, we act in such a manner that we do not feel that any external force is constraining us [*nous agissons en telle sorte que nous ne sentons point qu'aucune force extérieure nous y contraigne*]. For in order to be free it is not necessary that I am indifferent as to the choice of one or the other of two contraries [*que je sois indifferent a choisir l'un ou l'autre des deux contraires*].

The Latin is difficult. One issue here is how much importance to attach to the passive form of *feramur* (we are borne or carried away) and *ferri* (to be borne or carried). If we take the passive form seriously, as Geach did and Kenny advocates, then we get something along the lines of CSM's "inclinations/inclined" (which I have followed in translations given in the main text). If we do not, as Beyssade suggests, so that, despite their passive form, these words carry an active sense, we get the above rendering (somewhat in the spirit of the Greek middle voice, Beyssade explains). It is beyond my linguistic competence to try to settle this translation issue. Duc de Luynes's French translation, as Beyssade points out, employs a different wording, and (I think) she takes this to be an indication of a change of mind on Descartes's part. I wonder, however, whether we could not equally well think that the new wording is the result of Descartes's recognition of some ambiguity or awkwardness in the original Latin and his request that de Luynes reword so as to avoid this ambiguity or awkwardness. If so, the French version, although different, still gives us reason to read the Latin in such a way that its meaning is basically the same as the French. (Kenny, to whom Beyssade is in part responding, uses the French version, in "Descartes on the Will," 18, to elucidate the meaning of the Latin. My point here is that this could still be a sound strategy, even though there is a change in wording in the French version.)

25. In "Descartes on the Principle of Alternative Possibilities," C. P. Ragland argues for a similar conclusion along somewhat different lines by focusing on the question of whether the will is determined by internal motives or external forces (see 386ff., 393). It is compatible with the will's being a bidirectional power (to use my terminology) that it be internally determined, but not compatible with its being a bidirectional power that it be determined by external forces.

26. I think Descartes is making a similar point when he criticizes Gassendi's claim that blame for error "does not seem to lie with the will for not judging correctly, so much as with the intellect for not displaying the object correctly" (7:317; 2:220). Descartes responds:

I would . . . like to know what is your conception of the nature of falsity, and how you think it can be the object of the intellect. My own view is this. Since I understand falsity to be merely a privation of the truth, I am convinced there would be a total contradiction involved in the intellect's apprehending falsity under the guise of truth; but this would have to be the case if the intellect were ever to determine the will to embrace what is false. (7:378; 2:260)

I think what Descartes may be saying here is this: while the intellect's achievement of something (e.g., the clear and distinct perception of some truth) could determine the will to embrace something, its failure to achieve something could not determine the will to do anything. So when Gassendi implies that falsity in the intellect determines the will, he must be (incorrectly) thinking of the falsity as something positive, as an achievement, rather than as a privation. An intellect's perception may be deficient, but that deficiency cannot itself be causally efficacious. (This is not to deny, of course, that it won't be somehow salient, as when the captain's absence is in a way responsible for the sinking of the ship. But still, the sinking needed help from the storm.)

27. See Alanen, *Descartes's Concept of Mind*, chap. 7, sec. 7.

28. See texts mentioned in note 23 above.

29. For instructive discussion of this text, see Alanen, *Descartes's Concept of Mind*, chap. 7, sec. 5.

30. See "Descartes on the Will," 29. Kenny points out that such an interpretation fits well with an earlier letter that Descartes wrote to Mesland (4:115–18; 3:233–34). Alanen criticizes Kenny's interpretation in *Descartes's Concept of Mind*, chap. 7, sec. 8, pp. 242–43.

31. Lex Newman makes the same point in "Descartes on the Will."

32. Margaret Wilson, *Descartes*, 144–45.

33. Margaret Wilson makes a related point on p. 147 of *Descartes*.

34. Descartes makes a similar point about truth and the intellect in the Fifth Replies, where he writes, "Since I understand falsity to be merely a privation of the truth, I am convinced that there would be a total contradiction involved in the intellect's apprehending falsity under the guise of truth" (7:378; 2:260), but the situation is not exactly the same (see note 16 above). Descartes, prompted by something Gassendi said, is interested in how the intellect is situated vis-à-vis the truth, whereas we are interested in how the will is situated vis-à-vis the truth.

35. I think Descartes's view is that the considerations advanced here, when supplemented by the discovery that God is the author of my nature, provide a full justification for the belief. I discuss this in detail in chapter 3 (I). This fact may have something to do with Descartes's First Meditation characterization of his former beliefs as "highly probable opinions—opinions which, despite the fact that they are in a sense doubtful, as has just been shown, it is still much more reasonable to believe than to deny" (I.¶11; 7:22; 2:15).

36. I mean this only as an analogy. For interesting discussion of the ins and outs of taking the analogy more literally, see Menn, *Descartes and Augustine*, 318 n. 14.

37. This point is related to themes that Gary Hatfield insightfully develops in "The Senses and the Fleshless Eye."

38. He writes before the geometrical presentation of the *Meditations*, appended to the Second Replies, "I think it is fair for me to reject out of hand, and despise as worthless, the verdict given on my work by those who refuse to meditate with me and who stick to their preconceived opinions" (7:159; 2:112).

39. In *Descartes*, Margaret Wilson, if I understand her, seems to suppose God's not being a deceiver entails that it is practically possible for me to avoid error. She writes:

Is it always within our power to avoid forming an opinion when we perceive that the evidence for or against the proposition in question is less than adequate? It seems to me that the answer is as follows: it is empirically implausible to suppose that our belief-formation is within our power to this extent . . .

If these observations are correct, it may be necessary to conclude that after all God is a deceiver in the restricted sense at issue in the Fourth Meditation. That is, He has not made me such that it is within my power to control my assent; there are times when I just cannot help believing against the evidence, or despite the lack of evidence. (149)

That fact that God allows me to be in circumstances where it would be practically impossible (empirically impossible) for me to withhold my assent to something I do not perceive clearly and distinctly is not enough to make God a deceiver. In such circumstances, there is a sense in which my believing is "not within my power," but there is another sense in which it remains in my power. It is not as if the circumstances extinguish one half of my basic "bidirectional" ability; they are just hostile to its exercise.

40. Michael Della Rocca argues in "Judgment and Will" that there is a circularity in Descartes's establishment of the truth rule:

But . . . *why*, for Descartes, should we assent only to clear and distinct ideas? Without a good reason for this claim, Descartes will lack an effective way of putting to rest his doubt about clear and distinct ideas. The reason Descartes offers seems to be: we should assent to clear and distinct ideas and should not assent to non-clear and distinct because clear and distinct ideas are guaranteed to be true and non-clear and distinct are not. (157)

Della Rocca goes on to suggest that by assuming this, Descartes is arguing in a circle:

To assert or presuppose at this stage of Meditation IV—i.e. prior to the final resolution of the doubt about clear and distinct ideas—that clear and distinct ideas are guaranteed to be true is, it seems, simply to beg the question in a particularly direct way. To presuppose or assert that clear and distinct ideas are true in the course of trying to remove doubts about clear and distinct ideas is to argue in a circle. (158)

The issues here are delicate and interesting, and I do not have the space here to discuss them fully. I do want to note that it is not obvious to me that the thesis that everything I perceive clearly is true figures directly in Descartes's claim that one should assent only to what one clearly perceives. (1) When I am in a cogito-like state—perceiving clearly, say, that I exist or that the three angles of a triangle sum to two right angles—I cannot but give my assent. It is important, I believe, to Descartes's view that this assent comes spontaneously and freely and is not constrained, but it is still necessary. I believe that this is the source of the idea that I am doing as I ought to do when I assent. (2) When I am not in such a state, and so there is still some lack of clarity in my grasp of the subject matter, I should not give my assent: I cannot find a determinative reason to go one way or the other; in such a situation, it seems to me that if I do wind up landing on the truth, it is an accident or a matter of luck. That is enough to show me I would be using my will improperly if I were to affirm or deny, because "it is clear by the natural light that the perception of the intellect should always precede the determination of the will" (¶12; 7:60; 2:41). I do not think either (1) or (2) depends on the truth rule. (Notice, in particular, it does not follow from (*a*) the claim that when I don't perceive something clearly, I can see that if I get on to the truth, this must be a matter of luck, that (*b*) when I do perceive clearly, I can see that if I get on to the truth, this is not a matter of luck, but a matter of some guarantee involving perceiving clearly the truth.) In addition, it seems plausible to me, as a philosophical matter, that I can tell that when I am in a cogito-like state with respect to some subject matter, e.g., seeing clearly before my mind's eye the demonstration of the Pythagorean theorem, I *ought* to assent to what I see so clearly (as I must in fact do, according to Descartes), and that I can also tell that when I perceive something only obscurely, e.g., "whether the thinking nature . . . which I am is distinct from . . . corporeal nature or identical with it" (IV.¶10), I *should* refrain from affirming or denying, without having any commitment to the truth rule.

Further, in order to establish the truth rule via a claim about assent and clear perception, it seems to me that all that Descartes really needs is the claim that I *must* assent to something that I perceive very clearly (regardless of how we sort out the question about whether I *should* assent): surely if God had made me so that I *had* to give my assent to a falsehood, he would be a deceiver. (And I find it even less likely that Descartes's claim that I *must* assent to what I perceive clearly depends on the truth rule, than that his claim that I *should* assent to what I perceive clearly depends on the truth rule.) It is not obvious to me that the argument that Descartes provides in the text for the truth rule depends on his views about how I should assent. He does not seem to argue for the truth rule until the last paragraph of the Fourth Meditation, ¶17; the argument he gives there is curious and does not obviously depend on any claims he has made about how things should or must go with my will (although, I agree, one might reasonably believe that such claims are lurking somewhere beneath the surface). In this regard, it is worth pointing out that the article about the truth rule (Part I, a. 30) in the *Principles* comes before the articles dealing with error and how to avoid it (Part I, aa. 31–36 and 43–44).

41. If this line of interpretation is correct, it raises a question about perception that is clear but not distinct. I think that clarity is supposed to compel judgment and suffice for truth, and one might think that lack of distinctness, like obscurity, is a defect.

CHAPTER FIVE

1. That Descartes is not adding to his substantive account of material things, but instead is making the rather more metaphysical point that there is an essence or nature that goes with my distinct conception of body, is presumably what is puzzling Gassendi, who, after citing a bit of ¶5, remarks with some puzzlement, "This is all you have to say about the essence of material things, for the next few comments are part of the same argument." Descartes's response, while unhelpfully general, is at least compatible with the idea that the substantive work concerning the nature of body was done elsewhere:

Here after quoting one or two of my comments, you say that that is *all I have to say concerning the proposed question*. This obliges me to point out that you have not paid sufficient attention to the way in which what I wrote all fits together. I think this interconnection is such that, for any given point, all the preceding remarks and most of those that follow contribute to the proof of what is asserted. Hence you cannot give a fair account of what I have to say on any topic unless you go into everything I wrote about all the other related issues. (7:379; 2:261)

2. If one wants to take the doctrine of the creation of the eternal truths on board: the prior decisions God has made about what essences to create leave open now anything that the essences admit of.

3. See my "The Second Meditation and the Essence of the Mind," and Marleen Rozemond, "Descartes's Dualism."

4. In *Le Monde*, Descartes moves directly from what we can distinctly imagine to what God can do. After describing an imaginary "new world," he writes:

Were I to put into this new world the least thing that is obscure, this obscurity might well conceal some hidden contradiction I had not perceived, and hence, without thinking, I might be supposing something impossible. Instead, since everything I propose here can be distinctly imagined, it is certain that even if there were nothing of this sort in the old world, God can nevertheless create it in a new one. For it is certain he can create everything we can imagine. (11:36; 1:92)

I think the *Meditations* fills this picture out. In order for God to create something, there must be an essence or nature for him to make actual. If there is some hidden contradiction in the new world concealed by some obscurity, then the world does not have an essence or nature. Conversely, the fact that I can (distinctly) imagine this world is a sign that what I am imagining has an essence or, as Descartes will call it in the *Meditations*, a true and immutable nature. I don't think this reflects a change in doctrine; rather, I think it was not appropriate to Descartes's purposes in *Le Monde* to detail the metaphysics of the connection between what we can distinctly imagine and what God can create. For an interesting critical discussion of this passage, see Ernan McMullin, "Explanation as Confirmation in Descartes' Natural Philosophy."

5. See Rozemond, "Descartes's Dualism," and the authors she cites there, for helpful discussion of this point.

6. Descartes is making a further point in the Fifth Meditation as well. In the Sixth Meditation, the closure of the mind's essence comes in a context where I already know that my mind exists and so there is no occasion to take up what to make of the nature of a (possibly) nonexistent being. In the Fifth Meditation, I am attempting to close off body's essence before I know whether any bodies exist. This gives Descartes the opportunity to argue that my grasp of extended being—as shown in my ability to make geometrical judgments—shows me that there *is* such an essence, and so my ability to grasp an essence does not depend on my knowing that any beings exemplifying them really exist. This point is important to Descartes's strategic objectives. If one can have access to an essence without knowing whether anything possessing that essence really exists, then the way becomes open in principle for an instructive argument from God's essence to his existence.

7. It is interesting to note that Descartes follows the other, more traditional path in the case of the mind: there I lock onto the entity shown to exist in the cogito exercise, and ask, What is it, this thing that I know exists? Relatedly, there seems to be

this difference between how Descartes "closes off" the essence of body at the beginning of the Fifth Meditation and how he "closes off" the essence of the mind in the Sixth. In the Sixth, he appeals in a quasi-traditional way to an existing being and what he notices concerning it: "Thus, from the fact that I know that I exist and at the same time I notice that nothing else at all belongs to my nature or essence besides the one thing that I am a thinking thing, I can correctly conclude that my essence consists solely in the fact that I am a thinking thing" (VI.¶9; 7:78; 2:54). In the Fifth, since he does not yet know that body exists, he appeals rather to the distinctness of his cognition and argues that there is a true and immutable nature going with it (V.¶¶5–6), and later, in the Sixth, that God could create such a thing (VI.¶1).

8. Didn't he do this when he in some sense suspended doubt to consider the wax in the Second Meditation? I don't think he did. The point of the suspension was not to be sure that there existed some structure whose essence we were exploring (as in the Second Meditation the cogito exercise introduces a real being that carries the exploration of its essence, so that subsequent discussion is built around the question, What is that being?). In this respect the discussion of the wax is hypothetical: if there are any bodies, this is what their nature looks like. Descartes has a different reason for temporarily suspending doubt: at that point we need to think about the role that senses play in our cognition of individual body, and it is difficult to see how we could reflect on this while continuing with the dreaming skepticism.

9. I owe this way of putting the point to Joseph Almog.

10. This connecting between distinct cognition and perspicuously grasping something's essence is not obvious from the account of *distinct* that he will later give in *Principles* I, 45, but even in that text there is an emphasis on separateness that one might reasonably feel comes with knowing what something is: after all, having a perspicuous representation of what X is will tell one a good deal about what X is not. (I am not claiming that Descartes always uses the word *distinct* in this way even in the *Meditations*.) It is not clear to me whether Descartes's use of distinct is novel or a development of something found in the tradition. For some traditional employments of the idea of distinct cognition, see the entries Gilson gives under the entry "Distinct" in his *Index Scolastico-cartésian*, 84–86, and Stephen D. Dumont, "Theology as a Science and Duns Scotus's Distinction between Intuitive and Abstractive Cognition."

11. "Let us consider the things which people commonly think they understand most distinctly of all" and "In short, [the wax] has everything which appears necessary to enable a body to be known as distinctly as possible" (7:30; 2:20).

12. In *Le Monde*, in the course of presenting his conception of the physical world as extension in motion, he also appeals to the imagination (see 11:31–36; 2:90–92; for helpful discussion, see McMullin, "Explanation as Confirmation"). This is consistent with Descartes's view that "body (i.e., extension, shapes and motions) can ... be known by the intellect alone, but much better by the intellect aided by the imagination" (letter to Elizabeth, 28 June 1643, 3:691; 3:227). Descartes discusses the difference between imaginative and pure thought concerning body at the beginning of the Sixth Meditation, ¶¶2–3.

13. See note 7 above.

14. Earlier in the *Principles* (Part I, aa. 66 and 68), Descartes indicates that our sensations can "be clearly perceived provided we take care in our judgements concerning

them to include no more than what is strictly contained in our perception—no more than that of which we are intimately conscious [*cujus intime conscii sumus*]" (8A:32; 1:217). This is, I take it, meant as an account of the sensation red, not as an account of what it is for a body to be red. And the point that Descartes is making is, don't take something that properly belongs to the sensation red, and project that onto the world, as if there is something in the world, over and above extension and motion, answering to the red experience. In a. 68, he writes:

> In order to distinguish what is clear in this connection from what is obscure, we must be very careful to note that pain and colour and so on are clearly and distinctly perceived when they are regarded merely as sensations or thoughts. But when they are judged to be real things existing outside our mind, there is no way of understanding what sort of things they are. If someone says he sees colour in a body or feels pain in a limb, this amounts to saying that he sees or feels something there of which he is wholly ignorant, or, in other words, that he does not know what he is seeing or feeling. Admittedly, if he fails to pay sufficient attention, he may easily convince himself that he has some knowledge of what he sees or feels, because he may suppose that it is something similar to the sensation of colour or pain which he experiences in himself [*apud se experitur*]. But if he examines the nature of what it is that the sensations of pain or color represent [*repraesentat*] as existing in colored body or painful part, he will realize he is wholly ignorant of it. (8A:33; 1:217)

The mistake that Descartes is worried about here is akin to concluding from a double image that there must be two objects. When I have a double image, there is something I am seeing, say, my hand, but if I were to conclude from this that there is some real "double" thing existing outside my mind—a pair of hands, moving together in perfect synchronicity—I would have a hard time understanding what this "double" thing is.

15. One might think that there is this difference between color and shape, which, as far as I can determine, is not in play: whereas one might think that any finite body must have a determinate shape, it is implausible to think that any finite body must have the determinate structure that allows it to be sensed. I am not sure that Descartes would endorse this difference, given his view that the first element of matter does not have "determinate shape or size" (11:24; Gaukroger, 17); in any case, he does not appeal to such a difference in his account of the essence of material things.

16. For an insightful treatment of the philosophical issues surrounding Descartes's conception of body as extension, see Calvin Normore, "Descartes and the Metaphysics of Extension." For a detailed treatment of the scholastic background to the theory of body, see Dennis Des Chene, *Physiologia: Natural Philosophy in Late Aristotelian and Cartesian Thought.*

17. For discussion of this connection see my "Substance and Ends in Leibniz."

18. Descartes himself does not think that there are any triangles we can sense, but allows that insensible triangles could exist (7:381). To be clear, although Descartes holds that there can be a true and immutable nature of a triangle when there are no really existing or actually existing triangles, he does not seem to hold that there could be such a nature if nothing at all existed. In particular, he holds that the eternal truths and essences depend on the will of God; this is not, however, a commitment that he chooses to go into.

19. I think Descartes holds the same view concerning our cognition of our own minds, although that does not happen to be in view at the beginning of the Fifth Meditation.

20. The "for all we know" may be too weak. I do not wish to take a stand on whether Descartes thinks that the existence of beings with eaglelike heads and lion-like bodies amounts to the existence of griffins. I do think that he holds that the existence of a thousand-sided figure amounts to the existence of a chiliagon, but that may have something to do with the fact that we grasp the essence or nature of a chiliagon in a way that we don't grasp the essence or nature of a griffin. I want to leave open the possibility, for either the abstractionist or Descartes, that in situations where we operate with a superficial characterization of a thing, we depend on the world to fix the essence or nature. If that is right, then perhaps we already know that our idea of a griffin does not suffice to mark out an essence or nature.

21. There is some controversy over whether the true and immutable natures belong to the ideas or the things. I think the text flows more smoothly and makes better philosophical sense when we take the natures to belong to things, e.g., to a triangle, as opposed to ideas, an idea of a triangle. In particular, attributing the natures to the ideas rather than the things would have involved too much of a category shift for Descartes not to signal it more clearly. Moreover, the nature of an idea is to be a mode of thought; and if one asks, Doesn't an idea have some additional nature in virtue of its objective reality? I think the answer would have to be, Only to the extent that its object (e.g., a triangle) has a nature. For a concise review of this controversy, see Willis Doney, "On Descartes' Reply to Caterus."

22. See Anthony Kenny, *Descartes: A Study of His Philosophy*, chap. 7, especially p. 155; Edwin M. Curley qualifiedly endorses Kenny's interpretation in *Descartes against the Skeptics*, 149.

23. I sometimes italicize the specification of the natures (or, in the case of *winged horse*, putative nature), although Descartes makes use of no such device himself. Although this makes for ease of reading, it can create the misimpression of a shift from the level of the world and its properties to a level of representation (words, concepts, dicta).

24. See, e.g., Kenny, *Descartes*, 154, on Descartes's treatment of "winged horse."

25. The Burman passage came to my attention through Curley's *Descartes against the Skeptics*, 149–50. I am also grateful to discussion with Calvin Normore for helpful discussion.

26. There is a wrinkle here that I would like to put to the side. Perhaps there are some predications—e.g. Socrates is sitting—that do not require a true and immutable nature. Perhaps the "mutable" subject—sitting Socrates—would be enough for this truth. If the judgment that a chimera has the head of the lion, however, is a truth at all, it would be an eternal truth, and so, I am supposing, would require a true and immutable nature.

27. This paragraph owes a lot to some gentle prodding by Tyler Burge, reinforced by the comments of Calvin Normore.

28. See Aquinas, *De Ente and Essentia*, chap. 3, where natures seem prior to their act of existing.

29. This paragraph was prompted by questions at a conference from Paul Hoffman and Martha Bolton, and discussion afterward with Ed McCann.

30. What I mean by "substantive addition" to a nature here is different from what Descartes means by "augmenting an idea" at 7:371; 2:256. Augmenting the idea means changing the idea. Noticing that new things flow from the essence of triangle does not change my idea of a triangle.

31. Or how one perfection in God is related to God's other perfections. I later briefly take up how to understand this flowing in the case of God, given that God is simple.

32. Conversation with Janet Broughton prompted this paragraph.

33. The problem discussed here is similar to one raised by Anil Gupta and discussed by Walter Edelberg in "The Fifth Meditation" (see 507 n. 23, and the appendix, 532–33). I have found Edelberg's paper generally helpful for thinking about this topic, as well as Margaret Wilson's "True and Immutable Natures," in her *Ideas and Mechanism*, 94–107, which is in large part a response to Edelberg's paper.

34. This paragraph was prompted by an objection raised by Tyler Burge.

35. Curley (*Descartes against the Skeptics*, 161–64)—in reaction to Guéroult's suggestion that the ontological argument is not independent of the Third Meditation demonstration of God's existence because the ontological argument depends on the doctrine of the true and immutable natures, which in turn depends on the truth rule, which in turn depends on the Third Meditation argument for the existence of God—argues that Descartes does not really want, in this setting, a principle linking clear and distinct perception to the truth, but rather a principle that allows us to affirm of the thing itself what we can affirm of its nature: "The connection [that Descartes is interested in] is between belonging to a true and immutable nature and being true of something, not between clear and distinct perception and truth" (162). Although there are texts that might be read this way, it is unclear what philosophical question Curley supposes to be at stake here; that is, it is unclear why someone might be worried about the step from affirming that "the nature of the triangle is such that its three angles sum to two right angles," to affirming that "the triangle is such that its three angles sum to two right angles." Further, it is not clear to me how to understand, on Curley's interpretation, the line of reasoning that Descartes presents in V.¶6:

> All these properties are firmly [*sane*] true [*verae*], inasmuch as they are clearly cognized by me [*quandoquidem a me clare cognoscuntur*], and therefore they are something, and not merely nothing [*aliquid . . . non merum nihil*]; for [*enim*] it is obvious that anything that is true is something [*illud omne quod verum est esse aliquid*]; and I have already amply demonstrated all those things that I clearly cognize are true [*demonstravi illa omnia quae clare cognosco esse vera*]. (7:65; 2:45)

I gather that this is one of the passages Curley has in mind when he suggests that Descartes "expresses himself . . . in a most misleading way" (163; Curley puts the remark in the context of an imagined conversation with Guéroult, but I take it that this expresses his own position), but it seems to me that the problem may go deeper. The *enim* suggests that Descartes means to be giving an argument here, and it is hard to figure out, on Curley's interpretation, what this argument is or how it fits into the overall dialectic.

As I explain later, I don't think the ontological argument depends on the Third Meditation demonstration in the way Guéroult thought; but I think this is because the ontological argument does not depend on the doctrine of true and immutable natures in the way Guéroult thought (and not because Descartes misidentifies in ¶6 the principle on which it depends). I discuss the relation between the doctrine of true and immutable natures and the ontological argument at the end of the second part of this chapter.

36. This refers back to III.¶6.

37. It would also be possible to take the meditator to be a philosophical, dogmatic materialist of some stripe, in effect dropping the "for all she knows": in a world with no body there would be no reality or truth. I think this interpretation is unlikely. In the next chapter, I try to characterize the philosophical commitments that Descartes supposes the meditator to enter the *Meditations* with. They seem to me more modest than this, coming down to the thought that without senses I would not have access to reality.

38. Calvin Normore has suggested this way of thinking about objective reality over the years in various discussion groups and conversations.

39. In chapter 3 (II), I tried to make this vivid, by comparing, somewhat fancifully, someone who has the idea of extension with someone who lacks the idea of extension and so is, as we might put it, geometry blind. Someone who has the idea of extension can see that the longest side of triangle subtends (indeed, must subtend) the greatest angle, that the sum of any two sides of a triangle is (indeed, must be) greater than the third, and so on. The idea makes available a subject matter in which that cognitive agent discerns such properties. A certain ability to make judgments, a certain understanding, comes with the idea. By way of contrast, a person who lacks an idea of extension, lacks the ability to make such judgments, lacks such an understanding. We might imagine trying to make good her deficiency by trying to explain to her what a triangle is: We could explain that a triangle has three sides, and we might provide her with a list of truths about triangles. We might add to the list, for example, the fact that the largest side is opposite the greatest angle, that any two sides are longer than the remaining side. Such a person might be able to make rudimentary inferences of a certain sort: she might think to herself, "So a square (whatever that is) has more sides than a triangle (whatever that is and whatever a side is)." But she isn't, as we are imagining her, really connecting with the subject matter, or what purchase she has with the subject matter is not just mediated by, but is exhausted by, our instructions. From her point of view, the subject matter isn't anything real: it's more of a game that we play with her. For example, from her point of view, the list of triangle facts is more or less arbitrarily long. The only coherence it has is a sort of surface consistency. It is not possible for her to make new substantive discoveries about geometry (to make discoveries that Kant would later count as synthetic as opposed to analytic). Her knowledge does not bottom out in anything: she cannot tell from what she has been told whether triangles have a nature or essence and so cannot even tell whether they are the sort of things that can exist.

40. When Burman responds to Descartes's Third Meditation claim that "there can be no ideas which are not as it were of things" with the objection that we have an idea of nothing, Descartes answers:

> That idea is purely negative, and can be hardly called an idea. In this passage the author [i.e., Descartes] is taking the word "idea" in its strict and narrow sense. We

do also have ideas of common notions, which are not, strictly speaking, ideas of things. But this is a rather extended use of the word "idea." (5:153; 3:338)

How do (a) fictive ideas and (b) adventitious (sensory) ideas complicate the picture? (a) Fictive ideas are (nothing more than) the product of our manipulation of some real structure antecedently existing in one's mind; they depend on some reality already being given to our mind. (b) Adventitious ideas, or at least some adventitious ideas, make available what reality they do only in a confused manner. They make reality available to my mind but only obscurely and confusedly. "Materially false" sensory ideas (see III.¶19) raise special issues here because they come across as positive while representing a species of nonbeing. Let's say, for example, cold in bodies is the slowness of certain internal movements and, further, that the slowness is an absence of reality—a nonbeing of some sort. Then the sensory idea of cold brings a nonbeing into the mind, rather than reality. What I think Descartes would say is that, while it is true (in the envisioned case) that the sensory idea registers an absence (namely the absence of motion), it does not register pure nonbeing: the sensory idea of cold imports into the mind the corporeal structure of slow-moving particles. In other words, there is a positive reality, the particles, required in the background in order to give shape to the absence of motion. For an illuminating discussion of issues related to this topic, see Brown, "True and False Ideas."

41. This view has been interestingly developed by Lawrence Nolan in "The Ontological Status of Cartesian Natures." Nolan gives two main reasons for not taking these natures as primitive, in effect reading them in a Platonist manner. First, it is inconsistent "with Cartesian dualism by admitting created substances that are distinct from mind and bodies" and, second, "it commits Descartes to an account of natures which violates the method of universal doubt. If in the Fifth Meditation Descartes were positing abstract Platonic entities, then he would be guilty of smuggling in things which are at least as susceptible to methodic doubt as corporeal subjects" (171). I don't see a violation of dualism, so long as each of these natures is either a mental nature or a corporeal nature (it is not clear it is right to call these natures "created substances"—a created substance may be what ensues when certain of these natures exist formally). I think the texts from the *Principles* that Nolan cites in note 15 raise delicate issues too complicated to take up here.

42. I am grateful to helpful discussion with Janet Broughton, who brought this point to my attention.

43. Might it be the case that this "must" is to be located more in her, the judger, than in the structure, the triangle, as in "Given this structure I find myself confronted with, I must judge that its largest side is opposite its greatest angle"? This is hard to say. On the one hand, it would bring the sense of determination involved in ¶¶5 and 6 of the Fifth Meditation more in line with the "necessity" hovering about the conclusion of the cogito, "I must finally conclude that this proposition, *I am, I exist*, is necessarily true whenever it is put forward by me or conceived in my mind" (II.¶3; 7:25; 2:17). But, on the other hand, it would have to be reconciled with Descartes's comment, in the course of the ontological argument, "It is not that my thought makes it [that God exists] so, or imposes any necessity on anything; on the contrary, it is the necessity of the thing itself, namely the existence of God, which determines my thinking in this respect" (V.¶11; 7:67; 2:46).

44. On some interpretations of Descartes's doctrine of eternal truths, what's at issue is not whether one of these structures could have been different but whether there is such a structure. On these interpretations, God could have made it not be true that a triangle has three angles summing to two right angles by not creating the essence of a triangle, but God could not have made it not be true by creating that essence in a different way, so that, say, the three angles of a triangle sum to four right angles. See Calvin Normore, "Descartes's Possibilities."

45. Curley, *Descartes against the Skeptics*, 163, interprets the remark this way.

46. For further discussion of real or essential definition, see Secada, *Cartesian Metaphysics*, 57–59.

47. The point is somewhat technical, so let me give the Latin:

Praeterea, medium demonstrationis est quod quid est. Sed de Deo non possumus scire quid est, sed solum quid non est, ut dicit Damascenus. Ergo non possumus demonstrare Deum esse.

48. The Latin is:

Ad secundum dicendum quod cum demonstratur causa per effectum, necesse est uti effectu loco definitionis causae ad probandum causam esse: et hoc maxime contingit in Deo. Quia ad probandum aliquid esse, necesse accipere pro medio quid significet nomen, non autem quod quid est: quia quaestio quid est, sequitur ad quaestionem an est. Nomina autem Dei imponuntur ab effectibus, ut postea ostendetur: unde, demonstrando Deum esse per effectum, accipere possumus pro medio quid significet hoc nomen Deus.

The English translation I have used omits the *ut postea ostendetur* ("as will be shown later") in the English translation. The Latin gives I, Q. 13, A. 1 as the reference.

49. I am working with Aquinas's (what seems to me) simple and intuitive picture of the difference between *an est* and *quid est*. For a sense of how sophisticated and involved issues surrounding this topic became in the fourteenth century, see Stephen D. Dumont, "The *quaestio si est* and the Metaphysical Proof for the Existence of God according to Henry of Ghent and John Duns Scotus."

50. The Latin reads:

Praeterea, illa dicuntur esse per se nota, quae statim, cognitis terminis, cognoscuntur: quod Philosophus attribuit primis demonstrationis principiis, in I *Poster.*: scito enim quid totum et quid pars, statim scitur quod omne totum maius est sua parte. Sed intellecto quid significet hoc nomen Deus, statim habetur quod Deus est. Significatur enim hoc nomine id quod maius significari non potest: maius autem est quod est in re et intellectu, quam quod est in intellectu tantum: unde cum, intellecto hoc nomine Deus, statim sit in intellectu, sequitur etiam quod sit in re. Ergo Deum esse est per se notum.

Because they feel anachronistic to me, I have removed from the English translation of this objection and its reply the quotation marks that indicate use-mention distinctions.

51. The first is that not everyone understands by the word *God* a being than which none greater can be conceived; some, for example, have thought God to be corporeal.

52. The Latin reads:

Dato etiam quod quilibet intelligat hoc nomine Deus significari hoc quod dicitur,
scilicet illud quo maius cogitari non potest; non tamen propter hoc sequitur quod
intelligat id quod significatur per nomen, esse in rerum natura, sed in apprehensione intellectus tantum. Nec potest argui quod sit in re, nisi daretur quod sit in
re aliquid quo maius cogitari non potest, quod non est datum a ponentibus Deum
non esse.

53. This discussion was prompted by a question that Alvin Plantinga asked me in
a colloquium at Notre Dame; the account of Aquinas's position sketched here owes
something to a comment made by John O'Callaghan after the talk.

54. In their exchange over what it takes to "exist in the intellect," which seems to
end up involving only the comprehension of the phrase "that than which nothing
greater can be thought," Anselm and Gaunilo do not worry that there might be no
thing (essence, nature, reality) that corresponds to this construction.

55. "Anselmian" here is just a convenient label; in particular, I don't mean to be
taking a stand on whether the argument that Aquinas criticizes is a fair representation of Anselm's argumentation.

56. Blake D. Dutton makes a similar point in "The Ontological Argument: Aquinas's Objection and Descartes's Reply."

57. Why not just synthetic? Well, the judgments in question happen to be independent of sensory experience. But to stay with this anachronism, the nontrivial
character of the judgment is what Descartes is focused on, along with a seeing that
something must be so, where the "must" can be the "must" of "The butler must
have done it!" There are, of course, other features of the Kantian view of judgment,
e.g., his views about combination and synthesis, and through those views, his further views about the contribution of the judging subject to its judgment, that are
alien to Descartes's outlook. Even so, I find it helpful to think of Descartes as reflecting the same sort of phenomena that Kant was, our ability (to put it neutrally) to
make substantive, nontrivial judgments. According to Descartes, this ability reaches
to the subject matters of the mind and God, as well as to body.

58. What I am trying to resist in this paragraph is the idea that since God himself
is simple, all our judgments concerning God must ultimately be analytic. For Descartes, I take it, seeing how two of God's individual perfections are linked is a substantive matter of seeing how two different aspects of divine perfection fit together.
It is not, I think, a matter of our simply unpacking the concepts of the perfections,
any more than seeing that the three angles of a triangle sum to two right angles is a
matter of unpacking the concept of a triangle.

One might ask, then, what for Descartes is doing the work in philosophical theology that construction in intuition does in geometry for Kant. I speculate that at
bottom lies our sense of ourselves as dependent beings—my idea of myself as the
obverse of my idea of God (see III.¶24)—which is bound up with a set of commitments that leads to the claim that there must be an absolutely independent being
that is self-sustained in some positive sense of being self-sustained. (This sort of reasoning seems to be lying in the background of Descartes's presentation, based on
God's power, of the ontological argument in the First Replies at 7:119.)

59. The reason for the hedge "different or fuller" is Descartes's characterization of the relation of what he says in the First Replies:

> All this is manifest if we give the matter our careful attention; and it does not differ from anything I have written before, except for the method of explanation adopted. This I have deliberately altered so as to appeal to a variety of different minds. (7:119–20; 2:85)

60. I discuss the general distinction between necessary *per se* and necessary by reason of something else in "Spinoza's Views on Necessity in Historical Perspective."

61. There are other issues, which Descartes is not interested in, about the logical structure of the formula, roughly arising from the fact that a given perfection might be compatible with some perfections and not others. I believe that there was a fairly standard theory of perfection that handled these worries. Some perfections by their very nature were supposed to be limiting (if you were hot, you couldn't be cold; if you were here, you couldn't be there), and others were not. Moreover, the nonlimiting perfections were supposed to be compatible. I think Descartes is asking us to consider the being with all the nonlimiting perfections.

62. The idea that there are different ways of explaining—making plain—various aspects of God's nature (in the way that there are different ways of explaining why the Pythagorean theorem is true) and that some people will find some explanations more helpful than other explanations is a natural one. In Descartes, this natural idea seems bound up with his antiformal cast of mind: we are endowed with ideas of extension and of God that are very rich in content. There are various ways to elucidate that content. It is not clear to me that there is supposed to be some privileged formula that explains the content of the idea of either. In some settings it may make sense to start with a being that has all compatible perfections; in others, with a supremely powerful being; in still other contexts, with other formulas. In other words, it is not clear to me that there is a "definition" of divinity (or, for that matter, of extension) in the sense that Jean-Luc Marion seems to assume in his challenging and insightful "The Essential Incoherence of Descartes' Definition of Divinity." The approach here is closer to the one suggested by Jean-Marie Beyssade in "Idea of God," especially 180–82, and Kenneth P. Winkler in "Descartes and the Names of God."

63. What Descartes seems especially concerned to show is that characteristics we associate with God are not some arbitrary collection but have an internal coherence (a rhyme and reason to them). That they do have coherence, in his view, ultimately comes out in how we can reason about God and the sorts of inferences we can make concerning God. This shows us that there is a God essence or nature underlying our cognition of God, something that can really exist. One can imagine a different sort of challenge to God's possibility based on the logical consistency of the various perfections that God is supposed to have. Leibniz discusses this issue in "That a Most Perfect Being Exists," the first of "Two Notations for Discussion with Spinoza" (Loemker, 167–68; Gerhardt 7:261–62). Whether these two sorts of challenges to God's real possibility—one based on the thought that there might be no structure uniting God's perfections and the other based on the internal consistency of these perfections—come down to the same thing in the period is hard to say. To a modern ear, they feel like different sorts of worries. The thought that our idea of God is

arbitrary in a way that it does not bite on anything real seems to point in one direction (this is a way of taking Kant's criticism of rationalist theology). The thought that our idea of God is contradictory seems to point in a different direction (those who think there is an inconsistency in God's being the creator of this world, with all of its pain and suffering, and God's being omnipotent and benevolent, seem to be worried along these lines).

64. I have in mind Spinoza's reasoning for God's existence in 1p11 and 1p11s (Gebhardt 2:52ff.; Curley 417ff.), in particular the second demonstration he gives for 1p11. There he argues that no other being besides God can settle the question of whether God exists.

65. This last point seems to bear on an issue concerning the relation of the Fifth Meditation's argument for the existence of God to the Third Meditation's argument for the existence of God, raised by Martial Guéroult. Guéroult has contended that the order of reason dictates that the Third Meditation argument come before the Fifth Meditation one, because the latter depends on the former. While a full review of this controversy lies beyond the scope of my interests, let me simply note that one of the factors influencing Guéroult is the appearance of the truth rule in ¶6, which makes it seem that the ontological argument presented in ¶¶7–12 is dependent in some way on the central metaphysical results already established in the *Meditations*. Guéroult also connects this issue with a text from the Fourth Replies in which Descartes expresses a strong preference for the causal arguments: "But I think it is clear to everyone that a consideration of efficient causes is the primary and principal way, if not the only way, that we have of proving the existence of God" (2:166; 7:238). Gouhier, Kenny, and Curley (see the references given by Curley in *Descartes against the Skeptics*, 157–64, especially 157 nn. 20 and 21, on which I rely here) have rejected Guéroult's view, noting that Descartes presents the ontological argument as a freestanding demonstration in other venues, e.g., in the appendix to the Second Replies and especially in the *Principles* (in fact, in the *Principles* the ontological argument is placed before those corresponding to the Third Meditation demonstrations).

Descartes could in principle have used the ontological argument in the Third Meditation in place of the argument(s) that he did use there, but it would have been less illuminating with respect to what was on the meditator's mind at that juncture. As she was struggling with the evil-genius doubt, part of what she was trying to understand is why (some of) her cognition lines up with truth or reality. Learning that her idea of God could have come only from God provided her with a more direct, less circuitous, answer than the following: I see that a supremely perfect being has to exist; I see that it created everything else, including me; I see that it is not a deceiver, etc. This sort of argument will be less effective with, in particular, a meditator who is deeply suspicious of the suggestion that human beings have any access to God's essence. Thus, Descartes is fairly careful to develop the Third Meditation reasoning in a way that avoids any explicit commitment to the claim that our distinct cognition presents us with true and immutable natures—e.g., in ¶25 he claims only that the idea of God is true, and not that the nature presented by the idea is true. Conversely, when he does present the ontological argument, he deems it better to develop it in a setting where the meditator has available a larger understanding of what is going on as she works through the argument.

Depending on the context, one proof for a given conclusion may be more insightful and illuminating than another equally compelling proof for the same conclusion. In particular, the proof of God's existence that Descartes offers in the Third Meditation is more illuminating in that context than the ontological argument would have been. I think Descartes attaches great importance to such considerations (in part because he thinks of a proof as a set of cues for getting someone to see that something is so—more along the lines of a musical score than of truth-preserving abstract or formal object). So I agree with Guéroult that Descartes's way of proceeding is deliberate. But I disagree that the ontological argument depends on the truth rule in such a way that it cannot provide an autonomous means for enabling someone to see that God exists. Rather, I think that the ontological argument is not the right place to begin for someone who is preoccupied with the concerns of the Third Meditation. In particular, as soon as such a person exits the clear perception of God's existence afforded by the ontological reasoning, questions will flood in: Do my clear and distinct ideas plug me into truth/reality? How is it possible that I should have an idea that plugs me into as much truth/reality as my idea of God does? Until she is able to answer these questions—which requires covering more or less the ground covered by the Third Meditation proof for the existence of God and the doctrine of true and immutable natures—her position will not be fully stable.

66. Here I am in broad agreement with Janet Broughton, *Descartes's Method of Doubt*, 184–85.

67. Broughton, *Descartes's Method of Doubt*, chaps. 6 and 7.

68. There is something that is *prima facie* puzzling about Descartes's procedure here (in V.¶15; 7:70; 2:48; see also the passage cited in the letter to Regius, at 3:64–65; 3:147). One way to put the puzzle is this. Descartes holds that (before I recognize that God exists) upon exiting a cogito-like state where I see that three angles of a triangle sum to two right angles, I am to doubt that three angles of a triangle sum to two right angles. But if this is so, why does he think that upon exiting a cogito-like state where I see that God exists, I should continue believing that God exists? Is it because my remembered cogito-like state in which I saw that God exists is somehow more powerful than my remembered cogito-like state in which I saw that the three angles of a triangle sum to two right angles? That hardly seems likely. But if not, then why does the evil demon call into question the former and not the latter?

My answer has to do with how the second doubt functions. What is supposed to give it its efficacy, I think, is the absence of some understanding on the part of the meditator—the meditator's failure to understand her origin. This fits well with the shift in the First Meditation in ¶9 from a doubt based on "an omnipotent God" to ¶10, where Descartes says he will not "argue with" those who "would prefer to deny the existence of so powerful a God rather than believe everything else is uncertain," but that he will instead "grant them that everything said about God is a fiction" (7:21; 2:14). He then proceeds to cast the doubt as arising from the meditator's ignorance of her origin: "the less powerful they make my original cause, the more likely it is that I am so imperfect as to be deceived all the time." Now, what exactly does the meditator need to do in order to make good this deficiency? According to Descartes, she needs to perceive clearly certain things about her origin (that her nature is owed to a supremely perfect being, who is not a deceiver). Once she has succeeded in doing this, the doubt is rendered inefficacious. (This is not to deny that more ordinary worries associated with memory might apply at some point. If her philosophical theology becomes rusty, at some point we are going to think she no longer possesses her well worked-out understanding of her position as a knower, more or less in the way that I no longer now have the grasp of real analysis that I once did.)

I allow that there are other ways of understanding Descartes's second doubt—perhaps tying it more closely to the threat of an evil demon than to an absence of understanding one's position as a knower—that makes seem arbitrary his willingness to rely on remembered cogito-like states involving the perception of God's existence while he is unwilling to rely on (before he has recognized that God exists) remembered cogito-like states involving the perception of geometrical truths. I think it is a virtue of the interpretation offered here that we can (in my view) make some headway with this appearance of arbitrariness in what Descartes says in V.¶15 and in 3:64–65.

69. See, e.g., Louis Loeb, "The Cartesian Circle," 200–203.

70. This discussion was prompted by a helpful comment by Ken Winkler.

71. See Janet Broughton, "Skepticism and the Cartesian Circle," 599–600, and *Descartes's Method of Doubt*, 185, respectively.

CHAPTER SIX

1. I find it hard to say what language best captures Descartes's idea that there is a corporeal side to me as well as a cognitive side. I have used the word *part*, which is suggested by Descartes's comment in the Third Meditation, "I am now concerned only and precisely with that part of me which is a thinking thing" (7:49; 2:34). As will emerge, what I—the full human being—am is a cognitive agent united to a body. Does this make two elements (the mind, the body) "parts" of the whole? So we need to hear *part* in a broad enough way to be consistent with this underlying view.

2. Paragraph 8, which reads as a sort of preface to the account of human nature, runs:

> But now, when I am beginning to achieve a better knowledge of myself and the author of my being, although I do not think I should heedlessly accept everything I seem to have acquired from the senses, neither do I think that everything should be called into doubt. (7:77–78; 2:54)

3. When Arnauld asks him about a sheep's reaction to a wolf, Descartes replies:

> When people take a fall, and stick out their hands so as to protect their head, it is not reason that instructs them to do this; it is simply that the sight of the impending fall reaches the brain and sends the animal spirits into the nerves in the manner necessary to produce this movement even with the mind being unwilling [*vel mente invita*], just as it would be produced in a machine. And since we experience this for certain in our own selves, why should we be so amazed that the "light reflected from the body of a wolf onto the eyes of a sheep" should equally be capable of arousing the movements of flight in the sheep? (7:230; 2:161)

4. One way in which to draw the line between what Descartes would and would not have found problematic here is in terms of efficient causation. Aristotelian efficient

causes are fundamentally end pursuers ("no agent acts unless intending an end"). The intention of the end is, according to them, prior to the exercise of their agency, which is why Aquinas terms the final cause the cause of the causality of the other causes. By way of contrast, there is no end prior to a mechanistic efficient cause, directing the exercise of its agency: everything that a sheep does falls out of the conservation laws, as those laws apply to the internal motions of the sheep's body and the motions in the surrounding environment. If the mechanist is correct about how the sheep's body works, even a scholastic Aristotelian would agree that the sheep's pursuit of the end, say, safety, as it flees the wolf, is merely epiphenomenal. I discuss this contrast in more detail in "Spinoza on Final Causality" and in "Substance and Ends in Leibniz."

5. This emphasis on our ability to "trick" animals is interesting, because it suggests that one of the things on Descartes's mind is the way we can use animals as our tools, as it were. If someone were to propose, for example, that a computer chess program in some sense displays sufficient plasticity to satisfying his criterion for rationality, I think Descartes might counter that someone who was intimately familiar with the program could "trick" it. This perhaps suggests a similar line of response, with respect to the linguistic criterion, to a computer that passed the "Turing test": Would it still pass the test if one had full access to the program?

6. For a different reading of this passage, see Gordon Baker and Katherine J. Morris, *Descartes' Dualism*, 158.

7. We will consider this passage from ¶6 more carefully later.

8. I don't think it is intended as a full account, but rather the beginnings of an account, with a special focus on the imagination's role in knowledge. See note 19 below.

9. For the sake of clarity I am going to translate *imaginatio* as "imagining" instead of "imagination," to preserve a distinction between the activity of imagining and the faculty or power of imagining. See also ¶3, which begins, "Besides this, I consider that this power of imagining [*vim imaginandi*] which is in me, differing as it does from the power of understanding [*vim intelligendi*] . . ." The word that Descartes appears to be using for the activity of understanding in this discussion is *intellectio*, which will reappear in ¶10 of the Sixth Meditation. Descartes does not use the term in the other five meditations.

10. Earlier in the paragraph, it is clear that the theory requires that there be some body that is intimately present to me. But, I think, as far as the theory of imagining goes, I might be united to this body as a sailor to a ship, so it is not clear we should be thinking yet in terms of "the" (i.e., my human) body. It is easier to think, for example, that as far as imagining goes, I might use different bodies on different occasions.

11. Descartes uses the word *vis* (power) in VI.¶3 and the word *facultas* in VI.¶10 (for both imagination and sensation). I have not noticed a difference in the meaning of the terms.

12. To be clear, I am not suggesting that Descartes does not worry about these metaphors because he has a solution to the problem of how matter causes consciousness; rather, my suggestion is that it is not clear that he thinks there is a problem to be solved. If that is correct, then why doesn't he think there is a problem? Well, in that he is committed to the idea that God creates extension, he certainly thinks there is no problem in an immaterial being's causing the existence of a material being. In view of Descartes's views on divine omnipotence, I doubt that he would see any

difficulty in God's designing a nature of an immaterial being whose operation involves the use of a body; and I think he regards it as obvious, *a posteriori*, in view of the nature of imaginative cognition and sensory cognition, that God did just that. (That Descartes regards it as obvious that even imaginative cognition witnesses that I am joined to a body is perhaps in keeping with his comment that what might be called the fact of mind-body union is obvious: "Everyone recognizes [*à sçavoir*] that he is a single person with both body and thought so related by nature that the thought can move the body and sense [*sentir*] the things which happen to it" [3:694; 3:228].) And if we are still inclined to protest that the relationship is left blank—we want to know *how* this happens—I am not sure that Descartes thinks there is going be more, or needs to be more, of an explanation, than that the nature of the union is such that such and such happens. It is natural to protest that this would be to traffic in the very sort of explanations that Descartes the natural philosopher warns against. It is not obvious, however, that those warnings apply outside the realm of mechanism. When Descartes is thinking about either the nature of the mind alone or the nature of the union, he seems to be comfortable with Aristotelian modes of thinking in a way that his successors are not.

13. One could maintain, of course, that the level of involvement is just this: thought that is not "pure" is simply thought that is normally or characteristically (efficiently?) caused by body. But if we are thinking of body as an extrinsic cause of the cognition, this seems to yield a strained sense of pure, which one would have thought would be a property of the cognition itself rather than a function of its genesis. It may be that its corporeal genesis leaves a trace on the resulting thought that renders it not pure, but exactly what that trace is might be hard to see.

14. There is a reason to be fussy here and to stick with Descartes's formulation "intimately present to me" and use it to mark the sort of relationship between the cognitive faculty and body that is involved in imagining. The senses, we shall see shortly, witness a different and in a certain sense deeper relationship between the cognitive faculty and (its) body.

15. This squares with his statement to Gibieuf that the faculties of imagination and sensation "belong to the soul only in so far as it is joined to the body" (3:479; 3:203). When More asks Descartes whether, if separate souls or angels were entirely incorporeal and immediately apprehended one another's essences, this could properly be said to be sensing, Descartes responds:

> I reply that the human mind separated from the body does not have senses properly so called [*sensum proprie dictum non habere*]; but it is not clear by natural reason alone whether angels are created like minds distinct from bodies, or like minds united to bodies. (5:402; 3:380)

Both parts of Descartes's answer suggest a tight connection between the ability to sense and the possession of a body.

16. See Margaret Wilson, *Descartes*, 201–2:

> We have seen that Descartes does not believe it possible conclusively to demonstrate the existence of body or brain from the experiences of the *imagination*. The supposition of physical traces in the brain, which the mind "inspects," merely provides the "best explanation" of imagination that he is able to produce. It seems

safe to conclude, then, that for Descartes there is no *contradiction* in supposing that my phenomenal states of imagination occur although no body exists. And this means (I take it) that the experiences of *imagination* can be clearly and distinctly conceived in separation from anything physical.

On the interpretation I have presented, Descartes's hesitation about his account of imagination arises from doubt about whether he has got the real essence, the nature, of imagination correct; the hesitation does not hold any consequences for the metaphysical structure of imagination. The fact that he is not positive about his theory of imagination does not, I think, show that he believes that imagination can be clearly and distinctly conceived in separation from anything physical. What about the "experiences of imagination" and "phenomenal states of imagination" that Wilson refers to—can *they* be conceived apart from anything physical? Well, not if we think of the phenomenal/experiential "state" as ontologically parasitic on the activity of imagining. That is, not if an experience of imagination simply is an experience of a cognitive faculty that applies itself to a body that is intimately present to it and a phenomenal state of imagination simply is the phenomenal state of a cognitive faculty that applies itself to a body that is intimately present to it. In my view, "phenomenal states of imagination"—whatever we make of that dark notion—are, for Descartes, posterior to the power of imagination. Since the power is prior to exercises of it, it is not "reducible to" to such "phenomenal states" and their causal genesis.

17. Part of what makes it difficult to pursue the place of consciousness in Descartes's thought is the lack of easy equivalences between Latin (and French) vocabulary and the English word for consciousness (its own use a bit murky). So, for example, the Latin word closest to the English word *conscious*, *conscius*, appears only once in the *Meditations*, and the context there is not one in which he is concerned with our immediate awareness of our thoughts. (It comes up in the Third Meditation 7:49, where he argues that a thinking being that had the power to keep itself in existence would certainly be conscious—*conscius*—of this power.)

CSM do not make the task of tracking Descartes's views on consciousness any easier by their tendency to introduce the word *awareness* in their translations of Descartes's Latin cognitive terminology. Here are some examples, taken from the Second and Sixth Meditations.

> And yet may it not perhaps be the case that these very things which I am supposing to be nothing, because they are unknown to me, are in reality identical with the I of which I am aware [*novi*]? I do not know, and for the moment I shall not argue the point, since I can make judgements only about things which are known [*nota sunt*] to me. I know [*novi*] that I exist; the question is what is this I that I know [*novi*]? If the I is understood strictly as we have been taking it, then it is quite certain that knowledge of it does not depend on things of whose existence I am as yet unaware [*nondum novi*]. (7:27–28; 2:18–19)

The Latin words indicated here are all forms of *nosco*, which means "to know" or "to become acquainted with"; the first and last translations in terms of "awareness" seem inaccurate to me.

> Surely my awareness of my own self is not merely much truer and more certain than my awareness of the wax, but also much more distinct and evident. (7:33; 2:22)

The Latin here is *Nunquid me ispum non tantum multo verius, multo certius, sed etiam multo distinctius evidentiusque cognosco?* (Do I not know [*cognosco*] myself not only much more truly and certainly, but also much more distinctly and evidently?) In particular, the word underneath CSM's "awareness" is *cognosco*, which means to perceive or apprehend or to become acquainted with or get to know. (I believe that CSM often translate *cognosco* as "aware," partly in order to keep it distinct from *scio*; they seem to have revised their translation of the last paragraph of the Fifth Meditation so as to reflect this decision. It is worth trying to translate *cognosco* in a way that keeps it distinct from the translations of other cognitive terminology, and "aware of" is a reasonable choice; but there is a danger that one will hear the "aware of" in a way that gestures toward consciousness more than the original Latin does.)

> Considering the ideas of all these qualities which presented themselves to my thought, although the ideas were, strictly speaking, the only immediate objects of my sensory awareness [*sentire*], it was not unreasonable for me to think that the items which I was perceiving through the senses were things quite distinct from my thought, namely bodies which produced the ideas. For my experience was that these ideas came to me quite without my consent, so that I could not have sensory awareness [*sentire*] of any object, even if I wanted to, unless it was present to my sense organs; and I could not avoid having sensory awareness [*sentire*] of it when it was present. (7:75; 2:52)

I think that the most natural translation of *sentire* in this context would be "to sense" or "to perceive by the senses." (The first sentence raises other, more difficult translation issues that I will not go into here.)

CSM also sometimes introduce the word *experience* in ways uncalled for by the Latin:

> The first was that every sensory experience I have ever thought I was having while awake I can also think of myself as sometimes having while asleep. (7:77, 2:53)

The Latin here is *prima erat, quod nulla unquam, dum viligo, me sentire crediderim, quae non etiam inter dormiendum possim aliquando putare me sentire,* i.e., "the first was that there is nothing at all that I believed myself to sense when awake that I could not also take myself to sense sometimes while I was sleeping."

18. As we saw above, Descartes writes to Elizabeth, "The soul is conceived only by the pure intellect; body (i.e. extension, shapes, and motions) can likewise be known by the intellect alone, but much better by the intellect aided by the imagination" (4:691; 3:227).

19. I don't think that Descartes intends to offer a full account of imagining in ¶¶1–3 of the Sixth Meditation, as opposed to focusing on certain cognitive aspects of it. In the Sixth Meditation Descartes intends to treat only those imaginings that fall under the head of Article 20 of *The Passions of the Soul* ("Imaginings and other thoughts formed by soul") and not those imaginings that come under Article 21 ("Imaginings which are caused solely by the body"). For example, Descartes explicitly gives the imagination a role in human dreaming, which would seem to involve a broadening of the conception of imagination presented in the opening paragraphs of the Sixth Meditation. (He writes in the Fifth Replies, "When, for example, we are asleep and notice that we are dreaming, we need imagination in order to dream, but to notice that we are dreaming we need only the intellect" [7:359; 2:248], and the

same idea is suggested in the Third Meditation, ¶10.) It would appear then that the account of imagining in ¶¶1–3 is restricted to certain aspects of imagining, and that it is an open question whether as one moves to a broader conception it will still seem as natural to characterize imagination as something involving an "intellectual act" or as natural to deny that animals imagine.

In this regard, it is worth keeping in mind the sorts of abilities that are associated in the tradition with the imagination. Such theories are rich and complex, and fluid from thinker to thinker, but a rough picture will suffice for our discussion. "Imagination" was a term that medieval philosophers tended to use to cover a family of powers, one of which is the imagination proper. These powers are the interior sensitive powers, and were held to be corporeal, that is to say, their exercise was supposed to take place in a corporeal organ, and were found in animals. Aquinas, closely following Avicenna, identified four interior sensitive powers: (1) the common sense, (2) the phantasy or imagination, (3) estimative power (in animals), and (4) memory. These are powers found in nonintellectual beings, such as animals. The common sense is responsible for an animal's ability to coordinate and distinguish the species received by the proper senses, so as to determine, for example, that red is distinct from sweet. The phantasy or imagination had the function of storing the species for later use. The estimative power made available certain useful or harmful aspects of things sensed: sheep flee from wolves not because wolves are ugly but because they are perceived as dangerous, and birds go after straw not because it is pleasing to see but because it is perceived as useful for building a nest. Memory in animals was understood to be the spontaneous recollection of what is useful or harmful in appropriate situations.

All this holds good of animals. The situation becomes more complicated when we take into account human beings, who have imagination-based abilities that transcend in important respects what animals can do. Humans beings, unlike animals, can use their imaginations creatively so as, for example, to combine the form of gold with that of a mountain to yield the imaginary form of a golden mountain. Avicenna saw this as reason to posit a distinct power, but Aquinas held that the imaginative power suffices. More interesting examples, perhaps, are provided by the cognitive power or particular reason: Cognitive reason, our sense of what is harmful or useful, was seen as less instinctual than that of animals, a difference that was grounded in our ability to reason about particulars. Memory also works differently in our case, in that it is not purely automatic in the way that it is for animals: we search our memories in a way that they do not. This ability was termed reminiscence. Aquinas considers and rejects the suggestion that cognitive reason and reminiscence are sufficiently different from the base sensitive powers of estimation and memory that we ought to posit them as new powers:

> The cogitative and memorative powers in man owe their excellences not to that which is proper to the sensitive part but to a certain affinity and proximity to universal reason, which, so to speak, overflows [refluentiam: an overflowing or flowing back] into them. Therefore they are not distinct powers, but the same, yet more perfect than in the animals. (ST I, Q. 78, A. 4, ad 5)

Cognitive reason and reminiscence, for Thomas, seem almost to lie at the intersection of our animal nature and rational nature, something that will become unthinkable for Descartes.

Which of these abilities Descartes recognizes (and in what form), and the relation of those abilities that he does recognize to the imagination, is unclear to me. Baker and Morris point out in *Descartes' Dualism*, 127–28, that Descartes understands many of the phenomena associated with the estimative power in terms of what he calls the internal senses, presumably after Aquinas's interior senses, and suggest that the remaining three abilities, the common sense, (corporeal) memory, and imagination proper, are associated with the imagination.

20. This is how I understand Aquinas's rejection of Avicenna's thesis that there is a power in between imagination and the estimative power to compose new images: "But this operation is not to be found in animals other than man, in whom the imaginative power suffices thereto" (ST I, Q. 78, A. 4).

21. Descartes writes in ¶3, "[B]ut when it [the mind] imagines, it turns towards the body and looks at something in the body which conforms to an idea understood by the mind or perceived by the senses," which in the latter case sounds like memory. Descartes discusses memory in a letter to Mersenne of 6 August 1640:

> I do not think that there has to be a very large number of these folds [of memory] to supply all the things we remember, because a single fold will do for all the things which resemble each other. Moreover, in addition to the corporeal memory, whose impressions can be explained by these folds in the brain, I believe that there is also in our intellect another sort of memory, which is altogether spiritual, and is not found in animals. It is this that we mainly use. (3:143; 3:151)

22. Aquinas writes in ST I, Q. 78, A. 4:

> Now to receive and retain are, in corporeal things, reduced to diverse principles; for moist things are apt to receive, but retain with difficulty, while it is the reverse with dry things. Wherefore, since the sensitive power is the act of a corporeal organ, it follows that the power which receives the species of sensible things must be distinct from the power that preserves them. . . . Thus, therefore, for the reception of sensible forms, the proper sense and the common sense are appointed. . . . But for the retention and preservation of these forms, the phantasy or imagination is appointed, which are the same, for phantasy or imagination is as it were a storehouse of forms received through the senses.

23. Anton Pegis makes this argument persuasively in "The Separated Soul."

24. I discuss this Aristotelian background in somewhat more detail in my "On the Relationship between Mode and Substance in Spinoza's Metaphysics," 248–53.

25. Margaret Wilson has emphasized the importance of this exchange between Descartes and Gassendi, in *Descartes*, 178–85. Her reading of the discussion of the imagination differs from the one I have offered in that she thinks Descartes bases his claim that the brain is not involved in pure understanding on "phenomenological considerations" (185). I have tried instead to focus on considerations having to do with activities or operations and what they need. This approach fits with the fact that Descartes phrases his response to Gassendi in terms of what is of "use" to pure understanding. This is not to deny that "phenomenological considerations" may be at work here as well, in ways that Wilson would find objectionable.

26. Margaret Wilson offers an interpretation of Descartes's dualism that emphasizes the role of the intellect in an important and influential discussion in section 2

of chapter 6 of *Descartes* (see also sec. 3), to which my own discussion here is much indebted. If I understand her correctly, Wilson maintains in section 3 (186) that Descartes's "robust" dualism, according to which the goings-on in the pure intellect are not parallel to any corporeal goings-on, is not entailed by the argument Descartes gives in ¶9. I am trying to present a reading of ¶9 that sees it as more continuous with, if not precisely the lack of parallelism between intellectual happenings and bodily happenings, then at least the independence of cognitive activities from corporeal commitments.

27. See note 15 above.

28. In fact, in their translation, Anscombe and Geach break this paragraph into three separate paragraphs, along the lines that I am indicating.

29. See, e.g., *Passions of the Soul*, A.94. Descartes does not come back to these corporeal emotions in the *Meditations*; they do, however, provide much of the subject matter for the *Passions*.

30. Some have taken Descartes's claim, "Nor was it without sound reason [*nec sane absque ratione*] that, with respect to the ideas of all these qualities which presented themselves to my thought, and which alone I properly and immediately sense" as endorsing some sort of veil of perception with respect to these qualities, as if his point were that I properly sense the ideas as opposed to the qualities. (I discuss this passage in chapter 3 (I).) I think that his point is that hot, cold, and the like are the proper objects of the senses, and, for the purpose of this point, he is not intending to draw a distinction between the quality of hot and the idea of hot. Margaret Wilson offers a slightly different reading to the same general end in "Sense and 'Resemblance,'" 14–15.

31. Baker and Morris in *Descartes' Dualism*, 153, read the passage in this way, although they go on to argue that there is a higher-order perspective from which it becomes intelligible that there should be this unintelligibility.

32. On the distinction between thirst (sensation of throat dryness), hunger (sensation of stomach tugging), and pain (sensation of body damage), and the resulting desire to drink, desire to eat, and the passion of sadness, see the letter of 6 October 1645 to Princess Elizabeth (4:312; 3:271) and the letter of 1 February 1647 to Chanut (4:603; 3:306–7).

33. Descartes does not explicitly allude to natural impulse in his rehearsal in ¶6 of my reasons for thinking that I "sense certain things fully [*plane*] distinct from my cognition, namely bodies which produced the ideas." But it is natural to think that it is playing some role, and it does surface explicitly in the reasoning that Descartes sketches in III.¶8.

34. Let me put to the side interesting and important issues about what belongs to body in general as opposed what belongs to a specifically human body. Descartes touches on some of these in ¶¶17–18.

35. Descartes refers to it as *haec natura* (this nature) at 7:82, l. 25 and *naturam istam* (that nature) at 7:84, l. 4.

36. Locke writes of our "concern" for our bodies in the chapter in the *Essay* on personal identity (see II.27.18).

37. Sean Kelsey has provided helpful discussion on this point, in particular pointing out that it is likely that we are supposed, in this context, to be thinking of sailors as caring for their ships.

38. Descartes does write in ¶14 that "the fact that some of the perceptions are agreeable to me while others are disagreeable makes it quite certain that my body, or rather my whole self [*sive potius me totum*], in so far as I am a combination of body and mind, can be affected by the various beneficial or harmful bodies which surround it," and at the corresponding place in the *Principles* (II, 3), emphasizes the composite. But his preference to think in terms of the composite in these settings is explicable without attributing it to the view that it is incorrect to hold that body can be benefited or harmed: it does, after all, seem salient here that when the body is hurt the whole being suffers.

39. I think it would be possible to maintain that as far as this passage goes, the ideas of benefit, harm, and need—and, later, concepts like disease, drink, and body— apply to this machine only because it is united to a human mind. However, I do not see in Descartes a sensitivity to the sort of worry that might give one pause about claiming that a machine can drink and does so either to its benefit or detriment. (I suppose that, for Descartes, the vast majority of drinking that goes on in the world is done by machines; we are the exception.)

Spinoza follows Descartes in holding that one can develop, on a purely mechanistic basis, some notion of a mechanistic body's being better or worse off, that is, a notion of a body's "power of acting," which can be "increased or diminished, aided or restrained" (see *Ethics*, 3d3; Curley 493). What Descartes and Spinoza both seem to object to is the idea that we can locate within *res extensa* the sort of nature that could support the idea of a privation, defect, or disorder—the absence of some perfection or reality that is "supposed to" be in a thing by its nature. For further discussion, see my "Relationship between Mode and Substance."

40. I argue at the end of the next section that there is a rather close relationship between the claim in III.¶19 that sensory ideas are obscure and confused and the claim in VI.¶13 that "sensations of hunger, thirst, pain and so on are nothing but confused modes of cognition": Neither form of representation makes clear the sort of reality that they present (it seems clear that pain, hunger, and thirst represent privations, but it is hard to tell from the ideas why the body needs the sort of things that ideas point us toward, or how those things contribute to the well-being of the body). Further, part of the force of the claim that these representations are confused relies on a picture of what would count as the distinct representation of the same thing: the pattern of matter in motion that corresponds to external sensible qualities (colors, sounds, etc.), which representations are supposed to make obvious what counts as a reality or an absence thereof, and helps us to understand the mechanical condition of my body that goes with being damaged, needing food or drink, etc. Finally, the theory's account of the role of senses in the life of a human being helps us to understand why sensory representation is limited in the way it is, which limitations are, from the point of view of this role, advantageous.

In *Descartes' Philosophy Interpreted*, 2:110, Guéroult comes to a somewhat different conclusion on the question of whether there are two "conceptions of sensible obscurity and confusion" in the *Meditations* and holds that while "these two conceptions are not at all equivalent" they are not "incompatible."

41. Gilson writes on p. 187 of *Christian Philosophy of Aquinas*, "We must not regard a living being as a machine inert itself but with a soul as a motor. This is what

Descartes wanted to substitute for Aristotle's notion of a living being." Later he associates the "motor" sort of union with Plato, writing, "Plato only wished to unite the soul to the body as its motor because he did not place man's essence in the composite of soul and body, but in the soul alone using the body as an instrument. Hence we find him saying that the soul is in the body as a pilot in his ship" (193). I am sympathetic to the main point that Gilson wants to make in this context, namely, that the soul does not actualize the body (the "machine") in the way it does on Aquinas's theory. Still, Descartes hoped to make out a way in which the mind is united to a body more intimately than the way a sailor is united to his ship (VI.¶12). My suggestion is that he did this through making the goods, bads, and needs of the body in some deep and natural way the goods, bads, and needs of the cognitive agent, and this fact is made manifest to us through pain, hunger, thirst, so that the mind and the body in some deep and natural way share certain goods. I briefly consider at the end of this section why God might have done such a thing for (to?) the mind.

42. See the letter to Mesland of 2 May 1644, 4:120; 3:236. For a helpful discussion of this distinction see Dugald Murdoch, "Exclusion and Abstraction in Descartes' Metaphysics."

43. The idea that the (human) cognitive agent has this special ability to be concerned for its body is perhaps why Descartes in defending Regius can in good conscience maintain that certain thinkers at Utrecht who held that the mind and body form an *ens per accidens* "did not deny the substantial union by which the mind and body are conjoined nor a natural aptitude of each part to that union" (7:585; Rozemond's translation). For a fuller discussion, see Rozemond, *Descartes's Dualism*, 161, and Paul Hoffman, "Cartesian Composites," especially 260–65.

44. Margaret Wilson offers this passage as evidence that Descartes did not consistently adhere to what she terms the "Natural Institution" theory, which, as I understand it, involves the idea that the union consists in God's systematically joining sensory ideas to bodily states. In her illuminating and provocative discussion (*Descartes*, 206–9), Wilson seems to regard the Natural Institution theory as Descartes's most promising option, largely because of its austerity. I am not sure that Descartes does offer such a theory; below I attempt to provide an alternative reading of one of the main passages in which Wilson finds the theory (¶22). See also note 69 below.

45. I have described the problem as one where we cognitive agents interfere with the mechanistic goings-on. It is possible that Descartes holds that our bodies lack something that animal bodies have, and this needs to be made up for by us cognitive agents. It is hard to say, however, what body does not have in this regard that animal bodies have.

46. One question that I have not addressed, because it does not seem to arise squarely within the confines of the *Meditations*, is what to make of Descartes's suggestion that the mind is the substantial form of the human body, discussed in Paul Hoffman's seminal article, "The Unity of Descartes's Man." I am sympathetic to the interpretation that Hoffman presents there, and I conjecture that the dependence of the body on the mind for its natural continuance in existence may help to explain why Descartes thinks it is still appropriate to use the scholastic terminology in this case.

47. This is a point that Gilson has emphasized. See, e.g., *Christian Philosophy of Aquinas*, part 2, chap. 4, especially p. 191.

48. Paul Hoffman explores the question raised in this section in more depth in his "Descartes and Aquinas on Per Se Subsistence and the Union of Soul and Body." Hoffman suggests, plausibly, it seems to me, that one benefit Descartes might think mind receives from its union with body is the ability to know the natures of material things as existing individuals.

49. When Locke covers related ground in the *Essay*, he wonders about this point, writing:

> The privative causes I have assigned of positive ideas are according to the common opinion; but in truth it will be hard to determine whether there be really any ideas from a privative cause, till it be determined whether rest be any more a privation than motion. (II.8.6)

50. In recent years there has been a rich and interesting discussion in the secondary literature of Descartes's account of material falsity, sparked in large part by Arnauld's criticism of the account in the Fourth Objections (7:206–7) and Descartes's response (7:231–35). I have learned a lot, in particular, from Paul Hoffman's "Descartes on Misrepresentation," Deborah J. Brown's *Descartes and the Passionate Mind*, chap. 4, and her "True and False Ideas." While I hope the general approach to material falsity that I have sketched here squares with that exchange, working through the complex set of issues that it raises requires more discussion than I can allow here. I should say that I believe that part of Arnauld's puzzlement is at Descartes's apparent suggestion that cold could be a nonbeing and yet there could be an idea of it. Ideas, like forms (and, for that matter species), are principles of actuality or reality—of being as opposed to nonbeing. This is how I take Arnauld's remark, "But if cold is an absence [*privatio*], it cannot exist objectively in the intellect by means of an idea whose objective being is a positive entity [*cuius esse objectivum sit ens positivum*]" (7:206; 2:145).

51. Hot and cold are of special interest because of the role they played, along with wet and dry, in Aristotelian natural philosophy, which Descartes, as he remarks in *Le Monde*, does not use in his explanations because "these qualities themselves stand in need of explanation" (11:25–26; 1:89). I think Descartes supposes that if he can raise issues about exactly what our cognition of these qualities presents, he will have accomplished something important.

52. It might be suggested that Descartes is interested in the general idea of malfunction here and that his choice to cast the problem in terms of error and trickery is an accident of the cognitive setting in which the *Meditations* take place. As I explain toward the end of this section, I think there is more to Descartes's appeal to error and trickery than that: it is unclear that we can, in his metaphysics, get to the idea of real sensory deficiency except through a notion like inaccurate information.

Notice that Descartes puts the difficulty in terms of "error [*errores*]" and being "tricked [*delusus*]." This way of putting it may be merely a result of his desire to frame the problem he is interested in as one about God's veracity, but it raises the question of whether he recognizes anything along the lines of natural defect that does not ultimately involve falsity. I will return to this point briefly in the main text.

53. The point Descartes is making corresponds in a way to what he says in IV.¶13.

54. In Guéroult, *Descartes' Philosophy Interpreted*, vol. 2, chap. 17, sec. 2.

55. There is a delicate question about how the "me" works here—would I still be me if God gave me all the perfections found in an angel? I am speaking loosely here.

56. This passage has received a fair amount of attention in the secondary literature. See, for example, Daniel Garber, "Descartes, Mechanics, and the Mechanical Philosophy," and Alison Simmons, "Sensible Ends: Latent Teleology in Descartes' Account of Sensation," especially 58ff. I discuss this contrast in more detail in "Spinoza on Final Causality."

57. For an early modern statement of this view see Locke's *Essay* II.25.

58. I believe that Spinoza is offering a similar account of these matters in the Preface to Part IV of the *Ethics*.

59. For a helpful overview of the issues surrounding Descartes's thought about animals and functional explanation, see Gary Hatfield, "Animals."

60. In Guéroult, *Descartes' Philosophy Interpreted*, 2:148 and 149 respectively.

61. Simmons, "Sensible Ends," also develops an interpretation according to which teleological idioms apply to the human body primarily, and to animals only derivatively, "based on an (admittedly compelling) analogy with the organs of the human body" (62 n. 17).

62. See note 60 above.

63. Margaret Wilson offers related criticisms of Guéroult's interpretation in *Descartes*, 243–44 n. 22.

64. Guéroult cites two letters to Mesland, the one of 9 February 1645, AT 4:166–67, and one from late 1645 or early 1646, AT 4:346; and *Le Monde*, AT 11:15.

65. I owe these reservations concerning the exact import of Descartes's claim in the letter to Mesland to some unpublished work by Erin Eaker.

66. Leibniz, of course, did not believe that the mind could bring about motions in the pineal gland.

67. This is not to say that anything goes—not every adjustment in the architecture of the mind-body system counts as a new project.

68. I've consulted Margaret Wilson, *Descartes*, 206, for help with translation of this difficult passage.

69. Margaret Wilson finds evidence in this passage for the Natural Institution account of the mind-body union (see note 44 above), which, as I understand her, is the view that mind-body is "nothing but the arbitrarily established disposition of this mind to experience certain types of sensations on the occasions of certain changes in this body, and to refer these sensations to (parts of) this body" (*Descartes*, 211). She takes this theory to be in tension with other things Descartes says, including his suggestion that sensations "arise from" the body (211ff.).

I think we ought to take seriously Descartes's indication that the union is prior to sensation and read the "arbitrariness" of the dispositions in this light. Doing so requires that we give some content to an idea of a union independent of the sensory hookups themselves. I have tried to do this via the suggestion that through the union, the goods, bads, and needs of the body become the goods, bads, and needs of the cognitive agent. Whether this is enough content to prefer my way of going to the more "austere" Natural Institution theory is hard to say; it does seem to me that my interpretation fits better with the overall tenor of the Sixth Meditation.

Baker and Morris argue that the Natural Institution interpretation preferred by Wilson fails to give a proper place to Descartes's thinking about nature, because the mind-body connections are ordained by God, and God's ordinations "have a kind of necessity" (*Descartes' Dualism*, 167). Although I am broadly sympathetic to Baker and Morris's approach and their emphasis on the idea of nature, it is not clear to me that Wilson is committed to denying that once the "arbitrary" correlations have been established by God, they come to have a kind of necessity.

Bibliography

➤✦

TEXTS AND EDITIONS: DESCARTES

In general, I refer to Descartes's writings by Adam and Tannery (AT) volume and page, and by Cottingham, Stoothoff, and Murdoch (CSM) translation volume and page, so that "7:17; 2:12" is p. 17 of vol. 7 of Adam and Tannery and p. 12 of vol. 2 of the Cottingham, Stoothoff, and Murdoch translation.

Descartes, René. *Descartes: Philosophical Writings.* Edited and translated by Elizabeth Anscombe and Peter Geach. Indianapolis: Bobbs-Merrill, 1971.
———. *Descartes: The World and Other Writings.* Edited and translated by Stephen Gaukroger. Cambridge: Cambridge University Press, 1998. Cited as "Gaukroger."
———. *Oeuvres de Descartes.* Edited by Charles Adam and Paul Tannery. 11 vols. Paris: Libraire Philosophique J. Vrin, 1973–82.
———. *The Philosophical Writings of Descartes.* Edited and translated by John Cottingham, Robert Stoothoff, Dugald Murdoch, and (vol. 3 only) Anthony Kenny. 3 vols. Cambridge: Cambridge University Press, 1984–91.

TEXTS AND EDITIONS: SAINT THOMAS AQUINAS

For the original-language versions of the Aquinas writings I have used the following editions. I have also used the website http://www.corpusthomisticum .org/index.html.

S. Thomae Aquinatis. 1978. *Summa Theologiae.* 5 vols. Madrid: Biblioteca de Autores Cristianos, 1978. Cited as "ST."
Saint Thomas D'Aquin. 1951–61. *Contra Gentiles.* 5 vols. [Besançon]: P. Lethielleux.

I have used the following translations. In general, where I have altered a translation of Aquinas's writing, I have included the original Latin in the extract.

Aquinas, St. Thomas. *Aristotle's "De Anima" in the Version of William of Moerbeke and the Commentary of St. Thomas Aquinas.* Translated by Kenelm Foster and Silvester Humphries. 1951; rpt. New Haven: Yale University Press, 1959.
———. *De Ente and Essentia.* Translated by Robert P. Goodwin as "On Being and Essence." In *Aquinas: Selected Writings.* Indianapolis: Bobbs-Merrill, 1965.

————. *De Potentia.* Translated by the English Dominican Fathers. In *The Power of God.* London: Burns, Oates, and Washbourne, 1933.

————. *De Veritate.* Translated by Robert W. Mulligan, S.J., James V. McGlynn, S.J., and Robert W. Schmidt, S.J. In *Truth.* Chicago: Henry Regnery, 1952–54. Cited as "DV."

————. *In Boetium de Trinitate.* QQ. 5 and 6. Translated by A. Maurer. In *The Division and Methods of the Sciences.* Toronto: Pontifical Institute of Mediaeval Studies, 1963. Cited as "Maurer."

————. *Summa Contra Gentiles.* 5 vols. Translated by the English Dominican Fathers. In *The Summa Contra Gentiles of Saint Thomas Aquinas.* London: Burns, Oates, and Washbourne, 1923–28. Cited as "SCG."

————. *The Summa Theologica of St. Thomas Aquinas.* Translated by the Fathers of the English Dominican Province. 1911; Westminster, MD: Christian Classics, 1981.

OTHER PRIMARY SOURCES

Anselm. *St. Anselm's Proslogion with A Reply on the Behalf of the Fool by Gaunilo and The Author's Reply to Gaunilo.* Translated by M. J. Charlesworth. 1965; Notre Dame, IN: University of Notre Dame Press, 1979.

Aristotle. *De Anima.* In *The Complete Works of Aristotle: The Revised Oxford Translation,* edited by Jonathan Barnes, 1:641–92. Princeton: Princeton University Press, 1894.

Hume, David. A *Treatise of Human Nature.* Edited by L. A. Selby-Bigge, with text revision and notes by P. H. Nidditch. Oxford: Clarendon Press, 1975. Cited by book, part, and chapter.

Kant, Immanuel. *Critique of Pure Reason.* Translated by Norman Kemp Smith. New York: St. Martin's Press, 1965. Cited by page reference to the second "B" edition.

Leibniz, Gottfried Wilhelm. *Die Philosophischen Schriften.* Edited by C. J. Gerhardt. 1875–90; rpt. New York: Georg Olms Verlag, 1978. Cited as "Gerhardt."

————. "Two Notations for Discussion with Spinoza." In *Philosophical Papers and Letters,* edited and translated by Leroy E. Loemker, 167–69. 2nd ed. Boston: D. Reidel, 1976. Cited as "Loemker."

Locke, John. *An Essay Concerning Human Understanding.* Edited by Peter H. Nidditch. 1975; rpt. with corrections, Oxford: Clarendon Press, 1979. Cited by book, chapter, and section.

Spinoza, Baruch. *Spinoza Opera.* Edited by C. Gebhardt. Heidelberg: Carl Winters Universitätsbuchhandlung, 1925. Cited as "Gebhardt."

————. *Ethics.* In *The Collected Works of Spinoza,* translated by Edwin Curley, vol. 1. Princeton: Princeton University Press, 1985. Cited as "Curley."

SECONDARY SOURCES

Alanen, Lilli. *Descartes's Concept of Mind.* Cambridge: Harvard University Press, 2003.

Ariew, Roger. *Descartes and the Last Scholastics*. Ithaca, NY: Cornell University Press, 1999.

Ayers, Michael. *Locke: Epistemology and Ontology*. 2 vols. London: Routledge, 1991.

Baker, Gordon, and Katherine J. Morris. *Descartes' Dualism*. New York: Routledge, 1996.

Beyssade, Jean-Marie. "The Idea of God and the Proofs of His Existence." In *The Cambridge Companion to Descartes*, edited by John Cottingham, 174–99. Cambridge: Cambridge University Press, 1992.

Beyssade, Michelle. "Descartes's Doctrine of Freedom: Differences between the French and Latin Texts of the Fourth Meditation." In *Reason, Will, and Sensation: Studies in Descartes's Metaphysics*, edited by John Cottingham, 191–206. Oxford: Clarendon Press, 1994.

Broughton, Janet. *Descartes's Method of Doubt*. Princeton: Princeton University Press, 2002.

———. "Dreamers and Madmen." In *The History of Early Modern Philosophy: Mind, Matter, and Metaphysics*, edited by Christia Mercer and Eileen O'Neill, 1–23. New York: Oxford University Press, 2005.

———. "Skepticism and the Cartesian Circle." *Canadian Journal of Philosophy* 14 (1984): 593–615.

Broughton, Janet, and Carriero, John, eds. *A Companion to Descartes*. Oxford: Blackwell, 2008.

Brown, Deborah J. *Descartes and the Passionate Mind*. Cambridge: Cambridge University Press, 2006.

———. "Descartes on True and False Ideas." In *A Companion to Descartes*, edited by Janet Broughton and John Carriero, 196–215. Oxford: Blackwell, 2008.

Carriero, John. "Berkeley, Resemblance, and Sensible Things." *Philosophical Topics* 31 (2003): 21–46.

———. *Descartes and the Autonomy of the Human Understanding*. 1984; rpt. Hamden, CT: Garland, 1990.

———. "On the Relationship between Mode and Substance in Spinoza's Metaphysics." *Journal of the History of Philosophy* 33 (1995): 245–73.

———. "Painting and Dreaming in the First Meditation." In "Norms and Modes of Thinking in Descartes," edited by Tuomo Aho and Mikko Yrjönsuuri. *Acta Philosophica Fennica* 64 (1999): 13–46.

———. "The Second Meditation and the Essence of the Mind." In *Essays on Descartes' "Meditations,"* edited by Amélie O. Rorty, 199–221. Berkeley and Los Angeles: University of California Press, 1986.

———. "Spinoza on Final Causality." In *Oxford Studies in Early Modern Philosophy*, edited by Daniel Garber and Steven Nadler, 2:105–47. New York: Oxford University Press, 2005.

———. "Spinoza's Views on Necessity in Historical Perspective." *Philosophical Topics* 19 (1991): 47–96.

———. "Substance and Ends in Leibniz." In *Contemporary Perspectives on Early Modern Philosophy: Essays in Honor of Vere Chappell*, edited by Paul Hoffman, David Owen, and Gideon Yaffe, 115–40. Peterborough, Ont.: Broadview Press, 2008.

Clemenson, David. "Seventeenth-Century Scholastic Philosophy of Cognition and Descartes' Causal Proof of God's Existence." Ph.D. diss., University of Michigan, 1991.

Curley, Edwin M. *Descartes against the Skeptics*. Cambridge: Harvard University Press, 1978.

Deferrari, Roy J. *A Latin-English Dictionary of St. Thomas Aquinas*. Boston: Daughters of St. Paul, 1960.

Della Rocca, Michael. "Judgment and Will." In *The Blackwell Guide to Descartes' "Meditations,"* edited by Stephen Gaukroger, 142–59. Oxford: Blackwell, 2006.

Des Chene, Dennis. *Physiologia: Natural Philosophy in Late Aristotelian and Cartesian Thought*. Ithaca, NY: Cornell University Press, 1996.

Doney, Willis. "On Descartes' Reply to Caterus." *American Catholic Philosophical Quarterly* 67 (1993): 413–30.

Dumont, Stephen D. "The *quaestio si est* and the Metaphysical Proof for the Existence of God according to Henry of Ghent and John Duns Scotus." *Franziskanische Studien* 66 (1984): 335–67.

———. "Theology as a Science and Duns Scotus's Distinction between Intuitive and Abstractive Cognition." *Speculum* 64 (1989): 579–99.

Dutton, Blake D. "The Ontological Argument: Aquinas's Objection and Descartes's Reply." *American Catholic Philosophical Quarterly* 67 (1993): 431–50.

Edelberg, Walter. "The Fifth Meditation." *Philosophical Review* 99 (1990): 493–533.

Frankfurt, Harry. *Demons, Dreamers, and Madmen*. Indianapolis: Bobbs-Merrill, 1970.

Garber, Daniel. "Descartes, Mechanics, and the Mechanical Philosophy." *Midwest Studies in Philosophy* 26 (2002): 185–204.

———. "*Semel in vita*: The Scientific Background to Descartes' *Meditations*." In *Essays on Descartes' "Meditations,"* edited by Amélie O. Rorty, 81–116. Berkeley and Los Angeles: University of California Press, 1986.

Gilson, Étienne. *The Christian Philosophy of Saint Augustine*. New York: Random House, 1960.

———. *The Christian Philosophy of St. Thomas Aquinas*. 1956; Notre Dame, IN: University of Notre Dame Press, 1994.

———. Commentary on *René Descartes: Discours de la Méthode*. 5th ed. Paris: J. Vrin, 1976.

———. *Études sur le rôle de la pensée médiévale dans la formation du système cartésien*. 4th ed. Paris: J. Vrin, 1975.

———. *Index Scolastico-cartésian*. 2nd ed. 1966; Paris: J. Vrin, 1979.

Guéroult, Martial. *Descartes selon l'ordre des raisons, l'âme et Dieu*. 2 vols. Paris: Aubier-Montaigne, 1968. Translated by Roger Ariew as *Descartes' Philosophy Interpreted according to the Order of Reasons*, vol. 1, *The Soul and God*, vol. 2, *The Soul and the Body* (Minneapolis: University of Minnesota Press, 1983, 1985).

Hatfield, Gary. "Animals." In *A Companion to Descartes*, edited by Janet Broughton and John Carriero, 404–25. Oxford: Blackwell, 2008.

———. *Routledge Philosophy Guidebook to Descartes and the "Meditations."* New York: Routledge, 2002.

———. "The Senses and the Fleshless Eye: The *Meditations* as Cognitive Exercises." In *Essays on Descartes' "Meditations,"* edited by Amélie O. Rorty, 45–79. Berkeley and Los Angeles: University of California Press, 1986.

Hoffman, Paul. "Aquinas on Threats and Temptations." *Pacific Philosophical Quarterly* 86 (2005): 225–42.

———. "Cartesian Composites." *Journal of the History of Philosophy* 37 (1999): 251–70.

———. "Descartes and Aquinas on Per Se Subsistence and the Union of Soul and Body." In *Essays on Descartes*. Oxford: Oxford University Press, 2008.

———. "Descartes on Misrepresentation," *Journal of the History of Philosophy* 34 (1996): 371–81.

———. "The Unity of Descartes's Man." In *The Rationalists: Critical Essays on Descartes, Spinoza, and Leibniz*, edited by Derk Pereboom, 59–87. Lanham, MD: Rowman and Littlefield, 1999. Orig. pub. *Philosophical Review* 95 (1986): 339–70.

Joyce, James. *A Portrait of the Artist as a Young Man*. Dublin: Oxford University Press, 2000.

Kambouchner, Denis. *Les Méditations métaphysiques de Descartes*. Vol. 1. Paris: Quadrige/Presses Universitaires de France, 2005.

Kenny, Anthony. *Descartes: A Study of His Philosophy*. New York: Random House, 1968.

———. "Descartes on the Will." In *Cartesian Studies*, edited by R. J. Butler, 1–31. Oxford: Basil Blackwell, 1972.

———. *The Five Ways: St. Thomas Aquinas' Proofs of God's Existence*. London: Routledge, 1969.

Loeb, Louis. "The Cartesian Circle." In *The Cambridge Companion to Descartes*, edited by John Cottingham, 200–235. Cambridge: Cambridge University Press, 1992.

Malcolm, Norman. "Descartes's Proof That His Essence Is Thinking." In *Descartes: A Collection of Critical Essays*, edited by Willis Doney, 312–37. Notre Dame, IN: University of Notre Press, 1968. Orig. pub. *Philosophical Review* 74 (1965): 315–38.

Marion, Jean-Luc. "The Essential Incoherence of Descartes' Definition of Divinity." In *Essays on Descartes' "Meditations,"* edited by Amélie O. Rorty, 297–338. Berkeley and Los Angeles: University of California Press, 1986.

McMullin, Ernan. 2007. "Explanation as Confirmation in Descartes' Natural Philosophy." In *A Companion to Descartes*, edited by Janet Broughton and John Carriero, 84–102. Oxford: Blackwell, 2008.

Menn, Stephen. *Descartes and Augustine*. Cambridge: Cambridge University Press, 1998.

Murdoch, Dugald. "Exclusion and Abstraction in Descartes' Metaphysics." *Philosophical Quarterly* 43 (1993): 38–57.

Nelson, Roger B. *Proofs without Words*. Washington, DC: Mathematical Association of America, 1993.

Newman, Lex. "Descartes on the Will." In *A Companion to Descartes*, edited by Janet Broughton and John Carriero, 334–52. Oxford: Blackwell, 2008.

Nolan, Lawrence. 1997. "The Ontological Status of Cartesian Natures." *Pacific Philosophical Quarterly* 78 (1997): 169–94.

Normore, Calvin. "Descartes and the Metaphysics of Extension." In *A Companion to Descartes*, edited by Janet Broughton and John Carriero, 271–87. Oxford: Blackwell, 2008.

————. "Descartes's Possibilities." In *René Descartes: Critical Assessments*, edited by G.J.D. Moyal, 3:68–83. London: Routledge, 1991.

Patterson, Sarah. "Clear and Distinct Perception." In *A Companion to Descartes*, edited by Janet Broughton and John Carriero, 216–34. Oxford: Blackwell, 2008.

Pegis, Anton C. "The Separated Soul and Its Nature in St. Thomas." In *St. Thomas Aquinas: 1274–1974, Commemorative Studies*, edited by Armand A. Maurer, 1:131–58. Toronto: Pontifical Institute of Mediaeval Studies, 1974.

Ragland, C. P. "Descartes on the Principle of Alternative Possibilities." *Journal of the History of Philosophy* 44 (2006): 377–94.

Reid, Thomas. *Essays on the Intellectual Powers of Man*. Edited by Baruch Brody. Cambridge: MIT Press, 1969.

Rorty, Richard. *Philosophy and the Mirror of Nature*. Princeton: Princeton University Press, 1979.

Rozemond, Marleen. *Descartes's Dualism*. Cambridge: Harvard University Press, 1998.

————. "Descartes's Dualism." In *A Companion to Descartes*, edited by Janet Broughton and John Carriero, 372–89. Oxford: Blackwell, 2008.

Schmitter, Amy. "The Wax and I: Perceptibility and Modality in the Second Meditation." *Archiv für Geschichte der Philosophie* 82 (2000): 178–201.

Secada, Jorge. *Cartesian Metaphysics: The Late Scholastic Origins of Modern Philosophy*. Cambridge: Cambridge University Press, 2000.

Simmons, Alison. "Sensible Ends: Latent Teleology in Descartes' Account of Sensation." *Journal of the History of Philosophy* 39 (2001): 49–75.

Smit, Houston. "Aquinas's Abstractionism." *Medieval Philosophy and Theology* 10 (2001): 85–118.

Smith, Vincent Edward. *St. Thomas on the Object of Geometry*. Milwaukee: Marquette University Press, 1954.

Stroud, Barry. *The Significance of Philosophical Scepticism*. Oxford: Clarendon Press, 1984.

Thau, Michael. *Consciousness and Cognition*. New York: Oxford University Press, 2002.

Wilson, Catherine. *Descartes's "Meditations": An Introduction*. Cambridge: Cambridge University Press, 2003.

Wilson, Margaret Dauler. *Descartes*. Boston: Routledge and Kegan Paul, 1978.

————. "Descartes on Sense and 'Resemblance.'" In *Ideas and Mechanism: Essays on Early Modern Philosophy*. Princeton: Princeton University Press, 1999.

Winkler, Kenneth P. "Descartes and the Names of God." *American Catholic Philosophical Quarterly* 67 (1993): 451–66.

Index Locorum

✦

Only Descartes's works (including the Objections) are indexed here. Passages from the *Meditations* are referred to by meditation and paragraph number, followed by (in parentheses) the volume and page number in the Adam and Tannery translation (AT) and the volume and page number in the Cottingham, Stoothoff, and Murdoch translation (CSM) or, for vol. 3, the Cottingham, Stoothoff, Murdoch, and Kenny translation (CSMK). Other writings are referred to by AT and CSM/CSMK volume and page number and, where applicable, other identifiers: the recipient of correspondence, the part and article number of the *Principles*, and so on.

MEDITATIONS

Synopsis

AT 7:14–15 (CSM 2:10–11), 186–87
AT 7:15 (CSM 2:11), 443n.3

First Meditation

I.¶1 (AT 7:17; CSM 2:12), 27–28, 29, 337
I.¶¶1–3, 27–37
I.¶2 (AT 7:18; CSM 2:12), 30, 35
I.¶3 (AT 7:18; CSM 2:12), 27, 30, 34, 35, 73
I.¶¶3–4 (AT 7:18–19; CSM 2:12–13), 39
I.¶¶4–5, 37–46
I.¶5 (AT 7:19; CSM 2:13), 27, 39, 40, 156, 267
I.¶6 (AT 7:19–20; CSM 2:13–14), 47, 48, 49, 51, 293, 302, 309, 432n.9, 435n.25, 449n.5
I.¶¶6–7, 434n.17
I.¶¶6–8, 27, 47
I.¶7 (AT 7:20; CSM 2:14), 49, 54, 449n.5
I.¶8 (AT 7:20; CSM 2:14), 51, 436n.26
I.¶¶8–9, 432n.9
I.¶9 (AT 7:21; CSM 2:14), 54, 55, 223, 432n.7, 434n.17, 475n.68
I.¶¶9–10, 27, 53–60
I.¶10 (AT 7:21–22; CSM 2:14–15), 28, 43, 55–56, 60, 62, 475n.68

Second Meditation

Third Meditation

Fourth Meditation

OTHER WORKS

Correspondence

Discourse on Method

First Set of Objections and Replies

Second Set of Objections and Replies

Third Set of Objections and Replies

Fourth Set of Objections and Replies

Subject Index

>‹